CRIMINAL LAW AND ECONOMICS

ENCYCLOPEDIA OF LAW AND ECONOMICS, SECOND EDITION

General Editor: Gerrit De Geest
School of Law, Washington University, St Louis, MO, USA

1. Tort Law and Economics
   Edited by Michael Faure
2. Labor and Employment Law and Economics
   Edited by Kenneth G. Dau-Schmidt, Seth D. Harris and Orly Lobel
3. Criminal Law and Economics
   Edited by Nuno Garoupa

Future titles will include:

Antitrust Law and Economics
Edited by Keith Hylton

Procedural Law and Economics
Edited by Chris William Sanchirico

Regulation and Economics
Edited by Roger Van den Bergh

Contract Law and Economics
Edited by Gerrit De Geest

Methodology of Law and Economics
Edited by Thomas S. Ulen

Property Law and Economics
Edited by Boudewijn Bouckaert

Corporate Law and Economics
Edited by Joseph A. McCahery and Erik P.M. Vermeulen

Production of Legal Rules
Edited by Francesco Parisi

Intellectual Property Law and Economics
Edited by Ben Depoorter

Criminal Law and Economics

Edited by

Nuno Garoupa

UIUC College of Law, USA

ENCYCLOPEDIA OF LAW AND ECONOMICS, SECOND EDITION

Edward Elgar

Cheltenham, UK • Northampton, MA, USA

Published by
Edward Elgar Publishing Limited
The Lypiatts
15 Lansdown Road
Cheltenham
Glos GL50 2JA
UK

Edward Elgar Publishing, Inc.
William Pratt House
9 Dewey Court
Northampton
Massachusetts 01060
USA

A catalogue record for this book
is available from the British Library

Library of Congress Control Number: 2009930429

Mixed Sources
Product group from well-managed
forests and other controlled sources
www.fsc.org Cert no. SA-COC-1565
© 1996 Forest Stewardship Council
FSC

ISBN 978 1 84720 275 8

Printed and bound by MPG Books Group, UK

Contents

List of contributors vi
Introduction vii

1. Public enforcement of law 1
A. Mitchell Polinsky and Steven Shavell
2. Private enforcement of law 60
Reza Rajabiun
3. Criminal law and regulation 90
Anthony Ogus
4. Criminal law and torts 111
Antony Dnes
5. Criminal procedure 125
Thomas J. Miceli
6. Plea-bargaining and prosecution 145
Oren Gazal-Ayal and Limor Riza
7. Political economy of criminal procedure 171
Keith N. Hylton and Vikramaditya S. Khanna
8. The economics of capital punishment 207
Joanna M. Shepherd
9. Corporate crime 220
Wallace P. Mullin and Christopher M. Snyder
10. Organized crime 257
Vimal Kumar and Stergios Skaperdas
11. Corruption 271
Roger Bowles
12. Tax evasion and avoidance 290
Luigi Alberto Franzoni
13. Environmental crimes 320
Michael Faure
14. Cyber crime 346
Mark A. Cohen
15. Terrorism 375
Nuno Garoupa, Jonathan Klick and Francesco Parisi
16. Behavioral criminal law and economics 403
Richard H. McAdams and Thomas S. Ulen

Index 437

Contributors

Roger Bowles, University of York

Mark A. Cohen, Vanderbilt University and Resources for the Future

Antony Dnes, University of Hull Business School

Michael Faure, Maastricht University and University of Rotterdam

Luigi Alberto Franzoni, University of Bologna

Oren Gazal-Ayal, University of Haifa, Faculty of Law

Nuno Garoupa, University of Illinois College of Law

Keith N. Hylton, Boston University Law School

Vikramaditya S. Khanna, University of Michigan Law School

Jonathan Klick, University of Pennsylvania School of Law

Vimal Kumar, Indian Institute of Technology, Kanpur

Richard H. McAdams, University of Chicago Law School

Thomas J. Miceli, University of Connecticut

Wallace P. Mullin, George Washington University

Anthony Ogus, University of Manchester and University of Rotterdam

Francesco Parisi, University of Minnesota School of Law and University of Bologna

A. Mitchell Polinsky, Stanford Law School

Reza Rajabiun, York University

Limor Riza, University of Haifa, Faculty of Law

Steven Shavell, Harvard Law School

Joanna M. Shepherd, Emory University School of Law

Stergios Skaperdas, University of California, Irvine

Christopher M. Snyder, Dartmouth College

Thomas S. Ulen, University of Illinois College of Law

Introduction

Nuno Garoupa

The application of economic analysis to criminal law is based on the proposition that economic efficiency is useful for examining and designing rules and institutions. Criminal law is a fundamental area of public law concerned with certain acts (labeled as criminal) that are subjected to punishment. There is no simple definition of what a criminal act is, but as far as our economic analysis goes, there are two elements of a criminal act that make it distinct. First, a criminal act is intended to do substantial harm. For example, murder, rape, robbery are considered to be criminal acts. Tort wrongdoings also cause harm, but the nature of the harm is private, whereas with crimes the harm is overwhelmingly public. This difference is reinforced by the fact that a tort suit is brought by the victim (the plaintiff), whereas criminal prosecution is brought by the state.

A second important characteristic of a criminal act from an economic perspective is criminal intent or guilty mind (*mens rea*). There are gradations in criminal intent (which are relevant to guilt and punishment), but the intent to harm is a necessary part in a typical case involving personal injury. Whereas civil wrongs are concerned with harm caused by negligent or reckless behavior, criminal wrongs are necessarily the product of intentional, eventually cruel, behavior.

Criminal acts are subjected to punishment. The person who commits a crime exposes himself to the risk of punishment. Punishment can take several forms: a fine in excess of compensation, imprisonment and other forms of curtailing the criminal's freedom, execution in some jurisdictions. Whereas compensation in torts generally aims to make the victim (the plaintiff) better off at the expense of the injurer, punishment in criminal law makes the injurer worse off without usually directly benefiting the victim. Due to the fact that compensation and punishment have different objectives, they can be independent and punishment may be imposed on top of compensation (notwithstanding general principles of law such as double jeopardy or *Non bis in idem* or *Ne bis in idem* in civil law).

Another important element of punishing criminal acts is the standard of proof required by law. In a tort suit, the plaintiff must prove his case by the preponderance of the evidence, whereas in a criminal action the prosecutor must prove her case beyond a reasonable doubt. It is the case that proof beyond a reasonable doubt is a much higher standard than just showing that the plaintiff's case is more believable than his opponent's. As a consequence, rules in criminal procedure are significantly different from civil procedure.

Having distinguished a criminal act from other acts (criminal intent and public injury) and the legal consequences (punishment and a beyond a reasonable doubt standard of proof), we should understand the economic approach to criminal law as an effort to explain criminal behavior and the principles of criminal law from an economic viewpoint. There are two important venues in this approach.

Potential criminals are economically rational. They compare the gain from committing a crime with the expected cost, including the risk of punishment, the possibility of social stigma, and eventual psychological costs. A criminal is an individual for whom the gain from committing a crime more than compensates the expected cost. On the modeling of criminal behavior, the economic approach has faced the usual criticism of using the expected utility framework, in particular the usefulness of economic rationality. It assumes that individuals respond significantly to the incentives created by the criminal justice system. Nevertheless, there is some recent literature on behavioral criminal law and economics as we will note later. Overall, it seems crime rates are responsive to changes in punishment.

A criminal act is efficient if the criminal could compensate the victims and remain better off. However, economic efficiency does not say that a criminal act is fair or desirable. Non-efficiency-based criteria in relation to criminal issues are important and should not be disregarded. The advantage of an economic approach to crime is that it avoids interpersonal assessments and is more neutral in its analysis. Efficient criminal law has the capacity to make everyone better off (even though the distribution of wealth could be more unequal). Fairness criteria are usually difficult to define, and non-efficiency-based criteria of criminal justice are sometimes the expression of the preferences of a group of people. Policy makers and legal professionals should not forget that usually there is a trade-off between economic efficiency and other goals.

This volume draws together sixteen chapters, by leading scholars in the field, summarizing the theoretical and empirical work that has been done to date on criminal law and economics. The book opens with a chapter on the public enforcement of law by the founding fathers, A. Mitchell Polinsky and Steven Shavell. This chapter provides an overview of the field, starting with the Beckerian model of the late 1960s before moving on to more recent developments, including activity level; errors; the costs of imposing fines; general enforcement; marginal deterrence; the principal-agent relationship; settlements; self-reporting; repeat offenders; imperfect knowledge about the probability and magnitude of sanctions; corruption; incapacitation; costly observation of wealth; social norms; and the fairness of sanctions. It is an updated summary of the current state of the art in criminal law and economics with a view to future developments.

The following chapter provides a similar overview, but looking at the private enforcement of law, by Reza Rajabiun. Private enforcement is to be understood as detection or punishment imposed by private persons or organizations as a sanction against violation of legal rules without consent or action by public enforcers (such as the police, public prosecutors or regulators). Private enforcement is widespread in certain areas of public law. From an economic perspective, it is of interest to consider the extent to which private enforcement should be used in criminal law either as substitute for or as complement to public enforcement.

The boundaries between criminal law and other areas of the law are of importance in any legal system. The blurred line between criminal law and regulation deserves attention from legal economists, as a leading expert, Anthony Ogus, explains in his chapter, in particular determining the key differences between the principles and procedures of criminal liability and the criminal justice process and regulation. The line between criminal law and torts has also been the object of economic analysis. In his chapter, Antony Dnes, explains the theory and empirical work concerning the overlap of criminal acts with tort wrongdoings.

While explaining criminal law is a matter of importance for law and economics, procedure is instrumental in understanding how criminal law enforcement operates. A leading scholar on the law and economics of criminal procedure, Thomas Miceli, summarizes the current understanding. Criminal procedure concerns the rules governing the treatment of criminal defendants from the time of their arrest up to the determination of a final verdict. From an economic perspective, the goal of this process is to achieve the most accurate determination of guilt at the lowest possible cost. The process encompasses plea bargaining, the bail system, rules regarding the determination of guilt at trial, and appeal. Criminal procedure also affects deterrence because it ultimately determines the expected punishment imposed on offenders. However, uncertainty in enforcement necessarily leads to a conflict between the goals of deterrence and error avoidance. In the following chapter, Oren Gazal-Ayal and Limor Riza, expand the discussion on plea-bargaining and the nature of public prosecution. The final chapter on procedure is by Keith Hylton and Vikramaditya Khanna. They explain criminal procedure from a political economy perspective, in particular, the extent to which procedural rules and practices are tailored to regulate rent seeking behavior in the criminal law enforcement process.

Joanna Shepherd looks at capital punishment, a topic she has written about in some of the most relevant articles in the field. She reviews the empirical literature on the deterrence and brutalization effects of the death penalty, addressing the current controversies in this matter.

The following chapters of the book deal with particular areas within criminal law that deserve significant attention from legal economists. Wallace Mullin and Christopher M. Snyder look at corporate criminal liability, Vimal Kumar and Stergios Skaperdas discuss organized crime, Roger Bowles provides an overview of corruption and criminal law, Luigi Franzoni looks at tax evasion and avoidance, Michael Faure discusses environmental crime, Mark Cohen analyses the new cyber crimes, and Nuno Garoupa, Jonathan Klick and Francesco Parisi review terrorism from a criminal law perspective.

The volume concludes with a chapter by two leading experts on behavioral law and economics, Richard McAdams and Thomas Ulen. They discuss criminal law and economics in light of recent developments in the behavioral sciences.

The organization of the book allows different reading strategies. Those who look for a quick introduction should concentrate on the first chapters that discuss the economic model of criminal law and economics generally. Those who have a more concrete interest in a particular topic may find the more applied chapters of more interest. Furthermore, the authors go beyond providing an authoritative review of the current state of the art. They identify important gaps in the literature and discuss the new routes taken by recent research. This makes each chapter unique in condensing current knowledge with cutting-edge research, paving the way for future developments.

1 Public enforcement of law

*A. Mitchell Polinsky and Steven Shavell**

1. Introduction

Public enforcement of law – the use of governmental agents to detect and to sanction violators of legal rules – is a subject of obvious importance. Police and prosecutors endeavor to solve crimes and to punish criminals, regulators attempt to control violations of environmental, safety, consumer protection, and financial disclosure laws, and agents of the Internal Revenue Service seek to enforce the tax code.

The earliest economically oriented writing on the subject of public law enforcement dates from the eighteenth century contributions of Montesquieu (1748), Beccaria (1767), and, especially, Bentham (1789). Curiously, after Bentham, the subject of law enforcement lay essentially dormant in economic scholarship until the late 1960s, when Becker (1968) published a highly influential article. Since then, several hundred articles have been written on the economics of law enforcement.[1]

The main purpose of our chapter is to present the economic theory of public law enforcement in a systematic and comprehensive way.[2] The theoretical core of our analysis addresses the following basic questions: Should the form of the sanction imposed on a liable party be a fine, an

---

* Stanford Law School and National Bureau of Economic Research; and Harvard Law School and National Bureau of Economic Research. Research for this chapter was supported by the John M. Olin law and economics programs at Stanford Law School and Harvard Law School. An essentially identical version of this chapter appeared as 'The Theory of Public Enforcement of Law' in A. Mitchell Polinsky and Steven Shavell (eds), *Handbook of Law and Economics*, volume 1 (Amsterdam: North Holland, 2007), pp. 403–54. A previous essay was published by the *Journal of Economic Literature* under the title 'The Economic Theory of Public Enforcement of Law' in 2000. Reproduction has been kindly permitted by the American Economic Association.

1 See, for example, the references cited in Bouckaert and De Geest (1992, pp. 504–26), Garoupa (1997), Mookherjee (1997), and Polinsky and Shavell (2000a).

2 For other surveys of the theory of public enforcement, see Garoupa (1997) and Mookherjee (1997). For surveys of empirical research on law enforcement and crime, see Eide (2000) and Levitt and Miles (2007), and for a survey of empirical research on enforcement of environmental regulation, see Cohen (1999, pp. 78–95).

imprisonment term, or a combination of the two? Should the rule of liability be strict or fault-based? If violators are caught only with a probability, how should the level of the sanction be adjusted? How much of society's resources should be devoted to apprehending violators?

The chapter is outlined as follows. We begin in section 2 by considering the rationale for public enforcement of law, that is, by asking why society cannot rely exclusively on private enforcement of law to control undesirable behavior. We then state the problem of public enforcement of law in general terms in section 3. In sections 4 through 6, we analyze strict liability and fault-based liability when enforcement is certain, first considering monetary sanctions, next non-monetary sanctions, and then the two together. In sections 7 through 9, we perform the same analysis when enforcement is uncertain because it is costly. In section 10 we summarize the theory, and in section 11 we discuss enforcement practices in the light of the theory we have reviewed.

We subsequently examine a variety of extensions of our core analysis in sections 12 through 28. These concern mistake, the costs of imposing sanctions, marginal deterrence, the settlement process, self-reporting of violations, corruption of law enforcers, and the fairness of sanctions, among other topics. We conclude in section 29.

2. Why public enforcement rather than private enforcement?

Before proceeding, we should comment on the rationale for public, as opposed to private, law enforcement, where, by the latter, we mean the bringing of suits by victims of harm or those threatened by harm. An important element of the justification for private enforcement concerns information about the identity of violators. When victims of harm naturally possess knowledge of who injured them, allowing private suits for harm will motivate victims to initiate legal action and thus will harness the information they have for purposes of law enforcement. This may help to explain why, for example, the enforcement of contract law and tort law is primarily private in nature: a victim of a contract breach obviously knows who committed the breach, and a victim of a tort usually knows who the tortfeasor was. When, however, victims cannot easily identify who injured them, it may be desirable for public enforcement to be employed.

For public enforcement to be preferred in such circumstances, one still needs to explain why society cannot rely on rewards of some type to private parties other than victims (such as friends of violators or entrepreneurial private enforcers) to supply information and otherwise help in detecting violators. A difficulty with reliance on private enforcement of this sort is that if a reward is available to everyone, there might be wasteful effort devoted to finding violators (akin to excessive effort to catch fish from a common pool). Another problem is that private parties may find it hard to capture fully the benefits of developing expensive, but socially worthwhile, information systems to aid enforcement (such as computerized databases of fingerprint records). An additional obstacle to private enforcement is that force may be needed to gather information, capture violators, and prevent reprisal, yet the state frequently, if not usually, will not want to permit private parties to use force. For the preceding reasons, public enforcement often will be favored when effort is required to identify and apprehend violators.[3]

3. The general problem of public law enforcement

The general problem of public law enforcement may be viewed as one of maximizing social welfare. By social welfare, we refer to the benefits that individuals obtain from their behavior, less the costs that they incur to avoid causing harm, the harm that they do cause, the cost of catching violators, and the costs of imposing sanctions on them (including any costs associated with risk aversion). We will be explicit below about the definition of social welfare in the various contexts that we consider.

The state has four major policy choices to make in undertaking law enforcement. One is about the sanctioning rule. The rule could be *strict* in the sense that a party is sanctioned whenever he has been found to have caused harm (or expected harm). Alternatively, the rule could be *fault-based*, meaning that a party who has been found to have caused harm is sanctioned only if he failed to obey some standard of behavior or regulatory requirement.

A second choice of the state concerns the form of the sanction: monetary versus non-monetary (both may be employed together). We focus on imprisonment as the primary type of non-monetary sanction and we assume that monetary sanctions are socially less costly to employ than imprisonment.

A third choice involves the magnitude of the sanction.

And the fourth choice concerns the probability of detecting offenders

---

[3] The differences between public and private enforcement have been discussed by Becker and Stigler (1974), Landes and Posner (1975), and Polinsky (1980a); see also Shavell (1993) and Friedman (1995). In this chapter, we assume for simplicity that public enforcement is the exclusive means of enforcement, even though in practice private parties sometimes play a complementary role by supplying information to enforcement authorities and by bringing private suits. We also abstract from private parties' efforts to protect themselves from harm (and how such efforts might relate to public enforcement), though we mention this issue in the conclusion.

and imposing sanctions. This probability depends on the public resources devoted to finding violators and proving that they are liable.[4]

A. BASIC THEORY WHEN ENFORCEMENT IS CERTAIN

4. Monetary sanctions

In this section we analyze the optimal magnitude of monetary sanctions – which we call fines – assuming that enforcement is certain. We consider the two basic forms of liability, beginning with strict liability.

Suppose that individuals would obtain a gain from committing a harmful act, where the gain varies among them. If an individual does commit the act, he will have to pay a fine because he is strictly liable. Let

g = gain an individual obtains if he commits the harmful act;
$z(g)$ = density of gains among individuals;
h = harm caused by an individual if he commits the harmful act;[5]
f = fine; and
w = level of wealth of an individual.

The gain could be a literal benefit, for instance, the utility obtained from taking food from a cabin in the wilderness, or the savings from not investing in some precaution, such as not obtaining pollution control equipment.[6] The fine cannot exceed an individual's level of wealth, which is assumed to be the same for everyone.

An individual will commit the harmful act if and only if his gain from doing so exceeds the fine:[7] $g > f$.

Social welfare equals the gains individuals obtain from committing the harmful act less the harm caused.[8] Social welfare is not directly affected

---

[4] The framework for studying public law enforcement employed in this chapter derives, in many respects, from Bentham (1789). Becker (1968) first stated the enforcement problem in formal economic terms and added the choice of the probability of detection to Bentham's expression of the enforcement problem.

[5] If the harm is uncertain, h can be interpreted as expected harm instead of actual harm; see section 12.

[6] For simplicity, we assume that the gain is not itself available to pay the fine. This assumption would hold if the gain were non-monetary, as in the example of the utility benefit from taking food from a cabin. In many circumstances, the assumption would not be fitting, but the complications introduced by considering how the gain enhances an individual's ability to pay a fine would be distracting.

[7] We assume for simplicity that he does not commit the harmful act if he is indifferent.

[8] Some writers have questioned whether gains from committing harmful acts

by the imposition of fines because the payment of a fine is assumed to be a socially costless transfer of money.[9] Since the individuals who commit the harmful act are those whose gains exceed the fine, social welfare is

$$\int_{f}^{\infty} (g - h)z(g)dg. \tag{1.1}$$

The enforcement authority's problem is to maximize social welfare by choosing the fine f. We use an asterisk to denote the optimal value of the fine (and other variables below). It is clear from (1.1) that

$$f^* = h, \tag{1.2}$$

assuming that such a fine is feasible. Hence, individuals commit the harmful act if and only if their gain exceeds the harm, which is first-best behavior. Note, however, that there will be underdeterrence if the individual's wealth is less than h, in which case the optimal fine equals the individual's wealth.

Now consider the fault-based sanctioning rule, in which an individual who causes harm is sanctioned only if he failed to obey some standard of behavior. In the present framework, we assume that if an individual commits a harmful act, his gain must equal or exceed some threshold level of gain in order for him to escape liability; otherwise, he is considered to be at fault. Let

$\hat{g}$ = threshold level of gain under the fault-based sanctioning rule.

If an individual's gain is less than $\hat{g}$ he will commit the harmful act whenever $g > f$, while if his gain equals or exceeds $\hat{g}$, he will commit the harmful act regardless of his gain. In other words, the individual will commit the harmful act under fault-based liability if $g > \min(f, \hat{g})$. Thus, social welfare is

---

should necessarily be credited in social welfare; see, for example, Stigler (1970, p. 527) and Lewin and Trumbull (1990). If the gains from some type of harmful conduct were excluded from social welfare, the main consequence for our analysis would be that, for this type of conduct, society would want to achieve greater, possibly complete, deterrence. That, in turn, would tend to make a higher sanction and a higher probability of detection desirable.

[9] In practice, of course, some costs are incurred in collecting fines, such as the cost of identifying and confiscating the individual's assets if the individual resists paying the fine. We discuss the implications of such costs in section 16.

$$\int_{\min(f,\hat{g})}^{\infty} (g - h)z(g)dg. \tag{1.3}$$

The enforcement authority's problem is to maximize (3) by choosing the standard $\hat{g}$ and the fine f. It is straightforward to see that

$$f^* = \hat{g}^* = h \tag{1.4}$$

results in first-best behavior. In particular, if $g < h$, the individual would be at fault if he committed the harmful act, and would bear a fine equal to h, so he would not commit it. If $g \geq h$, he would not be at fault if he committed the harmful act and therefore would not have to pay anything, so he would commit the act. Note that f^* and $\hat{g}^*$ are not unique: first-best behavior also can be achieved by setting $\hat{g} > h$, with $f = h$, or by keeping $\hat{g} = h$ and setting $f > h$.

Although we have seen that the first-best outcome can be achieved under both strict liability and fault-based liability (when a fine equal to h is feasible), the two forms of liability differ in the information required to implement them. To apply strict liability, the state only needs to know the harm. Under fault-based liability, however, the state needs to know more: it also needs to ascertain the gain of the individual (to determine whether he was at fault).

To illustrate strict and fault-based liability, suppose that a firm contemplates whether to discharge a pollutant that would cause harm h, rather than to transport it to a waste disposal site at cost g. Under strictly imposed fines, the firm would incur a fine of h if it pollutes, so would not do so unless its savings from not transporting the waste, g, is greater than h. Under fault-based fines, a polluting firm would incur a fine of h only if the cost of transporting the waste g is less than h; thus, the firm would pollute only if $g \geq h$.

5. Non-monetary sanctions

In this section we analyze the optimal magnitude of non-monetary sanctions – which we assume to be prison sentences[10] – when enforcement is certain. Let

---

[10] It will be clear that most of what we have to say about imprisonment here and in subsequent sections would carry over, with only slight modification, to other forms of non-monetary sanctions, such as probation, electronic monitoring, community service, or, in the extreme, the death penalty.

s = length of prison sentence, where s is in $[0, s_M]$; and
$d(s)$ = disutility from prison sentence of length s; $d(0) = 0$; $d'(s) > 0$.

The maximum sentence s_M can be interpreted as life imprisonment, and is assumed to be the same for everyone.

Under strict liability, if an individual commits the harmful act, he will bear a prison sentence.[11] Thus, he will commit the act if and only if his gain from doing so exceeds the disutility of the prison sentence: $g > d(s)$.

Social welfare equals the gains individuals obtain from committing the harmful act, less the harm caused, and less the cost of imposing prison sentences. The cost of prison sentences is the sum of the disutility suffered by the sanctioned individuals and the cost to the state of maintaining a prison system. Let

c = cost to the state per unit of prison sentence; $c > 0$.

Thus, social welfare is

$$\int_{d(s)}^{\infty} [g - h - (d(s) + cs)]z(g)dg. \tag{1.5}$$

The enforcement authority's problem is to maximize social welfare by choosing the prison sentence s. From (1.5), the first-order condition can be written as

$$(h + cs)(dZ(d(s))/ds) = \int_{d(s)}^{\infty} [d'(s) + c]z(g)dg, \tag{1.6}$$

where $Z(.)$ is the cumulative distribution function for $z(.)$. The left-hand side is the marginal benefit of raising s: $h + cs$ is the social gain from deterring the marginal individuals, while $dZ(d(s))/ds$ is the number of such individuals deterred.[12] The right-hand side is the marginal cost of raising s:

11 Strict liability is in fact an unusual form of liability when the sanction is imprisonment. (An example of a strict liability criminal offense is the serving of liquor by a bar to under-age individuals.) As will be seen, fault-based liability tends to be superior to strict liability when the sanction is imprisonment.

12 The disutility of imprisonment and the benefit from committing the harmful act do not appear in (1.6) because they offset each other for the marginal person.

individuals who are not deterred incur additional disutility $d'(s)$ and cause the state to incur additional imprisonment costs c.

The optimal prison sentence could lead to either underdeterrence or overdeterrence due to the costs of prison sentences. To see why, suppose the sentence were such that individuals committed the harmful act if and only if their gain equaled the harm. If the sentence were raised above this level, some individuals would be deterred, which would reduce prison costs, but those who were not deterred would bear longer sentences. Depending on which effect is stronger, it may be desirable to raise, or lower, the sentence, leading to overdeterrence or underdeterrence. Note that a marginal change of the sentence from the initial level does not affect the gains net of the harm because the marginal individuals are those whose gains equal the harm.[13]

Regardless of whether the optimal prison sentence causes underdeterrence or overdeterrence, the strict sanctioning rule does not achieve the first-best outcome because it leads to the imposition of costly sanctions.

Now consider the fault-based sanctioning rule, with a standard $\hat{g}$. Analogously to the case of fines, an individual will commit the harmful act under fault-based liability if $g > \min(s, \hat{g})$. If $s < \hat{g}$, then there will be some individuals who commit the harmful act who will be found at fault, those for whom $s < g < \hat{g}$. Then social welfare would be

$$\int_{s}^{\infty} (g - h)z(g)dg - \int_{s}^{\hat{g}} (d(s) + cs)z(g)dg. \qquad (1.7)$$

If $s \geq \hat{g}$, then social welfare is

$$\int_{\hat{g}}^{\infty} (g - h)z(g)dg. \qquad (1.8)$$

The enforcement authority's problem is to maximize (1.7) or (1.8) by choosing the standard $\hat{g}$ and the sentence s. It is straightforward to see that

$$s^* = \hat{g}^* = h \qquad (1.9)$$

[13] The point that underdeterrence or overdeterrence may result when the prison sentence is optimally chosen was made by Polinsky and Shavell (1984, p. 94). See also Kaplow (1990b).

results in the first-best outcome. First observe that first-best behavior will occur. In particular, if $g < h$, the individual would be at fault if he committed the harmful act, and would bear a sentence equal to h, so he would not commit it. If $g \geq h$, he would not be at fault if he committed the harmful act and therefore would not bear any sentence, so he would commit the act. Second, given (1.9), costly sanctions will not be imposed because individuals will never choose to be at fault. Hence, the first-best outcome is achieved. Note that s^* and $\hat{g}^*$ are not unique: the first-best outcome also can be achieved by keeping $\hat{g} = h$ and setting $s > h$.

The preceding discussion shows that when sanctions are costly, the fault-based sanctioning rule is superior to the strict sanctioning rule. Not only does the fault-based rule lead to first-best deterrence, it does so without anyone actually incurring a costly sanction.[14]

6. Combined sanctions

In this section we consider the optimal mix of fines and imprisonment sanctions when they can be used together. Under the strict sanctioning rule, social welfare in this case is

$$\int_{f+d(s)}^{\infty} [g - h - (d(s) + cs)]z(g)dg. \tag{1.10}$$

First observe that it cannot be optimal to employ a prison sentence unless the fine has been set as high as possible, equal to individuals' wealth level w. To see why, suppose otherwise, that $f < w$ and $s > 0$. Then it would be possible to raise f and lower s so as to keep $f + d(s)$ constant, thereby leaving behavior unaffected but lowering the cost of imprisonment (see (1.10)).

Whether it is optimal to use a prison sentence in addition to a fine depends on whether a fine alone is sufficient to achieve first-best deterrence. If wealth levels are high enough, if $w \geq h$, then a fine equal to harm is feasible and there would be no need for a prison sentence. If, however, $w < h$, then relying on fines alone would lead to underdeterrence and it might be desirable to employ a prison sentence in addition to the maximal fine of w. To see whether a prison sentence would be desirable in these

---

14 This advantage of the fault-based rule was originally emphasized in Shavell (1987b), which also considered the possibility of error, and thus of the bearing of sanctions. On the latter issue, see section 15 below.

circumstances, consider the derivative of (1.10) with respect to the sentence s when $f = w$:

$$[h - w + cs][dZ(w + d(s))/ds] - \int_{w+d(s)}^{\infty} (d'(s) + c)]z(g)dg. \tag{1.11}$$

It follows that the condition for a positive prison sentence to be optimal is that

$$[h - w][dZ(w)/ds] > \int_{w}^{\infty} (d'(0) + c)]z(g)dg. \tag{1.12}$$

The left-hand side of (1.12) is the value of deterring the marginal individuals, while the right-hand side is the marginal cost of imposing prison sentences on individuals who are not deterred. If a positive prison sentence is socially desirable, it is determined from the first-order condition associated with (1.11).

Next consider the optimal mix of fines and imprisonment under the fault-based sanctioning rule. The key point is that, unlike under strict liability, it is always desirable to employ prison sentences to obtain compliance with the fault standard if fines alone are inadequate to do so. This is because, as noted above, sanctions are not actually imposed when the fault standard is complied with, so there is no social cost from using the threat of prison sentences to obtain compliance. Thus, any combination of fines and prison sentences that induces potential offenders to comply with the fault standard is optimal.

B. BASIC THEORY WHEN ENFORCEMENT IS UNCERTAIN

In this part we investigate the level of enforcement resources that the state should devote to detecting offenders. We assume that the higher the level of expenditures on enforcement, the greater is the probability of detection. Let

e = enforcement expenditures by the state; and
$p(e)$ = probability of detection given e; $p'(e) > 0$; $p''(e) < 0$.

We derive the optimal probability of detection[15] and, along with it, the optimal magnitude of sanctions.[16]

7. Monetary sanctions

In this section we analyze the optimal probability and magnitude of fines, first assuming that individuals are risk neutral and then that they are risk averse.

7.1 The risk-neutral case

Under the strict liability rule, an individual will commit the harmful act if and only if his gain from doing so exceeds the expected fine: $g > pf$. Social welfare, which now reflects the enforcement expenditures of the state, is

$$\int_{p(e)f}^{\infty} (g - h)z(g)dg - e. \tag{1.13}$$

The enforcement authority's problem is to maximize (1.13) by choosing enforcement expenditures e (and thus the probability of detection p), as well as the level of the fine f.

Before considering the complete problem, suppose that enforcement expenditures are fixed, resulting in the probability of detection p. It is obvious that if $pf = h$, namely, the expected fine equals the harm, (1.13) will be maximized over f since the first-best outcome will be achieved. In other words,

$$f^* = h/p, \tag{1.14}$$

assuming that such a fine is feasible. Individuals then commit the harmful act if and only if their gain exceeds the harm, which is first-best

---

[15] We implicitly assume that enforcement expenditures e determine a single probability of detection. Thus, we do not consider an issue identified by Lando and Shavell (2004), that it may be advantageous to concentrate enforcement resources on a subset of potential offenders (for example, by auditing taxpayers whose last names begin with certain letters) rather than to spread enforcement resources evenly.

[16] Although we assume that the probability of detection can be set independently of the level of sanctions, the two might be connected. This is because high sanctions may lead juries to be less likely to convict defendants, or may induce individuals to engage in greater efforts to avoid detection; on these points, see Andreoni (1991) and Malik (1990), respectively. See also Bar-Gill and Harel (2001) for a discussion of how the level of crime affects both the probability and magnitude of sanctions.

behavior.[17] Note, however, that there will be underdeterrence if individuals' wealth is less than h/p, in which case the optimal fine equals their wealth.

Now suppose that both enforcement expenditures and the fine are chosen by the state.[18] Then the optimal fine is maximal: $f^* = w$. To demonstrate this, suppose that f is less than w. Then f can be raised and e lowered so as to keep $p(e)f$ – the level of deterrence – constant. Because the behavior of individuals is unaffected but enforcement expenditures fall, social welfare rises (the first term in (1.13) does not change but e is lower). Hence, the optimal f cannot be less than w. In other words, because any particular level of deterrence can be achieved with different combinations of the fine and the probability of detection, society should employ the highest possible fine and a correspondingly low probability of detection in order to economize on enforcement expenditures.[19]

We next show that the optimal probability of detection is such that the expected fine is less than the harm, $p(e^*)w < h$ – that is, some degree of underdeterrence is desirable. Observe that the first-order condition determining optimal enforcement expenditures e^* is

$$[h - p(e)w][dZ(p(e)w)/de] = 1. \qquad (1.15)$$

The left-hand side is the marginal social benefit of the deterrent effect from a higher probability of detection. The right-hand side is the marginal cost of greater spending on enforcement. It follows from (1.15) that $p(e^*)w < h$. To explain this result, suppose that p were such that $pw = h$. Then there would be no first-order loss of social welfare from lowering p

17 The general formula (1.14), or its equivalent, was put forward by Bentham (1789, p. 173), was emphasized by Becker (1968), and has been noted by many others since then.

18 Consideration of this issue originated with Becker (1968); as we noted, early writers on law enforcement did not examine the issue of the choice of enforcement effort.

19 Although the general point that a low probability–high fine combination conserves enforcement costs is due to Becker (1968), he did not formally consider bounds on fines (and much of his analysis implicitly presumes that the optimal fine is not maximal). Carr-Hill and Stern (1979, pp. 300–04) and Polinsky and Shavell (1979, pp. 883–4) observed that Becker's argument implies that the optimal fine is equal to its upper bound. Many scholars have noted the unrealism of this result and have introduced additional considerations that imply that less-than-maximal fines are optimal. We will discuss several important factors of this type, including risk aversion, general enforcement, and marginal deterrence. See also Andreoni (1991), Bebchuk and Kaplow (1992, 1993), Malik (1990), and Polinsky and Shavell (1991, 2000b) for discussion of other such considerations.

because the individuals who would be induced to engage in the harmful activity would obtain gains equal to harm. But enforcement costs would be saved, making it desirable to lower the probability. How much p should be lowered depends on the resulting savings in enforcement expenses compared to the net social costs of underdeterrence.[20]

Under fault-based liability, analogues of the above conclusions hold. The optimal fine is maximal and the optimal probability of detection is such that the expected fine is less than the harm. Moreover, the optimal fault standard is less than the first-best standard. The explanation for these results is essentially that given above. The fine is maximal in order to reduce the probability of detection and thereby save enforcement costs, and some underdeterrence is desirable because this also allows savings in enforcement costs.

7.2 The risk-averse case

Now suppose that individuals are risk averse and that social welfare is the sum of expected utilities of individuals (in the risk-neutral case, social welfare was equivalent to the sum of utilities). For convenience, assume that the risk of being harmed is the same for everyone and that individuals buy insurance against harm, paying a premium equal to the expected harm. An individual's wealth is his initial wealth, less the taxes he pays, less the expected harm he suffers, and less the fine if he has to pay it. Let

$U(.)$ = utility of wealth; U is concave in wealth;
t = tax; and
λ = fraction of population that commits the harmful act.

Both t and λ are endogenous.

An individual will commit the harmful act if $g + (1 - p)U(w - t - \lambda h) + pU(w - t - \lambda h - f)$ is greater than $U(w - t - \lambda h)$, or equivalently, if

$$g > p[U(w - t - \lambda h) - U(w - t - \lambda h - f)]. \qquad (1.16)$$

Note that we are implicitly assuming that the gain g is non-monetary.[21] The condition (1.16) implicitly determines the fraction of the population λ that commits the harmful act. The tax t is such that the government breaks

[20] The point of this paragraph – that some underdeterrence is optimal – was first made by Polinsky and Shavell (1984).

[21] If the gain were monetary, then the condition would become $(1 - p)U(w + g - t - \lambda h) + pU(w + g - t - \lambda h - f) > U(w - t - \lambda h)$. The qualitative nature of the results in this section would not be affected.

even; hence t equals the enforcement cost e less the fine revenue collected, λpf.

Social welfare, the sum of individuals' expected utilities, equals

$$(1 - \lambda) U(w - t - \lambda h) + \int_{p[U(w-t-\lambda h) - U(w-t-\lambda h-f)]}^{\infty} [g + (1 - p) U(w - t - \lambda h) + pU(w - t - \lambda h - f)] z(g) dg - e, \quad (1.17)$$

since the individuals who commit the harmful act are those whose gains exceed the expected disutility of the fine.

Suppose initially that the probability of detection is fixed. Then the optimal fine in the risk-averse case tends to be lower than that in the risk-neutral case for two reasons. First, lowering the fine reduces the bearing of risk by individuals who commit the harmful act. Second, because risk-averse individuals are more easily deterred than risk-neutral individuals, the fine does not need to be as high to achieve any desired degree of deterrence.[22]

Now consider choosing both the probability and magnitude of fines. The optimal fine generally is not at its maximum when individuals are risk averse. This is because the use of a very high fine would impose a substantial risk-bearing cost on individuals who commit the harmful act. More precisely, reconsider the argument employed in the risk-neutral case. If f is less than the maximal fine (now $w - t - \lambda h$), it still is true that f can be raised and e lowered so as to keep deterrence constant. But due to risk aversion, the probability of detection that maintains deterrence falls *more* than proportionally, implying that the expected fine, and therefore fine revenue, falls. This reduction in fine revenue reflects the disutility caused by imposing greater risk on risk-averse individuals. If individuals are sufficiently risk averse, the decline in fine revenue associated with greater risk bearing could more than offset the savings in enforcement expenditures from reducing the probability of detection, implying that social welfare would be lower.[23]

---

22 It is possible, however, that the optimal fine is higher in the risk-averse case than in the risk-neutral case, for the following reason. A way to reduce the bearing of risk is to deter more individuals from committing the harmful act, for then fewer individuals will be subject to the risk of the fine. See Kaplow (1992).

23 The point that the optimal fine may be less than maximal when individuals

In effect, when individuals are risk averse, fines become a socially costly sanction (reflected in an increase in taxes) rather than a mere transfer of wealth. The more risk-averse individuals are, the better it is to control their behavior by using a lower fine and a higher probability of detection, even though this raises enforcement costs.

As in the risk-neutral case, there is a reason when individuals are risk averse to reduce enforcement costs by setting the probability such that some individuals will commit the harmful act even though their gain is less than the harm – meaning that there will be some underdeterrence.[24]

Under fault-based liability, the conclusions are different from those under strict liability. The differences are due to the fact that individuals are induced to comply with the fault standard and therefore do not bear risk. Consequently, the results are the same as those in the risk-neutral case: the optimal fine is maximal; the optimal probability is relatively low; and the optimal fault standard is such that there is some underdeterrence.

Because, as just emphasized, fines are not actually imposed under fault-based liability; fault-based liability is superior to strict liability, under which risk is borne. This advantage of fault-based liability is analogous to the advantage of fault-based liability over strict liability when imprisonment is used – a costly sanction is not actually imposed.

Another advantage of fault-based liability is that it may result in lower enforcement expenditures than under strict liability. Specifically, because fines are not imposed under fault-based liability, it becomes desirable to use a high (maximal) fine, which allows a relatively low probability of detection to be employed.

Of course, in reality, as we will be discussing below, mistakes may occur under fault-based liability, resulting in the imposition of risk. To the extent that risk exists under fault-based liability, the main result obtained under strict liability – that fines should not be maximal – carries over to fault-based liability.

---

are risk averse was proved initially by Polinsky and Shavell (1979) in a model with two levels of gain. See also Kaplow (1992), who demonstrates in an example that the fine may be less than maximal. It can be shown in the general model under discussion here that the optimal fine must be less than maximal if the cost of raising the probability of detection is sufficiently small (given that the wealth of individuals is not too low). The idea of the proof is that, if the cost of raising the probability were zero, the optimal probability would be one and the optimal fine less than maximal (equal to the harm). The conclusion follows by a continuity argument.

24 It also is possible, however, that overdeterrence would be optimal. The reason is that the imposition of risk can be reduced by discouraging individuals from engaging in the harmful activity.

8. Non-monetary sanctions

In this section we analyze the optimal probability and magnitude of prison sentences, first assuming that individuals are risk neutral, then that they are risk averse, and finally that they are risk preferring. The last case is of particular relevance for imprisonment sanctions, as will be explained.

8.1 The risk-neutral case

We assume here that $d(s) = s$, that is, that the disutility of imprisonment rises in proportion to the length of the sentence. This implies that individuals are indifferent between a sure sentence of s and an uncertain sentence with a mean of s. Thus, individuals display a risk-neutral attitude towards imprisonment sentences.

Under the strict liability rule, an individual will commit the harmful act if and only if his gain exceeds the expected sentence: $g > ps$. Social welfare is

$$\int_{p(e)s}^{\infty} (g - h - p(e)(s + cs))z(g)dg - e. \tag{1.18}$$

The enforcement authority's problem is to maximize (1.18) by choosing enforcement expenditures e and the length of the sentence s.

In this case the optimal sentence is maximal: $s^* = s_M$. As seen above, when the sanction is a fine, the optimal sanction is maximal. This is also true here even though the sanction is costly to impose. To demonstrate that $s^* = s_M$, suppose that s is less than s_M. Then s can be raised and e lowered so as to keep $p(e)s$ constant. The behavior of individuals is unaffected because $p(e)s$ has not changed. The social cost of imprisonment also is unaffected because $p(e)(s + cs)$ is constant. In other words, although the sentence is higher, proportionally fewer individuals are imprisoned. But because enforcement expenditures fall, social welfare rises. Hence, the optimal s equals s_M.

The optimal probability of detection is such that the expected prison sentence could lead to either underdeterrence or overdeterrence. This is essentially for the reasons discussed above (see section 5) when the probability of detection was fixed at one. Here, however, there is an additional factor favoring underdeterrence, namely that by lowering the probability, enforcement resources are saved.

Under fault-based liability, first observe that it must be optimal to have compliance with the fault standard. If the expected sentence were less than the standard, so that some individuals would choose to violate the standard and bear the expected sentence, then it would be optimal to lower the standard to the expected sentence. For then, the behavior of individuals would be the same, but the cost of imprisonment would be avoided.

Next observe that the expected sentence must equal the standard, rather than be higher. Otherwise, the probability of detection could be lowered without affecting behavior, but enforcement costs would be saved.

It is clear, too, that the optimal sentence must be maximal. This is for the now familiar reason that, otherwise, the sentence could be raised and the probability of detection lowered proportionally, without affecting behavior, but saving enforcement expenditures (imprisonment costs are zero because of compliance with the standard).[25] Given $s^* = s_M$, the optimal probability satisfies $p(e)s_M = \hat{g}$ because of our observation in the previous paragraph.

The optimal standard $\hat{g}^*$ is less than the harm h; in other words, there is some underdeterrence. This is true for a reason already discussed: by lowering the standard, enforcement costs are saved, but there is no first-order effect on social welfare due to more individuals committing the harmful act because their gain equals the harm.

Finally, as we previously emphasized, fault-based liability possesses the advantage over strict liability that costly sanctions are not actually imposed (in the absence of mistakes). Moreover, because the optimal sentence is maximal for this reason, a low probability of detection can be used.

8.2 The risk-averse case

We assume now that the disutility of the sentence $d(s)$ rises more than in proportion to the sentence. This could occur because of an increasing desire of a prisoner to join the outside world or a growing distaste for the prison environment as time in jail increases. This assumption implies that individuals prefer a sure sentence of s to an uncertain sentence with a mean of s. In other words, individuals are risk averse in imprisonment sentences.

Under the strict liability rule, an individual will commit the harmful act if and only if his gain exceeds the expected disutility of the sentence, $g > pd(s)$, and social welfare is

$$\int_{p(e)s}^{\infty} (g - h - p(e)(d(s) + cs))z(g)dg - e. \tag{1.19}$$

---

[25] Note, too, that the expected sentence remains constant, so even if imprisonment costs were borne, they would not change.

The optimal sentence is again maximal: $s^* = s_M$. The reasons given in the risk-neutral case are reinforced here. As s is raised and e lowered so as to keep $p(e)d(s)$ and the behavior of individuals constant, p declines proportionally more than s rises because of individuals' risk aversion. In other words, ps declines, which implies that the public cost of imprisonment pcs falls.[26] Hence, social welfare rises because both the cost of enforcement declines and the cost of imprisonment declines.

The optimal probability of detection is such that, as in the risk-neutral case, the expected prison sentence could lead to underdeterrence or overdeterrence.

Under fault-based liability, the results are essentially the same as in the risk-neutral case because, if the fault standard is complied with, risk is not borne. Thus, it is optimal to have compliance with the fault standard; the expected disutility of the sentence must equal the standard; the optimal sentence is maximal; there is some underdeterrence; and fault-based liability is superior to strict liability. A difference, however, is that the probability of detection needed to obtain compliance with the fault standard can be lowered because individuals are risk averse.

8.3 The risk-preferring case

Finally, suppose that the disutility of the sentence $d(s)$ rises less than in proportion to the sentence. This could occur because the disutility from the stigma of being in jail might be substantial from having spent even a short amount of time there, but not increase much with the length of imprisonment.[27] Individuals' discounting of the future disutility of imprisonment also makes earlier years of imprisonment more important than later ones. The present assumption implies that individuals prefer an uncertain sentence with a mean of s to a sure sentence of s; individuals are risk preferring in imprisonment sentences.

Under the strict liability rule, social welfare is again given by (1.19). The optimal sentence, however, might be less than maximal: $s^* \leq s_M$. Now, when the sentence is raised, the probability that maintains deterrence cannot be lowered proportionally, implying that the expected prison term rises. Because the resulting increased cost to the public of imposing imprisonment sanctions might exceed the savings in enforcement expenditures

---

[26] Note the contrast with the case of risk aversion in fines, in which the decline in the expected sanction pf meant a decline in revenue to the state and thus an increase in taxes. Here the decline in the expected sanction ps means a decline in expenses to the state and thus a decrease in taxes.

[27] Also, the first years of imprisonment may create special disutility due to brutalization of the prisoner.

from lowering the probability, the optimal prison term might not be maximal.[28]

Under fault-based liability, the results are again essentially the same as in the risk-neutral case.

9. Combined sanctions

Under the strict sanctioning rule, as we explained above, it never is optimal to employ a prison sentence unless the fine has been set as high as possible, since fines are socially cheaper sanctions. Whether it is optimal to use a prison sentence in addition to the maximal fine depends on the extent of underdeterrence that would result if fines were used alone, and the social cost of imprisonment.

Under the fault-based sanctioning rule, the key point is that it is always desirable to employ the maximal prison sentence in addition to the maximal fine, since neither sanction is actually imposed. By using maximal sanctions, the probability of detection can be set at a low level, thereby saving enforcement costs.

C. BASIC THEORY SUMMARIZED AND COMPARED TO PRACTICE

10. Summary of the basic theory

In this section we summarize the main points from parts A and B:

(a) When the probability of detection of a harmful act is taken as fixed and individuals are risk neutral, the optimal fine is the harm divided by the probability of detection, for this results in an expected fine equal to the harm. However, the risk aversion of individuals tends to lower the level of the optimal fine.

(b) When the probability of detection can be varied, relatively high sanctions may be optimal, for this allows a relatively low probability to be employed and thereby saves enforcement costs. Indeed, the optimal fine is maximal if individuals are risk neutral in wealth, and the optimal imprisonment term is maximal if individuals are risk neutral or risk averse in imprisonment. Optimal sanctions might not be maximal, however, when individuals are risk averse in wealth or risk preferring in imprisonment, both plausible assumptions, although the motive to set

---

[28] The results in this section were first presented by Polinsky and Shavell (1999) (although Shavell (1991b) notes the result in the case of risk neutrality).

sanctions at relatively high levels in order to reduce enforcement costs still applies.[29]

(c) Optimal enforcement tends to be characterized by some degree of underdeterrence relative to first-best behavior, because allowing underdeterrence conserves enforcement resources. More precisely, by lowering the probability of detection slightly from a level that would lead to first-best behavior, the state reduces enforcement costs, and although more individuals commit the harmful act, these individuals do not cause social welfare to decline substantially because their gains are approximately equal to the harm.

(d) The use of fines should be exhausted before resort is made to the costlier sanction of imprisonment.

(e) An advantage of fault-based liability over strict liability is that sanctions that are costly to impose – imprisonment, and fines when individuals are risk averse – are imposed less often under the former rule. Under fault-based liability, individuals generally are induced (in the absence of mistakes) to obey fault standards, and therefore ordinarily do not bear sanctions. Under strict liability, however, individuals who cause harm are sanctioned whenever they are caught.

(f) An advantage of strict liability over fault-based liability is that the former is easier to apply. Strict liability requires the state to determine only the harm done, whereas fault-based liability requires the state to ascertain optimal behavior (in order to set the fault standard) and to observe actual behavior (in order to apply the standard).

11. Theory versus practice

Having reviewed the basic theory of public enforcement of law, we briefly comment on the relationship between optimal enforcement and enforcement in practice.

First observe that important features of actual public law enforcement are congruent, at least in a broad sense, with what is theoretically desirable. Public enforcement is often characterized by low probabilities of detection. This is true for many criminal acts, and also is frequently the case in other spheres of public enforcement, such as traffic control and tax collection.[30] That probabilities of detection are low undoubtedly reflects the cost of raising the probability, a central factor in our discussion.

---

[29] There are other reasons why optimal sanctions might not be maximal. See, for example, the discussion of general enforcement in section 17.

[30] US Department of Justice (1997b, p. 205, table 25) indicates, for example, that the likelihood of arrest was 13.8 percent for burglary, 14.0 percent for automobile theft, and 16.5 percent for arson. Kenkel (1993, p. 145) estimates that

Corresponding to the low probabilities of detection are relatively high sanctions, often exceeding harm. For example, it seems that the sentence for theft typically outweighs the harm from that act, that the penalty for double parking frequently surpasses the resulting congestion costs, and that the sanction for tax evasion tends to exceed the social losses thereby created. Sanctions that are in excess of harm are needed for proper deterrence when the probabilities of enforcement are less than one, as they are in these examples.

The theory of optimal public enforcement of law also helps to explain why society uses the sanction of imprisonment when it does – for the category of harmful acts labeled criminal, notably, for theft, robbery, rape, murder, and so forth.[31] Because such acts cause substantial harm, yet often are detected with a low probability, the magnitudes of desirable penalties are high. If these penalties were solely monetary, they often would exceed the assets of the individuals who commit the acts, for individuals who commit crimes tend to have very low assets.[32] Imprisonment sanctions, therefore, usually will be required to maintain an adequate level of deterrence of acts classified as criminal.[33]

Note, too, that the standard of liability when imprisonment sanctions are imposed is generally fault-based – imprisonment is premised on the nature of the wrongful act, not merely on the fact that harm was done. This is socially desirable because, as we stressed, fault-based liability reduces the use of socially costly sanctions.

Although actual public enforcement is consistent in many respects with the theory of optimal enforcement, actual enforcement also appears to deviate in various ways from what is theoretically desirable. We note two discrepancies of general importance. First, substantial enforcement costs could be saved without sacrificing deterrence by reducing enforcement effort and simultaneously raising fines. This is possible in many enforcement contexts because fines are presently very low relative to the assets of

---

the probability of arrest for drunk driving is 'only about .003'. And according to Andreoni et al. (1998, p. 820), the audit rate for individual tax returns was 1.7 percent in 1995.

[31] See generally Posner (1985, pp. 1201–5), Shavell (1985, pp. 1236–41), and Shavell (2004, pp. 543–68).

[32] For example, in US Department of Justice (1988, p. 35) it is reported that 'the average inmate was at the poverty level before entering jail' and in US Department of Justice (1998, p. 4) it is stated that almost half of jail inmates reported incomes of less than $600 a month in the month before their most recent arrest.

[33] The use of imprisonment sanctions also makes sense in view of their incapacitative function: crimes cause substantial harm and may be difficult or expensive to deter (for the reason we just emphasized, as well as others), so that it often will be desirable to incapacitate individuals who have committed them. See section 25.

violators. For example, fines for most parking violations are less than $50, penalties for underpayment of income taxes are typically of the order of 20 percent of the amount not paid, and fines for corporate violations of health and safety regulations are frequently minuscule in relation to corporate assets. In such areas of enforcement, therefore, fines could readily be, say, doubled and enforcement costs reduced significantly, while maintaining deterrence at present levels.

Not only can present levels of deterrence be achieved more cheaply, it also seems that these levels are often too low. This is a reasonable supposition given the limited use of fines that we just noted and the low probabilities of their application. For example, the probability of a tax audit is approximately 2 percent; when combined with the modest penalties for underpayment, one would predict substantial tax avoidance.[34] Evidence also suggests that the expected fine for driving while intoxicated is of the order of one-quarter of the expected harm caused by such behavior,[35] and that monetary sanctions imposed on corporations equal on average only 33 percent of the harms caused.[36] Given the ample opportunities that exist for augmenting penalties, as well as the possible desirability of increasing enforcement effort, society probably should raise levels of deterrence in many areas of enforcement.

D. EXTENSIONS OF THE BASIC THEORY

This concludes the presentation of the basic theory of public enforcement of law. We now turn to various extensions and refinements of the basic analysis.

---

[34] In 1995 the audit rate for individual returns was 1.7 percent, as noted above, and the civil penalty for underpayment of taxes ordinarily is calculated as 20 percent of the underpayment that results from wrongful conduct (such as substantially misstating a valuation). See Andreoni et al. (1998, p. 820). Thus, for every dollar of underpayment, the expected payment, including the underpayment and the civil penalty, is only approximately $0.02 (= 0.017 × $1.20).

[35] See Kenkel (1993, p. 145). The expected fine is $12.82 and the expected harm is $47.77 (both in 1986 dollars). While the latter number may seem low, keep in mind that it is the product of the probability that a harm will occur as a result of drunken driving, and the level of harm if harm does occur. (To properly determine whether dangerous driving is underdeterred, one also would have to take into account the threat of liability from private suits brought by accident victims. But the deterrent effect of such suits will be dulled to the extent that drivers do not have sufficient assets to pay for the harms suffered by accident victims, or have liability insurance and therefore only partially bear the financial consequences of a lawsuit.)

[36] See Cohen (1989, pp. 617–18, 658). Cohen notes, however, that he did not take into account other sanctions imposed on corporate criminals, including restitution, civil penalties, and private tort suits.

12. Accidental harms

In our analysis above, we implicitly assumed that the acts that individuals commit result in harm with certainty. In many circumstances, of course, acts result in harm only with a probability. A driver who speeds only creates a likelihood of a collision; or a firm that stores toxic chemicals in a substandard tank only creates a probability of a harmful spill.

Essentially all of the results in the basic analysis carry over in a straightforward way when harms are accidental. If individuals are risk neutral, sanctions are monetary, and the expected sanction equals harm whenever harm turns out to occur, then induced behavior will still be socially optimal; further, the optimal magnitude of sanctions is maximal if individuals are risk neutral because this allows enforcement costs to be saved, but is not necessarily maximal if individuals are risk averse, and so forth. Our general conclusions in the basic analysis can thus be interpreted to apply both when harms occur for sure and when harms occur accidentally.

There is, however, a new issue that arises when harm is uncertain: a sanction can be imposed either on the basis of the commission of a dangerous *act* that increases the chance of harm – storing chemicals in a substandard tank – or on the basis of the *actual occurrence of harm* – only if the tank ruptures and results in a spill. In principle, either approach can be employed to achieve optimal deterrence. To illustrate, suppose that the substandard tank has a 10 percent chance of rupturing, in which case the harm would be $10 million; the expected harm from using the tank therefore is $1 million. If individuals are risk neutral and sanctions are imposed only when harm occurs, deterrence will be optimal if, as usual, the sanction equals the harm of $10 million. Alternatively, if sanctions are imposed on the basis of the dangerous act of using the substandard tank, deterrence will be optimal if the owner of the tank faces a sanction equal to the expected harm due to his use of the substandard tank, $1 million.

Several factors are relevant to the choice between act-based and harm-based sanctions. First, act-based sanctions need not be as high to accomplish a given level of deterrence, and thus offer an advantage over harm-based sanctions because of limitations in parties' assets. In the example in the preceding paragraph, the owner of the storage tank might be able to pay the $1 million required if sanctions are act-based (assuming for simplicity that individuals are always found liable) but not the $10 million required if sanctions are harm-based. Second, and closely related, because act-based sanctions need not be as high to accomplish deterrence, they tend to be preferable to harm-based sanctions when parties are risk averse. Third, act-based sanctions and harm-based sanctions may differ in the ease with which they can be applied. In some circumstances, act-based sanctions may be simpler to impose (it might be less difficult to determine whether an oil shipper properly maintains its vessels' holding tanks than to detect whether one of the vessels leaked oil into the ocean); in other circumstances, harm-based sanctions may be more readily applied (a driver who causes an accident might be caught more easily than one who speeds but does not cause an accident). Fourth, it may be hard to calculate the expected harm due to an act, but relatively easy to ascertain the actual harm if it eventuates; if so, this constitutes an advantage of harm-based liability.[37]

13. Precautions

In this section we consider a model in which harm is accidental, as in the previous section, and in which the probability of harm depends on the level of precautions taken by a potential injurer. Thus, the major difference from the basic model considered in earlier sections is that the act is continuously variable. The main results of the basic analysis carry over to the model of precautions. For simplicity, we focus on the case in which enforcement is certain. Let

x = level of precautions taken by a potential injurer; and
$q(x)$ = probability of harm given x; $q'(x) < 0$; $q''(x) > 0$.

The usual social objective of maximizing social welfare now can be expressed as minimizing social costs, that is, minimizing the sum of the cost of precautions and the expected harm: $x + q(x)h$. Let $x^* > 0$ be the solution to this problem.

First consider strict liability when the sanction is a fine equal to the harm. Then an individual's problem is to minimize $x + q(x)h$, so he will choose x^* (and obviously would not if the fine did not equal harm).

Next consider fault-based liability when the standard corresponds to x^* and the sanction is a fine equal to harm. If an individual takes less precaution than x^*, he bears costs of $x + q(x)h$, while if he takes precaution equal to or greater than x^*, he bears cost of x. It is straightforward to show that he will exercise precautions equal to x^*.[38]

Thus, as in the basic theory, strict liability and fault-based liability result in the first-best outcome when sanctions are monetary and are applied for sure. Similar reasoning would demonstrate that all of the other

---

37 Act-based versus harm-based enforcement is discussed in Shavell (1993).

38 Conditional on choosing $x \geq x^*$, his best choice clearly is x^*, as that minimizes his expense, which is x^*. If he chooses $x < x^*$, his expense is $x + q(x)h$, which exceeds $x^* + q(x^*)h > x^*$. Hence, x^* is strictly optimal for him.

primary conclusions in the basic theory would carry over to the model of precautions.

To illustrate, reconsider the case when individuals are risk neutral, liability is strict, and the sanction is a fine. Social costs are $x + q(x)h + e$. The level of precautions x is determined by the individual minimizing $x + q(x)p(e)f$. Again, the optimal fine must be the individual's wealth w (otherwise, f could be raised and e lowered without affecting deterrence) and the optimal p is such that $pw < h$.[39] Therefore, at the optimum, the level of precautions is less than the first-best level.

14. Activity level

We have been assuming that the sole decision that an individual makes is whether to act in a way that causes harm when engaging in some activity. In many contexts, however, an individual also makes a choice about his *activity level* – that is, not only does he choose whether to act in a harmful way while engaging in an activity, he also chooses whether to engage in that activity, or, more generally, at what level to do so. For example, in addition to deciding whether to comply with auto emissions controls (maintaining a catalytic converter), an individual also chooses how many miles to drive; the number of miles driven is the individual's level of activity. Similarly, not only does a firm decide whether to comply with workplace safety regulations, it also chooses its level of production; the output of the firm is its level of activity.

The socially optimal activity level is such that the individual's marginal utility from the activity just equals the marginal expected harm caused by the activity. Thus, the optimal number of miles driven is the level at which the marginal utility of driving an extra mile just equals the marginal expected harm per mile driven. The determination of the optimal level of activity presumes that individuals act optimally when engaging in the activity – for example, that they drive with appropriate care.

To illustrate this formally, let

r = level of activity; and
$U(r)$ = utility from activity level r; $U'(r) > 0$; $U''(r) < 0$.

---

[39] Let $x(e)$ be the x determined by the individual's optimization problem, given $f = w$ and enforcement expenditures e. The individual minimizes $x + q(x)p(e)w$, with the resulting first-order condition $1 + q'p(e)w = 0$. The social problem is to minimize $x(e) + q(x(e))h + e$. The first-order condition can be written as $x'(1 + q'h) + 1 = 0$. We know that $x' > 0$. Therefore, it must be that $1 + q'h < 0$. Solving for q' from the individual's first-order condition and substituting it into this expression implies that $pw < h$.

We suppose that an individual chooses how much precaution to take (see the previous section) while engaging in a harm-creating activity, with the level of harm being proportional to his level of activity.[40] Then social welfare is

$$U(r) - r[x + q(x)h]. \tag{1.20}$$

Note that the optimal level of precaution x^* minimizes $x + q(x)h$, and thus is as discussed in section 13. The optimal level of activity therefore is determined by

$$U'(r) = x^* + q(x^*)h; \tag{1.21}$$

that is, the marginal utility from the activity equals the social cost of the activity, which is the sum of the cost of precautions and the expected harm.

Will parties' choices about their activity levels and precautions be socially correct under the two standards for imposing sanctions? The answer is that under strict liability, their choices about both activity levels and precautions will be socially correct. This is clear since, assuming for simplicity that enforcement is certain and the sanction is a fine equal to harm, their objective also is to maximize (1.20). In particular, because they bear a fine equal to harm, they choose the optimal level of precautions x^* when engaging in their activity. And since they incur the full social costs of precautions plus expected harm when engaging in their activity, they choose the optimal level of activity.

Under the fault-based standard, however, parties will participate in activities to a socially excessive extent. To explain, observe that parties choose the optimal level of precautions x^* in order to avoid the fine, as seen in section 13. Because parties choose this level of precautions, they will not be found liable for having violated the standard if harm occurs. Hence, their choice of activity level r is determined by maximizing $U(r) - rx^*$, with the corresponding first-order condition

$$U'(r) = x^*. \tag{1.22}$$

Comparing this to (1.21), it is evident that r exceeds r^*. The reason is that the private marginal cost of increasing participation in the activity is only

[40] We are employing the model of precautions described in the previous section for convenience. It also would be possible to develop the points about activity level using the model from the basic analysis, in which the harm-producing action of an individual is not continuously variable.

the precaution cost x^*; it does not include the expected harm. Thus, for instance, if a person complies with auto emissions standards, he will not be concerned with the fact that the more he drives, the more pollution he causes (assuming that some pollution occurs even if one obeys emissions standards). Consequently, he will drive too much.

The implication of the preceding points in relation to firms is that under the strict sanctioning rule, the product price will reflect both the cost of precautions and the expected harm caused by production, so that the price will include the full social cost of production. Hence, the amount purchased, and thus the level of production, will be socially optimal. Under the fault-based rule, however, the product price will reflect the cost of precautions but not expected harm; thus, the amount sold, and the level of production, will be excessive.[41]

These conclusions about firms are of widespread applicability. Notably, safety regulations and other regulatory requirements are often framed as standards of care that have to be met, but which, if met, free the regulated party from penalties. Hence, regulations of this character are subject to the criticism that they lead to excessive levels of the regulated activity. Making firms strictly liable for harm would be superior to safety regulation with respect to inducing socially correct activity levels.

That parties choose an excessive level of activity under the fault-based rule – of which regulation is one variant – but not under the strict liability rule, constitutes a fundamental advantage of the latter rule. This advantage is stronger the greater is the harm from engaging in the activity (given that precautions are optimal when engaging in the activity). Thus, for activities for which expected harm is likely to be substantial, the disadvantage of the fault-based standard is significant.

More generally, the advantage of strict liability over fault-based liability applies to any dimension of behavior that affects expected harm but that is not included in the definition of fault. For example, suppose that pollution damage depends both on whether a scrubber is installed as well as on the degree of care with which it is cleaned. Because the existence of a scrubber is easy to verify but its maintenance might not be, a fault-based sanctioning system might, of necessity, reflect only the first dimension of behavior. Consequently, the firm will have a socially inadequate incentive to clean the scrubber under a fault standard. This problem does not arise under a strict sanctioning system because the firm has to pay for harm regardless of its cause.

---

41 Our discussion here about activity-level considerations in the context of public enforcement closely parallels the analysis of activity-level issues in the context of tort liability. See generally Shavell (1980) and Polinsky (1980b).

15. Errors

Errors of the two classic types can occur in public enforcement of law. First, an individual who should be found liable might mistakenly not be found liable – what we will refer to as 'mistaken acquittal'. Second, an individual who should not be found liable might mistakenly be found liable – 'mistaken conviction'. For an individual who has been detected, let

ε_A = the probability of mistaken acquittal; and
ε_C = the probability of mistaken conviction.

For example, suppose police randomly monitor drivers by stopping them and administering a blood-alcohol test. The test might understate the amount of alcohol in the driver's blood and result in mistaken acquittal, or overstate the amount and lead to mistaken conviction.

We initially consider the effect of mistake in the basic model of enforcement, assuming that the sanctioning standard is strict, the sanction is a fine, and individuals are risk neutral. Given the probability of detection p and the chances of mistaken acquittal and conviction, an individual will commit the wrongful act if and only if his gain net of his expected fine if he does commit it exceeds what he bears if he does not commit it:

$$g - p(1 - \varepsilon_A)f > -p\varepsilon_C f, \tag{1.23}$$

or, equivalently, if and only if[42]

$$g > (1 - \varepsilon_A - \varepsilon_C)pf. \tag{1.24}$$

Note initially that both types of error reduce deterrence: the right-hand side of (1.24) is declining in both ε_A and ε_C. Mistaken acquittal diminishes deterrence because it lowers the expected fine if an individual violates the law. Mistaken conviction also lowers deterrence because it reduces the difference between the expected fine from violating the law and not violating it. In other words, the greater is ε_C, the smaller the increase in the expected fine if one violates the law, making a violation less costly to the individual.[43]

---

[42] We assume that $1 - \varepsilon_A - \varepsilon_C > 0$, so that the probability that a guilty person will be found liable, $1 - \varepsilon_A$, exceeds the probability that an innocent person will be found liable, ε_C.

[43] This point was first emphasized by Png (1986).

Because mistakes dilute deterrence, they tend to reduce social welfare. Specifically, to achieve any level of deterrence, it may be necessary to raise the probability of detection or the magnitude of a costly sanction to offset the effect of errors.

Now consider the optimal choice of the fine. If the probability of detection is assumed to be fixed, the dilution in deterrence caused by errors requires a higher fine to restore deterrence, so the optimal fine is higher.[44] If both the probability and the fine are policy instruments, the optimal fine remains maximal despite mistakes. The explanation is essentially that given previously: If the fine f were less than maximal, then f could be raised and the probability p lowered so as to keep deterrence constant, but saving enforcement costs.

If individuals are risk averse, however, the possibility of mistakes does affect the optimal fine. As we emphasized in section 7.2, the optimal fine generally is less than maximal when individuals are risk averse – lowering the fine reduces the bearing of risk. Introducing the possibility of mistakes may increase the desirability of lowering the fine because, due to mistaken conviction, individuals who do not violate the law are subject to the risk of having to pay a fine. Indeed, because the number of persons who do not violate the law often would far exceed the number who do, the desire to avoid imposing risk on the former group can lead to a substantial reduction in the optimal fine.[45]

The possibility of mistakes generally affects the optimal probability of detection. On one hand, the deterrence-diluting effects of mistakes means, as we noted, that a higher probability of detection may be needed to achieve any given level of deterrence; this effect tends to raise the optimal expenditure on enforcement. On the other hand, because mistakes reduce the productivity of enforcement expenditures by a factor of $1 - \varepsilon_A - \varepsilon_C$ (see (1.24)), the cost of achieving a given level of deterrence is higher; this effect tends to reduce the optimal expenditure on enforcement. Either of these effects could dominate and lead to an optimal probability of detection that is higher or lower than in the absence of mistakes.

Next, consider imprisonment and mistake. As in the case of fines, mistakes of both type dilute the deterrent effect of imprisonment. Additionally, as in the case without mistakes, the optimal imprisonment term is maximal

---

44 Specifically, to achieve first-best behavior, it must be that $(1 - \varepsilon_A - \varepsilon_C)pf = h$, which implies that f must be higher the greater are either of the errors, ε_A or ε_C.

45 Building on Polinsky and Shavell (1979), Block and Sidak (1980, pp. 1135–9) emphasize the desirability of lowering sanctions on risk-averse individuals because of mistakes.

if individuals are risk neutral or risk averse in imprisonment, but is generally not maximal if they are risk preferring in imprisonment.[46]

The possibility of mistakes also affects individuals' decisions regarding their participation in activities. Everything else equal, mistaken acquittals lead to increased engagement in the activity, and mistaken convictions result in decreased engagement. The net effect could be a socially excessive or inadequate activity level.[47]

We have not yet commented on fault-based liability and mistake. In this context, an important implication of mistake is that some individuals will bear sanctions even if they comply with the fault standard. Consequently, both types of error reduce the incentive to comply with the fault standard in the basic model, for essentially the same reasons as under strict liability.

However, in the model with variable precautions, there is a possibility that error will lead to an excessive level of precautions – above the optimal level. Assume that the actual level of precautions x is observed with an error ε. If the observed level of precautions, $\bar{x} + \varepsilon$, exceeds the standard $\bar{x}$, the person will not be liable because he will not be found to be at fault. But if $x + \varepsilon$ is less than $\bar{x}$, then the person will be liable. The person will be found mistakenly liable if x is greater than or equal to $\bar{x}$ but $x + \varepsilon$ is less than $\bar{x}$; the person will be mistakenly acquitted if x is less than $\bar{x}$ but $x + \varepsilon$ equals or exceeds $\bar{x}$. Note that the probabilities of the two types of error depend on the person's choice of x. By choosing an x above $\bar{x}$, the person can reduce the risk of mistaken conviction, and it can be shown that he will be led to choose such an excessive x under fairly general conditions. In other words, individuals will often have a motive to take excessive precautions in order to reduce the chance of erroneously being found at fault.[48]

Errors also influence individuals' participation in the activity under

---

46 That the optimal term remains maximal if individuals are risk neutral or risk averse might seem surprising because one might expect that the chance of mistaken conviction would result in a lower optimal term. But the usual argument still applies: If the term were not maximal, it could be raised and the probability of detection could be lowered at least proportionally without sacrificing deterrence. Hence, the aggregate amount of jail time served by individuals who do not commit the harmful act would remain the same or fall, and enforcement expenditures would decline.

47 Recall, too, that if the probability of detection is fixed, the fine needs to be raised to offset the deterrence-diluting effects of mistakes. Raising the fine to this extent, however, leads to an inadequate incentive to engage in the activity. This problem, in turn, can be remedied by use of an appropriate subsidy for participating in the activity. For the details behind this point, see Png (1986).

48 This point was first emphasized by Craswell and Calfee (1986).

fault-based liability, similar to the effects of errors under strict liability. The main difference is that there is a general tendency for individuals to participate in the activity to an excessive extent under fault-based liability, for the reason explained in the previous section. Only if the chance of mistaken conviction is sufficiently high would this conclusion be reversed.

Finally, observe that the probabilities of error can be influenced by policy choices. For example, prosecutorial resources can be increased in order to reduce the probability of mistaken acquittal, or the standard of proof can be raised to reduce the chance of mistaken conviction (although this presumably increases the likelihood of mistaken acquittal). Because the reduction of both types of error increases deterrence, expenditures made to reduce errors may be socially beneficial.[49]

16. Costs of imposing fines

We inquire in this section about the implications of costs borne by enforcement authorities in imposing fines.[50] Our principal observation is that such costs should raise the level of the fine.

To elaborate, suppose that the probability of detection is fixed at p, that liability is strict, and that individuals are risk neutral. If fines are costless to impose, the optimal fine is h/p, the harm divided by the probability of detection (see (1.14)). Now suppose that the enforcement authority bears a cost each time a fine is imposed; let

k = cost of imposing a fine on an offender.

It is easy to verify that the optimal fine then is

$$f^* = h/p + k; \tag{1.25}$$

the cost k should be added to the fine that would otherwise be desirable. The explanation is that, if an individual commits a harmful act, he causes society to bear not only the immediate harm h, but also, with probability p, the cost k of imposing the fine – that is, his act results in an expected total social cost of $h + pk$. If the fine is set according to (1.25), the individual's expected fine is $h + pk$, which leads him to engage in the harmful act if and only if his gain exceeds the expected total social cost of the act.

There may be other costs associated with the imposition of fines. In

---

49 On the value of accuracy in adjudication, see Kaplow and Shavell (1994a).

50 We have already discussed the cost of imposing imprisonment sanctions – specifically, the cost to the state per unit of the imprisonment term, c.

particular, suppose that detection is followed by a costly second stage during which the state investigates and prosecutes an individual, and at the end of which a fine is imposed only with a probability. Let

s = cost of the investigation-prosecution stage; and
q = probability of a fine being imposed after the investigation-prosecution stage.

Hence, the probability that an individual will have to pay a fine is pq and the expected costs of imposing a fine, including the expected investigation-prosecution cost, become $ps + pqk$.

It is readily shown that the optimal fine now is

$$f^* = h/pq + s/q + k. \tag{1.26}$$

This formula illustrates a general principle: the optimal fine equals the costs incurred by society as a result of the harmful act divided by the probability – at the time that each component of cost is incurred – that the individual will have to pay the fine. Thus, h is divided by pq because, when the harm occurs, the probability of having to pay the fine is pq; and s is divided by q because, when the investigation-prosecution costs are incurred, the probability of having to pay the fine is q. If the fine is computed according to this principle, the expected fine will equal the expected social costs due to an individual committing a harmful act, including the harm caused and the expected sanctioning costs – that is, $h + ps + pqk$.

Note that under fault-based liability, the cost of imposing fines is significantly lower, if not zero. This is because, if individuals comply with the fault standard, they do not bear sanctions, in which case there are no costs associated with imposing sanctions. However, if individuals are found at fault (say because of errors), the fines imposed on them also should reflect the costs of imposing fines.

Finally, observe that not only does the state incur costs when fines are imposed, so do the individuals who pay the fines (such as legal defense expenses). The costs borne by individuals, however, do not affect the formula for the optimal fine. Individuals properly take these costs into account because they bear them directly.[51]

---

[51] The points developed in this section were first presented in Polinsky and Shavell (1992), although early writers on enforcement theory – including Becker (1968, p. 192) and Stigler (1970, p. 533) – recognized that sanctions should reflect enforcement costs.

17. General enforcement

In many settings, enforcement may be said to be *general* in the sense that several different types of violations may be detected by an enforcement agent's activity. For example, a police officer waiting along the side of a road may notice a driver who litters as well as a driver who goes through a red light or who speeds; or a tax auditor may detect a variety of infractions when he examines a tax return. To analyze this type of situation, suppose that a single probability of detection applies to all harmful acts, regardless of the magnitude of the harm.[52] (The contrasting assumption is that enforcement is *specific,* meaning that the probability is chosen independently for each type of harmful act.)

The main point that we want to make is that when enforcement is general, the optimal sanction rises with the severity of the harm and is maximal only for relatively high harms. To see this, assume that liability is strict, the sanction is a fine, and individuals are risk neutral. Let $f(h)$ be the fine given harm h. Then, for any general probability of detection p, the optimal fine schedule is

$$f^*(h) = h/p, \tag{1.27}$$

provided that h/p does not exceed the maximum feasible fine (say individuals' wealth level w); if h/p is not feasible, the optimal fine is maximal. This schedule is obviously optimal given p because it implies that the expected fine equals harm, thereby inducing first-best behavior, whenever that is possible.

The question remains whether it would be desirable to lower p and raise fines to the maximal level for the low-harm acts for which $f^*(h)$ is less than maximal. But if p is reduced for the relatively low-harm acts (and the fine raised for them), then p – being general – is also reduced for the high-harm acts for which the fine is already maximal, resulting in lower deterrence of these acts. The decline in deterrence of high-harm acts may cause a greater social loss than the savings in enforcement costs from lowering p. To express this point differently, p must be sufficiently high to avoid significant underdeterrence of high-harm acts (for which fines are maximal). But since this p also applies to less harmful acts, the fines for them do not need to be maximal in order to deter them appropriately.[53]

---

[52] It will be clear that the main point developed in this section does not depend on the assumption that the same probability applies to all acts. The only requirement is that the probabilities for different acts are linked, all a function of the same enforcement expenditure.

[53] Note that if p could be varied independently for a low-harm act and for a high-harm act – that is, if enforcement is specific rather than general – then it

The result that, when enforcement is general, sanctions should rise with the severity of harm up to a maximum also holds if the sanction is imprisonment and if liability is fault-based. The underlying reasoning is the same as that given above.[54]

18. Marginal deterrence

In many circumstances, an individual may consider which of *several* harmful acts to commit, for example, whether to release only a small amount of a pollutant into a river or a large amount, or whether only to kidnap a person or also to kill him. In such contexts, the threat of sanctions plays a role in addition to the usual one of deterring individuals from committing harmful acts: for individuals who are not deterred, expected sanctions influence *which* harmful acts individuals choose to commit. Notably, such individuals will have a reason to commit less harmful rather than more harmful acts if expected sanctions rise with harm. Deterring a more harmful act by having its expected sanction exceed that for a less harmful act is sometimes referred to as *marginal deterrence*.[55]

Other things being equal, it is socially desirable that enforcement policy creates marginal deterrence, so that those who are not deterred from committing harmful acts have a reason to moderate the amount of harm that they cause. This suggests that sanctions should rise with the magnitude of harm and, therefore, that most sanctions should be less than maximal. However, promoting marginal deterrence may conflict with achieving deterrence generally: for the schedule of sanctions to rise steeply enough to accomplish marginal deterrence, sanctions for less harmful acts might have to be so low that individuals are inadequately deterred from committing these acts.[56]

To illustrate the implications of marginal deterrence, consider the following example in which sanctions are monetary and liability is strict. Suppose that there are two harmful acts, with harms h_1 and h_2, where $h_1 < h_2$, that the probability of detection p is the same for both acts, and that individuals have the same level of wealth w. We will first consider a one-act

would be desirable to lower p and raise the fine for a low-harm act if the fine for it were less than maximal.

54 The basic point of this section was first made by Shavell (1991b); see also Mookherjee and Png (1992) for a closely related analysis.

55 The notion of marginal deterrence was remarked upon in some of the earliest writing on enforcement; see Beccaria (1767, p. 32) and Bentham (1789, p. 171). The term *marginal deterrence* apparently was first used by Stigler (1970).

56 For formal treatments of marginal deterrence, see Shavell (1992), Wilde (1992), and Mookherjee and Png (1994).

model in which there can be no marginal deterrence because each individual can commit only one type of harmful act. We will then compare the results in this case to a two-act model in which each individual can commit either of two harmful acts.

In the one-act model, suppose some individuals have the opportunity to commit an act causing harm of h_1 and other individuals have the opportunity to commit an act causing harm of h_2. It is optimal to set the fine for the high-harm act equal to w, for otherwise it would be possible to raise the fine for both acts and lower the probability of detection p without affecting deterrence, but saving enforcement costs. It also follows that the optimal p is such that pw is less than h_2, that is, there is some underdeterrence of the high-harm act. The reason is that if $pw = h_2$, there would be no first-order loss of social welfare in terms of gains and harm if p is lowered (since marginal individuals are those for whom $g = h_2$), but enforcement costs would be saved. Given the common probability p, the fine f_1 for the lesser offense then can be set such that $pf_1 = h_1$ (assuming such a fine is feasible), achieving first-best deterrence of this offense.

In the two-act model, each individual can commit an act causing harm of h_1 or an act causing harm of h_2. Again, it is optimal to set the fine for the high-harm act equal to w and for there to be underdeterrence of the high-harm act. Now, however, f_1 should be such that pf_1 is less than h_1, instead of equaling h_1. The essential reason for this result is that the reduction in f_1 from h_1/p leads some offenders to commit the act causing harm h_1 instead of the act causing higher harm h_2. This can be shown to raise social welfare even though the reduction in f_1 leads some individuals to commit the low-harm act who otherwise would not have committed either harmful act.[57] In other words, achieving marginal deterrence by reducing the expected fine for the low-harm act raises social welfare.

Two additional observations should be made about marginal deterrence. First, marginal deterrence can be promoted by increasing the probability of detection as well as the magnitude of sanctions for acts that cause greater harm. For example, kidnappers can be deterred more from killing their victims if greater police resources are devoted to apprehending kidnappers who murder their victims than to those who do not. (Note, though, that in circumstances in which enforcement is general,

---

[57] This conclusion essentially follows from two observations. First, because pw is less than h_2, some individuals who had been committing the high-harm act were causing a net loss of social welfare (their gain was less than h_2). Second, as f_1 is lowered marginally from h_1/p, individuals who are induced to commit the act causing harm h_1 (who either would have committed the high-harm act or not committed any harmful act) cause no net loss of social welfare (their gain equaled h_1).

the probability of detection cannot be independently altered for acts that cause different degrees of harm.) Second, marginal deterrence is naturally accomplished if the expected sanction equals harm for all levels of harm; for if a person is paying for harm done, he will have to pay appropriately more if he does greater harm. Thus, for instance, if a polluter's expected fine would rise from $100 to $500 if he dumps five gallons instead of one gallon of waste into a lake, where each gallon causes $100 of harm, his marginal incentives to pollute will be correct.[58]

19. Principal-agent relationship

Although we have assumed that an offender is an independent single actor, in fact the offender is often an agent of a principal. For example, the agent could be an employee of a firm or a subcontractor of a contractor. The enforcement problem is now how to maximize social welfare by choosing enforcement effort and the sanctions to be imposed on principals and agents. This maximization is carried out under the assumption that a principal chooses a contract with his agent that maximizes the principal's expected utility subject to two constraints: that the agent receive his reservation level of expected utility; and that the agent maximizes his own expected utility.

When harm is caused by an agent, many of our conclusions from the basic analysis carry over if the sanction is imposed on the principal. For example, given the probability of detection p, it is optimal for a risk-neutral principal to face a fine of h/p. Then the expected fine is equal to harm done. Consequently, the principal will behave socially optimally in controlling his agents, and in particular will contract with them and monitor them in ways that will give the agents socially appropriate incentives to reduce harm.[59]

---

[58] As we discussed in section 7.1, however, it generally is desirable for society to tolerate some underdeterrence in order to save enforcement costs, in which case expected sanctions will be less than harm. Then, consideration of marginal deterrence alters the structure of sanctions that would otherwise be best, as the comparison of the one-act model to the two-act model in this section showed.

[59] There is relatively little literature on the question of optimal enforcement when wrongdoers are agents of principals. Newman and Wright (1990) study the optimal monetary sanction to impose on a risk-neutral principal when liability is strict and is imposed for sure; they show that it equals harm. Polinsky and Shavell (1993) demonstrate the potential desirability of imposing criminal sanctions on an employee who causes harm, even when the employer is capable of paying for the harm. Arlen (1994) examines the effect of sanctions on corporations' incentives to monitor their employees, and she emphasizes the possibility that corporations may have perverse incentives not to monitor if they would become liable as a result

A question about enforcement that arises when there are principals and agents is how to allocate financial sanctions between them. First observe that the particular allocation of sanctions may not matter when, as would be the natural presumption, the principal and the agent can reallocate sanctions through their own contract. For example, if the agent finds that he faces a large fine but is more risk averse than the principal, the principal can assume it; conversely, if the fine would be imposed on the principal, he can bear that risk and not impose an internal sanction on the agent. Thus, the post-contract penalties that the agent suffers may not be affected by the particular division of sanctions initially selected by the enforcement authority.

The allocation of monetary sanctions between principals and agents would matter, however, if some allocations allow the pair to reduce their total burden. An important example is when a fine is imposed only on the agent and he is unable to pay it because his assets are less than the fine.[60] Then he and the principal (who often would have higher assets) would jointly escape part of the fine, diluting deterrence. The fine therefore should be imposed on the principal rather than on the agent (or at least the part of the fine that the agent cannot pay).

A closely related point is that the imposition of imprisonment sanctions on agents may be desirable when their assets are less than the optimal fine, even if the principal's assets are sufficient to pay the fine. The fact that an agent's assets are limited means that the principal may be unable to control him adequately through the use of contractually determined penalties, which can only be monetary. For example, a firm may not be able, despite the threat of salary reduction or dismissal, to induce its employees never to rig bids. In such circumstances, it may be socially valuable to use the threat of personal criminal liability and a jail sentence to better control agents' misconduct.[61]

20. Settlements

We have thus far assumed that when an individual who should be found liable is discovered, he will be sanctioned in some automatic fashion. In practice, however, an individual must be found liable in a trial, and before this occurs, it is common for an individual to settle in lieu of trial. (In the

---

of their discovering and reporting employee violations. Also, Shavell (1997b) finds that optimal sanctions on corporations could be above or below harm when employee assets are less than harm.

[60] See Sykes (1981) and Kornhauser (1982).

[61] This point is discussed by Segerson and Tietenberg (1992) and emphasized by Polinsky and Shavell (1993).

criminal context, the settlement usually takes the form of a *plea bargain*, an agreement in which the individual pleads guilty to a reduced charge.) Given the prevalence of settlements, it is important to consider how they affect deterrence and the optimal system of public enforcement, and whether settlements are socially desirable.

A general reason why a wrongdoer who has been caught might prefer an out-of-court settlement to a trial is that a settlement saves him time and/or money. Public enforcers presumably would prefer settlements for this reason as well. To amplify, consider a risk-neutral detected individual subject to a fine f and let

r = probability of conviction;
c_I = individual's litigation costs; and
c_P = prosecutor's litigation costs.

Assume that the parties agree on the probability of conviction. If the case goes to trial, the expected cost to the individual is $rf + c_I$, and the expected gain to the prosecutor, assuming his goal is to maximize expected penalties imposed net of his litigation costs, is $rf - c_P$. Thus, any settlement resulting in a fine between $rf - c_P$ and $rf + c_I$ would make both parties better off because the cost of litigation would be avoided. The same point would apply if the individual were subject to a jail sentence rather than a fine. Note, however, that if the parties disagree about the probability of conviction, a settlement might not occur – specifically, if the individual is relatively optimistic and believes that the probability of his being convicted is sufficiently less than the prosecutor thinks it is.

A second benefit of a settlement is that it eliminates the risks inherent in the trial outcome, a benefit to parties who are averse to such risks.[62]

The preceding advantages of settlement to the parties suggest that settlement is socially valuable, but the effect of settlement on deterrence is a complicating factor. Specifically, settlements dilute deterrence: for if individuals desire to settle, it must be because the expected disutility of sanctions is lowered for them. However, because settlements reflect the sanctions that would be imposed at trial, the state may be able to offset this settlement-related reduction in deterrence by increasing the level of

[62] These benefits of settlement are well recognized in the economic literature on civil litigation; see the surveys by Cooter and Rubinfeld (1989) and Spier (2007). For early discussions of settlement in the context of public enforcement, see Landes (1971) and Grossman and Katz (1983), and more recently, see, for example, Reinganum (1988), Polinsky and Rubinfeld (1989), Kobayashi and Lott (1992), and Miceli (1996).

sanctions. If so, settlements need not compromise the overall level of deterrence.[63]

Settlements may have other socially undesirable consequences. First, they may result in sanctions that are not as well tailored to harmful acts as would be true of court-determined sanctions. Second, settlements hinder the amplification and development of the law through the setting of precedents. Third, settlements also sometimes allow individuals to keep aspects of their behavior secret, which can reduce deterrence. Fourth, settlements for prison terms can result in increases in public expenditures on jail if individuals are risk averse in imprisonment.[64] A prosecutor whose goal is to maximize social welfare, as opposed to maximizing the expected sanction less prosecution costs, presumably would take these additional factors into account and sometimes refuse to settle even though the settlement saves litigation costs and avoids risk.[65]

21. Self-reporting

We have assumed that individuals are subject to sanctions only if they are detected by an enforcement agent, but in fact parties sometimes disclose their own violations to enforcement authorities. For example, firms often report violations of environmental and safety regulations, individuals usually notify police of their involvement in traffic accidents, and even criminals occasionally turn themselves in.

Self-reporting can be induced by lowering the sanction for individuals who disclose their own infractions. To avoid significantly reducing deterrence, however, the reward for self-reporting can be made relatively small. For example, suppose that the fine if an individual does not self-report is \$1,000 and that the probability of detection is 10 percent, so the expected fine is \$100. If the fine if one self-reports is \$99, individuals will self-report but deterrence will barely be reduced.

---

[63] The deterrence-diluting effects of settlement and other aspects of the social desirability of settlement have been discussed in the private litigation context by Polinsky and Rubinfeld (1988), Shavell (1997a), and Spier (1997). A related discussion in the public enforcement context appears in Polinsky and Rubinfeld (1989).

[64] For example, suppose a defendant faces a 50 percent chance of a five year sentence and a 50 percent chance of a 15-year sentence, with an expected sentence of ten years. If he is risk averse, he will strictly prefer a certain sentence of ten years. This implies that if prosecutors want to maintain deterrence, they must demand a settlement of more than ten years, say 12 years, which increases the cost of imprisonment.

[65] The question of what prosecutors maximize has received almost no attention from law and economics scholars, although two exceptions are Miceli (1996) and Glaeser et al. (2000).

To express this formally, assume for simplicity that individuals are risk neutral, and suppose that if an individual commits a violation and does not self-report, his expected fine is pf. Let

$$f' = \text{fine if a violator self-reports,}$$

and set

$$f' = pf - \varepsilon, \tag{1.28}$$

where $\varepsilon > 0$ is small. A violator will therefore want to self-report because f' is less than pf, but the deterrent effect of the sanction will approximate that if he did not self-report.

Given that self-reporting can be induced essentially without compromising deterrence, why is self-reporting socially advantageous? One reason is that self-reporting lowers enforcement costs because the enforcement authority does not have to identify and prove who the violator was. Environmental enforcers do not need to spend as much effort trying to detect pollution and establishing its source if firms that pollute report that fact.[66] Second, self-reporting reduces risk, and thus is advantageous if individuals are risk averse. Drivers bear less risk because they know that if they cause an accident, they will be led to report this to the police and suffer a lower and certain sanction (of approximately pf), rather than face a substantially higher sanction imposed only with some probability. Third, self-reporting may allow harm to be mitigated. Early identification of a toxic leak, for example, will facilitate its containment and clean-up.[67]

22. Repeat offenders

In practice, the law often sanctions repeat offenders more severely than first-time offenders. For example, under the US Sentencing Commission's

---

[66] In some contexts, however, self-reporting will not save enforcement costs. For example, suppose that a police officer waits by the side of a road to spot speeders. Then, were a driver to report that he had sped, this would not reduce policing costs, presuming that the officer still needs to be stationed at the roadside to watch for other speeders. Usually, though, there would be some cost savings as a result of self-reporting (for example, the police officer would not have to chase as many speeders).

[67] The basic theory of self-reporting in public enforcement is developed in Kaplow and Shavell (1994b); see also Malik (1993) and Innes (1999). Related literature concerns the reporting of income by individuals to tax authorities and the reporting of costs by regulated firms to regulatory authorities. See, for example, Andreoni et al. (1998) and Laffont and Tirole (1993).

sentencing guidelines for Federal crimes, both imprisonment terms and criminal fines are enhanced if an offender has a prior record. Civil money penalties also sometimes depend on whether the offender has a record of prior offenses. We explain here why such policies may be socially desirable.

Note first that sanctioning repeat offenders more severely cannot be socially advantageous if deterrence always induces first-best behavior. If the sanction for polluting and causing a $1,000 harm is $1,000, then any person who pollutes and pays $1,000 is a person whose gain from polluting (say the savings from not installing pollution control equipment) must have exceeded $1,000. Social welfare therefore is higher as a result of his polluting. If such an individual polluted and was sanctioned in the past, that only means that it was socially desirable for him to have polluted previously. Raising the sanction because of his having a record of prior convictions would overdeter him now.

Accordingly, only if deterrence is inadequate is it possibly desirable to condition sanctions on offense history to increase deterrence. But deterrence often will be inadequate because, as we emphasized in section 7.1, it will usually be worthwhile for the state to tolerate some underdeterrence in order to reduce enforcement expenses.

Given that there is underdeterrence, making sanctions depend on offense history may be beneficial for two reasons. First, the use of offense history may create an additional incentive not to violate the law: if detection of a violation implies not only an immediate sanction, but also a higher sanction for a future violation, an individual will be deterred more from committing a violation presently.[68] Second, making sanctions depend on offense history allows society to take advantage of information about the dangerousness of individuals and the need to deter them: individuals with offense histories may be more likely than average to commit future

---

[68] There is a subtlety in demonstrating the optimality of punishing repeat offenses more severely. Namely, if there is a problem of underdeterrence, one might wonder why it would not be optimal to raise the sanction to the maximum level for every offense (in which case repeat offenses would not be punished more severely). It must be shown that punishing all offenses maximally is inferior to punishing first offenses less than maximally and punishing repeat offenses more severely. See Polinsky and Shavell (1998) on the possible optimality of making sanctions depend on offense history because of the additional deterrence that such a policy creates. Miceli and Bucci (2005) supply a different reason for raising the fine for the second offense – that there is little additional social stigma associated with a second offense, so that a higher sanction is needed to maintain deterrence. Emons (2003), however, raises the possibility that it may be optimal to lower the sanction for the second offense.

violations, which might make it desirable for purposes of deterrence to impose higher sanctions on them.[69]

There is also an incapacitation-based reason for making sanctions depend on offense history. Repeat offenders are more likely to have higher propensities to commit violations in the future and thus more likely to be worth incapacitating by imprisonment.[70]

23. Imperfect knowledge about the probability and magnitude of sanctions

Although we have made the simplifying assumption that individuals know the probability of detection and the magnitude of sanctions, it is obvious that individuals frequently have imperfect knowledge of these variables. They generally possess only subjective probability distributions of the probability of a sanction and its magnitude. They might not know the true probability of a sanction for several reasons: because the enforcement authority refrains from publishing information about the probability (perhaps hoping that individuals will believe it to be higher than it is); because the probability depends on factors that individuals do not fully understand (the probability of a tax audit, for example, is influenced by factors that are kept secret from taxpayers); and because probabilities might be difficult for individuals to assess.[71] Also, individuals may have incomplete knowledge of the true magnitude of sanctions, particularly if sanctions are not fixed by law, but are to some degree discretionary.[72]

The implications of individuals' imperfect knowledge are straightforward to ascertain. First, to predict how individuals behave, what is relevant, of course, is not the actual probability and magnitude of a sanction, but perceptions of them.

---

[69] Note that this reason for making sanctions depend on offense history is different from the first reason: the second reason involves the assumption that offenders are different and that the optimal sanction for some offenders is higher than for others; the first reason applies even if individuals are identical. On the second, information-based, reason for making sanctions depend on offense history, see Rubinstein (1979), Polinsky and Rubinfeld (1991), and Chu et al. (2000).

[70] See section 25 for a discussion of the incapacitation rationale for the use of imprisonment sanctions.

[71] On the problems that individuals have in evaluating and using probabilities, see, for example, Kahneman et al. (1982).

[72] In addition, individuals could have imperfect information about the prevailing standard of liability, not being sure whether it is strict or fault-based. This type of mistake, about a discrete issue, seems less likely to be significant than errors in assessing the probability and magnitude of sanctions.

Second, to determine the optimal probability and magnitude of sanctions, account must be taken of the relationship between the actual and the perceived values. To illustrate, suppose that the perceived probability is a single value $\hat{p}(p)$, where $\hat{p}$ is increasing in the true probability p, and, similarly, that the perceived fine is $\hat{f}(f)$, where $\hat{f}$ is increasing in the true fine f. Thus, if the probability of detection p is fixed, the optimal fine is set such that $\hat{p}(p)\hat{f}(f) = h$, assuming such a fine is feasible. This might imply a higher or a lower fine than when perceptions are accurate.

Third, the result that the optimal fine should be maximal when individuals are risk neutral continues to hold. By raising the fine to the maximum, the perceived fine also will be maximal. The probability of detection then can be lowered, thereby saving enforcement costs without reducing deterrence.

Several other observations are worth making. One concerns lags in learning about changes in enforcement policy. For example, suppose that there is a delay of at least a year before individuals fully comprehend a change in the probability of enforcement. Then if enforcement resources are increased so as to make the probability, say, 15 percent rather than 10 percent, there might not be a significant increase in deterrence for some time, making such an investment less worthwhile.[73] Another observation involves the difficulty in learning about variations in enforcement policy when enforcement policy is described by a distribution. For instance, suppose that the sanction for some act, such as robbery, can vary (say from one month of jail time to ten years), and that individuals' perceptions are quite rough, not based on true averages, but mainly on the possible range of sanctions. Then increasing the average sentence within this range might have very little effect on deterrence. The processes by which individuals formulate probabilities of sanctions and their magnitudes are important, therefore, in determining optimal deterrence policy.[74]

---

[73] Similarly, suppose that individuals treat all probabilities of enforcement that are low, say below 1 percent, as if they were probabilities of 1 percent, because it is not possible for individuals to make discriminations finer than 1 percent. Then if the actual probability is 0.5 percent, spending more on enforcement to make the probability 1 percent would not be beneficial because deterrence would not increase.

[74] Bebchuk and Kaplow (1992) consider imperfect information about the probability of sanctions and emphasize that maximal sanctions may not be socially desirable. See also Kaplow (1990a), which takes into account learning about whether acts are subject to sanctions, and Sah (1991), which focuses on the process by which individuals form perceptions of the probability of detection.

24. Corruption

In this section we examine the possible corruption of law enforcement agents, how corruption lessens deterrence and distorts participation in harm-creating activities, and what policies may be employed to combat corruption.[75] One form of corruption is bribery, in which a law enforcer accepts a payment in return for not reporting a violation (or for reducing the mandated sanction for the violation). For example, in consideration of a bribe payment, a police officer may overlook a speeding violation or a building inspector may ignore a code infraction. (For simplicity, we do not distinguish between a bribe offered by an individual and an extortion demand made by the enforcer – a payment for not turning in the individual.) A second form of corruption is framing and framing-related extortion, in which an enforcement agent may frame an innocent individual or threaten to frame him in order to extort money from him.

One reason bribery is socially undesirable is that it dilutes deterrence of violations of law. This is because bribery results in a lower payment by an individual than the sanction for the offense. To be concrete, let

λ = fraction obtained by the enforcer of the surplus from a bribe agreement.

Therefore, because the surplus from a bribe agreement is the fine f, an individual pays a bribe of λf. To the degree that λ is less than one, there is underdeterrence.[76] Similarly, bribery leads to excessive participation in the harm-creating activity.

Framing and framing-related extortion also dilute deterrence of violations of law. The reason is that framing and extortion imply that those who act innocently face an expected sanction, so that the difference between the expected sanction if individuals commit a violation and if they do not is lessened. If, for example, individuals who violate the law face an expected fine of $1,000 and innocent individuals face an expected fine of $200 due to the risk of being extorted or framed, the additional cost to an innocent individual of committing the offense is $800 instead of $1,000. (This point is essentially the same as the observation in section

---

[75] The discussion in this section is based principally on Polinsky and Shavell (2001). We do not examine the corruption of the government procurement process, such as the payment of a bribe to a government agent in order to obtain a defense contract.

[76] Garoupa and Klerman (2004) discuss how the threat of an imprisonment sanction for the offense will lead the offender to pay a higher bribe than otherwise, thereby reducing the deterrence-diluting effect of bribery.

15 that mistaken convictions dilute deterrence.) Additionally, framing and framing-related extortion undesirably discourage participation in the harm-creating activity.

Because corruption dilutes deterrence and distorts activity decisions, its control may be socially desirable. One way to reduce corruption is to impose fines (or imprisonment sentences) on individuals caught engaging in bribery, extortion, and framing. For example, suppose there is a fine for bribery imposed on the enforcer with a probability. Let

f_B = fine imposed on the enforcer for engaging in bribery; and
p_B = probability that an enforcer is caught engaging in bribery.

Bribery will be deterred if the surplus from a bribe agreement is eliminated, that is, if $p_B f_B \geq f$. Otherwise, the bribe payment will be $p_B f_B + \lambda(f - p_B f_B)$, which exceeds λf, so that deterrence of the offense is greater due to the sanctioning of bribery. For previously discussed reasons, the optimal fine to impose on risk-neutral parties for engaging in bribery is maximal, and the optimal fine for enforcers who frame innocent individuals also is maximal. But, surprisingly, framing-related extortion should not be penalized.[77]

Corruption also can be reduced by paying enforcers rewards for reporting violations. Such payments will reduce their incentive to accept bribes because they will sacrifice their rewards if they fail to report violations. Indeed, sufficiently high rewards would eliminate all incentives to accept bribes. But high rewards may not be optimal because they give enforcers a greater incentive to frame innocent individuals, and high rewards tend to increase framing-related extortion payments (because enforcers sacrifice more by accepting the extortion payment). The optimal reward balances the beneficial effect of using rewards to offset the dilution of deterrence due to bribery with the detrimental effects associated with increased framing and extortion of innocent individuals.

A third way to control corruption is to pay enforcers more than their reservation wage (that is, to pay them an efficiency wage). Then they would have more to lose if punished for corrupt behavior and denied

---

[77] The kernel of the reason is that penalizing framing-related extortion will lead to one of two detrimental consequences: it will either fail to deter extortion and result in higher costs to innocent individuals (the sum of their expected extortion payment and the expected fine on them for paying extortion); or else it will cause enforcers to switch from extorting money from innocent individuals to actually framing them, which is socially worse. This result is demonstrated in Polinsky and Shavell (2001), which also discusses qualifications to this point.

future employment. There is, however, a social cost to the state of paying enforcers more than the wage necessary to attract them – the distortions caused by the additional taxes needed to make such payments.

The discussion to this point implicitly presumed that the fine for the harmful act is fixed. A question that naturally arises, however, is whether the deterrence-diluting effects of corruption can be offset by raising the fine on offenders. For example, suppose that the optimal fine would be $100 if a fine were always paid when an offender is caught, but that bribery results in a bribe payment equal to $50, one half of the fine. Could not the fine on an offender be increased to $200, so that the bribe would then be $100 and the effective penalty be exactly what is desired? In the basic risk-neutral model of enforcement, it is not possible to raise the fine because the optimal fine is maximal. More realistically, however, the optimal fine is less than maximal for a variety of reasons, including those related to risk aversion, marginal deterrence, and general enforcement. Then, while it would be possible to raise the fine to offset the deterrence-diluting effects of corruption, doing so would lead to social costs (for example, greater bearing of risk) and might not be desirable.[78]

25. Incapacitation

Our discussion of public enforcement has presumed that the threat of sanctions reduces harm by discouraging individuals from causing harm – that is, by deterring them. However, a different way for society to reduce harm is by imposing sanctions that remove parties from positions in which they are able to cause harm – that is, by *incapacitating* them. Imprisonment is the primary incapacitative sanction, although there are other examples: individuals can lose their drivers' licenses, preventing them from doing harm while driving; businesses can lose their right to operate in certain domains, and the like. We focus here on imprisonment, but what we say applies to incapacitative sanctions generally.

---

[78] Becker and Stigler (1974) focus on the control of bribery and consider paying rewards to enforcers or requiring them to post bonds that would be forfeited if they are caught engaging in bribery. Mookherjee and Png (1995) analyze bribery and conclude, given their assumption that fines are unbounded, that it is optimal to eliminate bribery. Bowles and Garoupa (1997) also discuss the control of bribery through sanctions. Hindriks et al. (1999) study bribery and extortion in the context of tax evasion, and examine rewards and penalties as methods of control. Other writing on corruption includes Pashigian (1975), Klitgaard (1988), Shleifer and Vishny (1993), Bardhan (1997), and Rose-Ackerman (1999); several of these articles focus on corruption in the awarding of government contracts and licenses rather than corruption in the imposition of sanctions for violations of law.

To better understand public enforcement when sanctions are incapacitative, suppose that their sole function is to incapacitate; that is, assume for simplicity that sanctions do not deter. (For instance, deterrence might not occur if, given the relevant range of the probabilities and magnitudes of the sanctions, individuals' gains from harmful acts exceed the expected sanctions.) Let

$h(t)$ = harm that would be caused by an individual at age t if not in jail.

We assume that $h(t)$ either is constant or declines with age.

Assuming that the social goal is to minimize the sum of the harm and the cost c of incarceration,[79] the optimal policy is to keep an individual in jail as long as $h(t) > c$. In other words, if the harm the individual would cause exceeds the cost of imprisonment, an individual should be put in prison and kept there as long as the harm continues to exceed the cost of imprisonment. He should be released otherwise. Put differently, the optimal prison term as a function of potential harm caused is zero up to a threshold – the point at which harm equals the cost of imprisonment – and then rises discontinuously to the length of time during which the person's harm if released would exceed imprisonment costs. Jail should only be used to incapacitate individuals who otherwise would have caused relatively high harm.

Two points about the incapacitative rationale are important to note. First, evidence exists suggesting that the harm caused by individuals declines with their age.[80] Thus, from the incapacitative standpoint, it often will be desirable to release older prisoners from jail. Second, as a matter of logic, the incapacitative rationale might imply that a person should be put in jail even if he has not committed a crime – if his danger to society makes incapacitating him worthwhile. This would be true, for example, if there were some accurate way to predict a person's dangerousness independently of his actual behavior. In practice, however, the fact that a person has committed a harmful act may be a good basis for predicting his future behavior, in which case the incapacitation rationale would imply that a jail term should be imposed only if the individual has committed an especially harmful act.

The optimal probability of detection is determined by a straightforward

---

[79] For simplicity, we are not taking into account here the gains that individuals obtain from committing offenses or the disutility that individuals bear from time in jail.

[80] See, for example, Wilson and Herrnstein (1985, pp. 126–47) and US Department of Justice (1997a, pp. 371, table 4.4, 378–79, table 4.7).

tradeoff. The higher the probability, the greater the number of individuals who will be incapacitated, resulting in social gains equal to the difference between the harm that individuals would cause and the cost of their incapacitation. But the higher the probability, the higher are enforcement costs. At some point, it is optimal to stop raising the probability, when the marginal social gains just equal the marginal cost of raising the probability.

Last, we briefly comment on the relationship between the nature of optimal enforcement when incapacitation is the goal versus when deterrence is the goal. First, when incapacitation is the goal, the optimal length of the prison term (which is determined by the condition that $h(t) > c$) is independent of the probability of apprehension. In contrast, when deterrence is the goal, the optimal sanction depends on the probability – the sanction generally is higher the lower is the probability. Second, when incapacitation is the goal, the probability and magnitude of sanctions are independent of the ability to deter. Thus, for example, if this ability is limited (consider individuals who commit crimes while enraged), a low expected sanction may be optimal under the deterrence rationale, but a high expected sanction still might be called for to incapacitate.[81]

26. Costly observation of wealth

In our prior discussions of optimal sanctions, we implicitly assumed that the enforcement authority could costlessly observe individuals' wealth levels. Knowing wealth levels, the enforcement authority then chose the sanctions to impose, fines and/or imprisonment sentences. In fact, however, individuals and firms may be able to hide assets from government enforcers, including by hoarding cash, transferring assets to relatives or related legal entities, or moving money to offshore bank accounts. In this section we consider optimal sanctions when an individual's level of wealth can be observed only after a costly audit or not at all.[82]

---

[81] See Shavell (1987a) for a theoretical examination of optimal incapacitation policy, Ehrlich (1981, pp. 315–16, 319–21) for a model used to estimate the relative importance of incapacitation and deterrence, and Levitt (1998) and Kessler and Levitt (1999) for empirical studies of incapacitation and deterrence. Economists have paid much less attention to incapacitation than to deterrence, despite the significance of the incapacitation rationale in criminal law enforcement.

[82] The discussion in this section is based on Polinsky (2006a, 2006b). See also Chu and Jiang (1993) and Levitt (1997), who consider the choice between fines and imprisonment when wealth cannot be discovered by the enforcement authority at any cost (in Chu and Jiang's case, this assumption is implicit), and Garoupa (1998), who investigates optimal fines when the enforcement authority is assumed to costlessly observe an underestimate of offenders' wealth levels.

Suppose first that the enforcement authority employs fines as sanctions and can audit an individual who claims that he cannot pay the fine. If the audit determines that the individual misrepresented his wealth level, he can be fined for having lied about his wealth. Assume for simplicity that this fine is independent of the degree of misrepresentation. The enforcement authority's problem is to choose, so as to maximize social welfare, the probability of detecting the offense, the fine for the offense, the probability of an audit conditional on the individual's claiming that he cannot pay the fine, and the fine for misrepresentation of wealth. Without loss of generality, we assume that if the latter fine is applicable, it is imposed instead of the fine for the offense (rather than in addition to the fine for the offense).

It can be demonstrated that the optimal fine for misrepresenting one's wealth level equals the fine for the offense divided by the audit probability, and therefore generally exceeds the fine for the offense. This is a natural generalization of the formula for the optimal fine, given the probability of detection, which is the harm divided by the probability. In effect, the 'harm' from the act of concealing one's wealth is the failure to pay the fine for the original offense, so the optimal fine for concealment is this harm divided by the applicable probability of being caught if one engages in it.

Assuming the harmful act is worth controlling, the optimal audit probability is positive, increases as the cost of an audit declines, and equals one if the cost is sufficiently low. Auditing is valuable because it reduces misrepresentation of wealth and thereby increases deterrence. If the optimal audit probability is less than one, however, some individuals who are capable of paying the fine for the offense will misrepresent their wealth levels. Unlike in the basic analysis in which wealth is assumed to be costlessly observable, the optimal fine for the offense now results in underdeterrence, due to the cost of auditing wealth levels. By reducing the fine for the offense from the level that would lead to first-best behavior, fewer individuals will misrepresent their wealth levels, so auditing costs decline. The reduction in deterrence has no first-order effect on social welfare because the marginal individuals who are induced to commit the offense have gains equal to the harm from the offense.

Next suppose that the enforcement authority simply cannot observe wealth, say because the cost of an audit is prohibitively high.[83] If the enforcement authority would have used fines alone if it could have

83 The following discussion introduces imprisonment as an alternative, or supplement, to fines. For simplicity, imprisonment was not considered above in the discussion of auditing.

observed wealth at no cost, it would have imposed a higher fine on higher-wealth individuals.[84] It obviously cannot do this now. Instead, it may be desirable to use the threat of an imprisonment sentence to induce individuals capable of paying a higher fine to do so. Specifically, if there are two levels of wealth, the enforcement authority might set the fine greater than the wealth level of the low-wealth individuals and impose an imprisonment sentence on any individuals who do not pay this fine. By using an imprisonment sentence in this way, high-wealth individuals can be induced to pay a higher fine, which is socially beneficial, though low-wealth individuals now will incur a socially costly sanction, imprisonment. In other words, when wealth is not observable, it may be desirable to impose a costly sanction – imprisonment sentences – on low-wealth individuals in order to better deter high-wealth offenders through a cheap sanction – fines.

Another possibility is that the enforcement authority would have used both fines and imprisonment if it could have observed wealth at no cost. Perhaps surprisingly, the inability to observe wealth is of no consequence in this case. The reason, in essence, is that the mix of fines and imprisonment that would be chosen when wealth is observable will impose a higher burden (though a lower fine) on low-wealth individuals. Thus, high-wealth individuals will naturally want to identify themselves. Specifically, they will prefer to pay a higher fine and bear a shorter imprisonment sentence than to masquerade as low-wealth individuals, who will bear longer imprisonment sentences and a higher overall burden. Consequently, the same mix of sanctions that would have been imposed on both groups if wealth were costlessly observable can be used when wealth is not observable.

In summary, information about wealth levels is useful only if the enforcement authority would want to impose a higher burden of sanctions on high-wealth individuals than on low-wealth individuals, for then high-wealth individuals would pretend to be low-wealth individuals if wealth could not be observed. This is the case if the enforcement authority would want to use fines alone. If, however, the enforcement authority would want to impose a lower burden of sanctions on high-wealth individuals than on low-wealth individuals, high-wealth individuals will voluntarily bear such sanctions even if they include a higher fine. This case is applicable when the enforcement authority would want to use fines and imprisonment together. Monitoring of wealth levels may be worthwhile in the first case, but is not needed in the second case.

---

[84] For now familiar reasons, it would have done this to reduce or eliminate the underdeterrence that otherwise would occur if the fine were the same as for low-wealth individuals.

27. Social norms

Although we have restricted attention to public enforcement of law, social norms and morality should be mentioned because they influence in significant ways the attainment of desired behavior.[85] By social norms (or moral rules), we mean conduct – such as keeping promises, not lying, and not harming others – that is associated with certain distinctive psychological and social attributes. In particular, social norms influence behavior partly through internal incentives: when a person obeys a moral rule, he will tend to feel virtuous, and if he disobeys the rule, he will tend to feel guilty. Social norms also influence behavior through external incentives: when a person is observed by another party to have obeyed a moral rule, that party may bestow praise on the first party, who will enjoy the praise; and if the person is observed by the other party to have disobeyed the rule, the second party will tend to disapprove of the first party, who will dislike the disapproval.

Because social norms affect behavior through the foregoing moral incentives, some socially desirable conduct can be encouraged reasonably well without employing the legal system.[86] For example, whether an individual cuts in line at the movie theater, keeps his lunch engagements, or lets his children make a nuisance of themselves at the supermarket, is controlled with rough success by internal and external moral incentives. Such conduct generally can be regulated satisfactorily by moral incentives alone because, among other things, internal incentives work automatically (we know when we have done the wrong thing), external incentives are likely to apply (if a person cuts in line, this will be noticed), and the benefits from violations are not large, so that they can be outweighed relatively easily by the force of the moral incentives.

The need for formal law enforcement stems from two principal considerations. First, much conduct that society desires cannot be controlled through moral incentives alone. One reason is that the private gains from undesirable conduct are often large. The utility obtained by a robber, a tax cheat, or a polluter may be substantial, and dominate the moral incentives. Another reason is that external moral sanctions might be imposed only with a low probability (the robber, tax cheat, or polluter might not be spotted by others). A second rationale for formal law enforcement is that the social harm from failing to control an act through moral incentives

---

[85] On social norms and the law, see generally McAdams and Rasmusen (2007). See also *University of Pennsylvania Law Review* (1996) and Posner (1997).

[86] For a comparison of social norms and law enforcement as means of controlling behavior, see Shavell (2002).

may be large. This makes the expense of law enforcement worth incurring (as in the case of robbery, but not of cutting in line at movie theaters).

Although we have been treating social norms and formal law enforcement as distinct ways of controlling behavior, law enforcement might also influence social norms.[87] For instance, enforcement of laws prohibiting discrimination based on race may change beliefs about proper conduct (reinforcing internal moral incentives) and lead to a greater willingness of individuals to express disapproval when they witness discriminatory behavior (enhancing external moral incentives). The importance of the effect of law on social norms may be limited, however, to the extent that social norms are mainly the result of early childhood experience and the messages conveyed by parents and other authority figures, such as educators.

28. Fairness

To this point we have not considered the possibility that individuals have opinions about the fairness of sanctions or the arbitrariness of enforcement.[88]

Suppose, first, that individuals believe that sanctions should be imposed on those who have committed certain bad acts and that the magnitude of sanctions should reflect the gravity of the acts. A formal assumption that captures this view is that individuals obtain fairness-related utility from the imposition of sanctions on those who committed the bad acts, where this utility is maximized at a *fairness-ideal* level of sanction that depends on the harmfulness (or a related aspect) of the acts. The fairness-ideal sanction may be lower or higher than the conventionally optimal sanction that we have discussed above. Note in particular that the fairness-ideal sanction does not depend on the probability of detection, whereas the conventionally optimal sanction is higher the lower is the probability of detection, suggesting that if the probability of detection is sufficiently low, the conventionally optimal sanction will exceed the fairness-ideal sanction. In any case, when fairness-related utility is taken into account along with the other elements of social welfare considered above, the optimal sanction will be a compromise between the fairness-ideal sanction and the conventionally optimal sanction.

---

87 See, for example, McAdams (1997) and Sunstein (1996).

88 The discussion in this section is based on Polinsky and Shavell (2000b) and Kaplow and Shavell (2002, pp. 291–378), the latter of which relates the economic analysis of fairness in enforcement to the philosophical literature. See also Miceli (1991) and Diamond (2002), who derive optimal sanctions taking both deterrence and the fairness of sanctions into account, but holding the probability of sanctions fixed. Waldfogel (1993) studies empirically whether actual sanctions are better explained by considerations of deterrence or fairness.

When both the probability and magnitude of sanctions may be varied, the conventional solution to the enforcement problem also is altered because of fairness considerations. As discussed previously, if individuals are risk neutral, the usual solution consists of the highest possible sanction and a relatively low probability. When the issue of fairness is added to the analysis, however, the usual solution generally is not optimal because a very high sanction will be seen as unfair, or more precisely, will result in the lowering of individuals' fairness-related utility. With respect to double parking, for example, even a sanction of \$100 might be considered unfair because double parking is regarded as only a slightly bad act.

A consequence of the desire to keep sanctions at fair levels, meaning quite constrained levels for acts that are not very bad or harmful, is that the socially optimal probability of detection changes. One possibility is that the optimal probability would be higher, perhaps much higher than the conventionally optimal probability: to achieve a desired level of deterrence with a lower fairness-restricted sanction, the probability has to rise. If the sanction for double parking cannot exceed \$100 because of fairness considerations, then, to create an expected sanction of \$10, the probability must be 10 percent, greatly exceeding the approximately 0.1 percent probability that would be optimal if risk-neutral individuals have wealth of \$10,000 and the fine is set at this level. Another possibility, though, is that the optimal probability would be lower than in the conventional case: the additional deterrence created by raising the probability might be relatively low because the sanction is relatively low; and the lower the deterrent benefit from raising the probability, the lower would be the social incentive to devote resources to enforcement.

Another concept of fairness concerns the probability of detection rather than the magnitude of sanctions. Suppose that individuals consider it unfair for some violators of law to be sanctioned when others who were lucky enough not to be caught are not sanctioned. Specifically, suppose that individuals experience fairness-related disutility if there is only a probability rather than a certainty of sanctions, and their disutility rises the lower the probability of detection. Then the optimal probability would be higher, and therefore the optimal sanction would be lower, than in the absence of this fairness-related component of social welfare.

A further notion of fairness involves the form of liability, whether liability is strict or based on fault. Individuals might prefer fault-based liability because sanctions are imposed on parties only if they behave in a socially inappropriate way. If individuals derive greater fairness-related utility from use of fault-based liability, then this form of liability is more likely to be optimal than we have suggested previously.

A final issue concerns the relevance of fairness considerations when firms, as opposed to individuals, are sanctioned. If sanctions are imposed on firms, then fairness-related utility may have to be reconsidered, presuming that what matters in terms of fairness is that the *individuals* responsible for harmful acts bear sanctions as opposed to the artificial legal entity of a firm. Specifically, one would want to identify the sanctions actually suffered by such persons within a firm if the firm bears a sanction. For example, if a firm demotes a person who negligently caused the firm to incur a sanction, then the person's loss from the demotion would be the fairness-relevant sanction, not the sanction imposed on the firm. Note, too, that the imposition of sanctions on firms often penalizes individuals who are unlikely to be considered responsible for the harm, namely shareholders and customers. To the extent that the fairness goal is to penalize responsible individuals within firms, and not firms as entities, the social value of sanctions in achieving fairness is attenuated.

29. Conclusion

Having reviewed the theory of public enforcement of law, we want to conclude by commenting on two types of private behavior that bear significantly on public law enforcement.

First, private parties may themselves take actions to prevent being harmed. For example, to reduce the risk of being criminally victimized, individuals might install locks on their possessions, carry weapons, or hire security personnel. These private efforts to prevent or deter harmful acts serve as a partial substitute for public efforts; moreover, private efforts are sometimes more efficient than public efforts (citizens may know better where to put locks), though they also may be less efficient (public authorities may know better how to assign police). These observations raise important questions about the relationship between private protection and public enforcement. Should private efforts to protect against being victimized be regulated? Does the state spend too little on public enforcement, relying on the fact that private actors often undertake their own defensive efforts? The optimal relationship between private and public efforts to control harmful activities deserves more careful examination.[89]

Second, private individuals may bring suits against parties who also may be subject to publicly imposed penalties. For example, a victim of an automobile accident may sue the driver who caused the accident, and this driver might also be sanctioned by the state for a driving infraction. Private lawsuits channel harm-creating behavior and thus constitute a substitute,

---

89 There is some literature that discusses the issues raised in this paragraph; see, for example, Clotfelter (1977, 1978) and Shavell (1991a).

at least to some extent, for public enforcement. This leads one to ask how public enforcement and parallel private litigation should be managed. Should the payment of a public penalty be an offset to private damages, and vice versa? Should the state regulate private litigation so as to better coordinate it with public enforcement? Is public enforcement or private litigation the socially cheaper way to accomplish desired behavior?

A full treatment of the control of harm-creating behavior would address both sets of issues just discussed.

References

Andreoni, J. (1991), 'Reasonable Doubt and the Optimal Magnitude of Fines: Should the Penalty Fit the Crime?', *RAND Journal of Economics*, **22**, 385–95.

Andreoni, J., B. Erard and J. Feinstein (1998), 'Tax Compliance', *Journal of Economic Literature*, **36**, 818–60.

Arlen, J.A. (1994), 'The Potentially Perverse Effects of Corporate Criminal Liability', *Journal of Legal Studies*, **23**, 833–67.

Bardhan, P. (1997), 'Corruption and Development: A Review of Issues', *Journal of Economic Literature*, **35**, 1320–46.

Bar-Gill, O. and A. Harel (2001), 'Crime Rates and Expected Sanctions: The Economics of Deterrence Revisited', *Journal of Legal Studies*, **30**, 485–501.

Bebchuk, L.A. and L. Kaplow (1992), 'Optimal Sanctions When Individuals are Imperfectly Informed about the Probability of Apprehension', *Journal of Legal Studies*, **21**, 365–70.

Bebchuk, L.A. and L. Kaplow (1993), 'Optimal Sanctions and Differences in Individuals' Likelihood of Avoiding Detection', *International Review of Law and Economics*, **13**, 217–24.

Beccaria, C. (1767), *On Crimes and Punishments, and Other Writings*, R. Davies et al., trans. R. Bellamy (ed.) (New York: Cambridge University Press, 1995).

Becker, G.S. (1968), 'Crime and Punishment: An Economic Approach', *Journal of Political Economy*, **76**, 169–217.

Becker, G.S. and G.J. Stigler (1974). 'Law Enforcement, Malfeasance, and Compensation of Enforcers', *Journal of Legal Studies*, **3**, 1–18.

Bentham, J. (1789), 'An Introduction to the Principles of Morals and Legislation', in *The Utilitarians* (Garden City, NY: Anchor Books, 1973).

Block, M.K. and J.G. Sidak (1980), 'The Cost of Antitrust Deterrence: Why Not Hang a Price Fixer Now and Then?', *Georgetown Law Journal*, **68**, 1131–9.

Bouckaert, B. and G. De Geest (eds) (1992), *Bibliography of Law and Economics* (Dordrecht: Kluwer Academic Publishers).

Bowles, R. and N. Garoupa (1997), 'Casual Police Corruption and the Economics of Crime', *International Review of Law and Economics*, **17**, 75–87.

Carr-Hill, R.A. and N.H. Stern (1979), *Crime, the Police and Criminal Statistics* (London: Academic Press).

Chu, C.Y.C. and N. Jiang (1993), 'Are Fines More Efficient than Imprisonment?', *Journal of Public Economics*, **51**, 391–413.

Chu, C.Y.C., S. Hu and T. Huang (2000), 'Punishing Repeat Offenders More Severely', *International Review of Law and Economics*, **20**, 127–40.

Clotfelter, C.T. (1977), 'Public Services, Private Substitutes, and the Demand for Protection Against Crime', *American Economic Review*, **67**, 867–77.

Clotfelter, C.T. (1978), 'Private Security and the Public Safety', *Journal of Urban Economics*, **5**, 388–402.

Cohen, M.A. (1989), 'Corporate Crime and Punishment: A Study of Social Harm and Sentencing Practice in the Federal Courts, 1984–1987', *American Criminal Law Review*, **26**, 605–60.

Cohen, M.A. (1999), 'Monitoring and Enforcement of Environmental Policy', in H. Folmer and T. Tietenberg (eds), *The International Yearbook of Environmental and Resource Economics 1999/2000* (Cheltenham, UK and Northampton, MA, USA: Edward Elgar), pp. 44–106.

Cooter, R.D. and D.L. Rubinfeld (1989), 'Economic Analysis of Legal Disputes and their Resolution', *Journal of Economic Literature*, **27**, 1067–97.

Craswell, R. and J.E. Calfee (1986), 'Deterrence and Uncertain Legal Standards', *Journal of Law, Economics, & Organization*, **2**, 279–303.

Diamond, P.A. (2002), 'Integrating Punishment and Efficiency Concerns in Punitive Damages for Reckless Disregard of Risks to Others', *Journal of Law, Economics, & Organization*, **18**, 117–39.

Eide, E. (2000), 'Economics of Criminal Behavior', in B. Bouckaert and G. De Geest (eds), *Encyclopedia of Law and Economics* (Cheltenham, UK and Northampton, MA, USA: Edward Elgar), pp. 345–89.

Ehrlich, I. (1981), 'On the Usefulness of Controlling Individuals: An Economic Analysis of Rehabilitation, Incapacitation and Deterrence', *American Economic Review*, **71**, 307–32.

Emons, W. (2003), 'A Note on the Optimal Punishment for Repeat Offenders', *International Review of Law and Economics*, **23**, 253–9.

Friedman, D.D. (1995), 'Making Sense of English Law Enforcement in the Eighteenth Century', *University of Chicago Law School Roundtable*, **2**, 475–505.

Garoupa, N. (1997), 'The Theory of Optimal Law Enforcement', *Journal of Economic Surveys*, **11**, 267–95.

Garoupa, N. (1998), 'Optimal Law Enforcement and Imperfect Information when Wealth Varies Among Individuals', *Economica*, **65**, 479–90.

Garoupa, N. and D. Klerman (2004), 'Corruption and the Optimal Use of Nonmonetary Sanctions', *International Review of Law and Economics*, **24**, 219–25.

Glaeser, E.L., D.P. Kessler and A.M. Piehl (2000), 'What Do Prosecutors Maximize? An Analysis of the Federalization of Drug Crimes', *American Law and Economics Review*, **2**, 259–90.

Grossman, G.M. and M.L. Katz (1983), 'Plea Bargaining and Social Welfare', *American Economic Review*, **73**, 749–57.

Hindriks, J., M. Keen and A. Muthoo (1999), 'Corruption, Extortion and Evasion', *Journal of Public Economics*, **74**, 395–430.

Innes, R. (1999), 'Remediation and Self-Reporting in Optimal Law Enforcement', *Journal of Public Economics*, **72**, 379–93.

Kahneman, D., P. Slovic and A. Tversky (eds) (1982), *Judgment under Uncertainty: Heuristics and Biases* (Cambridge and New York: Cambridge University Press).

Kaplow, L. (1990a), 'Optimal Deterrence, Uninformed Individuals, and Acquiring Information About Whether Acts are Subject to Sanctions', *Journal of Law, Economics, & Organization*, **6**, 93–128.

Kaplow, L. (1990b), 'A Note on the Optimal Use of Nonmonetary Sanctions', *Journal of Public Economics*, **42**, 245–7.

Kaplow, L. (1992), 'The Optimal Probability and Magnitude of Fines for Acts That Definitely are Undesirable', *International Review of Law and Economics*, **12**, 3–11.

Kaplow, L. and S. Shavell (1994a), 'Accuracy in the Determination of Liability', *Journal of Law and Economics*, **37**, 1–15.

Kaplow, L. and S. Shavell (1994b), 'Optimal Law Enforcement with Self-Reporting of Behavior', *Journal of Political Economy*, **102**, 583–606.

Kaplow, L. and S. Shavell (2002), *Fairness Versus Welfare* (Cambridge, MA: Harvard University Press).

Kenkel, D.S. (1993), 'Do Drunk Drivers Pay Their Way? A Note on Optimal Penalties for Drunk Driving', *Journal of Health Economics*, **12**, 137–49.

Kessler, D. and S.D. Levitt (1999), 'Using Sentence Enhancements to Distinguish between Deterrence and Incapacitation', *Journal of Law and Economics*, **42**, 343–63.

Klitgaard, R. (1988), *Controlling Corruption* (Berkeley, CA: University of California Press).

Kobayashi, B.H. and J.R. Lott, Jr (1992), 'Low-probability-high-penalty Enforcement Strategies and the Efficient Operation of the Plea-bargaining System', *International Review of Law and Economics*, **12**, 69–77.
Kornhauser, L.A. (1982), 'An Economic Analysis of the Choice Between Enterprise and Personal Liability for Accidents', *California Law Review*, **70**, 1345–92.
Laffont, J. and J. Tirole (1993), *The Theory of Incentives in Procurement and Regulation* (Cambridge, MA: MIT Press).
Landes, W.M. (1971), 'An Economic Analysis of the Courts', *Journal of Law and Economics*, **4**, 61–107.
Landes, W.M. and R.A. Posner (1975), 'The Private Enforcement of Law', *Journal of Legal Studies*, **4**, 1–46.
Lando, H. and S. Shavell (2004), 'The Advantage of Focusing Law Enforcement Effort', *International Review of Law and Economics*, **24**, 209–18.
Levitt, S.D. (1997), 'Incentive Compatibility Constraints as an Explanation for the Use of Prison Sentences Instead of Fines', *International Review of Law and Economics*, **17**, 179–92.
Levitt, S.D. (1998), 'Why Do Increased Arrest Rates Appear to Reduce Crime: Deterrence, Incapacitation, or Measurement Error?', *Economic Inquiry*, **36**, 353–72.
Levitt, S.D. and T. Miles (2007), 'Empirical Study of Criminal Punishment', in A.M. Polinsky and S. Shavell (eds), *Handbook of Law and Economics*, volume 1 (Amsterdam: North-Holland), pp. 455–95.
Lewin, J.L. and W.N. Trumbull (1990), 'The Social Value of Crime?', *International Review of Law and Economics*, **10**, 271–84.
Malik, A.S. (1990), 'Avoidance, Screening and Optimum Enforcement', *RAND Journal of Economics*, **21**, 341–53.
Malik, A.S. (1993), 'Self-reporting and the Design of Policies for Regulating Stochastic Pollution', *Journal of Environmental Economics and Management*, **24**, 241–57.
McAdams, R.H. (1997), 'The Origin, Development, and Regulation of Norms', *Michigan Law Review*, 96: 338–433.
McAdams, R.H. and E. Rasmusen (2007), 'Norms and the Law', in A.M. Polinsky and S. Shavell (eds), *Handbook of Law and Economics*, volume 2 (Amsterdam: North-Holland), pp. 1573–618.
Miceli, T.J. (1991), 'Optimal Criminal Procedure: Fairness and Deterrence', *International Review of Law and Economics*, **11**, 3–10.
Miceli, T.J. (1996), 'Plea Bargaining and Deterrence: An Institutional Approach', *European Journal of Law and Economics*, **3**, 249–64.
Miceli, T.J. and C. Bucci (2005), 'A Simple Theory of Increasing Penalties for Repeat Offenders', *Review of Law & Economics*, **1**, 71–80 (available at http://www.bepress.com/rle/vol1/iss1/art5).
Montesquieu (1748), *The Spirit of the Laws* (Berkeley, CA: University of California Press, reprinted 1977).
Mookherjee, D. (1997), 'The Economics of Enforcement', in A. Bose, M. Rakshit and A. Sinha (eds), *Issues in Economic Theory and Policy: Essays in Honor of Tapas Majumdar* (New Delhi: Oxford University Press), pp. 202–49.
Mookherjee, D. and I.P.L. Png (1992), 'Monitoring vis-à-vis Investigation in Enforcement of Law', *American Economic Review*, **82**, 556–65.
Mookherjee, D. and I.P.L. Png (1994), 'Marginal Deterrence in Enforcement of Law', *Journal of Political Economy*, **102**, 1039–66.
Mookherjee, D. and I.P.L. Png (1995), 'Corruptible Law Enforcers: How Should They Be Compensated?' *Economic Journal*, **105**, 145–59.
Newman, H.A. and D.W. Wright (1990), 'Strict Liability in a Principal-Agent Model', *International Review of Law and Economics*, **10**, 219–31.
Pashigian, B.P. (1975), 'On the Control of Crime and Bribery', *Journal of Legal Studies*, **4**, 311–26.
Png, I.P.L. (1986), 'Optimal Subsidies and Damages in the Presence of Judicial Error', *International Review of Law and Economics*, **6**, 101–05.

Polinsky, A.M. (1980a), 'Private versus Public Enforcement of Fines', *Journal of Legal Studies*, **9**, 105–27.

Polinsky, A.M. (1980b), 'Strict Liability vs. Negligence in a Market Setting', *American Economic Review: Papers and Proceedings*, **70**, 363–70.

Polinsky, A.M. (2006a), 'The Optimal Use of Fines and Imprisonment When Wealth is Unobservable', *Journal of Public Economics*, **90**, 823–35.

Polinsky, A.M. (2006b), 'Optimal Fines and Auditing When Wealth is Costly to Observe', *International Review of Law and Economics*, **26**, 323–35.

Polinsky, A.M. and D.L. Rubinfeld (1988), 'The Deterrent Effects of Settlements and Trials', *International Review of Law and Economics*, **8**, 109–16.

Polinsky, A.M. and D.L. Rubinfeld (1989), 'A Note on Optimal Public Enforcement with Settlements and Litigation Costs', *Research in Law and Economics*, **12**, 1–8.

Polinsky, A.M. and D.L. Rubinfeld (1991), 'A Model of Optimal Fines for Repeat Offenders', *Journal of Public Economics*, **46**, 291–306.

Polinsky, A.M. and S. Shavell (1979), 'The Optimal Tradeoff between the Probability and Magnitude of Fines', *American Economic Review*, **69**, 880–91.

Polinsky, A.M. and S. Shavell (1984), 'The Optimal Use of Fines and Imprisonment', *Journal of Public Economics*, **24**, 89–99.

Polinsky, A.M. and S. Shavell (1991), 'A Note on Optimal Fines When Wealth Varies Among Individuals', *American Economic Review*, **81**, 618–21.

Polinsky, A.M. and S. Shavell (1992), 'Enforcement Costs and the Optimal Magnitude and Probability of Fines', *Journal of Law and Economics*, **35**, 133–48.

Polinsky, A.M. and S. Shavell (1993), 'Should Employees be Subject to Fines and Imprisonment Given the Existence of Corporate Liability?', *International Review of Law and Economics*, **13**, 239–57.

Polinsky, A.M. and S. Shavell (1998), 'On Offense History and the Theory of Deterrence', *International Review of Law and Economics*, **18**, 305–24.

Polinsky, A.M. and S. Shavell (1999), 'On the Disutility and Discounting of Imprisonment and the Theory of Deterrence', *Journal of Legal Studies*, **28**, 1–16.

Polinsky, A.M. and S. Shavell (2000a), 'The Economic Theory of Public Enforcement of Law', *Journal of Economic Literature*, **38**, 45–76.

Polinsky, A.M. and S. Shavell (2000b), 'The Fairness of Sanctions: Some Implications for Optimal Enforcement Policy', *American Law and Economics Review*, **2**, 223–37.

Polinsky, A.M. and S. Shavell (2001), 'Corruption and Optimal Law Enforcement', *Journal of Public Economics*, **81**, 1–24.

Posner, R.A. (1985), 'An Economic Theory of the Criminal Law', *Columbia Law Review*, **85**, 1193–231.

Posner, R.A. (1997), 'Social Norms and the Law: An Economic Approach', *American Economic Review: Papers and Proceedings*, **87**, 365–69.

Reinganum, J.F. (1988), 'Plea Bargaining and Prosecutorial Discretion', *American Economic Review*, **78**, 713–28.

Rose-Ackerman, S. (1999), *Corruption and Government: Causes, Consequences, and Reform* (Cambridge: Cambridge University Press).

Rubinstein, A. (1979), 'An Optimal Conviction Policy for Offenses that May Have Been Committed by Accident', in S.J. Brams, A. Schotter and G. Schwödiauer (eds), *Applied Game Theory* (Wurzburg: Physica-Verlag), pp. 406–13.

Sah, R.K. (1991), 'Social Osmosis and Patterns of Crime', *Journal of Political Economy*, **99**, 1272–95.

Segerson, K. and T. Tietenberg (1992), 'The Structure of Penalties in Environmental Enforcement: An Economic Analysis', *Journal of Environmental Economics and Management*, **23**, 179–200.

Shavell, S. (1980), 'Strict Liability versus Negligence', *Journal of Legal Studies*, **9**, 1–25.

Shavell, S. (1985), 'Criminal Law and the Optimal Use of Nonmonetary Sanctions as a Deterrent', *Columbia Law Review*, **85**, 1232–62.

Shavell, S. (1987a), 'A Model of Optimal Incapacitation', *American Economic Review: Papers and Proceedings*, **77**, 107–10.
Shavell, S. (1987b), 'The Optimal Use of Nonmonetary Sanctions as a Deterrent', *American Economic Review*, **77**, 584–92.
Shavell, S. (1991a), 'Individual Precautions to Prevent Theft: Private versus Socially Optimal Behavior', *International Review of Law and Economics*, **11**, 123–32.
Shavell, S. (1991b), 'Specific versus General Enforcement of Law', *Journal of Political Economy*, **99**, 1088–108.
Shavell, S. (1992), 'A Note on Marginal Deterrence', *International Review of Law and Economics*, **12**, 345–55.
Shavell, S. (1993), 'The Optimal Structure of Law Enforcement', *Journal of Law and Economics*, **36**, 255–87.
Shavell, S. (1997a), 'The Fundamental Divergence Between the Private and the Social Motive to Use the Legal System', *Journal of Legal Studies*, **26**, 575–612.
Shavell, S. (1997b), 'The Optimal Level of Corporate Liability Given the Limited Ability of Corporations to Penalize Their Employees', *International Review of Law and Economics*, **17**, 203–13.
Shavell, S. (2002), 'Law versus Morality as Regulators of Conduct', *American Law and Economics Review*, **4**, 227–57.
Shavell, S. (2004), *Foundations of Economic Analysis of Law* (Cambridge, MA: Harvard University Press).
Shleifer, A. and R.W. Vishny (1993), 'Corruption', *Quarterly Journal of Economics*, **108**, 599–617.
Spier, K.E. (1997), 'A Note on the Divergence Between the Private and the Social Motive to Settle under a Negligence Rule', *Journal of Legal Studies*, **26**, 613–21.
Spier, K.E. (2007), 'Litigation', in A.M. Polinsky and S. Shavell (eds), *Handbook of Law and Economics*, volume 1 (Amsterdam: North-Holland), pp. 259–342.
Stigler, G.J. (1970), 'The Optimum Enforcement of Laws', *Journal of Political Economy*, **78**, 526–36.
Sunstein, C.R. (1996), 'Social Norms and Social Roles', *Columbia Law Review*, **96**, 201–66.
Sykes, A.O. (1981), 'An Efficiency Analysis of Vicarious Liability Under the Law of Agency', *Yale Law Journal*, **91**, 168–206.
University of Pennsylvania Law Review (1996), 'Symposium: Law, Economics, and Norms', *University of Pennsylvania Law Review*, **144**, 1643–2339.
US Department of Justice (1988), *Report to the Nation on Crime and Justice, Technical Appendix* 2nd edition (Washington, DC: US Department of Justice, Bureau of Justice Statistics, NCJ-112011).
US Department of Justice (1997a), *Sourcebook of Criminal Justice Statistics – 1996* (Washington, DC: US Department of Justice, Office of Justice Statistics, Bureau of Justice Statistics, NCJ-165361).
US Department of Justice (1997b), *Uniform Crime Reports for the United States, 1996* (Washington, DC: US Department of Justice, Federal Bureau of Investigation).
US Department of Justice (1998), *Profile of Jail Inmates 1996* (Washington, DC: US Department of Justice, Office of Justice Programs, NCJ-164620).
Waldfogel, J. (1993), 'Criminal Sentences as Endogenous Taxes: Are they "Just" or "Efficient"?', *Journal of Law and Economics*, **36**, 139–51.
Wilde, L.L. (1992), 'Criminal Choice, Nonmonetary Sanctions, and Marginal Deterrence: A Normative Analysis', *International Review of Law and Economics*, **12**, 333–44.
Wilson, J.Q. and R.J. Herrnstein (1985), *Crime and Human Nature* (New York: Simon and Schuster).

2 Private enforcement of law

Reza Rajabiun[1]

1. Introduction

Polinsky and Shavell in Chapter 1 define public enforcement as the use of government agents to detect and sanction violators of legal rules. These agents include inspectors, tax auditors, police, regulators, and prosecutors. This chapter complements their analysis by focusing on the study of private enforcement of law, defined as follows:

> Private enforcement allows for private persons or organizations to sanction violators of legal rules in courts without consent or action by public enforcers (such as the police, public prosecutors, or regulators). Private enforcers include the victims of offences, as well as the legal representatives of their claims.

Private enforcement is an integral part of policy debates on socio-economic problems ranging from the application of human rights codes, mitigation of environmental hazards, to the regulation of anticompetitive practices. This chapter studies how economic theorists describe private enforcement procedures and institutions, how they differ from public enforcement, and how they can contribute to the efficient implementation of legal rules.

The 'economic approach' to the study of law pioneered by Becker (1968, 1993) emphasizes that systems of public enforcement tend to coexist with procedures for private enforcement. Even in jurisdictions with highly competent and sophisticated bureaucracies, victims often search for alternative rights of access to courts or other independent adjudication venues to seek remedies. Typically, private access rights exist along with public responsibilities and prosecutorial discretion to enforce legal rules, for instance in the case of bid rigging or price fixing without prior disclosure, or in the presence of civil claims for sexual assault or abuse. Access by non-state entities to enforce legal rules and prosecute offenders also requires the presence of a court system and other necessary public infrastructure for implementing judgments.

---

[1] The author thanks Nuno Garoupa, Alena Kimakova, Steffan Riddell and Brenda Spotton Visano for valuable comments and suggestions.
Corresponding address: rezarajabiun@osgoode.yorku.ca.

In this context, victims of injustice face a delegation problem when trying to make a claim, enforce legal rules, and punish offenders. In the case of public enforcement, the problem involves providing information to government agents with the authority to determine if the case merits further investments. With private enforcement, the victim, or her lawyer, must make the necessary investments instead. Government agents in the form of judges can of course refuse private access rights by a victim to the public judicial infrastructure, as can public prosecutors and regulators (based on evidentiary, economical, or ideological reasons) in the case of public enforcement.

Naturally, victims would typically want to defray the costs of legal enforcement and deterrence to the public sector. This is especially true if the victims are poor, and the offenders either too rich or too poor, and hence difficult to punish by the victims or their private representatives (judgment proof). Furthermore, the public sector can exhibit economies of scale and scope, and thus cost savings in the implementation of legal rules compared to a private system prone to duplication and coordination problems. On the other hand, reaching a certain threshold in terms of the size and complexity of a jurisdiction, the informational benefits of decentralization may weigh more heavily in favour of private rather than public enforcement (Fearon and Busch, 2006). Hence, smaller jurisdictions may have good financial reasons to assign exclusive rights to enforce legal rules to public inspectors and prosecutors, and pay for the deterrence through the general tax pool, while larger jurisdictions may adopt a mixed public-private enforcement system. Nevertheless, the economic approach suggests that, even in the presence of benevolent public agents, budget and information requirements of public enforcement ration the 'rule of law' in jurisdictions that do not provide sufficient scope for private legal actions by victims. For economists, pecuniary legal claims that function independently of the incentives and resources of government agents represent a 'high powered' incentive scheme that may remedy the expected inadequacies of a centralized public enforcement system (Weber, 1946; Aghion and Tirole, 1997).

Effective implementation of formal legal rights and prohibitions requires investments in funds to acquire information, prosecute offences, and punish the convicted. The financial problem exists regardless of the substantive norms under consideration, whether the application of human rights codes, mitigation of environmental hazards, trading of corporate securities, or the regulation of anticompetitive practices. The required investment can be made through public agents such as state prosecutors or regulators. Importantly, even the most well-intentioned and informed regulators, prosecutors, or judges depend upon the cooperation of either victims of crime or knowledgeable informants to complete their tasks. In case of enforcement rationing and low deterrence levels by a centralized public enforcement system, the responsibility for investigation, prosecution, and punishment will fall on the victims or their representatives. The key difference between public and private enforcement consequently lies in the availability of a procedural option for victims and their representatives to access the public judicial infrastructure in search of compensatory remedies without consent, action, or investment by agents of the state, such as prosecutors, inspectors, regulators, or administrators.

As detailed long ago by Weber (1946), and formalized more recently by Aghion and Tirole (1997), public agents are typically paid fixed salaries, generating the possibility that they will have 'low powered' incentives to implement the formal authority of the law. Private enforcers, on the other hand, seek pecuniary legal claims, or the 'bounty'. Mookherjee (2006) provides a review of the economic literature on the design of mechanisms for controlling principal-agent problems characterized by low-powered incentives in hierarchical organizations that arise because of a separation of ownership and control.

Drew (1995) characterizes private enforcement in modern legal thought as ultimately deriving from legal mechanisms which existed prior to the centralization of power by monarchies in Europe during the Middle Ages. With the rise of republicanism in the 18th century, the clan-based and feudal regimes for enforcement of contract and property law were gradually superseded by codified statutes and centralized administrative agencies in most of continental Europe. The evolution of legal procedures in England differed somewhat from the European trends due to the increased use of private prosecutors. Friedman (1996) explores this historical anomaly, and attributes its formation to the profit motive of the monarchy. However, as it became increasingly problematic in the English bounty system to control the urban populations, the regime was abandoned and replaced by public policing and prosecution agencies in the 19th century.

In the United States, private systems for the regulation of liability, from industrial accidents to anticompetitive practices, operated for most of the 19th century. Glaeser and Shleifer (2003) argue that the adoption of the new technologies that relied on economies of scale and the institution of limited liability enhanced the asymmetries among potential victims and offenders, motivating the 'rise of the regulatory state'.

Expanding the powers of public prosecutors and administrators to detect and sanction violators of legal rules outside Western Europe and North America was typically a product of colonial efforts to subdue local populations. A large body of research reviewed by Wolf (1982) and

Merry (1992) has studied the co-evolution of colonial and local regulatory regimes.

The inefficiencies associated with the public enforcement of trade regulations were criticized by the forerunners of modern economic thought. For instance, the Physiocrats in the French court focused on the perverse incentives created by the enforcement of monopoly rights granted by the monarchy, while authors of the Scottish Enlightenment like Adam Smith pointed out the costs of trade regulations on local and colonized economies (Smith, 1776; Landreth and Colander, 2002). Liberal thinkers stressed the potential unintended consequences of the exercise of centralized political authority to regulate socio-economic behaviour. Thomas Malthus (1800), on the other hand, blamed the private rights of access by the indigent to common law courts as the cause of 'The High Price of Provisions'.

Economists of the late 19th and early 20th centuries often found the liberal appeals to private systems of regulation to be 'unscientific' and instead followed the Malthusian tradition. Clark (1894), an influential figure in the development of economic analysis in the United States, for instance categorized appeals to law to organize economic processes into 'anarchist' and 'socialist' groups, and dismissed attempts to limit the powers of the state as 'self terminating'. In the German-speaking world, scholars such as Eugen von Böhm-Bawerk (1851–1914) and Max Weber (1864–1920) developed bodies of systematic evidence about modern and pre-modern legal systems. Contemporary studies in law and economics combine the formalist and empiricist methodologies to describe and analyze features of real legal systems (see Williamson, 2000; Greif, 1998, 2005).

The framework for most formal rational choice models follows from the seminal study by Becker (1968) on the 'economic approach' to the study of crime and punishment. In his analysis, the institution of private enforcement functions as a theoretical construct (ideal type in the language of the empirical or 'historical' school in the German language tradition). The theoretical ideal serves as a benchmark for the analysis of public legal systems. Consequently, what we call 'first generation' models in this chapter implicitly assume that the two distinct mechanisms function as substitutable institutions, potentially able to completely replace each other (see Gerschenkron, 1962, for the seminal introduction of this concept in his historical criticism of deterministic Marxian models of economic history). Hence, the adoption of one negates the need for another in this class of models. More recently, some researchers have instead characterized private enforcement as an instrument that complements the resources and information available to the public and enhances the credibility of legal rules present in statutes and precedent (see Aoki, 1994, for an analysis of institutional complementarities in terms of contingent delegation of tasks to public and private bureaucracies). The 'second generation' models view law and regulation as mechanisms that can replicate 'missing markets', or as insurance against undesirable states of the world (Laffont, 2000, 2005).

Ahead of detailing the rich distinctions within the economic models of enforcement, it is imperative to highlight their similarities in terms of the 'economic approach' to the study of behaviour (Becker, 1993). In both classes of models, private enforcement of the law serves as a proxy for a system of regulation where all individual interactions are monetized, and both individuals and groups rationally exchange rights and privileges, compensating each other for the consequences of their actions. In this view, legal institutions function analogously to a Pigouvian tax system on negative externalities (for example, pollution). The tax punishes socially undesirable behaviour by imposing small fines applied frequently, instead of resorting to heavy but infrequent criminal sanctions. The next section looks at the historical origins of problems that motivated this analytical dichotomy between public and private enforcement procedures. Section 3 reviews theories that describe the two enforcement mechanisms as institutional substitutes, while Section 4 looks at models that emphasize complementarities between actions by public and private enforcers. Section 5 concludes by presenting a number of specific applications of the economic approach to the study of enforcement mechanisms. An extended reference section follows, with suggestions for further reading.

2. The crime-tort puzzle

Becker (1968) provides an exploration of crime and punishment using the usual tools for the analysis of industrial organization. His application of marginal analysis shows that legal systems that impose small but frequent punishments are superior to those that tend to deploy 'hang them all' strategies (with heavy, but infrequent punishments) for inducing compliance with the law. Moreover, Becker (1968) demonstrates that budget-maximizing behaviour of public enforcers encourages the adoption of 'hang them all' strategies promoted famously by Jeremy Bentham (1789) in his *Introduction to the Principles of Morals and Legislation* aimed at preventing vice and promoting virtue. Fyodor Dostoevsky (1821–1881) criticized the usefulness of heavy punishments due to the perverse economic incentives they create in offenders, enforcers, and victims. The economic approach uses the instruments of formal modelling, and more recently empirical testing, to study these perverse incentives and design efficient mechanisms for implementing legal rules.

In the ideal type of private enforcement system implicitly underlying most economic models, a price system generates a stable equilibrium level of illegal activity. Moreover, the theory assumes that the marginal expected utility calculation of potential offenders determines the level of expected offences. Consequently, rational criminals commit offences as long as they believe that the marginal expected private benefits from their actions are greater than the expected costs of punishment. The primary variables considered by offenders in the Becker (1968) model are the probability of apprehension and conviction, and the potential punishment if convicted. Two distinct trends in the development of US legal institutions shortly after World War II explain the choice of variables, model structure, and the puzzle raised in this chapter.

2.1 Criminalization

In some areas of crime and punishment, the evolution of the US system contradicts the prediction of price theory that economic considerations should stimulate the formation of efficient systems of enforcement that equate the social costs and private benefits of illegal actions. Importantly, Becker's (1968) analysis appears to be inspired both by a concern for the increased criminalization of a wide range of activities, and by the basic observation that criminal law typically involved heavy punishments, including execution, prison terms, and the social stigma of having a criminal past. He estimated that, as of 1965, 2 per cent of the US labour force was already in prison, on parole, or subject to the resultant restrictions on their participation in the labour market. Recent data show that the trend identified by Becker (1968) has persisted: Department of Justice statistics reveal that the number of persons in prison, on parole, or on probation in the US tripled between 1980 and 2005. As of 2005, this amounted to approximately 7 million of America's labour force of 150 million (approximately 5 per cent of the labour force).[2]

As an illustration of the level of criminalization, the courts apply heavy criminal punishments for numerous non-violent offences, for example illegal drug possession or prostitution. Economists usually do not view these crimes as socially costly. Moreover, US courts have handed down heavy sentences to young offenders (who are deemed incompetent to form requisite criminal intent in most other jurisdictions) with increasing consistency. The persistence of heavy criminal punishments in the US and some developing country jurisdictions remains puzzling to observers who apply the fundamental methods of price theory to the analysis of legal institutions. Friedman (1999, 2000) observed that, even if we ignore

2 US Department of Justice, *Sourcebook of Criminal Justice Statistics*, see: http://www.albany.edu/sourcebook/.

the immorality of execution, torture, or imprisoning people for extended periods of time, economic considerations reveal that such harsh punishments are inefficient relative to private enforcement alternatives that principally apply smaller, but more frequent punishments in terms of fines:

> Replacing a criminal punishment with another that both is more severe and has a lower ratio of punishment costs to amount of punishment while reducing the probability of conviction to maintain the same level of deterrence, lowers both punishment cost and enforcement cost. Hence, imprisonment is always dominated by execution and both are dominated by fines and other alternatives. Modern legal systems do not fit that pattern. (Friedman, 1999, p. 259)

Although some legal systems continue to utilize execution and long-term imprisonment liberally, many other jurisdictions have moved away from these forms of punishment and switched to fines and other alternatives. Prominent examples of this transition include Western Europe, Japan, and Canada after World War II, Latin America and Eastern Europe after the political changes of the 1980s and 1990s, and South Africa following apartheid. The new lawmakers in these jurisdictions did not preserve their sovereign rights to engage in execution, torture, and long imprisonment for non-violent acts in order to control the population. These states have instead increasingly instituted economic control through taxes and administrative regulations, and have not retained the heavy criminal punishments readily available under previous regimes. For violent offences, although imprisonment remains as an effective solution, these jurisdictions also abolished execution, an important symbolic gesture in the choice of punishment strategies. Hence, many modern legal systems have started to converge towards the patterns of institutional change suggested by price theory.

This observation justifies the need to separate the analysis of enforcement along two classes of models. The methodology of the first generation of models implies that public and private enforcement institutions could replace each other in practice. In other words, this theory assumes that public and private enforcement mechanisms are substitutable processes for the enforcement of law, and the presence of one negates the power of the other. A crucial assumption on which this result rests is that orthodox theory of optimal punishment 'treats the enforcement apparatus – police, courts, prosecutors, and legislature – as a philosopher-king, with imperfect knowledge but only the best of motives' (Friedman, 1999, p. 262). Hence, if there is a divergence of incentives between public enforcers and victims (or their representatives) due to political or financial motives, we cannot expect the outcomes under public and private enforcement to be identical.

In reality, we often see a mix of private and public prohibitions applied to remedy similar or related behaviour. Different entities, including the victims and offenders, their representatives, public prosecutors, or even the news media, get involved in gathering information about illegal practices. In case of sufficient grounds for a legal claim, the public or private prosecutors then must invest their funds and efforts in prosecution and punishment of offenders. Second-generation models explore how private access rights function to enhance the inherently limited capacity of public regulatory institutions to channel information necessary to identify and prosecute offences.

2.2 Privatization

Although choices made regarding criminal law procedures and punishments in the United States did not follow the predictions of price theory, a second broad trend in the development of legal procedures in the US is readily explained, and justified, by the analysis of Becker (1968). Following World War II, criminalization coincided with the radical and rapid expansion of private rights of standing in courts to claim civil liability based on a wide range of norms and statutes. Specifically, private claims were allowed in the regulation of civil rights, labour market practices, environmental monitoring, securities regulation, and antitrust. The new enforcement regimes meant that victims had the option of directly prosecuting offenders, as long as they could convince a lower court judge of the merits of their case. Victims hence did not have to seek the approval of public prosecutors or other administrative agencies in their pursuit of pecuniary claims.

The procedures adopted to enforce the laws, however, did not eliminate the role of the government, but simply changed the channels for communication of information from potential victims to bypass the police, inspectors, and public prosecution offices. In the case of civil rights, a well-documented popular hostility to the laws of the central government in some regions meant that public enforcement lacked credibility. Nevertheless, government agencies at all levels remained active in developing standards for the implementation of the new Federal legislative mandates. Moreover, the radical expansion of cases was supported by increased investments in courts and training of the judiciary, as well as bailiffs, sheriffs, and court-appointed creditors that implement civil judgments. Private enforcement mechanisms hence did not replace the public sector, but instead enhanced the government's credibility by giving its legislation more ubiquitous authority.

As an important illustration, consider the case of enforcement of public antitrust/competition laws, which is a task delegated almost exclusively to national competition bureaus or antimonopoly agencies in most jurisdictions, with the notable exception of the United States. When the Clayton Act was passed in 1914, citizens and other legal entities were granted the right to enforce provisions of the Sherman Act through civil actions, and claim triple the actual damages. Public enforcement since the adoption of the Sherman Act had been highly erratic, and it was almost completely abandoned in the early 1930s as the Federal government started to adopt policies aimed at stimulating agglomeration and cartelization (Cole and Ohanian, 2004). Private actions were nonetheless rare before World War II, despite the formal legislative mandate established by the Clayton Act of 1914.

Following World War II, there was a rapid transition from a primarily public enforcement approach to one relying principally upon knowledge and investments by private enforcers. The reason for this transition in choice of legal procedure remains a mystery for US antitrust historians. Records of the Administrative Office of the US Courts document that the ratio of civil cases filed by private claimants to those initiated by public prosecutors increased from approximately 1:1 in 1945 to 10:1 by the 1970s before stabilizing at around 7:1 in the 1980s and 1990s. Moreover, as documented by Salop and White (1986), the private claimants were typically downstream firms and competitors of the offenders. These entities are likely to have more detailed and accurate knowledge about what constitutes anticompetitive practices in specific industries, and often have commercial incentives other than the expected damages to stop them. Despite the availability of a damage multiplier and relatively lax rules for the formation of class actions, their data suggested that final consumers did not play a significant part in the enforcement process. This observation potentially highlights the difficulties in employing private enforcement mechanisms, when the benefits of a particular offence are concentrated, and their costs dispersed across a large population facing high coordination costs to engage in collective action through the courts. Due to the asymmetry in organizational ability, and hence also financial means, to engage in legal action on the part of consumers, private enforcement must be viewed as a high-powered mechanism for the acquisition of information that complements public regulatory institutions.

By the 1970s, the trend towards greater rights of access to courts generated a good deal of political resistance by the usual suspects, including industrial and professional service/labour lobby groups involved in a movement now colloquially called 'tort reform' in the United States. In addition to groups that expected to lose from the emergent enforcement procedures, private actions faced significant resistance from lawyers and economists associated with Federal Courts and antitrust bureaucracy. As documented by Breit and Elzinga (1985), despite their many differences on the desirability of horizontal and vertical collusion, the so-called Chicago and Harvard schools of antitrust thought of the late 1970s and 1980s vehemently opposed private standing rights before the courts. This normative consensus stands in sharp contrast to the results obtained by Becker (1968, p. 199) in his application of the usual price-theoretical framework for the analysis of industries to the study of enforcement institutions:

> If compensation were stressed, the main purpose of legal proceedings would be to levy fines equal to the harm inflicted on society by constraints of trade. There would be no point to cease and desist orders, imprisonment, ridicule, or dissolution of companies. If economists' theory about monopoly is correct, and if optimal fines were levied, firms would automatically cease any constraints of trade, because the gain to them would be less than the harm they cause and thus less than the fines expected. On the other hand, if Schumpeter and other critics are correct, and certain constraints of trade raise the level of economic welfare, fines could fully compensate society for the harm done, and yet some constraints would not cease, because the gain to participants would exceed the harm to others.

Becker's (1968) arguments were purely theoretical and did not recognize the emergence of a private enforcement system in the US after World War II. Since the early 1980s, many other jurisdictions in Europe, Latin America, and Asia have adopted competition laws that aim to regulate restrictive trading practice (for example, collusion without disclosure) in their emerging market economies (Palim, 1998). Although these jurisdictions often replicated the substantive elements of the Sherman Antitrust tradition, almost none has managed to develop a regime that accommodates private actions by victims. Consequently, similar legal rules are enforced through radically different procedures, motivating appeals to private rights of action by both local and foreign entities in courts. In many cases, private actions are not possible, despite repeated manifestation of such rights in formal laws. Examples of the existing wedge between formal legal and real political authority in the area of competition law can be found in Brazil (Gidi, 2003), Canada (Roach and Trebilcock, 1996), and in the member states of the European Union (European Commission, Ashurst Report).[3]

The widely quoted decision by the European Court of Justice (ECJ) in *Courage v. Crehan* summarizes the economic arguments for employing private enforcement mechanisms, in this case to enhance the authority of existing agreements among the member states of the European Union:

---

[3] http://ec.europa.eu/comm/competition/antitrust/others/actions_for_damages/study.html. Study on the Conditions of Claims for Damages in Case of Infringement of EC Competition Rules (2004), European Commission.

> The full effectiveness of Article [81] of the Treaty and, in particular, the practical effect of the prohibition laid down in Article [81(1)] would be put at risk if it were not open to any individual to claim damages for loss caused to him by a *contract* or by conduct liable to restrict or distort competition.
>
> Indeed, the existence of such a right strengthens the working of the Community competition rules and discourages agreements or practices, which are *frequently covert*, which are liable to restrict or distort competition. From that point of view, actions for damages before the national courts can make a significant contribution to the maintenance of effective competition in the Community.[4]

The particular justification used by the ECJ for supporting private access rights through local judiciaries highlights the point of departure of the second-generation models in Section 4 that describe public and private enforcement as potentially complementary mechanisms. Significantly, the argument by the ECJ does not suggest that private actions are desirable because they save the state financial expenditures on enforcement. The ECJ justifies private enforcement with the presumption that information about practices that threaten inter-state legal commitments are costly to acquire and disseminate, and especially so for a public bureaucracy. In stark contrast to the ECJ's opinion stands Landes and Posner's (1975) pessimistic characterization of private access rights as a form of 'blackmail'. In both theories though, private enforcement institutions serve to convey information that would otherwise be unavailable to the public.

3. First-generation models of private enforcement

Coase (1960) criticized the manner in which economists and other social scientists characterized the notion of social cost from the top-down perspective of a benevolent state (Cooter and Ulen, 2004, p. 96). To remedy the problem, he constructed a bottom-up view of legal institutions and economic behaviour comprised of two general classes of mechanisms used to regulate socio-economic behaviour. Liability regimes employ adjudication venues such as courts after a harmful act has taken place, as well as public standards of precautionary care. Hence, liability allows for bargaining between offenders and their victims over the distribution of the costs and benefits of an action after victims and offenders have observed some information about the actual level of harm. Usually, negotiations take place before a case is filed with the public courts or with private arbitrators, based on the expectations the parties have formed about

---

[4] Case C-453/99. Emphasis added. For a critique of efforts to implement private access rights in the European Union jurisdictions, see Depoorter and Parisi (2005).

the costs and benefits of adversarial litigation. In case bargaining in this bilateral setting fails, a court could take on the case, collect and verify information about the level of harm from the offence, judge if the evidence shows a violation of applicable standards, and determine the punishment. A fundamentally different approach to instituting legal authority are property regimes, which comprise 'bright line' rule (versus liability standards) and heavy punishments against violators of the prohibitions. Easy to interpret and costly sanctions motivate stronger commitments to negotiations prior to a potentially risky act than liability regimes relying on monetary compensations. For property regimes to function efficiently, the transaction costs of exchanging usage and exclusion rights must be sufficiently low. Since transaction costs are generally positive, a residual role remains within this framework for liability regimes that monetize compensation and encourage negotiations between victims and offenders after the act.

Becker (1968) argued that the central variable in determining the level of offences are the resources devoted to control by police, courts, and prisons. Higher expenditures increase the probability of detection, apprehension, conviction, and punishment of wrongdoers. Punishments are assumed to take on the form of fines or imprisonment.

Becker (1968, p. 198) argued that

> . . . if the case for fines were accepted, and punishment by optimal fines became the norm, the traditional approach to criminal law would have to be significantly modified. First and foremost, the primary aim of all legal proceedings would become the same: not punishment or deterrence, but simply the assessment of the 'harm' done by defendants. . . . A criminal action would be defined fundamentally not by the nature of the action but by the inability of a person to compensate for the 'harm' that he caused. Thus an action would be 'criminal' precisely because it results in uncompensated 'harm' to others. Criminal law would cover all such actions, while tort law would cover all other (civil) actions.

Becker and Stigler (1974) focus on the interactions between public enforcers and potential offenders and highlight the possibility of perverse incentives in public enforcement systems. They show that higher punishments induce rent-seeking behaviour in a centralized enforcement agency and may lead to collusion and/or cooperation between enforcers and criminals to split the punishment from illegal actions, defined generally in terms of a fine. This trade can take place explicitly through cash bribes. Alternatively, the collusion can be implicit, for instance based on a promise of future employment by the offender to the public employees. Administrative improvements and political control will only partially mitigate the problem.

The possibility of Coasian bargaining (Cooter and Ulen, 2004, p. 74) between enforcers and offenders is of course also present in a private litigation system as the parties reach a settlement. However, the limitations of public and private enforcement systems manifest themselves under different conditions: Public enforcement will tend to be less effective in terms of punishment and deterrence when offenders have sufficient resources to bribe public officials. On the other hand, offenders who are poor, or have gained little from their crimes, will have little to share with government agents, and thus public enforcement is likely to be more effective in such cases. The standard solution to the incentive problem by public agents is to simply add more levels of public enforcers within a hierarchy to monitor each other. This top-down monitoring solution allows supervisors to control the communications and transactions by the police, prosecutors, or industry regulators better than a flatter organizational structure.

As bottom-up monitoring through private actions became more popular in the United States, Landes and Posner (1975) retorted to Becker and Stigler's (1974) justification for private access rights as a means to enforce public norms. The argument by Landes and Posner (1975) focused on the actual distribution of enforcement activities between public prosecutors and private litigants in the US legal system. They assume/hypothesize that common law institutions should be able to learn to adopt efficient procedures over time, thus assigning enforcement responsibility to public and private actors based on their capacities. They ask a question that goes against the grain of the standard economic framework: If private enforcement is always more efficient, why do we see so many appeals to public enforcers when a law is broken? Public enforcers are regularly called upon to control violent crimes, environmental infractions, or trust law violations. Indeed, why would any community resort to public enforcement if it were such an inefficient procedure for detecting and punishing offenders of legal rules?

Landes and Posner (1975) conjectured that a private system is more efficient for offences detected and punished at near zero costs, such as contract or property offences, whereas a public system should be utilized for offences that are hard to detect and punish. Their arguments against the value of extending private enforcement include: (a) the impossibility of constructing legal rules that give victims optimal incentives to prosecute, (b) the prospects for scale economies in public enforcement, and (c) the potential for the tragedy of commons if private enforcers have access to a publicly subsidized judicial infrastructure.

Part (a) of the Landes-Posner (1975) impossibility theorem conjectures that once an amount of punishment is set in a system of private prosecutions, there is no way to control the probability of punishment. With predefined punishments, the profit-maximizing behaviour of private litigants will drive the level of punishment. Given the tragedy of commons considered under part (c), public subsidies to courts lead to over-enforcement and over-deterrence. On the other hand, public enforcement does not lead to the same perverse incentives. The primary intuition for this result is the important observation that public prosecutors have great discretion and power to decide which rules to integrate into legal practice, and hence which offences are punished and deterred. The discretion allows government agents to avoid enforcing inefficient and/or unjust laws in courts subsidized by the tax pool, as in the traditional commons tragedy argument. The behaviour of private litigants consequently would be much harder to control when victims or their legal agents access the judicial infrastructure. Probably the most evocative critique of the economic approach is that which labels private enforcement as 'blackmail':

> Were blackmail, a form of private enforcement, lawful, the public monopoly of enforcement would be undermined. Over-enforcement of the law would result if the blackmailer were able to extract the full fine from the offender . . . Alternatively, the blackmailer might sell his incriminating information to the offender for a price lower than the statutory cost of punishment to the criminal, which would reduce the effective cost of punishment to the criminal below the level set by the legislature. (Landes and Posner, 1975, p. 42)

Becker and Stigler (1974) had argued that public agents have perverse incentives in interpreting and punishing offences, specifically because they tend to apply harsh punishment to offenders whose actions cause little social harm, and cooperate with those entities engaged in more harmful acts. The actual level of enforcement then can deviate from the social optimum in an idiosyncratic manner. Landes and Posner (1975) contribute to the discussion by pointing out that actions by private persons or organizations in search of pecuniary claims under a private regime can similarly lead to such deviations. The analogy of 'blackmail' nonetheless also captures the idea that private enforcers can have 'high powered' incentives to enforce the law. This notion supports the hypothesis that information about offences with potentially significant social costs may remain secret in the absence of private rights of standing before the courts.

Notably, this characterization of private enforcement as a mechanism for the acquisition and dissemination of information appears similar to the opinion of the European Court of Justice decision in *Courage v. Crehan*, detailed earlier in the case of prohibitions against anticompetitive practices that constrain the application of treaty obligations among European Union member states. In contrast to the ECJ of the late 1990s, however,

Landes and Posner (1975) clearly believe that revealing information about illegal practices using private enforcement limits the efficient application of legal rules and sanctioning of offenders. Breit and Elzinga (1985) show that the aversion to private access rights shown by Landes and Posner (1975) was quickly accepted by antitrust analysts with strong historical associations to the US Federal government (for example, the so-called Harvard and Chicago schools of thought).

Friedman (1984) offers an elegant and readily tractable treatment of the criticism of the economic approach offered by Landes and Posner (1975), specifically with respect to the 'over-enforcement' hypothesis claimed in the case of private enforcement. He notes that the Landes and Posner (1975) results follow directly from their assumptions that: (a) only monetary punishments are possible, (b) courts simply impose the maximum fine, and (c) the collection of fines is costless. Friedman (1984) points out that a more general and realistic approach would account for the idea that collection costs (including litigation costs) tend to be an increasing function of the expected punishments that offenders face.

For Landes and Posner (1975), punishment represented both a disincentive to the criminal, and an incentive to the private enforcer, not accounting for the costs associated with the collection of a punishment. This meant that the same variable would determine two parameters of their models, generating the 'impossibility theorem' and suggesting that an ideal system of private enforcement will always be inferior to a public one that allows for public prosecutorial discretion. Expected and actual punishments are typically 'decoupled' in legal systems, for instance in jurisdictions where private claimants have to incur the costs of collecting the fine. When collection costs increase with the level of punishments imposed on offenders, private enforcers have incentives not to over-enforce, and hence over-deter, offences. Indeed, as the example of antitrust litigation in the US showed, private enforcers may face excessively weak incentives to prosecute entities that are asymmetrically resourceful relative to their victims, requiring a damage multiplier to motivate private actions. Easing procedures for the formation of class actions by victims is another method for increasing the efficacy of private enforcement mechanisms when there are significant asymmetries in the collective action capacities of offenders and victims.

Friedman (1984) further claims that the assumption that collection costs increase with expected punishments accentuates the results by Becker and Stigler (1974) about the perverse incentives for public enforcers to target actions with relatively little social harm, and cooperate/collude with entities engaged in more costly practices. The fact that such perverse incentives can also arise under private enforcement systems that employ 'hang them all strategies' for punishing offenders was not incorporated into Friedman's (1984) model. For instance, the People's courts of revolutionary Soviet Union and China were forums that used private information and prosecution, as well as heavy punishments, to sanction violators of legal rules. Friedman (1999) addresses this problem by highlighting the infamous use of financially motivated private enforcers in Imperial Britain in the 18th century to prosecute or deport offenders of minor crimes to overseas colonies, as well as the possibility that excessive tort liability can lead to the demise of useful industries.

Garoupa and Klerman (2002) build on the suggestion by Friedman (1999) that economic models have failed to adequately detail the incentives of enforcers. Specifically, they relax the orthodox assumption that public enforcers act in a benevolent manner, and explore how the presence of rent-seeking behaviour by agents of the government influences the standard results from the Becker-Friedman model. Their analysis suggests that if offenders have sufficient wealth, rent-seeking public enforcers discourage minor crimes more aggressively than a social welfare-maximizing government, and are less attentive to crimes with potentially large social costs. Similarly, competitive private enforcement is always at least as good as monopolistic private enforcement. Competitive private enforcement is, however, typically inferior to public enforcement when the level of harm is very high or when public enforcement has a cost advantage. Garoupa and Jellal (2002) model the presence of an agency problem between government and the enforcement agency. They show that if raising public funds is very costly, private enforcement could be superior to public enforcement, an insight of particular importance in the design of legal institutions in developing countries.

Further imperfections that are likely to affect the comparisons between public and private enforcement include, for example, victims of an offence facing resource constraints. When capital markets are inefficient, victims, or their legal agents, cannot borrow against their legal claims, leading to under-enforcement in private systems. This critique builds on historical insights from the era of modern industrialization in Western Europe and the Americas. As described by Polanyi (1944) and Glaeser and Shleifer (2003), technological innovation and economies of scale led to significant inequalities in resources, and thus limited the efficacy of a decentralized system that organized property and liability.

Similarly, injury to victims can be diffuse, resulting in collective action problems in organizing and uniting resources needed to investigate, prosecute, and punish resourceful offenders (see Friedman, 2000).

A significant limitation of the first-generation models is that they do not account for the features of political institutions that impact on the choice between high frequency/low punishment mechanisms of private enforcement on the one hand, and low frequency/'hang them all' public enforcement strategies promoted by Bentham and his followers on the other. Persson and Siven (2007) address this problem by focusing on the impact of mass voting on the choice of enforcement procedures. They observe that models of crime that follow Becker (1968) typically assume that courts have an aversion to convicting people who are not guilty or making Type I errors (that is, false positives). Their analysis shows that voting pressures by citizens, who internalize the possibility that public enforcers will (falsely) investigate, prosecute, and punish them, limits the scope for maximal punishments. When the probability of wrongful conviction is large, democratic systems allow the voters to communicate their fears of wrongful conviction to lawmakers, motivating the adoption of more efficient procedures characterized by smaller, but more frequent, sanctions.

The analysis by Persson and Siven (2007) provides an explanation for the rather rapid transition from systems of heavy criminal punishment in Western Europe after World War II, Eastern Europe after the collapse of socialism, post-apartheid South Africa, and in the new democracies of Latin America since the 1980s. Top-down monitoring by public enforcers, both capitalist and socialist, generated too many false positives from a social perspective.

The adaptive (Bayesian) political economy framework of Persson and Siven (2007) suggests that when subgroups of the population are routinely targeted by the public enforcers and have little political voice, inefficient low frequency/heavy punishment strategies can be sustainable over time. When heavy punishments are concentrated on narrow population groups, for example on political dissidents, ethnic or religious minorities, 'hang them all' strategies persist with democratic voter support. For example, the US experience with high incarceration rates and the prevalence of ethnic minorities in convicted offenders can be explained in this context.

It should be noted that this review of first-generation models is not comprehensive and the reader should refer to the reference section at the end of this chapter for further research. For example, Polinsky (1980), Miceli (1991, 1994), and Garoupa (1997) provide different models of public versus private enforcement. Another class of research that has focused primarily on private enforcement in a historical and institutional context includes Macaulay (1963), Landa (1981), Greif (1989), Milgrom et al. (1990), Ellickson (1991), and Clay (1997).

4. Second-generation models of private enforcement

The models reviewed in the last section invariably viewed public and private enforcement as mechanisms that can replace each other, or function as substitutable procedures for a given type of offence. This means that the presence of one procedure negates the need for the other by assumption, motivating some observers to describe private mechanisms as a threat to the power of the state. This section focuses on models that explicitly explore the possibility that private enforcement procedures extend the authority of government under budget and informational scarcities facing bureaucratic administrations, and thus introduces the possibility of overlapping jurisdictions for a given type of offence.

As an illustration of the gap addressed by second-generation models, consider the example of environmental pollution by a subgroup of power plants in excess of the statutory or self-regulatory industry standard. Three general procedures are available for the acquisition and dissemination of information about the violations by the specific subgroup: (A) The government inspects and enforces punishment on behalf of those harmed by the pollution. (B) The state legislative bodies or the industry set the standard of care as in part (A), but private persons or organizations bring the cases to courts or negotiate with violators directly over the costs of their actions. Private litigants may be the direct victims of the negative consequences of the pollution, for example in terms of their health or property, or competing firms in the industry. The second group of litigants arguably differs from the first because of the high level of specialized knowledge that they may have gained in the course of their business. (C) Lawmakers can institute a system with overlapping jurisdictions between public and private enforcers.

Landes and Posner (1975) argued that when there are effective private rights of standing in courts, public prosecutors and administrators lose their monopoly position in choosing which laws to enforce. Without prosecutorial discretion, legal rules on the books would be over-enforced, and many actions with little social harm would be subject to blackmail by private enforcers in search of pecuniary awards. However, when public enforcers face budget and information scarcities, and victims do not have independent access to courts, offences with large social costs may go under-punished, and hence under-deterred. Indeed, public prosecutors and administrators commonly encourage 'blackmail', for instance by using confidential informants and leniency programmes to acquire information they need about the practices of a wide range of possible offenders.

To see the difference between first- and second-generation models, consider Rose-Ackerman (1991, p. 54) who characterizes the relationship between tort law and regulation by stressing that the 'fundamental differences between tort law and regulation centred not on substantive standards, or on the distribution of benefits and harms, but on procedures'. Her procedural view outlines the conditions under which the tort system complements statutory regulations. Torts and statutory regulation can be complementary when: (1) tort doctrines are stopgap measures which are applied when more stringent statutory standards are unavailable, (2) statutes are considered to reflect minimum requirements, and more strict tort doctrines are available, and (3) a regulatory standard is set at a socially optimal level, and a less strict tort standard applies (Rose-Ackerman, 1991, p. 55). However, the analysis of Rose-Ackerman (1991) does not allow for asymmetries between public and private enforcers in terms of resources, information, or incentives.

Laffont and Martimort (1998) do not directly address the problem of private enforcement, but instead emphasize the political difficulties in the implementation of 'separation of power' strategies, especially when they are efficient from an economic perspective. They focus on the internal organization of the government as the determinant of the 'efficient' allocation of regulatory rights and the design of communication channels for the acquisition of costly private information about undesirable practices. They assume that the power to 'capture' the government results from the presence of costly and asymmetric information between the regulators and the regulated. They show that a decentralized form of government is only good if it does not improve the communication channels between local state entities and pressure groups relative to a centralized form of government. This argument follows the belief that centralized agencies tend to be more separated from day-to-day issues concerning specific interest groups. On the other hand, decentralization improves the capacity of the regulatory system to acquire the information necessary to function efficiently.

Importantly, this approach to describing regulatory systems (also see Laffont 2000 and 2005) stresses that reorganizing regulatory power (in terms of centralization or decentralization) is not feasible precisely when it is optimal from an economic perspective. The presence of asymmetric information leads to endogenous political resistance by those who benefit from the *status quo* organization of regulatory rights and prohibitions. In the context of private enforcement, this conjecture provides an explanation for situations in which formal access rights to private persons or organizations exist in legislations, but judges and public prosecutors effectively block standing rights by victims. The remainder of this section reviews three different approaches offered by recent studies that extend the basic Laffont-Martimort framework to the study of private enforcement.

Hirart, Martimort and Pouyet (2004) contribute to this discussion by distinguishing between *ex ante* regulations and *ex post* litigation. *Ex ante* regulation involves setting standards of precautionary care against future harm, and designing an incentive scheme that induces firms to abide by the rules. *Ex post* litigation means verification of the public standards through courts that are functionally independent from the regulatory administration. Their framework does not assume away the possibility of overlapping jurisdictions, as do first-generation models. It presumes instead that (a) firms have private information about their levels of risky behaviour with respect to third parties, and (b) the role of the public enforcers is primarily limited to setting the relevant standard of precautionary efforts. Their analysis shows that when the level of precaution by firms engaged in potentially risky activities is only imperfectly observable by the public regulators, high-risk offenders act as if they were engaged in activities with low expected social costs. Private enforcement serves as a form of co-insurance against possible risky behaviour by a subgroup of potential offenders who can easily mask the costs of their actions from external observers.

Aubert et al. (2006) focus on the differences between two alternative methods to motivating private enforcers to reveal their valuable information about offences to agents of the government. Their analysis suggests that reduced fines/leniency are less effective than positive rewards/bounties in helping the government acquire information from external sources, specifically in the area of public enforcement of antitrust/competition regulations. Positive rewards are especially important because they reduce incentives to collude before the illegal actions have taken place. Positive rewards for valuable information deter offences because members of a colluding firm must incur additional costs to hide their illegal actions internally from their own employees.

Chen (2006) offers a third approach to modelling private enforcement within the Laffont-Martimort framework by depicting private enforcement as a 'divide and conquer' strategy that allows a state to control the power of a bureaucracy. Inspired by the widespread use of the suggestion box in Imperial Chinese history, this analysis compares private enforcement to an open channel for communication of information about offences to the political authorities. The emperors used a suggestion box to allow information to circumvent the large and powerful ministries responsible for the day-to-day implementation of government edicts. The boxes provided the possibility of a channel for either government officials or other private persons to communicate information about illegal practices to the political elites. This possibility generated stronger incentives for compliance with the law by the offenders and constrained the discretion of mid- and low-level bureaucrats and judges who often protected resourceful criminals from investigation, prosecution, and punishment.

The analysis highlights that an effective/open communication channel for private enforcement must contain two elements: (a) a right to secret reporting so that bureaucratic intermediaries do not block the flow of information, and (b) a system of positive rewards for informants taking the trouble to reveal their valuable secrets.

In the Chen (2006) and Aubert et al. (2006) models, private enforcement is used to simply acquire more information by the state at lower costs. Government personnel consequently retain an option to block the flow of this information, either to their supervisors, or to the public. As highlighted by the ECJ in *Courage v. Crehan*, private enforcement is desirable not only because it lowers the costs of information acquisition. Courts also induce an element of separation of power in available procedures for the production of socially valuable information, hence increasing the expected costs to private interests that aim to influence regulatory decisions.

5. Some applications

5.1 Competition law/antitrust

A commonly cited application of the complementarities between public and private enforcers relates to the regulation of anticompetitive agreements and abusive practices. Post-World War II private enforcement of *per se* prohibitions against anticompetitive agreements, for instance bid rigging and price fixing in procurement contracts, became the principal mechanism for the implementation of the (long neglected) rules of the Sherman and Clayton statutes in the US. More recently, the lack of private rights of access has become an important issue in the European Union, as well as in a number of developing and transition jurisdictions that adopted competition statutes in the 1980s and 1990s. As detailed by Gidi (2003) in the case of Brazil and the Ashurst Report for member states of the European Union, even where formal standing rights for non-state actors to enforce rules against anticompetitive agreements are present, actual private actions are rare outside the United States. Further evaluations of private rights of access to competition law enforcement include Roberts (2000), Jones (2004), Ginsberg (2005), Depoorter and Parisi (2005), Wurmnest (2005), Brokelmann (2006) and Klees (2006).

A review of the literature reveals a number of inefficiencies in the construction of competition law as an exercise in the regulation of concentrations by a centralized administration, and thus helps explain contemporary calls for mixed enforcement regimes. First, in the presence of diffuse and costly information, public agents have a limited capacity to identify anticompetitive agreements and abusive practices. Private enforcement deals with this problem with the promise of a bounty for agents with specific knowledge about explicit or tacit arrangements. Second, the literature suggests that even when the right information is available to public servants, they may not have the right incentives to implement the legal rules in an efficient manner. Specifically, public enforcement of antitrust laws may lead to over-deterrence of potentially beneficial business arrangements (Williamson, 1983), and under-deterrence of more costly practices, as in Becker and Stigler (1974) and Friedman (1984).

Even without regulatory capture, economizing practices by public enforcers reveal the presence of incentives to divert resources to actions against firms less likely to be able to defend themselves. First-generation models suggest that private enforcers improve the available information set to the legal system, and help direct investments in enforcement activity to harmful acts that public agents may choose to ignore. Second-generation models further point out that a mixed enforcement regime can increase the transaction costs of capture relative to a purely public or private arrangement for the identification of offenders and their prosecution.

5.2 Sexual assault and domestic abuse

Sexual assault against women is a common crime perpetrated by men who are often acquainted with their victims before the fact. Many assaults go under-reported, and consequently under-punished and under-deterred in public legal systems. Since public prosecutors in modern societies tend to be male, female victims may be less inclined to report offences if they suspect that the police or prosecutors will be biased in their interpretation of the facts. Moreover, victims are also likely to internalize the high burden of proof required by criminal courts to convict assailants. Police departments try to deal with this problem through a number of measures, including hiring more female officers, or by setting up special victim's units with qualified personnel. In this context, improving enforcement entails opening the communication channels between victims and public enforcers of criminal law.

However, studies by Becker and Stigler (1974) and Garoupa and Klerman (2002) point out that administrative improvement will not be sufficient in dealing with all classes of offences. Assaults likely to be ignored under a public system include those committed by the public enforcers themselves, or those committed by judgment-proof offenders with access to enough resources to immunize themselves against public prosecution either by paying bribes directly, or by buying the services of resourceful lawyers. When communication channels between victims and enforcers are not adequately open, the resulting under-enforcement of the law generates incentives for victims to seek out private remedies. Rationing by public enforcers hence justifies the purchase of instruments like pepper sprays and guns. Private civil actions are an alternative to these instruments of violence that appear necessary when state institutions do not adequately constrain the tendencies of offenders. Allen (1996) argues for the use of civil liability in the case of sexual offences arising in the course of professional relationships. However, civil rights of action against judgment-proof offenders without adequate resources to compensate their victims are unlikely to generate adequate deterrence by themselves. Optimal enforcement hence requires the overlapping jurisdiction of effective criminal and civil prohibitions.

The issue of domestic abuse can be analyzed within a similar framework. As in the case of sexual assault, asymmetries in the physical capacity of men and women, as well as plausibly a wide range of other economic and psychological factors, allow such abusive practices to go under-reported and under-deterred (Type II errors or false negatives). In contrast to sexual assault where some proportion of offenders are not known to their victims, domestic abuse takes place in situations with significant investments in relationship-specific capital, for instance in children. These investments generate incentives for the victims not to reveal information about their ordeals, sometimes even to their own family members. If public divorce rules do not associate the *ex post* distribution of jointly owned assets, including children, with evidence of previous abuse, then the victims face a serious dilemma about revealing such information. With or without divorce, exposing the secret can impose emotional and financial costs on the entire family. For instance, if the offender is found criminally liable, and hence subject to the imprisonment and/or labour market restrictions associated with such a label, it will most likely translate into lower family income. The hesitance of victims to provide information to the police or public prosecutors in these cases clearly illustrates the limitations of public enforcement in this area. To encourage victims to report abuse, it may be necessary to link the distribution of marital property, or future earnings of the abuser, to the presence of domestic abuse in divorce proceedings. In jurisdictions where prenuptial agreements are common, rules that invalidate such private contracts in case of abuse could be codified in their terms, or be incorporated by family court judges and private arbitrators in divorce proceedings.

It should be also noted that given the private nature of the abuse and the resulting high degree of informational asymmetry between the family and outsiders, the potential for false positives increases in a system that provides monetary incentives to allege abuse. Consequently, the delineation of evidentiary standards will play an important role in minimizing false positives.

5.3 Martial law

Most jurisdictions keep sets of emergency measures on hand for application in situations when the normal legal enforcement mechanisms are no longer effective. By declaring martial law, local rulers or foreign invaders indicate that the standards of punishment have changed from ones that emphasize investigation and negotiation through the courts, bureaucracy, or legislative bodies, to those imposed in a discretionary manner by the military or the police. Shifting to heavy and randomized punishments under martial law may be desirable to counter instability. However, as suggested by Persson and Siven (2007), a switch towards 'hang them all' strategies also increases the probability of false positives as soldiers and the police are encouraged to engage in the collective punishment of a population, or publicly torture political opponents to induce compliance with their will. As martial law persists, false positives motivate investment by victims to defend themselves against persecution by the authorities and the costs of collateral damage in terms of life and property.

One way of dealing with this problem is to set up instruments of public law – such as those which now apply to Bosnian war crimes – to motivate political and military leaders not to engage in collective and randomized punishments. A second option would be to execute the alleged perpetrators – as was the case for Benito Mussolini or Nicolae Ceausescu. Mongerald (2006) suggests the imposition of corporate civil liability enforceable by victims of illegal destruction of life and property as a complementary method for checking the practices of professional and mercenary armies that are deployed around the world.

5.4 Environmental pollution

Hirart et al. (2004) describe private enforcement as an instrument for the verification of environmental standards set by a regulatory authority. Their analysis suggests that optimal *ex ante* regulation fails to be effective in the absence of courts that are able to generate information about adherence to standards of care by industry necessary to avoid large-scale damage. Private enforcement thus complements the efforts of state inspectors and regulators constrained by their budgets and information. Price (1985) looks at the interaction between public and private enforcers during the implementation of clean water regulations in the United States, after the adoption of Federal environmental statues during the late 1970s. The rise in cases brought to court by private citizens under the Clean Water Act forced public enforcers to 'grapple with the question of whether to view private enforcers as compatriots or competitors' (Price, 1985, p. 31). Federal administrators appear to have viewed private enforcers as compatriots, at least immediately following the adoption of legislations.

Interestingly in this case, private enforcers appeared to exhibit a strong interest in complementing public regulatory activities, despite the fact that these litigants could not expect any pecuniary reward. This was because all fines paid by violators in the private action cases were allocated to the public treasury instead of to the litigants – as would happen in private tort, property, or antitrust claims. In the case of clean water regulations, just the legal right to file a grievance through the courts appears to have been sufficient to generate a mixed enforcement regime where private persons and organizations with information about violations specialized in enforcing the standards, and the public administrators in setting them.

5.5 Corporate Finance

Hay and Shleifer (1998) explore the possibility of using private rights of action in securities markets. They argue that because public securities regulators interact more frequently with firm managers, efficient enforcement of information disclosure rules often requires private legal actions by subgroups of outside investors. In the absence of private access rights, the pattern of interactions between regulators and managers lowers the incentives of prudent investors to extend financing, and limits the prospects for the development of informationally efficient capital markets. Djankov et al. (2008) construct empirical indicators of public and private enforcement procedures for 72 industrialized and developing jurisdictions. Their analysis reveals that the ability of governments to impose fines or prison sentences is not correlated with the growth of securities markets and does not appear to limit the capacity of insiders to 'tunnel' or 'self-deal' company cash flows for their private benefit. In contrast, the growth of financial markets and access of firms to external finance benefit from the presence of an easy burden of establishing standing by external investors in courts. The optimal approach to structuring corporate regulations involves the complementary use of (a) public enforcers who set standards for disclosure of information about managerial practices, and (b) access rights by private enforcers with the best information and incentives to identify and punish offenders of legal rules.

References

Acemoglu, D. and Robinson, J. (2006), 'De Facto Political Power and Institutional Persistence', *American Economic Review*, **96**, 2, 325–9.

Aghion, P. and Tirole, J. (1997), 'Formal and Real Authority in Organizations', *Journal of Political Economy*, **105**, 1, 1–29.

Allen, T. (1996), 'Civil Liability for Sexual Exploitation in Professional Relationships', *Modern Law Review*, **59**, 1, 56–77.

Aoki, M. (1994), 'The Contingent Governance of Teams: Analysis of Institutional Complementarity', *International Economic Review*, **35**, 3, 657–76.

Arthur, B. (1997), 'The Economy as an Evolving Complex System', Santa Fe Institute Series on Complexity.

Arendt, H. (1951), *The Origins of Totalitarianism*, New York: Harcourt, Brace.
Arendt, H. (1958), *The Human Condition*, Chicago: University of Chicago Press.
Arrow, K. (1951) *Social Choice and Individual Values*, Cowles Foundation Monographs Series, New York: Wiley.
Aubert, C., Rey, P. and Kovacic, W. (2006), 'The Impact of Leniency and Whistle-blowing Programs on Cartels', *International Journal of Industrial Organization*, **24**, 1241–66.
Axelrod, R. (1997), *The Complexity of Cooperation: Agent-Based Models of Competition and Collaboration*, Princeton, NJ: Princeton University Press.
Barabasi, A.L. (2002), *Linked: The New Science of Networks*, New York: Perseus.
Beck, T., Demigguc-Kunt, A. and Maksimovic, V. (2005), 'Financial and Legal Constraints to Growth: Does Firm Size Matter?', *Journal of Finance*, February, 137–77.
Becker, G. (1968), 'Crime and Punishment: An Economic Approach', *Journal of Political Economy*, **76**, 169–217.
Becker, G. (1993), 'Nobel Lecture: The Economic Way of Looking at Behaviour', *Journal of Political Economy*, **101**, 3, 385–409.
Becker, G. and Stigler, G. (1974), 'Law Enforcement, Malfeasance and Compensation of Enforcers', *Journal of Legal Studies*, **3**, 1–18.
Bentham, J. (1789), *An Introduction to the Principles of Morals and Legislation*, available at: http://socserv2.socsci.mcmaster.ca/~econ/ugcm/3113/bentham/index.html.
Bentham, J. (1995), *The Panopticon Writings*, Miran Bozovic (ed.), London: Verso.
Besanko, D. and Spulber, D. (1990), 'Are Treble Damages Neutral? Sequential Equilibrium and Private Antitrust Enforcement', *American Economic Review*, **80**, 4, 870–87.
Black, J. (2000), 'Proceduralizing Regulation: Part I', *Oxford Journal of Legal Studies*, **20**, 4, 597–614.
Bohnet, I and Frey, B. (2001), 'More Order with Less Law: On Contract Enforcement, Trust, and Crowding', *American Political Science Review*, **95**, 131–44.
Boisot, M. and Child, J. (1996), 'From Fiefs to Clans and Network Capitalism: Explaining China's Emerging Economic Order', *Administrative Science Quarterly*, **41**, 4, 600–28.
Breit, W. and Elzinga, G. (1985), 'Private Antitrust Enforcement: The New Learning', *Journal of Law and Economics*, **28**, 2, 405–43.
Brokelmann, H. (2006), 'Enforcement of Articles 81 and 82 EC under Regulation 1/2003: The Case of Spain and Portugal', *World Competition*, **29**, 4, 535–54.
Brunt, M. (1990), 'The Role of Private Actions in Australian Restrictive Practices Enforcement', *Melbourne University Law Review*, **17**, 582–613.
Buchanan, J. and Lee, D. (1992), 'Private Interest Support for Efficiency Enhancing Antitrust Policies', *Economic Inquiry*, **30**, 2, 218–24.
Buchanan, J. and Yoon, Y. (2000), 'Symmetric Tragedies: Commons and Anticommons', *Journal of Law and Economics*, April, 1–13.
Caballero, R., Cowan, K., Engel, E. and Micco, A. (2004), 'Effective Labour Regulation and Microeconomic Flexibility', MIT Working Paper.
Chen, Z. (2006), 'Private Enforcement against Collusion in Mechanism Design', MPRA (Munich Personal RePEc Archive) Paper No. 873.
Clark, J. B. (1894), 'The Modern Appeal to Legal Forces in Economic Life: Presidential Address to American Economic Association', http://socserv2.socsci.mcmaster.ca/~econ/ugcm/3ll3/clarkjb/clarkjb001.html.
Clay, K. (1997), 'Trade Without Law: Private-Order Institutions in Mexican California', *Journal of Law, Economics and Organization*, **13**, 1, 203–31.
Coase, R. (1960), 'The Problem of Social Cost', *Journal of Law and Economics*, **3**, 1–44.
Cole, H. and Ohanian, L. (2004), 'New Deal Policies and the Persistence of the Great Depression: A General Equilibrium Analysis', *Journal of Political Economy*, **112**, 3, 779–816.
Cooter, R. and Ulen, T. (2004), *Law and Economics*, Pearson/Addison Wesley.
Depoorter, B. and Parisi, F. (2005), 'Modernization of European Antitrust Enforcement: The Economics of Regulatory Competition', *George Mason Law Review*, **13**, 2, 309–24.
Dewey, J. (1926), 'The Historical Background of Corporate Legal Personality', *Yale Law Journal*, **35**, 5, 655–73.

Djankov, S., Glaeser, E. La Porta, R. Lopez-de-Silanes, F. and Shleifer, A. (2008), 'The Law and Economics of Self Dealing', *Journal of Financial Economics*, **88**, 3, 430–65.
Drew, K.F. (1995), 'Private vs. Public Enforcement of the Law in the Early Middle Ages: Fifth to Twelfth Centuries', *Chicago Kent Law Review*, **70**, 1583–92.
Eisenberg, T. and Miller, G. (2007), 'The Market for Contracts', New York University Law and Economics Working Paper, 06-45.
Ellickson, Robert C. (1991), *Order without Law: How Neighbors Settle Disputes*, Cambridge, MA: Harvard University Press.
Farrell, J. (2005), 'Deconstructing Chicago on Exclusive Dealing', University of California, Berkeley Competition Policy Center Working Paper.
Fearon, G. and Busch, L.A. (2006), 'Auditing and Competitive Bidding in the Public Sector', *Journal of Public Economics*, **90**, 657–78.
Fernandez, R. and Rodrik, D. (1991), 'Resistance to Reform: Status Quo Bias in the Presence of Individual Specific Uncertainty', *American Economic Review*, **81**, 1146–55.
Foucault, M. (1978), *The History of Sexuality*, volume I, New York: Random House, Vintage Books.
Foucault, M. (1979), *Discipline and Punish: The Birth of the Prison*, New York: Random House, Vintage Books.
Friedman, D. (1979), 'Private Creation and Enforcement of Law – A Historical Case', *Journal of Legal Studies*, 399–415.
Friedman, D. (1984), 'Efficient Institutions for the Private Enforcement of Law', *Journal of Legal Studies*, **13**, 379–97.
Friedman, D. (1996), 'Beyond the Tort/Crime Distinction', *Boston University Law Review*, **76**, 103–12.
Friedman, D. (1999), 'Why Not Hang Them All? On the Virtues of Inefficient Punishment', *Journal of Political Economy*, **107**, 6, 5250–5269.
Friedman, D. (2000), *Law's Order*, Princeton, NJ: Princeton University Press.
Galanter, M. (1981), 'Justice in Many Rooms: Courts, Private Ordering, and Indigenous Law', *Journal of Legal Pluralism*, **19**, 1–47.
Garfinkel, M. and Skaperdas, S. (eds) (1996), *The Political Economy of Conflict and Appropriation*, Cambridge: Cambridge University Press.
Garoupa, N. (1997), 'The Theory of Optimal Law Enforcement', *Journal of Economic Surveys*, **11**, 3.
Garoupa, N. (2005), 'On the Optimal Choice of Enforcement Technology: An Efficiency Explanation for ECHR', Working Paper, CEPR, London.
Garoupa, N. and Jellal, M. (2002), 'A Note on Optimal Law Enforcement under Asymmetric Information', *European Journal of Law and Economics*, **14**, 5–13.
Garoupa, N. and Klerman, D. (2002), 'Optimal Law Enforcement with a Rent Seeking Government', *American Law and Economics Review*, **4**,1, 116–40.
Gerschenkron, A. (1962), *Economic Backwardness in Historical Perspective*, (Cambridge, MA: Harvard University Press).
Gidi, A. (2003), 'Class Actions in Brazil: A Model for Civil Law Countries', *American Journal of Comparative Law*, **51**, 311–408.
Ginsburg, D. (2005), 'Comparing Antitrust Enforcement in the United States and Europe', *Journal of Competition Law and Economics*, **1**, 3, 427–39.
Glaeser, E. and Shleifer, A. (2003), 'The Rise of the Regulatory State', *Journal of Economic Literature*, **41**, June, 401–25.
Greif, A. (1989), 'Reputation and Coalitions in Medieval Trade: Evidence on the Maphribi Traders', *Journal of Economic History*, **49**, 857–82.
Greif, A. (1998), 'Historical and Comparative Institutional Analysis', *American Economic Review*, Papers and Proceedings, 80–84.
Greif, A. (2005), 'Commitments, Coercion and Markets: The Nature and Dynamics of Institutions Supporting Exchange', in *The Handbook of Institutional Economics*, C. Menard and M. Shirley (eds.), Springer.

Grossman, G. and Helpman, E. (1996), 'Rent Dissipation, Free Riding and Trade Policy', *European Economic Review*, **40**, 795–803.

Hadfield G. and Talley, E. (2006), 'On Public versus Private Provision of Corporate Law', *Journal of Law, Economics, and Organization*, **22**, 2, 414–41.

Hay, J. and Shleifer, A. (1998), 'Private Enforcement of Public Laws: A Theory of Legal Reform', *American Economic Review*, **88**, 2, 398–403.

Hayek, F.A. (1940), 'Socialist Calculation: The Competitive "Solution"', *Economica*, **125**, 125–49.

Hayek, F.A. (1945), 'The Use of Knowledge in Society', *American Economic Review*, **35**, 519–30.

Heller, M. (1998), 'The Tragedy of the Anticommons: Property in the Transition from Marx to Markets', *Harvard Law Review*, **111**, 621–88.

Hillman, A. (2004), 'Nietzschean Development Failures', *Public Choice*, **119**, 263–80.

Hirart, Y. and Martimort, D. (2004), 'Environmental Risk Regulation and Liability under Adverse Selection and Moral Hazard', University of Toulouse Working Paper.

Hiriart, Y., Martimort, D. and Pouyet, J. (2004), 'On the Optimal Use of Ex Ante Regulation and Ex Post Liability', *Economic Letters*, **84**, 2, 231–5.

Jones, C. (2004), 'Exporting Antitrust Courtrooms to the World: Private Enforcement in a Global Market', *Loyola Consumer Law Review*, **16**, 4, 409–30.

Kant, I. (1795), *Perpetual Peace: A Philosophical Sketch*, see: http://www.constitution.org/kant/perpeace.htm.

Kennedy, D. (2003), 'Laws and Developments', in *Law and Development: Facing Complexity in the 21st Century*, John Hatchard and Amanda Perry-Kessaris (eds), Routledge-Cavendish.

Klees, A. (2006), 'Breaking the Habits: The German Competition Law after the 7th Amendment to the Act Against Restraints of Competition', *German Law Journal*, **7**, 4, 399–420.

Kratochwil, F. (1989), *Rules, Norms and Decisions: On the Conditions of Practical and Legal Reasoning in International Relations and Domestic Affairs*, New York and Cambridge: Cambridge University Press.

Laffont, J.J. (2000), *Incentives and Political Economy*, Oxford: Oxford University Press.

Laffont, J.J. (2005), *Regulation and Development*, Cambridge: Cambridge University Press.

Laffont, J.J. and Martimort, D. (1998), 'Transaction Costs, Institutional Design and the Separation of Power', *European Economic Review*, **42**, 673–84.

Laffont, J.J. and Tirole, J. (1993), *A Theory of Incentives in Procurement and Regulation*, Cambridge, MA: MIT Press.

Landa, J. (1981), 'A Theory of the Ethnically Homogeneous Middleman Group: An Institutional Alternative to Contract Law', *Journal of Legal Studies*, **10**, 349–62.

Landes, W. and Posner R. (1975), 'The Private Enforcement of Law', *Journal of Legal Studies*, **4**, 1–46.

Landreth, H. and Colander, D. (2002), *History of Economic Thought*, fourth edition, Boston-Toronto: Houghton Mifflin Company.

Lange, O. (1949), 'The Practice of Economic Planning and the Optimum Allocation of Resources', *Econometrica*, **17**, supplement, 166–71.

Lerner, J. and Schoar, A. (2005), 'Does Legal Enforcement Affect Financial Transactions? The Contractual Channel in Private Equity', *Quarterly Journal of Economics*, **120**, 1, 223–46.

Luhmann, N. (1984), *Social Systems*, Stanford, CA: Stanford University Press.

Macaulay, S. (1963), 'Non-contractual Relations in Business: A Preliminary Study', *American Sociological Review*, **28**, 55–67.

Malthus, T.R. (1800), 'An Investigation of the Cause of the Present High Price of Provisions', http://socserv.mcmaster.ca/econ/ugcm/3ll3/malthus/highpric.txt.

McAfee, P.R., Mialon, H. and Mialon, S. (2008), 'Private v. Public Antitrust Enforcement: A Strategic Analysis', *Journal of Public Economics*, **92**, 1863–75.

Merry, S. (1992), 'Anthropology, Law and Transnational Processes', *Annual Review of Anthropology*, **21**, 357–77.

Miceli, T. (1991), 'Optimal Criminal Procedure: Fairness and Deterrence', *International Review of Law and Economics*, **11**, 3–11.
Miceli, T. (1994), 'Prisons and Parole: Minimizing the Cost of Non-monetary Sanctions as Deterrent', *Research in Law and Economics*, **16**, 197–211.
Milgrom, P., North, D. and Weingast, B (1990), 'The Role of Institutions in the Revival of Trade: The Law Merchant, Private Judges, and the Champagne Fairs', *Economics and Politics*, **2**, 1–23.
Milgrom, P., Qian, Y and Roberts, J. (1991), 'Complementarities, Momentum, and the Evolution of Modern Manufacturing', *American Economic Review,* Papers and Proceedings, **81**, 84–8.
Milgrom, P. and Roberts, L. (1990), 'Rationalizability, Learning, and Equilibrium in Games with Strategic Complementarities', *Econometrica*, **59**, 1255–77.
Mongerald, Eric (2006), 'Corporate Civil Liability for Violations of International Humanitarian Law', *International Review of the Red Cross*, **88**, 665–91.
Mookherjee, Dilip, (2006), 'Decentralization, Hierarchies and Incentives: A Mechanism Design Perspective', *Journal of Economic Literature*, **2**, 367–90.
Murphy, Russell (2004), 'Crime, Confiscation, and Growth: For and against Leviathan', *Public Choice*, **118**: 325–39.
Naysnerski, W. and Tietenberg, T. (1992), 'Private Enforcement of Federal Environmental Law', *Land Economics*, **68**, 1, 28–48.
North, D. (1990), *Institutions, Institutional Change and Economic Performance*, New York and Cambridge: Cambridge University Press.
Ogus, A. (1995), 'Rethinking Self-regulation', *Oxford Journal of Legal Studies*, **15**, 1, 97–108.
Olson, M. (1968), *The Logic of Collective Action*, Cambridge, MA: Harvard University Press.
Olson, M. (2000), *Power and Prosperity*, New York: Basic Books.
Palim, M. (1998), 'The Worldwide Growth of Competition Law: An Empirical Analysis', *Antitrust Bulletin*, **43**, 1, 105–45.
Persson, M. and Siven, C.H. (2007), 'The Becker Paradox and Type I versus Type II Errors in the Economics of Crime', *International Economic Review*, **48**, 1, 211–33.
Polanyi, K. (1944), *The Great Transformation*, New York: Farrar Rinehart.
Polinsky, Mitchell. (1980), 'Private versus Public Enforcement of Fines', *Journal of Legal Studies*, **9**, 105–27.
Polinsky, M. and Shavell, S. (2009), 'Public Enforcement of Law', see Chapter 1 this volume.
Popper, Karl (1945), *The Open Society and its Enemies*, London: Routledge.
Power, Michel (1997), *The Audit Society: Rituals of Verification*, Oxford: Oxford University Press.
Price, C. (1985), 'Private Enforcement of the Clean Water Act', *Natural Resources and Environment*, **1**, 31–3.
Qian, Y., Roland, G. and Xu, C. (1999), 'Why is China Different from Eastern Europe? Perspectives from Organization Theory', *European Economic Review*, **43**, 1085–94.
Qian, Y., Roland, G. and Xu, C. (2006), 'Coordination and Experimentation in M-Form and U-Form Organizations', *Journal of Political Economy*, **114**, 2, 366–402.
Rivkin, J., (2001), 'Reproducing Knowledge: Replication without Imitation at Moderate Complexity', *Organization Science*, **12**, 3, 274–93.
Roach K. and Trebilcock, M. (1996), 'Private Enforcement of Competition Laws', *Osgoode Hall Law Journal*, **34**, 3, 461–508.
Roberts, J. (2000), 'International Comparative Analysis of Private Rights of Access', Industry Canada, Competition Bureau.
Rodden, J. and Rose-Ackerman, S. (1997), 'Does Federalism Preserve Markets?' *Virginia Law Review*, **83**, 7, 1521–72.
Rose-Ackerman, S. (1991), 'Tort Law as a Regulatory System', *American Economic Review*, **81**, 2, 54–8.
Salop, S.C. and White, L.J. (1986), 'Economic Analysis of Private Antitrust Litigation', *Georgetown Law Journal*, **74**, 1004–64.

Santos, B. de Sousa (1987), 'Law: A Map of Misreading; Toward a Postmodern Conception of Law', *Journal of Law and Society*, **14**, 279–302.
Shavell, S. (1984), 'A Model of the Optimal Use of Liability and Safety Regulation', *Rand Journal of Economics,* **15**, 271–80.
Schelling, T. (1956), 'An Essay on Bargaining', *American Economic Review*, **46**, 281–306.
Schelling, T. (1960), *Strategy of Conflicts*, Cambridge, MA: Harvard University Press.
Simon, H.A. (1962), 'The Architecture of Complexity', *Proceedings of American Philosophical Society*, **106**, 467–82.
Simon, H.A. (1997), *Administrative Behavior*, second edition, New York: Free Press.
Smith, A. (1776), *An Inquiry into the Nature and Causes of the Wealth of Nations*, London: W. Strahan & T. Cadell.
Spagnolo, G. (2004), 'Managerial Incentives and Collusive Behaviour', *European Economic Review*, **49**, 1501–23.
Stark, D. (1996), 'Recombinant Property in East European Capitalism', *American Journal of Sociology*, **101**, 993–1027.
Stiglitz, J.E. (1989), *Whither Socialism?*, Cambridge, MA: MIT Press.
Stasavage, D. (2002), 'Credible Commitment in Early Modern Europe: North and Weingast Revisited', *Journal of Law, Economics, and Organization*, **18**, 1, 155–86.
Tirole, J. (2001), 'Corporate Governance', *Econometrica*, **69**, 1, 1–35.
Varagovic, I. Louis, E. and Diaz-Guileras, A. (2005), 'Efficiency of Informational Transfer in Regular and Complex Networks', *Physical Review*, E. 71, 036122, 9 pages (1–9).
Weber, M. (1946), *From Max Weber: Essays in Sociology*, Chapter VIII, H. Gerth and C.W. Mills, translators and editors, Oxford: Oxford University Press.
Weinrib, E. (1995), *The Idea of Private Law*, Cambridge, MA: Harvard University Press.
Weyrauch, O.W. and Bell, M.A. (1993), 'Autonomous Lawmaking: The Case of the "Gypsies"', *Yale Law Journal*, **103**, 2, 323–99.
Williamson, O. (1983), 'Credible Commitments: Using Hostages to Support Exchange', *American Economic Review*, **73**, 4, 519–40.
Williamson, O. (2000), 'The New Institutional Economics', *Journal of Economic Literature*, **38**, 2, 595–613.
Wolf, E. (1982), *Europe and The People Without History*, Berkeley, Los Angeles, London: University of California Press.
Wurmnest, W. (2005), 'A New Era for Private Antitrust Litigation in Germany? A Critical Appraisal of the Modernized Law against Restraints of Competition', *German Law Journal*, **6**, 8, 1173–90.

3 Criminal law and regulation

Anthony Ogus[1]

1. Scope and focus of chapter

Few problems are encountered in delineating the scope of the criminal law since, as a matter of legal definition, it is the law prescribing liability for those offences which are prosecuted in the criminal justice system. Characterising particular forms of undesirable conduct as 'criminal' and subjecting them to the processes of the criminal law is thus one way of controlling such conduct.

'Regulation', in contrast, is not a legal term of art and its meaning varies according to the discipline of the discourse and the context (Mitnick, 1980, chapter 1). For the purposes of legal-economic analysis, it can be treated as having the following characteristics (Ogus, 2004a, pp. 2–3): it is public law, predominately enforced as well as formulated by an agency of the state;[2] and it aims to induce outcomes which would not be reached by free market activity. It is therefore designed to overcome some perceived instance of market failure. As such, it can be usefully classified as 'economic regulation' where there is inadequate competition in the relevant market and 'social regulation', which is used to correct externalities and information asymmetry.

Now, of course, there are several regulatory methods of inducing individuals and firms to reach desired outcomes. Behaviour inconsistent with the outcomes may be made the subject of a tax or charge. Or regulatees may be required, as a matter of law, to refrain from such behaviour. The obligation may be incorporated as a condition for the lawful exercise of a licensed or authorised activity, with non-compliance leading to the suspension or revocation of that licence or authority. Breach of the obligation may, in the alternative, be the subject of a formal order by a court or other

1 I am grateful to Michael Faure, Niels Philipsen and the editor of this volume for comments on earlier drafts.

2 The governance of regulation is predominantly determined by administrative law, as to which there are major differences between legal cultures: most civil law jurisdictions have a coherent body of principles developed on the basis of what is required in the public interest and applied in a system of specialist tribunals; the common law approach involves the ordinary courts judging the legality of regulatory decision-making, primarily through judicial review. See Bell (2006).

public authority, with the threat of imprisonment, daily financial payments, or the seizure of assets in the event of continued non-compliance. Most obviously, the enforcement agencies may themselves have power to issue financial penalties, or to bring an action in the civil justice courts for such penalties. Last, but by no means least, the case can be taken to the criminal courts and the offender punished under the criminal law.

Across different jurisdictions and even within jurisdictions, there are widely differing approaches to the methods and practices of enforcing regulation, particularly by means of the criminal law. In some jurisdictions, criminal prosecutions are reserved for flagrant or very serious breaches while in others, for example, the United Kingdom, in theory at least they constitute the principal sanction for most regulatory contraventions; and indeed, there is evidence that enforcement agencies are increasingly relying on them (Baldwin, 2004). The latter approach has been criticised on the ground that it is unduly heavy-handed and unnecessarily expensive (Macrory and Woods, 2003; Ogus, 2004b; Hampton, 2005) and this has given rise to an important policy debate on the merits of using the criminal law for regulatory enforcement (Macrory, 2006). Clearly the policy question can be, and has been, addressed from an economic perspective and in this chapter I review the relevant literature.

To structure the review, I examine some of the key differences between the principles and procedures of criminal liability and the criminal justice process and their non-criminal equivalents. I begin (section 2) with the ex post character of most criminal offences, moving then to discussion of sanctions (section 3), followed by the conditions of liability (section 4) and procedural arrangements (section 5). I turn finally (section 6) to a consideration of the institutional characteristics of enforcement authorities and how they impact on efficient enforcement.

2. Ex post deterrence versus ex ante prevention

For the vast majority of criminal offences, liability arises only ex post engagement in the undesired, generally harm-creating, activity. The inducement to comply with the law thus rests on the assumption that the costs incurred by offenders as a result of the liability (D), when discounted by the probability of being caught (p), will be sufficient to deter them from engaging in the undesired activity because pD exceeds the benefit (U) to the offender of the offence (Becker, 1968).

In many cases, the costs arising from detected offences are significantly broader than the penalties imposed by the law since they include also the 'hassle' and personal inconvenience arising from encounters with enforcement officials, legal and other defence expenditures, as well as any loss of market reputation resulting from the detection. It follows that some of the costs to the trader will be incurred even if there is no formal condemnation by a tribunal or other authorised institution. Because not all cases reach the ultimate stage of a court condemnation, involving the imposition of the formal sanction, it might be helpful to rewrite the ex ante additional cost arising from the contravention as $qE + pD$ where qE represents the probability and the associated costs of the relevant act being detected, and pD the probability of a formal condemnation and its associated costs, including notably the prescribed sanction (Ogus, 2006, pp. 102–5). The condition of compliance thus becomes $U < qE + pD$.

The theory of deterrence developed for the criminal law applies equally to many forms of regulation although, as we shall see in subsequent pages, differences between the regulatory and criminal processes have major implications for the efficiency of the deterrence. However, some regulatory forms operate to prevent, rather than deter, the undesired outcome.

The classic example is where an individual or firm must, prior to supplying a service or product, first obtain formal approval from some public agency, and to secure the approval the applicant must show that the product or service satisfies certain standards (Ogus, 2004a, chapter 10). The idea may be that the screening process should ensure that undesired outcomes do not occur, but the economic arguments for prevention, rather than deterrence, are not always compelling and must be carefully considered (Moore, 1961; Shavell, 1984 and 1993). If the benefits of particular ex ante regimes do exceed their costs, that may provide a public interest justification for their existence, as an alternative to the more familiar private interest, rent-seeking explanation based on public choice analysis (Svorny, 2000).

A prima-facie case for ex ante prevention can be made out for situations where ex post deterrence is likely to be ineffective. One possibility is that the sanction and other associated costs of ex post liability might be insufficiently high relative to the benefit which the offender acquires from committing the crime. Although the financial level of the penalty might be increased, that could exceed the offender's assets and hence have little impact. Another possibility is inadequate enforcement, and hence a low value of p.

In principle, both of these problems can be overcome, the first by substituting a non-financial penalty, such as imprisonment, and the second by allocating additional resources to monitoring behaviour. However, both policies are costly and the task is, then, to compare the benefit-cost ratio (the amount of social harm avoided from deterring the undesired outcome, relative to the administrative costs incurred) of a deterrence policy with the equivalent ratio for a regulatory preventative policy, which as we shall see, gives rise to large administrative costs.

For the purpose of this comparison, the amount of harm caused by the undesired activity may have relevance. The larger the amount, the more likely it is that risk-averse politicians, concerned with public reactions to the risk of very large losses, will opt for a regulatory ex ante preventative policy, thus suggesting that, in this context, some additional weighting must be attributed to the benefit of preventing such losses (Posner, 2004, p. 199).

Another variable relevant to the comparison and discussed in the literature (Malik, 1990; Nussim and Tabbach, 2007) is that of detection avoidance. Under an ex post deterrence regime, potential offenders are motivated to use resources in avoiding detection and thus punishment. This is not only wasteful, since no social benefits accrue from the behaviour; it also impedes deterrence.[3] Under an ex ante prevention regime, the opportunities for avoidance are much more limited.

The prevention of harm is, in principle, secured in ex ante licence regimes by the systematic scrutiny of all market participants Of course, such a system generates very high administrative costs, compared with a deterrence regime, under which the enforcement agency is concerned only to investigate cases of suspected contravention and therefore will monitor the behaviour of only a proportion of the market participants.[4] The principal trade-off to be considered by policy-makers thus appears to be between the higher social benefits of prevention at higher administrative costs and the lower social benefits of deterrence at lower administrative costs. In fact, the comparison is significantly more complex.

Take, first, the administrative costs of enforcement. Although deterrence systems involve less monitoring, those contraventions which are detected will give rise to the additional costs of prosecuting offenders and imposing sanctions on them. Under an ex ante regime, although these costs will not arise in relation to those deemed by the screening process to be unfit for a licence, monitoring of the market activity has to take place to ensure that unlicensed suppliers are not participating (Ogus and Zhang, 2005). Furthermore, since licensing excludes some suppliers from the market, the process can be exploited by private interests to create artificial barriers to entry, thus reducing competition and generating welfare losses (Maurizi, 1974; Gellhorn, 1976): there is much empirical evidence of anti-competitive practices being linked to licensing regimes (surveyed

---

[3] As Nussim and Tabbach (2007) point out, it may also lead to the paradox that a more severe punishment might induce more crime, because potential offenders will make greater efforts to avoid detection.

[4] The cost of such monitoring can be further reduced by risk assessment and profiling.

in Svorny, 2000). Since the satisfying of conditions for a licence generally calls for some discretionary decision-making, this confers power on officials and in some circumstances can give rise to bribery and other corrupt transactions (Manion, 1996).

In short, given the heavy administrative and welfare losses which are consequent on most ex ante preventive regimes, the onus of proof must be on those who contend that, in relation to particular areas of regulation, the benefits exceed those costs. Such may be the case where ex post deterrence is likely to prove to be ineffective or where very high social losses can result from a single contravention and, for this latter purpose, 'social losses' should be construed to include fear generated by the regulated activities.

3. Sanctions

A major difference between criminal and non-criminal methods of enforcing regulatory obligations arises from the sanctions, both formal and informal, which are available. The penalties which a criminal court can impose on conviction for an offence include imprisonment and community service as well as fines and the confiscation of assets. In the absence of a criminal prosecution, the administrative authorities may, exceptionally, have powers to revoke or suspend a licence, or to obtain from a court an injunction, or equivalent order prohibiting further non-compliance, breach of which may lead to proceedings for contempt or a per diem financial charge. In most, but not all, jurisdictions, financial penalties may be imposed by a civil court or (generally to only a modest level) by the administrative authorities themselves. Other sanctions include the issuing of adverse publicity ('naming and shaming'), and the seizure or immobilisation (for example, 'wheel-clamping') of assets.

From a deterrence perspective we need to analyse the impact of these different regimes and to hypothesise on the circumstances in which use of the criminal justice sanctions might be optimal. We note first that the cost to the offender following conviction in the criminal process will generally[5] be significantly higher than that which follows non-criminal procedures. This is not only because the formal sanctions available in the criminal process are, in broad terms, more severe – notably with reference to imprisonment and very large fines; it is also because stigma attaches to a criminal conviction much more than to other forms of condemnation

---

5 The administrative power to revoke or suspend a licence may be an exception.

(Funk, 2004).[6] Indeed, there is empirical evidence that loss of market reputation following criminal proceedings may be of greater consequence to some firms than the penalty imposed (Baldwin, 2004, pp. 361–4; Karpoff et al., 2005).

Now if, for the purpose of Becker's model of deterrence, the criminal process can be used to ensure that the offender, on conviction, will face costs ($pD + qE$) sufficiently high to exceed the utility (U) to be derived from the contravention, why should it not be invoked in all cases? There are four important answers to that question and it is a consideration of these which should lead us to the means of identifying when criminal sanctions might be optimal for regulatory contraventions.

Two arguments relate to the lowering of costs which are generated by the imposition of criminal penalties. The first has regard to the costs incurred by the offender. Although it is of the very essence of a deterrence system that individuals and firms should incur costs if they offend, social welfare is increased if the same level of deterrence can be achieved when those costs are smaller, rather than larger. Secondly, account has to be taken of administrative costs. Of course, some criminal penalties, notably imprisonment, are much more expensive to apply than administrative or civil penalties; but more significant is the comparison of process costs, since (as we shall see) the procedural requirements of criminal liability are much more exacting than their administrative and civil equivalents. In short, the goal should be the minimisation of costs, consistent with the securing of adequate deterrence.

The third consideration is that of marginal deterrence (Friedman and Sjostrom, 1993; Mookherjee and Png, 1994): other things being equal, the severity of penalties should increase proportionately with the severity of the harm caused by illegal activities. This is because offenders intent on committing a less serious offence should not be motivated, perversely, to commit a more serious offence for the same penalty. If a severe criminal penalty is handed out for a relatively minor regulatory contravention, then more severe penalties, at additional administrative costs, will have to be handed out for more serious contraventions.

Fourthly, excessively severe penalties can lead to over-deterrence (Bierschbach and Stein, 2005). It may be the case that with mainstream crimes, such as theft, assault or arson, there is little or no social utility in the behaviour which constitutes the offence, but regulatory offences

[6] The economic interpretation is that since procedural safeguards reduce the number of erroneous decisions, a criminal conviction conveys more reliable information than decisions from other institutions: Galbiati and Garoupa (2007).

are different (Selznick, 1985, p. 363). The latter normally arise during the course of everyday activities, including industrial and commercial undertakings, which enhance social welfare. Of course, with insufficient precautions, those activities may generate harm which exceeds the social benefit, hence the regulatory control, but if the prospect of a severe penalty induces the firm either to reduce the amount of the activity or to invest in an excessive level of care, or both, social welfare losses are incurred.

If the discussion above indicates why criminal penalties should not be used for all regulatory contraventions, there are other powerful arguments suggesting that administrative sanctions are preferable for most such contraventions. Take, first, the question of the offender's knowledge and information concerning legal obligations (Craswell and Calfee, 1986). This is generally not a problem in relation to mainstream crime, covering the familiar range of offences to the person and property, because, as the Latin expression (*mala in se)* used to distinguish them from regulatory offences (*mala prohibita*) indicates, these are inherently wrongful (Wiley, 1998): all individuals, except those who are mentally disabled, are presumed to have a sufficient understanding of the law. Most regulatory contraventions, in contrast, involve complex obligations and many regulatees, particularly if they are individuals or small firms, in the absence of some interaction with regulatory agencies, have only a sketchy knowledge of what is required (for empirical evidence, see, for example, Frick and Walters, 1998; Environment Agency 2005). Where a regulatory contravention occurs through inadvertence or ignorance as to legal requirements, it is inefficient to secure future compliance by the costly imposition of a criminal penalty if the communication of appropriate information by the regulatory agency will be equally effective in securing this outcome (May and Wood, 2003).[7]

It is, of course, far too easy for an offender to plead inadvertence or ignorance and the cost to the authorities in securing the evidence to rebut the claim will be disproportionately high. As we shall see, that is a justification for applying strict liability in the application of administrative sanctions, but the consideration can also lead us to a further generalisation, distinguishing between first offenders and second (and subsequent) offenders (Ogus et al., 2006). If the empirical evidence referred to in the last paragraph is reliable, it is not likely that imposing a penalty on first offenders will ensure future compliance better than dismissing the case with advice and/or an informal warning (Scholz and Gray, 1997; Nyborg

---

[7] Although the strategy imposes no formal sanction leading to costs D, it should not be forgotten that mere detection can impose large informal costs (E) on the offender and ex ante qE may not be insignificant relative to U.

and Telle, 2004). Note, too, that a heavy-handed approach, for little or no additional benefit, will not only generate increased administrative costs; it will also involve significant additional costs to regulatees. And these are likely to include 'indignation costs' which may motivate them to initiate appeals against decisions, leading to yet more administrative costs (Bardach and Kagan, 1982).

The argument does not apply where a regulatory contravention gives rise to large losses: here even a first offence should be deterred. But subject to that important caveat, the reasoning leads to the conclusion that generally, in a regulatory context, substantial, particularly criminal, penalties should not be imposed for a first offence. That reasoning helps to explain the empirical finding that, in most jurisdictions, in the absence of deliberate wrongdoing or serious harm, regulatory agencies tend to be lenient towards first offenders and the insight has formed the basis of the theoretical analysis in the literature.

Fenn and Veljanovski (1988) reason that, since the monitoring costs of enforcement agencies are high, it is in their interest to secure a commitment to future compliance by an agreement not to prosecute a past offence. Of course, for the offender to be motivated to adhere to the agreement, there must still be a credible threat to prosecute on the occasion of the second bite of the cherry. But since the firm in question will be aware that it is now 'under observation', the probability of being apprehended is significantly increased – compared to its first contravention. And hence a higher perceived value to the pD of a formal conviction might be plausible.

To similar effect, Harrington (1988) has modelled the relationship between an enforcement agency and firms as a game in which profit-maximising firms have to decide whether or not to comply with the law, and the agency, aiming to maximise compliance, has to decide whether or not to punish a firm which decides not to comply (see also McCannon, 2006). For the purposes of the game, the agency classifies all firms into two groups, G_1 and G_2: the first is monitored only rarely, while the second is monitored regularly and, if found to contravene, receives a substantial penalty. Initially, the agency does not have sufficient information on which to classify firms. The first monitoring enables it to do so. If a firm is found to comply, it is classified as G_1.[8] If it is found to have committed a contravention, it is classified as G_2; it will not be punished, but it will know that another contravention will lead to the prescribed punishment and the

[8] The game can be played opportunistically by a firm, ensuring that it is seen to comply on the first inspection, and only then deciding to contravene. Hence the importance of some residual monitoring.

chance of the contravention being detected is now relatively high, given that it will be subjected to regular monitoring. So it must be seen regularly to comply, thus enabling it to be reclassified as G_1. Institutional arrangements which facilitate the game being played to these outcomes should lead to the goals of firms and agencies being met at lowest cost.

Both of these models can be accommodated within the well-known 'enforcement pyramid' of Ayres and Braithwaite (1992, p. 35). The horizontal axis of the pyramid represents the percentage of apprehended contraventions for a given offence, and the vertical axis the steps of increasing severity which can be taken in the treatment of the offender from, at the base, an informal warning to, at the apex, a substantial criminal penalty. In accordance with the economic models, the marginal benefits of the enforcement agency proceeding up the pyramid until it is satisfied that it has secured a particular offender's compliance should exceed the marginal costs.

Reference to this pyramid also reveals the problem of excessive reliance on criminal, as opposed to administrative, sanctions in deterring regulatory contraventions (Woods and Macrory, 2003; Ogus, 2004b). Although the costs (D) to the offenders increase with each higher stage, so also will there be a significant reduction in the ex ante probabilities, p and q, that the relevant next stage will be reached. In relation to the criminal sanction at the apex of the pyramid, p is likely to be small,[9] particularly because of the disproportionately high cost to the agency of procuring evidence sufficient to satisfy the procedural standards of liability in the criminal courts (see further on this below). If criminal liability constitutes the only significant penalty, then, for deterrence purposes, this must be sufficiently large when discounted by p to exceed the profit to the offender from the contravention. Since courts are typically reluctant to impose large penalties for most regulatory contraventions (Macrory, 2006, pp. 30–31), such a system is likely to suffer from under-deterrence. Clearly this problem should not arise if the agency is able to impose an administrative financial penalty at an intermediate point in the pyramid, where p will have a relatively high value (for empirical evidence, see Brown, 1992).

The economic models formulated for the purpose of determining the optimal criminal fine and incorporating variables of the offender's wealth and the probability of apprehension and conviction (for example, Polinsky and Shavell, 2002) are obviously applicable to administrative financial penalties, but there are some special considerations arising from

---

[9] In Europe, p rarely exceeds 0.05: see the empirical studies cited in Ogus and Abbot (2002, pp. 497–8).

variations in the mode of exacting such penalties. There is a spectrum of possibilities ranging from a financial charge automatically imposed for each contravention and a discretionary, but fixed, penalty payable to an officer of the agency when a contravention is detected, to a discretionary variable penalty selected after a reviewing of the circumstances of the case (Macrory, 2006, pp. 41–52).

Clearly, as the selection of sanction moves across the spectrum from fixed and automatic to variable and discretionary penalties, so there is increased deterrence targeting, but at greater administrative cost. The trade-off between these benefits and costs will vary according to the volume of cases, the amount of social harm resulting from contraventions, the level of information of regulatory requirements to be expected of offenders, and the degree of variation in their wealth. The greater the social harm relative to the number of contraventions, the greater the degree of wealth variation and the lower the information level of regulatees, the greater the benefit from targeting, thereby justifying the higher administrative cost. Account has also to be taken of the fact that the larger the penalty imposed, the higher the costs of erroneous decisions, and therefore the greater the benefit from more elaborate procedures (see further on this section 5, below).

Mention can also be made here of the deterrence effectiveness of regulatory sanctions which have little or no equivalent within the criminal process. We have already seen that the latter generates stigma which may be important in raising the costs above those arising from the formal penalty to a level necessary for deterrence purposes. While an administrative imposition will not by itself have this effect, a similar outcome can be achieved by the regulatory agency publicising the fact in some appropriate media (Whitman, 1998). Likewise, the confiscation or immobilisation of assets can facilitate deterrence where the limited wealth of offenders renders them insensitive to financial penalties but where the costs arising from draconian penalties such as imprisonment are not justified by the level of harm inflicted by the contravention (Bowles et al., 2000 and 2005). Empirical evidence suggests that, in this respect, the wheel-clamping of private vehicles is a particularly effective sanction (Halcrow, 2007, Appendix D2).

None of this is to deny the importance of criminal liability as a residual deterrent for certain categories of regulatory offences and regulatory offenders, notably where a single contravention gives rise to a significantly large amount of harm and for repeated contraventions when other sanctions provide inadequate deterrence. As Garoupa and Gomez-Pomar (2004) demonstrate, resort to a criminal sanction may be economically justifiable also where the institutional characteristics of the enforcement agency, for example, the existence of conflicts of interests or political influence, result in a less than optimal level of deterrence; so also where the regulatory penalty is larger than the reward received by the agency and where, therefore, there is a possibility of collusion between the agency and offenders.

4. Conditions of liability: *mens rea*

Prosecutions for criminal offences are subject to very different liability regimes and procedural arrangements than those giving rise to administrative sanctions. Most obviously, criminal liability normally requires proof of intention or at least some form of blameworthiness (*mens rea*), while these conditions are generally absent from regimes governing administrative sanctions. What explanations are there for this different approach?

The traditional legal rationalisation of *mens rea* relates to the moral basis of the criminal law (Ashworth, 2000): since criminal liability implies moral obloquy, it is necessary to ensure that the offenders assume some degree of mental responsibility for their acts. In their (perhaps unnecessary) strenuous efforts to avoid this simple explanation, exponents of law and economics have proffered several economic arguments, none of which is entirely convincing.

Perhaps the best known are those of Posner (1985) who articulates three economic rationalisations for *mens rea*. The first arises from his defining crime as a 'pure coercive transfer', which deliberately avoids voluntary market transactions that could have been accomplished at relatively low transactions costs. Since there is little or no social utility in the act, the amount of the offender's gain is irrelevant and all crimes therefore should be deterred. This is contrasted with what Posner calls 'impure coercive transfers', which includes what in the context of this chapter are regulatory offences. Although these acts to some extent bypass the market, that aspect is ancillary to the main purpose which has social utility. In the 'pure' case, the actor intentionally uses resources to inflict the harm which avoids the market transaction; in the impure case, most of the resources are deployed for market-related purposes and the harm is only incidental. Now, although this analysis might be helpful in identifying mainstream crime with the absence of social utility, it provides an imperfect justification for the *mens rea* requirement as used in the criminal law, because the latter covers a far wider range of mental states (for example, acting with the knowledge that the harm is highly likely to result[10]) than deliberate

---

[10] See, for example, in English law *R v. Woollin* [1999] 1 AC 82.

or intentional harm, which is the central feature of Posner's argument (Parker, 1993; Finkelstein, 2000).

The other two economic rationalisations are linked to the goal of optimal enforcement. An intended harm is more likely to occur, more likely to be concealed and (perhaps) more likely to lead to very substantial losses, compared with unintended harm; and therefore there is a strong argument for concentrating resources on deterring such activity. These contentions are subject to the same objection, that they identify *mens rea* too closely with intention. But quite apart from that, they lead only to the proposition that intentional wrongdoers should face a heavier penalty than unintentional wrongdoers. It does not follow that that penalty should necessarily be imposed by the criminal law.

Very different economic rationalisation of *mens rea* are offered by Parker (1993) and Hamdani (2007), focusing on the information costs to the offender of responding to legal obligations. Parker, having observed that the prospect of high penalties will induce potential offenders to invest resources in acquiring information relevant to criminal liability, argues that such investment will be economically excessive where the penalty is high relative to the social harm caused by the act. In such circumstances, the requirement of *mens rea* discourages the investment and is therefore economically justified. Normatively, the reasoning may convince, but it is less easy to use it as a rationalisation for the difference between mainstream crime and regulatory offences, since most mainstream crimes seem not to fit the pattern of a relatively high penalty combined with relatively low social harm.

Hamdani's approach provides, perhaps, a better explanation. As he notes, strict liability, that is liability without *mens rea* typically adopted in administrative processes, induces potential offenders to acquire information relevant to liability which would not readily be available at low cost to them as a consequence of ordinary market processes. The requirement of *mens rea*, in contrast, creates an incentive to remain ignorant in such circumstances. As a broad generalisation, it is probably the case that information relevant to mainstream offences is typically available at low cost, while this is not the case for many regulatory offences given their complexity and technical content.

5. Procedural arrangements

A criminal penalty can be imposed only by a court – this is a requirement of human rights law (Guinchard, 2005) – and only following completion of prescribed procedures. These vary between jurisdictions and particularly across legal cultures, but the procedures generally include: (for more serious offences) trial by jury; a burden of proof on the prosecution to a standard higher than that used in non-criminal cases; and rules of evidence protecting the defendant. In contrast, some administrative sanctions, for example, small fines and financial charges, can be imposed without an oral hearing or other formality, although an alleged offender, unwilling to make the payment, might be provided with the opportunity to offer reasons why the sanction is inappropriate, perhaps by way of appeal to a court or tribunal. Even with this last qualification, it is clear that there are very major procedural differences between criminal and administrative processes: what are the economic justifications?

The principal purpose of the procedural arrangements is to reduce the number of errors that can result from the adjudication process, including notably the wrongful imposition of a penalty on those who are innocent, and the costs that arise from such imposition. But since the procedures designed to reduce errors are themselves costly, there is in principle an optimal level of error reduction where the benefits of such reduction approximate to their costs (Posner, 1973; Lando, 2003). For the differences between criminal and administrative procedures to be economically justified, we therefore need to identify the relevant variables and variations in the values to be attributed to them.

Take, first, the benefits to be derived from reducing wrongful penalty impositions, sometimes referred to as Type I errors. Most obviously, the innocent parties themselves benefit from the procedural arrangements since the penalties and other losses associated with them are avoided (B_1) and it seems appropriate to add a set of less concrete benefits (B_2), in that society gains from increased confidence in the quality of justice generated by its institutional processes (Polinsky and Shavell, 2000).

To be set against these benefits are the costs. These may include any increase in administrative resources which have to be spent on the adjudicative process (C_1). Further costs (C_2) arise from the impairment of the deterrence function of the law, resulting from the fact that some guilty defendants will avoid the penalty (Type II errors). It is important to appreciate that the reduced deterrence resulting in C_2 occurs for two related but independent reasons.[11] Some of the 'guilty' cases processed will not satisfy the higher procedural standards and will fail for that reason. Others will not be prosecuted because, with limited resources, the enforcement agency will concentrate those resources on clear-cut cases requiring less prepara-

[11] Posner (1973, p. 412) and Png (1986) rightly argue that reducing Type I errors should enhance deterrence because it will increase the net punishment cost of committing the crime relative to that of abstaining from the crime, but this effect will surely be outweighed by the considerations mentioned in the text.

tion (Polinsky and Shavell, 1989; Miceli, 1991 and for empirical evidence, Ogus et al., 2006).

To compare the incidence of these benefits and costs in relation to criminal and administrative procedures, take, first, by way of example, the question of burden of proof, which in criminal law is on the prosecution but which in many administrative systems is, in practice at least, on the suspected offender. A simple guideline here is to place the burden on the party who can supply the information at lower cost, and it may be that, in this respect, the regulatee-regulator relationship has different characteristics from the criminal defendant-prosecutor relationship (Lewis and Poitevin, 1997). But there are other variables involved. The criminal law approach operates to avoid substantial adjudication and post-adjudication administrative costs, including the imposition of penalties, in cases where liability is indeterminate: placing the burden on the defendant would therefore significantly increase C_1. It also reduces Type I error costs (B_1) at the expense of Type II error costs (C_2) (Lee, 1997).

In the context of the criminal justice system, the burden of proof rule is economically appropriate because adjudication and post-adjudication administrative costs are particularly heavy, and because, given the stigma attaching to criminal law convictions, Type I error costs are assumed to be significantly higher than Type II error costs: it is 'better that ten guilty persons escape, than one innocent suffer' (Blackstone, 1836, p. 358). Adjudication and post-adjudication administrative costs are generally less onerous in a regulatory non-criminal context, but the principal economic justification for the alternative burden of proof rule must be that, given typically relatively modest penalties and an absence of stigma, Type I error costs are not so significant and, indeed, may be outweighed by Type II error costs (Posner, 1973, pp. 414–16).

The analysis has similar implications for other procedural protections conferred on criminal defendants, including notably the standard of proof which is particularly important, since there is a striking contrast between the criminal rule ('beyond all reasonable doubt') implying a level of accuracy above 0.95 and the equivalent administrative standard, which is just above 0.5 (Kokott, 1998, p. 134).[12] Other relevant rules include those restricting the evidence on which the prosecution can rely (on which see Schrag and Scotchmer, 1994; and for a survey of the relevant literature, Parker and Kobayashi, 2000). A quite different economic approach to

[12] The text reflects the rules in common law jurisdictions; civil law jurisdictions have a different approach. For an economic analysis of the comparison see Demougin and Fluet (2005).

these phenomena is offered by Hylton and Khanna (2007). They argue that while the analysis above explains the pro-defendant bias in American criminal procedure, it does not justify the extent of the protections and the latter are better explained by reference to public choice considerations. From this perspective, since the protections increase the costs to self-interested actors of using the criminal process for their own ends, they help to reduce the rent-seeking and deterrence costs associated with abuses of prosecutorial authority.

6. Institutional considerations

In terms both of rule-making and of enforcement, there are many institutional differences between regulatory processes and criminal justice processes, but we need only highlight those which are the most significant for the purposes of this chapter. Undoubtedly, the major such difference relates to the separation of powers. The rules governing criminal liability are, in theory at least, determined by the legislature; compliance with the law is principally monitored by a police force; they may undertake prosecutions, but in many jurisdictions this is the responsibility of an independent authority; and liability is determined by a court (often by a jury) and the appropriate penalty is selected by the judiciary. In contrast, in relation to regulatory controls, although the legislature establishes the principles, the detailed rules are typically formulated by a regulatory agency (which may be more or less independent of government); and that same agency is normally responsible for monitoring behaviour and initiating administrative enforcement proceedings. These roles may, in some areas and to some extent, be shared by the regulated industry under co-regulation or self-regulation arrangements. In some jurisdictions, liability for, and selection of, the administrative sanction is the responsibility of an independent authority or tribunal, but in others they are undertaken by the regulatory agency,[13] with the offender having access to an independent authority only by way of appeal.

Generalising on these arrangements, it may be said that regulatory institutions and functions (rule-making, monitoring, enforcement and adjudication) are, to a large degree, vertically integrated, whereas in the criminal sphere they are separated. The integration generates considerable savings in the coordination and information costs of regulatory processes, but of course it also has adverse consequences. An independent assessment of the

[13] The character of agencies differs across jurisdictions and legal cultures, as a consequence of divergent approaches to administrative law: see above, n. 2. The civil law tradition is for agencies to be part of, or close to, central government; the common law tradition is of greater autonomy: Ogus (2002).

application of the rules can reduce intertemporal inconsistency and hence error costs (Stephenson, 2006). Further, some form of competition of, or overlapping between, decision-makers can inhibit corrupt transactions (Rose-Ackerman, 1978; Bowles, 2000).

For an economic appraisal of these arrangements, we can begin with rule-making. Mainstream crime tends to be governed by general principles rather than specific rules. On the assumption that they will be properly interpreted to meet the circumstances of individual cases, general principles avoid the over-deterrence and under-deterrence arising from specific rules,[14] but the superior targeting comes at the price of increased administrative costs (Ehrlich and Posner, 1974; see also Stephenson, 2006, who models the legislative choice in terms of diversifying risk across time and issues). Given the higher error costs, particularly of Type I, associated with criminal justice adjudication, it is appropriate to reduce these by general principles, albeit at an increased administrative cost.

As we have seen, the incidence of administrative and error costs in a regulatory context varies significantly and specific rules with much technical detail therefore predominate. Delegation to the regulatory agency for fleshing out the skeletal legislative principles can be justified in terms of economising both on information costs and on the costs of rule promulgation, given the likelihood of frequent amendment (Mashaw, 1985). Of course, this gives rise to a principal-agent problem (Schwartz et al., 1994), but judicial review and other administrative law devices can contain this (Bishop, 1990; and for a survey of the substantial literature on this question, see Spiller, 1998). The delegation of rule-making to regulatory agencies can also be explained on public choice grounds (Fiorina, 1982; Aranson et al., 1983): politicians can benefit from a generalised legislative response to the competing demands of pressure groups; the burden of the costs arising from disappointment at the outcome of implementation can be shifted to those responsible for drafting the detailed rules.

The public interest arguments for delegation to agencies can be extended to justify co-regulation and self-regulation (Tuohy and Wolfson, 1978): the regulated industry generally has superior technical knowledge and expertise to that of agencies; and there are even greater economies in the costs of rule promulgation. This is because it is cheaper to publish and disseminate the rules, which may be only informal, within the private community. At the same time, and obviously, the principal-agent problem

---

[14] The deterrence effect of uncertain standards is analysed in Craswell and Calfee (1986). They conclude that where the uncertainty is small, over-compliance is likely to occur, but broad uncertainty is likely to lead to under-compliance.

becomes acute with such arrangements, given the motivation of the regulated industries to exploit their (partial) rule-making and perhaps enforcement powers to generate rents for themselves (Shaked and Sutton, 1981). To meet it requires effective accountability to a public agency ('enforced self-regulation': Ayres and Braithwaite, 1992) or competition between different self-regulatory agencies (Ogus, 1995).

The borderline between rule-making and enforcement is not always easy to define because the more general the regulatory requirement, the greater the agency's discretion and the more important interpretation becomes in the enforcement process. We have also seen, in these pages, that discretion in deciding whether or not to take formal proceedings in relation to contraventions plays an equally significant role, because supplying information, particularly to first offenders, can provide a less costly means than deterrence of securing compliance.

Indeed, explicit, or more usually implicit, bargaining between regulator and regulatee can help to generate a wide range of efficient outcomes (Yeung, 2004). In analogy to plea-bargaining, agencies may agree to informal standards, lower than those required by the law, in return for a commitment to compliance (Kambhu, 1989; see also Johnston, 2001, who indicates the importance of the device in relation to environmental regulation where there may be information problems and some uncertainty regarding future requirements). Law (2006), drawing on an empirical study, shows how enforcement agencies, with a limited budget, can gain the cooperation of regulatees by offering benefits other than a decision not to prosecute for a contravention. The agency may have technical expertise not available to small firm regulatees and can assist the latter by supplying information as to low-cost methods not only of meeting regulatory requirements but also of attaining higher quality output more generally.

Of course, the phenomenon of arm's-length bargaining between offender and enforcement agency raises the possibility of private agreement which serves to benefit both parties, but not the public interest. In the absence of adequate controls involving transparency and accountability, this can lead to corrupt transactions with major negative externalities (Polinsky and Shavell, 2001; Garoupa and Klerman, 2004), as well as high costs to business and incentives to move towards the unofficial economy (Johnson et al., 1998). These problems are so prevalent in less developed countries that the costs of discretion within the regulatory institutional arrangements may outweigh the benefits (Ogus, 2004c). An independent argument for rules rather than discretion in less developed countries is the human capital argument that discretion generates demand for a better educated workforce, which might be in limited supply (Schaefer, 2002).

A final issue concerns the role of enforcement agencies in formally determining that a regulatory contravention has occurred and selecting and imposing the administrative sanction. To be sure, there is here an overlap with the characteristics of financial penalty, considered above: an 'on the spot' fine can hardly be administered otherwise than by the agency responsible for detecting the contravention. In other respects, the issue turns on the familiar trade-off between error costs and administrative costs. There are, of course, large savings of the latter if the same institution is responsible for different stages in the enforcement process. But such arrangements can also generate large error costs, and decision-makers can be prone to commit such errors if the agency itself benefits from the volume of formal condemnations recorded for contraventions (Posner, 1973, pp. 416–17). Such benefits may arise in two forms: an enhancement of the public reputation of the agency for effective performance of its enforcement responsibilities; and additions to the agency's income if financial payments accrue directly to it. The normative implications are clear: although there is little that can be done to moderate the first benefit, the second should not be permitted; and, in any event, the offender must be able to initiate some form of appeal against, or review of, the decision. The optimal trade-off between administrative and error costs is dependent on several important variables. These include notably: the probability of error which itself is a function of the procedural arrangements, in particular the facilities for appeals and the size of the penalties imposed.

References

Aranson, P., E. Gellhorn and G. Robinson (1983), 'A Theory of Legislative Delegation', *Cornell Law Review*, **68**, 1–67.

Ashworth, A. (2000), 'Is the Criminal Law a Lost Cause?', *Law Quarterly Review*, **116**, 225–56.

Ayres, I. and J. Braithwaite (1992), *Responsive Regulation: Transcending the Deregulation Debate*, New York: Oxford University Press.

Baldwin, R. (2004), 'The New Punitive Regulation', *Modern Law Review*, **6**, 351–83.

Bardach, E. and R.A. Kagan (1982), *Going by the Book: The Problem of Regulatory Unreasonableness*, Philadelphia: Temple.

Becker, G.S. (1968), 'Crime and Punishment: An Economic Approach', *Journal of Political Economy*, **7**, 169–217.

Bell, J. (2006), 'Comparative Administrative Law', in M. Reimann and R. Zimmermann (eds), *The Oxford Handbook of Comparative Law*, Oxford: Oxford University Press, chapter 39.

Bierschbach, R.A. and A. Stein (2005), 'Overenforcement', *Georgetown Law Journal*, **93**, 1743–81.

Bishop, W. (1990), 'A Theory of Administrative Law', *Journal of Legal Studies*, **19**, 489–530.

Blackstone, W. (1836), *Commentaries on the Laws of England*, volume IV, 19th edition (London: Sweet and Maxwell).

Bowles, R.M. (2000), 'Corruption', in B. Bouckaert and G. De Geest (eds), *Encyclopedia of Law and Economics*, Volume V, Cheltenham, UK and Northampton, MA, USA: Edward Elgar, pp. 460–91.

Bowles, R., M. Faure and N. Garoupa (2000), 'Economic Analysis of the Removal of Illegal Gain', *International Review of Law and Economics*, **20**, 537–49.

Bowles, R., M. Faure and N. Garoupa (2005), 'Forfeiture of Illegal Gain: An Economic Perspective', *Oxford Journal of Legal Studies*, **25**, 275–95.
Brown, R.M. (1992), 'Administrative and Criminal Penalties in the Enforcement of Occupational Health and Safety Legislation', *Osgoode Hall Law Journal,* **30**, 691–735.
Craswell, R. and J.E. Calfee (1986), 'Deterrence and Uncertain Legal Standards', *Journal of Law, Economics and Organization*, **2**, 279–303.
Demougin, D. and C. Fluet (2005), 'Deterrence versus Judicial Error: A Comparative View of Standards of Proof', *Journal of Institutional and Theoretical Economics*, **161**, 193–206.
Ehrlich, I. and R.A. Posner (1974), 'An Economic Analysis of Legal Rulemaking', *Journal of Legal Studies* **3**, 257–86.
Environment Agency (2005), '*SME-nvironment 2005*', available at www.netregs.gov.uk/commondata/acrobat/2005_uk_summary_1197319.pdf.
Fenn, P. and C. Veljanovski (1988), 'A Positive Economic Theory of Regulatory Enforcement', *Economic Journal*, **98**, 1055–70.
Finkelstein, C. (2000), 'The Inefficiency of Mens Rea', *California Law Review*, **88**, 895–920.
Fiorina, M.P. (1982), 'Legislative Choice of Regulatory Forms: Legal Process or Administrative Process', *Public Choice*, **39**, 33–66.
Frick, K. and D. Walters (1998), 'Worker Representation on Health and Safety in Small Enterprises: Lessons from a Swedish Approach', *International Labour Review*, **137**, 367–89.
Friedman, D. and W. Sjostrom (1993), 'Hanged for a Sheep: The Economics of Marginal Deterrence', *Journal of Legal Studies*, **22**, 345–66.
Funk, P. (2004), 'On the Effective Use of Stigma as a Crime-Deterrent', *European Economic Review*, **48**, 715–28.
Galbiati, R. and Garoupa, N. (2007), 'Keeping Stigma Out of Administrative Law: An Explanation of Consistent Beliefs', *Supreme Court Economic Review*, **15**, 273–83.
Garoupa, N. and F. Gomez-Pomar (2004), 'Punish Once or Punish Twice: A Theory of the Use of Criminal Sanctions in Addition to Regulatory Penalties', *American Law and Economics Review*, **6**, 410–33.
Garoupa, N. and D. Klerman (2004), 'Corruption and the Optimal Use of Nonmonetary Sanctions', *International Review of Law and Economics*, **24**, 219–25.
Gellhorn, W. (1976), 'The Abuse of Occupational Licensing', *University of Chicago Law Review*, **44**, 6–29.
Guinchard, A. (2005), 'Fixing the Boundaries of the Concept of Crime: The Challenge for Human Rights', *International and Comparative Law Quarterly*, **54**, 719–34.
Halcrow Group Ltd (2007), 'Costs and Benefits of DfT's Compliance Activity', Report for Department of Transport (unpublished).
Hamdani, A. (2007), 'Mens Rea and the Cost of Ignorance', *Virginia Law Review*, **93**, 415–58.
Hampton, P. (2005), *Reducing Administrative Burdens: Effective Regulation and Enforcement*, London: Cabinet Office.
Harrington, W. (1988), 'Enforcement Leverage When Penalties are Restricted', *Journal of Public Economics*, **37**, 29–53.
Hylton, K.H. and V.S. Khanna (2007), 'A Public Choice Theory of Criminal Procedure', *Supreme Court Economic Review*, **15**, 61–118.
Johnson, S., D. Kaufmann and P. Zoido-Lobaton (1998), 'Regulatory Discretion and the Unofficial Economy', *American Economic Review*, **88**, 387–92.
Johnston, J.S. (2001), 'The Law and Economics of Environmental Contracts', in E.W. Orts and K. Deketelaere (eds), *Environmental Contracts: Comparative Approaches to Regulatory Innovation in the United States and Europe*, The Hague: Kluwer, chapter 12.
Kambhu, J. (1989), 'Regulatory Standards, Noncompliance and Enforcement', *Journal of Regulatory Economics*, **1**, 103–14.
Karpoff, J., J.R. Lott and E.W. Wehrly (2005), 'The Reputational Penalties for Environmental Violations: Empirical Evidence', *Journal of Law and Economics*, **48**, 653–76.
Kokott, Juliane (1998), *The Burden of Proof in Comparative and International Human Rights Law*, The Hague: Kluwer Law International Publishers.

Lando, H. (2003), 'The Optimal Standard of Proof in Criminal Law When Both Fairness and Deterrence Matter', available at http://papers.ssrn.com/paper.taf?abstract_id=238334.
Law, M.T. (2006), 'How do Regulators Regulate? Enforcement of the Pure Food and Drugs Act, 1907–38', *Journal of Law, Economics, and Organization*, **22**, 459–89.
Lee, T.R. (1997), 'Pleading and Proof: The Economics of Legal Burdens', *Brigham Young University Law Review*, 1–34.
Lewis, T. and M. Poitevin (1997), 'Disclosure of Information in Regulatory Proceedings', *Journal of Law, Economics, and Organization*, **13**, 50–74.
Macrory, R. (2006), *Regulatory Justice: Sanctioning in a post-Hampton World*, London: Cabinet Office.
Macrory, R. and M. Woods (2003), 'Modernising Environmental Justice', *Town and Country Planning*, **72**, 304–5.
Malik, A.S. (1990), 'Avoidance, Screening and Optimum Enforcement', *Rand Journal of Economics*, **21**, 341–53.
Manion, M. (1996), 'Corruption by Design: Bribery in Chinese Enterprise Licensing', *Journal of Law, Economics and Organization*, **12**, 167–95.
Mashaw, J. (1985), 'Prodelegation: Why Administrators Should Make Political Decisions', *Journal of Law, Economics, and Organization*, **1**, 81–100.
Maurizi, A. (1974), 'Occupational Licensing and the Public Interest', *Journal of Political Economy*, **82**, 399–413.
May, P. and R. Wood (2003), 'At the Regulatory Front Lines: Inspectors' Enforcement Styles and Regulatory Compliance', *Journal of Public Administration Research and Theory*, **13**, 117–39.
McCannon, B.C. (2006), 'Compliance, Repeat Offenses, and Strategic Enforcement', available at SSRN: http://ssrn.com/abstract=896933.
Miceli, T.J. (1991), 'Optimal Criminal Procedure: Fairness and Deterrence', *International Review of Law and Economics*, **11**, 3–10.
Mitnick, B.M. (1980), *The Political Economy of Regulation*, New York: Columbia University Press.
Mookherjee, D. and I.P.L. Png (1994), 'Marginal Deterrence in Enforcement of Law', *Journal of Political Economy*, **102**, 1039–66.
Moore, T. (1961), 'The Purpose of Licensing', *Journal of Law and Economics*, **4**, 93–117.
Nussim, J. and A.D. Tabbach (2007), 'Controlling Avoidance: Ex-Ante Regulation Versus Ex-Post Punishment', *Bar Ilan University Public Law Working Paper No. 07-2*.
Nyborg, K. and K. Telle (2004), 'The Role of Warnings in Regulation: Keeping Control with Less Punishment', *Journal of Public Economics*, **88**, 2801–16.
Ogus, A. (1995), 'Rethinking Self-regulation', *Oxford Journal of Legal Studies*, **15**, 97–108.
Ogus, A. (2002), 'Regulatory Institutions and Structures', *Annals on Public and Cooperative Economics*, **73**, 627–48.
Ogus, A. (2004a), *Regulation: Legal Form and Economic Theory*, Oxford: Hart Publishing.
Ogus, A. (2004b), 'Enforcing Regulation: Do We Need the Criminal Law?', in H. Sjögren and G. Skögh (eds), *New Perspectives on Economic Crime*, Cheltenham, UK and Northampton, MA, USA: Edward Elgar, pp. 42–56.
Ogus, A. (2004c), 'Corruption and Regulatory Structures', *Law and Policy*, **26**, 329–46.
Ogus, A. (2006), *Costs and Cautionary Tales: Economic Insights for the Law*, Oxford: Hart Publishing.
Ogus, A. and Abbot C. (2002), 'Pollution and Penalties', in T. Swanson (ed.), An Introduction to the Law and Economics of Environmental Policy: Issues in Institutional Design, *Research in Law and Economics*, **20**, 493–512.
Ogus, A., M. Faure and N. Philipsen (2006), *Best Practices for Consumer Policy: Report on the Effectiveness of Enforcement Regimes*, Paris: OECD.
Ogus, A. and Q. Zhang (2005), 'Licensing East and West', *International Review of Law and Economics*, **25**, 124–42.
Parker, J.S. (1993), 'The Economics of Mens Rea', *Virginia Law Review*, **79**, 741–811.

Parker, J.S. and B.H. Kobayashi (2000), 'Evidence', in B. Bouckaert and G. De Geest (eds), *Encyclopaedia of Law and Economics*, Volume V, Cheltenham, UK and Northampton, MA, USA: Edward Elgar, pp. 290–306.
Png, I.P.L. (1986), 'Optimal Subsidies and Damages in the Presence of Judicial Error', *International Review of Law and Economics*, **6**, 101–5.
Polinsky, A.M. and S. Shavell (1989), 'Legal Error, Litigation, and the Incentive to Obey the Law', *Journal of Law, Economics, and Organization*, **5**, 99–108.
Polinsky, A.M. and S. Shavell (2000), 'The Fairness of Sanctions: Some Implications for Optimal Enforcement Policy', *American Law and Economics Review*, **2**, 223–37.
Polinsky, A.M. and S. Shavell (2001), 'Corruption and Optimal Law Enforcement', *Journal of Public Economics*, **81**, 1–24.
Polinsky, A.M. and S. Shavell (2002), 'Enforcement Costs and the Optimal Magnitude and Probability of Fines', *Journal of Law and Economics*, **35**, 133–48.
Posner, R.A. (1973), 'An Economic Approach to Legal Procedure and Judicial Administration', *Journal of Legal Studies*, **2**, 399–458.
Posner, R.A. (1985), 'An Economic Theory of the Criminal Law', *Columbia Law Review*, **85**, 1193–231.
Posner, R.A. (2004), *Catastrophe: Risk and Response*, New York: Oxford University Press.
Rose-Ackerman, S. (1978), *Corruption: A Study in Political Economy*, New York: Academic Press.
Schaefer, H.-B (2002), 'Legal Rules and Standards', *German Working Papers in Law and Economics*, Paper 2.
Scholz, J.T., and W.B. Gray (1997), 'Can Government Facilitate Cooperation? An Informational Model of OSHA Enforcement', *American Journal of Political Science*, **41**, 693–717.
Schrag, J. and S. Scotchmer (1994), 'Crime and Prejudice: The Use of Character Evidence in Criminal Trials', *Journal of Law, Economics, and Organization*, **10**, 319–42.
Schwartz, E., P.T. Spiller and S. Urbiztondo (1994), 'A Positive Theory of Legislative Intent', *Law and Contemporary Problems*, **57**, 51–74.
Selznick, P. (1985), 'Focussing Organisational Research on Regulation', in R. Noll (ed.), *Regulatory Policy and the Social Sciences*, Berkeley, CA: University of California Press, pp. 363–8.
Shaked, A. and J. Sutton (1981), 'The Self-regulating Profession', *Review of Economic Studies*, **47**, 217–34.
Shavell, S. (1984), 'Liability for Harm versus Regulation of Safety', *Journal of Legal Studies*, **13**, 357–74.
Shavell, S. (1993), 'The Optimal Structure of Law Enforcement', *Journal of Law and Economics*, **36**, 255–87.
Spiller, P.T. (1998), 'Agency Discretion and Accountability in Regulation', in P. Newman (ed.), *The New Palgrave Dictionary of Economics and the Law*, Volume 1 London and Basingstoke: Macmillan, pp. 30–35.
Stephenson, M.C. (2006), 'Legislative Allocation of Delegated Power: Uncertainty, Risk, and the Choice between Agencies and Courts', *Harvard Law Review*, **119**, 1036–70.
Svorny, S. (2000), 'Licensing, Market Entry Regulation', in B. Bouckaert and G. De Geest (eds), *Encyclopaedia of Law and Economics*, Volume III, Cheltenham, UK and Northampton, MA, USA: Edward Elgar, 296–328.
Tuohy, C. and A. Wolfson (1978), 'Self-Regulation: Who Qualifies?', in P. Slayton and M.J. Trebilcock (eds), *The Professions and Public Policy*, Toronto: University of Toronto Press, pp. 111–22.
Whitman, J.Q. (1998), 'What is Wrong with Inflicting Shame Sanctions?', *Yale Law Journal*, **107**, 1055–92.
Wiley, J.S. (1998), 'Not Guilty by Reason of Blameworthiness: Culpability in Federal Criminal Interpretation', *Virginia Law Review*, **85**, 1021–157.
Woods, M. and R. Macrory (2003), *Environmental Civil Penalties: A More Proportionate Response to Regulatory Breach*, London: UCL Centre for Law and the Environment.
Yeung, K. (2004), *Securing Compliance: A Principled Approach*, Oxford: Hart Publishing.

4 Criminal law and torts

Antony Dnes

1. Introduction

Economic analysis examines crime as a special case of rational maximizing behavior, in which certain harmful acts may be deterred through the careful construction of expected penalties relative to the gains from crime. Of considerable interest is the source of separate criminal law, since deterrence could often be created by an obligation to pay ex-post damages –in either contract, or tort – that is, deterrence may be said to be a characteristic of several areas of law where control of an externality is at stake. Both tort law and criminal law may be described as minimizing social cost. Just why do we need to use the coercive power of the state to augment penalties in some areas of behavior? Of related interest is the observation that criminal law moves with the times, and to some extent, with cultures (Friedman, 2007). There are at once great similarities, through history and across civilizations, with a near universal criminalization of murder, theft and violence against the person, and observable differences, such as the harsher treatment of drug offenses in some countries, or the prosecution of some nationals for certain offenses carried out abroad. Just what does criminal justice do?

In considering the particular distinguishing characteristics of criminal law, we need carefully to separate normative economic analysis from positivistic observations. Much of the literature, such as it is, focuses on good reasons for separating criminal law (Posner, 1985; Shavell 1985 and 1993; Bowles et al., 2005). This is often portrayed as normative analysis, telling us the sensible way to create deterrence in certain difficult situations: principally when wrongdoers hide their activities. Normative analysis of the optimal design of criminal law is actually more of an example of normative analysis as positive theory (NPT), which is often encountered in regulatory economics (Viscusi et al., 2005) and is implicitly followed in Bowles et al. (2005). There has been little work assessing the correspondence between theory and the allocation of cases across the tort-criminal divide, that is, testing NPT (Dnes and Seaton, 1997). There is an additional line of analysis in more general legal studies that is concerned that criminal law may be used inappropriately, typically by the state to reinforce more general policies in some area (Klein, 1999; Dnes, 2005): a mixture of normative criticism and positivistic observation of practices.

We also need to recognize some variety in the nature of torts, in particular distinguishing intentional from unintentional torts, and of criminal offenses, where recklessness may be a major issue. Landes and Posner (1987) argue that the absence of the defense of contributory negligence in cases of intentional tort is explained by a wish to deter avoidance expenditure by potential victims, given that least-cost prevention will always result from the injurer not forming the intention in the first place. An implication is that this principle should carry over to criminal law, although we can question whether contributory negligence is always irrelevant in crimes of violence since the defense of provocation is very similar to contributory negligence. In an analysis of punitive damages in tort, Biggar (1995) shows that, when bargaining is possible between parties, above average (that is, punitive) damages are required to prevent victims incurring wasteful avoidance expenditures when they in fact face above average injuries. Biggar's observation extends to criminal law as a version of Posner's point that sufficient penalties create deterrence, which removes the need for wasteful avoidance by potential victims.

2. The nature of criminal activity

Most generally, a person is considered to have committed a crime by intentionally carrying out an act prohibited by statute or common law, and for which the coercive power of the state is drawn upon in imposing a penalty.[1] Historically, the common law comes first, although statutes should not be underestimated, particularly in the almost military rule governing much of colonial America in the run-up to independence (Friedman, 2007). Despite a modern trend towards codification of the criminal law, in several common-law jurisdictions, many serious crimes (for example, murder) remain essentially common-law crimes. It is not obvious why many injurious acts are regarded as crimes when others are not. Indeed, some non-injurious acts, such as unfinished robberies, can be 'victimless' crimes. Also, in the past, many actions now treated as crimes were treated as torts. Both tort and criminal law use ex-post penalties to deter harmful acts: We need to examine the key features of criminal law that set it apart from its civil counterpart (Posner, 1985).

The standard of proof is different in the case of crime. First, the prosecution must prove its case beyond reasonable doubt, which is a tougher criterion than the one used in civil disputes. In a tort case, by contrast, it is enough to show that the defendant was negligent by the standards

---

[1] In this chapter, I use examples from common-law countries, principally England and the American jurisdictions.

of a reasonable person in causing the injury. The tougher criterion in a criminal case suggests caution in applying the penalties that the court may impose, which are potentially severe. Punishment in a criminal case goes beyond compensating the victim and imposes harm on the criminal, and punishing the wrong person is likely to create considerable welfare loss as well as undermining individual integrity.[2] Severe, often non-monetary punishment may be implied by a need to create deterrence when offenses are frequently hidden, or when the magnitude of harm exceeds the financial resources of the wrongdoer.

Secondly, in most cases, the prosecution must show that the criminal intended to commit the crime: there must be *mens rea,* a 'guilty mind'. The intent to cause harm is, almost universally across common-law countries, required to be *subjective* intent. There is a strong requirement that the wrongdoer knew what the result of the specific harmful act would be, or was possibly reckless over the consequences. Criminal law tends to avoid finding *mens rea* just because some other 'reasonable' person in the same situation would have recognized a risk, or would have clearly intended the harm by a similar action.[3] This again contrasts with civil cases: for example, the torts of nuisance and negligence are defined independently of the state of mind of the tortfeasor. In nuisance, either there was 'unreasonable user' or not; in negligence, either one did or did not take 'reasonable', that is, cost-effective, steps to avoid doing some harm. Such contrasts, and especially the emphasis in criminal law on subjective intent, suggest that an important element in criminalizing an activity is the deterrence of a certain type of person, who is likely to impose harm deliberately on members of society or knowingly to take large risks. From a normative perspective, we

---

2 Although Lando (2006) argues that punishing the wrong person can still have a deterrent effect on wrongdoers.

3 English law did for a while allow an objective element to creep into assessing *mens rea* in criminal damage cases by holding a party guilty if they failed to consider a risk that would have been obvious to a reasonable person. There has now been a retreat back toward a largely subjective focus in *R v. G and R* [2003] UKHL 50; 3 WLR 1060 (Lord Bingham of Cornhill: 'But it is not clearly blameworthy to do something involving risk to another if . . . one genuinely does not perceive the risk. Such a person may fairly be accused of stupidity or lack of imagination, but neither of these failings should expose him to conviction of serious crime . . .'). So, once more, the common law in England asserts blame for ignoring a high risk of which one is aware, or for failing to consider an obvious and apparent risk of which one should be aware, given all the facts in the case and not in comparison with another individual. Objectivity has however been introduced by statute, as a 'reasonable person' standard for interpreting consent, in sexual offences, most likely simply as a public policy move to increase the number of convictions.

are rightly less concerned with individuals who blunder into the same acts, because they do not pose the same kind of long-term threat.

In terms of a spectrum of harm, many injurious acts resulting from negligence are the subject of tort actions. However, intentional harm and severe forms of negligence, like 'recklessness' over risk taking or gross negligence over professional duties, are dealt with by the potentially more severe sanctions of the criminal law. One explanation of this distinction is that criminal law aims to suppress the criminal frame of mind, which is identified by the demonstration of intent. 'Recklessness' (and 'gross negligence') are commonly interpreted by the courts as amounting to a form of intent, for example, if a person drops a rock from a freeway bridge onto a car, killing the driver, that person may have ignored a serious risk that was obvious to them (advertent recklessness) or not cared a hoot about an obvious risk (inadvertent recklessness).

The major exception to the requirement to show *mens rea* is the case of the strict-liability crime, such as possession of narcotics. In a drugs case, possession may reasonably be taken to imply intent to use the items, although it would anyway be virtually impossible to distinguish accidental from deliberate possession. Therefore, these examples of strict-liability crimes are not really inconsistent with the general requirement for intent to be proved. A defense in these cases can be that one did not know of the possession, which is consistent with treating possession as indicative of intent absent proof to the contrary. Strict-liability crimes originated for relatively minor offenses, as explicitly considered by the US Supreme Court in 1922.[4] Later, of course, the tendency has grown for statute law to impose strict liability: for example, in parts of the US Sarbanes-Oxley Act dealing with CEO responsibility for financial information.

The third major distinguishing characteristic of criminal law is that the harm has an element of public harm about it, as perceived by Blackstone (1765). Crime disrupts social codes of behavior that are thought to be beneficial to all. Crimes like murder, assault or robbery, for example, are disturbing to many people and not just to their victims. In fact, by standard utilitarian analysis, we should not prosecute murder on the basis of harm to the victim, who has died and feels no pleasure or pain: the legal problem with murder is its inherent threat to the wider population, as the murderer may strike again and is generally likely to have characteristics threatening to good public order. Even if we knew the murderer would never strike again, one would not want to do business with him, and there

---

[4] See *United States v. Balint*, 258 US 658 (1922) (penalties for dealing in adulterated drugs in interstate commerce).

are issues of creating deterrence in any normal society.[5] In this context, it is interesting to note that early common-law punishments for crimes often included substantial elements of naming and shaming: perhaps a period in the stocks for those disrespectful of authority in seventeenth-century society, or possibly the branding of a burglar. The widespread social harm from burglary or violence appears to go beyond mere diffuse damages, which would arise in tort law.[6]

There is a wider public interest in prosecuting the criminal than in suing the typical tortfeasor. The victim of a crime (or a relative in a case of murder) has an incentive to sue to reclaim personal losses only. However, this will not obtain compensation for the fear and anxiety experienced by dispersed observers of the crime. Notice that the victim can often take an action in tort against a criminal, although such actions may be prohibited by statute, in the case of England, or may run up against American Constitutional protections preventing double jeopardy (Klein, 1999). Also, consider the distinction between negligence, a tort, and gross negligence, such as drunkenness while driving a train, where the criminal law steps in. The gross element appears to reflect the wider social concerns: the anesthetist who might be prone to leaning an elbow on the air line; the train driver who might incline toward drinking alcohol on the job.

---

5 One needs to say 'normal' as there are some nutty arguments about in legal teaching that purport to dismiss deterrence as a function of criminal law by noting, for example, an account circulating at Trinity College, Cambridge, that the punishment of the murderer of the only other person in the Gobi Desert could serve no purpose for deterrence, assuming that the two individuals were the limit of a society, but one could find other reasons for punishing. Such arguments are not as smart as some think: who will do the punishing? Once one allows for any authority, it seems the society is increased beyond two; and without the authority it seems there would be no deterrence nor reason for it, looking to the future – nor any possibility for it, given that there were only two people, viewed in the past. A variant on 'two men' is the 'last man' argument, in which it is alleged that there would be no reason to punish to create deterrence, if we knew for sure that the murderer is the last of his class. It is then argued that, still, we probably feel a (Kantian) need to punish. The problem is actually that if we do not punish the last murderer, we create a problem analogous to the 'chain store paradox': failure to punish the ultimate murderer causes the penultimate one to become the last one for deterrence purposes, so that, by backwards induction, all deterrence would fail. Therefore the ultimate murderer must be credibly subject to punishment to support deterrence at earlier stages of the 'game'. Such arguments anyway overlook the enormous issue of uncertainty: even if my rebuttals were wrong, just how many full information, two-man – or end game – societies are there? The proper approach to the deterrence hypothesis is through examining empirical work, such as Dezhbakhsh et al. (2003).

6 Note my discussion of *Boomer v. Atlantic Cement Co.*, 257 NE 2d 870 (CA of NY 1970) in Dnes (2005).

It may also be that there is generally a low probability of apprehension in the case of many criminal acts, particularly as the criminal intends to hide the crime.[7] Therefore, relatively severe penalties may be needed to deter the harm, along with organized detection if, as Becker (1968) suggests, the conditional probability of conviction given arrest is relatively highly effective in deterring the risk-taking criminal. In general, if there is only a 50 percent chance of catching the thief of a car valued at $1,000, the fine must be set at just over $2,000 if the expected value of stealing is to be negative. Action in tort would for the most part succeed only in reclaiming $1,000 damages. The difference is that, in tort, we tend to know when the accident or nuisance has occurred. Criminals are often members of impoverished sections of the community who would not be able to pay damages, particularly as they often sell stolen property at below market value. Then, the only real way to create a deterrent is to impose a custodial or other non-monetary sanction. These considerations suggest that the coercive power of the state is useful in deterring criminal behavior, either through enhanced penalties, or because of a need for organized detection.[8]

Homicide is an interesting offense raising the important issue of distinguishing gross negligence, or recklessness – both criminalized as forms of manslaughter – from regular negligence where the tortfeasor simply fails to take cost-effective precautions. The standard legal answer is that some risk taking attracts opprobrium owing to the greatness of the gap between the injurer's avoidance costs and the expected damage.[9] The argument is one based on the size of the cost-benefit margin. Unless this refers to the inability of the offender to pay damages owing to his wealth constraint and the non-linearity affecting gambles with life, it is not obvious that the cost-benefit margin gives a reason for criminal penalties. We may find it reprehensible, but if there were sufficient wealth, that is, if people placed modest values on taking serious risks of fatal injury, liability for compensatory damages would be sufficient to deter the negligent taking of high risks, just as in the case of smaller risks.

---

[7] Note again the importance of subjective intent: if we are worried about the criminal's mind inclining toward hiding harm, then it is indeed subjective intent that matters.

[8] Friedman's (2000) *Law's Order* points out that the police service could be privatized.

[9] Learned Hand J in *Conway v. O'Brien*, 111 F. 2d 611 (2nd Cir. 1940); Lord Hewitt CJ in *R v. Bateman* [1925] 94 LJKB 791 talked of matters going beyond compensation so as to amount to a crime against the state and deserving punishment.

It is the presence of a non-linearity that is crucial in defining gross negligence and recklessness in the criminal law. The treatment of manslaughter never permits an individual to take a gamble when it is objectively highly likely that fatal injury will result. This recognizes the inability of anyone to accept liability to pay compensation that would induce the victim to undergo the activity associated with the risk, and sets the optimal level of manslaughter to zero (ignoring enforcement costs). However, the law does not treat the fatal accidents associated with manslaughter as certain. When fatal acts are virtually (or 'morally') certain, the criminal law treats this as evidence of intent for murder.[10]

Cases of manslaughter involve risks to life that victims would never take and which the law tries to suppress. The more successful the law is at suppressing manslaughter, the more can potential victims refrain from taking avoidance measures that would often be highly disruptive to their lives. As Biggar (1995) points out, potential victims must often take steps like not going out at certain times to avoid undeterred intentional torts or crimes. The penalty for manslaughter is typically less than for murder because less deterrence is required. The need for less deterrence follows from the lack of specific intent and from the lower benefits to the injurer from the act. Owing to the lack of premeditation, the injurer is less likely to hide the act, so manslaughter will tend to be revealed by circumstances. Also, the benefit will be a lower, indirect one (for example, avoiding costs of staying alert in practicing one's profession) rather than a larger, direct one (killing to obtain a legacy).

Finally, most crime is socially wasteful and represents a classic form of rent-seeking behavior (Tullock, 1967), which may in itself give some rationale for its special treatment. Criminals devote resources to pure redistribution of existing goods without creating anything new, and criminal law may be seen as forcing their transactions back into the market place. Their potential victims also devote resources to security devices, to paying insurance companies, and, indeed, to funding the cost of the police service. Similarly, a thief may value a stolen item at an amount (say $1) that is below its owner's valuation (of say $0.50). We cannot be sure that resources move to their highest-valued uses when items are stolen. Crime is typically doubly wasteful.

---

[10] In *R v. Moloney* [1985] 1 All ER 1025, Lord Bridge required awareness of 'moral certainty', that is, overwhelming probability, before recklessness amounted to *mens rea* for murder. The standard of proof requires the defendant to have been aware of the risk. This covers the type of case where someone fires a gun indiscriminately in a crowded room, which would be treated as murder in England and as second-degree murder in most states in the USA.

3. Empirically testing the tort-criminal boundary

Dnes and Seaton (1997) carried out statistical work aimed at correctly identifying the tort criminal boundary, based on the characteristics of negligence and manslaughter cases. Essentially, they tested the predictive power of NPT. In cases of manslaughter, they expected to find difficulty in detection, direct costs and direct benefits to the injurer, the non-linearity affecting the value of risk to life, the desirability of discouraging avoidance expenditure by the victim, and the possibility of encouraging the injurer to avoid provocative environments (situational deterrence).[11] These six characteristics should be found much less frequently in simple negligence cases. Dnes and Seaton examined 64 English manslaughter and negligence cases recorded on the Lexis database, 32 of which were 32 manslaughter cases for which the Court of Appeal in England upheld a guilty verdict. Generally, the predicted characteristics did show across the cases, although there were many exceptions.

Dnes and Seaton compared the characteristics of the manslaughter cases with 32 fatal-accident cases where the Court of Appeal in England upheld judgment for the plaintiff. The characteristics judged important in manslaughter did not feature at all heavily in cases of negligence, with some exceptions: for example, in *Pearce v. Secretary of State for Defence*,[12] the plaintiff claimed terminal cancer was caused by participation in the testing of atom bombs in the 1950s, which implies the non-linearity is present and that the injury was hard to detect. The cases were all fairly close to classic negligence cases like *Lambert v. Lewis*,[13] in which a coupling broke, detaching a trailer from a Land Rover: detection was obvious, there were no direct benefits or costs to the driver, the non-linearity did not operate as this was a small risk, the situation was that of normal life, and we would want the victim to invest in care (for example, keeping a safe distance on the road).

Dnes and Seaton obtained probit estimates of equation (4.1) to assess the importance of each of the characteristics in explaining the classification of cases across the tort-manslaughter boundary.

---

[11] Why should law create deterrence in manslaughter cases where people lose self-control? Surely they cannot be deterred? Penalties for manslaughter may make those who feel they are vulnerable to loss of self-control take care to keep out of provocative situations. The cool-headed neighbor might complain of smoke and call the environmental health authority if persuasion failed. However, the hot-headed neighbor might be deterred from complaining, knowing how he could over-react if then engaged in an argument. Situational deterrence may be compared to controlling the scale of a tort.

[12] [1988] 2 All ER 348.

[13] [1981] 1 All ER 1185.

$$y_i^* = \alpha + \_\_{j} = {}_{1,K} \beta_j D_{ji} + u_i \tag{4.1}$$

where,

y_i = 1 if $y_i^* > 0$ and is otherwise zero
D_{ji} = dummy variable representing the *j*th characteristic for the *i*th case.

Therefore y_i shows whether a case is defined as manslaughter ($y_i = 1$) or as unintentional tort ($y_i = 0$).

The five independent variables used in the probit estimation were those characteristics that are hard to categorize solely as manslaughter or tort variables: difficulty in detection, direct benefits to the injurer, the presence of the non-linearity affecting the value of risk to life, the desirability of discouraging avoidance expenditure by the victim, and situational deterrence. The results indicated that manslaughter cases were more likely to have higher levels of all the variables. Situational deterrence was the only statistically insignificant variable, possibly because it turned out to be correlated quite strongly with other variables, especially the presence of the non-linearity. All variables had a positive impact on the probability of the case being manslaughter, with the non-linearity showing the greatest impact followed by benefit to the injurer, detection difficulty and avoidance costs for the victim. Cost to the injurer was excluded from the estimation because it only characterizes manslaughter.

Dnes and Seaton (1997) then classified the 64 cases as manslaughter or negligence based on the probit analysis of case characteristics. They predicted 86 percent of the cases correctly: only three manslaughter cases were incorrectly classified as negligence. In general, the presence of any three criminal characteristics was sufficient to classify a case as criminal, although two characteristics were sometimes sufficient as long as they were drawn from detection costs, benefit to the injurer, and avoidance costs for the victim. Only six negligence cases were incorrectly classified as manslaughter. One of the cases concerned a claim of damages against the police force for the death of a prisoner in custody, where a criminal prosecution had failed. Dnes and Seaton also found their model predicted well for a sample of 34 classic (that is, case-book) manslaughter and negligence cases.

4. Misuse of criminal law: hybrids

Posner's (1985) NPT analysis of the distinction between criminal and tort law could lead us to adopt an essentially public-interest view of regulation, when positivistic analysis should be taking a private interest view (Stigler, 1971). Regulatory economists have observed much use of the coercive power of the state to attain sub-group aims, which is consistent with Posner's (2007) claim that the common law tends to evolve efficiently, owing to the incentive to appeal holdings creating a deadweight loss, whereas statute law is used by special-interest groups in rent seeking. There are examples of criminal law being used inappropriately in place of civil law, and cases of civil law being used as a substitute for criminal law. Usually the substitution concerns tort law, although sometimes it is contract, and invariably we can see some emanation of the state, in the terminology of judicial review, that has found it easier to substitute across the criminal-civil divide.

Sometimes the use of criminal law is staggeringly inappropriate: as in the case of the BBC license fee in the UK. A government decision was consciously taken in pre-war Britain to provide, via the BBC monopoly, not the broadcasting that people wanted, but, rather, the broadcasting that was seen as good for them – to be paid for by a tax on the ownership of broadcast receivers (Coase, 1950). Broadly speaking, and notwithstanding the subsequent breakdown of the monopoly after emergence of more populist independent broadcasters and their proliferation on digital services, a person found to own a television set without a license will be fined, and will then have a criminal record. The most that could ever have been claimed for this policy is that the coercive power of the state is used to avoid a coordination problem, similar to a problem of paying for public goods. It is difficult to avoid the conclusion that the state is using its coercive power simply to reduce the cost of pursuing those taking BBC services, offered to all, and subsequently failing to pay for them. Similar issues appear to arise in privatized public-transport services in the UK, where bylaws continue to exist as part of the deal in transferring the services to the private sector. In one recent case, a young woman was taken to court after being found with her feet on the seating of a train and ended up with a criminal record. Appropriate responses might have included refusing to sell her any more tickets, or claiming back from her the cost of damage done. The use of criminal law, although convenient for company policy, cannot be justified by the underlying economics.

A further example of the use of criminal law in place of civil law is the punishment of violations of environmental regulations as crimes, with fines and possibly prison sentences. We can show that fines for pollution, if they are set using a polluter-pays principle, are equivalent to strict liability in tort, and achieve no more than the application of a negligence standard: the difference being that fines are paid, whether or not the firm takes cost-effective avoidance care, on any remaining pollution for which the firm would rather pay the fine than incur higher marginal costs of avoidance. In Figure 4.1, optimal avoidance is given by a point like A*, where marginal

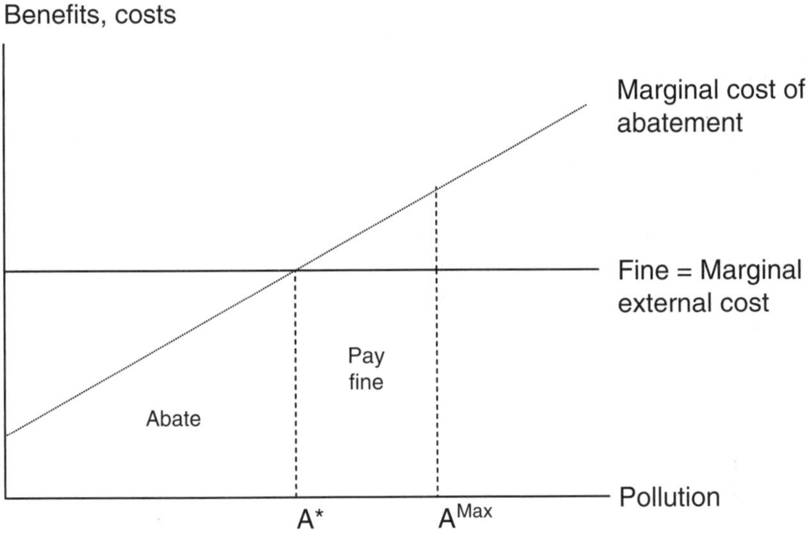

Figure 4.1 Fines and abatement

avoidance cost begins to exceed marginal external cost, which has been set as a unit pollution fine. A fine is paid over the A* to A^{Max} level of operation: that is, over the range where we should not wish precautions to be taken. If tort law governed the situation, the firm would not be negligent if it ended avoidance at the optimal level, A*, and no damages would be paid. This comparison shows that a distributional effect is the main consequence of introducing criminal law, as administrative law, simply as a matter of using the coercive power of the state to encourage desirable behavior. In this example, tort law would achieve the same allocation of resources but would leave environmental costs where they fall, once the efficient level of abatement is reached. Criminal law would be appropriate to punish intent to hide damage.

Just as we can find inappropriate use of criminal law in place of tort law, so we can find examples where an emanation of the state makes use of tort law, or possibly some other branch of civil law, to avoid more costly procedures in criminal law. In the US, a considerable debate has grown up around this phenomenon of 'hybrid cases', owing to concerns that it may undermine constitutional protections for defendants in criminal cases. The US Supreme Court has generally been protective of defendants in these cases, taking the view that if the penalty element in the case is sufficiently large, then the case looks like a criminal one and defendants should have constitutional rights to such things as legal representation protected.

Examples include: civil *in rem* forfeiture proceedings,[14] fines for the violation of environmental standards,[15] exclusion of an alien,[16] and the preventive custody of the mentally abnormal.[17]

Constitutional lawyers worry that if a case looks sufficiently close to a criminal one, then it should be surrounded by the same safeguards. In particular, issues have arisen around applying the Fifth Amendment's clause prohibiting double jeopardy, and the Eighth Amendment's clause prohibiting excessive fines. We see interplay between constitutional law, judicial review by the Supreme Court, and the tort-criminal boundary. Broadly, it is argued that once a constitution exists,[18] the authorities should not circumvent it by making use of civil-law procedures that are not intended for punishing citizens for criminal violations. The hybrid action appears to have been growing significantly in recent years (Klein, 1999).

5. Foreign crimes and long-arm laws

Uniquely, English common law has always prosecuted murderers and bigamists regardless of where the offense took place. That is, if a UK citizen (the English common law is now the basis for the 1957 Homicide Act applying to all of the UK) murders somebody in another jurisdiction, he may be prosecuted and punished in the UK upon return or extradition. This makes sense as an approach and should be commended more widely, again focusing on the significance of the subjective intent of the villain. Given the risk of the murderer's returning to his home country, there is a wider benefit from prosecuting the overseas murder.[19]

It is possible that the UK approach to overseas murder reflects a desire to stop murderers simply taking their victims outside of the national territory, perhaps to some no man's land, to carry out the dastardly killing. What makes it more likely that it is indeed the more sophisticated wider concern with the subjective intent of the ex-patriot citizen is that the

---

14 *One Plymouth Sedan v. Pennsylvania,* 380 US 693 (1965) (forfeiture of an article used in crime).

15 *US v. Ward,* 448 US 242 (1980) (civil penalty for water pollution raising issue of punitive damages).

16 *Kennedy v. Mendoza-Martinez,* 372 US 144 (1963) (rejecting revocation of citizenship without trial following conviction for evading the military draft).

17 *Kansas v. Hendricks,* 521 US 346 (1997) (proceedings for lifelong commitment to a mental institution, following completion of a sentence for a criminal offense, raises issues of due process).

18 We could make this point for less formal constitutions.

19 Whereas the extradition of a foreign national for a crime committed in the extraditing country's territory is straightforwardly interpreted as maintaining deterrence for all citizens regardless of origin.

avoidance of a jurisdictional loophole would simply require a rule that the ex-patriot could be prosecuted from home, if there were no *foreign* jurisdiction with an interest in prosecution.

Both the UK and USA have laws prohibiting their nationals from behaving corruptly at home and abroad. So, within the common-law world, we can gather up examples of several crimes that might be thought to be high-profile instances of harmful acts likely to undermine trust within society. We see a long-arm procedure in place reinforcing the idea that those criminal-law sanctions, although often costly, form the appropriate mechanism to create deterrence. It may be that the approach of prosecuting crimes regardless of location is not extended further owing to cost factors.

6. Conclusions

The study of the tort-criminal boundary is not widely studied, but we have identified a brand of normative analysis as positive theory (NPT) that gives good reasons for separating criminal law. Broadly, the emphasis is on the nature of criminal intent, and the manner in which widespread impacts may have very high values attached to them. There is a need to develop non-monetary punishments that can be supported by the coercive power of the state. It is possible to construct empirical tests of the classification of cases across the tort-criminal boundary.

We have also seen that inappropriate use of criminal sanctions is common enough, and, actually, most countries probably have many examples of the substitution of tort for criminal law, and vice versa. There is, therefore, a public-policy case for the constitutional regulation of the use of criminal law, to cases involving the wider public interest that we have identified in terms of intent and a need for non-monetary penalties.

References

Becker, G. (1968), 'Crime and Punishment: An Economic Approach, *Journal of Political Economy*, **69**, 169–217.

Biggar, Daryl (1995), 'A Model of Punitive Damages in Tort', *International Review of Law and Economics*, **15**, 1–24.

Blackstone, William (1765), 'Commentaries on the Laws of England (1765–1769)', Oxford: Clarendon Press, http://www.lonang.com/exlibris/blackstone/index.html.

Bowles, Roger, Faure, Michael, and Garoupa, Nuno (2005), 'The Scope of Criminal Law and Criminal Sanctions: An Economic View and Policy Implications', paper presented at the annual conference of the European Association of Law and Economics.

Coase, R.H. (1950), *British Broadcasting: A Study in Monopoly*, London: London School of Economics and Political Science/Longmans.

Dezhbakhsh, Hashem, Rubin, Paul H. and Shepherd, Joanna M. (2003), 'Does Capital Punishment have a Deterrent effect? New Evidence from Post-Moratorium Panel Data', *American Law and Economics Review*, **5**, 344–76.

Dnes, Antony (2005), *The Economic Analysis of Law*, Mason, Ohio: Thomson South Western.
Dnes, Antony W. and Seaton, Jonathan (1997), 'An Economic Exploration of the Tort-criminal Boundary using Manslaughter and Negligence Cases', *International Review of Law and Economics*, **17**, 537–51.
Friedman, David (2000), *Law's Order*, Princeton, NJ: Princeton University Press.
Friedman, Lawrence M. (2007), *A History of American Law*, New York: Touchstone.
Klein, Susan R. (1999), 'Redrawing the Criminal-civil Boundary', *Buffalo Criminal Law Review*, **2**, 679–721.
Landes, William and Posner, Richard (1987), *The Economic Structure of Tort Law*, Cambridge, MA: Harvard University Press.
Lando, Henrik (2006), 'Wrongful Conviction and Deterrence', *Journal of Legal Studies*, **35**, 327–37.
Posner, Richard (1985), 'An Economic Theory of Criminal Law', *Columbia Law Review*, **85**, 1193–231.
Posner, Richard (2007), *Economic Analysis of Law*, seventh edition, Boston: Wolters Kluwer.
Shavell, S. (1985), 'Criminal Law and the Optimal Use of Nonmonetary Sanctions as a Deterrent', *Columbia Law Review*, **85**, 1232–62.
Shavell, S. (1993), 'The Optimal Structure of Law Enforcement', *Journal of Law and Economics*, **36** (1), 255–87.
Stigler, George (1971), 'The Theory of Economic Regulation', *Bell Journal of Economics and Management Science*, **2**(1), 3–21.
Tullock, Gordon (1967), 'The Welfare Costs of Tariffs, Monopolies and Theft', *Economic Inquiry*, **5**, 224–32.
Viscusi, Kip, Vernon, John, and Harrington, Joseph (2005), *Economics of Regulation and Antitrust*, Cambridge, MA: MIT Press.

5 Criminal procedure

*Thomas J. Miceli**

Introduction

Criminal procedure is the legal process by which a criminal defendant's guilt or innocence is ascertained. It thus encompasses the set of procedures and rules that apply to criminal defendants from the time of arrest through the adjudication of guilt, and, in the event of a conviction, the imposition of a legal sanction. Key features of this process include pretrial bargaining between the defendant and prosecutor (potentially resulting in a plea bargain), the bail system, the standard for determining guilt at trial, rules of evidence (including constitutional protections of the defendant's rights), and the appeal process. An economic approach to criminal procedure views these various elements within a common framework whose goal is to minimize the sum of the cost of legal error plus the administrative cost of operating the system.[1]

Regarding legal error, two types are possible: type 1 errors, or conviction of innocent defendants, and type 2 errors, or acquittal of guilty defendants. We will argue that the rules governing conduct of a criminal trial can best be understood as reflecting a strong bias against committing type 1 errors. This bias, for example, explains the strict standard of proof for conviction (beyond a reasonable doubt), as well as the various legal protections afforded to defendants, such as the exclusionary rule and the right against self-incrimination.[2] As for administrative costs, the pervasive use of plea bargaining to dispose of criminal cases in the American

* I acknowledge the insightful comments of Richard Adelstein and Nuno Garoupa.

[1] For previous economic analyses of criminal procedure that adopt a similar perspective, see Posner (2003, chapter 21), Lewisch (2000), Ehrlich (1998) and Wittman (1974). This chapter focuses on the American procedural system, though the basic elements are common to European (civil law) systems as well. One difference is the greater prevalence of plea bargaining in the United States, as will be discussed.

[2] But see Hylton and Khanna (2007), who offer a different rationale for the generally pro-defendant bias in criminal procedure. Specifically, they argue that this bias discourages individuals and the government from using criminal law to pursue their own self-interest, thereby saving on rent-seeking costs.

criminal justice system can best be understood as an effort to conserve scarce prosecutorial and judicial resources.

Since criminal procedure concerns the adjudication of guilt, it is a key component of the overall process of law enforcement. Thus, an economic approach to procedure must also recognize its impact on deterrence.[3] To some extent, this creates conflicts because the optimally deterring sanction will not always coincide with the sanction that best serves the other goals of the procedural system. The ongoing debate regarding the appropriate scope of judicial discretion in sentencing reflects this conflict (Miceli, 2008; Shepherd, 2007).

The remainder of the chapter is organized as follows. The next section reviews competing perspectives on how the procedural system as a whole operates – specifically, is it more like a market or is it more like a regulatory system? Subsequent sections then turn to specific aspects of the system. We first consider plea bargaining, which is the manner in which the vast majority of criminal convictions are achieved in the American legal system. We then consider the bail system, which sets the terms under which a criminal defendant can remain free. We next turn to the trial process, focusing on the standard of proof and rules of evidence. Finally, we consider the implications of criminal procedure for deterrence.

Criminal procedure: competing perspectives

Easterbrook (1983) has offered an economic perspective on criminal procedure that views it like a market system whose goal is to establish the efficient 'price' of crime. He argues that the considerable discretion of prosecutors in determining what cases to pursue, and on what charge, as well as the sentencing discretion of judges, are key elements of this system in that they allow these agents to make decentralized decisions based on their case-specific information. The result is a pricing system that operates like a market to achieve efficient deterrence of crime. It follows that efforts to curtail discretion, such as mandatory sentencing guidelines, can only interfere with the smooth operation of the system, in the same way that government regulations impede the efficient operation of otherwise competitive markets.

Schulhofer (1988) has criticized this market-oriented view of criminal procedure by emphasizing the unfairness in sentencing that is a necessary by-product of unlimited prosecutorial and judicial discretion. Specifically,

---

[3] For general models of law enforcement that focus on deterrence, see Becker (1968) and Polinsky and Shavell (2000a). For a model that explicitly incorporates some aspects of the procedural system, see Miceli (1991).

he argues that '[d]iscreton leads to unwarranted disparities in the treatment of similarly situated offenders' (Schulhofer, 1988, p. 80). Moreover, discretion actually undermines deterrence, first, by creating ex ante uncertainty among potential offenders regarding the consequences of their actions, and second, by preventing judges from imposing harsh sentences on especially dangerous offenders. As a result, the market 'fails' to establish the efficient price for crime.

More fundamentally, Schulhofer challenges the market analogy by arguing that the procedural system lacks the basic equilibrating mechanisms that are crucial to the determination of market prices. In particular, agents do not receive signals of departures from the equilibrium price, nor do they have incentives to act in ways that restore equilibrium. Further, Garoupa and Stephen (2007) point to the existence of significant market failures inherent in the system, such as asymmetric information and agency costs. Given these problems, limits on judicial and prosecutorial discretion may therefore be necessary to promote efficiency in sentencing, suggesting that the procedural system is better viewed as a regulatory system than as a market.

Adelstein (1981) offers an institutional perspective that views the procedural system as pursuing the objective assumed by Easterbrook – namely, setting the efficient price for crime – but recognizes the imperfections identified by Schulhofer. The result is an evolutionary process (rather than a market) that involves an interplay between legislatures, which seek to send clear signals to would-be offenders ex ante, and prosecutors and judges, who seek to fit punishments to crimes ex post. Whereas predictability promotes deterrence, discretion promotes proportionality, both of which are goals of the criminal process, but which, given the imperfections of criminal enforcement, are generally in conflict. Adelstein's theory therefore suggests that the procedural system continually evolves, albeit imperfectly, to maintain a balance between these goals. Wittman's (1974) theory of procedure highlights a similar trade-off between efficiency and fairness in the rules determining criminal punishment.

The economic objective of the procedural system

It is not essential to accept the argument that the procedural system has evolved according to market forces in order to view it as having an economic logic. This logic, whether it arose spontaneously or by design, involves maximizing an objective function that includes (1) the benefit of punishing the guilty (which may include deterrence and/or retribution), (2) the cost of punishing the innocent, and (3) administrative costs. Unfortunately, the first two of these goals are fundamentally in conflict, given uncertainty about a defendant's guilt. This uncertainty, and the problems it poses for the procedural system, can be illustrated as follows.

When a suspect is apprehended, the prosecutor cannot observe whether he is in fact guilty of the crime in question. Instead, he or she observes an imperfect signal, θ, which can be interpreted as the probability that the defendant is guilty based on the available evidence. (Equivalently, θ can be interpreted as the defendant's probability of conviction at trial.) We will refer to θ as the 'strength of the case' against the defendant. We assume that, on average, evidence gathering is effective in the sense that the stronger is the case against a defendant, the more likely it is that he is truly guilty. To capture this, we suppose that θ is a random variable drawn from a distribution $F_j(\theta)$, where j denotes the defendant's true status: $j = G$ indicates that he is truly guilty and $j = I$ indicates that he is truly innocent. Further, we assume that

$$F_I(\theta) > F_G(\theta) \text{ for all } \theta. \tag{5.1}$$

That is, the distribution is shifted rightward (in the sense of first-order stochastic dominance) for truly guilty defendants. It follows that observing a high value of θ is more likely if the defendant is truly guilty, but it is not impossible when the defendant is innocent (as when there is strong circumstantial evidence or if the defendant has been framed). Conversely, a low θ is more likely if the defendant is innocent, but not impossible if he is guilty (as when he has covered his tracks well or has framed someone else).

In this setting, it should be evident that reaching a verdict based solely on θ, whether by plea or trial, will result in two types of errors: conviction of the innocent, referred to as a type 1 error, and acquittal of the guilty, referred to as a type 2 error. For example, if all defendants with θ exceeding a threshold $\hat{\theta}$ are found guilty, then the probability of a type 1 error is $1 - F_I(\hat{\theta})$, while the probability of a type 2 error is $F_G(\hat{\theta})$. Further, if the only policy lever available is the standard of guilt, $\hat{\theta}$, then it is impossible to lower one of these probabilities without raising the other (see Figure 5.1). In other words, there is a fundamental trade-off between the two types of errors.

With this trade-off in mind, we first consider the primary manner in which guilt is determined in the American criminal justice system: the plea bargain. Later we consider the determination of guilt by trial.

Plea bargaining

Early models of plea bargaining viewed it primarily as a means for the prosecutor to conserve scarce resources by avoiding the cost of having to take all defendants to trial (Landes, 1971). In this perspective, the prosecutor and defendant reach a mutually beneficial agreement whereby

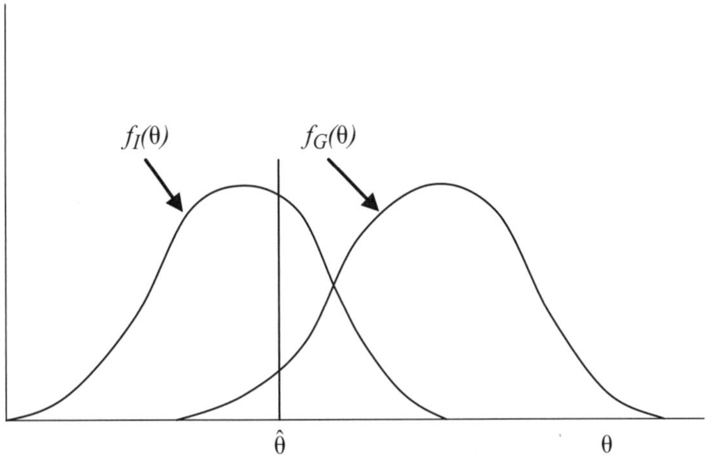

Figure 5.1 The distributions of evidence against innocent and guilty defendants and the standard of proof for conviction, $\hat{\theta}$

the defendant pleads guilty in return for a lesser penalty than he would have received on conviction at trial (the so-called sentence discount). This outcome is the result of a bargaining process in which each side acts to further his or her own self-interest.

Landes assumed that the prosecutor maximizes the expected punishment imposed on the defendant, less the cost of trial. The prosecutor is therefore concerned with achieving the greatest possible punishment, given his resource constraint, regardless of the factual guilt or innocence of the defendant.[4] For a defendant whose probability of conviction at trial is θ, the prosecutor's expected return from trial is thus $\theta s - C_p$, where s is the penalty on conviction, and C_p is the cost of trial. Given this objective, the prosecutor would only be willing to let the defendant plead guilty in return for a sentence of s_0 if $s_0 \geq \theta s - C_p$.

The defendant, in turn, will only accept this offer if it entails a lower cost than going to trial. The expected cost of trial for the defendant is his expected punishment plus legal costs, or $\theta s + C_d$. He will therefore only accept the offer of s_0 if $s_0 \leq \theta s + C_d$. A mutually acceptable plea offer is

4 Grossman and Katz (1983) and Reinganum (1988) adopt an objective function for the prosecutor that also includes the cost of wrongful punishment, thus presumably bringing the objective of the prosecutor more in line with that of society.

therefore possible if there exists an s_0 such that $\theta s + C_d \geq s_0 \geq \theta s - C_p$. It is clear that such an s_0 always exists since $\theta s + C_d > \theta s - C_p$. Intuitively, because the parties agree on the expected outcome at trial, θs, they have a joint interest in avoiding the trial costs. The model therefore predicts that a large percentage of cases should result in a plea bargain, which is in fact what we observe.

The actual sentence emerging from the plea bargain in this model is ambiguous, as it depends on the bargaining strengths of the parties. All we can say with certainty is that it will lie somewhere between the 'threat points' $\theta s - C_p$ and $\theta s + C_d$. As an example, the Nash bargaining solution, which gives each player half of the surplus, implies a sentence of

$$s_0 = \theta s + (C_d - C_p)/2. \tag{5.2}$$

Note that this may be larger or smaller than s, the penalty on conviction at trial. It will tend to be smaller the lower is the probability of conviction, θ, the smaller is the defendant's cost of trial, C_d, and the larger is the prosecutor's cost of trial, C_p.

A shortcoming of the preceding model is that it does not explain why cases *ever* go to trial. One explanation is that the plaintiff and defendant disagree about the probability of conviction at a trial. Specifically, let θ_p and θ_d be the prosecutor's and defendant's assessments, respectively, of the probability of conviction. The condition for a plea bargain to be possible now is $\theta_d s + C_d \geq \theta_p s - C_p$, or

$$C_p + C_d \geq (\theta_p - \theta_d)s. \tag{5.3}$$

Thus, if $\theta_p - \theta_d$ is positive and large, a plea bargain is no longer feasible. Intuitively, if both sides are optimistic about their chances of winning at trial (meaning that θ_p is high and θ_d is low), then a mutually acceptable plea agreement will not exist (Cooter and Rubinfeld, 1989).

A different explanation for why some trials occur is asymmetric information (Reinganum, 1988). Suppose, in particular, that defendants know their own probability of conviction at trial, but the prosecutor only observes, say, the average probability across all defendants, $\bar{\theta}$. The condition for a mutually acceptable plea bargain in this case is

$$\theta s + C_d > \bar{\theta} s - C_p,$$

or

$$\theta > \bar{\theta} - \frac{C_p + C_d}{s}. \tag{5.4}$$

Thus, only defendants with relatively high probabilities of conviction will accept a bargain, while those with low probabilities will opt for trial. In this way, plea bargaining achieves a kind of 'sorting' of defendants based on the strength of the cases against them. Note that both the 'mutual optimism' and asymmetric information models predict that trials are more likely the larger are the stakes of the case (s), and the lower are the costs of trial ($C_p + C_d$).

Plea bargaining as a sorting device

The possibility of sorting implied by the asymmetric information model suggests that, in addition to saving on trial costs, plea bargaining might also be used to reduce legal error. Based on this insight, Grossman and Katz (1983) developed a model in which plea bargaining achieves perfect sorting of innocent and guilty defendants by means of self-selection. To illustrate, suppose that all guilty defendants have a probability of conviction at trial equal to θ_G, while all innocent defendants have a probability of conviction equal to θ_I, where $\theta_G > \theta_I$. In this setting, any plea offer s_0 that satisfies $\theta_G s + C_d > s_0 > \theta_I s + C_d$ will be acceptable to guilty defendants but not acceptable to innocent defendants. As a result, all guilty defendants will plead guilty, while all innocent defendants will go to trial. In other words, a perfect separating equilibrium occurs in which no innocent defendants are induced to plead guilty.[5]

There are, however, two significant drawbacks of this outcome. First, it implies that *any* convictions at trial are wrongful since only the innocent opt for trial. One response is simply for the court to acquit all defendants, but this would undermine the equilibrium because guilty defendants would no longer find it preferable to plead guilty. Thus, in order to support the equilibrium, the court must knowingly convict some innocent defendants (that is, there must be some type 1 errors), or sorting must be imperfect (that is, some guilty defendants must opt for trial).

The second problem with the perfect sorting equilibrium is that, in the real world, innocent and guilty defendants cannot be neatly partitioned based on their probabilities of conviction. This is readily apparent from the specification depicted in Figure 5.1 where the distributions of θ for innocent and guilty defendants overlap. As a result, it is not possible to choose a plea offer s_0 that can perfectly separate those who are factually innocent

---

[5] The possibility that some innocent defendants might plead guilty is one of the concerns courts have voiced when considering the acceptability of plea bargaining. See, for example, *Brady v. United States*, 397 US 742 (1970). Also see Adelstein (1978) and Garoupa and Stephen (2007).

from those who are factually guilty. Thus, the same fundamental trade-off between type 1 and type 2 errors exists under plea bargaining as at trial.

Cost shifting

In the context of civil litigation, it is often argued that a shift to the British (or loser pays) rule for legal costs might promote settlement, thereby saving judicial resources (Cooter and Rubinfeld, 1989). However, no such proposal has apparently been made for criminal litigation. This is probably true for several reasons. First, theory predicts an ambiguous effect of such a change on the settlement rate: on one hand, a loser-pays rule will tend to make trials more likely by increasing the stakes of the case, but on the other, it will tend to promote plea bargains by making trials riskier affairs (assuming litigants are risk averse). Thus, there is no necessary saving in litigation costs. Second, as noted, promoting plea bargains (as opposed to civil settlements) is not necessarily socially desirable given the possibility that some innocent defendants might be induced to plead guilty. Finally, many (perhaps most) criminal defendants cannot afford to pay their own legal costs, let alone the possibility of having to pay the state's costs in the event of a conviction.[6]

Empirical evidence on plea bargaining

Empirical evidence on plea bargaining confirms many of the predictions emerging from the above theory. For example, Elder (1989) found that plea bargains are more likely when the outcome of a trial is more certain, reflecting the above prediction that when the prosecutor and defendant assess the same probability of conviction, a bargain is always possible.[7] He also found that cases involving higher stakes (more severe punishments) are more likely to go to trial, a prediction of both the mutual optimism and asymmetric information models. Finally, Elder found that plea bargains lead to shorter sentences compared to convictions at trial. Although this was not predicted unambiguously by the model (see equation (5.2)), it is consistent with the conventional notion of sentence discounts.

A comparative perspective

In contrast to its prevalence in the United States, plea bargaining is (in principle) prohibited by the inquisitorial (civil law) systems of continental

---

[6] A related issue is the effect public financing of the legal costs of indigent defendants has on plea bargaining. See Garoupa and Stephen (2007).

[7] Also see the studies by Landes (1971), Rhodes (1976), and Forst and Brosi (1977).

Europe (Adelstein, 1998; Garoupa and Stephen, 2007). In particular, prosecutors are theoretically required to try all cases on the maximum possible charge under the principle of compulsory prosecution. Since trials cannot be avoided by guilty pleas, the problem of allocating scarce resources across a large caseload has been addressed by these systems in other ways. One is by simplifying trials and weakening some procedural protections of defendants' rights compared to the US system, thereby lowering trial costs (Langbein, 1979). Another is by allowing prosecutors to dispose of less serious cases by cursory means that amount to little more than thinly veiled plea bargains.[8]

From a normative perspective, the question is whether plea bargaining or compulsory prosecution better promotes the goals of criminal procedure. In this vein, Adelstein and Miceli (2001) have argued that the two systems can be understood as efficient responses to a different set of values. Consider first the aversion to type 1 errors (punishment of the innocent). Given the reality that some wrongful convictions are unavoidable, plea bargaining actually *lowers* the cost of type 1 errors by allowing innocent defendants, against whom there is strong evidence, to plead guilty to a lesser charge. Easterbrook (1983, p. 320) defends this practice, arguing that there is 'no reason to prevent [an innocent] defendant from striking a deal that seems advantageous. If there is injustice here, the source is not the plea bargain. It is, rather, that innocent people may be found guilty at trial.'

Conversely, if society places a high value on convicting the guilty (avoiding type 2 errors), then we would expect it to favor compulsory prosecution precisely because it does not allow the guilty to seek to reduce their punishment by pleading guilty to a lesser charge. Consistent with this view is that continental systems typically do not give defendants the right against self-incrimination, a right which, as we will argue below, actually helps make innocent defendants' denials of guilt more believable. Taken together, these conclusions imply 'that plea bargaining is more likely to evolve in systems that emphasize the protection of innocent defendants,

---

[8] Garoupa and Stephen (2007) note that some civil-law countries (for example, France, Italy, Poland, and Argentina) have in fact explicitly introduced plea bargaining, despite severe criticism by traditionalists. An empirical analysis of this experiment in Italy by Boari and Fiorentini (2001), however, shows that plea bargaining has failed to produced the promised cost savings. Indeed, after five years, no more than 8 percent of criminal dispositions were achieved by plea bargains (compared to about 90 percent in the United States). The authors attribute this to institutional aspects of the inquisitorial system, and the reluctance of Italian prosecutors to adopt the new procedures.

and systems that stress punishing the guilty are more likely to be able to sustain a regime of compulsory prosecution' (Adelstein and Miceli, 2001, p. 60).

The bail system

A fundamental question facing the procedural system is what to do with criminal defendants between their arrest and trial (or guilty plea). The trade-off is between a defendant's right to freedom (based on the presumption of innocence), plus the cost of detention on one hand, and the cost to society should the defendant flee and possibly commit further crimes on the other. The solution is the bail system, which requires defendants to post a monetary bond as a condition for remaining free. An economic analysis of this system views the amount of bail as being determined by the above trade-off (Landes, 1973).

One criticism of the bail system is that it favors wealthier defendants who can more easily raise the necessary funds. Although bail bondsmen help to mitigate this problem, one suspects that the resulting agency problem increases the flight risk of defendants using bondsmen. Another criticism is the claim that courts set higher bail rates for minority compared to white defendants, holding the flight risk constant. Ayres and Waldfogel (1994) provide some evidence that this type of discrimination occurs.

Finally, the Bail Reform Act of 1984 made it easier to detain defendants judged to be especially dangerous. Passage of this act during a period of high crime rates in the United States is consistent with the above theory to the extent that Congress judged the increased cost of detention as being outweighed by the social interest in avoiding further crimes.[9] The result, however, is an increase in the expected punishment for both guilty and innocent defendants (Posner, 2003, p. 579), which we will see below has an ambiguous effect on deterrence.

The standard of proof at trial

The standard of proof for conviction at trial represents a threshold for the probability of guilt beyond which the court convicts the defendant. Essentially, it represents a decision rule for transforming a probabilistic assessment of the defendant's guilt into a dichotomous verdict. In this section, we examine the choice of the optimal standard of proof, $\hat{\theta}$, in light of the goal of minimizing the cost of type 1 and type 2 errors. We also

---

9 See Shepherd (2007, pp. 569–70) for evidence on crime rates in the US from 1960–2000, and Friedman (2000, pp. 108–11) on legislative responses to increasing crime rates over this period.

examine how this approach sheds light on the differing standards of proof in criminal and civil trials.

As noted above, in the context of the model depicted in Figure 5.1, the probability of a type 1 error (false conviction) is $1 - F_I(\hat{\theta})$, while the probability of a type 2 error (false acquittal) is $F_G(\hat{\theta})$. Suppose society attaches a cost of $c_1(s)$ to the former and $c_2(h)$ to the latter, where s is the sanction imposed on conviction, h is the social harm caused by the crime in question, and c_1 and c_2 are increasing functions. Thus, the cost of false convictions is presumed to be increasing in the magnitude of the wrongfully imposed punishment, and the cost of false acquittals is presumed to be increasing in the severity of the crime that goes unpunished. (Again, this could reflect either a deterrent or a retributive motive for punishing the guilty.) Taking s and h as given, the problem is to choose $\hat{\theta}$ to minimize the expected cost of the two types of errors:

$$[1 - F_I(\hat{\theta})]c_1(s) + F_G(\hat{\theta})c_2(h). \tag{5.5}$$

The resulting first-order condition is

$$- F_I'(\hat{\theta})\, c_1(s) + F_G'(\hat{\theta})c_2(h) = 0,$$

or

$$\frac{F_I'(\hat{\theta})}{F_G'(\hat{\theta})} = \frac{c_2(s)}{c_1(h)}. \tag{5.6}$$

The interpretation of this condition is that the marginal rate of transformation between the two types of errors should be set equal to the ratio of the social cost of those errors (Miceli, 1990; Yilankaya, 2002; Lando, 2006).

Conducting comparative statics on this condition yields[10]

$$\frac{\partial\hat{\theta}}{\partial s} > 0, \text{ and } \frac{\partial\hat{\theta}}{\partial h} < 0. \tag{5.7}$$

That is, the standard of proof should increase with the severity of the sanction imposed on conviction, and decrease with the severity of the harm caused by the offense in question. These results make sense since a given change in the standard of proof has opposing effects on the number of type 1 and type 2 errors. Thus, as the cost of type 1 errors increases,

[10] This assumes that the second-order condition for a minimum is satisfied. Specifically, $-F_I''c_1+F_G''c_2>0$.

the standard of proof should be raised in order to reduce the frequency of these errors. Conversely, as the cost of type 2 errors increases, the standard should be relaxed in order to reduce the frequency of these errors.

Although the actual standard of proof in criminal cases – beyond a reasonable doubt – does not vary based on these aspects of the case, the way it is applied in practice might. For example, it would be interesting to ascertain whether judges and juries define 'reasonable doubt' differently depending on what the punishment on conviction would be, or how severe the crime in question was.[11] Dawson (1969, p. 201) provides some anecdotal evidence on the former point by noting that 'there is judicial resistance to imposition of mandatory maximum sentences that seem unduly long in relation to the circumstances of the case'. Shepherd (2007, p. 558) likewise observes that '[n]ot wanting to impose a long sentence on a seemingly low-risk defendant, a prosecutor may decide not to prosecute, or a judge or jury may dismiss charges or acquit'.

One issue on which the model does shed light is the question of why there is a different standard of proof in civil versus criminal cases (Posner, 2003, pp. 618–20). The criminal standard of 'beyond a reasonable doubt' suggests a very high value for $\hat{\theta}$ (near certainty), which implies a strong bias against type 1 errors. This makes sense in the context of criminal cases because conviction often involves imprisonment, and, even in the case of probation or a fine, carries with it the stigma associated with a criminal record (Rasmusen, 1996). This is consistent with a high value of s in the above model.

In contrast, the relative costs of the two types of errors in civil cases are roughly equal, given that most disputes involve monetary damages, and there is no reason to believe that plaintiffs or defendants systematically place a higher value on a given dollar loss. This is consistent with the use of a 'preponderance of the evidence' standard in most civil cases, which sets the threshold for conviction at just over 0.50.

Rules of evidence

Rules of evidence dictate what evidence is permissible at trial and how it may be gathered. We consider two important constitutional rules aimed at protecting the rights of criminal defendants in the United States: the

---

[11] Posner (2003, p. 620) notes that, when asked to quantify proof beyond a reasonable doubt, judges and juries generally choose numbers between 0.75 and 0.95. However, I know of no empirical study of the factors that determine how the particular threshold is chosen.

exclusionary rule and the right against self-incrimination. We also consider the defense of entrapment.

Search and seizure

The Fourth Amendment protects people against unreasonable searches and seizures by the police in an effort to acquire evidence in connection with a criminal investigation. The prohibition, however, is not complete; the use of a reasonableness standard suggests a balancing of costs and benefits in order to determine which searches are allowed and which are not (Posner, 2003, pp. 711–14). To illustrate, suppose that a person is suspected of having committed a crime. The expected benefit of a search is the product of the probability of uncovering evidence that will lead to a conviction, P, times the social gain from a conviction, B. The cost of a search, C, is the impaired privacy of the suspect, including any loss in the suspect's reputation from the cloud of suspicion that inevitably falls on anyone who is the target of a criminal investigation. Based on these factors, the search is reasonable if and only if

$$C < PB. \tag{5.8}$$

Thus, searches that involve a substantial invasion of privacy (high C) are not allowed, whereas those that would lead to conviction of someone who has committed a particularly heinous crime (high B) are allowed.[12]

The law enforces this standard in two ways. The first is the requirement of a search warrant, which gives an impartial judge the opportunity to evaluate the inequality in (5.8) before authorizing a search. The second is the 'exclusionary rule', which prohibits the use of evidence at trial that was obtained unlawfully. There is much dissatisfaction with this rule, however, because many believe that it unduly benefits guilty defendants. An often-proposed alternative is to impose tort liability on the police for illegally seized evidence. The economic argument for this remedy is that it would allow a court to set the amount of liability in proportion to the cost of the invasion of privacy, thus allowing the police in effect to 'buy' the efficient amount of evidence from victims of the search. A counter-argument is that juries may be unwilling to award damages after the fact to defendants who were convicted based on evidence that was seized illegally.

---

[12] See Garoupa (2007) for a more formal analysis of the trade-off between protecting the privacy rights of criminal suspects and crime prevention. He develops this analysis in the context of the European Convention on Human Rights, which strengthens procedural protections of criminal defendants, reflecting an increase in C in condition (5.8).

The rule against self-incrimination

The Fifth Amendment gives criminal defendants the right to refuse to incriminate themselves. What this means is that a defendant's refusal to testify cannot be held against him in court. Again, some have criticized this right as primarily protecting the guilty, but an economic analysis shows that, under some circumstances, the right to remain silent can actually benefit innocent defendants by making their denials of guilt more believable (Seidmann and Stein, 2000; Mialon, 2005). This point can be demonstrated as follows.

Suppose that the right of silence were not available. Then, juries would be entitled to draw an inference of guilt from a defendant's refusal to testify since truly innocent defendants would presumably always be willing to assert their innocence. Knowing this, however, guilty defendants would have a strong incentive to deny their guilt as well, despite the risk of being discovered in a lie. The result is a 'pooling' equilibrium in which innocent and guilty defendants adopt the same strategy, thereby making denial of guilt at trial an uninformative signal to juries. In contrast, the right to silence allows guilty defendants to refuse to testify without creating a presumption of guilt. In doing so, they separate themselves from innocent defendants, thus making the latter's denials of guilt more believable.

A simple model helps to make this point clear. Let λ be the probability that a given defendant is innocent – that is, λ is the fraction of innocent defendants in the population of all defendants, and $1 - \lambda$ is the fraction of guilty defendants.[13] Also, assume that all innocent defendants testify (since, as noted, they have nothing to lose from doing so), but guilty defendants may or may not testify, depending on how the court is allowed to interpret their silence.

Consider first the case where there is no right to silence. Since the court would then be allowed to infer guilt from a defendant's silence (given the presumed behavior of innocent defendants), all guilty defendants presumably would testify as well, even at the risk of being caught in a lie. As a result, however, the court would be able to infer nothing from the defendant's mere act of testifying – that is, the probability of a defendant's innocence would simply be equal to the prior probability of innocence, λ.

Now consider the impact of a right to silence. In this case, the court is not allowed to draw any inferences about a defendant's guilt or innocence by his refusal to testify. Thus, while all innocent defendants will continue to testify, some guilty defendants will now choose to remain silent rather than take the stand and lie. Let g be the fraction of guilty defendants who

[13] In this case, the probability of conviction, θ, is assumed to be the same for all defendants.

choose to testify. As a result, the conditional probability that a defendant is innocent, given that he testifies, is

$$\lambda' \equiv \Pr(\text{innocent} \mid \text{testify}) = \frac{\lambda}{\lambda + (1 - \lambda)g}. \tag{5.9}$$

Clearly, $\lambda' > \lambda$ as long as $g < 1$; that is, as long as some guilty defendants choose not to testify, the conditional probability that the defendant is innocent given that he testifies is larger than the prior probability of innocence.[14] In this sense, the right to remain silent, by allowing guilty defendants to remain silent without penalty, actually helps innocent defendants by making their denials of guilt more believable. As an example, if $\lambda = 0.10$ and $g = 0.15$, then $\lambda' = 0.43$. Thus, the right to remain silent results in a fourfold increase in the probability that a defendant's testimony denying his guilt is believable.

Entrapment

Entrapment is a defense that a criminal defendant can raise based on the claim that he would not have committed the crime but for the solicitation of the police.[15] Thus, although the defendant is not technically innocent of the crime, he should nevertheless be acquitted. This argument makes sense both in terms of fairness (the defendant is not really a criminal), and also deterrence (since there is no behavior to deter). Thus, efforts to entrap otherwise law-abiding people are socially wasteful.

This argument does not imply, however, that solicitation of crimes is never a useful law enforcement tool. Indeed, if solicitation focuses on apprehending individuals who otherwise *would* have committed the crime but in circumstances where it would have been much harder to detect them, then the strategy substantially lowers the cost of law enforcement. The problem, of course, is proving in court that the individual who was nabbed by a police sting was pre-disposed to commit the crime anyway. This raises the same issues of proof discussed above regarding the determination of guilt.

Appeals

We have argued that the primary function of criminal trials is to minimize the cost of legal errors. The fact that such errors are unavoidable, however,

---

14 Note that criminal penalties for perjury enhance this conclusion by making it costly to lie under oath.

15 See Miceli (2007), Hay (2005), McAdams (2005), Shavell (2004, pp. 564–5), and Posner (2003, p. 221).

provides an important economic rationale for the appeals process (Shavell, 1995; Posner, 2003, pp. 600–602).[16] The structure of appeals in the Anglo-American legal system involves losing defendants having the right to seek redress from a higher court. One might ask whether this is preferred to a system in which a higher-level court chooses which cases to review. The advantage of litigant-initiated appeal is based on the notion that litigants (and their counsel) are presumably in a better position to observe when the trial court's decision was erroneous (based on their private information), resulting in a filtering of cases at the appeals court level. Specifically, litigants whose cases were decided in error are more likely to be willing to incur the cost of appeal because they have a greater chance of winning. This sorting is socially desirable because it limits the work of appeals courts to cases that were more likely to have been incorrectly decided. In contrast, if appeals courts selected the cases that they would hear, this sorting would be less effective because the higher court lacks the case-specific information available to litigants.

The preceding suggests that appeals courts can be an effective means of correcting legal errors, but this gain must be weighed against the cost of adding an extra layer (or layers) to the legal process. Appeals are therefore only socially desirable if the expected gain from error correction (which in the criminal context generally involves reversal of type 1 errors) exceeds the additional administrative cost. To illustrate, suppose that legal error at the trial level, if uncorrected, imposes a cost of \$500,000 on society. Also, let the cost of appeal be \$150,000, and let the probability that the appeals court corrects the error be 60 percent. In this example, appeal is socially desirable because the expected gain of \$300,000 = (0.60)(\$500,000) exceeds the cost of \$150,000.

Implications for deterrence

To this point, the discussion has focused on minimizing the cost of legal error plus the cost of administration as the primary function of the procedural system, but the system also affects deterrence through a variety of avenues. First and most obviously, the procedural system determines the punishment of those defendants found guilty, whether at trial or by plea. Thus, the particular goal of criminal punishment embodied in the system will affect the behavior of potential offenders according to Becker's (1968) rational offender model.

---

[16] The appeals process also serves a lawmaking function, as common-law rules are promulgated primarily through appellate decisions. See Cooter and Rubinfeld (1989, pp. 1091–94).

Miceli (1991) explicitly compares the goals of deterrence and fairness in the Becker model with legal error.[17] His results show that these goals are complementary in some respects, and contradictory in others. Specifically, more severe punishments deter crime and promote retribution (appropriate punishment of the guilty) up to a point, but they also potentially reduce fairness when punishments are perceived to be excessive,[18] and when the risk that truly innocent defendants are being punished becomes high. Indeed, as we noted above, there is anecdotal evidence that judges and juries are reluctant to convict defendants in the face of mandatory sentences that seem unduly harsh in relation to the circumstances of the case.

The role of the prosecutor in determining criminal punishment is also substantial since, as we have seen, the vast majority of criminal convictions are the result of plea bargains, and it is the prosecutor who ultimately decides whom to charge, and what charge to bring. Prosecutors use this discretion to conserve on limited judicial resources, but also as a check on legislatures. For example, a prosecutor who believes that the legislatively determined sanction for a particular crime is overly harsh may offer the defendant a lesser penalty in return for pleading guilty to a reduced charge (Reinganum, 1988; Miceli, 1996; Shepherd, 2007). Bjerk (2005) provides empirical evidence for this type of behavior in response to three-strikes laws for repeat offenders. Specifically, he found that prosecutors systematically react to such laws by charging offenders covered by the laws with lesser, uncovered offenses.

Apart from determining the actual punishment imposed on convicted defendants, the procedural system affects deterrence by reducing legal error. Generally, error in the determination of guilt mitigates the deterrent effect of criminal punishment by reducing the expected cost of committing a crime, or, equivalently, by reducing the benefit of being innocent (Posner, 2003, pp. 618–19). To see how, note that the expected sanction from committing a crime is $(1 - \lambda)\theta_G s$, where, recall, $1 - \lambda$ is the probability that the true offender is apprehended, θ_G is the probability of convicting a guilty defendant, and s is the sanction on conviction. The fact that there is legal error, however, means that there is also an expected cost of

[17] Also see Harris (1970) and Polinsky and Shavell (2000b).

[18] The problem of excessive punishment becomes especially problematic given the need in the Becker model to scale up sanctions to reflect the uncertainty of enforcement. As a result, those offenders who are caught are in effect punished for the harm that they caused as well as for the harms caused by others who escaped detection. This prescription, which is a key element of the model of deterrence, clearly violates proportionality and also potentially runs afoul of the Eighth Amendment prohibition of cruel and unusual punishments (Adelstein, 1981).

not committing a crime. This is given by $\gamma\theta_I s$, where γ is the probability that a given individual is wrongly apprehended for a crime,[19] and θ_I is the probability that an innocent person is convicted. The net expected cost of committing a crime is therefore $(1-\lambda)\theta_G s - \gamma\theta_I s = [(1-\lambda)\theta_G - \gamma\theta_I]s$. The deterrent effect of criminal punishment will therefore be increasing in both the effectiveness of the police in apprehending the true offender, $(1-\lambda)-\gamma$, and in the effectiveness of the procedural system in sorting the innocent from the guilty, $\theta_G - \theta_I$, holding the actual sanction, s, fixed.

Conclusion

This article has provided an economic perspective on criminal procedure, defined to be the rules governing the treatment of criminal defendants from the time of arrest up to the rendering of a final verdict. The primary function of this procedure is to arrive at the most accurate verdict at the least possible cost. Because of the uncertainty about a defendant's guilt, however, there is an unavoidable conflict between the goals of punishing the guilty (whether for purposes of deterrence or retribution) and exonerating the innocent. Although popular perception of the criminal process often views the numerous safeguards of defendants as protecting the guilty, they in fact reflect a strong aversion to wrongfully convicting the innocent (type 1 error). The price for this protection is that some guilty defendants will escape punishment (type 2 errors). Ongoing policy debates regarding issues like judicial discretion in sentencing and evidence admissibility reflect this fundamental tension.

References

Adelstein, Richard (1978), 'The Negotiated Guilty Plea: A Framework for Analysis', *New York University Law Review*, **53**, 783–833.

Adelstein, Richard (1981), 'Institutional Function and Evolution in the Criminal Process', *Northwestern University Law Review*, **76**, 1–99.

Adelstein, Richard (1998), 'Plea Bargaining: A Comparative Approach', in Peter Newman (ed.), *The New Palgrave Dictionary of Economics and the Law*, volume 3, New York: Stockton Press, pp. 46–50.

Adelstein, Richard and Thomas Miceli (2001), 'Toward a Comparative Economics of Plea Bargaining', *European Journal of Law and Economics*, **11**, 47–67.

Ayres, Ian and Joel Waldfogel (1994), 'A Market Test for Race Discrimination in Bail Setting', *Stanford Law Review*, **46**, 987–1047.

Becker, Gary (1968), 'Crime and Punishment: An Economic Approach', *Journal of Political Economy*, **76**, 169–217.

[19] Note that γ generally does not equal λ. Whereas γ is the probability that a *particular* innocent person is apprehended, λ is the probability that *someone* who is innocent is apprehended. Thus, we would expect γ to be considerably smaller that λ. See Wittman (1974).

Bjerk, David (2005), 'Making the Crime Fit the Penalty: The Role of Prosecutorial Discretion under Mandatory Minimum Sentencing', *Journal of Law and Economics*, **48**, 591–625.
Boari, Nicola and Gianluca Fiorentini (2001), 'An Economic Analysis of Plea Bargaining: The Incentives of the Parties in a Mixed Penal System', *International Review of Law and Economics*, **21**, 213–31.
Cooter, Robert D. and Daniel L. Rubinfeld (1989), 'Economic Analysis of Legal Disputes and their Resolution', *Journal of Economic Literature*, **27**, 1067–97.
Dawson, Robert (1969), *Sentencing: The Decision as to Type, Length, and Conditions of Sentencing*, Boston: Little, Brown and Co.
Easterbrook, Frank (1983), 'Criminal Procedure as a Market System', *Journal of Legal Studies*, **12**, 289–332.
Ehrlich, Isaac (1998), 'Criminal Justice', in Peter Newman (ed.), *The New Palgrave Dictionary of Economics and the Law*, volume 1, New York: Stockton Press, pp. 553–60.
Elder, Harold (1989), 'Trials and Settlements in the Criminal Courts: An Empirical Analysis of Dispositions and Sentencing', *Journal of Legal Studies*, **18**, 191–208.
Forst, Brian and Kathleen Brosi (1977), 'A Theoretical and Empirical Analysis of the Prosecutor', *Journal of Legal Studies*, **6**, 177–91.
Friedman, Lawrence (2000), *Law in America*, New York: The Modern Library.
Garoupa, Nuno (2007), 'On the Optimal Choice of Enforcement Technology: An Efficiency Explanation of Privacy Rights', *Revue Economique*, **58**, 1353–62.
Garoupa, Nuno and Frank H. Stephen (2007), 'Law and Economics of Plea-bargaining', Working Paper, Manchester School of Law.
Grossman, Gene and Michael Katz (1983), 'Plea Bargaining and Social Welfare', *American Economic Review*, **73**, 749–57.
Hay, Bruce (2005), 'Sting Operations, Undercover Agents, and Entrapment', *Missouri Law Review*, **70**, 387–431.
Harris, John (1970), 'On the Economics of Law and Order', *Journal of Political Economy*, **78**, 165–74.
Hylton, Keith and Vic Khanna (2007), 'Toward a Public Choice Theory of Criminal Procedure', *Supreme Court Economic Review*, **15**, 61–118.
Landes, William (1971), 'An Economic Analysis of the Courts', *Journal of Legal Studies*, **14**, 61–108.
Landes, William (1973), 'The Bail System: An Economic Approach', *Journal of Legal Studies*, **2**, 79–105.
Lando, Henrik (2006), 'A Derivation of Probabilities of Correct and Wrongful Conviction in a Criminal Trial', *Review of Law and Economics*, **2**(3), www.bepress.com/rle/vol2/iss3/art3.
Langbein, John (1979), 'Land without Plea Bargaining: How the Germans do it', *Michigan Law Review*, **78**, 204–25.
Lewisch, Peter (2000), 'Criminal Procedure', in Boudewijn Bouckaert and Gerrit DeGeest (eds), *Encyclopedia of Law and Economics,* Volume VII, Cheltenham, UK and Northampton, MA: Edward Elgar, pp. 241–60.
McAdams, Richard (2005), 'The Political Economy of Entrapment', *Journal of Criminal Law and Criminology*, **96**, 107–85.
Mialon, Hugo (2005), 'An Economic Theory of the Fifth Amendment', *RAND Journal of Economics*, **36**, 833–48.
Miceli, Thomas (1990), 'Optimal Prosecution of Defendants whose Guilt is Uncertain', *Journal of Law, Economics & Organization*, **6**, 189–201.
Miceli, Thomas (1991), 'Optimal Criminal Procedure: Fairness and Deterrence', *International Review of Law and Economics*, **11**, 3–10.
Miceli, Thomas (1996), 'Plea Bargaining and Deterrence: An Institutional Approach', *European Journal of Law and Economics*, **3**, 249–64.
Miceli,Thomas (2007), 'Criminal Solicitation, Entrapment, and the Enforcement of Law', *International Review of Law and Economics*, **27**, 258–68.
Miceli, Thomas (2008), 'Criminal Sentencing Guidelines and Judicial Discretion', *Contemporary Economic Policy*, **26**, 207–15.

Polinsky, A. Mitchell and Steven Shavell (2000a), 'The Economic Theory of Public Enforcement of Law', *Journal of Economic Literature*, **38**, 45–76.
Polinsky, A. Mitchell and Steven Shavell (2000b), 'The Fairness of Sanctions: Some Implications for Optimal Enforcement Policy', *American Law and Economics Review*, **2**, 223–37.
Posner, Richard (2003), *Economic Analysis of Law*, sixth edition, New York: Aspen Publishers.
Rasmusen, Eric (1996), 'Stigma and Self-fulfilling Expectations of Criminality', *Journal of Law and Economics*, **39**, 519–43.
Reinganum, Jennifer (1988), 'Plea Bargaining and Prosecutorial Discretion', *American Economic Review*, **13**, 115–34.
Rhodes, William (1976), 'The Economics of Criminal Courts: A Theoretical and Empirical Investigation', *Journal of Legal Studies*, **5**, 311–40.
Schulhofer, Stephen (1988), 'Criminal Justice Discretion as a Regulatory System', *Journal of Legal Studies*, **17**, 43–82.
Seidmann, Daniel and Alex Stein (2000), 'The Right to Silence Helps the Innocent: A Game-theoretic Analysis of the Fifth Amendment Privilege', *Harvard Law Review*, **114**, 430–510.
Shavell, Steven (2004), *Foundations of Economic Analysis of Law*, Cambridge, MA: Belknap Press.
Shavell, Steven (1995), 'The Appeals Process as a Means of Error Correction', *Journal of Legal Studies*, **24**, 1–28.
Shepherd, Joanna (2007), '*Blakely's* Silver Lining: Sentencing Guidelines, Judicial Discretion, and Crime', *Hastings Law Journal*, **58**, 533–89.
Wittman, Donald (1974), 'Two Views of Procedure', *Journal of Legal Studies*, **3**, 249–56.
Yilankaya, Okan (2002), 'A Model of Evidence Production and Optimal Standard of Proof and Penalty in Criminal Trials', *Canadian Journal of Economics*, **35**, 385–409.

6 Plea-bargaining and prosecution

*Oren Gazal-Ayal and Limor Riza**

1. Introduction

In a speech delivered to American prosecutors in 1940, the US Attorney General and later Supreme Court Justice Robert H. Jackson said: 'The prosecutor has more control over life, liberty, and reputation than any other person in America. His discretion is tremendous' (Jackson, 1940, p. 3). Since then, prosecutorial power in the US and around the world has been increasing steadily. Moreover, in the passing decades, plea-bargaining has become the prevailing method of case disposal in the United States and in an increasing number of other countries around the globe.

While this increase in prosecutorial power has usually been criticized by legal scholars, it has generally been viewed favorably in the law and economics scholarship. Prosecutors have the power to charge people and they can use that power, refrain from doing so, or use it as a bargaining chip, in order to promote the goals of the criminal justice system.[1] This chapter reviews the law and economics of prosecutorial discretion and of plea-bargaining.

2. Legal background

Public or private prosecution

Historically, common law prosecution of criminal cases was left to private entities – mainly the victims of the offense (Cockburn, 1977, p. 15; Beattie 1986, p. 35; Friedman, 1979; 1984). During the nineteenth century, dissatisfaction with the old system led to the creation of the public prosecution system which currently dominates the criminal justice system. There are sound economic reasons for the failure of a system that relies on private criminal prosecution. Criminal prosecution is a public good. If private prosecutors do not receive compensation, at least when the prosecution is successful, only a few will be willing to bear the costs of such an action.

---

* University of Haifa, Faculty of Law. We thank the German-Israeli Foundation for Scientific Research and Development for generous financial support.

1 The economic literature on crime views deterrence as the main goal of criminal law (see, for example Becker, 1968), giving less weight to the other goals of criminal law, such as retribution, incapacitation and rehabilitation.

If compensation is granted to such private entities, wasteful competition between competing prosecutors is likely to emerge. In addition, apprehending violators and gathering information often require the use of force, and invasion of privacy; allowing private citizens to make use of forceful measures is likely to result in abuse of power (Polinsky and Shavell, 2000).

Friedman (1995) argues that the old common law system was functional because in some cases private prosecutors benefited from prosecuting. In some cases, victims had sufficient self-interest in prosecuting violators in order to prevent future offenses against them (Friedman, 1995). In other cases, defendants settled the case by paying the prosecutor, and in return, the charges were dropped or not filed at all, even though such compounding of the offense was not always legal (Friedman, 1995, pp. 486–7). While such incentives could induce some private enforcement, they are hardly effective when most defendants are indigent and where many crimes are victimless. Since all modern criminal justice systems rely on public prosecutions, the following discussion concentrates only on public prosecution. Analysis of private enforcement can be found in Chapter 2 of this volume.

Charging discretion – in general

Charging discretion refers to the prosecutor's power to decide whether to prosecute a person and which charges to file. In common law countries, prosecutors have the power to refrain from prosecuting when they lack sufficient evidence or when they believe that other reasons, often termed 'public interests', justify such refrainment. This 'opportunity principle' is in contrast to the 'legality principle' which is employed in many civil law countries, requiring prosecution when sufficient evidence of guilt exists. Where charging discretion exists, prosecutors often use the power to match the caseload to their limited resources. This last factor plays a major role in the economic analysis of prosecution, as discussed below.

While prosecutorial discretion in non-adversarial systems is still limited, these civil law countries have increasingly conferred discretionary charging powers on prosecutors. It seems that by now, in most of the Western jurisdictions, prosecutors have much discretion in deciding whether to file charges for minor offenses. The difference between the approaches of the two types of systems – the adversarial and the inquisitorial systems – is more substantial in their attitudes to discretion for more serious offenses. In the United States, prosecutors' filing powers are usually subject to grand jury review or judicial approval in preliminary hearing, while the decision not to prosecute is fully in the prosecutors' hands. Most Continental European countries adopt the opposite rule, granting the decision to prosecute to the prosecutors while limiting only the decision to refrain from prosecution. In most common law jurisdictions outside the United States, prosecutors' charging decisions, as well as their decisions not to file charges are usually not subject to review even in the most severe cases.[2]

It should be noted though that discretion sometimes exists even where it is officially banned. In Italy, for example, prosecution is always compulsory; however, prosecutors can set their priorities and defer the prosecution of some cases to allow handling of other cases. This can often amount to de-facto dismissals (Grande, 2002, pp. 195–6).

Plea-bargaining – in general

After charging a person, the prosecutor can decide whether to proceed to trial or to offer the defendant a plea-bargain. A plea-bargain is a settlement of a criminal case. It commonly includes the defendant's agreement to plead guilty to some or all of the charges in return for leniency. This leniency usually takes the form of less severe or fewer charges (charge-bargains) or some concession regarding the punishment (sentence-bargains). Although judges have an increasing role in plea-bargaining in many systems, plea-bargains are mostly treated as agreements between defendants and prosecutors. In such a format, sentence-bargaining is somewhat uncertain. In most systems, the parties cannot determine the sentence for the court, and hence sentence-bargaining results only in recommendations that the court might reject. Still courts tend to follow these recommendations.[3] Unlike sentence-bargaining, courts have very limited power to review charge-bargaining in common law jurisdictions. With charge

---

[2] In Canada, prosecutorial discretion is generally unrestricted (Saunders and McMunagle, 2002, p. 202; Piccinato, 2004, p. 10). It is only subject to a limited review based on the Canadian Charter of Rights and Freedoms (Stuart, 1995; Gorman, 2000; Piccinato, 2004, pp. 9–10). Similarly, in Australia, the power to decide whether to prosecute or not, and which charges to pursue, is bestowed almost entirely in the hands of prosecutors (Commonwealth Director of Public Prosecutions, 2004).

[3] In some countries, such as England and Wales, prosecutors do not present sentence recommendations to the court. Therefore, in England and Wales sentence-bargains are made only between the judge and the defendant, and prosecutors retain only the power to charge-bargain (Sanders and Young, 2007, chapters 8.2–8.4). In Germany, plea-bargaining takes place in court, with the active participation of the judge, prosecutor and defense attorney (Langer, 2004, pp. 39–46; Turner, 2006, pp. 217–22). In other jurisdictions, like Italy and France, the prosecutors are in charge of the sentence offer, while judges can only accept or reject the deal as a whole. When judges reject the agreed sentence, they must allow the defendant to opt for a trial (Langer, 2004, pp. 46–53, 58–62). In the United States, most jurisdictions allow the parties to present a sentence recommendation but

bargaining, prosecutors can easily assure that the agreed sentence is reasonable by 'making the crime fit the penalty' (Bjerk, 2005). To gain from both worlds, many plea-bargains involve both sentence-bargaining and charge-bargaining, and thus reduce the risk that courts will reject the sentence recommendations.

Plea-bargaining has become ubiquitous. About 95 percent of convictions in the United States follow guilty pleas, most of which are a direct result of plea-bargaining (Bureau of Justice Statistics, 2005, table 4.2). In England and Wales, trials in magistrates' courts occur only in 8 percent of the cases, while guilty pleas and convictions in the absence of defendants account for the rest.[4] In the crown courts, 61.5 percent of the cases result in guilty pleas while only 14.3 percent result in conviction by jury (Sanders and Young, 2007).[5] In other common law countries, the picture is similar.[6]

Strictly speaking, plea-bargaining does not exist in non-adversarial systems. These systems do not have the pleading stage, which allows defendants, through a guilty plea, to save the prosecutors from bringing the evidence required for conviction at trial. Yet in the last few decades, several countries in Continental Europe have developed procedures which bear similarities to plea-bargaining. First, in minor offenses, prosecutors often have the power to offer suspects monetary or other non-incarceration sanctions and if the offer is accepted, a trial is avoided (Van den Wyngaert et al., 1993).[7] Second, in several countries, including Italy and France, prosecutors can offer defendants a settled sentence which can even include short terms of incarceration, subject to the court's approval. Third, in Germany, judges have become involved in inducing an admission of guilt, which suffices, de facto, to assure a quick conviction, in return for a sen-

some also allow them to condition the guilty plea on the acceptance of the agreed sentence.

4 Seventy-four percent of the cases result in a guilty plea and 17.5 percent were proved in the defendant's absence.

5 The remaining 22.5 percent result in an acquittal.

6 In Australia, 97 percent of convictions in summary federal offenses resulted from guilty pleas in 2003–4. In indictable federal offenses, the rate was 86 percent (Australian Law Reform Commission, 2005, §2.26). The rate of guilty pleas in Israel ranges from about 80 percent in district courts to 90 percent in the magistrates' courts.

7 Procedures called penal order (*Strafbefehl*, *Ordonnace pénale*), conditional dismissals, transaction or compound fine (see also Albrecht, 2001, p. 13: Aebi et al., 2006, p. 90). In some countries, like Germany, courts must approve the offer first; in others, like the Netherlands and Denmark, courts' approval is not required.

tence discount (Albrecht, 2001, p. 18; Langer, 2004, p. 39; Turner, 2006, p. 214). These new developments have not attracted much attention in the economic literature; hence, this chapter focuses mainly on plea-bargaining in common law countries.

Other discretionary powers

Prosecutors' discretion is not limited to charging and bargaining. Prosecutors (and, in some jurisdictions, the police)[8] have discretion in many other phases of the process including the gathering of evidence, the selection of charges, selection of the instance before which the case is brought and more (Jackson, 2004, pp. 112, 114). Yet charging and bargaining decisions are the most troubling and controversial instances of prosecutorial discretion and thus most economic literature has concentrated on these two stages.

Historical background of plea-bargaining

Plea-bargaining evolved only in the nineteenth century (Langbein, 1979, p. 261; Fisher, 2003). Until then, trials were rapid and inexpensive; thus, plea-bargaining was unnecessary. With the appearance of lawyers in courts, the criminal procedure became much more complex, and courts and prosecutors started looking for ways to encourage guilty pleas (Alschuler, 1979; Fisher, 2003). As the adversary system and evidence law continued to develop, and, hence, jury trials became too convoluted, the need to turn to non-trial alternatives, such as plea-bargaining, increased.

Langbein (1978) identifies similarities between the development of medieval European law of torture and plea-bargaining. Both, he claims, were developed to overcome the excessive trial's safeguards against false accusations placed at trial. In the Middle Ages, a conviction required either two witnesses or a voluntary confession. Since these rules hampered the system's ability to convict many clearly guilty people, the law allowed a bypass. When the indications against defendants were sufficiently convincing, torture replaced the voluntary confessions. The current plea-bargaining process is a somewhat refined version of the torture system since it coerces and induces defendants to plead guilty in order to overcome the highly regulated, complex and expensive criminal trial. Moreover, plea-bargaining, like torture, is highly coercive and thus risky

[8] For example, in some jurisdictions in Canada the power to initiate a criminal prosecution is granted to the police (MacKenzie, 1999). The police also have discretion as to whether to arrest a person, how to investigate a case, and often, whether to forward the case to the prosecution.

for innocent defendants. Langbein (1978) concludes that a simplified trial process is required to assure societies' ability to supply a trial for every defendant. Schulhofer (1984) suggests a simplified bench trial as an alternative to the reliance on plea-bargaining and shows that such a system has been proven workable in Philadelphia. Yet others argue that reducing the cost of trial must result in less accurate trials, and thus raise the rate of wrongful convictions, to the detriment of innocent defendants (Scott and Stuntz, 1992a, p. 1932). When trials are less accurate, prosecutors' incentives to assure that only guilty defendants are prosecuted will also be weakened. Thus, a costly and accurate trial with the option to settle in its shadow protects innocent defendants better than a cheaper and less accurate trial (Scott and Stuntz, 1992a, p. 1950).

3. Economic analysis of charging and plea-bargaining

Plea-bargaining and resource constraints

It is often argued that plea-bargains result in excessive leniency for defendants. After all, the criminal law sets the standards that society has chosen for punishing an offender, and the trial is designed to implement these standards in each case, and to assure that offenders receive the optimal sanction. Since prosecutors have to offer defendants something in return for the guilty plea, 'plea-bargaining results in leniency that reduces the deterrent impact of the law' (US National Advisory Commission, 1973, p. 44).

Landes (1971) set the basic framework for the economic analysis of plea-bargaining which has refuted this argument. He shows how plea-bargaining can help prosecutors maximize the number of convictions weighted by their respective sentences. By settling cases, the prosecutor avoids the risk of acquittal and saves trial resources which can be used in other cases. Hence, prosecutors are willing to settle for a lower sentence when the probability of conviction, post-trial sentence and settlement costs are lower and when the trial costs are higher. Defendants' willingness to accept offers similarly depends on their estimation of the probability of conviction, the post-trial sentence, the trial costs, settlement costs and their attitude to risk. In the end, since trials are more costly than plea-bargains for both parties, a mutually beneficial settlement can usually be reached. A trial can take place only if the defendant's evaluation of the probability of acquittal at trial is higher than the prosecutor's, or the defendant is a risk lover. Landes (1971) also examines his model empirically showing, inter alia, that the difference between trial cost and settlement cost is positively correlated to the parties' tendencies to go to trial. Landes's model was developed and empirically tested in other studies such as those of Rhodes

(1976), Weimer (1978) and Forst and Brosi (1977) For example, Weimer's (1978) study of Alameda County data shows that the plea-bargain offer increases with the increase in the probability of conviction and severity of the anticipated post-trial sentence and that defendants demand for trials decreases when the plea discount increases.

Easterbrook (1983), relying on the line of literature which followed Landes (1971), presents one of the most comprehensive justifications for prosecutorial discretion. He argues that criminal procedure works like a market system. Prosecutors try to maximize deterrence (or the other goals of criminal enforcement) but they are subject to limited resources. They cannot prosecute all possible cases and proceed with each case to a full trial. Absolute prosecutorial discretion allows them to select cases based on the marginal return in deterrence, and settle cases with a similar aim in mind. 'This selection method is presumptively efficient for the same reasons a competitive market is likely to be efficient' (Easterbrook, 1983, p. 299). Prosecutors can react to changes in the demand for trials, in the supply of trial services, in the need to deter certain crimes or offenders and in other factors, and accordingly change the allocation of resources between the different offenses. Similarly, they can adapt their willingness to settle to the relative costs of trial and settlements. Regulation can never be so adaptive and hence will result in much less efficient allocation of resources. Thus, regulation or review of prosecutorial discretion by either judges or grand juries is inefficient. Only absolute discretion can assure that prosecutors' choice of cases and plea-bargaining decisions will optimize the use of resources and maximize deterrence along with other goals of the criminal justice system.

Easterbrook (1983) convincingly argues that if prosecutors want to use discretion to the benefit of all, they can do so. However, prosecutors are not perfect agents of the public interest. While Easterbrook addresses this reservation, he also trivializes it by arguing that any attempt to supervise prosecutors would result in a similar agency problem of the supervising agent, be it a judge, a jury or someone else. This is where Schulhofer (1988) challenges him, arguing that prosecutors are motivated by a favorable public perception, by the desire to avoid the risk of an embarrassing trial loss, by their relationship with successful private practitioners and more. Though these factors might sometimes be correlated with the public interest, often they are not. These agency costs can only be solved by a regulatory system that does not rely too heavily on discretion and free market powers (these agency costs are discussed in detail below). Such regulation should include judicial review of the decision to prosecute and internal prosecutorial review of the decision not to charge.

In sum, the exchange between Easterbrook (1983) and Schulhofer

(1988) reflects the two main positions in the plea-bargaining debate. On the one hand, discretion allows prosecutors to allocate resources better and thus helps them promote criminal justice goals. On the other hand, if prosecutors' interests are not aligned with the public interest, such discretion could be counter-productive. Much of the economic literature of prosecutorial discretion and plea-bargaining has therefore concentrated on tools to control potential deviations of prosecutors from the public interest, as elaborated below.

Plea-bargaining and settlements in private law litigations

At first glance, plea-bargaining seems to share many similarities with settlements in private law. In both cases, the parties evaluate the expected result of the judicial process (probability of a successful prosecution/civil action and the expected court order if the action is successful) and the costs of the proceedings themselves. Each party then calculates the odds and costs and sets its willingness to pay or accept accordingly in the shadow of the trial. Usually, the trial costs and risk averseness lead the parties to settle, unless over-optimism prevents such meeting of the minds. The result is thus beneficial for both parties and, absent externalities, is socially desired.

Yet plea-bargains differ substantially from other legal settlements in many important respects. First, the criminal prosecutors do not attempt to maximize expected profits from trial. Since trials do not result in monetary profit, there is no commensurability between severity of sentence and costs of the proceedings. If prosecutors try to maximize sentences (an issue discussed below), they must do so subject to a fixed budget constraint, while parties to civil litigation usually try to maximize the payoffs from the process, taking into account both the costs and trial result. Second, prosecutors, as agents of society, do not necessarily have an interest in maximizing the sentence in each case, since excessive sentences are costly to the public they represent. Thus, while plaintiffs in civil disputes usually try to maximize the court's award, prosecutors are often interested in less than the harshest sentence they can get. Third, prosecutors are unique players since their decisions in one case are likely to affect many other cases. For example, after a failed plea-bargaining, prosecutors might invest more than otherwise justified in a trial, in order to deter future defendants in similar cases from going to trial; such considerations are only rarely relevant for parties in civil law dispute. Fourth, while attorneys for plaintiffs are closely reviewed by their clients and the market for legal services, the public can hardly review each prosecuted case, and there is virtually no market for disciplining prosecutors. Hence, agency problems in criminal proceedings have distinctive characteristics.

Like prosecutors, defendants in criminal cases also differ from their civil case counterparts. For one, their direct trial costs are usually of limited importance. For sufficiently wealthy defendants, trial costs are usually a negligible factor in the face of potential incarceration. For indigent defendants, legal representation costs are usually borne by the state. At the same time, the criminal process has very different but no less substantial costs for such defendants. Pretrial detention, bail, the tension and stigma of being charged are all highly costly to the defendant and thus their willingness to settle is influenced more by these factors than by the direct cost of legal services and trial. The reliance on publicly funded lawyers also results in a unique agency problem in criminal cases. The limits on the parties' ability to settle, especially due to judicial supervision of plea-bargains, are also unique to this type of settlements. All in all, plea-bargaining is distinct from civil law settlements in many respects, and thus requires separate treatment (Bibas, 2004).

4. Plea bargaining and wrongful convictions

The innocence problem

While the public's objections to plea-bargaining concentrate on the perceived lenient outcome (Cohen and Doob, 1989–90; Herzog, 2003), most legal scholars are more concerned with the innocence problem; that is, the risk that innocent defendants accept plea-bargain offers.

Those legal scholars who fear that innocent individuals may plead guilty often raise two arguments. First, it is argued that innocent defendants might plead guilty for fear of harsher consequences of a wrongful conviction at trial. Second, it is argued that innocent defendants might agree to plead guilty even when it is not in their interest. This section concentrates on the first of these two concerns, leaving the issue of irrational decisions for later.

Alschuler (1968) shows how a rational innocent defendant might plead guilty. He refers to a certain rape defendant who accepted a charge-bargain for a simple battery to avoid the risk of trial, even though the chances of conviction at trial were very low. This defendant preferred a certain conviction, which was likely to result in a probation sentence, to even a small risk of a rape conviction that could be followed by years of imprisonment. This might surely be a rational choice, even for an innocent defendant. Still, it means that plea-bargaining could lead an innocent defendant to plead guilty.

Yet as Church (1979) demonstrates, plea-bargaining was not the source of grievance for this assumedly innocent defendant. The defendant agreed to plead guilty because he feared that he would inaccurately be convicted at trial, and decided that the plea-bargain could mitigate this risk. If plea-bargaining was banned, he would have had to face the risk of a much graver sentence after trial. More generally, innocent defendants might sometimes prefer plea-bargaining to a trial, and thus plead guilty; however, as grave as that choice might be, banning plea-bargaining in order to force these defendants to face a risky trial cannot protect them (Scott and Stuntz, 1992b). For the innocent, the problem is not the plea-bargain offer, but the imperfect trial which drives him to accept the offer.

Similarly, it has often been shown that the trial process itself is more costly to defendants than the post-trial punishment (Feeley, 1979). Especially for minor offenses, defendants suffer more from the anxiety of awaiting adjudication, the cost of the bail bond and the loss of time than from the sentence itself after conviction. This is especially true for defendants in pretrial detention. Empirical studies confirm that detention increases defendants' willingness to plead guilty (Landes, 1974; Kellough and Wortley, 2002, p. 196; CJA, 2005, p. 7; CJA, 2007, p. 7).[9] Thus, in many cases, defendants can be better off accepting a plea-bargain even if they know that a trial will result in an acquittal. When the process is the punishment, as Feeley (1979) describes it, innocent defendants should be encouraged to bypass this process, and plea-bargaining can help them do so (Bowers, 2008).

This position has been heavily criticized by opponents of the plea-bargaining system. Alschuler (1981, p. 699) and Schulhofer (1992, p. 1986) argue that plea-bargaining with innocent defendants creates an externality that is disregarded by advocates of plea-bargaining. The moral force of the criminal conviction is undermined if innocent defendants can be regularly convicted, while inconveniencing an innocent person by requiring him to stand trial is not equally damaging to society. Alschuler (1981) also argues that society is better off with few wrongful trial convictions than with many wrongful plea-bargaining convictions, even if the latter result in much lower sentences and are thus preferred by the innocent defendants.

---

[9] New York City Criminal Justice Agency (CJA) finds that detention mainly indicated the likelihood of conviction (although it is not a predominant condition). It points out that '[d]etention can increase the likelihood of conviction . . . by increasing the pressure on a defendant to plead guilty' (CJA, 2007, p. 7). Moreover, '[a] defendant facing a conditional discharge, a fine, or a sentence of time served – unlike a defendant facing serious jail or prison time – can gain immediate release by pleading guilty. This creates a strong incentive to do so' (ibid.). In a former brief the CJA mentioned that '[w]e had guessed that prosecutors link their bail request to probability of conviction . . . or that they attempt to encourage guilty pleas through detention resulting from high bail . . .' (CJA, 2005, p. 7).

In the end, the dispute is normative in nature. As long as wrongful convictions carry no special moral cost (except for the direct cost to the innocent defendant), a plea-bargain, like any other contract, is a transaction that benefits both prosecutors and wrongly charged defendants. But if wrongful convictions are morally costly per se, restrictions on plea-bargaining might be justified.

Plea-bargaining as a screening mechanism

Grossman and Katz (1983) added to Landes 1971) analysis by showing how plea-bargains can be beneficial to both prosecutors and defendants even absent any cost savings, simply because the parties might be risk averse. More importantly, they demonstrate how asymmetric information leads innocent defendants to opt for trials. Prosecutors try to adjust the offered sentence to the probability of conviction and the post-trial sentence. Similarly, defendants – wishing to minimize the expected sentence – adjust their willingness to settle to these two factors – probability of conviction and expected sentence. However, defendants know whether they are actually guilty or not. Since trials are designed to reveal the truth, an innocent defendant would correctly estimate that his chances at trial are better than the prosecutor's offer suggests. As a result, innocent defendants tend to reject offers, while guilty defendants tend to accept them.[10] Thus, plea-bargaining is a mechanism which screens innocent defendants from guilty ones (see also Kobayashi and Lott, 1992; 1996).

Reinganum (1988) examines two alternative prosecutorial discretion regimes: restricted discretion regimes, where prosecutors must offer all defendants of similar offences a similar plea-bargain, and unrestricted regimes, which allow prosecutors to adjust their offer freely. In her model, both parties have asymmetric information: only the defendant knows whether he is guilty and only the prosecutor knows how strong her case is, and both factors affect the probability of conviction. The prosecutor finds that where the arrest process fails to sufficiently distinguish between innocent and guilty defendants, unrestricted discretion is preferable. However, when prosecutors can rightly estimate that arrestees are guilty often enough, the restricted regime which offers the same plea-bargaining offer to similar defendants is preferable. In this regime, innocents tend to reject the offers made by prosecutors, while guilty defendants accept them.

Innocent defendants are more likely than guilty ones to reject

---

[10] The screening device is more effective if all defendants – guilty and innocent – are equally risk averse. Higher risk aversion of innocent defendants increases their willingness to plea-bargain and thus offsets the effect of private information.

plea-bargain offers for another reason. They might do so because in some cases prosecutors further investigate the case after rejection. Such investigation may reveal their innocence to the prosecutor, leading her to drop the charges (Baker and Mezzetti, 2001).

Behavioral studies indicate other factors creating a similar screening mechanism. Studies using experimental settings show that innocent defendants tend to be more optimistic about the chances of acquittal at trial even when there is no rational reason for such relative optimism (Gregory et al., 1978; Bordens, 1984).[11] Adding to these findings, Tor et al. (2006) experimentally show that innocent defendants are more averse to guilty pleas even absent such relative optimism, because they deem such plea-bargains as unfair. As a result, innocent defendants tend to select trials much more often than guilty ones.

The reluctance of innocent defendants to plead guilty has substantial normative implications. Recall that several opponents of plea-bargaining, including Alschuler (1981) and Schulhofer (1992), argue that plea-bargaining is normatively unacceptable since it induces innocent defendants to plead guilty. But if innocent defendants are much less likely to plead guilty than initially thought, this concern might be overstated. In fact, because of the screening mechanism, plea-bargaining probably reduces the proportion of wrongful convictions, since guilty defendants are easily convicted through plea-bargaining while innocent defendants select trials which sometimes result in acquittals. One can argue that this should lead scholars who emphasize the need to avoid wrongful convictions to support plea-bargaining.

Interestingly, supporters of plea-bargaining, like Church (1979) and Easterbrook (1983), who commend the process for its ability to insure innocent defendants from the harsh consequences of trial conviction, should be more skeptical of their views, too. Since innocent defendants often reject plea-bargains, it is mainly the guilty ones that benefit from this type of insurance. Given that guilty defendants tend to accept generous plea discounts while innocent defendants are inclined to opt for trials, the expected sentence for a defendant is higher if he is innocent. For example, consider cases in which the chances of conviction at trial are 50 percent. Assume that prosecutors offer defendants in such cases plea-bargains for a quarter of the post-trial sentence. Assume further that innocent defendants, because they are averse to pleading guilty, reject the offers, and guilty

---

[11] It might be that the illusion of transparency, that is people's overestimation of others' ability to discern their truthfulness or untruthfulness, can explain this relative optimism (Gilovich et al., 1998).

defendants accept them. As a result, half of the innocent defendants are convicted and receive the full sentence (an average of half the full sentence per defendant) while all the guilty ones receive only one quarter of the full sentence. The expected sentence an innocent defendant faces is thus twice as long as the one imposed on a guilty one ceteris paribus, because the former is averse to a guilty plea. In fact, the trial penalty, that is, the excess sentence imposed on defendants who select trials instead of pleading guilty, is often much higher than as in this example. Thus, innocent defendants probably face a much higher average sentence compared to equally situated guilty defendants. Those who emphasize the importance of plea-bargaining for innocent defendants seem to disregard this aggravating effect (Tor et al., forthcoming).

There is another aspect to the innocence problem which lies in plea-bargaining's effect on prosecutorial screening decisions. With plea-bargaining, prosecutors know that they can settle virtually every case, even weak cases. All they need to do is to adjust the offered charges and sentence to the probability of trial conviction and the expected post-conviction sentence. Thus, they have much less interest in screening away weak cases. Yet some cases are weak because the defendant is innocent. The availability of plea-bargaining allows prosecutors to proceed with these cases, and hence to increase the risk of wrongful conviction.

One way to discourage the prosecution of weak cases is by limiting the level of concession prosecutors can give in return for a guilty plea (Gazal-Ayal, 2006). By imposing such a limitation, defendants in weak cases would refuse to settle. That way, prosecution of a weak case would typically result in a trial, while strong cases would usually be settled. Since prosecutorial resource constraint does not allow them to try too many cases, they would refrain from bringing weak cases in the first place (Bar-Gill and Gazal-Ayal, 2006). While such a limitation can be effective, it seems that when charge-bargaining is available it is extremely hard for judges in an adversarial system to review the size of concession offered to the defendant.

5. Bounded rationality and agency costs

Prosecutors' agency costs

The early models of plea-bargaining and prosecutorial discretion, starting with Landes (1971), assume that prosecutors are perfect agents of society. If this were true, prosecutorial discretion could do nothing but good. For example, if society is strongly averse to wrongful conviction, prosecutors would share that aversion and only prosecute and settle cases where a defendant's guilt is sufficiently certain. Similarly, they would only settle when social benefits outweigh social costs. If restricted discretion were socially beneficial, prosecutors, as perfect agents of society, would restrict themselves. Hence, under this assumption, regulation of prosecutorial discretion is unnecessary. Yet prosecutors' interests do not always coincide with the social interest. Their interests depend on structural factors which differ across jurisdictions (Garoupa and Stephen, 2006).

In many American jurisdictions, chief prosecutors are publicly elected officials. As such, they are likely to be excessively concerned with more apparent aspects of their work. The conviction rate is such a factor (Stuntz, 2001, p. 534). The electorate probably also cares about the severity of the sentences and the charging policies. However, it is much more difficult for the electorate to examine these policies (Alschuler, 1968). Hence, such prosecutors are often interested in plea-bargains even if that requires them to offer excessive plea discounts. Prosecutors' risk aversion or the psychology of loss aversion might further encourage prosecutors to secure plea agreements through excessively lenient offers, which undermines the public interest in deterrence (Schulhofer, 1988). Additionally, in weak cases, where innocence is most likely, they are likely to offer a large plea discount to assure acceptance of the offer (Alschuler, 1968; Bowers 2008).[12] For a society that prefers convictions only when reasonable doubt is removed, these large discounts are an adverse consequence of plea-bargaining.[13]

The agency problem is not restricted to elected prosecutors. Non-elected prosecutors often wish to reduce their workload, and thus settle more cases, while others might take cases to trial to gain trial experience (Bibas, 2004). Boylan and Long (2005) argue that such personal incentives have a noticeable effect on assistant district attorneys in the federal system.

---

12 But see Boylan (2005), who shows that the future career success of chief federal prosecutors in the US is positively correlated with the total sentence imposed in their district. Boylan argues that sentence length, as opposed to the conviction rate, is the relevant performance metric. Note that these prosecutors are not elected officials.

13 Bowers (2008) argues that innocent defendants are often people with past encounters with the law, since prosecutors and the police are biased against such suspects. These defendants are more likely to be detained, and thus to have an interest in a faster process. Additionally, these defendants care less about the stigma and more about the actual sentence. Hence plea-bargaining actually protects these innocent defendants from the possibility of harsh post-trial convictions. However, this analysis disregards the effect of plea-bargaining on the initial charging decision and the decision not to drop charges. As we have shown, prosecutors will not proceed to trial in such weak cases if excessive plea concessions are not allowed, since this would commit much of their limited resources to costly trials and likely acquittals.

They show empirically that federal prosecutors try more cases in districts where private sector salaries are high. In these districts, prosecutors are more interested in gathering trial experience, which can make them more attractive to private law firms. If prosecutors want trial experience and jury convictions, they might refrain from plea-bargaining in the strongest cases, although the cost of such bargaining is likely to be minimal, and prefer plea-bargaining in the weak cases to avoid losses in trials (Bibas, 2004). All in all, these studies show that prosecutors' personal interests affect their plea-bargaining policies.

While some thought has been given to the potential prosecutor-public interest disjunction, there is almost no economic study analyzing the prosecutor-police relationship. Most models assume unity between prosecutors and police, while in practice such relationships range from a hierarchal model of prosecutorial control to a model of coordination between two separate bodies (Richman, 2003; Jackson, 2004, p. 116). Similarly, the economic literature on the structural relationship between prosecutors and the executive is very limited. Van Aaken et al. (2004) and Voigt et al. (2005) hypothesize that when prosecutors enjoy more independence from the executive, they are more likely to effectively enforce the law on public figures. Yet little has been written about the effect of such structural independence on the enforcement in other cases or the efficacy of the criminal justice system, in general.

Defendants and their lawyers

While prosecutors are professional repeat players, defendants are not. Psychological pitfalls might often lead defendants to wrong decisions in plea-bargaining. As we showed above, innocent defendants tend to overestimate their chances of acquittal at trial, leading them to reject beneficial plea-bargain offers. But this is just one example of a broader phenomenon. Bibas (2004) surveys a set of heuristics, biases and other psychological pitfalls that are likely to impair defendants' ability to bargain rationally in the shadow of a trial. If such biases are as substantial as argued (and empirical data here are greatly needed), plea-bargaining might be much less attractive than economics suggests. If the probability of trial conviction and the expected post-conviction sentence are only loosely correlated to defendants' willingness to accept plea-bargain offers, the distribution of sentences after plea-bargaining deviates substantially from the socially desirable distribution (assuming trials distribute sentences in a desirable fashion).

This problem might not be as severe in the majority of cases, where defendants are represented by counsel. Like prosecutors, defense attorneys are often repeat players and thus can counteract their clients' biases. Yet here again, several agency problems are of major concern. While some defendants are wealthy enough to hire highly reputed lawyers, most defendants cannot. They often have to make do with much less costly defense attorneys and urgently, with little means or time to inquire about their quality. These lawyers commonly charge defendants a relatively small fixed fee in advance. After payment, their main personal interest is to secure a quick disposition of the case. Thus, these lawyers, who usually have substantial control over defendants' positions, are often interested in encouraging their clients to quickly plead guilty, whether this serves their clients' interests or not (Blumberg, 1967; Alschuler, 1975).

This agency problem might be more acute when indigent defendants are represented by appointed lawyers. The fee-structure of state-funded lawyers can alter these lawyers' incentives, and there are several studies which show that it actually does (Gray et al., 1996; Moore, 1998, Fenn et al., 2007). It is hard to find a rule that assures efficient incentives for such lawyers (Garoupa and Stephen, 2006). Lawyers who receive a flat fee per case might be mainly interested in a quick disposition of each case. These lawyers have even less interest in keeping their reputation with defendants; they are interested in pleasing the agency who nominated them, who is often equally interested in plea-bargains. For example, in some places, the judge nominates the defense attorney, and since judges are often interested in removing cases from the docket, there is a high risk that lawyers encourage guilty pleas even when it is not in their clients' best interest (Alschuler, 1975; Moore, 1998).[14] A similar preference for plea-bargaining exists when the per-hour fee is subject to a cap, which de-facto assures that lawyers will not be paid for the time they spend on a full trial (Stuntz, 1997, pp. 10–11). Empirical studies support this conclusion. When lawyers' fees were altered from a per-hour system to a flat-fee system in Scotland, the rate of defendants who changed their plea to 'guilty' after accessing legal aid increased substantially (Tata and Stephen, 2006).[15] Some even argue that the extremely high rate of plea-bargaining is at odds with what we would expect from defendants who are averse to losses, and it can only be explained by defense lawyers' manipulation (Birke, 1999).

---

[14] Blumberg (1967, pp. 35–8) shows that most defendants pleaded guilty based on their counsel's advice. Schulhofer and Friedman (1993, pp. 112–22) argue that indigent defendants in a criminal procedure should be allowed to choose their representatives and receive vouchers from the state to finance their legal aid. This voucher system thus assures that lawyers need to safeguard their reputations and align their interests with the interest of their indigent clients. Dnes and Rickman (1998, pp. 260–62) also propose vouchers as a payment system for legal aid.

[15] Introducing the flat-fee system sharply reduced the amount of contact defense lawyers had with their clients and also their prior investigation of evidence. Moreover, plea-bargaining patterns were changed; defendants pleaded guilty at a later stage (Tata and Stephen, 2006).

However, an hourly payment is not a panacea either. If paid by the hour, attorneys might push too often for trials or delay plea-bargaining, regardless of the defendant's interests (Garoupa and Stephen, 2006). A more subtle way of assuring quality is an institutional one, using public defender's office employees. Where public defenders operate within a hierarchal office, quality can be preserved through monitoring by the head of the office.[16] Moreover, public defenders are paid a fixed salary, and thus their economic interest in quickly resolving many cases is mitigated (Alschuler, 1975). Yet even in such offices, the caseload often encourages public defenders to prefer guilty pleas, as several studies show (Alschuler, 1975, p. 1255; Schulhofer, 1992, 1989–90; Bibas, 2004, p. 2477).

If the defendant's bounded rationality and agency problems are too substantial, plea-bargaining cannot be relied upon. Plea-bargaining has no mechanism to assure that innocent defendants would be acquitted or that the guilty would be punished proportionally unless the parties bargain rationally in the shadow of a trial, which is constructed to achieve these goals (Bibas, 2004). Thus, calls for a ban on plea-bargaining often rest on these agency problems (Alschuler, 1981; Schulhofer, 1988). True, defendants might make mistakes and lawyers might misrepresent them in trials too. However, misrepresentation in an open trial might cost defense lawyers more disrepute than such behavior in the less observable plea-bargaining. Moreover, plea-bargaining allows the defense attorney to save substantial time resources when that is in their interest. By encouraging the defendant to plead guilty, defense attorneys can avoid most of the costs of the process. Cutting corners at trial is much less beneficial, and hence the incentives to do so are much smaller (Schulhofer, 1988). On the other hand, a trial is a much more complex process than plea-bargaining, and hence defendants' ability to monitor their lawyers is substantially reduced at trial (Scott and Stuntz, 1992a; Bibas, 2004). It is, thus, still highly debatable whether the defendant-attorney agency problem is more severe in trials or in plea-bargaining.

6. Prosecutorial discretion's effects on criminal justice systems

As we have shown in the historical review, the pressure to adopt plea-bargaining and encourage the practice has resulted from an increase in criminal trial complexity. Trial complexity and high caseload also force prosecutors to screen away cases that otherwise would have been

---

[16] The head of such an office might be interested in assuring high quality services because his office is monitored by the press, unlike the job of an individual defender.

prosecuted. In many jurisdictions, both charging discretion and plea-bargaining are used to overcome limited prosecutorial and trial resources. Yet Stuntz (1997) shows that in such a discretionary system, trial complexity does not only benefit suspects that now escape prosecution; it also hurts other defendants who would have otherwise escaped charges. More specifically, in a discretionary system, trial complexities harm weaker and poorer defendants, while benefiting strong and affluent ones. Since prosecutors already have more potential cases than they can prosecute, when some cases are more costly to prove, prosecutors simply choose other cases instead. When prosecutors are subject to resource constraints, the main effect of more regulation of trials is distributive, not quantitative. This distributive effect is not random. The defendants' right to confront witnesses is much more valuable to those who have resources to prepare a decent cross-examination. The defendant's right to remain silent is much more useful to the minority who know that speaking to the police is usually damaging.[17] The defendant's right to exclude illegally obtained evidence has a much greater effect where the defense lawyer can be paid to investigate police misconduct. As a result, complex trial regulation mainly benefits strong, experienced and wealthier defendants. Subsequently, it pushes prosecutors to divert their limited resources to the prosecution of weaker, indigent less sophisticated defendants. Moreover, defendants in detention or indigent defendants who have to bear the high cost of making bail are not interested in prolonging the process, even if they can afford it. Their main interest is in shortening the process. Their willingness to plead guilty makes their cases even more attractive to prosecutors, and makes the costly prosecutions of wealthier defendants who can easily raise bail much less attractive comparatively. Even when a wealthier or more sophisticated defendant is prosecuted, the high cost of the expected trial assures that he receives a much more generous plea-bargain offer than other defendants facing similar charges. As a result, prosecutorial discretion and plea-bargaining, combined with a highly regulated and costly trial, result in a much more discriminatory system than one with a simplified trial process with more limited charging and bargaining discretion.

Stuntz (2001) brings legislators' incentives into the picture. Legislators might be interested in satisfying a constituency which wants a more 'tough on crime' approach. Thus, legislators consistently increase sentences and criminalize more activities by enacting broader criminal statues.

---

[17] According to a field study carried out in the US during the 1990s, the vast majority of suspects – ranging from 78 percent to 96 percent – waive the right to remain silent (Leo, 1996, p. 281; 1998, p. 275).

Sentencing guidelines and minimum sentences laws can restrict judges from undercutting such policies. If prosecutors have no charging and bargaining discretion, such a policy quickly results in overcrowded prisons, which legislators will need to finance. But in systems which rely on prosecutorial discretion, the effect of this policy is very different. In such a system, broader and harsher criminal statues result mainly in more power for prosecutors to decide who should be sentenced and for how long. This policy simply vests prosecutors with more bargaining chips to extract guilty pleas and avoid expensive trials. Legislators know that prosecutors would not force every convicted defendant to serve the disproportional sentences required by law, but only the few that insist on a trial. They know that trivial misconducts, which are criminalized, would not result in prosecution unless the prosecutor suspects that the defendant has committed a more severe crime but the prosecutor faces difficulties in proving it. Hence, expanding substantive criminal law is a tool to empower prosecutors in plea-bargaining and overcome the costs of a criminal trial. Substantive criminal law is no longer designed to assure that trials result in the socially desired outcome; it is designed to allow prosecutors to reach such an outcome in plea-bargaining. In such a system, the 'shadow of trial', which is the only tool to discipline prosecutors in plea-bargaining, loses its meaning (Stuntz, 2004).

Bjerk (2005) shows empirically how prosecutors use the tools provided by legislators. In many American jurisdictions, legislators have enacted 'three strike laws', that is, laws which require judges to impose a minimum incarceration sentence for third-time felons. Prosecutors have several ways to bypass these laws. One of them is to reduce the felony charges in cases qualifying for the minimum sentence to misdemeanors. Bjerk (2005) finds that after the enactment of such three-strike laws, third-time felons were 70 percent more likely to have their charges reduced to misdemeanor, while no such change could be observed with regard to other felons. Walsh (2004) examines another method of circumvention of the three-strikes rule, which is to drop previous 'strikes', and shows that prosecutors mainly use this tool when they believe that the circumstances do not justify such harsh treatment. These results show that often prosecutors are not interested in the most severe sentence they can impose on defendants. If a prosecutor is interested in a sentence of one or two years of imprisonment but a trial conviction would result in ten years, the prosecutor can easily extract a guilty plea even from defendants who have a reasonable chance of proving their innocence and even from defendants who believe that the offered sentence is much higher than is socially desired. Such excessive trial sentences thus result in very few trials. Absent trials, there are almost no effective checks on prosecutorial discretion.

This raises the obvious concern of prosecutorial mistakes and misconduct, when their interest is not fully aligned with the public interest. For example, prosecutors might invest too little in verifying that a defendant is guilty, when they can easily extract a guilty plea without this further investigation in the shadow of the broad and harsh criminal law. The excessive scope of criminal law also allows pretextual prosecution, meaning the bringing of charges that usually do not result in prosecution because the prosecutor believes that these defendants deserve punishment for something else which cannot be proven (Richman and Stuntz, 2005). While these tools can be used to promote deterrence and other goals of the criminal law, absent a public process and an appeal procedure, prosecutors are often free from criticism which might help monitor their use, and overcome the prosecutor's agency problem.

Such prosecutorial power raises an additional concern. Though prosecutors can use plea-bargaining and charging discretion to prevent an unwarranted increase in the prison population, there is nothing that forces them to do so. Misner (1996) concentrates on this external cost of prosecutorial discretion and proposes allocation of specific prison space to the prosecutors; this would force prosecutors to take into account the costs of prisons when they decide to prosecute. Several jurisdictions, most notably Minnesota, solved the problem of increasing overcrowding in prisons differently, by requiring the sentencing commission to take into account the prisons' capacity in deciding about the presumptive sentence.[18]

7. Judicial participation in plea-bargaining

The analysis thus far rests on the assumption that bargaining is conducted between the defendant and the prosecutor, while the judge, if involved at all, only reviews the agreement reached. In practice though, in many systems, including several American states, the judge takes an active part in the negotiation, often a pivotal one (Alschuler, 1976; Turner, 2006). For example, in England and Wales, defendants can charge-bargain with prosecutors but sentence-bargaining is only conducted with the judge, who can

[18] According to the Minnesota Sentencing Guidelines, prison capacity should be taken into consideration before sentencing. The requirement to consider prison overcrowding is listed as the third principle of the guidelines presented at its outset. These guidelines state that '[b]ecause the capacities of state and local correctional facilities are finite, use of incarcerative sanctions should be limited to those convicted of more serious offenses or those who have longer criminal histories. To ensure such usage of finite resources, sanctions used in sentencing convicted felons should be the least restrictive necessary to achieve the purposes of the sentence' (Minnesota Sentencing Guidelines, 2007).

inform the defendant of the sentence he should expect if he pleads guilty (Sanders and Young, 2007, chapter 8). Judges often participate in plea-bargaining in many other jurisdictions, including Germany and Israel.

The economic literature has generally overlooked this phenomenon (Garoupa and Stephen, 2006). Plea-bargaining has been treated as an agreement between defendants and prosecutors only. Yet bargaining with a judge is something quite different. Prosecutors can only determine the post-plea sentence where judges also control the post-trial sentence. When prosecutors are interested in avoiding a trial, they can only encourage defendants to plead guilty by offering them a settlement which is better than the expected result of the trial; when a judge is interested in a guilty plea, he can also alter the result of the expected trial. If judges had no interest in guilty pleas, that might not raise concerns; however, judges are probably very interested in guilty pleas since guilty pleas reduce their workload. Defendants might rightfully fear displeasing the judge in the bargaining process. Here, again, one cannot rely on the shadow of the trial to regulate the result of plea-bargaining.

That does not mean that judicial involvement in plea-bargaining has no value. Prosecutorial plea offers often cannot assure the defendant of a specific sentence, because most systems give judges the final say regarding the sentence. Judicial participation can reduce the risks for defendants by assuring that the offered post-plea sentence will be respected and by supplying authorized information about the expected post-trial sentence. Additionally, judicial participation can reduce over-optimism and the self-serving bias of parties which might hinder successful bargaining (Loewenstein et al., 1993; Babcock et al., 1995).[19] Judges thus can serve as de-facto mediators, and, like other mediators, can help the parties to overcome their cognitive biases (Mnookin, 1993). Several jurisdictions, such as Connecticut and Israel, allow judges to participate in plea-bargaining only if they are not going to preside over the case if plea-bargaining fails, thus allowing the parties to benefit from mediation while preventing the judges from coercing guilty pleas.

8. Plea-bargaining and prosecutorial discretion in civil law countries

Unlike plea bargaining in adversarial systems, economic research into the parallel procedures in civil law countries is scarce.[20] The differences

---

[19] Over-optimism refers to the general tendency of people to believe that positive, but not negative, events will happen to them. Self-serving bias refers to people's tendency to interpret information in a light favorable to them (Jolls et al., 1998).

[20] One reference to plea-bargaining in civil law countries can be found in

between the two types of system make much of the plea-bargaining literature irrelevant to civil law systems. For example, in Italy, parties are allowed to apply for a consensual punishment which does not exceed a sentence of five years (Langer, 2004, pp. 49–50). This process is often called *patteggiamento* or bargaining, and seems to be similar to sentence-bargaining in common law countries. In the Italian system, judges are allowed to overturn prosecutorial refusal to offer a sentence discount and defendants do not even have to admit their guilt in order to get such a bargain (Langer, 2004, p. 51). These features should have encouraged the parties to make use of the process.

Yet the process is generally regarded as a failure. Full trials still occur in 85 percent of cases in Italy, in sharp contrast to the roughly 10 percent trial rate in common law countries. The Italian system still suffers from an excessive caseload and delays. One possible explanation for the failure of plea-bargaining to clear the market is the compulsory prosecution rule. In common law countries, if too many defendants choose to go to trial, prosecutors can offer larger plea concessions and drop more cases. On the other hand, in Italy, the legality principle does not allow prosecutors to drop cases, and the law does not allow charge-bargaining or more than a one-third reduction in sentence-bargaining. Since too few defendants agree to this limited concession, the cases still pile up. Defendants thus know that prosecutors cannot bring their case to trial promptly and hence prefer to reject the offer. As the number of defendants who reject such offers increases, the delays increase too, and the benefits from bargaining are further reduced. It thus might be that plea-bargaining is much less attractive to defendants in systems with compulsory prosecution. This is just one example of the difficulty in applying models developed in common law countries in the analysis of plea-bargaining in civil law jurisdictions. A more thorough economic analysis and empirical research should be tailored to the study of plea-bargaining in civil law systems.

References

Adelstein, Richard and Thomas J. Miceli (2001), 'Toward a Comparative Economics of Plea-bargaining', *European Journal of Law and Economics*, **11**, 47–67.

Aebi, Marcelo Fernado, Kauko Aromaa, Bruno Aubusson de Cavarlay, Gordon Barclay, Beata Gruszczyñska, Hanns von Hofer, Vasilika Hysi, Jörg-Martin Jehle, Martin Killias, Paul Smit and Cynthia Tavares (2006), *The European Sourcebook of Crime and Criminal Justice Statistics* (2006), Boom Juridische uitgevers, available at www.europeansourcebook.org/esb3_Full.pdf.

Adelstein and Miceli (2001), who argue that the difference in criminal justice values in the two types of system makes plea-bargaining a welfare-increasing process in common law countries but not in civil law countries.

Albrecht, Hans Jörg (2001), 'Simplification of Criminal Procedure: Settlements out of Court – A Comparative Study of European Criminal Justice Systems', Research Paper 19, Pretoria: South African Law Commission, available at www.doj.gov.za/salrc/rpapers/rp19.pdf.

Alschuler, Albert W. (1968), 'The Prosecutor's Role in Plea-bargaining', *University of Chicago Law Review*, **36**, 50–112.

Alschuler, Albert W. (1975), 'The Defense Attorney's Role in Plea-bargaining', *Yale Law Journal*, **84**, 1179–315.

Alschuler, Albert W. (1976), 'The Trial Judge's Role in Plea Bargaining, Part I', *Columbia Law Review*, **76**, 1059–154.

Alschuler, Albert W. (1979), 'Plea-bargaining and its History', *Law & Society Review*, **13**, 211–45.

Alschuler, Albert W. (1981), 'The Changing Plea-bargaining Debate,' *California Law Review*, **69**, 652–730.

Australian Law Reform Commission (2005), 'Sentencing of Federal Offenders – Issue Paper 29', available at www.austlii.edu.au/au/other/alrc/publications/issues/29/#Heading24.

Babcock, Linda, George Loewenstein, Samuel Issacharoff and Colin Camerer (1995), 'Biased Judgments of Fairness in Bargaining', *American Economic Review*, **85**, 1337–43.

Baker, Scott and Claudio Mezzetti (2001), 'Prosecutorial Resources, Plea-bargaining, and the Decision to Go to Trial', *Journal of Law, Economics and Organization*, **17**, 149–67.

Bar-Gill, Oren and Oren Gazal-Ayal (2006), 'Plea Bargains Only for the Guilty', *Journal of Law and Economics*, **49**, 353–64.

Beattie, J.M. (1986), *Crime and the Courts in England 1660–1800*, New Jersey: Princeton University Press.

Becker, Gary S. (1968), 'Crime and Punishment: An Economic Approach', *Journal of Political Economy*, **76** (2), 169–217.

Bibas, Stephanos (2004), 'Plea-bargaining Outside the Shadow of Trial', *Harvard Law Review*, **117**, 2463–547.

Birke, Richard (1999), 'Reconciling Loss Aversion and Guilty Pleas', *Utah Law Review*, **1999**, 205–54.

Bjerk, David (2005), 'Making the Crime Fit the Penalty: The Role of Prosecutorial Discretion under Mandatory Minimum Sentencing', *Journal of Law and Economics*, **48**, 591–625.

Blumberg, Abraham S. (1967), 'The Practice of Law as Confidence Game: Organizational Cooperation of a Profession', *Law & Society Review*, **1**, 15–39.

Bordens, Kenneth S. (1984), 'The Effects of Likelihood of Conviction, Threatened Punishment, and Assumed Role on Mock Plea Bargaining Decisions', *Basic and Applied Social Psychology*, **5**, 59–74.

Bowers, Josh (2008), 'Punishing the Innocent', *University of Pennsylvania Law Review*, **156**, 1117–79, available at http://ssrn.com/abstract=983819.

Boylan, Richard T. (2005), 'What do Prosecutors Maximize? Evidence from the Careers of U.S. Attorneys', *American Law and Economics Review*, **7** (2), 379–402.

Boylan, Richard T. and Cheryl X. Long (2005), 'Salaries, Plea Rates, and the Career Objectives of Federal Prosecutors', *Journal of Law and Economics*, **48**, 627–51.

Bureau of Justice Statistics (2005), *State Court Sentencing of Convicted Felons, 2002 – Statistical Tables*, Washington DC: Department of Justice, available at www.ojp.usdoj.gov/bjs/pub/pdf/scscf02.pdf.

Church, Thomas W. (1979), 'In Defense of Bargain Justice', *Law & Society Review*, **13**, 509–25.

CJA (New York City Criminal Justice Agency) (2005), 'Prosecutor's Bail Requests and the CJA Release Recommendation: What Do They Tell the Judge?', Research Brief No. 9 (August 2005), available at www.cjareports.org/reports/brief9.pdf.

CJA (New York City Criminal Justice Agency) (2007), 'Bail, Detention, & Nonfelony Case Outcome', Research Brief No. 14 (May 2007), available at www.cjareports.org/reports/brief14.pdf.

Cockburn. J.S. (1977), *Crime in England 1550–1800*, London: Methuen & Co. Ltd.

Cohen, Stanley A. and Anthony N. Doob (1989–90), 'Public Attitudes to Plea-bargaining', *Criminal Law Quarterly*, **32**, 85–109.
Commonwealth Director of Public Prosecutions (2004), 'Prosecution Policy of the Commonwealth', available at www.cdpp.gov.au/Prosecutions/Policy/Default.aspx.
Dnes, Antony and Neil Rickman (1998), 'Contracts for Legal Aid: A Critical Discussion of Government Policy Proposals', *European Journal of Law and Economics*, **5**, 247–65.
Easterbrook, Frank H. (1983), 'Criminal Procedure as a Market System', *Journal of Legal Studies*, **12**, 289–332.
Feeley, Malcolm M. (1979), *The Process is the Punishment*, New York: Russell Sage Foundation.
Fenn, Paul, Alastair Gray and Neil Rickman (2007), 'Standard Fees for Legal Aid: An Empirical Analysis of Incentives and Contracts', *Oxford Economic Papers*, 1–20.
Fisher, George (2003), *Plea-bargaining's Triumph: A History of Plea-bargaining in America*, Stanford, CA: Stanford University Press.
Forst, Brian and Brosi, Kathleen B. (1977), 'A Theoretical and Empirical Analysis of the Prosecutor', *Journal of Legal Studies*, **6**, 177–91.
Friedman, David D. (1979), 'Private Creation and Enforcement of Law: A Historical Case', *Journal of Legal Studies*, **8**, 399–415.
Friedman, David D. (1984), 'Efficient Institutions for the Private Enforcement of Law', *Journal of Legal Studies*, **13**, 379–97.
Friedman, David D. (1995), 'Making Sense of English Law Enforcement in the Eighteenth Century', *University of Chicago Law School Roundtable*, **2**, 475–505.
Garoupa, Nuno and Frank H. Stephen (2006), 'Law and Economics of Plea-bargaining', available at http://papers.ssrn.com/sol3/papers.cfm?abstract_id=917922.
Gazal-Ayal, Oren (2006), 'Partial Ban on Plea Bargains', *Cardozo Law Review*, **27**, 2295–349.
Gilovich, Thomas, Kenneth Savitsky and Victoria Husted Medvec (1998), 'The Illusion of Transparency: Biased Assessments of Others' Ability to Read One's Emotional States', *Journal of Personality and Social Psychology*, **75**, 332–46.
Gorman, Wayne (2000), 'Prosecutorial Discretion in a Charter-dominated Trial Process', *Criminal Law Quarterly*, **44**, 15–33, reprinted in R.B. Saunders and J.A. McMunagle (2002), *Criminal Law in Canada: An Introduction to the Theoretical, Social and Legal Contexts*, Toronto: Carswell, pp. 213–17.
Grande, Elisabetta (2002), 'Criminal Justice: The Resistance of a Mentality', in Jeffrey S. Lena and Ugo Mattei (eds), *Introduction to Italian Law*, The Hague/London/New York: Kluwer Law International.
Gray, Alastair, Paul Fenn and Neil Rickman (1996), 'Controlling Lawyers' Costs through Standard Fees: An Economic Analysis', in Richard Young and David Wall (eds), *Access to Criminal Justice: Legal Aid, Lawyers & The Defence of Liberty*, UK: Blackstone Press Limited.
Gregory, W.L., J.C. Mowen and D.E. Linder (1978), 'Social Psychology and Plea-bargaining: Applications, Methodology, and Theory', *Journal of Personality and Social Psychology*, **36**, 1521–30.
Grossman, Gene M. and Michael L. Katz (1983), 'Plea-bargaining and Social Welfare', *American Economic Review*, **73** (4), 749–57.
Herzog, Sergio (2003), 'The Relationship between Public Perceptions of Crime Seriousness and Support for Plea-bargaining Practices in Israel: A Factorial-survey Approach', *Journal of Criminal Law and Criminology*, **94**, 103–31.
Jackson, John D. (2004), 'The Effect of Legal Culture and Proof in Decisions to Prosecute', *Law, Probability and Risk*, **3**, 109–31.
Jackson, Robert H. (1940), 'The Federal Prosecutor', *American Institute of Criminal Law and Criminology*, **31**, 3–6.
Jolls, Christine M., Cass Sunstein and Thaler Richard (1998), 'A Behavioral Approach to Law and Economics', *Stanford Law Review*, **50**, 1471–550.
Kellough, Gail and Scot Wortley (2002), 'Remand for Plea: Bail Decisions and Plea-bargaining as Commensurate Decisions,' *British Journal of Criminology*, **42**, 186–210.

Kobayashi, Bruce H. and John R. Lott (1992), 'Low-probability-high-penalty Enforcement Strategies and the Efficient Operation of the Plea-bargaining System', *International Review of Law and Economics*, **12**, 69–77.

Kobayashi, Bruce H. and John R. Lott (1996), 'In Defense of Criminal Defense Expenditures and Plea-bargaining', *International Review of Law and Economics*, **16**, 397–416.

Landes, William M. (1971), 'An Economic Analysis of the Courts', *Journal of Law and Economics*, **14** (1), 61–107.

Landes, William M. (1974), 'Legality and Reality: Some Evidence on Criminal Procedure', *Journal of Legal Studies*, **3**, 287–337.

Langbein, John H. (1978), 'Torture and Plea-bargaining', *University of Chicago Law Review*, **46**, 3–22.

Langbein, John H. (1979), 'Understanding the Short History of Plea-bargaining', *Law & Society Review*, **13**, 261–72.

Langer, Máximo (2004), 'From Legal Transplants to Legal Translations: The Globalization of Plea-bargaining and the Americanization Thesis in Criminal Procedure', *Harvard International Law Journal*, **45** (1), 1–64.

Leo, Richard A. (1996), 'Criminal Law: Inside the Interrogation Room', *Journal of Criminal Law and Criminology*, **86**, 266–303.

Leo, Richard A. (1998), 'Miranda and the Problem of False Confessions', in Richard A. Leo and George C. Thomas III (eds), *The Miranda Debate: Law, Justice and Policing*, Boston, MA: Northeastern University Press, pp. 271–82.

Leo, Richard A. (2001), 'Questioning the Relevance of Miranda in the Twenty-first Century', *Michigan Law Review*, **99**, 1000–1029.

Loewenstein, George, Samuel Issacharoff, Colin Camerer and Linda Babcock (1993), 'Self-serving Assessments of Fairness and Pretrial Bargaining', *Journal of Legal Studies*, **22**, 135–59.

MacKenzie, Gavin (1999), 'Lawyers and Ethics: Professional Responsibility and Discipline', reprinted in R.B. Saunders and J.A. McMunagle (2002), *Criminal Law in Canada: An Introduction to the Theoretical, Social and Legal Contexts*, Toronto: Carswell, pp. 204–9.

Minnesota Sentencing Guidelines Commission (2007), 'Minnesota Sentencing Guidelines and Commentary', available at www.msgc.state.mn.us/guidelines/guide07.DOC.

Misner, Robert L. (1996), 'Recasting Prosecutorial Discretion', *Journal of Criminal Law and Criminology*, **86** (3), 717–77.

Mnookin, Robert H. (1993), 'Why Negotiations Fail: An Exploration of Barriers to the Resolution of Conflict', *Ohio State Journal on Dispute Resolution*, **8**, 235–56.

Moore, Michael K. (1998), 'State Bar of Texas – Committee on the Provision of Legal Services to the Poor in Criminal Matters – Executive Summary – The Status of Indigent Defense in Texas: The Prosecutor's Perspective', available at www.uta.edu/pols/moore/indigent/proexsum.PDF.

Piccinato, Milica Potrebic (2004), 'Plea Bargaining', Department of Justice Canada, available at www.justice.gc.ca/en/ps/inter/plea/PleaBargaining-EN.pdf.

Polinsky, A. Mitchell and Steven Shavell (2000), 'The Economic Theory of Public Enforcement of Law', *Journal of Economic Literature*, **38**, 45–76.

Reinganum, Jennifer F. (1988), 'Plea-bargaining and Prosecutorial Discretion', *American Economic Review*, **78** (4), 713–28.

Rhodes, William M. (1976), 'The Economics of Criminal Courts: A Theoretical and Empirical Investigation', *Journal of Legal Studies*, **5**, 311–40.

Richman, Daniel (2003), 'Prosecutors and their Agents, Agents and their Prosecutors', *Columbia Law Review*, **103**, 749–832.

Richman, Daniel C. and William J. Stuntz (2005), 'Al Capone's Revenge: An Essay on the Political Economy of Pretextual Prosecution', *Columbia Law Review*, **105**, 583–639.

Sanders, Andrew and Richard Young (2007), *Criminal Justice*, Oxford: Oxford University Press.

Saunders, R.B. and J.A. McMunagle (2002), *Criminal Law in Canada: An Introduction to the Theoretical, Social and Legal Contexts*, Toronto: Carswell.

Schulhofer, Stephen J. (1984), 'Is Plea-bargaining Inevitable', *Harvard Law Review*, **97**, 1037–107.
Schulhofer, Stephen J. (1988), 'Criminal Justice Discretion as a Regulatory System', *Journal of Legal Studies*, **17**, 43–82.
Schulhofer, Stephen J. (1992), 'Plea Bargaining as Disaster', *Yale Law Journal*, **101**, 1979–2009.
Schulhofer, Stephen J. and David D. Friedman (1993), 'Rethinking Indigent Defense: Promoting Effective Representation through Consumer Sovereignty and Freedom of Choice for all Criminal Defendants', *American Criminal Law Review*, **31**, 73–122.
Scott, Robert E. and William J. Stuntz (1992a), 'Plea-bargaining as Contract', *Yale Law Journal*, **101**, 1909–68.
Scott, Robert E. and William J. Stuntz (1992b), 'A Reply: Imperfect Bargains, Imperfect Trials, and Innocent Defendants', *Yale Law Journal*, **101**, 2011–15.
Stuart, Don (1995), 'Prosecutorial Accountability in Canada', in Philip Stenning (ed.), *Accountability for Criminal Justice: Selected Essays*, Toronto: Toronto University Press, reprinted in R.B. Saunders and J.A. McMunagle (2002), *Criminal Law in Canada: An Introduction to the Theoretical, Social and Legal Contexts*, Toronto: Carswell.
Stuntz, William J. (1997), 'The Uneasy Relationship between Criminal Procedure and Criminal Justice', *Yale Law Journal*, **107**, 1–76.
Stuntz, William J. (2001), 'The Pathological Politics of Criminal Law', *Michigan Law Review*, **100**, 505–600.
Stuntz, William J. (2004), 'Plea Bargaining and Criminal Law's Disappearing Shadow', *Harvard Law Review*, **117**, 2548–69.
Tata, Cyrus and Frank Stephen (2006), '"Swings and Roundabouts": Do Changes to the Structure of Legal Aid Remuneration Make a Real Difference to Criminal Case Management and Case Outcomes?', *Criminal Law Review*, **2006** (8), 722–41.
Tor, Avishalom, Oren Gazal-Ayal and Stephen M. Garcia (forthcoming), 'Fairness and the Willingness to Accept Plea Bargain Offers', *Journal of Empirical Legal Studies*, **7**.
Turner, Jenia Iontcheva (2006), 'Judicial Participation in Plea Negotiations: A Comparative View', *American Journal of Comparative Law*, **54**, 199–267.
United States National Advisory Commission on Criminal Justice Standards and Goals (1973), Washington, DC: United States Government Printing Office.
Van Aaken, Anne, Eli Salzberger and Stefan Voigt (2004), 'The Prosecution of Public Figures and the Separation of Powers: Confusion within the Executive Branch – A Conceptual Framework', *Constitutional Political Economy*, **15**, 261–80.
Van den Wyngaert, Christine with C. Gane, H.H. Kuhne and F. McAuley (eds) (1993), *Criminal Procedure Systems in the European Community*, London: Butterworths.
Voigt, Stefan, Lars Feld and Anne van Aaken (2005), 'Power over Prosecutors Corrupts Politicians: Cross Country Evidence Using a New Indicator', available at www.dur.ac.uk/john.ashworth/EPCS/Papers/Voigt_%20Feld_vanAaken.pdf.
Walsh, Jennifer E. (2004), 'Tough for Whom? How Prosecutors and Judges Use their Discretion to Promote Justice under the California Three-strikes Law', available at www.cdaa.org/CDAAMember/WalshMono.pdf.
Weimer, David L. (1978), 'Plea-bargaining and Decision to Go to Trial: The Application of a Rational Choice Model', *Policy Science*, **10**, 1–24.

7 Political economy of criminal procedure

Keith N. Hylton and*
*Vikramaditya S. Khanna***

1. Introduction

This chapter presents a public choice theory of criminal procedure.[1] Alternatively, one could describe the argument of this chapter as a 'rent-seeking' theory of criminal procedure. We are especially concerned with the panoply of rules that make it more difficult to convict criminal defendants and obstruct the work of prosecutors. The rules appear to be perverse at first glance, because any well-functioning society should aim to suppress crime as effectively as possible. What purpose is served by rules that reduce the likelihood that a guilty defendant will be punished?

The core idea of this chapter is that criminal procedure is best understood as a set of rules designed to thwart attempts to use the state's law enforcement power in a predatory fashion or in order to transfer wealth generally. Our argument is most easily grasped if one imagines a society consisting of predatory factions or predatory prosecutors who attempt to use the law enforcement process as a mechanism for wealth extraction or enhancement. A social planner, in such a society, might find it valuable to construct a set of rules that cabin the predator; and since predators are wily sorts, the rules may have to take a number of different forms and change over time to meet new challenges.

This chapter's core idea, expressed simply as a concern for abuse, is not new. Many courts have noted that procedural protections in criminal law constrain the potential for abuse by government agents. Among criminal law theorists, Herbert Packer argued in 1964 that the due process model

* Professor of Law and Paul J. Liacos Scholar, Boston University.
** Professor of Law, University of Michigan.

[1] The arguments in this chapter are based on Keith N. Hylton & Vikramditya Khanna, *A Public Choice Theory of Criminal Procedure*, 15 SUP. CT. ECON. REV. 61–118 (2007). By 'public choice', we mean the study of government from the rational actor or market perspective. See, generally, JAMES M. BUCHANAN & GORDON TULLOCK, THE CALCULUS OF CONSENT: LOGICAL FOUNDATIONS OF CONSTITUTIONAL DEMOCRACY (University of Michigan Press, 1962); MANCUR OLSON, THE LOGIC OF COLLECTIVE ACTION: PUBLIC GOODS AND THE THEORY OF GROUPS (Harvard University Press, 1965).

of criminal law envisions a set of rules designed to reduce the efficiency of criminal prosecution in order to constrain the potential for abuse.[2] However, surprisingly little attention has been invested by criminal law specialists in explaining the importance of public choice theory relative to other theories, precisely how criminal procedural rules constrain abuse, and in using public choice theory to explain the case law on criminal procedure. We will address these issues in this chapter.

For the most part we focus on a set of core procedural protections that can be considered long-established norms. We are thus less focused on Warren Court innovations (for example, *Gideon v. Wainwright*, *Miranda v. Arizona*), though the approach developed here would be useful in justifying some of those as well. Some key propositions of this chapter can be set out right away. With respect to the reasonable doubt rule, the double jeopardy clause, and the ex post facto clause, this chapter's theory implies the following. First, the primary function of the reasonable doubt rule is to make it difficult for the criminal law enforcement process to be used for predatory purposes. Second, the essential purpose of double jeopardy doctrine is to prevent prosecutors from substituting toward successive prosecutions in order to avoid fundamental single-trial procedural constraints such as the reasonable doubt rule. Third, the ex post facto clause is violated only by those changes in the punishment process that create a potential for abuse by increasing the risk of targeted enforcement. These propositions by no means exhaust the implications of public choice theory for criminal procedure. However, they do get across the types of specific-function theories motivated by our general approach.

Since the public choice approach has received relatively little attention in the theoretical literature on criminal law, we will devote most of this chapter to setting out the theory in detail. To the extent that the public choice approach has been explored earlier in the literature, it is largely in the margins and in passing remarks, with little effort to offer a taxonomy of predation and its implications for criminal procedure case law. This chasm is especially troubling in view of the important status of criminal procedure doctrine in modern constitutional law.

We begin in Section 2 by discussing some of the prior literature that hints at or suggests a public choice approach to criminal procedure. In Section 3, we briefly describe a few core pro-defendant criminal procedural protections. Following that, we re-examine the traditional justification for these protections, set out in the Supreme Court's decision in *In Re*

---

[2] Herbert Packer, *Two Models of Criminal Procedure*, 113 U. Pa. L. Rev. 1 (1964).

Winship.[3] In Sections 4 and 5, we explore the costs of rent-seeking in the criminal law enforcement process and the means by which these costs are controlled through basic features of criminal procedure. In Section 6, we apply the theory to some case law, focusing on double jeopardy. Section 7 concludes.

2. Previous literature suggesting a public choice approach to criminal procedure

The public choice approach has been remarkably underdeveloped in the criminal procedure literature. Indeed, with the exception of David Friedman's 'Why Not Hang Them All? The Virtues of Inefficient Punishment',[4] there have been virtually no attempts to use public choice theory, either in the criminal law literature or in the law and economics literature on law enforcement, as a comprehensive analytical approach to criminal procedure.[5]

In spite of the near absence of the public choice approach in the law books and journals on criminal procedure, pieces or hints of public choice theory can be found in some of the criminal law literature and related sources. In this section, we discuss three notable examples: works by John Langbein,[6] Henry Packer,[7] and John Hart Ely.[8] Langbein's approach is historical and implies a public choice explanation for some key procedural innovations of the eighteenth century. Packer's approach is policy-oriented and uses public choice reasoning to describe one model of the criminal justice system. Ely's approach focuses on constitutional rather than criminal law. However, since much of criminal procedure law is constitutional today, Ely's approach has clear implications for criminal procedure.

---

3 397 U.S. 358 (1970).

4 107 J. Pol. Econ. 259 (1999).

5 One notable exception is Gary S. Becker & George J. Stigler, *Law Enforcement, Malfeasance, and Compensation of Enforcers*, 3 J. Leg. Stud. 1 (1974). More recently, Hugo Mialon has authored articles on the economics of constitutional law. See, for example, Hugo M. Mialon and Paul Rubin, *The Economics of the Bill of Rights*, 10 AM. L. & ECON. REV. 1, 1–60 (2008); Hugo M. Mialon & Sue H. Mialon, *The Effects of the Fourth Amendment: An Economic Analysis*, 24 J. L. Econ. & Organ. 22 (2008). However, we have limited our discussion in the text to literature that presents a public choice account of the criminal law.

6 John H. Langbein, The Origins of Adversary Criminal Trial (Oxford University Press, 2003).

7 Herbert L. Packer, The Limits of the Criminal Sanction 149–73 (Stanford University Press, 1968).

8 John Hart Ely, Democracy and Distrust: A Theory of Judicial Review (Harvard University Press, 1980).

2.1 Langbein

Langbein's *The Origins of Adversary Criminal Trial* is focused, as the title suggests, on the events leading to the employment of lawyers by defendants in criminal trials. Criminal trials were largely private affairs well into the 1800s. Until the early 1700s, criminal defendants were prohibited from employing defense lawyers. A series of scandals, first in treason trials and later in ordinary felony trials, led to reforms that eventually permitted defense counsel.

Langbein's book is not primarily directed to providing a theory of the function of pro-defendant criminal procedures. However, his detailed history of adversary trial suggests a theory that is consistent with the public choice rationale provided in this chapter. The scandals leading to the allowance of defense counsel could all be described as examples of predatory abuse of the criminal process. The scandalous treason trials recounted by Langbein involved the crown's prosecution of political enemies.[9] The felony trial scandals involved efforts by opportunists to secure false convictions in order to collect rewards offered by the state.[10] These scandals led judges to permit criminal defendants to employ lawyers in order to improve their chances against opportunistic plaintiffs.

Although Langbein's historical account of the events leading to adversary trial could be cited as empirical support for our functional theories of core procedural protections, the focus of this chapter is different from that of Langbein. Instead of examining historical incidents of predation, we start with the procedural rules and examine the extent to which they could be used to obstruct predation in the criminal punishment process.

2.2 Packer

In his essay titled 'Two Models of Criminal Procedure', Herbert Packer sets out alternative models of the criminal law enforcement process, one labeled the 'Crime Control Model' and the other labeled the 'Due Process Model'. The crime control model presents a normative vision of efficient criminal law enforcement. Packer describes an assembly-line process that seeks to apprehend violators quickly and punish them without delay. Lengthy criminal trials and appeals would be discouraged. A presumption of guilt would apply to defendants that pass an initial administrative screening by enforcement agents.

Packer's due process model is almost diametrically opposed to the crime control model. It envisions a system in which procedural safeguards make

---

9 Langbein, *supra* note 6, at 67–79.

10 Id., at 148–58.

the criminal enforcement process inefficient and time-consuming. The defendant is given a presumption of innocence in this model. The reason for procedural safeguards is that

> [p]ower is always subject to abuse – sometimes subtle, other times, in the criminal process, open and ugly. Precisely because of its potency in subjecting the individual to the coercive power of the state, the criminal process must, in this model, be subjected to controls that prevent it from operating with maximal efficiency.[11]

The due process model is in some respects similar to the public choice theory provided here. Both theories point to the potential for abuse or predation as a reason for pro-defendant procedural constraints. However, Packer's discussion of the due process model suggests that he is ultimately concerned with rights that the state should respect rather than the costs of violating those rights. In addition, although Packer uses his crime control and due process models to explain trends in criminal law, he never attempts to use either model to provide a detailed, positive theory of the core planks of criminal procedure doctrine. In both of these senses – the focus on utilitarian versus rights-based arguments and the priority given to justifying established institutions and law – our approach differs from Packer's.

2.3 Ely

In *Democracy and Distrust*, John Hart Ely offered a theory of constitutional interpretation that suggests a public choice account of some parts of constitutional law, including the law of criminal procedure.[12] According to Ely, courts have interpreted the constitution in order to prevent legislative majorities from extracting wealth from legislative minorities. An approach to interpretation that discourages such wealth extraction promotes democracy under Ely's theory because it forces elected representatives to take into account the interests of minority groups within their communities. It should be clear that this theory can result in implications for criminal procedure law that are consistent with the public choice model.

Still, the public choice model is a more direct and simpler rationale than Ely's democracy-forcing theory. Occam's razor should lead us to prefer the simpler and sparser theory. Moreover, there are several respects in which the public choice model may be preferable.

First, the democracy-forcing theory is a contradiction in its own terms.

---

11 PACKER, *supra* note 7, at 166.

12 See, for example, ELY, *supra* note 8, at 173–8.

Democracy ordinarily has been understood as a system in which the majority gets its way. It is a contradiction to argue that a purer form of democracy would require judges to block the decisions of majorities when those decisions trample over the rights of minorities. The US Constitution contains provisions that clearly thwart the will of legislative majorities. Those provisions are by no means designed to generate a purer form of democracy. They are designed to prevent some specific and predictable failures that are planted in the seedbed of majority vote regimes.

The democracy-forcing theory, consistent with much of modern constitutional law doctrine, alters the direction and shape of the shields that protect legislative minorities in the Constitution. The democracy-forcing theory suggests that it is important to identify and monitor the treatment of 'discrete and insular' minorities. The discrete and insular status of the protected minorities distinguishes them from minorities based on attributes such as age or income distribution. Age and income form status groups whose membership fluctuates. The legislative minorities that should be protected under the democracy-forcing theory, in contrast, are hard-cast in the form of race, ethnicity, religion, or some other feature which is unlikely to be passed off quickly. According to the democracy-forcing theory, judges should be especially quick to block the decisions of majorities when they extract wealth from identifiably different ethnic, racial, or religious minority groups. By implication, a decision to transfer wealth from one particular economic class does not necessarily raise alarm bells under the model.

The public choice theory of this chapter focuses on rent-seeking conduct rather than the identification of legislative minorities that are deserving of constitutional protection. The public choice theory, which we argue is embodied in criminal procedure, identifies particularly troubling wealth extraction methods and attempts to block those methods, whether or not they aim to expropriate some identifiable legislative minority. The public choice theory implies all of the 'distrust' based theories for protecting legislative minorities, but goes further by suggesting a broad suspicion or distrust of expropriation efforts in general.

Finally, the democracy-forcing model, with its emphasis on hard-cast legislative minorities, does not necessarily imply the specific-function theories articulated in this chapter. Whether it would do so depends on the distribution of such minorities in the society. A largely homogeneous society should not need the pro-defendant protections under the democracy-forcing model. However, under the public choice approach, the core pro-defendant procedural protections observed in the law would exist irrespective of the society's degree of homogeneity.

3. Some core criminal procedural protections and the traditional justification

We have argued to this point that the pre-existing literature, though showing an awareness of the public choice model as a possible explanation for criminal procedure law, has largely sidestepped the task of using the model to provide a detailed justification for key procedural conventions and the case law. The courts, on the other hand, have been forced to provide a rationale for procedural protections because of the need to decide cases. The rationale emphasized in the courts was set out in full in the Supreme Court's *In Re Winship* decision. In *Winship*, the Court held that the reasonable doubt standard was required in criminal trials by the due process clause of the Constitution. The Court argued, as a justification, that the reasonable doubt standard was best because false convictions in the criminal process are more costly to society than false acquittals. Further, the reasonable doubt standard would generate fewer false convictions than the preponderance standard (and correlatively more false acquittals). We will refer to this traditional justification as the 'error-cost' rationale.

Criminal procedure is a vast topic and space will not permit us to explore all of the procedural protections given to criminal defendants. In this section, we will focus on the reasonable doubt standard and a few other core protections, such as double jeopardy, and examine them against the traditional error-cost justification offered in the American case law. We will start with a brief survey of core procedural protections.

3.1 Core procedural protections

The reasonable doubt standard requires that the moving party (that is, the prosecution) prove that the defendant is guilty, beyond a reasonable doubt, of the criminal offense(s) with which he is charged.[13] Although the reasonable-doubt formulation seems to have first appeared in 1798,[14] the notion that the standard of proof in criminal trials should favor defendants has ancient origins. Blackstone, in his description of the criminal process, noted that 'all presumptive evidence of felony should be admitted cautiously: for the law holds, that it is better that ten guilty persons escape, than one innocent suffer'.[15] Coke, considerably earlier, said that 'the evidence against a prisoner should be so manifest, as it could not be contradicted'.[16] In 1970, the Supreme Court constitutionalized this

---

13 In Re Winship, 397 U.S., at 361.

14 See C. McCormick, Evidence § 341, at 576–8 (1992).

15 4 William Blackstone, Commentaries, at 358.

16 Id., at 349–50.

long-established norm by holding in *In Re Winship* that the due process clause protects the defendant against conviction except upon proof beyond a reasonable doubt.[17]

The reasonable doubt standard stands in contrast to the 'preponderance of the evidence' standard, used most frequently in civil cases.[18] It requires that the moving party prove that the defendant is liable on the preponderance of the evidence or, put simply, is more likely liable than not.

The prohibition against double jeopardy stems from the Fifth Amendment of the US Constitution, which states 'nor shall any person be subject for the same offense to be twice put in jeopardy of life or limb'.[19] In some respects, this protection is similar to the doctrines of res judicata and collateral estoppel that are found in non-criminal cases.[20] However, there are some differences. In particular, one that has garnered much attention is the rule, unique to criminal proceedings, that normally prohibits prosecutorial appeals of initial trial acquittals, but permits defense appeals of initial trial convictions.[21]

Other procedural protections in the criminal context are the right to a jury trial,[22] the right to confront witnesses,[23] the ex post facto punishment

---

[17] In Re Winship, 397 U.S., at 364.

[18] Concrete Pipe and Products Of California, Inc. v. Construction Laborer's Pension Trust for Southern California, 508 U.S. 602, 622 (1993) (noting that preponderance of the evidence is the 'most common standard in the civil law'); Apprendi v. New Jersey, 530 U.S. 466 (2000) (noting that the preponderance of the evidence standard can be used for sentencing as long as the sentence is not more severe than the statutory maximum for the offense established by the jury's verdict).

[19] U.S. CONST. amend.V.

[20] See Robin W. Sardegna, *No Longer in Jeopardy: The Impact of* Hudson *v.* U.S. *on the Constitutional Validity of Civil Monetary Penalties for Violations of the Securities Laws under the Double Jeopardy Clause,* 33 VAL. U. L. REV. 115, 117 (1998) (noting that the civil procedure doctrines of res judicata and collateral estoppel are similar to prohibitions of the double jeopardy clause).

[21] See Vikramaditya S. Khanna, *Double Jeopardy's Asymmetric Appeal Rights: What Purpose do they Serve?*, 82 B.U.L. REV. 341 (2002); U.S. v. Ball, 163 U.S. 662, 671 (1896); Joshua Steinglass, *The Justice System in Jeopardy: The Prohibition on Government Appeals*, 31 IND. L. REV. 353 (1998); Kate Stith, *The Rise of Legal Error in Criminal Cases: Some Consequences of the Asymmetry in the Right to Appeal*, 57 U. CHI. L. REV. 1 (1990); Peter Westen & Richard Drubel, *Toward a General Theory of Double Jeopardy*, 1978 SUP. CT. REV. 81. On the non-criminal side, the analogous doctrines (for example, collateral estoppel) do not present such asymmetry in appeal rights. See Cooper v. Federal Reserve Bank of Richmond, 467 U.S. 867, 874 (1984) (noting that if the requirements are met, both res judicata and collateral estoppel are available to plaintiffs and defendants).

[22] U.S. CONST. AMEND. VI.

[23] Id.

rule,[24] and the excessive punishments prohibition.[25] This does not exhaust the list of protections that impose a pro-defendant bias. Although we will focus on a few core protections, we claim that the public choice theory provides the best explanation for most of them. However, before presenting the public choice account, we will first examine the traditional explanation for procedural protections.

3.2 Traditional justification for core criminal procedural protections

3.2.1 Reasonable doubt standard as example The reasonable doubt standard is the quintessential example of a pro-defendant protection. The traditional justification, captured in Blackstone's 'ten guilty men' statement, is that in the criminal process we should be more concerned with false convictions than false acquittals.[26] Elaborating, the US Supreme Court in *Winship* identified three types of harm associated with false convictions: loss of liberty, stigma, and dilution of the moral force of the criminal law.[27]

We can classify the costs of false convictions and false acquittals as sanctioning costs, deterrence costs, and disutility costs.[28] Sanctioning costs are the costs of punishment, which include the loss of liberty and stigma effects. Deterrence costs refer to the practical effect of the dilution in the law's moral force caused by false convictions. For example, if the law punishes the innocent, then it weakens deterrence by giving people less incentive to comply. Disutility costs refer to the disutility individuals suffer when they know that the law fails to punish the guilty or that it sometimes punishes the innocent.

---

[24] U.S. CONST. ART. I, § 9, CL. 3.

[25] U.S. CONST. AMEND. VIII.

[26] See 4 WILLIAM BLACKSTONE, COMMENTARIES *358; *see also* In Re Winship, 397 U.S., at 372 (Harlan, J., concurring).

[27] In Re Winship, 397 U.S. at 363–4. Although the Court did not conduct an examination of false acquittal costs, those costs presumably consist only of the third type of harm, dilution of the law's moral force.

[28] In theory, one could consider the impact on the expressive effects of the law too. The expressive effect of the law is the effect it has on behavior without threatening a sanction. See Richard H. McAdams, *A Focal Point Theory of Expressive Law,* 86 VA. L. REV. 1649 (2000), Robert Cooter, *Expressive Law and Economics*, 27 J. LEG. STUD. 585 (1998). However, the law's expressive effect is probably more closely connected to the perceived legitimacy of the law – that is, whether it is corrupt or easy to corrupt – rather than a particular trade-off between types of errors. See Jason Mazzone, *When Courts Speak: Social Capital and Law's Expressive Capital*, 49 SYRACUSE L. REV. 1039 (1999).

Translating *Winship* into these terms, the Supreme Court has said in effect that the additional sanctioning, deterrence, and disutility costs of moving from the reasonable doubt to the preponderance standard would outweigh the potential benefits. This is what we have referred to before as the traditional error-cost justification for the reasonable doubt rule.

3.2.2 Error-cost analysis of legal standards: a diagrammatic exposition In order to get a better understanding of the error-cost analysis of legal standards, consider Figure 7.1,[29] which shows the relationship between error probabilities, evidence, and standards of proof. The vertical axis measures the probability of guilt. The horizontal axis measures the amount of evidence (of guilt). The 45 degree line OP captures the functional relationship between the probability of guilt and the quantity of evidence against the defendant. The vertical line *PE* reflects the preponderance-of-evidence standard. If the amount of evidence is below (to the left) of the *PE* line, the defendant will be found innocent, and if the evidence is above the *PE* standard then the defendant will be found guilty. Error probabilities under the *PE* standard are shown by the areas OBE and PBA in Figure 7.1. The probability of a false acquittal is given by OBE, to the left of the *PE* standard. The probability of a false conviction is given by PBA, to the right of the *PE* standard. Figure 7.1 also shows the same relationship under the reasonable doubt standard, where the vertical line labeled *RD* reflects the reasonable doubt standard.

Two intuitive points follow from Figure 7.1: the probability of a false acquittal and the overall likelihood of error are both larger under the reasonable doubt standard. In moving from the preponderance to the reasonable doubt standard, we reduce the probability of a false conviction by the area ABDC, and we increase the likelihood of a false acquittal by the larger area BDFE. It follows that if the social costs of false acquittals and false convictions are equal, society should prefer the preponderance standard to the reasonable doubt rule. However, if the costs of false convictions and false acquittals are not equal, examining the overall probability of error will be insufficient to tell us whether the reasonable doubt rule is preferable to the preponderance rule.

Society should prefer the reasonable doubt standard to the preponderance standard if the expected social costs are lower under the

---

[29] The figure is based on the analysis in Gordon Tullock, The Logic of the Law 65–7 (1987 ed.). Perhaps the first to examine the error-cost question in the context of criminal law was John Kaplan in his classic article 'Decision Theory and the Factfinding Process'. See John Kaplan, *Decision Theory and The Factfinding Process,* 20 Stan. L. Rev. 1065 (1968).

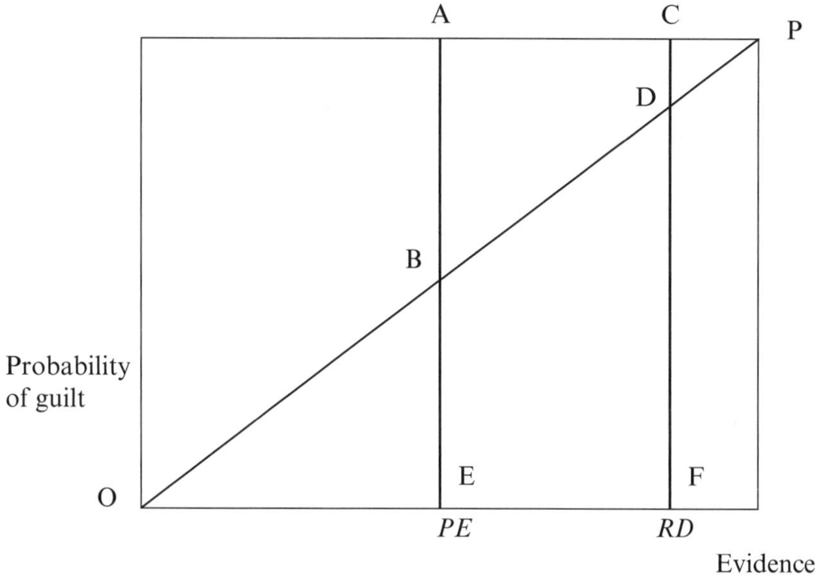

Figure 7.1 *Relationship between probability of guilt and quantity of evidence*

reasonable doubt standard. Thus, the reasonable doubt standard is preferable if the reduction in false conviction costs resulting from a move from the preponderance to the reasonable doubt standard exceeds the incremental false acquittal costs. In terms of Figure 7.1, the reasonable doubt rule is preferable if the change in the probability of a false conviction (ABDC) multiplied by the cost of a false conviction exceeds the incremental false acquittal probability (BDFE) multiplied by the cost of a false acquittal. Given the difference in the probabilities, the actual cost of a false conviction must be substantially greater than the cost of a false acquittal in order to justify a switch from preponderance to reasonable doubt.

The Supreme Court identified the key components of the false conviction cost in its *Winship* opinion: additional sanctioning and disutility costs (and perhaps deterrence costs due to loss accuracy or of the law's moral force). The cost of a false acquittal can be considered primarily the cost of under-deterrence (due to the reduction in the expected punishment).

3.2.3 A brief empirical examination The *Winship* opinion asserts that the additional sanctioning, deterrence and disutility costs of the preponderance standard exceed the under-deterrence costs of the reasonable doubt standard. Is there empirical support for this claim?

There are data that enable a rough, back-of-the-envelope test. If we use the sum of losses due to injuries and property theft (including fraud) as a conservative definition of the aggregate harm from crime, David Anderson's study of the costs of crime suggests the annual aggregate crime cost is of the order of $1 trillion.[30] If we measure sanctioning costs by adding the opportunity costs of the inmate's time while locked up plus the costs of maintaining inmates in prison, Anderson's study suggests that the annual sanctioning cost for *all convictions* is roughly $70 billion.[31]

These numbers imply that the aggregate costs of crime, which can be treated as under-deterrence costs, are of the order of 15 times greater than the sanctioning costs for all convictions. In view of the magnitude of this differential, it seems improbable that the savings from a measure that reduces crime by enhancing the likelihood of punishment, such as moving to the preponderance standard, would be swamped by incremental sanctioning,

---

[30] See David Anderson, *The Aggregate Burden of Crime*, 42 J. L. Econ 611 (1999) (estimating cost of crime at $1,102 billion, which represents the sum of 'risks to life and health', 'crime-induced production', and 'opportunity costs' (for criminals and victims)). The 'risks to life and health' reflect the value of crime-related lives lost (approximately 72,111 lives lost per year, valued at about $6.1 million each) and the value of non-fatal injuries, id., at 624–6. The $6.1 million per life measure appears to be about the average value from many previous studies, id., at 626. The value of non-fatal injuries is also based on an average of prior studies valuing non-fatal injuries, id., at 626. The 'crime-induced production' reflects the estimated amount of resources spent on items that result from or are associated with crime and hence cannot be spent on other items. See id., at 616–7. 'Examples include the production of personal protection devices, the trafficking of drugs, and the operation of correctional facilities.' Id., at 616. Andersen provides a fairly detailed list of these expenditures, id., at 620. The 'opportunity costs' associated with crime in the text represent the value of the days victims were unable to work due to the crime event, the time and effort spent by criminals in undertaking crime, and the time and effort of victims in attempting to prevent crime (for example, locking things), id., at 623–4.

[31] See id., at 620, 624 (this figure represents the sum of 'crime-induced production: corrections' and 'criminal lost workdays: in prison'). Obviously, these numbers miss some important costs. Indeed, they do not include the stigma costs, part of the liberty costs, and the moral disutility costs of diluting the moral force of the criminal law referred to by the Court in *Winship*. However, we are using the numbers only to determine whether the sanctioning and deterrence costs of errors, as commonly understood, would justify the reasonable doubt rule. An important part of our analysis is to show the rough magnitude of other costs that need to be considered to justify the reasonable doubt rule if standard sanctioning and deterrence costs do not.

stigma, and disutility costs. Indeed, the empirical evidence on the responsiveness of crime to changes in prison population suggests that this is unlikely.

Surveying evidence on the responsiveness of crime to incarceration, Donohue and Siegelman estimate that the elasticity of crime with respect to incarceration is 0.15 and Levitt finds an elasticity of 0.30.[32] Using the lower figure, an increase in sanctioning costs of 200 percent (that is, tripling the prison population and increasing sanctioning costs from $70 to $210 billion) should be associated with a reduction in crime of the order of 30 percent ((200)(0.15) = 30). This yields a deterrence benefit of $300 billion (($1 trillion cost of crime)(0.30) = $300 billion). Since the additional sanctioning cost of tripling the prison population ($140 billion) is less than the deterrence benefit ($300 billion), a switch to the preponderance standard appears desirable on traditional error-cost grounds.

We have discussed only deterrence and sanctioning costs, but there are stigma and disutility costs that should be considered too. Obviously, these are difficult to quantify. Still, our analysis suggests how large these other costs must be to justify the reasonable doubt standard on the traditional error-cost account. It would appear that these costs need to be at least of the same order of magnitude as the incremental sanctioning costs generated by the preponderance rule. For example, return to the scenario just considered: a tripling of the prison population, caused by a switch from the reasonable doubt to the preponderance standard, which produces a deterrence benefit of $300 billion and an incremental sanctioning cost of $140 billion. To justify choosing the reasonable doubt standard over the preponderance standard, the stigma and disutility costs generated by the preponderance standard would have to add $160 billion to the change in total sanctioning costs.

The required magnitude of stigma and disutility costs is so large in relation to sanctioning and deterrence costs that one is compelled to view it with suspicion. If the stigma and disutility costs noted in *Winship* prove to be too small to justify the reasonable doubt rule, what other costs excluded from this analysis should be considered? We explore this question next.

4. Public choice theory and criminal procedural protections

In our view, the traditional error-cost justification offered for core criminal procedural protections, such as the reasonable doubt rule, is incomplete. In

---

32 See John J. Donohue III & Peter Siegelman, *Allocating Resources among Prisons and Social Programs in the Battle against Crime*, 27 J. Leg. Stud. 1, 13 (1998); Steven Levitt, *The Effect of Prison Population Size on Crime Rates: Evidence from Prison Overcrowding Litigation*, 111 Q. J. Econ. 319 (1996).

this section, we will set out the groundwork for a public choice approach. Specifically, we will offer an overview of the types of predation or rent-seeking practices that are likely to occur in connection with the criminal enforcement process, and the costs generated by these practices.

We contend that the reasonable doubt standard is designed primarily to make it harder for individuals and groups to use the criminal law enforcement process as a mechanism for wealth extraction. Moreover, most of the key pro-defendant procedural protections serve this purpose. This reduces the social costs generated by rent-seeking efforts to influence law enforcement and enhances the deterrent effect of the law.

Our argument should not be viewed as a rejection of error-cost analysis in general. Rather, it should be viewed as a substantial modification of the error-cost analysis of legal standards. In terms of the general approach associated with Figure 7.1, we contend that the false conviction costs should include the costs of rent-seeking in the criminal law enforcement process. If these costs are included, it appears far more likely that the cost (on average) of a false conviction substantially exceeds the cost of a false acquittal – and substantial excess is necessary given the greater frequency of false acquittals under the reasonable doubt standard. We explain below how rent-seeking happens in law enforcement and the costs that it generates.

4.1 Rent-seeking in law enforcement

Rent-seeking is essentially self-interested, profit-motivated conduct observed within an institutional framework, such as the political or legal process, rather than in the market. In the law enforcement context, the core of the theory can be captured with a simple profit function for the prosecutor. Suppose the probability of a conviction from the prosecutor's perspective is p_p, the payoff to the prosecutor from a successful prosecution is π, and the cost of prosecution is c_p. The payoff to the prosecutor is itself a function of the amount that a prosecution target would bid to avoid punishment, and the amount that third parties would gain from the punishment of the target. Let v represent the loss to the target, which is the same as his bid to avoid punishment, and let g represent the gain to third parties. The profit function of the prosecutor can therefore be expressed as

$$p_p\pi(g, v) - c_p \,. \tag{7.1}$$

This implies that the profit-motivated enforcer will have an incentive to target individuals who will offer substantial bids to avoid punishment, and to select targets that third parties will pay substantial amounts to see punished.

Rent-seeking in the law enforcement process can occur in a variety of forms. However, we think two general types capture its observed forms. One is inter-group wealth expropriation, which arises when one group attempts to gain an advantage from law enforcement at the expense of other members of society.[33] In terms of the prosecutor's profit function (see equation (7.1)), these are third parties who are willing to bid g in order to see the prosecutor go after their preferred targets. The other type of rent-seeking is simple corruption, which occurs when an individual uses bribery or some other means, in connection with law enforcement, to extract wealth from society. In terms of the prosecutor's profit function, these are cases in which individual targets will be compelled to bid v in order to avoid punishment.

4.1.1 Inter-group wealth expropriation Inter-group wealth expropriation can be effected in a number of ways. For example, there is lobbying, which results in targeted or selective enforcement. The familiar case is where prosecutors disproportionately bring charges against members of group B because of lobbying efforts, or simply to curry the favor of the dominant group A. This permits group A members to shift the burden of criminal enforcement onto group B or to impose costs on group B which result in some benefit to group A – for example, the maintenance of a caste system. Indeed, in regimes in which prosecutors are elected, candidates for the position will have incentives to seek support from group A by promising to direct enforcement efforts against group B. [34] Perhaps the best-known example of this in United States history is law enforcement in the South during the Jim Crow period, which involved prosecutors refusing to enforce the law against white citizens, while using the threat of criminal punishment to coerce black citizens.[35]

Another example of wealth expropriation in the enforcement process is where prosecutors ask for payoffs to avoid bringing charges against

---

[33] See, for example, Angela O. Davis, *The American Prosecutor: Independence, Power, and the Threat of Tyranny*, 86 Iowa L. Rev. 393, 459 (2001).

[34] See, for example, William J. Stuntz, *The Pathological Politics of Criminal Law,* 100 Mich. L. Rev. 505, 520–34 (2001); Tracey L. McCain, *The Interplay of Editorial and Prosecutorial Discretion in the Perpetuation of Racism in the Criminal Justice System,* 25 Colum. J.L. & Soc. Probs. 601, 648, n. 81 (1993) (decisions to prosecute are susceptible to political influence because most prosecutors are elected); Dwight L. Greene, *Abusive Prosecutors: Gender, Race & Class Discretion and the Prosecution of Drug-Addicted Mothers*, 39 Buff. L. Rev. 737, 777 (1991) (noting career motivations of prosecutors as an influence on decisions).

[35] See Richard Epstein, Forbidden Grounds 91–7 (1992); William J. Stuntz, *Race, Class, and Drugs*, 98 Colum. L. Rev. 1795, 1839 (1998).

members of politically marginal groups. For example, a self-interested prosecutor, who knows that politically powerful groups will have him removed from office if he threatens their interests, would then focus his extraction efforts on the politically marginal. The difference between this version of inter-group wealth extraction and the first is slight: in the first, the dominant group initiates the wealth extraction process and in the second, the prosecutor initiates the process. In the first case, the dominant group pays the prosecutor the smallest amount necessary to accomplish their ends, allocating the surplus to themselves. In the second, the prosecutor who initiates the wealth extraction process allocates the surplus to himself.

Yet another example of wealth expropriation is the passing of laws with disproportionate burdens on different groups. In order to effect wealth expropriation, the laws need not apply directly to group *B* members. The dominant group (*A*) may find that certain activities are carried out only, or predominantly, by group *B* members, or that group *B* members carry out these activities in a different manner from others. With this information, the dominant group may prohibit or place special burdens on the activity when carried out in a particular manner. For example, white majorities in the western United States enacted facially neutral statutes in the late 1800s that had the effect of prohibiting Chinese laundries, both to limit competition from them and to limit the independent work options of Chinese laborers.[36]

These cases are united by the common theme of one group benefiting at the expense of others through the use of the governmental process, whether law enforcement or legislation. As our concern is with law enforcement, we will not discuss in much depth the passing of laws with disproportionate burdens. However, the legislative and law enforcement processes provide alternative routes through which a predatory dominant group could extract wealth from others. In this sense, the legislative and law enforcement processes are substitutes in the eyes of the wealth extractor. The laws controlling rent-seeking in these governmental processes can be understood as complements, in the sense that they prevent a predatory dominant group from shifting its expropriation efforts from one governmental process to another.

4.1.2 Simple corruption The other type of rent-seeking, simple corruption, involves the effort of a single individual or group to extract

---

[36] See David E. Bernstein, Lochner, *Parity and the Chinese Laundry Cases*, 41 WM. & MARY L. REV. 211 (1999).

wealth from the general population. We have in mind two cases: that of an enforcement agent (police officer or prosecutor) who threatens to apprehend and charge an individual unless he pays the agent, and that of an enforcement agent who is willing to accept bribes from the general public or individuals to enforce or not to enforce the law in a particular way.[37] In general, these payoffs can take two forms. One, ex ante bribery, occurs when an individual bribes an enforcement agent before he commits a crime in exchange for an agreement by the agent not to enforce the law against him. In the other form, ex post bribery, the individual bribes the agent after he commits the crime.

There are many examples of simple corruption and its forms. A common example of ex post bribery is a police officer who accepts bribes in return for not issuing a ticket to a speeding motorist. Ex ante bribery appears to be less common, though there are many examples of it too. In most towns in the US, local government business is carried out by boards made up of residents with deep and strong connections to many of the parties who appear before them. In these settings, it is hard to distinguish the ordinary reciprocal exchanges that are part of normal social intercourse from ex ante bribery.

Because the criminal law enforcement process can be used by groups or by individuals as a means to extract wealth, we should anticipate a steady stream of efforts to use it for that purpose. In light of this, it becomes important to get a sense of the precise costs generated by such behavior and methods for constraining them.

4.2 Costs associated with rent-seeking in the criminal process

We have so far considered the private interests of the enforcement agent or agency. The social welfare effects of rent-seeking are much broader and are by no means captured by the prosecutor's profit interests. We will consider the broader effects as additional costs from rent-seeking in law enforcement. We divide our discussion of the costs of rent-seeking in law enforcement into two parts: first, the costs related to the act of lobbying, and second, the costs related to the effect of lobbying on the deterrent force of the criminal law.

---

[37] One could argue that the simple corruption category is the same as our second example of wealth expropriation, and we concede that the difference is more a matter of degree than of character. In the second example, the enforcement agent maintains his position through the support of local dominant groups. In the simple corruption story, the enforcement agent is either unconcerned with maintaining support from local dominant groups (in the case of the actively predatory enforcer), or passively accepts bribes in exchange for not enforcing the law.

4.2.1 Direct costs Rent-seeking in the criminal process involves lobbying efforts to influence the selection and prosecution of cases. The process of lobbying itself generates costs that are from a societal perspective often wasteful.

As a useful analogy, consider efforts to obtain a monopoly. Expenditures to obtain a monopoly may be desirable when a firm secures a dominant position by improving its product or reducing its costs. However, some expenditures to obtain a monopoly are socially wasteful; consider, for example, lobbying efforts to obtain a government privilege, such as an exclusive license or tariff protection.[38]

In the context of criminal law enforcement, efforts by group *A* to lobby the prosecutor to enforce selectively against group *B* are often wasteful forms of wealth extraction. Of course, the result is not an entire waste if targeting group *B* reduces the overall costs of crime.[39] However, there is little reason to believe that lobbying for selective enforcement will always bring about an efficient result. For example, group *A* will have no interest in inducing the prosecutor to go after cases of crime involving only members of group *B* as victims. Further, group *A* members may discourage the prosecutor from enforcing the law when members of their own group commit crimes against group *B*.

So far we have focused on the costs associated with inter-group expropriation efforts, but analogous arguments apply in the context of simple corruption. Corruption creates costs in terms of the resources spent in bribing the enforcement agent to enforce or not to enforce the law in some way and the efforts of the agent in positioning himself to take bribes. However, there is an important feature of the corruption model that suggests that rent-seeking costs can be much larger than appears initially. The enforcement process is *vertically fragmented*, in the sense that it moves through a chain beginning with a police officer (and next his superiors), moving to a prosecutor, and on to a magistrate or judge, and so on. If each one of these agents demands bribes to enforce or not enforce the law, then the total social waste will be considerably larger than in a vertically integrated enforcement regime in which a single agent controls the process from arrest to punishment.[40]

---

38 See Dennis C. Mueller, Public Choice II 229–46 (rev. ed. 1989).

39 It might be that lobbying coincides with what is socially desirable. See Gordon Tullock, *Efficient Rent-Seeking*, in Toward a Theory of the Rent-Seeking Society 97–112 (James M. Buchanan, R.D. Tollison & Gordon Tullock eds, 1980).

40 See Andrei Shleifer & Robert W. Vishny, *Corruption*, 108 Q. J. Econ. 599 (1993). The vertical fragmentation of law enforcement means that each individual

4.2.2 Deterrence and other costs from rent-seeking Rent-seeking in the criminal process, if successful, has the effect of skewing law enforcement. In this section, we discuss three ways in which rent-seeking reduces the net social benefits of law enforcement: first, by reducing the direct sanctions imposed on offenders; second, by reducing indirect sanctions imposed on offenders through stigma and reputation costs; and, third, by increasing the cost of enforcing the law.

SOME DETERRENT EFFECTS OF SELECTIVELY ENFORCING THE LAW Selective enforcement of the law due to lobbying can have corrosive effects on deterrence. Consider, for example, where lobbying by group *A* members results in selective law enforcement against group *B* members, with little regard for the actual guilt of the defendants, and disproportionately less enforcement against group *A* members.

In this scenario, deterrence is likely to drop for both groups *A* and *B*. Group *A* members are under-deterred because they are facing low expected sanctions for engaging in undesirable activities. The deterrent effect on group *B* members would also be reduced because they are now punished whether they have been 'good' or 'bad'. In other words, the incentive to comply with the law is reduced for group *B* members because the payoffs from compliance and non-compliance have gotten closer.

An enforcement policy chosen by group *A* members that reduces deterrence may seem irrational, because it could lead to additional crimes being committed against group *A* members. However, there are scenarios in which such a policy could be chosen rationally by group *A*.

To see this we note that, in general, deterrence can be achieved through *substitution* effects or *scale* effects. Substitution effects occur when a change in the effective sanction leads potential offenders to substitute legitimate, law-complying conduct for illegitimate, undesirable conduct. Scale effects occur when enforcement causes potential offenders to stay out of certain areas, or off the streets at certain times. A selective enforcement policy in which group *B* is targeted implies, within a fixed budget setting, a diversion of resources from *substitution-oriented policies* to *scale-oriented policies*. This is analogous to shifting from a strategy of ticketing every motorist that speeds (inducing substitution toward slow driving) to a strategy of ticketing motorists who meet the profile of a speeder, whether

agent is in a position similar to that of successive owners of the pieces of a toll road. One of the standard results is that the sum of the tolls charged by successive owners will be larger than the toll charged by a single owner of a road. This is known in the monopolization literature as the double-marginalization problem, see Joseph J. Spengler, *Vertical Integration and Antitrust Policy*, 58 J. POL. ECON. 347 (1950).

or not they are speeding (inducing drivers who fit the profile to stay off the roads).

Keeping this in mind, we can then return to our example of *A*s and *B*s. If groups *A* and *B* are geographically segregated, then group *A* may choose to reduce potential crimes by *B*s on *A*s by apprehending all *B*s who venture into their territory, whether or not the *B*s are complying with the law.[41] Such a policy would make it costly for *B*s to move among *A*s, encouraging the *B*s to stay in their own territory. In other words, group *A* members may choose to rely on scale effects to reduce the risks posed to them by group *B* offenders. Such a policy, in a fixed budget setting, could easily result in a weakening at the substitution-effect level in deterrence among *B*s.[42]

OTHER COSTS: STIGMA, EXPRESSIVE, AND ENFORCEMENT COST EFFECTS Rent-seeking probably reduces the stigma, associated with criminal punishment. If the criminal label carries some stigma then that becomes part of the total sanction for criminal behavior and influences deterrence. Anything that reduces the stigma, without causing a countervailing increase in the official sanction, reduces deterrence.

The stigma from being labeled a criminal stems in part from a belief that the person so labeled has violated a societal norm meriting condem-

---

[41] See, for example, David A. Harris, *The Stories, The Statistics, and the Law: Why 'Driving While Black' Matters,* 84 MINN. L. REV. 265, 271(1999) (discussing law enforcement's tendency to subject black drivers in upscale neighborhoods to traffic stops). One implication of the theory here is that 'racial profiling' may be socially undesirable. For some empirical evidence on racial profiling, see John Knowles, Nicola Persico & Petra Todd, *Racial Bias in Motor Vehicle Searches: Theory and Evidence*, 109 J. POL. ECON. 203 (2001).

[42] Another scenario might be where lobbying by group *A* members leads to selective enforcement against group *B* members, focusing on those who are guilty, but again with disproportionately less enforcement against group *A* members. In this case, the same potential under-deterrence problem for group *A* members exists because again they face low expected sanctions. However, for the group *B* members, the situation has changed. The deterrent effect on group *B* members may still remain or be enhanced because in this case if a group *B* member complies with the law, he is probably not going to be prosecuted and if he fails to comply, he is more likely to be prosecuted. The overall impact on deterrence is ambiguous in this case. However, given that *A* members are assumed to control the enforcement process, one probable scenario is where their law enforcement agent (the prosecutor) is unable, because of unfamiliarity or indifference, to distinguish complying from non-complying members of group *B*. With a prosecutor unable or unwilling to distinguish the 'good' from the 'bad' among group *B*, a policy of targeting only the bad in group *B* would be infeasible. This suggests that the outcome discussed in the text, in which deterrence falls unambiguously, is a plausible outcome of selective enforcement.

nation.[43] If, however, being labeled a criminal is perceived by members of one's social circle as indicative of a biased use of the law, then the stigma from the criminal label diminishes.[44] For similar reasons, rent-seeking is likely to reduce any expressive or symbolic features of the criminal law.

In addition to stigma and expressive effects, rent-seeking may have enforcement-cost effects. If law enforcement is perceived to be biased, then it is likely that some people will refuse to assist law enforcement. This would increase the difficulty and costs associated with apprehensions and prosecutions, which in turn reduces the likelihood that wrongdoers will be sanctioned.

5. Procedural protections as methods of constraining rent-seeking

In this section, we describe the precise function of pro-defendant procedural protections. Our description suggests a positive theory for the basic procedural rules.

5.1 Procedural protections

Procedural protections constrain rent-seeking in the criminal process by making the process costly for both law enforcement agents and for society. Prosecutors, who are rewarded when conviction rates are high, bear much of the brunt of the costs of these procedures.[45]

The primary function of pro-defendant procedural protections is to alter the 'relative prices' of various enforcement approaches in a way that makes predation unprofitable (or less profitable). In general, the rules increase the probability that a prosecutor and a bribing party will be unable to find a mutually acceptable bribe, thus making the set of contractible bribes zero or close to it.

---

43 See generally Paul H. Robinson & John M. Darley, *The Utility of Desert,* 91 Nw. U. L. Rev. 453 (1997).

44 Eric Posner, Law and Social Norms 97–100 (2000) (noting that criminal offenders can signal loyalty to a subcommunity by violating the law and being punished by the dominant group. The subcommunity is more likely to view criminal punishment as a signal of loyalty to the subcommunity, the more the subcommunity believes the criminal justice system is 'infected with a political agenda').

45 J. Mark Ramseyer & Eric B. Rasmussen, *Why is the Japanese Conviction Rate So High?,* 30 J. Leg. Stud. 53 (2001) (arguing that because of the stigma in Japan of acquitting defendants and the corresponding detrimental career effects it may have for prosecutors and judges, they prosecute only strong cases); Fred C. Zacharias, *Structuring the Ethics of Prosecutorial Trial Practice: Can Prosecutors Do Justice?*, 44 Vand. L. Rev. 45, n. 264 (arguing that '[t]o the extent a prosecutor's conviction rate is all that counts, the institutional incentives point toward minimizing the responsibility to "do justice".').

A simple model can be used to convey the argument at a general level. Recall that the profit function of the prosecutor is

$$p_p\pi - c_p\,, \qquad (7.2)$$

where p_p is the probability of a conviction from the prosecutor's perspective, and c_p is the cost of prosecution. The payoff to the prosecutor, π, is a function of the gain to third parties (g) and the loss to the potential defendant (v) – that is, $\pi = \pi(g, v)$. Suppose the defendant's prediction of the probability of conviction is p_d. In addition, let the cost of a criminal prosecution be c_d for the defendant. The cost function for the defendant is

$$p_d v + c_d\,. \qquad (7.3)$$

Pro-defendant protections have the effect of reducing p_p and increasing c_p, though in a non-uniform manner across potential defendants. In particular, the reduction of p_p and increase in c_p are both substantially larger for innocent defendants than for guilty defendants. This change in relative prices induces prosecutors to shift their prosecution efforts away from the innocent and toward the guilty. In many cases, the relative price change should cause the prosecutor's expected profit to turn negative for innocent defendants ($p_p\pi - c_p < 0$), thus removing any credible threat of prosecution.

Bribes will be exchanged between the defendant and the prosecutor when two conditions are met: (1) the prosecutor can credibly threaten prosecution ($p_p\pi - c_p > 0$), and (2) the expected cost of a prosecution to the defendant exceeds the expected profit to the prosecutor ($p_d v + c_d > p_p\pi - c_p$).

It follows that pro-defendant procedural protections make bribery less likely through two incentive effects. First, the procedural protections destroy the credibility of the prosecution threat against innocent defendants. Second, in those cases where the threat remains credible against innocent defendants, procedural protections can reduce the defendant's expected probability of conviction to a level that may in large part eliminate the scope for mutually beneficial bribes.

Consider the effects of procedural protections on inter-group expropriation through selective enforcement. On the prosecutor's side, procedural protections raise the cost of targeting innocent parties as well as the costs of letting the guilty go free. If the prosecutor at the behest of group *A* targets innocent group *B* members, he is unlikely to be successful given the pro-defendant procedures. In terms of the profit function in equation (7.1), this reduces the amount, g, that a third party would be willing to bid for targeted enforcement. If the prosecutor maintains his promise to target group *B*, he will have few successful prosecutions, and will probably lose his job. This suggests that the prosecutor will demand a high bribe in order to adopt a selective enforcement policy. Moreover, given the risk of losing his job, potential bribers will doubt the credibility of the prosecutor's promise to selectively enforce. In view of the greater difficulty of implementing a successful selective enforcement policy and the doubtful credibility of a prosecutor who promises to do so, the potential briber's willingness-to-pay should fall substantially.[46]

Next, consider the effects of procedural protections on simple corruption – that is, individual attempts to use law enforcement as a path to wealth. Procedural protections make it difficult for such corruption to flourish. A prosecutor who on his own initiative threatens to arrest individuals on false charges would find it difficult to mount a credible threat against his victims in the presence of procedural protections. In terms of the prosecutor's profit function, this reduces the maximum bid that a potential defendant will offer to avoid punishment ($p_d v + c_d$). Moreover, the prosecutor's ability to credibly promise *not to enforce* the law against a particular defendant should fall. If the prosecutor charges the wrong person or no one at all, he most likely will be unsuccessful in obtaining a conviction. Given his difficulty in charging and convicting an alternate (innocent) candidate, the cost to the prosecutor of promising not to enforce against a particular defendant is relatively high, and the promise cannot be considered fully credible. The prosecutor's power to shake down individuals for money in exchange for a promise not to bring charges is severely diminished in the regime with procedural protections. Moreover, the potential defendant's willingness to pay a bribe falls since he is less likely to be convicted in the first place if he is innocent, and any promise by the prosecutor not to enforce against a guilty defendant cannot be regarded as credible.[47]

---

[46] For analyses of bribery and law enforcement, see A. Mitchell Polinsky & Steven Shavell, *Corruption and Optimal Law Enforcement,* 81 J. PUB. ECON. 1 (2001). See also ROBERT KLITGAARD, CONTROLLING CORRUPTION (1988); Susan Rose-Ackerman, CORRUPTION: A STUDY IN POLITICAL ECONOMY (1978); Pranab Bardhan, *Corruption and Development: A Review of Issues*, 35 J. ECON. LIT. 1320 (1997); and Andrei Schleifer & Robert W. Vishny, *Corruption*, 108 Q.J. ECON. 599 (1993).

[47] We do not discuss what might happen if the defendant suffered a large stigma simply from being charged or indicted for certain kinds of wrongdoing. See *In re Fried*, 161 F.2d 453, 458 (2nd Cir. 1947) (noting that '[f]or a wrongful indictment is no laughing matter; often it works a grievous, irreparable injury to the person indicted. The stigma cannot be easily erased.'). See also, Eric Rasmusen, *Stigma*

We can see in greater detail how procedural protections dampen corruption in the context of the two core procedural protections: the reasonable doubt standard and the double jeopardy rule. Both reduce the prosecutor's ability to selectively enforce. In this sense, they clearly fall within our analysis because they simultaneously raise the cost to the prosecutor of implementing a selective policy and lower the value to the potential beneficiary of seeking such a policy. The reasonable doubt rule accomplishes this task by directly reducing the probability of a guilty verdict and increasing the amount of evidence necessary for conviction. In terms of the prosecutor's expected profit function, the reasonable doubt rule increases c_p and reduces p_p. The double jeopardy rule aids in this task by preventing the prosecutor from substituting toward successive prosecutions against the same defendant in order to avoid the effects of the reasonable doubt rule. If (in equation (7.1)) p_p is too low to credibly threaten prosecution in a one-shot trial, the threat of successive prosecutions could restore credibility to the prosecutor's strategy. For example, suppose the prosecutor is permitted to prosecute the defendant twice. In this case, one might observe:

$$p_p\pi - c_p < 0\,, \tag{7.4}$$

$$[p_p + (1 - p_p)\,p_p)]\pi - c_p > 0\,, \tag{7.5}$$

where c_p represents the prosecution cost for two trials, which implies that the prosecutor's threat could be credible against innocent defendants.

Under this theory, the reasonable doubt and double jeopardy rules have complementary functions. No matter how low the probability of successful targeting is reduced as a result of the reasonable doubt rule, the prosecutor may still have an incentive to adopt a selective enforcement policy if he can bring successive actions against a defendant. In the extreme case in which the prosecutor can bring an infinite number of successive actions against the defendant, he is likely to eventually get a conviction, no matter how small the probability of conviction in the individual trial. The more worrisome case, however, is where the prosecutor learns from a previous mistake and uses the information from a 'test trial' to boost the probability of conviction to a near certainty in the second trial.[48] The double jeopardy rule appears in this framework to serve the function of prevent-

---

and Self-fulfilling Expectations of Criminality, 39 J. L. & ECON. 519 (1996). In such cases, the potential for corruption and wealth extraction are greater because the prosecutor can gain or impose costs without actually having to win at a trial.

[48] See *Developments in the Law – Corporate Crime: Regulating Corporate Behavior through Criminal Sanctions*, 92 HARV. L. REV. 1227 1341–9 (1979).

ing enforcement agents from substituting toward a successive prosecution strategy in order to avoid the constraints imposed by the reasonable doubt rule and other single trial protections.

5.2 Penalty restrictions

Another way to constrain the costs associated with abuses of prosecutorial or punishment authority is to put restrictions on the size of penalties or the process by which they are levied. David Friedman has described the size and process restrictions as 'inefficient punishments'.[49] Friedman distinguishes inefficient punishments, like prison, from efficient punishments, like the death penalty administered quickly or a large monetary penalty equal to the defendant's wealth. [50] The argument is that efficient punishments do not impose large direct costs on the state and hence prosecutors may have an incentive to use them to extract wealth from defendants.[51] However, inefficient punishments impose substantial costs on the state and therefore present obstacles to the use of the criminal process as a means of extracting wealth. [52]

Two types of penalty restrictions are relevant here: the prohibition of retroactive punishments and of cruel and unusual punishments.[53] The latter restriction fits with the analysis here as well as Friedman's. As Friedman notes, the state could easily adopt a low-cost system of punishment; defendants could be executed, enslaved, or put into laboratories for scientific experimentation and the harvesting of organs and tissue.[54] Instead, we observe a system in which the state forgoes the opportunity to extract all of the defendant's wealth, and incarceration prevents the state from taking full advantage of the convict's labor. The constitutional prohibition on cruel and unusual punishments is in part responsible for this choice, although the choice seems to have been made in some countries where there is no such explicit prohibition.[55]

---

49 See Friedman, *supra* note 4, at 259.

50 See id., at 260–61.

51 See id., at 261.

52 See id., at 263–4.

53 See U.S. CONST. ART I, § 9, CL. 3 ('No Bill of Attainder or ex post facto Law shall be passed'). A similar prohibition applies to the states: 'No State shall . . . pass any Bill of Attainder . . .'. Id., ART. I, § 10, CL. 1; U.S. CONST. AMEND. VIII ('Excessive bail shall not be required, nor excessive fines imposed, nor cruel and unusual punishments inflicted.').

54 See Friedman, *supra* note 4.

55 Malaysia, Morocco, Senegal, and the Ivory Coast do not have a rule prohibiting cruel and unusual punishment. Yet, the governments in those countries have not gone to the extreme of trying to profit from punishing the guilty.

The historical evidence is consistent with this view of the constraining function of the cruel and unusual punishment clause.[56] The first restrictions on excessive penalties in English law appeared in the Magna Carta, in chapters regulating discretionary fines.[57] The discretionary fines, or 'amercements',[58] obviously had the potential to be used as a source of revenue for the state, and as a source of private income in a period in which much of criminal prosecution was undertaken by private parties.[59] It was their abuse that led the authors of the Magna Carta to devote three chapters to their control.[60] These provisions later evolved into the modern prohibitions of excessive and disproportionate punishments.[61]

In terms of the profit function introduced in equation (7.1), Friedman's argument is easy to understand. Inefficient punishments work not by altering the cost of prosecution, c_p, but by modifying the payoff to the prosecutor, π. The prosecutor's payoff increases in the amount that a defendant would bid to avoid punishment and the amount that third parties would bid to take the defendant's wealth. The payoff should decline as a function of the cost of punishment, since any increase in the cost of punishment reduces the net reward from using the criminal law to extract wealth. Consider, for example, a wealthy individual who would pay an enormous amount to avoid conviction for some criminal violation. If the law permits the prosecutor (or the state) to strip the defendant of his wealth, the payoff to the prosecutor can be approximated by the monetary loss to the defendant, $\pi = v$. For a wealthy potential defendant, the prosecutor's profit function would then be

$$p_p v - c_p , \tag{7.6}$$

which could be positive even if the likelihood of conviction is extremely low.

Penalty restrictions increase the cost of punishment to the state, dampening incentives for wealth extraction, and at the same time reduce the amount a potential defendant would be willing to pay in order to avoid being charged with a crime. The prohibition on cruel and unusual

56 See Anthony F. Grannuci, *'Nor Cruel and Unusual Punishments Inflicted:' The Original Meaning*, 57 CAL. L. REV. 839, 844–8 (1969).

57 See id., at 845.

58 Id.

59 On privately initiated enforcement, see, for example, Friedman, *supra* note 4, at 264.

60 See Grannuci, *supra* note 56, at 845–6.

61 See id.

punishments reduces the potential for the state or prosecutor to punish innocent individuals in order to profit from their punishment. By raising the cost of punishment, the prohibition enhances the likelihood that the state will punish only the guilty – the same substitution effect induced by the reasonable doubt rule. It also dampens incentives individuals have to become prosecutors in order to enrich themselves.

The prohibition of retroactive punishments constrains rent-seeking at the legislative level. In the absence of such a restriction, a predatory enforcement regime could retroactively impose a criminal penalty on the activity of a particular group and use the new law as leverage to expropriate their wealth. The ex post facto and bill of attainder clauses in the Constitution both apply to this type of activity. The ex post facto clause applies specifically to legislative attempts to punish retroactively.[62] The bill of attainder clause applies to legislative attempts to punish particular individuals without a trial.[63]

The distinction between penalty restrictions and procedural protections suggests that these types of rules, both designed to dampen rent-seeking, serve as complements: procedural protections work better in the short run, while penalty restrictions work better in the long run. The procedural protections described earlier – the reasonable doubt rule and the double jeopardy rule – operate in the short run to remove incentives for the prosecutor to selectively enforce the law. However, if the background institutional structure is one that allows the state to profit from the punishment of individuals, we should worry about how long the prosecutor will be able to stay out of the predatory enforcement game. Just as the potential for profit induces entry of new businesses in the private sector, the potential for profit in enforcement should induce entry of a similar sort in the public sector. Creative prosecutors would find ways to modify the procedural rules, plea bargain around them, or to lobby the legislature until the desired changes were enacted.[64] Penalty restrictions constrain this

---

62 See Harold J. Krent, *The Puzzling Boundary between Criminal and Civil Retroactive Lawmaking,* 84 GEO. L.J. 2143 (1996); Wayne A. Logan, *The Ex Post Facto Clause and the Jurisprudence of Punishment,* 35 AM. CRIM. L. REV. 1261 (1998).

63 See Jane Welsh, *The Bill of Attainder Clause: An Unqualified Guarantee of Process,* 50 BROOK. L. REV. 77 (1983); Thomas B. Griffin, *Beyond Process: A Substantive Rationale for the Bill of Attainder Clause,* 70 VA. L. REV. 475 (1984). We will focus our discussion on the ex post facto clause for the sake of brevity. Note that both clauses induce a reactive type of rent-seeking, as they seem to invite defendants to challenge virtually every effort to punish on the ground that it is either a disguised bill of attainder or retroactive penalty.

64 See, for example, Stuntz, *supra* note 34, at 509–15.

long-term erosion process by reducing the potential for profit in criminal law enforcement.[65]

5.3 Some implications for the jury

Although we have focused on rent-seeking in the enforcement process rather than in the legislative process, the jury serves as an important constraint against both types of rent-seeking. A prosecutor who brings politically motivated charges against members of politically weak groups faces the risk, under the jury system, of being unable to gain a unanimous verdict from a jury consisting of some members from the weak group. Indeed, the theory of this chapter suggests an important rationale for the requirement of unanimity among jurors in criminal trials. The need to obtain a unanimous verdict makes it more difficult for the prosecutor to selectively target politically marginal groups or individuals in the law enforcement process. The need to obtain a unanimous verdict from the jury also gives the jury the power to nullify statutes designed to expropriate wealth from politically marginal groups.

Our theory provides some insight into the original function of challenges to the jury's composition, including the controversial problem of peremptory challenges. Challenges to individual jurors could be based on cause, or could be peremptory, in the sense of not being based on any of the accepted grounds.[66] Peremptory challenges were granted only to the defendant.[67] Although peremptory challenges have come under attack recently as a form of invidious discrimination,[68] the original purpose is somewhat easier to see in the context of a rent-seeking model. The peremptory, in its original design, gave the defendant a zone of unquestioned authority in the choice of jurors, as long as he did not use it to an excessive degree. If a wily predatory sheriff had managed to choose conviction-

---

[65] The procedural constraints we have discussed might reduce the incentive to lobby law enforcers, but might lead parties to more lobbying on the legislative side. Penalty restrictions, to the extent they are part of constitutional law, reduce incentives for legislative lobbying. In addition, any set of restraints that forces rent-seeking groups to use more costly methods of extracting wealth should have the desired effect of dampening rent-seeking incentives. At a minimum, the restraints considered here have that effect.

[66] Blackstone Commentaries, *supra* note 17, at 361–3.

[67] Id., at 362.

[68] See J.E.B. v. Alabama ex rel. T.B., 511 U.S. 127, 140 (1994) (the Equal Protection Clause prohibits gender discrimination in the use of peremptory challenges); Batson v. Kentucky, 476 U.S. 79, 89 (1986) (the prosecutor's peremptory challenges based solely on race were unconstitutional under the Equal Protection Clause).

prone jurors in a way that would be difficult to challenge on the accepted grounds, the defendant could fall back on his peremptory challenges. To the extent that this obstruction stood in the way of any effort to selectively enforce the law, the sheriff would have a much smaller incentive to try to control the composition of the jury.

6. Applications of positive theory

We have been concerned so far with explaining broad institutional features. In this section, we extend the argument by taking a look at the case law associated with pro-defendant protections, focusing on double jeopardy law. Since criminal procedure is a vast area, we can provide only a sketch here. We claim that this chapter's framework provides a good positive theory of substantial parts of criminal procedure doctrine.

6.1 Double jeopardy

As a general matter, double jeopardy reduces the prosecutor's power to selectively enforce or abuse his discretion in a manner complementary to the reasonable doubt standard. Double jeopardy complements the reasonable doubt rule by preventing the prosecutor from bringing successive prosecutions against the same defendant with the hope of eventually learning how to convict the defendant on weak evidence.[69] In brief, our claim is that the essential purpose of double jeopardy doctrine is to prevent prosecutors from substituting toward successive prosecutions in order to avoid fundamental single-trial procedural constraints such as the reasonable doubt rule. This proposition explains puzzles in double jeopardy doctrine as well as its overall structure.[70]

One of the important puzzles in double jeopardy doctrine is the tension between the decisions in *Blockburger v. United States*[71] and *Diaz v. United States*.[72] *Blockburger* established the principle that, for double jeopardy purposes, a greater offense is treated as the same as each of its lesser-included offenses. Thus, under the *Blockburger* test, it would be a violation of the double jeopardy rule to retry an individual for murder after that individual is acquitted on a charge of attempted murder (arising from the

---

[69] Benton v. Maryland, 395 U.S. 784, 796 (1969).

[70] On the puzzles of double jeopardy law, see Akhil Reed Amar, *Double Jeopardy Law Made Simple*, 106 Yale L. J. 1807 (1997).

[71] 284 U.S. 299 (1932).

[72] 223 U.S. 442 (1912). As Amar notes, the principle of *Diaz* was affirmed later by the Supreme Court in Garret v. United States, 471 U.S. 773 (1985). See Amar, *supra* note 70, at 1813.

same set of facts).[73] However, in *Diaz*, the Court permitted an individual to be retried for murder, after having been convicted of attempted murder, in a case in which the victim died after the first trial from injuries received in the initial attack.[74] Under a strict application of the *Blockburger* test, *Diaz* would have to be considered a mistake.

The tension between *Blockburger* and *Diaz* (and between *Blockburger* and several other decisions) appears to be a puzzle under a strict interpretation of *Blockburger*. However, under the anti-substitution thesis implied by our framework, there is no tension between *Blockburger* and *Diaz*. *Blockburger* prohibits a particular substitution strategy: the use of a later trial on either a greater or lesser-included offense in order to take two shots at convicting a defendant on one particular set of facts. The '*Diaz* exception' (if one wishes to call it that) applies to a case in which there is clearly no evidence that the prosecutor has adopted such a strategy. *Blockburger* and *Diaz* are easily reconciled under the anti-substitution principle.

A simple model of the problem under consideration may clarify this argument. Suppose a crime consists of elements $\{A, B, C\}$. Each element must be proved in order to hold the defendant guilty. For example, in the case of murder, A might be the intent element, B the attempt element, C the actual killing of the victim. Attempted murder would then require only the proof of elements A and B. *Blockburger* holds that, in general, it is violation of double jeopardy to first prosecute the defendant for $\{A, B\}$ and then later prosecute him for $\{A, B, C\}$. This seems sensible in light of the potential for predation. The predation potential is especially clear in the case in which the government loses on the $\{A, B\}$ prosecution and then brings $\{A, B, C\}$. If the government wins $\{A, B\}$ and then brings $\{A, B, C\}$, the predation concern is somewhat less, but still important.

Diaz is distinguishable from the standard case of successive prosecutions for two reasons: the government won in the first case, and the new element was only prospective at the time of the first trial. In terms of the model, at the time of trial, the crime could be described as consisting of A and B with only a chance of C. The government did not have a real choice between $\{A, B\}$ and $\{A, B, C\}$, and given the absence of such a choice, the government's decision to bring $\{A, B\}$ should not be called an example of strategic predation. When C was later realized, a prosecution based on $\{A, B, C\}$, offsetting for the punishment already inflicted, preserves the deterrent effect of the law without introducing risks of government predation.

---

[73] See Amar, *supra* note 70, at 1813.

[74] The state was prepared to offset against the murder sentence time served under the attempted murder conviction. See id.

Consider another puzzle involving the splitting of possible charges. Suppose one charge consists of circumstances *A*, *B*, and *C*, and another of the circumstances *A*, *B*, and *E*. For example, suppose one charge is robbery and the other is murder, arising from the same set of events, and element *B* requires proof of the defendant's presence at the scene of the crime.[75] The defendant is tried under the *ABC* charge first, and the government loses because it cannot prove element *B*. Can the government turn around and bring the *ABE* charge? *Blockburger* would seem to imply that the answer is yes, because the charges do not involve the same elements. However, the Supreme Court held in *Ashe v. Swenson* that, under the double jeopardy clause, the government was collaterally estopped from attempting to prove element *B* in the second prosecution.[76]

The tension between *Blockburger* and *Ashe* disappears under this chapter's anti-substitution principle. If prosecutors were free to split up their charges into separate yet overlapping bundles – {*A*, *B*, *C*}; {*A*, *B*, *E*}; {*B*, *C*, *D*} – without having to fear that they would be barred by the double jeopardy rule, then this would clearly be a desirable way of skirting the single-trial constraints imposed by the reasonable doubt rule. It follows that double jeopardy doctrine should be understood to prevent this kind of prosecution stratagem. If the *Blockburger* doctrine is read to incorporate the anti-substitution rule proposed here, then there is no apparent conflict between *Blockburger* and the collateral estoppel rule of *Ashe*.

Our claim that the overall structure of double jeopardy doctrine is consistent with the model of this chapter is supported by two other features of the doctrine: the asymmetry of appeal rights and the treatment of mistrials.

Consider the treatment of appeal rights. In *Kepner v. U.S.*, the Supreme Court held that appeal rights are asymmetric,[77] in the sense that the defense generally can appeal any conviction, but the prosecution's right to appeal acquittals is severely limited.[78] If we incorporate concerns over rent-seeking, then a strong rationale for asymmetric appeal rights emerges.

---

75 Amar, *supra* note 70, at 1827.

76 397 U.S. 436 (1970); for discussion see Amar, *supra* note 70, at 1827–8.

77 Kepner v. United States, 195 U.S. 100, 105 (1904).

78 Sanabria v. United States, 437 U.S. 54, 64 (1978) (holding that even if legal rulings on the exclusion of evidence leading to acquittals were erroneous, the prosecution could not appeal); Fong Foo v. United States, 369 U.S. 141, 143 (1962) (holding that the prosecution could not appeal an acquittal where the judge, who lacked the authority to do so, directed a verdict of acquittal before the prosecutor has rested his case); Carroll v. United States, 354 U.S. 394, 400 (1956); United States v. Ball, 163 U.S. 662 (1896) (holding that a defendant may not be prosecuted more than once for an offense).

The asymmetric appeal rights rule of *Kepner* has the effect of making the jury's initial determination of acquittal final. By denying prosecutors the option to have a jury's acquittal determination reviewed by an appellate court, the *Kepner* asymmetry rule enhances the power of the jury relative to that of the prosecutor. Given the unanimity requirement and the jury's composition after the defendant's challenges, the *Kepner* rule increases the difficulty facing any prosecutor who mounts a selective enforcement campaign.

The treatment of mistrials is another area of double jeopardy doctrine that shows a concern for constraining prosecutorial abuse. The kind of abuse we are concerned with here is that the prosecution may think, at some point in the initial trial, that a conviction is not likely and may then try to have a mistrial declared by the court to try to get another shot at the defendant.[79] If we permitted the prosecution to do this and bring another trial, then the prosecution would have a tremendous incentive to have mistrials declared whenever it thought it might not win the initial trial.

The law appears to reflect these concerns in the way it addresses whether another trial will be permitted following a mistrial. One could characterize the law's approach to this problem as one that depends on the defense's attitude towards a mistrial. Thus, if the defense seeks or does not oppose a motion for a mistrial, then the prosecution will normally be permitted to bring another suit.[80] This is consistent with our substitution thesis because if the *defense* is seeking a mistrial, the prosecution is not likely to be using the mistrial process to seek another trial to go after the defendant. An exception to this is observed where the defense seeks a mistrial based on something the prosecution did that appears deliberately calculated by the prosecution to induce the defense to seek a mistrial.[81] This is also consistent with the rent-seeking framework because in such cases there is a clear

---

[79] See Ashe v. Swenson, 397 U.S. 436, 447 (1970); Stephen Schulhofer, *Jeopardy and Mistrials*, 125 U. PA. L. REV. 449, 468–9 (1977).

[80] See United States v. DiFrancesco, 449 U.S. 117, 130 (1980); see also Oregon v. Kennedy, 456 U.S. 667, 676 (1982).

[81] See Arizona v. Washington, 434 U.S. 497, 508 (1978); United States v. Dinitz, 424 U.S. 600, 611 (1976) (stating that '[the Double Jeopardy law] bar retrials where "bad-faith" conduct by judge or prosecutor threatens the harassment of an accused by successive prosecutions [or] a more favorable opportunity to convict the defendant; [W]here a defendant's mistrial motion is necessitated by judicial or prosecutorial impropriety designed to avoid an acquittal, reprosecution might well be barred'); United States v. Jorn, 400 U.S. 470, 485 (1971) (stating that '[t]hus, where circumstances develop not attributable to prosecutorial or judicial overreaching, a motion by the defendant for mistrial is ordinarily assumed to remove

risk that the prosecutor could have induced the defense's motion for a mistrial in order take advantage of information gleaned from the initial trial.[82]

On the other hand, when the defense opposes a mistrial motion, the courts have adopted a more cautious stance to permitting another trial – the prosecution must prove a 'manifest necessity' for the next trial.[83] In addition, the factors that go to showing whether 'manifest necessity' is present appear to be designed to ascertain whether the prosecutor was trying to abuse the criminal process – for example, by getting a mistrial in order to avoid a loss in the initial trial.[84] For example, a hung jury leading to a mistrial does not present the same specter of potential abuse as does the injection of prejudicial error by the prosecutor to obtain a mistrial. [85] In the former case, the prosecution is often granted another trial, while the latter case will normally not result in another trial.[86] Further, when the reason for the mistrial was a move by the defense, without prosecutorial provocation, then the scope for prosecutorial abuse is also low and another trial is usually granted.[87] These factors are all consistent with an approach that seeks to constrain the prosecutor's ability to substitute successive prosecutions in order to avoid the effect of pro-defendant procedural protections.

---

any barrier to reprosecution, even if the defendant's motion is necessitated by prosecutorial or judicial error').

[82] See Commonwealth v. Starks, 416 A.2d 498, 500 (1980) (arguing that prosecutorial overreaching '. . . signals the breakdown of the integrity of the judicial proceeding, and represents the type of prosecutorial tactic which the double jeopardy clause was designed to protect against'). This exception to the bar on the application of double jeopardy where a defendant seeks a mistrial is a very narrow one. See Green v. United States, 451 U.S. 929, 931 (1981) (Marshall, J., dissenting) (stating that 'I suspect that a defendant seeking to prevent a retrial will seldom be able to prove the Government's actual motivation'). Few courts have found intentional prosecutorial inducement. See Commonwealth v. Warfield, 227 A.2d 177 (Pa. 1967) (defendant was indicted for murder and voluntary manslaughter and the trial judge suppressed the defendant's confession, yet the District Attorney revealed in his opening statement that the defendant had made a confession to the police. After the defendant moved for a mistrial, the District Attorney admitted that he sought to induce the defendant to seek a mistrial).

[83] See Arizona v. Washington, 434 U.S. 497, 505 (1978); Wayne R. LaFave, Jerold H. Israel & Nancy J. King, Criminal Procedure 1176–80 (3d ed., St. Paul, Minn.: West Group 2000).

[84] See Schulhofer, *supra* note 104, at 468–9.

[85] See Steinglass, *supra* note 21, at 361.

[86] Id., at 487.

[87] See Joshua Dressler, Understanding Criminal Procedure 607 (1997).

6.2 *Ex post facto clause*

The ex post facto clause bars retroactive application of certain changes in the criminal law.[88] The standard justifications are that it provides *notice* to defendants of the conduct that is illegal and the sanction for it, as well as constraining the government from passing arbitrary or vindictive legislation against a particular defendant.[89] The prohibition is only concerned with matters that amount to 'punishment'[90] and applies more frequently in the context of legislative decisions as compared to judicial decisions.

Given that a concern for potential government oppression has always been one of the justifications for the ex post facto clause, the key contribution of the rent-seeking framework is its identification of a particular justification as central to efforts to understand case outcomes. The two standard justifications, notice and prevention of abuse, provide alternate approaches to explaining the case law. Under the notice approach, just about every change in the criminal punishment process, whether in the law or in evidentiary requirements, could violate the prohibition against ex post facto rules if applied retroactively. Under the 'abuse' or rent-seeking approach, only those changes in the punishment process that create a potential for abuse, by increasing the risk of targeted enforcement, should be deemed violations of the ex post facto clause.

We have argued that the case law is more consistent with the latter view.[91] The most obvious illustration of this is that the ex post facto provision is understood today to be violated if a penalty is enhanced, but not if it is reduced. Obviously, any change in a penalty could be viewed as a violation of the ex post facto clause under the notice theory. The abuse theory, however, would imply a concern only for penalty enhancements.

Since it is clear that an enhancement of the penalty, applied retroactively, violates the ex post facto clause, much of the modern case law involves less clear changes such as rules governing the provision of benefits to prisoners (such as the timing of parole hearings) or the type of evidence

---

[88] See JOHN E. NOWAK & RONALD D. ROTUNDA, CONSTITUTIONAL LAW 428 (5th ed. 1995); Lindsey v. Washington, 301 U.S. 397 (1937).

[89] See WAYNE R. LAFAVE & AUSTIN W. SCOTT, JR. CRIMINAL LAW 97–100 (2d. ed).

[90] Sometimes 'civil' sanctions may amount to 'punishment' for purposes of ex post facto inquiry. See Landgraf v. U.S.I. Film Products, 511 U.S. 244 (1994) (finding that the punitive damage awards of the 1991 Civil Rights Act were similar enough to criminal sanctions to apply the ex post facto clause). However, this is not a frequent occurrence so that normally the legislative label is determinative (that is, if it is labeled 'civil' by the legislature then it will most likely not amount to 'punishment'). See Kansas v. Hendricks, 521 U.S. 346 (1997).

[91] Hylton & Khanna, *supra* note 1, at 100–04.

admitted into court. The modern decisions suggest that the Supreme Court applies a balancing test that weighs the likelihood and potential severity of abuse against the administrative efficiencies. In the case of a reduction in certain benefits provided to prisoners, the administrative efficiencies come in the form of cost reductions to the state. This is weighed against the potential for targeted punishment against a person or class. In the case of evidence requirements, the potential for abuse is weighed against gains in the administration and accuracy of trials.[92]

6.3 Void-for-vagueness

The void-for-vagueness doctrine serves as a constraint on legislators and law-enforcement agents that curtails their discretion. The early cases struck down laws that were deemed vague, in the sense that they granted law enforcement agents broad discretion in deciding what is legal and what is not.[93] Such discretion gives enforcement agents wide power to extract wealth through the criminal law enforcement process. This raises the specter of rent-seeking.

The purpose of the void-for-vagueness doctrine was confused to some extent by the Supreme Court's rationale in *Papachristou v. City of Jacksonville*, a decision striking down a Florida vagrancy ordinance. Rather than focusing solely on the enormous discretion the statute gave to law enforcers, the Court spoke at length about the class-stratification consequences of the ordinance. The Court noted that '[t]hose generally implicated by the imprecise terms of the ordinance – poor people, non-conformists, dissenters, idlers – may be required to comport themselves according to the life-style deemed appropriate by the Jacksonville police and the courts'.

The Court's class-stratification worries in *Papachristou* led to the belief on the part of some litigants and commentators that a vague law should be upheld if it raised no class-stratification issues. So, for example, an ordinance giving law enforcers greater discretion to arrest gang members should be viewed positively in the absence of any race or class-stratification issues. If such an ordinance appeared to play no role as a mechanism for inter-group wealth expropriation, this reasoning would suggest that it should be upheld.

However, this view misses the fundamental point that the void-for-vagueness doctrine aims at suppressing the risk of what we described

---

[92] Id., at 102–04.

[93] Papachristou v. City of Jacksonville, 405 U.S. 156 (1972); Fields v. City of Omaha, 810 F.2d 830 (8th Cir. 1987).

earlier as 'simple corruption' – the use of the power to enforce as a path to enrichment. Excessively vague statutes give discretion to law enforcers to shake down law-abiding citizens for bribes. This fundamental concern underlying void-for-vagueness doctrine remains a valid one, as suggested by the Court's decision upholding the doctrine in *Chicago v. Morales*.[94]

7. Conclusion

Perhaps the most enduring statement of criminal procedure is Blackstone's claim that it is better to let ten guilty men go free rather than punish one innocent man. The public choice theory we have offered in this chapter is in accord with this claim. The Supreme Court later elaborated on this notion in its *Winship* decision by framing the problem as one of avoiding certain false conviction costs, such as stigma and disutility costs. It is this formulation that we find inadequate. We contend that public choice theory provides the best basis for understanding the key institutional features of criminal procedure. Moreover, the public choice theory suggests functions for each of the most important protections – such as the double jeopardy, ex post facto, and reasonable doubt rules – that align well with the actual case law.

---

[94] Hylton & Khanna, *supra* note 1, at 104–06. The approaches in Papachristou and Morales are good examples of how Ely's approach differ from ours. Ours is closer to Morales and Ely's to Papachristou.

8 The economics of capital punishment

Joanna M. Shepherd

Introduction

This chapter surveys the existing empirical literature on whether capital punishment deters crime. I briefly discuss standard economic theory's predictions of capital punishment's impact on crime and provide a concise history of the death penalty in the United States. Then I extensively review both the early and recent empirical literature testing the relationship between capital punishment and crime. Most recent empirical studies of capital punishment find evidence supporting the deterrence hypothesis. However, a few recent studies have raised questions about the sensitivity of some of the previous results. Other recent research also shows that deterrence does not occur in many states and for many types of executions. Indeed, in a substantial number of states, executions may instead increase crime.

Although the heated debate over capital punishment raises many moral, legal, and religious issues, economists' greatest contribution has been an extensive analysis of whether capital punishment deters crime. This chapter reviews the growing empirical literature that examines this deterrent effect.

Because almost all Western industrialized nations have abolished capital punishment, the recent empirical literature focuses exclusively on capital punishment's effect in the United States.[1] In this chapter, I briefly discuss theoretical predictions of capital punishment's impact on crime, provide a concise history of the death penalty in the US, and review both the early and recent empirical literature.

1. Theoretical predictions

According to standard economic theory, the possibility of being executed is one of many potential costs that criminals consider when they are deciding whether to engage in crime. When the use of capital punishment

[1] There are a few early studies of the deterrent effect in other countries. For example, Wolpin (1978) found evidence of deterrence in England. Avio (1979) found no evidence of a deterrent effect in Canada, but Layson (1983) found evidence of deterrence in Canada.

increases, the costs of committing murder increase, and, according to the theory, some potential criminals will refrain from committing murder.

Although the basic theory is straightforward, three alternate theories suggest that, instead, capital punishment may have no effect on crime, or may even cause crime to increase. First, executions are rare. In 2006, there were 16,692 homicides, but only 60 executions. Because recent literature suggests that many individuals treat events with low probability as having a zero probability (Cooter and Ulen 2004, p. 351), executions might be expected to have little impact on crime. On the other hand, the substantial publicity surrounding many executions may exaggerate criminals' perceptions of the probability of being executed.

Second, for some criminals, the existence of state-sanctioned executions may reduce the moral aversion or social stigma associated with committing a murder. By reducing the moral and social costs of committing murders, executions may cause some criminals to murder more people than they would otherwise. This possibility has been called capital punishment's 'brutalization effect' (Bowers and Pierce, 1975; Shepherd, 2005).

Third, the threat of execution may induce some criminals to commit more murders in order to avoid being executed. A person who has already committed a murder that would subject him to execution may have an incentive to murder potential witnesses who could provide incriminating evidence against him and increase the likelihood of a death sentence.

Whether capital punishment deters murder is ultimately an empirical question.

2. History of the death penalty

In order to provide a context for my discussion of the empirical studies, I now briefly discuss the history of the death penalty in the United States in the twentieth century.

During the first half of the twentieth century, executions were frequent. For example, more executions occurred during the 1930s than in any other decade in American history: an average of 167 executions each year. However, over the next few decades, various social forces combined to reduce capital punishment's use. Two primary concerns were, first, that capital punishment was applied in a racially discriminatory way and, second, that its application was arbitrary. Echoing these concerns, the US Supreme Court declared current capital statutes unconstitutional in three cases in 1972: *Furman v. Georgia*, *Jackson v. Georgia*, and *Branch v. Texas*, collectively referred to as the *Furman* decision (408 US 238). The Court held that the statutes resulted in arbitrary sentencing, constituting cruel and unusual punishment under the Eighth Amendment to the US Constitution. The decision's effect was to void 40 states' death penalty statutes and to commute the sentences of more than 600 death row inmates.

After *Furman*, the states quickly began to draft new death penalty laws. The Supreme Court approved several of the new statutes in 1976 in *Gregg v. Georgia*, *Jurek v. Texas*, and *Proffitt v. Florida*, known collectively as the *Gregg* decision (428 US 153). After the enactment of the new death penalty statutes that satisfied the Constitution, death rows quickly filled. The moratorium on executions ended in January, 1977, with the execution of Gary Gilmore in Utah. The number of annual executions steadily increased after 1977, peaking in 1999 with 98 executions. After 1999, as questions about capital punishment's fairness have again surfaced and as capital punishment has lost some public support, the number of executions has declined. Between 1977 and 2006, there have been a total of 1,057 executions.

Despite the recent resurgence in executions, the use of the death penalty varies widely across states. As of 2007, 13 states do not have statutes that permit capital punishment: Alaska, Hawaii, Iowa, Maine, Massachusetts, Michigan, Minnesota, New York, North Dakota, Rhode Island, Vermont, West Virginia, and Wisconsin. Of the 37 states that currently have capital-punishment statutes, three have performed no post-moratorium executions: Kansas, New Hampshire, and New Jersey. Moreover, the use of the death penalty varies widely across regions. Executions have been concentrated in the South for most of this century, and the concentration there has recently become even stronger. Southern states accounted for approximately half of the 3,859 executions between 1930 and 1968 (Zimring and Hawkins 1986, p. 30). Of the executions since 1977, over 75 percent have occurred in the South. Researchers exploit the variation in the frequency of executions both in the states and over time to distinguish capital punishment's effect on murders from other influences.

3. Early empirical studies

The empirical debate in the economics literature began with Isaac Ehrlich's two papers in 1975 and 1977. Ehrlich was the first to examine deterrence using regression analysis. His 1975 paper examines US time-series data for the period 1933–69. Controlling for other deterrent variables, demographic variables, economic variables, and a time variable, Ehrlich finds a statistically significant negative relationship between the murder rate and execution rate. He estimates that each execution results in approximately seven or eight fewer murders. Ehrlich's later paper, from 1977, studies cross-sectional data from the 50 states in 1940 and 1950. Again, with similar control variables as in his 1975 paper, his findings indicate a substantial deterrent effect of capital punishment on murder.

Ehrlich's finding triggered an avalanche of econometric analyses of capital punishment and deterrence. The papers that immediately followed Ehrlich use his original data (national time-series for 1933–69 or state-level cross-section data for 1940 and 1950) and variants of his econometric model. The results were mixed. Many find that capital punishment has a deterrent effect, but others do not. For example, using Ehrlich's data, the following find a deterrent effect: Yunker (1976), Cloninger (1977), and Ehrlich and Gibbons (1977). In contrast, Bowers and Pierce (1975), Passel and Taylor (1977), and Hoenack and Weiler (1980) find no deterrence when they use the same data with alternative specifications. Similarly, McAleer and Veall (1989), Leamer (1983), and McManus (1985) find no deterrent effect when different variables are included over the same sample period. Finally, Black and Orsagh (1978) obtain mixed results depending on which cross-section year they use.

In the late 1980s and 1990s, a second generation of econometric studies extended Ehrlich's national time-series data or used more recent cross-sectional data. As before, some of the papers find deterrence while others do not. For example, Layson (1985) and Cover and Thistle (1988) use an extension of Ehrlich's national time-series data, covering up to 1977. Although Layson finds a significant deterrent effect of executions, Cover and Thistle correct for data flaws – non-stationarity – and find no deterrent effect. Chressanthis (1989) employs national time-series data covering 1966 through 1985 and finds a deterrent effect. In contrast, Grogger (1990) uses daily data for California during 1960–63 and finds no deterrent effect.

Most of the early studies, both the first wave and the second generation, use the same types of data: either national time-series or cross-section data. However, these aggregated data have limitations. Analyses of national time-series data may suffer from aggregation bias; whenever several states are grouped together, changes in the murder rates of one state within the group may dilute opposite changes in the murder rates of another state. Likewise, cross-sectional data do not allow for fixed-effects estimation to control for jurisdiction-specific characteristics that could be related to murder. Moreover, both time-series and cross-section data have few observations, which may produce spurious results or make strong statistical conclusions impossible.

Noting these possible limitations, several authors (Cameron, 1994; Avio, 1998) and a specially convened National Academy of Sciences panel called for new research using more disaggregated data, and, ideally, panel data.

4. Recent empirical studies

Since the mid-1990s, researchers have conducted studies that attempt to fix flaws in the earlier studies. Most recent studies have overcome many of the fundamental problems associated with national time-series and cross-section data by using panel data. The panel data that are normally used are a combination of time-series and cross-section data, looking at the experiences of each of many states or counties over time. Use of panel data often enables researchers to estimate any deterrent effect more precisely because panel data produces more observations, allows fixed-effects estimations to control for important jurisdictional differences among US states or counties, and minimizes aggregation bias.

Many papers have recently been published in economics journals, law and economics journals, and law reviews. The methodology of many of the recent empirical studies resembles other empirical studies of crime. The new studies typically measure capital punishment's effect by estimating a murder supply equation that has some measure of murders as the dependent variable. Independent variables include the relevant capital punishment variables, along with a host of other control variables that typically include economic, demographic, political, and law enforcement variables. Moreover, most of the panel data studies include time and state fixed effects that both control for any factors that affect all states but vary over time and control for any unobservable variables that systematically differ among states.

Many of the estimations address the potentially endogenous relationship between executions and murders; it is conceivable not only that the number of executions could affect the number of murders, but also that more murders could cause governments to respond to a public outcry for more executions. Accordingly, scholars often estimate a system of equations to minimize potential bias.

In the following review of the recent empirical studies, I group articles by their primary focus.

4.1 Testing for deterrence

Many of the recent papers focus on whether capital punishment deters crime. In contrast to earlier papers, the recent papers use both new datasets that offer more disaggregated data and more sophisticated empirical methods.

In the earliest of the recent papers, Brumm and Cloninger (1996) use cross-sectional data covering 58 cities in 1985 to test for a deterrent effect. They estimate a covariance structure model in which the perceived risk of punishment is treated as an endogenous latent variable, with two measures of sanctions as its indicators. Their results provide support for the deterrence hypothesis: they find that the perceived risk of punishment, including the probability of execution, is negatively and significantly correlated with the homicide rate.

A paper by Dezhbakhsh et al. (2003) takes a different approach. It examines whether deterrence exists using county-level panel data from 3,054 US counties over the period 1977 to 1996. This is the only study to use county-level data, significantly increasing the number of observations and allowing the researchers to control for the demographic, economic, and jurisdictional differences among US counties that can affect murder rates. The estimation of a simultaneous-equations system to control for endogeneity between murders and executions produced results supporting the deterrence hypothesis; both death row sentences and the executions themselves are associated with decreases in the murder rate. Moreover, the results are robust to many different ways of performing the statistical analysis.

In another study of the deterrent effect, Mocan and Gittings (2003) use state-level panel data from 1977 to 1997 to examine the relationship among executions, commutation and other removals from death row, and murder. Controlling for a variety of state-level characteristics in a series of estimations, their results strongly support the deterrence hypothesis. The findings suggest that each additional execution decreases homicides by about five, and that both commuting death-row prisoners' sentences and removing them from death row cause more murders. Specifically, each commutation results in approximately five extra murders and each removal from death row generates one additional murder. Moreover, further supporting their conclusions, they find that executions, commutations, and removals have no impact on other crime rates. Their results are robust to a series of alternative specifications.

Another recent paper by Katz et al. (2003) uses state-level panel data covering the period 1950 to 1990. Although their primary focus is on the relationship between prison conditions and crime rates, they also test for a relationship between the execution rate and murder rates. They find only limited evidence of a deterrent effect: some specifications show no relationship between murders and executions, but other estimations do indicate a deterrent effect.

Similarly, Lott and Landes (1999) use state-level panel data from 1977 to 1995 to examine whether right-to-carry concealed handgun laws deter multiple-victim public shootings. Included in their analysis are tests of the deterrent effect of executions on murder. The authors find that right-to-carry concealed handgun laws do result in fewer multiple-victim public shootings. They also find that executions have a significant deterrent effect on the overall murder rate. Specifically, a 1 percent increase in the execution rate is associated with a 7 percent decline in the overall murder rate.

Zimmerman (2004) uses state-level panel data from 1978 to 1997 to test for a deterrent effect. His simultaneous-equations system uses instrumental variables that are motivated by the theory of public choice as it relates to the criminal justice system and bureaucratic behavior. The results strongly support the deterrence hypothesis: Zimmerman's estimates imply that a state execution deters approximately 14 murders on average.

4.2 The impact of moratoriums

Other papers have attempted to isolate the deterrent effect from other factors affecting murders by examining state and federal moratoriums on executions. Many factors that affect crime – for example, law enforcement, judicial, demographic, and economic variables – change only slightly over a short period of time. Therefore, changes in a state's murder rate quickly following a change in its death penalty law are likely the result of the legal change.

Cloninger and Marchesini (2001) exploit Texas's unofficial moratorium on executions during 1996 to analyze both the moratorium's effect on murder rates and the effect on murder rates of ending the moratorium. They conduct a portfolio analysis that is similar to the event-study methodology used in the financial literature. They find both that the moratorium appears to have caused additional homicides and that murder rates significantly decreased after the moratorium was lifted.

Cloninger and Marchesini (2006) apply a similar methodology to explore the impact of Illinois's unofficial moratorium on executions in 2000 and the commutation of all death sentences in the state in 2003. They find that these two actions substantially increased Illinois's homicide rate. Specifically, they estimate that there were 150 additional homicides in Illinois during the years immediately following these two events

Similarly, Dezhbakhsh and Shepherd (2006) test for deterrence by exploiting the natural experiment offered by the moratorium on executions in all states from 1972–6 resulting from the US Supreme Court's decisions. They use a state-level panel dataset from 1960–2000 that includes data from before, during, and after the moratorium. Comparisons of murder rates before and after the moratorium reveal that about 91 percent of states experienced an increase in murder rates after they suspended the death penalty, and about 70 percent of states experienced decreases in murder rates after reinstating the death penalty. Moreover, regression analyses that disentangle the impact of the moratorium on murders from the impact of executions on murders also support the existence of deterrence. The results suggest that the moratorium was associated with increases in murders, while executions are associated with decreases in murders.

4.3 Variations of the murder-execution relationship

A group of studies have extended the basic deterrence studies and focused on the details of the relationship between murders and executions. Several studies have focused on which execution method provides the most effective deterrent, and other studies have examined the types of murders that are deterred.

Ekelund et al. (2006) use state-level panel data for the period 1995–99 to explore the relationship between executions, single murders, and multiple murders. They find that executions strongly deter single murders. Moreover, they find that executions by electrocution are associated with greater reductions in murders than executions by lethal injection. In contrast, they find that executions have no statistically significant impact on multiple murders, suggesting that these murders are not deterrable.

In another analysis of which execution methods have the strongest deterrent effects, Zimmerman (2006) employs state-level panel data from 1978–2000. His results suggest that the deterrent effect of capital punishment is driven primarily by executions conducted by electrocution, as these executions are associated with significant decreases in murder rates. In contrast, none of the other four methods of execution has a statistically significant impact on murder rates.

Shepherd (2004) uses state-level, monthly panel data from 1977–99 to examine both the types of murders deterred by capital punishment and the impact on deterrence of execution delays. Despite beliefs that certain types of murder are not deterrable because they are products of uncontrollable rage, this study's empirical analysis indicates that the combination of death row sentences and executions is associated with decreases in all types of murders: murders between intimates, acquaintances, and strangers, crime-of-passion murders and murders committed during other felonies, and murders of both African-American and white people. Moreover, the results also suggest that shorter waits on death row increase deterrence. The results indicate that, on average, a 2.75-year reduction in the death-row wait before each execution is associated with the deterrence of one extra murder.

Fagan et al. (2007) explore the impact of capital punishment on a subset of murders in Texas: homicides that have been defined statutorily as death eligible. Using state-level panel data over the years 1976–2003, they found no evidence of a deterrent effect on such murders.

4.4 Sensitivity analysis

As most of the recent papers have found some evidence of deterrence, they have generated substantial interest in the sensitivity of the deterrence findings. In addition to the extensive sensitivity analyses that appear in several of the papers themselves, other recent papers have focused either on the robustness of previous studies' results or on the nuances of capital punishment's deterrent effect. These papers focus on deterrence findings in both early and recent papers.

The first of the recent sensitivity analyses was Ehrlich and Liu (1999), which tested the robustness of Ehrlich's deterrence findings from the 1970s. Using Ehrlich's original state-level, cross-section data from 1940 and 1950, the paper tests for improper functional form, heteroscedasticity, heterogeneity, measurement errors, simultaneity, and contemporaneous correlation. All of the results support the deterrence hypothesis.

Liu (2004) investigates the endogenous nature of states' decisions to enact death penalty laws, and the resulting selection bias in many econometric models. He presents a theoretical model that shows that the effect of deterrent variables will differ between states with and without death penalty laws, and proposes an econometric model that will control for this selection bias. Using Ehrlich's original state-level, cross-section data, a system of equations, and switching regression techniques to minimize simultaneity, the results confirm the deterrent findings of Ehrlich's earlier study. The results are also consistent across several alternative specifications.

Narayan and Smyth (2006) explores whether the results of early studies that used national time-series data are spurious because they did not account for the data's stationarity properties. Using national-level time-series data over the years 1965–2001, they employ a cointegration and error-correction framework that allows estimation of both the short-run and long-run elasticities between capital punishment and murder. They find only limited support for the deterrence hypothesis. In both the short run and the long run, only the probability of receiving a death sentence explains national variations in the homicide rate; the probability of execution is statistically insignificant in all but a few specifications.

Fagan (2006) addresses the reliability of both early and recent studies. After discussing several technical and conceptual problems that could be present in all early deterrence studies, he undertakes his own sensitivity analysis of the estimation in a recent paper, Mocan and Gittings (2003). Although he is able to replicate their results perfectly, he finds that the results do not hold when he performs the same analysis on different data sources, excludes Texas from the estimation, includes different variables, or uses alternate functional forms and econometric methods. He concludes that the impact of capital punishment on murders is still uncertain.

Berk (2005) explores whether the small number of executions in most states and years influences the earlier deterrence findings. He asserts that, because the majority of states perform few, if any, executions each year, any deterrent effect must be driven by a few individual states and years. To confirm this, he examines the 1977–97 state-level, panel data from Mocan and Gittings (2003) to compare the relationship between murders and executions when a state has very few executions with when there are several executions. He finds that the negative relationship between executions and murders exists only when there are several executions in a state each year. In addition, when he eliminates from the data states such as Texas with especially large numbers of executions, he finds no evidence of deterrence.

Shepherd (2005) also recognizes the relevance of state-specific deterrence, in the first study to measure the different deterrent effects among the US states. Using three different datasets – annual county-level data from 1977–96, annual state-level data from 1960–2000, and monthly state-level data from 1977–99 – the paper finds that the impact of executions differs substantially among US states. Executions deter murders in some states, but actually increase murders in many others. In general, a deterrent effect exists only in the few states with a large number of executions since the end of the 1970s Supreme Court moratorium. In contrast, in the many states with few executions since the moratorium, executions generally increase the number of murders or have no significant impact. Shepherd concludes that, in most states, executions do not deter crime, but instead induce additional murders.

A later study by Donohue and Wolfers (2005) also analyzes the state-by-state variation in capital punishment's deterrent effect and concludes that there is no deterrent effect in most states. In addition, this study critiques the empirical analyses of several previous papers. Although Donohue and Wolfers find that they were able to replicate the results from the previous papers perfectly, they find that some of the previous results are not robust to alternative specifications, including different sample periods, comparison groups, control variables, functional forms, or estimators. They assert that executions are so rare that it is impossible reliably to distinguish their effect on the murder rate from the effects of the other factors that influence murder rates. They therefore conclude that whether capital punishment deters murder is still an unanswered question.

5. Responses to criticisms

Several of the authors whose work was challenged by Donohue and Wolfers (2005) have written responses. Mocan and Gittings (2006) argue that Donohue's and Wolfers's re-analysis of their original 2003 article (Mocan and Gittings 2003) errs by assuming that an execution or commutation occurs in the same year that a prisoner receives his death sentence. Mocan and Gittings perform the same sensitivity analyses that Donohue and Wolfers used to critique their paper, but with an econometric model that allows for a several-year lag between death sentences and executions or commutations. They find that the results of these sensitivity analyses confirm their earlier findings that deterrence exists.

Similarly, Dezhbakhsh and Rubin (2007) respond to Donohue's and Wolfers's criticisms of two of their previous papers (Dezhbakhsh et al., 2003; Dezbakhsh and Shepherd, 2006). Dezhbakhsh and Rubin argue that econometric tests indicate that Donohue and Wolfers made an important statistical error in the primary sensitivity analysis that Donohue and Wolfers used to criticize Dezhbakhsh et al. (2003).

Dezhbakhsh and Rubin also repeat all of the sensitivity analyses that Donohue and Wolfers used to challenge the 2006 study (Dezbakhsh and Shepherd 2006). Donohue and Wolfers reported the results for only a subset of the sensitivity analyses, most of which showed no deterrent effect. In contrast, Dezhbakhsh and Rubin report the results from all 80 alternative specifications that Donohue and Wolfers discuss, finding that almost 75 percent of the results provide statistically significant evidence of a deterrent effect.

Cloninger and Marchesini (2007) is also a brief response to Donohue and Wolfers. The paper claims that the homicide measure that Donohue and Wolfers used to critique the portfolio analysis in the authors' previous two papers (Cloninger and Marchesini, 2001; Cloninger and Marchesini, 2006) is invalid (Cloninger and Marchesini, 2007, p. 6).

6. Current state of the literature

Most recent empirical studies of capital punishment find evidence supporting the deterrence hypothesis. However, a few recent studies have raised questions about the sensitivity of some of the previous results. Other recent research also shows that deterrence does not occur in many states and for many types of executions. Indeed, in a substantial number of states, executions may instead increase crime.

Because findings on deterrence continue to evolve, it is likely that future research will continue to focus on the issue. Regardless of the state of the literature on deterrence, it should be recognized that even were there a strong, consistent deterrent effect, this would appropriately contribute only a small piece to the puzzle of whether the US should join the rest of the Western world in abolishing the death penalty. Issues of morality, justice, constitutionality, racial and gender discrimination, and arbitrariness are equally important considerations.

References

Avio, Kenneth L. (1979), 'Capital Punishment in Canada: A Time-Series Analysis of the Deterrent Hypothesis', *Canadian Journal of Economics*, **12**, 647–76.

Avio, Kenneth L. (1998), 'Capital Punishment', in P. Newman (ed.), *The New Palgrave Dictionary of Economics and the Law*, London: Macmillan Reference Limited.

Berk, Richard (2005), 'New Claims about Executions and General Deterrence: Deja Vu All Over Again?', *Journal of Empirical Legal Studies,* **2** (2), 303–30.

Black, T., and T. Orsagh (1978), 'New Evidence on the Efficacy of Sanctions as a Deterrent to Homicide', *Social Science Quarterly*, **58**, 616–31.
Bowers, W.J., and J.L. Pierce (1975), 'The Illusion of Deterrence in Isaac Ehrlich's work on Capital Punishment', *Yale Law Journal*, **85**, 187–208.
Brumm, H.J., and D.O. Cloninger (1996), 'Perceived Risk of Punishment and the Commission of Homicides: A Covariance Structure Analysis', *Journal of Economic Behavior and Organization*, **31**, 1–11.
Cameron, S. (1994), 'A Review of the Econometric Evidence on the Effects of Capital Punishment', *Journal of Socio-Economics*, **23**, 197–214.
Chressanthis, G.A. (1989), 'Capital Punishment and the Deterrent Effect Revisited: Recent Time-series Econometric Evidence', *Journal of Behavioral Economics*, **18** (2), 81–97.
Cloninger, D.O. (1977), 'Deterrence and the Death Penalty: A Cross-sectional Analysis', *Journal of Behavioral Economics*, **6**, 87–107.
Cloninger, D.O., and R. Marchesini (2001), 'Execution and Deterrence: A Quasi-controlled Group Experiment', *Applied Economics*, **35** (5), 569–76.
Cloninger, D.O., and R. Marchesini (2006), 'Execution Moratoriums, Commutations and Deterrence: The Case of Illinois', *Applied Economics*, **38** (9), 967–73.
Cloninger, D.O., and R. Marchesini (2007), 'Reflections on a Critique', *Applied Economic Letters*.
Cooter, R., and T. Ulen (2004), *Law and Economics*, Boston: Pearson Addison Wesley.
Cover, J.P., and P.D. Thistle (1988), 'Time Series, Homicide, and the Deterrent Effect of Capital Punishment', *Southern Economic Journal*, **54**, 615–22.
Dezhbakhsh, H., and J.M. Shepherd (2006), 'The Deterrent Effect of Capital Punishment: Evidence from a Judicial Experiment', *Economic Inquiry*, **44** (3), 512–35.
Dezhbakhsh, H., and P.H. Rubin (2007), 'From the "Econometrics of Capital Punishment" to the "Capital Punishment" of Econometrics: On the Use and Abuse of Sensitivity Analysis', Emory University Working Paper.
Dezhbakhsh, H., P.H. Rubin, and J.M. Shepherd (2003), 'Does Capital Punishment Have a Deterrent Effect? New Evidence from Post Moratorium Panel Data', *American Law and Economics Review*, **5**, 344–76.
Donohue, J., and J. Wolfers (2005), 'Uses and Abuses of Empirical Evidence in the Death Penalty Debate', *Stanford Law Review*, **58**, 789–842.
Ehrlich, I. (1975), 'The Deterrent Effect of Capital Punishment: A Question of Life and Death', *American Economic Review*, **65** (3), 397–417.
Ehrlich, I. (1977), 'Capital Punishment and Deterrence: Some Further Thoughts and Additional Evidence', *Journal of Political Economy*, **85**, 741–88.
Ehrlich, I., and J. Gibbons (1977), 'On the Measurement of the Deterrent Effect of Capital Punishment and the Theory of Deterrence', *Journal of Legal Studies*, **6** (1), 35–50.
Ehrlich, I., and Z. Liu (1999), 'Sensitivity Analysis of the Deterrence Hypothesis: Let's Keep the Econ in Econometrics', *Journal of Law and Economics*, **42** (1), 455–88.
Ekelund, R., J. Jackson, R. Ressler, and R. Tollison (2006), 'Marginal Deterrence and Multiple Murders', *Southern Economic Journal*, **72** (3), 521–41.
Fagan, J. (2006), 'Death and Deterrence Redux: Science, Law and Causal Reasoning on Capital Punishment', *Ohio State Journal of Criminal Law*, **4**, 255–320.
Fagan, J., F. Zimring, and A. Geller (2006), 'Capital Punishment and Capital Murder: Market Share and the Deterrent Effects of the Death Penalty', *Texas Law Review*, **84**, 1803–67.
Grogger, J. (1990), 'The Deterrent Effect of Capital Punishment: An Analysis of Daily Homicide Counts', *Journal of the American Statistical Association*, **85** (410), 295–303.
Hoenack, S.A., and W.C. Weiler (1980), 'A Structural Model of Murder Behavior and the Criminal Justice System', *American Economic Review*, **70**, 327–41.
Katz, L., S.D. Levitt, and E. Shustorovich (2003), 'Prison Conditions, Capital Punishment, and Deterrence', *American Law and Economics Review*, **5** (2), 318–43.
Layson, S. (1983), 'Homicide and Deterrence: Another View of the Canadian Time Series Evidence', *Canadian Journal of Economics*, **16**, 52–73.

Layson, S. (1985), 'Homicide and Deterrence: A Reexamination of the United States Time-Series Evidence', *Southern Economic Journal*, **52** (1), 68–89.
Leamer, E. (1983), 'Let's Take the Con out of Econometrics', *American Economic Review*, **73** (1), 31–43.
Liu, Z. (2004), 'Capital Punishment and the Deterrence Hypothesis: Some New Insights and Empirical Evidence', *Eastern Economic Journal*, **30** (2), 237–58.
Lott, J.R., Jr, and W.M. Landes (1999), 'Multiple Victim Public Shootings', University of Chicago Law and Economics Working Paper.
McAleer, M., and M.R. Veall (1989), 'How Fragile are Fragile Inferences? A Re-evaluation of the Deterrent Effect of Capital Punishment', *Review of Economics and Statistics*, **71**, 99–106.
McManus, W. (1985), 'Estimates of the Deterrent Effect of Capital Punishment: The Importance of the Researcher's Prior Beliefs', *Journal of Political Economy*, **93**, 417–25.
Mocan, H.N., and R.K. Gittings (2003), 'Pardons, Executions, and Homicides', *Journal of Law and Economics*, **46** (2), 453–78.
Mocan, H.N., and R.K. Gittings (2006), 'The Impact of Incentives on Human Behavior: Can We Make It Disappear? The Case of the Death Penalty', NBER Working Papers 12631.
Narayan, P.K., and R. Smyth (2006), 'Dead Man Walking: An Empirical Reassessment of the Deterrent Effect of Capital Punishment Using the Bounds Testing Approach to Cointegration', *Applied Economics*, **38**, 1975–89.
Passell, P., and J.B. Taylor (1977), 'The Deterrent Effect of Capital Punishment: Another View', *American Economic Review*, **67**, 445–51.
Shepherd, J.M. (2004), 'Murders of Passion, Execution Delays, and the Deterrence of Capital Punishment', *Journal of Legal Studies*, **33** (2), 283–321.
Shepherd, J.M. (2005), 'Deterrence versus Brutalization: Capital Punishment's Differing Impacts among States', *Michigan Law Review*, **104**, 203–55.
Wolpin, Kenneth I. (1978), 'Capital Punishment and Homicide in England: A Summary of Results', *American Economic Review: Papers and Proceedings*, **68**, 422–7.
Yunker, J.A. (1976), 'Is the Death Penalty a Deterrent to Homicide? Some Time Series Evidence', *Journal of Behavioral Economics*, **5**, 45–81.
Zimmerman, P.R. (2004), 'State Executions, Deterrence, and the Incidence of Murder', *Journal of Applied Economics*, **7** (1), 163–93.
Zimmerman, P.R. (2006), 'Estimates of the Deterrent Effect of Alternative Execution Methods in the United States: 1978–2000', *American Journal of Economics and Sociology*, **65** (4), 909–41.
Zimring, F.E., and G. Hawkins (1986), *Capital Punishment and the American Agenda*, New York and Cambridge: Cambridge University Press.

9 Corporate crime

*Wallace P. Mullin and Christopher M. Snyder**

1. Introduction

The law and economics literature usually categorized under the heading of corporate crime is actually broader than this (already quite broad) heading. The literature goes beyond crimes (commission of willful illegal acts) to study corporate torts (accidental harms) as well. It is appropriate to study torts as well as crimes because the categorization of acts into torts or crimes is not pre-ordained but is a public-policy choice, which can be informed by economic analysis. The literature is also broader in another way, studying crimes committed not just by incorporated enterprises but by a broad range of business enterprises including closely held firms, non-profit institutions, and government agencies. Many of the economic principles derived in the literature are general enough to apply equally to these different types of enterprise.

Consistent with the broad approach of the literature, then, this chapter will discuss crimes and torts committed by legal enterprises. An enterprise is distinct from an individual (and thus corporate crime is distinct from 'ordinary' crime), in that an enterprise is a hierarchical group of individuals, with low-level employees acting under the direction of a manager (or possibly a tier of managers) who in turn works for the firm's directors and owners. The fundamental issue analyzed by law and economics scholars has been the appropriate level of the hierarchy to target with sanctions in order to deter crime most efficiently. Should sanctions target just the individual within the corporation who was identified as carrying out the criminal act (if it is even possible to identify such an individual)? Or should the whole enterprise be sanctioned in addition or instead, with the burden of the sanctions falling on the enterprise's directors or owners? Should the enterprise be allowed to indemnify a sanctioned employee for fines and legal expenses or vice versa? Such questions are of practical interest because corporate criminal laws in the US and elsewhere have a dual structure of liability, with sanctions targeting both employees and enterprises, and it is useful to determine whether the laws have been designed

* The authors thank Phillip Stocken for insights on the accounting literature, Eric Zitzewitz on the corporate finance literature, and editor Nuno Garoupa for helpful comments. The authors are solely responsible for errors.

efficiently. In addition, all the standard law and economic questions about 'ordinary' crimes and torts – the appropriate level of liability relative to harms caused, the choice between strict liability and negligence rules – can also be asked about corporate crime.

This chapter is complementary to previous surveys on corporate crime published in the 2000 predecessor of this volume, including Kraakman (2000), Lott (2000), and section 11 of Polinsky and Shavell (2000). This chapter also complements other contributions in this volume. Many of the issues regarding corporate crime by legal enterprises could also be analyzed in the context of organized crime, or crimes committed by illegal enterprises. We devote relatively little attention to private versus public enforcement, or administrative enforcement versus criminal enforcement, since those issues are addressed elsewhere in this volume.

We begin by providing updated stylized facts on the nature of corporate crime in Section 2. We then move to the heart of the chapter, the survey of the theoretical corporate crime literature in Sections 3 and 4. Here we highlight the central economic principles that have emerged from this literature regarding the socially optimal structure of sanctions. We will capture a bit of the formalism in this literature by couching our discussion in the context of a principal-agent model. The principal-agent model is particularly attractive because it is the simplest formal way to capture the hierarchical structure that separates corporate from 'ordinary' crime.

The final part of the chapter (Section 5) focuses on a particular category of corporate crime – securities and accounting fraud – in more detail. This category has received considerable recent attention after the Enron, WorldCom and other major fraud cases and the passage of the Sarbanes-Oxley Act in 2002 in response. Another reason for focusing on this category is that it is inherently corporate, whereas other categories (environmental violations, consumer-product fraud, etc.) can be carried out by any sort of enterprise or even individuals. We will survey some of the new theoretical issues raised by securities and accounting fraud and some recent empirical research in the area.

2. Stylized facts

This section updates some stylized facts to help provide an empirical frame of reference for the more abstract analysis in later sections. Our descriptive analysis is closely related to the third section of Cohen (1996) (see also Cohen 1989, 1991, 1992a, 1992b), using a similar data source to update his figures for 1984–90 to the more recent period 2002–06.

The data come from various tables in the US Sentencing Commission's *Sourcebook of Federal Sentencing Statistics* for each of the years 2002–06.

Table 9.1 Enterprises sentenced under Federal Guidelines in past five years

	2002	2003	2004	2005	2006
Total number of cases	252	200	130	187	217
Breakdown by crime category					
Fraud	41%	32%	28%	28%	33%
Environmental	19%	25%	25%	28%	19%
Antitrust	9%	7%	5%	8%	7%
Products	8%	7%	8%	4%	4%
Characteristics of case					
Managerial tolerance	31%	32%	42%	31%	40%
Self-reported	1%	1%	6%	2%	1%
Cooperated with investigation	51%	40%	44%	60%	49%
Court ruling					
Monetary sanction imposed	92%	86%	88%	91%	87%
Inability to pay	43%	37%	28%	36%	42%
Compliance program ordered	15%	12%	16%	19%	20%

Notes: Enterprises sentenced under Chapter 8 of the US Sentencing Commission Guidelines. Dates are fiscal years. 'Breakdown by crime category' entries are percentages of the year's cases falling into each category. 'Products' category includes food, pharmaceuticals, agriculture, and consumer products. 'Characteristics of case' entries are percentages of the cases with non-missing data exhibiting the characteristic. 'Managerial tolerance' is the percentage of cases in which both the enterprise employed ten or more people and its management was involved or tolerated the crime. In the 'Court ruling' entries, 'Monetary sanction' is the percentage of cases in which a fine and/or restitution was ordered and 'Inability to pay' is the number of cases in which the enterprise was unable to pay the entire monetary sanction as a percentage of those in which some monetary sanction was ordered.

Source: US Sentencing Commission (various years), tables 51, 53, and 54.

The data cover all enterprises sanctioned under Chapter 8 of the US Sentencing Commission Guidelines, averaging about 200 cases a year (see the first row of Table 9.1). Broadly speaking, the figures in Table 9.1 vary considerably over time but exhibit no appreciable trends. Around a third of the cases involved fraud, 20 percent involved environmental violations, around 7 percent involved antitrust, and about an equal fraction involved a general 'product' category which includes food, drugs, other consumer products, and agriculture. The remaining cases are scattered across categories, including immigration, bribery, and gambling.

Around a third of the cases (40 percent in 2006) involved managerial tolerance of behavior of lower-level employees. This figure suggests that different models of corporate crime may apply to different cases. In some cases, the employee directly responsible for committing the crime may have been acting in their own interest as against the interest of his employer, but in at least some cases employees seem to have acted with complicity from higher-ups. This finding relates to Alexander and Cohen's (1999) study of about 100 criminal firms matched against an equal number of others according to industry and size. The authors find that the probability of crime decreases with the percentage of the firm's equity held by directors and officers. Their interpretation is that offering more equity to managers aligns their interests with shareholders', and so the higher crime rate in firms in which managers hold less equity is likely to be against the shareholders' interests. Their result may characterize the majority of observations in their sample but does not rule out the possibility that the reverse is true in a minority (consistent with Table 9.1). Further, their result characterizes shareholder preferences given existing criminal sanctions and does not rule out the possibility that shareholders would prefer crime with lower (or no) sanctions.

Table 9.1 indicates that it is rare for enterprises to self-report crimes – only in 1–2 percent of cases – but common for them to cooperate with the investigation once under way – in around half of the cases. The court's judgment almost always involves some monetary sanction. In around 20 percent of the cases, a compliance program is also ordered. Limited enterprise liability appears to be a significant consideration. In around a third of the cases in which a monetary sanction was ordered, the firm could not pay the entire amount, suggesting the importance of the analysis of the judgment-proof firms, which we will discuss in Section 3.4.

Table 9.2 shows few trends in the mean monetary sanction levied on enterprises, around $5 million (in 2006 dollars) over the period. The distribution is highly skewed. For example, the median enterprise sanction in our 2006 sample was $127,800 and the mean was $5.6 million. The mean sanctions vary considerably across categories within a year and across years within a category, often driven by a few notorious cases with huge sanctions. Antitrust cases tend to generate the highest fines, with a mean as high as $46.6 million in 2006.

3. Five theoretical principles

We will organize our discussion of the theoretical literature around five broad economic principles that emerge from the literature concerning the design of socially efficient sanction schemes. Some of the principles are clearly and widely stated in the literature. Others come from our own

Table 9.2 Monetary sanctions on enterprises sentenced under Federal Guidelines

	2002	2003	2004	2005	2006
Means for all cases	5.6	2.6	7.9	4.6	5.6
Means by crime category					
Fraud	8.5	2.2	0.8	0.6	3.9
Environmental	0.5	0.7	1.6	0.8	0.6
Antitrust	6.0	6.8	11.2	41.3	46.6
Products	17.1	8.4	25.7	0.1	1.5
Other	0.2	0.8	0.9	1.1	0.6

Notes: Entries are mean monetary sanctions (fine and/or restitution) across all cases in category in which a positive monetary sanction was imposed. Figures are in millions of 2006 US dollars, adjusted for inflation using the consumer price index. Dates are fiscal years.

Source: US Sentencing Commission (various years), table 52.

synthesis of the literature. In at least one case – for example, the principle that the sanction should be set equal to the harm – we will see that the principle is less robust than the literature might suggest, requiring a discussion of important caveats and nuances, although the principle still serves as a useful benchmark.

To facilitate the discussion and to give a flavor of the content of the theoretical literature, the principles will be presented in the context of a formal model – a principal-agent model of the enterprise. General analyses of corporate crime in a principal-agent model are provided by Kornhauser (1982), Sykes (1984), Newman and Wright (1990), Polinsky and Shavell (1993), Davis (1996), and Garoupa (2000). Our model introduced in Section 3.1 will follow the structure of Garoupa (2000) closely (with some slight changes in assumptions and notation) since his comprehensive analysis nests much of the previous work.

3.1 Model

The enterprise consists of a principal and an agent. One interpretation is that the principal represents the shareholders and the agent an upper-level manager, say the chief executive officer (CEO) of the corporation. Another interpretation is that the principal is an upper-level manager and the agent is an employee whom the manager supervises.

The agent exerts two sorts of effort: productive effort x and what we will call 'criminal effort' a. Criminal effort can be thought of either as deliberate action which causes a harm or as cutting back on precaution which helps prevent an accidental harm. The enterprise's gross return is

$\Pi(x, a)$, assumed to be weakly increasing in both arguments. Productive effort obviously benefits the enterprise. Criminal effort may also increase profits by cutting the cost of hazardous waste disposal in the case of environmental crime or by increasing revenue in the case of the antitrust crime of price fixing. Let $C(x, a)$ be the agent's cost of effort and $B(a)$ his private benefit from criminal effort, which is weakly increasing in a. The model allows the crime to benefit the enterprise directly, benefit the agent directly, or both. For example, dumping hazardous waste in a nearby river rather than in a legal site further away may save the enterprise disposal fees, fuel, and the opportunity cost of the transportation equipment and the agent's time. It may directly benefit the agent to the extent he is the residual claimant of cost savings (say he has to pay the disposal or fees or transportation costs himself or can use the time saved for leisure). Even if $B(a) = 0$, implying that the agent does not benefit directly from criminal effort, as we will see, he may still benefit indirectly through the incentive scheme offered by the principal.

Criminal effort a is socially harmful because it increases the probability $p(a)$ of a harm h to a third party. Assume for now that the state can detect and sanction the harm perfectly but cannot observe a. Therefore, the state can impose a strict-liability rule but not a negligence rule. (In later sections we will adjust the model to allow for imperfect detection and negligence rules.) Let s_p be the monetary sanction on the principal and s_a on the agent, and let $s = s_p + s_a$ be the total sanction under the strict-liability rule. To allow for the possibility of internal transfers, let s_i be the payment from the agent to the principal if the state issues sanctions. A positive value of s_i means that the principal internally sanctions the agent over and above any state sanction; a negative value means that the principal indemnifies the agent for the state sanction (partially or wholly).

The principal cannot control the agent's efforts directly but only indirectly through the incentives provided by the employment contract. Suppose the contract consists of a fixed wage w plus a share β of enterprise profit $\Pi(x, a)$. High values of β provide the agent with incentives to exert effort but are costly to the principal because she retains a smaller profit share for herself. The contract can be thought of as involving explicit profit sharing, perhaps in the form of stock, stock options, or performance bonuses, or can be less explicit, such as a greater likelihood of continued employment or better external job-market prospects if the firm is observed to perform well.

To start, we take the simple case in which all parties (principal, agent, and harmed third party) are risk neutral and leave the more complicated case of risk aversion to be discussed later. The expected payoff of a risk-neutral principal is

$$(1 - \beta)\Pi(x, a) - p(a)(s_p - s_i) - w \tag{9.1}$$

and of a risk-neutral agent is

$$\beta\Pi(x, a) + B(a) - C(x, a) - p(a)(s_a + s_i) + w. \tag{9.2}$$

Social welfare equals the sum of these payoffs minus expected social harm:

$$\Pi(x, a) + B(a) - C(x, a) - p(a)h. \tag{9.3}$$

The equilibrium contract consists of values of β, w, and s_i maximizing the principal's expected payoff in equation (9.1) subject to two constraints. First, since the principal cannot control the agent's efforts directly, the agent will choose x^* and a^* to maximize his expected payoff in equation (9.2). This is called the incentive-compatibility constraint. Second, the agent will only accept the contract and thus participate in the enterprise if his expected payoff in (9.2) exceeds the payoff from the agent's next best opportunity, which we will normalize to zero for simplicity. This is called the participation constraint.

In the next several subsections, we will use the model to present some basic economic principles behind the optimal sanction scheme.

3.2 *Principle: structure of sanctions may be irrelevant*

The first principle is the irrelevance of the structure of state sanctions if the enterprise is able to transfer funds frictionlessly between the principal and the agent using the internal payment s_i. That is, only the total sanction $s_p + s_a$ matters, not how this total is divided into a principal and an agent sanction. A consequence is that the state need not be worried about whether enterprise liability (holding only the principal liable and not the agent, so $s_p > 0$ and $s_a = 0$) is better than agent liability (holding only the agent liable and not sanctioning the principal, so $s_a > 0$ and $s_p = 0$) or vice versa or indeed whether some sophisticated combination is optimal. All lead to the same outcome as long as they have the same total sanction. To our knowledge, Kornhauser (1982) was the first to formally establish the irrelevance principle.

The irrelevance principle holds because, for any total sanction, the principal and agent can effect any division of this by varying s_i. To take a numerical example, suppose that the state targets the enterprise with a sanction of \$100 (and no sanction for the agent). Suppose further that the principal and agent find it jointly optimal to split the sanction between themselves, which they can do by requiring the agent to pay the principal an internal sanction of $s_i = 50$. If instead the state directed the \$100 sanction solely at the agent, the enterprise could obtain the optimal (50,50) division by now having the principal indemnify the agent ($s_i = -50$).

The irrelevance principle can be seen as another instance of the Coase Theorem (Coase 1960), stating that if bargaining is efficient, parties can unravel external rules (property-rights regimes in the usual context, sanction schemes in the present context) to their mutual benefit. In the present context, efficient bargaining requires that the transfer s_i can be set frictionlessly, which in turn requires that both parties have sufficient wealth so they are not liquidity constrained and that there be no state prohibition against such internal payments (we will discuss prohibition of indemnity payments later). If one or the other parties has limited wealth thus constraining the set of possible transfers s_i, then the division of total sanctions between principal and agent will matter. We will discuss this further in Section 3.4 on judgment proofness.

3.3 *Principle: set the sanction equal to the harm*

A second principle in the literature is that the socially optimal rule is to set the sanction equal to the harm h from the crime. Our view is that this rule is a useful benchmark, but we will spend some time arguing that it is less robust than generally understood.

To demonstrate that the sanction should be set equal to harm at least under some conditions, assume the agent in the model in Section 3.1 is risk neutral. It is easy to see what the equilibrium contract is. The principal provides the correct incentives for the agent to exert effort by giving him a 100 percent share of profits ($\beta = 1$) and passing the liability for the principal's sanction completely down to the agent by setting $s_i = s_p$. The principal then extracts all the expected surplus from the enterprise through the fixed wage w, effectively selling the enterprise to the agent for an up-front payment. Substituting these contractual terms into equation (9.2), the agent's objective function becomes

$$\Pi(x, a) + B(a) - C(x, a) - p(a)(s_p + s_a) + w, \tag{9.4}$$

which is identical to the social planner's objective in equation (9.3) – and thus would generate the social optimum – if the total sanction is set equal to harm: $s_p + s_a = h$. Thus the sanction-equals-harm principle holds.

Note the special condition under which the principle holds in this model: the agent is assumed to be risk neutral. This assumption effectively eliminates the hierarchical nature of the enterprise because it allows the principal to exit the scene by selling out his interest to the agent. With only the agent, the setting reverts to an 'ordinary' crime committed by an individual. For 'ordinary' crimes, it is well understood, dating back to Becker (1968), that crime is optimally deterred by setting the sanction equal to the harm, because this forces the potential criminal to internalize the social costs of his actions.

We can argue in fairly general terms why setting the sanction equal to harm is not socially optimal once we depart from the special assumptions that the agent is risk neutral and has unlimited liability. Social welfare involves the sum of three parties' surpluses: the principal, agent, and harmed third party. Without any sanctions, the principal just cares about her own surplus. If the state imposes a sanction *h* on the principal, she perfectly internalizes the third party's surplus. In either case, the agent is left out of the principal's objective function, and so it may not match the social planner's objective, which does include the agent. Thus the equilibrium may not be socially optimal. For all of the articles deriving a proposition regarding the social optimality of setting the sanction equal to the harm – Newman and Wright (1990), Polinsky and Shavell (1993), Garoupa (2000) – it is possible to identify a way in which the model was finessed to leave out the agent's surplus. Accounting for the agent's surplus, Shavell (1997) shows that the optimal sanction may not equal the harm. Other papers have found that the optimal sanction should be less than harm in other settings and for other reasons, including Chu and Qian (1995) (in which a reduced sanction encourages the enterprise to hire a monitor that will report credibly on the agent's negligence) and Pitchford (1995) (in which a reduced sanction feeds back through reduced debt repayments to increase the firm's residual profit claim and ultimately its precaution level).

To summarize the implications of this section for practical policy, the benchmark result that the socially optimal sanction equals harm, which holds for 'ordinary' crimes committed by an individual, may serve as a starting point for calculating the optimal sanction for a corporate crime but will not be precisely correct. Which direction and how much to adjust the sanction away from the benchmark of the harm *h* would require detailed knowledge of individual surplus functions among other things. No practical rules of thumb have yet been provided by the law and economics literature, leading Shavell (1997) to conclude, '. . . the best course for society ordinarily is probably to set damages equal to harm'.

To simplify the discussion, so far we have ignored a well-understood reason for sanctions to diverge from *h*, that is, to adjust for the state's inability to detect crime (and convict the criminal) perfectly. A principle that applies to 'ordinary' as well as corporate crime, again from Becker (1968), is that the sanction should be scaled up by the inverse of the detection probability. To take a numerical example, if the harm is \$100 and the probability of detection 1/3, the optimal sanction should equal \$300. More generally, if σ is the probability that the state detects harm when it occurs, the sanction should scale harm h up by the multiple $1/\sigma$.

3.4 Principle: sanction party that is not judgment-proof

The irrelevance principle suggests that the partition of a given total sanction between the principal and agent does not matter because the enterprise will use internal transfers to unravel any partition. The chief reason the literature has forwarded for the partition to have real consequences is that one or the other party is judgment proof. A judgment-proof party has limited internal resources, preventing it from paying the full amount of a sanction, allowing it to escape the liability for the unpaid portion. Judgment proofness effectively puts a ceiling on the sanction the state can levy on the party. See Shavell (1986), Pitchford (1995), and MacMinn (2002) for further discussion of the judgment-proof problem in a general context and White (1998) in the context of corporate crime.

It is straightforward to adjust the model from Section 3.1 to allow for judgment proofness, although the exact form it takes depends on specifics such as the priority of claims in bankruptcy. Assuming a bankrupt enterprise gives first priority to suppliers and workers and pays fines out of the remaining funds, and that the enterprise has no retained earnings other than those earned in the current period, the effective enterprise sanction s_p is constrained to be no greater than $(1 - \beta)\,\Pi(x, a) + s_i - w$. Turning to the agent, assuming he has savings ℓ in addition to his current-period earnings, the effective agent sanction s_a is constrained to be no greater than $\beta\Pi(x, a) - s_i + w + \ell$. The savings term can be negative ($\ell < 0$), reflecting the possibility that the agent consumes some of his assets before the fines are imposed. In addition to savings, a positive term $\ell > 0$ can reflect harm that the state can impose on an assetless agent by imprisoning him. (If this interpretation is followed, the modeler should be careful to subtract the agent's harm from being imprisoned, in addition to the costs to the state of running the prison system, from social welfare.)

The literature has derived the principle that if the agent's judgment proofness prevents him from bearing the full amount of a sanction, the principal should be sanctioned as well and vice versa. To take a numerical example, suppose that the state finds it optimal to levy a sanction of \$100 on an enterprise and is deciding how to partition it between the principal and agent. If the agent with internal resources of \$40 and otherwise limited liability is made solely liable for the \$100, it will end up only paying out \$40 and the enterprise will escape \$60 of the liability. The result will be that the enterprise will have too much incentive to cause harm (or equivalently too little incentive to invest in precaution to avoid harm) since it is not bearing the full \$100 sanction. Instead, supposing the principal is unconstrained in its internal resources, the state could divide the sanction, with $60 of the liability going to the principal and $40 to the agent. Other options might be equivalent. The principal could be made solely liable for the $100 and assuming the principal will require the agent to pay some internal sanction between $0 and $40. Or the state could place the $100 liability initially with the agent but then require the principal to make up any unpaid portion due to the agent's inability to pay.

If the agent is an individual manager or employee of the enterprise, the prospect that he will be judgment proof is a very realistic one. As we will see in the empirical section, sanctions for all categories of crime can average in the millions of dollars. Even with moderate harms, if the state's probability of detection is low, as discussed in the previous section, the resulting sanction may be scaled up considerably, quickly resulting in a sanction too high for the typical individual to afford. If the principal represents the shareholders of a corporation, it is often more likely that such a principal would have more internal resources and would be less likely to be judgment proof than the agent. This is not always the case. The principal in some instances may be an individual or a small enterprise that hires a larger enterprise as an agent. For example, the agent may be a large firm specializing in disposal of hazardous waste, as in Ringleb and Wiggins (1990), or a large retailer selling a smaller manufacturer's product.

The discussion in this section can be summarized in the principle that sanctions should be directed away from judgment-proof parties and toward parties with deep pockets. In most real-world settings, this means that sanctions should tend to be directed toward the principal rather than the agent, thus arguing for enterprise liability rather than agent liability. If the state has recourse to a conditional liability scheme, whereby the agent is liable up to his ability to pay and the principal for the remainder (as outlined in one of the options in the numerical example above) or vice versa, then the judgment-proofness principle becomes less important as a guide to public policy.

3.5 Principle: body best able to control agent should sanction him

The principles discussed so far do not provide an especially strong guide as to where within the enterprise the state should place liability. The principle presented in this section related to the ability to control the agent is in our view the strongest and clearest principle. Simply stated, the state should impose enterprise (principal) liability – thereby delegating control of the agent to the enterprise – when the enterprise is better able to control the agent than the state can. The state should impose agent liability, thereby intervening in the control of the agent, only if the state has some advantage over the enterprise in controlling the agent. Stated in these terms, the principle seems almost tautological: the party better able to control the agent should control the agent. Further discussion is required to understand which party is better able to control the agent and under what conditions.

In many instances, the principal can better control the agent than the state can. The principal may be involved in the day-to-day operations of the enterprise and may routinely observe the agent's conduct. The principal may be able to provide incentives based on the fine-grained information she obtains, perhaps in a formal legal contract, perhaps in an informal contract enforced by long-run reputation. The state as an outsider may understand little about the operation of the enterprise and may have none of this fine-grained information. The state may not know enough to identify which specific agent from a team or hierarchy was responsible for the crime, and indeed it may be the case that no single individual but the whole team or hierarchy may have contributed. In such instances, the state should sanction the enterprise and rely on the enterprise to do its own internal sanctioning based on its better ability to monitor and control its agents. If no further considerations intervene, the presumption based on the control principle is that the state should impose enterprise liability.

There are circumstances under which the state is a better monitor and controller of the agent and thus under which agent liability is socially optimal. The principal may have limited ability to punish the agent. For example, the principal may have the power only to fire the agent but not to force payments from him. The state may be able to force such payments by garnishing future wages earned at other firms. Even if the agent is judgment proof, the state may be able to increase the punishment level by imprisoning him. Moreover, criminal sanctions imposed by the state may carry more severe additional reputational penalties than internal firm sanctions. The state may have better investigative powers to determine what criminal effort a was undertaken by the agent and condition punishments on that.

Segerson and Tietenberg (1992) and Polinsky and Shavell (1993) provide formal models in which agent liability can be socially optimal under some circumstances. Reputational penalties are discussed in more detail in Section 4.3. The merits of conditioning sanctions on intent, effort, and/or criminal attempts are discussed in more detail in Sections 4.1 and 4.2. See Khalil, Martimort, and Parigi (2007) for a general theoretical analysis of the monitoring of an agent by several principals, with applications to financial contracting.

The ability to control the agent shows up in various places in the formal model from Section 3.1. In the basic model, the principal can increase the agent's incentives to take appropriate effort (x) and crime (a) actions by giving him a larger profit share β. The principal can also adjust the internal sanction s_i. An increase in s_i (recalling this is a payment from agent to principal) would lead the agent to choose a lower level of a. Moving beyond the basic model, one could assume that by expending some cost, say m, the principal can increase its ability to monitor the agent's criminal effort a, perhaps providing a signal $\tilde{a}$ of a that is increasingly precise as m is increased. The principal may improve its control of the agent by building in payments conditional on $\tilde{a}$ in the agent's incentive contract. Alternatively, monitoring may allow the principal to exclude certain extreme behaviors, which could be modeled as a reduction in the domain of possible a the agent could choose.

The government could likewise expend resources to improve its monitoring of the agent. The state may have better or worse monitoring powers than the enterprise, and so have a different mapping from its monitoring expenditures m into signals $\tilde{a}$ of the agent's behavior. As noted in Section 3.4, the state's ability to imprison and to seize an agent's savings may allow it to punish a judgment-proof agent more harshly than his employer could.

The control principle clarifies why, given that enterprise liability seems efficient in many contexts, the state does not just pick a single scapegoat enterprise A with deep pockets and make it liable for all corporate crimes and torts in the economy. Presumably enterprise A has little or no ability to monitor and control the employees of other enterprises and so making A liable would not deter crime and torts by these other enterprises. Generally speaking, an enterprise should only be liable for the actions of its own employees or employees of affiliated enterprises. Consistent with this idea, the doctrine of *respondent superior*, which is the basis in the common law for enterprises to be jointly and severally liable for corporate crimes and torts committed by their agents, explicitly requires the agent's wrong to have been committed in the scope of work for a principal as a condition for that principal to be held liable. See Kraakman (2000) for further discussion.

Perverse incentives may be created if the principal can escape liability by demonstrating that it did not have the ability to control the agent. If, as in the model sketched above in this section, the principal's control over the agent is captured as an expenditure m on a monitoring system, the principal would be led to underinvest in m. To avoid these perverse incentives, the state may base its sanctioning policy on what reasonable control mechanisms should have been in place for such an enterprise rather than on the actual level of control the enterprise had in a particular case. Alternatively, the state can induce the principal to adopt appropriate monitoring systems through direct fiat or by having a negligence standard for monitoring systems.

A caveat to the control principle is that even if the state is better than the principal at monitoring the agent, the state may still not want to focus sanctions exclusively on the agent and ignore the principal. Sanctioning the principal will lead it to internalize the social harm from its overall level of production or other activity and to bring this level more in line with the social optimum (see Shavell 1980).

The principle here applies to more complicated hierarchies than just principal-agent structures. In practice, an enterprise may have external parties such as lawyers, auditors, insurers, and banks that are crucial to its operations and may serve as independent monitors of the enterprise's and its employees' activities. Kraakman (1984, 1986, 2000) refers to these parties as 'gatekeepers'. Especially when deterrence is limited by the enterprise's judgment proofness, deterrence may be improved by exposing these gatekeepers to criminal liability. As the control principle suggests, extending liability to gatekeepers will tend to be worthwhile when they are good monitors and controllers of the enterprise and agent. Besides the cites in Kraakman (2000), additional recent work on the gatekeeper idea include Mattiacci and Parisi (2003), Ganuza and Gomes (2007), and a large body of work by John Coffee, including Coffee (2003, 2004).

3.6 Principle: state should exploit the Prisoner's Dilemma

The literature on self-reporting (including Malik 1993, Kaplow and Shavell 1994, Levitt and Snyder 1997, and Innes 1999a, 1999b) suggests that integrating self-reports into law enforcement may be of some value: for example, economizing on enforcement costs or providing early warnings that can be used to mitigate further damage. However, the main message of this literature is that self-reporting is of limited value in increasing deterrence because, in order to induce the individual to self-report, there are limits to how harshly he can be punished.

Reporting may be more useful for corporate crimes than for crimes committed by individuals because the former involves multiple parties (at the very least two, the principal and the agent) who can be played off against each other in a version of the Prisoner's Dilemma. A characteristic of the Prisoner's Dilemma and related games is that parties would be jointly better off cooperating on one set of actions (being silent), but self-interest leads them to choose another (informing on the other player). A number of deterrence schemes proposed in the corporate-crime literature can be shown to derive their value from setting up a version of the Prisoner's Dilemma game between the enterprise and agent, inducing each to report on the other. These schemes are able to reward reporting without having to reduce sanctions very much. The state may try to induce the enterprise to report on the agent (as in the monitoring literature), the agent to report on the enterprise (as in the whistleblowing literature), or have parties race to report each other (as in the corporate-leniency literature). See Feess and Walzl (2004) for a game-theoretic analysis of self-reporting in criminal teams.

Turning first to the monitoring literature, Arlen (1994), Chu and Qian (1995), and Arlen and Kraakman (1997) provide models in which partially forgiving enterprise sanctions can increase its incentive to monitor its agent when such monitoring can increase the likelihood of uncovering the agent's criminal acts (see Garoupa 2000 for a synthesis). Ex post – after the agent has undertaken the criminal act – the enterprise may have little hesitation in reporting on the agent if this information is used against the agent alone and not against the enterprise. If the state uses the information to penalize the enterprise as well, however, this moves the enterprise from the Prisoner's Dilemma game to the self-reporting game, reducing the enterprise's incentive to set up a monitoring system and to make honest reports. Arlen (1994) finds the perverse result that increased corporate liability can reduce the enterprise's incentive to monitor so much that it results in more corporate crime. Arlen and Kraakman (1997) note further that it is not enough for the state to be neutral toward an honestly reporting enterprise. Reporting may be costly enough for the enterprise ex post that it cannot commit to report the results of its monitoring unless given a leniency reward sufficient to offset the cost.

The antitrust literature has studied whether and how to use corporate-leniency programs to unravel cartels by effectively setting up a Prisoner's Dilemma among the cartels' members which has them 'race to the courthouse'. Spagnolo (2008) provides an overview of the evolution of policy and the relevant academic literature, which includes Spagnolo (2000, 2004), Ellis and Wilson (2003), Hinloopen (2003), Motta and Polo (2003), and Harrington (2007). Spagnolo (2004) abstracts from the hierarchical nature of firms, treating them as unitary actors, and analyzes leniency toward a firm that blows the whistle on the cartel. He studies socially optimal leniency programs under the constraint that they be self-financing, implying that rewards to whistleblowing firms can be no greater than the total fines on offenders. He derives conditions under which the optimal policy places severe sanctions on offenders, coupled with rewards only for the first reporting firm. Intuitively, the sanction and leniency scheme maximizes the wedge between the payoff from cooperating in the cartel and the payoff from cheating on the cartel and then reporting the cartel to the authorities. Spagnolo's (2004) result that only the first reporting firm receives leniency provides a rationale for this feature in the 1993 US Department of Justice leniency program. Interestingly, there is a limit to how high the offender sanctions should be set. Otherwise the cartel could exploit the leniency program as a disciplining device to sustain collusion. The cartel could threaten to blow the whistle on itself and subject its members to high sanctions if any firm undercut the high collusive price.

Net (positive) transfers to self-reporting firms are ruled out in the Department of Justice leniency program. Aubert, Rey, and Kovacic (2006) examine the theoretical benefits of relaxing this constraint and offering bounties to agents who blow the whistle on their colluding employers. Such rewards make cartels less profitable because a colluding firm has to 'bribe' its employees not to become whistleblowers. Aubert, Rey, and Kovacic (2006) also note that communication is necessary for cartel success (see Cramton and Palfrey 1990 for a theoretical argument and Genesove and Mullin 2001 for an empirical illustration through the experience of the Sugar Institute). But that communication produces evidence – a paper trail – that can be used in a prosecution or in a leniency application.

Miller (2007) provides an empirical evaluation of the 1993 US Department of Justice leniency program. He advances a formal model allowing him to map unobservables (including parameters of the rates of cartel formation and dissolution) into observables (the number of detected cartels), generating testable predictions about the effects of leniency programs. His empirical estimates indicate that the 1993 leniency policy had substantial effects on deterrence – lowering the rate of cartel formation by over 40 percent – and detection – raising the rate at which formed cartels are detected by over 60 percent.

Dyck, Morse, and Zingales (2007) assembled detailed data from press accounts of all reported fraud cases for large US corporations over the past decade (230 cases in all). Parties with an explicit mandate to detect fraud (regulators and auditors) were responsible for only 36 percent of detections; other sources – including in order of importance employees, the media, financial analysts, and competitors – made up the rest. Employee whistleblowers receive a penalty (firing, quitting under duress, or altered responsibilities) far more often than a reward. In industries in which employee whistleblowers do receive monetary rewards (the Federal Civil False Claims Act provides the whistleblower with a share of the money recovered from frauds against the government), such as healthcare, employees account for a significantly larger share of detections. Bowen, Call, and Rajgopal (2007) analyze a sample of corporations accused of accounting misreporting, comparing those for which the misreporting was revealed by whistleblowing to a control sample. Although it is difficult to infer causation, the authors find significant differences between the two samples regarding firm size, past stock performance, and industry concentration, among other variables. Whistleblowing increased the probability of the restructuring of the board of directors, including removal of the CEO, removal of insiders, and an increase in attendance at board meetings.

Recently, there have been growing concerns that the ability to set up a Prisoner's Dilemma between the enterprise and agent shifts too much power to prosecutors. In 2007, the indictments were dismissed for 13 of the 16 employees of one of the big-four US accounting firms, KPMG, for illegal tax-shelter activity. The judge found that federal prosecutors inappropriately used the threat of indicting KPMG – which could be a death sentence for an accounting firm – to coerce it into cutting off indemnification of its employees' legal fees. As a result of this case and other negative publicity, the US Department of Justice modified its guidelines on prosecution of enterprises, supplanting the 2003 Thompson Memorandum with the 2006 McNulty Memorandum (see US Department of Justice 2003 and 2006).

4. The structure of sanctions in finer detail

In this section, we delve into some of the finer details of the structure of sanctions that have been analyzed in the literature.

4.1 Strict liability versus negligence

According to the doctrine of *respondent superior*, which guides common law toward corporate crime, enterprises face a strict-liability rather than a negligence rule for the crimes and torts of their agents. Kraakman (2000) provides an extensive survey, which we will summarize in this section, of the relative merits of enterprise strict liability versus the alternative of a negligence rule, which requires the enterprise to exert due care in monitoring and controlling the agent's criminal behavior.

Many of the textbook arguments for strict liability over and above negligence for 'ordinary' torts and crimes (see Shavell 1980 for an early reference) carry over to the case of an enterprise in the corporate-crime context. Even if the enterprise has difficulty controlling its agents' criminal or precautionary behavior, strict liability will still lead the enterprise to internalize some of the harm of its commercial activities and to curtail these activities appropriately. A negligence rule would allow the enterprise to escape any liability by exceeding a standard of care and thus lead the enterprise to undertake socially too much of the commercial activity leading to the harm. Furthermore, determining the appropriate standard for something as complicated as enterprise monitoring of agents is terribly difficult and may lead to considerable uncertainty if it is left to the courts to make ex post determinations. In the face of this uncertainty, enterprises may undertake inefficiently too little commercial activity.

On the other hand, certain unique features of the corporate-crime context may weigh in favor of a negligence rule. As pointed out by Arlen (1994), and discussed in Section 3.6, enterprises will have too little incentive to monitor their employees and report on their misdeeds if that information increases the chance that the harm is discovered and the enterprise faces liability. A negligence rule specifying a reasonable level of monitoring could provide the enterprise with better monitoring incentives. Even if there is no issue of hiding crimes, as Arlen and Kraakman (1997) note, the enterprise may have difficulty committing to internal monitoring and sanctioning schemes. Once the agent has undertaken the crime or tort, carrying out monitoring and sanctioning functions may simply add an ex post cost for the enterprise and under a strict liability rule would not save it any fines. Under a negligence rule, the enterprise would be better able to commit to monitoring and sanctioning the agent because by so doing it may be able to avoid liability.

Hybrid regimes are also possible. Chu and Qian (1995) study a legal rule under which the enterprise is strictly liable for harm if and only if the agent is found to be negligent. Such a rule may capture the practical distinction between a corporate crime and a corporate tort because some sort of intentionality or negligence is required for crimes. Under this legal rule, the enterprise faces a tradeoff in setting up a monitoring system. By hiring an honest monitor, the enterprise can incorporate the monitor's reports of the agent's effort into an incentive scheme that provides stronger incentives for the agent to behave in a non-negligent way. The drawback of honest reporting is that this increases the chance that the court uncovers any agent negligence. The social optimum is always designed to induce the enterprise to hire an honest monitor, sometimes accomplishing this by reducing the negligence standard below the first-best level or reducing the enterprise's vicarious liability below the full social harm.

4.2 Civil versus criminal penalties

A number of articles have questioned whether corporate wrongs should be tried under criminal law or whether civil law would be a better forum. Fischel and Sykes (1996) note that, while good economic arguments can be advanced for applying criminal liability to individuals, the arguments are less strong for enterprises. One of the main benefits of the criminal-law system is that the state has recourse to imprisonment as a punishment in addition to fines. Imprisonment can be valuable if the defendent's judgment proofness limits the highest effective fine that can be levied against him. Since enterprises are not physical entities that can be imprisoned, the main benefit of imprisonment is irrelevant in their case.

In arguing for the virtue of applying civil rather than criminal law to enterprises, Fischel and Sykes (1996) list a number of drawbacks of the criminal law. (See also Parker 1996; Lynch 1997; Simpson 2002; and James, Kirkbride, and Letza 2005). (a) Pre-specified criminal penalties may not be as flexibly tied to the harm from each particular act as are civil penalties. (b) Civil law does a better job of tracking total fines levied jointly against principals and agents to ensure that the fines together do not greatly exceed the harm caused. Criminal proceedings against the enterprise and agents may result in 'double damages' being assessed, leading to a situation of overdeterrence. (c) The social stigma associated with a criminal conviction may be much higher than with a civil penalty, and when added to the explicit criminal penalties may also lead to overdeterrence. Overdeterrence has a number of social costs, including possibly excessive litigation, excessive internal monitoring by the enterprise, and underinvestment and underproduction by the enterprise. (d) Criminal law often involves at least an implicit negligence standard. Fischel and Sykes (1996) prefer strict liability, citing the difficulty in computing an appropriate standard without introducing judicial error. Faced with an uncertain standard, a textbook result is that parties will engage in excessive precaution. (e) The standard of proof may be inordinately high in criminal cases (beyond a reasonable doubt), and the civil standard (preponderance of the evidence) more appropriate for corporate wrongs.

Arguments can also be advanced in the opposite direction, favoring criminal penalties for enterprises. Although prison is not an option for them, enterprises can be put on probation, including being excluded from certain lines of business and from future government contracts. Probation may be a useful option for punishment in addition to fines. Indeed, of the 217 cases sentenced in 2006 according to Chapter 8 of the US Sentencing Guidelines, organizations were ordered to serve over a month of probation in three-quarters of the cases (US Sentencing Commission, 2006, table 53). Another argument in favor of criminal penalties for enterprises is based on Section 3.3, where we saw that the socially optimal level of enterprise liability may not be as simple as the social harm (or a multiple of harm inversely proportional to the conviction probability). The optimum might involve a complicated combination of factors that would be better analyzed in advance and set into guidelines rather than being determined on an ad hoc basis by a judge in a particular case. Fischel and Sykes (1996) themselves note that a benefit of the criminal-law system is that deterrence can be enhanced by levying criminal penalties on detected attempts as well as realized harms (civil penalties generally require an actual harm to be compensated).

4.3 Reputational penalties

As noted in the previous section, in addition to any explicit state sanctions, the enterprise may suffer implicit market or reputational penalties after detection of a wrong. The reputational penalties can be modeled by adding the term r to the principal's objective function from equation (9.1):

$$(1 - \beta)\Pi(x, a) - p(a)(r + s_p - s_i) - w. \tag{9.5}$$

As Garoupa (2000) shows, starting from a sanction scheme (s_p^*, s_a^*) that delivers the first-best in the absence of reputational penalties, the principal's sanction s_p^* would need to be reduced by r in order to return to the first-best in the presence of reputational penalties. If the reputational penalties are ignored, overall sanctions will be too high, resulting in overdeterrence (see Lott 1996 for further analysis).

Reputational penalties may be beneficial if limited liability of principal or agent prevented the original sanction scheme (s_p^*, s_a^*) from delivering the first best. Additional reputational penalties may help move the sanction scheme closer to an unconstrained social optimum.

Empirical research tends to find reputational penalties only for crimes against parties in a position to extract such a penalty (for example, fraud) and not for crimes against unrelated third parties (for example, environmental violations). For corporations involved in fraud, Karpoff and Lott (1993) find that the loss in stock market value after the announcement of the crime swamps the anticipated criminal penalties, a difference attributed to reputational penalties. For environmental violations, Karpoff, Lott, and Wehrly (2005) attribute most of the decline in the stock-market value of convicted firms to regulatory and legal actions rather than reputational penalties. Alexander (1999) confirms this variety of results in a study of cross-section of crime categories. Reputational penalties also require the signal of wrongdoing to be sufficiently informative. Helland (2006) finds that, except in a limited set of cases, allegations of fraud against officers and directors in private securities class actions do not yield a reputational penalty for them, suggesting that such allegations do not carry much credence in the market.

4.4 Agent indemnification

Indemnification payments offer a way for the enterprise and agent to share the costs of being prosecuted and convicted of a corporate crime. Referring to the model in Section 3.1, a positive value of s_i indicates that the agent must indemnify the enterprise's losses and a negative value indicates that the enterprise must indemnify the agent's losses. This section will focus on the latter sort of indemnification (that is, where the enterprise indemnifies the agent) because this is a widespread practice among corporations.

Agent indemnification can either be provided directly by the firm or by purchase of third-party directors and officers (D&O) insurance. State incorporation laws differ as to what costs the firm may indemnify, but most allow firms to reimburse agents' legal costs and losses from settlements, judgments, and fines.

Public policy is ambivalent toward agent indemnification. Certain policies strongly encourage it; for example, Delaware law requires a firm to provide directors and officers insurance as a condition for incorporation there. On the other hand, officials have recently begun questioning the wisdom of allowing firms to use indemnification to shift all liability away from the agent – see, for example, the speech by the Chairman of the US Securities and Exchange Commission, William Donaldson (Donaldson 2003).

One can see the economic intuition for both sides. The benefit of allowing agent indemnification is that the larger enterprise with perhaps diversified owners is likely to be able to bear risk more efficiently than the agent. It is thus in a position to insure the agent through indemnification against the risk of mistaken prosecutions or judicial error in assessing sanctions. Besides the direct utility provided by insurance, allowing agent indemnification may avoid some of the social costs due to overdeterrence. The drawback of allowing indemnification is that it may remove a powerful tool for crime deterrence. Referring to the model, the agent may get a direct private benefit $B(a)$ from crime, but most of his benefit may come indirectly through his share β of the enterprise's increased profit $\Pi(x, a)$. The agent may put much more weight on the sanction s_a targeted directly at him. Thus it may be very difficult for the enterprise to induce the agent to engage in criminal behavior unless it unravels the agent's sanction by making an indemnification payment equal to this amount: $s_i = -s_a$.

The common law tries to capture the social benefits of agent indemnification while avoiding some of the drawbacks by declaring liability that stems from willful agent misconduct to be uninsurable under the law (Johnston 1978; see also Harrington and Niehaus 1998). The public policy question then reduces to determining standards for the willfulness of criminal conduct above which indemnification would be forbidden. The standards would need to be sufficiently high or else promises to indemnify or to make D&O insurance payments would not have much credibility and the social benefits of indemnification would be lost. The difficulty in denying insurance coverage for willful misconduct is illustrated by the case of Bank of America, fined \$13 billion for its role in the WorldCom fraud. Lloyd's of London agreed to pay its share of Bank of America's insured liability, but Swiss Re and Kemper held out and had to be sued by Bank of America (Fleming and Mollenkamp 2005).

Mullin and Snyder (2009) study the social optimality of forbidding agent indemnification in a model in which the enterprise benefits from its agent's crime (at least in the absence of state sanctions). The enterprise seeks to induce the agent to commit the crime through the design of the incentive scheme. A crucial feature of the model (see Beckenstein and Gabel 1986 and Schinkel and Tuinstra 2006 for related assumptions about antitrust enforcement) is that the state has a probability of making type I prosecution errors – possibly convicting an honest party – as well as the usual type II errors – failing to convict a guilty party. As suggested by Stone (1980), Kraakman (1984), and Privileggi, Marchese, and Cassone (2001), holding constant the level of sanctions, the state can deter more corporate crimes if it forbids agent indemnfication. Forbidding indemnification removes an instrument that would be used in a contract to induce crime.

Nevertheless, Mullin and Snyder (2009) show that forbidding indemnification is socially inefficient. The result follows from employee risk aversion. Banning indemnification prevents the firm from insuring the employee against type I prosecution errors. Since the employee is risk averse, the loss of this insurance is socially costly. Crime can be deterred more efficiently by sanctioning only the firm because a firm sanction is just a transfer between the risk-neutral firm and government involving no loss of social surplus.

It might be countered that the state is not always free to increase the effective level of enterprise sanctions, in particular when the enterprise's limited liability makes it judgment proof. However, as long as state sanctions receive priority over indemnification payments in bankruptcy proceedings, a judgment-proof firm that is unable to meet its fine obligations would also be unable to meet its indemnification obligations even if the law did not explicitly forbid indemnification. Hence judgment proofness is not an argument for actively forbidding indemnification.

Mullin and Snyder (2009) do find a role for forbidding indemnification: when there is scope for the agent to cooperate with prosecutors to raise the probability the enterprise is convicted. For some parameters, it is beneficial for prosecutors to forgive a portion of the agent's sanction as a reward for cooperation. A fully indemnified employee gains nothing from this reward, so forbidding indemnification is necessary to secure the agent's cooperation. This is conceptually similar to issues surrounding corporate leniency policies.

Regarding the enterprise's choice between (a) indemnifying the agent itself or (b) buying third-party insurance such as D&O insurance, Holderness (1990) suggests that a benefit of bringing in a third-party insurer is to add an independent monitor of the agent's criminal behavior, effectively bringing in another gatekeeper, to use Kraakman's (1986) term.

Holderness (1990) offers a range of empirical evidence in support of this hypothesis as against a risk-shifting hypothesis.

5. Securities fraud

This section discusses an important special case of corporate crime: securities fraud, a violation of a public corporation's duty to report mandated financial information that has been audited according to accepted accounting principles. In the United States, the main reporting requirements are quarterly 10-Q reports and more extensive annual 10-K reports filed with the Securities and Exchange Commission.

We devote a separate section to securities fraud for several reasons. The recent wave of high-profile corporate scandals – including, most notoriously, Enron – involved securities fraud (see Healy and Palepu 2003 for an analysis of the accounting issues involved in the Enron case). In response to these scandals, the US Congress passed a major reform of securities laws, the Sarbanes-Oxley Act of 2002. The scandals and policy reforms have generated considerable academic research; indeed, securities fraud is the most active area of corporate-crime research, generating a body of research in the accounting and corporate-finance fields as well as law and economics. Finally, securities fraud is perhaps the canonical corporate crime. While individuals or non-corporate enterprises can commit an environmental crime, for example, by dumping pollution in a river, a securities fraud generally involves a public corporation.

In the rest of the section, we will discuss some conceptual issues regarding securities fraud, connecting this special case back to our previous general analysis of corporate crimes. To provide a theoretical framework, we will analyze a recent paper by Bar-Gill and Bebchuk (2002) in some detail. We will then survey the empirical literature on the causes and consequences of financial misreporting and survey preliminary evidence on the effects of the Sarbanes-Oxley Act on the US financial market. See Arlen and Carney (1992) for an earlier survey of the law and economics of securities fraud.

5.1 Conceptual issues

Securities frauds add several interesting wrinkles to the conceptual framework we presented earlier for general corporate crimes. Rather than the harm h accruing to some external party that obviously needs protection from the state as in the model in Section 3.1, the harmed party is often an existing or new investor in the corporation, so an existing or prospective principal in the hierarchy. The harm is typically that the investor overpays for a security relative to the full-information price. (There are exceptions: under-reporting earnings in Aboody and Kasznik 2000 lowers the exercise price for the manager's options and in Liberty and Zimmerman 1986 improves management's position in labor negotiations.) The manager may derive one of a number of benefits from inflating the firm's position: retaining his job and the associated private benefits for a longer period (for example, Fudenberg and Tirole 1995), obtaining a higher stock price for inside trades (for example, Bar-Gill and Bebchuk 2002) or as an agent for current rather than future shareholders (for example, Dye 1988), or jamming a principal's observation of his effort in order to increase incentive pay (for example, Goldman and Slezak 2006).

Given that the harmed party is potentially a sophisticated market participant and the harm seems more like an income transfer than a true loss of social welfare, it needs to be argued why the state would need to intervene in the market and mandate information disclosure and auditing procedures. Diamond and Verrecchia (1991), Baiman and Verrecchia (1996), and especially the Verrecchia (2001) survey identify several channels through which misreporting may lead to true social-welfare losses. Misreporting may reduce the liquidity of the market, lowering an individual's surplus from holding securities. Misreporting may distort the market signals and divert financial capital away from high-value uses toward low-value ones. Misreporting may reduce the value of information in structuring managers' incentive contracts. Misreporting may reduce the ability to use incentive contracts based on the reported information to provide incentives to management.

Even though there may be social losses from misreporting, it is not clear why the private market could not solve the problem without intervention from state mandates. Grossman and Hart (1980) argue that if information is verifiable ex post, an information cascade may arise, resulting in full revelation of managers' private information. Suppose a manager had private information about the firm's sales growth. Managers whose information was above some threshold would have an incentive to share this with the market to boost the stock price. But managers just below the threshold would prefer to announce as well to separate themselves from the average firm that did not make an announcement. In this way, all, except perhaps for the manager with the worst news, would announce their private information. Information only cascades in this way under special assumptions, including costless announcements and perfect verifiability ex post of the announced information. Indeed, one role of the state in the market would be to provide a mechanism for such ex post verification.

Even if conditions for an information cascade are absent, the private market may still provide full revelation. A fundamental principle of the economics of contracts, the revelation principle, says that investors, as principals of the firm, can structure an optimal contract so that the manager has incentives to announce his private information truthfully. (See Myerson 1979 for general theory on the principle and Arya, Glover, and Sunder 1998 and Lambert 2001 for its application to the specific context of financial disclosure). For the revelation principle to hold, the reporting agent must be able to communicate his information completely, the principal must have access to a full range of contracting options, and the principal must be able to commit to the contractual mechanism. In practice, transactions costs may prevent fully flexible communication and contract design. Commitment may be even more problematic. In the face of significant ex-post auditing and reporting costs, the principal and agent would have an incentive to renegotiate the contract. Commitment would be especially difficult if the manager working by himself or the manager and current investors working together could expropriate the surplus of a third party – new investors – by misreporting. When the conditions for the revelation mechanism do not hold, optimal contracts can involve at least some earnings smoothing (shifting revenue recognition earlier if earnings are expected to be low and delaying revenue recognition in high-earnings periods), if not outright fraudulent misreporting, rather than truthful reporting (see Dye 1988, Fudenberg and Tirole 1995, and Goldman and Slezak 2006 for theoretical models).

Additional factors may constrain the extent of misreporting. A corporation that continually inflates earnings period after period will be increasingly likely to have its misreporting detected. Sunder's (1997) 'law of the conservation of income' suggests that corporations cannot continually inflate earnings without the deficit eventually being detected. Maintaining a long-run reputation may provide incentives for honest reporting (Benabou and Laroque 1992, Stocken 2000). The addition of an auditor may improve the quality of financial statements and reporting. The auditor serves as what we referred to in Section 3.5 as a gatekeeper. The auditor may not be a perfect control on misreporting because he may shirk on auditing effort (Dye 1993) and may be captured by the management through promises of continued retainer for auditing or additional consulting services (Pagano and Immordino 2007).

5.2 Theoretical model

To make some of the ideas from the previous section more concrete, it is worthwhile discussing a theoretical model in more detail. We will cover Bar-Gill and Bebchuk (2002) here because it is one of the most complete and useful frameworks on securities fraud in the law and economics literature.

The timeline for their model begins with the manager's undertaking actions, which are costly to the firm, that facilitate over-reporting earnings later. Such investments might include, as Enron did, setting up special-purpose entities to hide liabilities, or choosing trading partners on the basis of willingness to structure transactions flexibly rather on the basis of price. The manager's investment is analogous to the criminal action a in Section 3.1. The manager then learns whether the firm's type – its baseline revenue will be at the end of the game – is high or low. The manager then issues an earnings report. If the firm's type is high, the manager will report this truthfully. If the firm is the low type, the manager is more likely to be able to misreport this as high, the more he invested initially in facilitating misreporting. The manager then trades his own stock, and these trades may or may not be observable to the market, depending on the model variant.

Next, the firm is presented with a follow-on investment opportunity, which will require raising outside equity to fund. The funds raised by this secondary offering depend on the earnings report. Since the high type is partially pooled with the low type, it does not obtain as high an equity price as under full information. If the discount is sufficiently high, it may forgo the follow-on investment opportunity, even though this may be commonly know to have positive net present value. On the other hand, a misreporting low type may receive a sufficient price premium over full information that it undertakes the secondary equity offering even though the follow-on project has negative net present value. Finally, baseline revenue and the revenue from the follow-on project are realized and paid to investors.

There are several sources of real social costs of misreporting in the model. The manager's ex-ante investment in facilitating misreporting is a real cost. An additional cost is that capital is misdirected away from positive net present value projects for the high-revenue firms and toward possible negative net present value projects for low-revenue firms. The authors find that the manager invests more in facilitating misreporting the lower is a parameter measuring the stringency of legal and accounting controls, the more stock the manager owns, and the less public his insider trades.

5.3 Empirical studies of misreporting

A large literature, much of it in accounting and corporate finance, analyzes the characteristics of firms accused of misreporting financial information compared to a matched sample of control firms (usually the match is to a firm in the same industry that is closest in size). It is impossible to uncover all instances of misreporting since much of it is presumably hidden. Instead, most studies use a sample of firms (around 200 in a typical study) required by the Securities and Exchange Commission to restate earnings during a certain period of time because of a violation of generally accepted accounting principles. The studies take the restatement as an indication of the earlier misreporting by the corporation, so in the subsequent discussion we will use 'restatement' and 'misreporting' synonymously. Many studies find significant differences between the characteristics of misreporting firms and matched controls, whether in the design of the manager's compensation scheme or in the firm's financial or corporate-governance structure. Healy and Palepu (2001) survey the earlier literature.

Regarding the structure of managerial compensation, CEO's stock options appear to be the sole piece of his compensation package related to misreporting (Burns and Kedia 2006; Efendi, Srivastava, and Swanson 2007). Erickson, Hanlon, and Maydew (2006) find no relationship between executive compensation and misreporting, but this may in part be due to their small sample (50 observations) because they restrict attention to violations rising to the level of criminal fraud. Regarding the firm's financial structure, Richardson, Tuna, and Wu (2003) find a correlation between outstanding debt levels (and also the market's expectations of future growth) and the probability of restatements. Regarding the firm's corporate-governance structure, Dechow, Sloan, and Sweeney (1996) find many significant differences between misreporting and control firms, including the CEO's also being chairman of the board, the founder of the firm continuing as CEO, the absence of an audit committee, dominance of the board by insiders, and the absence of an outside blockholder. Further analysis by Agrawal and Chadha (2005) finds fewer significant correlates between misreporting and corporate governance (first, having no director with financial experience on the board or audit committee and, second, having a member of the founding family as CEO).

A number of studies find a relationship between the timing of activities by a manager or the stock market and misreporting. Efendi, Srivastava, and Swanson (2007) find restatements are more likely if the firm recently raised new debt or equity. Beneish (1999) finds that the managers of restating firms are more likely to sell equity holdings and exercise stock appreciation rights. Desai, Krishnamurthy, and Venkataraman (2006) find that restatements are preceded by a run-up in short selling, and this short selling is more intense when accounting accruals appear to be inflated, suggesting that some market participants are able to anticipate the market's response to what they see is suspect financial reporting.

Core (2001) notes that it is difficult to infer causation from empirical studies of restatements because the structure of managerial compensation, corporate governance, and financial structure are determined jointly with misreporting. These structures might be designed to mitigate the problem of misreporting rather than the cause of it. Core (2001) also points to the possibility of substantial measurement error. One overlooked source of error is in assuming that the window during which the firm is misreporting ends exactly with the issuance of the formal restatement. Often a long period intervenes during which the firm may institute reforms to remedy reporting violations. The consequences of errors in measuring event windows can be severe. Karpoff, Lee, and Martin (2007) painstakingly track restating firms throughout the entire relevant period and show that 93 percent of responsible managers lose their jobs as a result, most being fired. If instead of observing event windows, they had used the assumptions maintained in previous studies, they would have missed almost half of the firings of responsible managers because these happened far in advance of the formal restatement. Leaving aside Core's (2001) criticisms, the body of empirical findings is consistent with the model and conclusions of Bar-Gill and Bebchuk (2002). Misreporting appears to be used to increase the price at which the manager sells his equity and to reduce the firm's cost of raising new capital. The manager's stock holdings (stock options more specifically) appear to increase incentives to misreport.

5.4 Sarbanes-Oxley Act and other securities laws

We will focus on the Sarbanes-Oxley Act because it is such a major recent reform, although at the end of the subsection we will also review studies of earlier reforms and some macroeconomic evidence on the efficiency of securities laws. See Seligman (2003) for a history of US securities laws and Zitzewitz (forthcoming) for a survey of economic analyses of these laws. Enriques and Volpin (2007) survey corporate governance reforms in Europe.

The provisions of the Sarbanes-Oxley Act, summarized in Coates (2007), generally strengthened auditing requirements, in particular creating a new regulatory body (the Public Company Accounting Oversight Board) and requiring CEOs and auditors to certify material weaknesses in their accounting control systems. To maintain independence between auditors and the audited firm, the act requires firms to rotate their auditing partners every five years and restricts auditors from providing consulting services for client firms, which used to be a significant source of revenue and a possible lever for management to control auditors' reports.

While the tradeoffs involved in the act are clear – enhancing the credibility of financial reports at the cost of increased compliance, auditing, and liability expenses – the net effect is more controversial, with Coates (2007) seeing it as positive but Romano (2005) calling it 'quack corporate governance'. Empirical work is challenging because the act affected all public firms at once, so it is difficult to find a control sample to compare with affected firms. The study by the Committee on Capital Markets Regulation (2006) offered evidence that the market for initial public offerings was drying up in the US compared to Europe, but it is difficult to separate the time-series effect of Sarbanes-Oxley from secular trends in increased competition for financial services outside the US. Rezaee and Jain (2006) and Zhang (2007) find mixed results in their study of the aggregate US stock-market reaction to passage of the act. Chhaochharia and Grinstein (2007) compare the abnormal returns of a portfolio of firms that were already compliant with the act's provisions before its passage to those that were not. They find a 6–20 percent abnormal return, suggesting net benefits to shareholders. Dividing the sample by firm size, they find negative abnormal returns for small firms that were previously non-compliant, suggesting substantial fixed costs of complying with the new provisions that are a larger relative burden for small firms. Hochberg, Sapienza, and Vissing-Jorgensen (2007) find that firms whose management lobbied harder against the act had greater positive abnormal stock returns from its passage, providing additional evidence that the act generally produced at least small net benefits. Li, Pincus, and Rego (2008) find that firms' abnormal stock returns to Sarbanes-Oxley legislative events were positively related to measures of firms' earnings management, and they conclude that investors anticipated that Sarbanes-Oxley would constrain earnings management.

Several studies have looked at policy changes preceding Sarbanes-Oxley. Choi (2006) and Johnson, Nelson, and Pritchard (2006) examined the Private Securities Litigation Reform Act of 1995, aimed at discouraging nuisance class-action lawsuits by imposing sanctions on lawsuits judged to be frivolous, limiting attorney fees, insulating forward-looking statements from suits, among other provisions. The studies generally suggest that the act has been successful in reducing frivolous lawsuits, but at the margin some meritorious suits seem to have been discouraged as well, with some evidence of a resulting decline in deterrence of securities fraud. Greenstone, Oyer, and Vissing-Jorgensen (2006) analyzed the effects of mandated disclosure in the Securities Act amendments of 1964.

La Porta, Lopez-de-Silanes, and Shleifer (2006) analyze the effectiveness of the broad suite of securities laws in a cross-section of 49 countries. They find that mandatory disclosure laws and low standards for establishing liability are the most important factors in determining the level of development of a country's stock market; the stringency of public enforcement does not appear to matter. The results suggest that securities laws work best if they facilitate private contracting rather than substituting for it through public monitoring.

6. Conclusion

The volume of cites provided in this chapter across the literatures of law and economics, accounting, and corporate finance may overwhelm the reader new to the area of corporate crime. Besides this chapter, earlier surveys in the 2000 predecessor of this volume – Kraakman (2000), Lott (2000), and section 11 of Polinsky and Shavell (2000) – are useful introductions to the topic. A good view of the modeling techniques would be provided by reading Polinsky and Shavell (1993) and Garoupa (2000). On securities fraud, Arlen and Carney (1992) provide a useful survey and Bar-Gill and Bebchuk (2002) an accessible but comprehensive formal model. The body of empirical work is relatively extensive on securities fraud. Chhaochharia and Grinstein (2007) provide a good example of this work, and it is topical because it covers the effects of the major recent policy reform in the US, the Sarbanes-Oxley Act.

Bibliography

Aboody, David, and Kasznik, Ron (2000), 'CEO Stock Option Awards and the Timing of Corporate Voluntary Disclosures', **29**, *Journal of Accounting and Economics*, 73–100.

Agrawal, Anup, and Chadha, Sahiba (2005), 'Corporate Governance and Accounting Scandals', **48** *Journal of Law and Economics*, 371–406.

Alexander, Cindy R. (1999), 'On the Nature of the Reputational Penalty for Corporate Crime: Evidence', **42** *Journal of Law and Economics*, 489–526.

Alexander, Cindy R. (2004), 'Corporate Crime, Markets and Enforcement: A Review', in Sjogren, Hans and Skogh, Goran (eds), *New Perspectives on Economic Crime*, Cheltenham, UK and Northampton, MA, USA: Edward Elgar, pp. 20–41.

Alexander, Cindy R., Arlen, Jennifer, and Cohen, Mark A. (1999), 'The Effect of Federal Sentencing Guidelines on Penalties for Public Corporations', **12** *Federal Sentencing Reporter*, 20–26.

Alexander, Cindy R., and Cohen, Mark A. (1996), 'New Evidence on the Origins of Corporate Crime', **17** *Managerial and Decision Economics*, 421–35.

Alexander, Cindy R., and Cohen, Mark A. (1999), 'Why Do Corporations Become Criminals? Ownership, Hidden Actions, and Crime as an Agency Cost', **5** *Journal of Corporate Finance*, 1–34.

Alexander, Janet Cooper (1996), 'Rethinking Damages in Securities Class Actions', **48** *Stanford Law Review*, 1487–537.

Arlen, Jennifer (1994), 'The Potentially Perverse Effects of Corporate Criminal Liability', **23** *Journal of Legal Studies*, 833–67.

Arlen, Jennifer (1998), 'Corporate Crime and its Control', in Newman, Peter (ed), *New Palgrave Dictionary of Economics and the Law*, New York: Macmillan, pp. 492–7.

Arlen, Jennifer, and Carney, William J. (1992), 'Vicarious Liability for Fraud on Securities Markets: Theory and Evidence', **25** *University of Illinois Law Review*, 691–740.

Arlen, Jennifer, and Kraakman, Reiner (1997), 'Controlling Corporate Misconduct: An Analysis of Corporate Liability Regimes', **72** *New York University Law Review*, 687–779.

Arya, Anil, Glover, Jonathan, and Sunder, Shyam (1998), 'Earnings Management and the Revelation Principle', **3** *Review of Accounting Studies*, 7–34.

Aubert, Cécile, Rey, Patrick, and Kovacic, William (2006), 'The Impact of Leniency and Whistle-blowing Programs on Cartels', **24** *International Journal of Industrial Organization*, 1241–66.

Baiman, Stanley, and Verrecchia, Robert E. (1996), 'The Relation among Capital Markets, Financial Disclosure, Production Efficiency, and Insider Trading', **34** *Journal of Accounting Research*, 1–22.

Bar-Gill, Oren, and Bebchuk, Lucian Arye (2002), 'Misreporting Corporate Performance', Harvard Law School John M. Olin Center Discussion Paper no. 400.

Baysinger, Barry D. (1991), 'Organization Theory and the Criminal Liability of Organizations', **71** *Boston University Law Review*, 341–76.
Baysinger, Barry D. and Butler, Henry N. (1985), 'The Role of Corporate Law in the Theory of the Firm', **28** *Journal of Law and Economics*, 179–91.
Beckenstein, Alan R. and Gabel, H. Landis (1986), 'The Economics of Antitrust Compliance', **52** *Southern Economic Journal*, 673–92.
Becker, Gary S. (1968), 'Crime and Punishment: An Economic Approach', **76** *Journal of Political Economy*, 169–217.
Benabou, Roland, and Laroque, Guy (1992), 'Using Privileged Information to Manipulate Markets: Insiders, Gurus, and Credibility', **107** *Quarterly Journal of Economics*, 921–58.
Beneish, Messod D. (1999), 'Incentives and Penalties Related to Earnings Overstatements that Violate GAAP', **74**, *Accounting Review*, 425–57.
Black, Bernard, Cheffins, Brian, and Klausner, Michael (2006), 'Outside Director Liability', **58** *Stanford Law Review*, 1055–159.
Black, Bernard, and Kraakman, Reinier (1996), 'A Self-enforcing Model of Corporate Law', **109** *Harvard Law Review*, 1911–82.
Block, Michael K. (1991), 'Optimal Penalties, Criminal Law, and the Control of Corporate Behavior', **71** *Boston University Law Review*, 395–420.
Bowen, Robert M., Call, Andrew C., and Rajgopal, Shiva (2007), 'Whistle-blowing: Target Firm Characteristics and Economic Consequences', University of Washington Business School Working Paper.
Burns, Natasha, and Kedia, Simi (2006), 'The Impact of Performance-based Compensation on Misreporting', **79**, *Journal of Financial Economics*, 35–67.
Byam, John I. (1982), 'The Economic Inefficiency of Corporate Criminal Liability', **73** *Journal of Criminal Law and Criminology*, 582–603.
Calkins, Stephen (1997), 'Corporate Compliance and the Antitrust Agencies' Bi-Modal Penalties', **60** *Law and Contemporary Problems*, 127–67.
Chhaochharia, Vidhi, and Grinstein, Yaniv (2007), 'Corporate Governance and Firm Value: The Impact of the 2002 Governance Rules', **62** *Journal of Finance*, 1789–825.
Choi, Stephen J. (2006), 'Do the Merits Matter Less after the Private Securities Litigation Reform Act?', **23** *Journal of Law, Economics, and Organization*, 598–626.
Chu, C.Y. and Qian, Yingyi (1995), 'Vicarious Liability under a Negligence Rule', **15** *International Review of Law and Economics*, 305–22.
Coase, Ronald H. (1960), 'The Problem of Social Cost', **3** *Journal of Law and Economics*, 1–44.
Coates, John C. (2007) 'The Goals and Promise of the Sarbanes-Oxley Act', **21** *Journal of Economic Perspectives*, 91–116.
Coffee, John C., Jr (1980), 'Corporate Crime and Punishment: A Non-Chicago View of the Economics of Criminal Sanctions', **17** *American Criminal Law Review*, 419–76.
Coffee, John C., Jr (1981), '"No Soul to Damn: No Body to Kick": An Unscandalized Inquiry into the Problem of Corporate Punishment', *Michigan Law Review*, 386–459.
Coffee, John C., Jr (2003), 'The Attorney as Gatekeeper: An Agenda for the SEC', **103** *Columbia Law Review*, 1293–1316.
Coffee, John C., Jr (2004), 'Gatekeeper Failure and Reform: The Challenge of Fashioning Relevant Reforms', **84** *Boston University Law Review*, 301–64.
Cohen, Mark A. (1989), 'Corporate Crime and Punishment: A Study of Social Harm and Sentencing Practice in the Federal Courts, 1984–1987', **26** *American Criminal Law Review*, 605–60.
Cohen, Mark A. (1991), 'Corporate Crime and Punishment: An Update on Sentencing Practice in the Federal Courts, 1988–1990', **71** *Boston University Law Review*, 247–80.
Cohen, Mark A. (1992a), 'Environmental Crime and Punishment: Legal/Economic Theory and Empirical Evidence on Enforcement of Federal Environmental Statutes', **82** *Journal of Criminal Law and Criminology*, 1054–108.
Cohen, Mark A. (1992b), 'Sentencing Guidelines and Corporate Criminal Liability in the US', **4** *Business and the Contemporary World*, 140–57.

Cohen, Mark A. (1996), 'Theories of Punishment and Empirical Trends in Corporate Criminal Sanctions', **17** *Managerial and Decision Economics*, 399–412.
Committee on Capital Markets Regulation (2006), 'Interim Report', revised December 5, 2006, accessed at www.capmktsreg.org/pdfs/11.30Committee_Interim_ReportREV2.pdf.
Core, John E. (2001), 'A Review of the Empirical Disclosure Literature: Discussion', **31** *Journal of Accounting and Economics*, 4414–56.
Cox, James D. (1997), 'Private Litigation and the Deterrence of Corporate Misconduct', **60** *Law and Contemporary Problems*, 1–38.
Cramton, Peter C. and Palfrey, Thomas R. (1990), 'Cartel Enforcement with Uncertainty about Costs', **31** *International Economic Review*, 17–47.
Davis, Michael L. (1996), 'The Impact of Rules Allocating Legal Responsibilities between Principals and Agents', **17** *Managerial and Decision Economics*, 413–20.
Dechow, Patricia, Sloan, Richard G., and Sweeney, Amy P. (1996), 'Causes and Consequences of Earnings Manipulation: An Analysis of Firms Subject to Enforcement Actions by the SEC', **13** *Contemporary Accounting Research*, 1–36.
DeMott, Deborah A. (1997) 'Organizational Incentives to Care about the Law', **60** *Law and Contemporary Problems*, 39–66.
Desai, Hemang, Krishnamurthy, Srinivasan, and Venkataraman, Kumar (2006), 'Do Short Sellers Target Firms with Poor Earnings Quality? Evidence from Earnings Restatements', **11** *Review of Accounting Studies*, 71–90.
Diamond, Douglas W., and Verrecchia, Robert E. (1991), 'Disclosure, Liquidity, and the Cost of Capital', **46** *Journal of Finance*, 1325–59.
Dickens, William T., Katz, Lawrence F., Lang, Kevin, and Summers, Lawrence H. (1989), 'Employee Crime and the Monitoring Puzzle', **7** *Journal of Labor Economics*, 331–47.
Donaldson, William H., Chairman (2003), 'Remarks before the New York Financial Writers Association', June 5, 2003, accessed at www.sec.gov/news/speech/spch060503whd.htm.
Dyck, Alexander, Morse, Adair, and Zingales, Luigi (2007), 'Who Blows the Whistle on Corporate Fraud?', University of Chicago Working Paper.
Dye, Ronald A. (1988), 'Earnings Management in an Overlapping Generations Model', **26** *Journal of Accounting Research*, 195–235.
Dye, Ronald A. (1993), 'Auditing Standards, Legal Liability, and Auditor Wealth', **101** *Journal of Political Economy*, 887–914.
Easterbrook, Frank H., and Fischel, Daniel R. (1991a), 'Optimal Damages in Securities Cases', **52** *University of Chicago Law Review*, 611–52.
Easterbrook, Frank H., and Fischel, Daniel R. (1991b), *The Economic Structure of Corporate Law*, Cambridge, MA: Harvard University Press.
Edgerton, Henry W. (1927), 'Corporate Criminal Responsibility', **36** *Yale Law Journal*, 827–44.
Efendi, Jan, Srivastava, Anup, and Swanson, Edward P. (2007), 'Why do Corporate Managers Misstate Financial Statements? The Role of Option Compensation and Other Factors', **85** *Journal of Financial Economics*, 667–708.
Ellis, Christopher J., and Wilson, Wesley W. (2003), 'Cartels, Price-fixing, and Corporate Leniency Policy: What Doesn't Kill Us Makes Us Stronger', University of Oregon Department of Economics Working Paper.
Enriques, Luca, and Volpin, Paolo (2007), 'Corporate Governance Reforms in Continental Europe', **21** *Journal of Economic Perspectives*, 117–40.
Epple, Dennis and Raviv, Artur (1978), 'Product Safety: Liability Rules, Market Structure, and Imperfect Information', **68** *American Economic Review*, 80–95.
Erickson, Merle, Hanlon, Michelle, and Maydew, Edward L. (2006), 'Is There a Link between Executive Equity Incentives and Accounting Fraud?', **44** *Journal of Accounting Research*, 113–43.
Feess, Eberhard, and Walzl, Markus (2004), 'Self-reporting in Optimal Law Enforcement when there are Criminal Teams', **71** *Economica*, 333–48.
Finch, Vanessa (1994), 'Personal Accountability and Corporate Control: The Role of Directors' and Officers' Liability Insurance', **57** *Modern Law Review*, 880–915.

Fischel, Daniel R., and Sykes, Alan O. (1996), 'Corporate Crime', **25** *Journal of Legal Studies*, 319–50.
Fleming, Charles and Mollenkamp, Carrick (2005), 'Insurers, Banks Clash over Claims for Enron, WorldCom Settlements', *Wall Street Journal*, December 25, A1.
Fudenberg, Drew, and Tirole, Jean (1995), 'A Theory of Income and Dividend Smoothing Based on Incumbency Rents', **103** *Journal of Political Economy*, 75–93.
Gans, Joshua S. (1998), 'Incentive Contracts, Optimal Penalties and Enforcement', Melbourne Business School Working Paper no. 98–06.
Ganuza, Juan Jose, and Gomez, Fernando (2007), 'Should we Trust the Gatekeepers? Auditor's and Lawyer's Liability for Clients' Misconduct', **27** *International Review of Law and Economics*, 96–109.
Garoupa, Nuno (2000), 'Corporate Criminal Law and Organization Incentives: A Managerial Perspective', **21** *Managerial and Decision Economics*, 243–52.
Genesove, David, and Mullin, Wallace P. (2001), 'Rules, Communication, and Collusion: Narrative Evidence from the Sugar Institute Case', **91** *American Economic Review*, 379–98.
Goldman, Eitan, and Slezak, Steve L. (2006), 'An Equilibrium Model of Incentive Contracts in the Presence of Information Manipulation', **80** *Journal of Financial Economics*, 603–26.
Greenstone, Michael, Oyer, Paul, and Vissing-Jorgensen, Annette (2006), 'Mandated Disclosure, Stock Returns, and the 1964 Securities Acts Amendments', **121** *Quarterly Journal of Economics*, 399–460.
Grossman, Sanford, and Hart, Oliver (1980), 'Disclosure Laws and Takeover Bids', **35** *Journal of Finance*, 323–34.
Harrington, Joseph E. (2007), 'Optimal Corporate Leniency Programs', **56** *Journal of Industrial Economics*, 215–46.
Harrington, Scott E., and Niehaus, Gregory R. (1998), *Risk Management and Insurance*, New York: McGraw Hill.
Harvard Law Review Editors (1946), 'Criminal Liability of Corporations for Acts of their Agents', **60** *Harvard Law Review*, 283–98.
Hay, Bruce, and Spier, Kathryn E. (2005), 'Manufacturer Liability for Harm Caused by Consumers to Others', **95** *American Economic Review*, 1700–11.
Healy, Paul M., and Palepu, Krishna G. (2001), 'Information Asymmetry, Corporate Disclosure, and the Capital Markets: A Review of the Empirical Disclosure Literature', **31** *Journal of Accounting and Economics*, 405–40.
Healy, Paul M., and Palepu, Krishna G. (2003), 'The Fall of Enron', **17** *Journal of Economic Perspectives*, 3–26.
Helland, Eric (2006), 'The Reputational Penalties and the Merits of Class-action Securities Litigation', **49** *Journal of Law and Economics*, 365–95.
Hinloopen, Jeroen (2003), 'An Economic Analysis of Leniency Programs in Antitrust Law', **151** *De Economist*, 415–32.
Hochberg, Yael V., Sapienza, Paola, and Vissing-Jorgensen, Annette (2007), 'A Lobbying Approach to Evaluating the Sarbanes-Oxley Act of 2002', National Bureau of Economic Research Working Paper no. 12952.
Holderness, Cliff (1990), 'Liability Insurers as Corporate Monitors', **10** *International Review of Law and Economics*, 115–29.
Innes, Robert (1999a), 'Remediation and Self-reporting in Optimal Law Enforcement', **72** *Journal of Public Economics*, 379–93.
Innes, Robert (1999b), 'Self-Policing and Optimal Law Enforcement When Violator Remediation is Valuable', **107** *Journal of Political Economy*, 1305–25.
James, Annabelle, Kirkbride, James, and Letza, Steve (2005), 'Does the Criminal Law have a Role in the Corporate Setting?', **1** *International Journal of Business Governance and Ethics*, 259–76.
Johnson, Marilyn F., Nelson, Karen K., and Pritchard, A. C. (2006), 'Do the Merits Matter More? The Impact of the Private Securities Litigation Reform Act', **23** *Journal of Law, Economics, and Organization*, 626–52.

Johnston, Joseph F., Jr (1978), 'Corporate Indemnification and Liability Insurance for Directors and Officers', **33** *The Business Lawyer*, 1993–2053.

Joyce, Jon M. (1989) ,'The Effect of Firm Organizational Structure on Incentives to Engage in Price-Fixing', **7** *Contemporary Policy Issues*, 19–35.

Kadish, Sanford H. (1963), 'Some Observations on the Use of Criminal Sanctions in Enforcing Economic Regulations', **30** *University of Chicago Law Review*, 423–49.

Kaplow, Louis, and Shavell, Steven (1994), 'Optimal Law Enforcement with Self-reporting Behavior', **102** *Journal of Political Economy*, 583–606.

Karpoff, Jonathan M., Lee, D. Scott, and Martin, Gerald S. (2007), 'The Consequences to Managers for Financial Misrepresentation', Texas A&M University Working Paper.

Karpoff, Jonathan, and Lott, John R., Jr (1993), 'The Reputational Penalty Firms Bear from Committing Criminal Fraud', **36** *Journal of Law and Economics*, 757–802.

Karpoff, Jonathan, Lott, John R., Jr, and Wehrly, Eric (2005), 'The Reputational Penalties for Environmental Violations: Empirical Evidence', **48** *Journal of Law and Economics*, 653–75.

Kennedy, Christopher (1985), 'Criminal Sentences for Corporations: Alternative Fining Mechanisms', **73** *California Law Review*, 443–82.

Khalil, Fahad, Martimort, David, and Parigi, Bruno (2007), 'Monitoring a Common Agent: Implications for Financial Contracting', **135** *Journal of Economic Theory*, 35–67.

Khanna, V. S. (1996) 'Corporate Criminal Liability: What Purpose Does it Serve?', **109** *Harvard Law Review*, 1477–534.

Kornhauser, Lewis (1982), 'An Economic Analysis of the Choice between Enterprise and Personal Liability for Accidents', **70** *California Law Review*, 1345–92.

Kraakman, Reinier (1984), 'Corporate Liability Strategies and the Costs of Legal Controls', **93** *Yale Law Journal*, 857–98.

Kraakman, Reinier (1986), 'Gatekeepers: The Anatomy of a Third-party Enforcement Strategy', **2** *Journal of Law, Economics and Organization*, 53–104.

Kraakman, Reinier (1991), 'Toward Unlimited Shareholder Liability for Corporate Torts', **100** *Yale Law Journal*, 1879–934.

Kraakman, Reinier (2000), 'Vicarious and Corporate Civil Liability', in Bouckaert, Boudewijn and De Geest, Gerrit (eds), *Encyclopedia of Law and Economics*, Volume II, Cheltenham, UK and Northampton, MA, USA: Edward Elgar, pp. 669–81.

La Porta, Rafael, Lopez-de-Silanes, Florencio, and Shleifer, Andrei (2006), 'What Works in Securities Laws?', **61** *Journal of Finance*, 1–32.

Lambert, Richard A. (2001) 'Contracting Theory and Accounting', **32** *Journal of Accounting and Economics*, 3–87.

Laufer, W.S. (1996), 'Corporate Culpability and the Limits of the Law', *Business Ethics Quarterly*, 311–24.

Lederman, Eliezer (1985), 'Criminal Law, Perpetrator and Corporation: Rethinking a Complex Triangle', **76** *Journal of Criminal Law and Criminology*, 285–340.

Lee, Frederic P. (1928), 'Corporate Criminal Liability', **28** *Columbia Law Review*, 1–28.

Leigh, L.H. (1982) 'The Criminal Liability of Corporations and Other Groups: A Comparative View', **80** *Michigan Law Review*, 1508–28.

Leung, S.F. (1991), 'How to Make the Fine Fit the Corporate Crime? An Analysis of Static and Dynamic Optimal Punishment Theories', **45** *Journal of Public Economics*, 243–56.

Levitt, Steven, and Snyder, Christopher M. (1997), 'Is No News Bad News? Information Transmission and the Role of Early Warning in the Principal Agent Model', **28** *RAND Journal of Economics*, 641–61.

Li, Haidan, Morton Pincus, and Sonja Rego (2008), 'Market Reactions to Events Surrounding the Sarbanes-Oxley Act of 2002 and Earnings Management', **51** *Journal of Law and Economics*, 111–34.

Liberty, Susan E., and Zimmerman, Jerold L. (1986), 'Labor Union Contract Negotiations and Accounting Choices', **61** *Accounting Review*, 692–712.

Lofquist, William S. (1993), 'Organizational Probation and the U.S. Sentencing Commission', **525** *Annals of the American Acadamy of Political and Social Science*, 157–69.

Lofquist, William S., Cohen, Madeline, and Rabe, Gary (1996), *Debating Corporate Crime: An Interdisciplinary Examination of the Causes and Control of Corporate Misconduct*, Cincinatti, OH: Anderson Publishing.

Lott, John R., Jr (1996), 'The Level of Optimal Fines to Prevent Fraud When Reputations Exist and Penalty Clauses are Unenforceable', **17** *Managerial and Decision Economics*, 363–80.

Lott, John R., Jr (2000), 'Corporate Criminal Liability', in Bouckaert, Boudewijn and De Geest, Gerrit (eds), *Encyclopedia of Law and Economics*, Volume V, Cheltenham, UK and Northampton, MA, USA: Edward Elgar, pp. 492–501.

Lynch, Gerard E. (1997), 'The Role of Criminal Law in Policing Corporate Misconduct', **60** *Law and Contemporary Problems*, 23–65.

Macey, Jonathan R. (1991), 'Agency Theory and the Criminal Liability of Organizations', **71** *Boston University Law Review*, 315–40.

Malik, Arun (1993), 'Self-reporting and the Design of Policies for Regulating Stochastic Pollution', **24** *Journal of Environmental Economics and Management*, 241–57.

MacMinn, Richard (2002), 'On the Judgment Proof Problem', **27** *Geneva Papers on Risk and Insurance Theory*, 143–52.

Mattiacci, Giuseppe Dari, and Parisi, Francesco (2003), 'The Cost of Delegated Control: Vicarious Liability, Secondary Liabiity and Mandatory Insurance', **23** *International Review of Law and Economics*, 453–75.

Miller, Nathan H. (2007) 'Strategic Leniency and Cartel Enforcement', University of California, Berkeley Working Paper.

Morehead Dworkin, Terry (2007), 'Sox and Whistleblowing', **105** *Michigan Law Review*, 1757–80.

Motta, Massimo, and Polo, Michele (2003), 'Leniency Programs and Cartel Prosecution', **21** *International Journal of Industrial Organization*, 347–79.

Mullin, Wallace P., and Snyder, Christopher M. (2009), 'Should firms be allowed to Indemnify their Employees for Sanctions?', *Journal of Law, Economics, and Organization*; doi:10.1093/jleo/ewn027, 1–24.

Myerson, Roger (1979). 'Incentive-compatibility and the Bargaining Problem', **47** *Econometrica*, 61–73.

Newman, Harry A., and Wright, David W. (1990), 'Strict Liability in a Principal-agent Model', **10** *International Review of Law and Economics*, 219–31.

Pagano, Marco, and Immordino, Giovanni (2007), 'Optimal Regulation of Auditing', **63** *CESifo Economic Studies*, article 1.

Parker, Jeffrey S. (1989), 'Criminal Sentencing Policy for Organizations: The Unifying Approach of Optimal Penalties', **26** *American Criminal Law Review*, 513–604.

Parker, Jeffrey S. (1996), 'Doctrine for Destruction: The Case of Corporate Criminal Liability', **17** *Managerial and Decision Economics*, 381–98.

Parker, Jeffrey S., and Atkins, Raymond A. (1999), 'Did the Corporate Criminal Sentencing Guidelines Matter? Some Preliminary Empirical Observations', **42** *Journal of Law and Economics*, 423–53.

Pitchford, Rohan (1995), 'How Liable Should a Lender Be? The Case of Judgment-proof Firms and Environmental Risk', **85** *American Economic Review*, 1171–86.

Polinsky, A. Mitchell, and Shavell, Steven (1993), 'Should Employees be Subject to Fines and Imprisonment Given the Existence of Corporate Liability?', **13** *International Review of Law and Economics*, 239–57.

Polinsky, A. Mitchell, and Shavell, Steven (2000), 'Public Enforcement of Law', in Bouckaert, Boudewijn and De Geest, Gerrit (eds), *Encyclopedia of Law and Economics*, Volume V, Cheltenham, UK and Northampton, MA, USA: Edward Elgar, pp. 307–344.

Privileggi, Fabio, Marchese, Carla, and Cassone, Alberto (2001), 'Agent's Liability versus Principal's Liability when Attitudes toward Risk Differ', **21** *International Review of Law and Economics*, 181–95.

Rezaee, Zabihollah, and Jain, Pankaj K. (2006), 'The Sarbanes-Oxley Act of 2002 and Security Market Behavior: Early Evidence', **23** *Contemporary Accounting Research*, 629–54.

Richardson, Scott, Tuna, Irem, and Wu, Min (2003), 'Predicting Earnings Management: The Case of Earnings Restatements', University of Pennsylvania Wharton School Working Paper.
Ringleb, Al, and Wiggins, Steven N. (1990), 'Liability and Large-scale, Long-term Hazards', **98** *Journal of Political Economy*, 574–95.
Romano, Roberta (2005) 'The Sarbanes-Oxley Act and the Making of Quack Corporate Governance', **114** *Yale Law Journal*, 1521–612.
Salzburg, Stephen A. (1991), 'The Control of Criminal Conduct in Organizations', **71** *Boston University Law Review*, 421–38.
Schinkel, Maarten Pieter, and Tuinstra, Jan (2006), 'Imperfect Competition Law Enforcement', **24** *International Journal of Industrial Organization*, 1267–97.
Segerson, Kathleen, and Tietenberg, Tom (1992), 'The Structure of Penalties in Environmental Enforcement: An Economic Analysis', **23** *Journal of Environmental Economics and Management*, 179–200.
Seligman, Joel (2003), *The Transformation of Wall Street: A History of the SEC and Modern Corporate Finance* (third edition), Chicago, IL: Aspen Publishers.
Shavell, Steven (1980), 'Strict Liability Versus Negligence', **9** *Journal of Legal Studies*, 1–25.
Shavell, Steven (1986), 'The Judgment Proof Problem', **6** *International Review of Law and Economics*, 45–58.
Shavell, Steven (1997), 'The Optimal Level of Corporate Liability Given the Limited Ability of Corporations to Punish their Employees', **17** *International Review of Law and Economics*, 203–13.
Simpson, Sally S. (2002), *Corporate Crime, Law, and Social Control*, Cambridge, UK: Cambridge University Press.
Spagnolo, Giancarlo (2000), 'Self-defeating Antitrust Laws: How Leniency Programs Solve Bertrand's Paradox and Enforce Collusion in Auctions', Fondazione Eni Enrico Mattei Working Paper no. 52.00.
Spagnolo, Giancarlo (2004), 'Divide et Impera: Optimal Leniency Programmes', CEPR Discussion Paper no. 4840.
Spagnolo, Giancarlo (2008), 'Leniency and Whistleblowers in Antitrust', in P. Buccirossi (ed.), *Handbook of Antitrust Economics*, Cambridge, MA and London, UK: MIT Press, 259–304.
Stessens, Guy (1994) 'Corporate Criminal Liability: A Comparative Perspective', **43** *International and Comparative Law Quarterly*, 493–520.
Staw, B.M. and Szwajkowski, E. (1975), 'The Scarcity-munificence Component of Organisational Environments and the Commission of Illegal Acts', **20** *Administrative Science Quarterly*, 345–54.
Stocken, Phillip C. (2000), 'Credibility of Voluntary Disclosure', **31** *RAND Journal of Economics*, 359–74.
Stone, Christopher D. (1975), *Where the Law Ends: The Social Control of Corporate Behavior*, New York: Harper and Row.
Stone, Christopher D. (1980), 'The Place of Enterprise Liability in the Control of Corporate Conduct', **90** *Yale Law Journal*, 1–77.
Straachan, J.L., Smith, D.B. and Beedles, W.L. (1983), 'The Price Reaction to (Alleged) Corporate Crime', **18** *Financial Review*, 121–32.
Sunder, Shyam (1997), *A Theory of Accounting and Control*, Cincinatti, OH: South-Western Publishing.
Sykes, Alan O. (1984), 'The Economics of Vicarious Liability', **93** *Yale Law Journal*, 1231–80.
Ulen, Thomas S. (1996) 'The Economics of Corporate Criminal Liability', **17** *Managerial and Decision Economics*, 351–62.
US Department of Justice, Office of the Deputy Attorney General, Larry D. Thompson, Memorandum (2003), 'Principles of Federal Prosecution of Business Organizations', accessed at www.usdoj.gov/dag/cftf/business_organizations.pdf.
US Department of Justice, Office of the Deputy Attorney General, Paul J. McNulty,

Memorandum (2006), 'Principles of Federal Prosecution of Business Organizations', accessed at www.usdoj.gov/dag/speeches/2006/mcnultymemo.pdf.
US Sentencing Commission (various years), *Sourcebook of Federal Sentencing Statistics*, available online at www.ussc.gov/annrpts.htm.
Verrechhia, Robert E. (2001), 'Essays on Disclosure', **32** *Journal of Accounting and Economics*, 97–180.
Webb, Dan K., Molo, Steven F., and Hurst, James F. (1994), 'Understanding and Avoiding Corporate and Executive Criminal Liability', **49** *Business Lawyer*, 617–68.
White, James J. (1998), 'Corporate Judgment Proofing: A Response to Lynn LoPucki's The Death of Liability', **107** *Yale Law Journal*, 1363–412.
Yale Law Journal Editors (1979), 'Structural Crime and Institutional Rehabilitation: A New Approach to Corporate Sentencing', **89** *Yale Law Journal*, 353–75.
Zhang, Ivy X. (2007), 'Economic Consequences of the Sarbanes-Oxley Act of 2002', **44** *Journal of Accounting and Economics*, 74–115.
Zitzewitz, Eric (forthcoming), 'Retail Securities Regulation in the Aftermath of the Bubble', in N. Rose (ed.), *Economic Regulation and its Reform: What Have We Learned?*, Cambridge, MA: National Bureau of Economic Research.

10 Organized crime*

Vimal Kumar and Stergios Skaperdas

Introduction

The core function of organized crime is the selling of protection. Protection can be real, against third-party crime, or manufactured by the organized crime groups themselves. Mafias and gangs emerge in areas of weak state control, because of prohibition and geographic, ethnic, or social isolation. Although competition is considered good in economics, in the case of organized crime the predatory competition that is more likely to take place is harmful. The costs of organized crime include the resources expended on the activity, more ordinary productive and investment distortions, as well as other dynamic effects on occupational choice.

From highly sophisticated mafias to youth street gangs, organized crime is present in almost every country in the world. In addition to the better publicized Italian and American mafias,[1] examples include the Yakuza in Japan, the Triads in Hong Kong, Shanghai's Green Gang, Colombian and Mexican drug cartels, numerous groupings in post-Soviet states, youth gangs in Los Angeles, New York, Soweto, or Sao Paulo, as well as many other less well-known – even some, given the nature of the business, unknowable – groups.

Organized crime engages in much regular economic activity, the production and distribution of a wide variety of goods and services that are typically both legal and illegal – from construction and restaurant services to drugs, gambling, and prostitution. For that reason we might be tempted to think that mafias and gangs are just like any typical business firm and are therefore subject to the same economic analysis that ordinary firms are. However, the defining activity of an organized crime group – in the absence of which its other activities could not take place at all or their nature would drastically change – is the provision of *protection*. Protection is not an ordinary economic activity. It is supposed to protect the ownership of

* The original title of this chapter was 'On the Economics of Organized Crime'. It has been changed to the current title for editorial purposes.

1 For the Italian mafias, see Hess (1973), Arlacchi (1986), and Gambetta (1993), whereas for the American mafias, see Reuter (1995) and Jacobs (1999). For the Russian mafia and Japanese Yakuza, see Varese (2001) and Hill (2006), respectively.

other goods and services and make their contractual exchange enforceable. And, that enforceability does not come from the laws and courts – to which an ordinary security firm and its clients have access – but ultimately from the barrel of a mafioso's gun. The problem, of course, is that that gun can be turned not just against potential transgressors but also against those it is supposed to protect. That is the peculiarity of protection and it makes organized crime groups less akin to ordinary business firms and more similar to the traditional provider of protection and security, the state. However, the type of states that organized crime groups have similarities with are the early, proprietary, tribute-extracting, autocratic chiefdoms and states that are far removed from today's modern states. That is, it would be better to think of mafiosi as feudal lords than anything close to bureaucrats.

We will first trace the origins of organized crime to conditions of anarchy, to power vacuums that are created by geography, political, social and ethnic distance, as well as legal vacuums that might be created by the prohibition of certain goods and services within modern states. We will then discuss the hierarchical organization of organized crime and its market structure. In particular, we will distinguish between two types of competition that may exist between organized groups that have very different implications for economic efficiency. One type is ordinary economic competition in terms of the price and quality of the service that is provided, which in this case, as just mentioned, is protection. The other type of competition is predatory competition for turf among competing groups, which has deleterious economics effects. After discussing some consequence of organized crime, we conclude.

1. Origins of organized crime

In a fundamental way, organized crime emerges in conditions that are antithetical to a major assumption of much economic modeling: the perfect and costless enforcement of property rights. If that assumption were to strictly hold, there would be no possibility for a mafioso to ask for protection money, for the potential victim could costlessly take the extortionist to court and win. The mafioso can exist only when property rights are costly to enforce or imperfect. The more costly and imperfect property rights enforcement is, the lower the efficacy of the state as manifested in its laws, courts, police, other government agencies. Organized crime is more likely to emerge then in conditions under which either the state is weak or when the state effectively cedes control by, for example, prohibiting certain activities that are then picked up by organized crime. That is, organized crime is more likely to emerge in conditions that are close to anarchy (absence of rule) and where there is a power vacuum.

Simple *geographic distance and inaccessibility* from the centers of power is a major factor that reduces state authority. No states have, or have had in the past, an absolute monopoly of the use of force within their territories. In addition to ordinary crime, there are and have been areas within which it is too costly for the state to extend direct control. Jungles, mountains, or deserts have thus been breeding grounds of brigandage and rebellions. Geography then can play a role in creating a vacuum of power that can be filled by organizations that play the role of quasi-states. The Amazon jungle, for example, has been a place in which Brazil, Peru, Ecuador, and Colombia have had difficulty extending state power over their respective areas. Private armies, financed by landlords or drug traffickers, guerillas, and paramilitaries have been continually fighting among themselves and, sometimes, against governments for control over territories.

Another type of distance from the center of power that matters is that of *ethnic and social distance.* American youth gangs have traditionally flourished in low-income areas, often populated by a homogeneous ethnic group – Irish, African-American, Hispanic. Many residents of such areas typically have viewed themselves as being apart and discriminated against by the larger society (see Jankowski, 1991). The police and the justice system have also been often viewed at best as indifferent to their welfare and at worst as agents of repression. Therefore, ordinary crime becomes difficult to control in such areas, and gangs step in to fill the gap that is created, but also further contribute to violence in a more organized fashion. The townships of apartheid South Africa were perhaps extreme examples of alienation of a population from state authorities and, unsurprisingly, the levels of insecurity and violence there were extremely high (see, for example, Carver, 1992). The same broad process may be occurring in European cities, where conditions are ripe in areas of high unemployment or concentrations of poor immigrant groups that may feel alienated from the larger society. However, that type of alienation can carry over to ordinary, adult organized crime, where a whole ethnic group like the Chechens in Russia is both stigmatized and identified by the larger society with organized crime (see Lieven, 1998).

A power vacuum can also be created by *revolutions, wars, and major political change.* With the previous political authority and institutions gone and new effective ones typically taking time to develop, there can be long periods of time during which people can face basic physical insecurity in addition to more complex problems of uncertainty and insecurity over contract enforcement. It is perhaps then no accident that the Sicilian mafia grew significantly during the years immediately following the unification of Italy in an area that was previously under authoritarian rule for many centuries and in which republican institutions were unfamiliar compared to other parts of Italy. For the former Soviet Union, it has been argued

(Solnick, 1998) that the power vacuum preceded its break-up and was actually the precipitating cause of the break-up itself. Bureaucratic control weakened considerably over the years, with individual bureaucrats or coalitions of bureaucrats seizing control of the organizational assets they were supposed to be managing. Actually, the word 'mafiya' was used to describe the networks of corruption lurking inside regional and central ministries (Handelman, 1994). There appears to be some continuity in membership in these old Soviet-era mafiyas and the mafias and gangs of the post-Soviet world.

Thus far, we have considered potential sources of state weakness that can contribute to the development of organized crime. However, the state itself can create such conditions by effectively ceding control of contract enforcement through the *prohibition of production and distribution of certain goods and services.* Drugs, prostitution, alcohol, arms, gambling have been important areas of action for mafias and gangs. Exclusive government monopolies in the sale of salt, matches, or tobacco in the past have also invited smuggling and protection by organized crime groups. More recently, human trafficking across international borders has become a lucrative business for many organized groups. The distribution of nuclear material or even of nuclear weapons by such groups can not be ruled out in the present or future.

When the production and sale of a good or a service is prohibited, and there is reasonable demand at high prices, as there is for drugs, some demand is bound to be filled at high prices. Along the supply chain from primary producer to final consumer, however, there are a host of contractual enforcement and financing problems that have to be solved without recourse to the police, the legal system, or to mainstream financial institutions. That is, with prohibition, private parties cannot write and enforce contracts through the normal legal channels, and thus an effective power vacuum is created around the production, distribution, and financing of the prohibited commodity and its inputs. Cocaine is an example of a prohibited commodity for which there is a multiplicity and variety of contractual enforcement problems that exist along its supply chain (see Clawson and Lee, 1998). These problems cannot be solved realistically through each individual agent along this chain just taking their own defensive and private enforcement measures. The conditions cry for an ultimate enforcer, a 'hegemon', at least over substantial parts of the supply chain. The reasons for such an arrangement are similar to those that make states have the notional, if not always the de facto, monopoly of enforcement within their territories. For now, we could compactly characterize the rationale for a single enforcer within a certain area as being due to 'increasing returns' in enforcement.

We would like to stress at this point that drugs or any other economic activity of organized crime cannot exist without providing protection and enforcement, whereas organized crime groups can exist solely by providing protection and not engaging in other activities. This is similar to the customary Weberian definition of the state as the monopolist in the use of force, despite the fact that states do a lot more than providing internal and external security.

2. Internal organization

Organized crime groups are typically hierarchical organizations. Whereas some youth gangs, like Chicano gangs in east Los Angeles, have a flat organizational structure with leadership that is only informally recognized, others, like many New York gangs, have a formal hierarchical structure with considerable differentiation of duties among its members (Jankowski, 1991, chapter 3). The Sicilian mafia is hierarchically organized and that is recognized to be so through formal procedures (Gambetta, 1993, chapter 5).

Although precise knowledge of the internal functions of most organized groups is hard to come by, Levitt and Venkatesh (2000) were able to obtain detailed information on the organization and finances of a Chicago drug-selling gang. According to Levitt and Venkatesh, there was a core group at the top of the organization concerned with long-term strategy and responsible for maintaining a relationship with drug suppliers and other affiliates. At the next level of the hierarchy are local leaders who hire an enforcer, a treasurer, and a runner whose job is to run risky tasks. The enforcers recruit foot soldiers (between 25 and 75, who serve as street-level drug sellers). The functioning of the organization is similar to that of a franchised company. The local leaders receive drug supplies through the central leadership, and pay a fee and receive protection against law enforcement and rival gangsters; the central leaders obtain drug supplies from the central leadership.

Since, as argued in the previous section, mafias and gangs emerge out of a power vacuum to provide protection, why don't those who need the protection band together as equals in a 'social contract' and provide the needed protection themselves? Why do they have to pay a mafioso who may actually artificially create his own demand and extort more than it would cost each one in the group of equals if they were to band together? In principle, for example, the shopkeepers and residents within a few city blocks could agree to form community policing groups against common crime. They could create patrols of residents and shopkeepers. Whereas this practice could occur in certain cases, too often the mafias prevail. Forming such self-governing protection groups involves substantial coordination costs and as group size increases, the free-rider problem becomes more serious. These problems can be overcome with a small enough group of residents and shopkeepers who know one another. However, the main problem in such groups forming and surviving appears to be the presence of powerful mafias that are looking to expand their protection rents as well as their other business. It is one thing to have community policing against common theft. It is an entirely different matter to have the same residents and shopkeepers go into battle against the heavily armed deputies of Al Capone. Thus, residents and shopkeepers succumb. They pay up, and smile, wave, and chat to their local protector. They are the only protectors they have and they'd better keep them happy.

For someone to become a member of such an organization, it will be necessary to have at least once applied force decisively against opponents or, as can happen with youth gangs, against members of the organization itself. That is, mafiosi and gang members need to demonstrate the ability to use force and have sufficient ruthlessness in using it. Naturally, then, members of organized crime groups tend to be recruited from those who have a certain comparative advantage in violence. (Levitt and Venkatesh, 2000, report an annual death rate in their data sample of 7 percent, a figure which is shockingly high.) Once someone is within the organization, however, it is unclear whether greater capacity and predisposition for violence can help much more for advancement within the hierarchy. Other skills become important at the higher echelons: the ability to plan and execute tasks, sophisticated political and administrative skills, or how well you can motivate those who work for you. These are skills that are necessary in any other organization.

As with ordinary organizations, motivating the employees is a critical determinant of an organization's success. Inculcating loyalty and pride in work is a concern of virtually all organizations. Abiding by norms and informal constraints reduces infighting and other transaction costs within the organization. (Part of the discussion that follows also draws from Skaperdas and Syropoulos, 1995.) It is likewise with gangs and mafias, as they appear to develop and articulate cultures and ideologies, systems of beliefs about the world that have a certain internal logic to which, at least outwardly, all its members appear to subscribe. A core element of the ideology of many American youth gangs (Jankowski, 1991, chapter 3) is that American society systematically discriminates against their kind. Nearly all gangs believe that their ethnic group has been denied access to conventional opportunities that would allow them to live better lives. Their members subscribe to a social Darwinist perspective according to which predatory behavior is how one gets ahead in society everywhere. The gang, then, contributes to the advancement of its members and their ethnic group, just as the more powerful networks contribute to the welfare of their own members in the larger society. With such a worldview, the activities of the gang that are considered reprehensible in the mainstream are thus rationalized by gang members. The poverty of their surroundings and the hostility of media and authorities help reinforce such beliefs.

The main job of the mafioso is not much different from that of the feudal knight: he provides protection or, to put it more respectably, security. In rural Sicily, the mafioso used to perform straightforward intermediary and judicial functions that were conferring legitimacy from the community. It is therefore not surprising that the traditional Sicilian mafioso's self-image, even in cases of acts of extreme brutality, was that of a 'sacrifice which he makes for the benefit of the public weal' (Hess, 1973, p. 68) – like killing in times of war, it's a dirty job but it has to be done for the overall benefit.

Similarly, whether out of genuine conviction, guilt, or narrow self-interest, many major organized crime figures have also been involved in charity and public service. The leader of the Shanghai Green Gang, Du Yuesheng, became a major community leader and philanthropist (Martin, 1996). Pablo Escobar (of the Colombian Medellin cartel) and his associates donated several hundred new homes to poor slum dwellers in Medellin and constructed some 80 illuminated sports arenas in the area. Articles in the local newspaper – produced by Escobar's uncle – contrasted Escobar's public spirit with the indifference of other businessmen and of the Colombian political establishment at large (Clawson and Lee, 1998, p. 48). Genuine propaganda or not, the outward projection of the provider-of-public-good image is often an important component of organizations that have matured enough to compete with the state itself. In the case of Escobar the gambit did not succeed as he was killed in a highly publicized government raid – perhaps he should have been as conciliatory with the Colombian state as he was with the Medellin area. For the Sicilian mafia, however, the adaptation of seeing itself as a public servant worked reasonably well for more than a century.

3. Market structure: two types of competition

Since organized crime yields profits both from protection activities and from the production and distribution of goods and services, we might expect potential new entrants who attempt to gain a slice of the business from existing groups. New entrants could be deterred by existing groups in two broad ways. One is the regular way, available to legitimate business firms, of lowering price, enhancing quality, and other measures to keep existing and new customers happy. Organized crime groups, however, have another way of competing with one another that is not typically available to ordinary business firms: They can 'knee-cap' – or mete out worse punishments than that to – customers and competitors alike, so that they can compel them to do what they want them to do, without having to change price or quality. We discuss these two types of competition next.

For the first type of competition, the organized crime group can be thought of as providing protection to customers – say shopkeepers in their area – against crime in exchange for a fee. (For models of this type of competition, see Grossman, 1995, and Dixit, 2004.) The protection service provided can vary in terms of quantity and quality: how often the group checks on the shop, how much knowledge ('intelligence') they have about potential local thieves, what other measures they undertake to prevent theft, what they do in terms of restitution to the victim if theft takes place, and so on. The higher the level of the protection service, the higher the cost to the organized groups can be expected to be. Then, a group that tries to maximize profits would like to receive the highest possible fee from a shopkeeper for delivering service while incurring minimum cost.

An organized crime group – according to this approach – could be considered as offering packages of protection services that come with different prices or fees, one of which could be accepted by the shopkeeper. When the organized group has a monopoly in the area, it offers a protection service–price package that maximizes its own profit subject to the condition that is just (barely) acceptable to the shopkeeper. That is, a monopolistic group would receive almost all the surplus from providing the protection service to the shopkeeper. If we were to include more than one shopkeeper, the monopolistic organized crime group could either offer one level of service at a given price to all shopkeepers, with some of them accepting the package and others not, or it could price-discriminate and offer a dedicated package to each shopkeeper that is just accepted by every shopkeeper. In either case, according to standard economic theory, the outcome would be economically inefficient, because in the first case the price is too high and the level of protection too low, whereas in the second case different customers face different prices.

If, however, a competitor were to enter the 'market' for protection services, the original monopolist would be forced to reduce price and increase the level of protection services offered (see Grossman, 1995, for the particular mechanics) and thus increase economic efficiency. As with other similar economic models of competition, the greater the number of competitors, the higher the level of efficiency. The shopkeepers would need to pay less and the protection services they would receive would be higher, the higher the number of organized crime groups competing to provide the service.

The type of model just outlined fits well the private security services industry, an industry that has expanded significantly in the US and elsewhere over the past two decades. Applying the same model, though, to organized crime involves the adoption of at least two assumptions that are empirically difficult to fulfill. The first assumption is that organized crime groups cannot take extra-legal measures like creating their own demand for protection services. Ordinary security firms do not typically go threatening their potential customers with burning down their shop if they do not buy protection services from them. Mafiosi can, and are known to, make such threats and sometimes carry them out. A shopkeeper can take a legitimate security firm to court for making such threats and the firm will have to pay lawyers' bills and possibly face sanctions as a result. A shopkeeper could theoretically take a mafioso to court, but the mafioso has additional extra-legal means to respond: ransacking the shop, burning it down, physically threatening the shopkeeper and his family. The second assumption of the model outlined above is that competitors cannot take extra-legal measures against one another so as to prevent competition. Organized groups, however, typically try to keep one another off their respective turfs. Some famous films have been made out of mafia wars, but such turf battles are real and central to the survival and profitability of organized crime groups. With organized crime groups having a typically geographically non-overlapping potential clientele, the price and service competition we have outlined above effectively could not take place.

That leads us to the second type of competition that is possible among organized crime groups, and it is precisely this that involves competition for turf, an area within which a group has a near-monopoly in the use of force. This type of competition resembles more closely the competition among lords, kings, and emperors that took place for most of human history since the agricultural revolution. It takes the form of an arms race with your neighbors. If you have a large enough army, you can deter your neighbors or take some of their turf; if not, you lose turf or you can be taken over completely. The market structure that could best describe organized crime, then, is a curious sort of monopolistic competition, whereby each gang has a local monopoly of protection within a certain area and this local monopoly is maintained by the gang's capability of mobilizing and using force against other gangs. The absence locally of alternative providers of protection implies that the gang can use its enforcement powers internally to extract a price for its protection that is not just at its monopoly level but is extortionist – the gang can name its price and its quantity, especially if the gang's time horizon is short or the area's population does not have the resources to move into areas without gangs.

With profit maximization and free entry, in the long run we should expect the profits of gangs and mafias to be reduced to those available elsewhere in the economy. Does the greater competition that comes with free entry and the absence of excess profits imply a better economic outcome, though, as it does in the case of the first type of competition? The answer is different here. Remember that competition takes place through resources devoted to fighting that then become unavailable for production. Therefore, greater competition implies that more resources are used in fighting and fewer are used in production. Hence greater competition in the protection business reduces total production and efficiency.[2] If cooperation or consolidation among gangs could occur, economic efficiency would in principle be enhanced as fewer resources could be devoted to predation. However, it is doubtful how much of the saving in costs would be passed down to the community in the areas controlled by the cooperating gangs. And, as the institutional safeguards for cooperation are weak – often based on personalized leadership that breaks down when a leader disappears from the scene – there is an inherent unpredictability and instability in the world of organized crime.

4. Some economic consequences

We have just discussed some of the effects of competition among organized crime groups. Whereas for the first type of competition, more competition induces lower economic costs (or higher efficiency), the second type of competition induces greater economic costs when there is more of it. It is important to be clear analytically about the type of inefficiency that is identified in that second type of competition, and, as we have argued, more empirically relevant one for organized crime. It is not the allocative inefficiency that exists because of the suboptimal, but productive, employment of factors of production, although that can occur too. What has been discussed is the unproductive employment of economic resources that could be used elsewhere for directly productive purposes, in what has been variously labeled 'appropriative', 'redistributive', 'conflictual', or 'predatory' activities. Gang and mafia members spend their time making their presence felt in the neighborhood, defending against one another, and preparing to fight one another. Guns, locks, and steel bars also fall into this category of activities. They can be considered to contribute to security in an indirect way, but the same amount of security is compatible with many different levels of expenditure on such appropriative activities. Intense competition of many gangs can involve the expenditure of a lot more resources than complete hegemonic domination by one large mafia, and this in turn can involve the expenditure of

2 For models of this type of competition, see Konrad and Skaperdas (2006) and Skaperdas (2001).

a lot more resources than those of a modern state with an effective police and judicial system.

Although the loss of efficiency due to appropriation in areas with organized crime can be substantial, the spillover effects that organized crime has on regular economic activity can be even higher. Legal businesses that have to pay for protection face higher costs of operation, invest less, and bias the investments they make against anything that can be easily destroyed (Konrad and Skaperdas, 1998). For the same businesses, regular contracting through the mainstream legal system can become difficult even if it concerns perfectly legal matters, since the mafia can intentionally and actively discourage recourse to the legal system as it represents a challenge to its authority and a reduction in the rationale for its existence. There can be substitute contracting and other informal constraints, of course, as the mafia provides protection after all and has substantial enforcement powers within its area. In fact, the mafia could enforce contracts more effectively than the state can because it can impose penalties that are much more severe; for example, physical punishment and even death. However, the arbitrariness that typically accompanies such penalties and the multitude of uncertainties that surround contract fulfillment in a mafia's territory are unlikely to be outweighed by the severity of penalties the mafia can impose. As a result of the multiple uncertainties and incomplete information that exists, violence, destruction of property, and death are more likely to occur in organized crime territory.[3]

The long-term effects of organized crime could be even more devastating than its immediate, static effects. The area's most able, entrepreneurial, and responsible youth may choose to become mafiosi and gangbangers,[4] as Jankowski (1991, chapter 4) argues to be the case in American inner cities. Those are precisely the individuals who under different circumstances would provide very different types of community support and leadership. Once human beings develop human capital expertise in one area, it is very costly for them to change later in life. Former guerillas, demobilized soldiers after wars, and gang members have difficulties adapting to conventional lives and occupations later in life. Many find brigandage, robbery, or reversion to organized crime a familiar and more profitable lifestyle than its alternatives. Even after the destruction of organized crime in an area, it can take more than a generation before normalcy prevails.

---

3 Bester and Warneryd (2006) show how open conflict can be an equilibrium phenomenon in a model with appropriation, whereas Garoupa (2000) and Konrad and Skaperdas (1997) show how violence is possible as a result of credibility problems in the business of organized crime.

4 A member of a (typically, youth) gang.

In summary, the costs of organized crime include the resources expended on appropriation and predation, instead of production; various more conventional productive and investment distortions; the contractual problems that develop outside the realm of modern governance; and the incentives for the development of human skills that are biased towards appropriation instead of towards production.

Potential criminals, like any individuals, can be considered rational as in any other economics setting. They compare the benefits with the expected costs of committing a crime. Therefore, society can deter crime by making illegitimate activities costlier. To achieve this, a society typically increases the probability of crime detection and the severity of associated punishment, which results in an increase in the cost associated with crime. An organized crime group is able to coordinate all its members' activities and, as a consequence, crimes committed by them become difficult to detect.[5] They are also able to protect their members against potential punishment by bribing government officials, threatening potential witnesses, and, in some cases, employing violence against judges and magistrates. Top-echelon members of organized crime groups are further removed from direct crime and thus enjoy virtual immunity from the negative consequences of the crimes they perpetrate. Not surprisingly, there have been only a few successful campaigns in the past against organized crime groups.

In the US, the Racketeer Influenced and Corrupt Organization Act or RICO, as it is commonly known, has been the most effective tool against crimes committed by organized crime groups. The act lists various activities (such as extortion, bribery, loan sharking, illegal drug sales, prostitution, or murder), relaxes the definition of conspiracy, and provides penalties for criminal acts performed as a part of an ongoing criminal organization. The act focuses on the patterns of criminal acts as opposed to individual crimes. Thus, under RICO, the head of a crime organization can be prosecuted even if he has never been personally engaged in any criminal activity. The punishments under RICO can be exceptionally harsh. Apart from a long prison sentence, a convicted person forfeits all interests and claims over the criminal enterprise, as well as over the property that constitutes the racketeering activity or which has been obtained from the racketeering activity. Further, RICO allows the victims of organized crime to recover from the convicted person in civil court. The RICO is designed, first, to make detection of criminal enterprises easier and ultimately, to cripple and eradicate organized crime enterprises.

---

5 See Garoupa (2007) for an intra-organizational view of organized crime.

5. Concluding remarks

Despite all the technological improvements, economic growth, and expansion of the scope of governments over the past two centuries, organized crime is present even in the richest of countries. Evidently there are still cracks in the power of modern states that are created not just by the prohibition of commodities like drugs but also by the divisions of ethnicity, race, and class that modern societies still have. As long as these cracks, which create local power vacuums, exist, organized crime will continue to emerge to fill them. Well-publicized attempts to dislodge or eliminate organized crime are not likely to be successful unless they address the forces that create those vacuums of power.

References

Arlacchi, P. (1986), *Mafia Business*, London: Verso.

Bester, Helmut and Warneryd, Karl (2006), 'Conflict and the Social Contract', *Scandinavian Journal of Economics*, July, **108**(2), 231–49.

Carver, T. (1992), 'South Africa; The Other Frontline', *The New Statesman and Society*, **5**, 22–3.

Clawson, P.L. and Lee, R.W. III (1998), *The Andean Cocaine Industry*, New York: St Martin's Griffin.

Dixit, Avinash K. (2004), *Lawlessness and Economics: Alternative Modes of Governance*, Princeton: Princeton University Press.

Gambetta, D., (1993), *The Sicilian Mafia*, Cambridge, MA: Harvard University Press.

Garoupa, Nuno (2000), 'The Economics of Organized Crime and Optimal Law Enforcement', *Economic Inquiry*, **38** (2), 278–88.

Garoupa, Nuno (2007), 'Optimal Law Enforcement and Criminal Organization', *Journal of Economic Behavior and Organization*, July, **63** (3), 461–74.

Grossman, H.I. (1995), 'Rival Kleptocrats: The Mafia versus the State', in G. Fiorentini and S. Peltzman (eds), *The Economics of Organized Crime*, Cambridge, UK and New York: Cambridge University Press.

Handelman, S. (1994), 'The Russian "Mafiya"', *Foreign Affairs*, **73** (2), 83–96.

Hess, H. (1973), *Mafia and Mafiosi: The Structure of Power*, Lexington, MA: D.C. Heath & Co.

Hill, Peter B.E. (2006), *The Japanese Mafia: Yakuza, Law, and the State*, Oxford: Oxford University Press.

Jacobs, James B. (with Colleen Friel and Robert Radick) (1999), *Gotham Unbound: How New York City was Liberated from the Grip of Organized Crime*, New York: New York University Press.

Jankowski, M.S. (1991), *Islands in the Street: Gangs and American Urban Society*, Berkeley, CA: University of California Press.

Konrad, K.A. and Skaperdas, S. (1997), 'Credible Threats in Extortion', *Journal of Economic Behavior and Organization*, **33**, 23–39.

Konrad, K.A. and Skaperdas, S. (1998), 'Extortion', *Economica*, **65**, 461–77.

Konrad, Kai A. and Skaperdas, Stergios (2006), 'The Market for Protection and the Origin of the State', Manuscript.

Levitt, Steven and Venkatesh, Sudhir A. (2000), 'An Economic Analysis of a Drug-selling Gang's Finances', *Quarterly Journal of Economics*, **115** (3), 755–89.

Lieven, Anatol (1998), *Chechnya: The Tombstone of Russian Power*, New Haven, CN: Yale University Press.

Martin, B.G. (1996), *The Shanghai Green Gang: Politics and Organized Crime, 1919–1937*, Berkeley, CA: University of California Press.

Reuter, P. (1995), 'The Decline of the American Mafia', *Public Interest*, (120), 89–99.
Skaperdas, Stergios (2001), 'The Political Economy of Organized Crime: Providing Protection When the State Does Not', *Economics of Governance*, (2), 173–202.
Skaperdas, S. and Syropoulos, C. (1995), 'Gangs as Primitive States', in G. Fiorentini and S. Peltzman (eds), *The Economics of Organized Crime*, Cambridge, UK and New York: Cambridge University Press.
Solnick, S.L. (1998), *Stealing the State: Control and Collapse in Soviet Institutions*, Cambridge, MA: Harvard University Press.
Varese, Federico (2001), *The Russian Mafia: Private Protection in a New Market Economy*, Oxford: Oxford University Press.

11 Corruption
*Roger Bowles**

1. Introduction
Corruption takes many forms and is encountered in a bewilderingly wide range of settings. It can be an elusive notion ranging as it does across a wide spectrum of activities from complex dealings involving politicians, government officials and business executives to simple bribery to activities which fade imperceptibly into 'parochial corruption' (Kingston, 2007) or 'custom and practice'. It can be confined to a small number of specific individuals or pervade a whole organisation and can be in the form of a one-off casual event or embedded in a longer-term relationship. That it is widespread in many countries is not in any doubt. The World Bank estimates that more than $1 trillion is lost each year to pay bribes, draining the world economy of investment and developing countries of funds to reduce poverty and address development objectives.[1] The United Nations (UN) has set up a Convention against Corruption,[2] the Organisation for Economic Co-operation and Development (OECD) has a convention against bribery and many countries have set up anti-corruption commissions (Doig et al. 2005).

Definitions of corruption tend to rely on the notion of dishonesty, and particularly on the idea of a betrayal of public trust. They often refer to the improper use of influence or power for purposes of private gain. Public officials and politicians, for example, are particularly susceptible because they are in a position to 'misuse' their power or position to grant favours in exchange for bribes, campaign funding, votes or whatever. They are by no means alone in having the capacity to subvert a position of trust for private financial gain, however: corporate managers, for example, can

* The research on which this chapter is based was supported in part by an EC-funded project on Mainstreaming Methodology for Estimating the Costs of Crime (MMECC). Participants in the project have influenced my thinking on the costs of crimes including corruption-related offences, although they bear no responsibility for the contents of this chapter. The contents of the chapter do not in any way reflect the views or policies of the EC or any other organisation.

1 From the web site of the Anti-Corruption Commission of the International Chambers of Commerce.

2 http://www.unodc.org/unodc/crime_convention_corruption.html.

collude with others to enrich themselves at the expense of shareholders. For the purposes of this chapter we are going to exclude this kind of fraud. We confine ourselves, as is customary (Ogus, 2004), to a relatively narrow definition of corruption that has a focus on misuse of public office and we exclude corporate corruption.

It is a characteristic of the economic approach, which we follow, to treat corruption as an issue of incentives and organisation rather than as a matter of public morals and norms (Bardhan, 2006). We treat corruption as a mutual activity, as a transaction with willing traders as both buyer and seller. Both parties are assumed to be driven by their own private interests as well as, or instead of, the 'public interest'. This does not necessarily imply moral unworthiness, but it does mean that the design of government organisations needs to reflect private incentives if the bodies are to be proof against opportunism and exploitation.

Many definitions of corruption, implicitly at least, identify the initial breach of trust as the key point at which damage is done to a public institution. From a moral perspective this may be right: the breach of public trust is a serious matter and may be very costly to remedy. But such a breach is not of itself the only costly consequence. From a social cost perspective, the harm from corruption can be split into at least two components. One is the 'institutional damage' which occurs at the point when the possibility of a corrupt transaction is aired: the breach of trust, say, by an official asking for a bribe or indicating willingness to accept one. This single action may damage irrevocably the integrity and reputation of the agency. The second component is the substantive social cost of the corrupt transaction itself: for example, the cost to taxpayers of having goods supplied to government at a price above the market rate and any further adjustments that might be triggered on the part of agents anticipating a repetition of the corruption.

Our purpose in this review is to focus on the costs of corruption. We do this by bringing together contributions on the rent-seeking facet of corruption with the literature on the costs of other types of crime. We suggest that such a fusion offers a useful framework for the analysis of anti-corruption policy.

2. The literature on corruption

The breadth of the topic of corruption is reflected in the wide ambit of its coverage in the economics literature. It is a matter that has been treated in many sub-branches of the discipline, as evidenced by the very large number of *Journal of Economic Literature* (JEL) categories to which the papers in the bibliography to this chapter refer. Mainstream micro and macro, economic organisation, law and economics, development economics, applied micro and applied macro economics, public economics, public choice are just some of the subject areas within which substantial numbers of papers on corruption have been published: useful surveys include Andvig (1991) and the large collection in Fiorentini and Zamagni (1999). It goes without saying that there has been a great deal written about corruption outside the discipline of economics. The disciplines of law, philosophy and political science are a few examples and of course corruption is a mainstream matter of interest to non-academic audiences.

Even from a 'law and economics' perspective, corruption has been studied from many different angles. It can be treated variously as a crime (Kugler et al., 2005; Bowles and Garoupa, 1997; Chang et al., 2000; Polinsky and Shavell, 2001), as a transaction cost (Murphy et al., 1993), as an issue of asymmetric information (Laffont and Martimort, 1997), as an agency cost (Bac, 1996) or as a violation of an allocation of rights. It crops up sometimes in an abstract way and at other times in an empirical form. In some settings, it takes a one-shot, casual form, while in others it is more deeply embedded within organisations (Laffont, 1990; Kofman and Lawarree, 1993) and/or takes a repeated form (Mishra, 2006).

In order to give some shape to this vast area we exploit some of these distinctions. But we start by trying to capture some of the common themes underpinning most analysis of corruption.

3. Illustration of the three-party structure of a corruption model

The basic structure of most economic analysis of corruption can be illustrated in a simple three-party model. The notion of a betrayal of trust requires some form of collusion between an employee of an organisation with responsibilities to the public and someone outside the organisation seeking a good or service from it. The benefits of the collusion are split in some way between the two parties at the expense of the organisation itself and ultimately society at large, the third player or interest.

To give concrete expression to the setting, suppose an official in a passport office demands payment of a bribe (over and above the cost of the visa) to issue a visa without further delay. Provided that the official sets the bribe at a level below the amount the citizen is prepared to pay then the visa is issued and both parties have 'gained'. If the maximum amount the citizen is prepared to pay for the visa is p (in addition to the cost of the official fee) then a well-informed official could charge a bribe $b(<p)$, leaving both parties better off. The citizen enjoys a surplus of $(p–b)$ while the official keeps the bribe, b.

This is, of course, a simplification for purposes of modelling. For both sides, there may be reasons why this overstates the gains. The citizen has an entitlement to obtain a visa without paying a bribe, and is thus worse off than she would be had the entitlement been respected. The official may incur some moral qualms or 'psychic costs' in taking a bribe. This reduces their net gain from taking a bribe, but may not be sufficient to prevent them taking the bribe.

The gain (b) may appear not to affect anyone else but usually in reality it will. The official may still honestly pass the revenue from the visa fee to his office, in which case there may seem just to be a transfer payment from the citizen to the official: the transaction seems 'victimless'. But in fact these sorts of transactions take longer when bribes are involved than when they are not and this gives rise to costs to third parties, such as those waiting in line for a visa: Murphy et al. (1993). Irrespective of how the negotiations are conducted, the net result will be that the official ties up time in the transaction and this will reduce the number of other visa applications the official can handle. This reduces productivity and causes greater delay for other visa applicants.

In addition to the transactions costs there will likely be further rounds of costs. We look more closely at the composition of these costs in the following section. For the immediate purpose of setting out the structure of our three-player model we will summarise the transactions costs (or 'rent-seeking costs' as they might be termed) as RSC and the other downstream costs of corruption as D. The transactions costs (RSC) will be shared by the parties to the corruption while the downstream costs (D) fall on third parties.[3] For the citizen involved in the corruption, RSC will depend on the opportunity cost of time, previous experience of bribery transactions and so on. In any event, these costs will reduce the net rent (p) being shared by the conspirators. The scale and distribution of the downstream costs will be highly context-specific, as will the relationship between the size of the rent and the third-party costs.

From a social perspective, there is, in essence, a principal-agent problem. The corruption choices of the agent (the official) are not observable. Typically, the official will be paid a salary that is not (and cannot be) linked to her choices about taking bribes. The incentive to avoid corruption may thus be rather weak. There are several strategies that might be considered as a means of mitigating this moral hazard.

One is to re-design the employment contract of the official. This might entail a model based on the 'tax farming' approach used historically in many societies (Azabou and Nugent, 1988; Besley and Maclaren, 1993). The tax collector (or in our case, the visa issuer) pays a lump sum in exchange for the right to collect taxes (issue visas) according to the laws of

---

[3] The corrupt official may, of course, be able to pass most of her share on to her employers.

the land. A good deal of public sector reform in recent decades has been motivated by this sort of approach, although it is important to keep in mind that such changes may be motivated by their incentive effects as well as their anti-collusion properties. In practice, there may be substantial cultural and other barriers to implementing radical solutions of this kind.

Another approach is to use enforcement powers under the criminal law to tackle corrupt practices directly. This treats corruption like any other offence and involves investigation of officials, with the prospect of prosecuting those who are found to be taking bribes. Models based on the approach of Becker (Becker, 1968; Becker and Stigler, 1974) can be readily adapted for a corruption setting by treating the corruption decision for an official as a simple gamble (Cadot, 1987; Bowles and Garoupa, 1997; Garoupa, 2000; Garoupa and Jellal, 2007; Polinsky and Shavell, 2001). The official's share of the rent (b) net of any transaction costs represents the potential gain while the expected cost is the product of the probability of the corruption being detected (π) and the sanctions imposed in the event of conviction. If we assume for simplicity that transactions costs are zero and that the sanction is a fine of size f, then the corruption choice for a risk-neutral official with no psychic costs of taking a bribe is:

$$\text{Accept bribe iff: } (1 - \pi).b > \pi.f \qquad (11.1)$$

This basic structure can of course be modified in many different ways. For example:

- the size of the bribe can be endogenised (since it will quite plausibly be a function of the probability of conviction and the size of the sanction) or fixed at some reference level that reflects the surplus gain to each side of the corrupt transaction such as the Shapley value;
- moral restraints can be introduced that limit the net gain to the official of taking a bribe;
- the sanction can be expanded to allow for loss of job and pension rights and other elements.

The decision rule in equation (11.1) can be used to estimate the incidence of corruption on various assumptions about the effectiveness of anti-corruption technology, as captured through the relationship of the probability of detection to the resources going into anti-corruption work. But in any event, an informed judgement about the net return to investment in corruption-reduction will require evidence about the degree of harm being caused by corruption. Particularly if, as is likely, it is very costly to prevent corruption, it is essential to have a good sense of the savings that will result.

4. The costs of corruption

4.1 Typology of costs

The approach we take here to measuring the costs of corruption makes use of a blending of the 'rent-seeking' analysis of corruption referred to above and the empirically based research that has been done on the economic and social costs of crime. This latter has focused primarily on 'street crime' such as burglary, theft and assault. Its literature normally identifies three principal components of the economic and social costs of crime (Cohen, 2000, 2005; Brand and Price, 2000; Dubourg et al., 2005; Mayhew, 2003 and others), namely: costs to victims, costs in anticipation of crime and costs of the criminal justice system. In effect, then, we are arguing for a four-way classification of the costs of corruption that incorporates rent-seeking costs plus the three components just listed. We consider each category in turn.

4.1.1 Rent-seeking costs In the model of the previous section, corruption centred on the possibility of the official and the citizen sharing a rent (p) created by the citizen being prepared to pay a sum in excess of the visa fee. The rent-seeking costs are the costs the two sides invest in securing, sharing and protecting their interest in this rent. Corrupt transactions are illegal, with the result that the normal protection of obligations under contract law does not apply. The parties have to spend time agreeing first that a bribe is to be paid, then how much it is to be, how the agreement is to be made self-enforcing and possibly also how it is to be kept secret (Rose-Ackerman, 1999).

For a one-off transaction this rent-seeking activity can take considerable time, since the official has to probe the citizen to make an estimate of their reservation price (p). There may be haggling over the size of the bribe, particularly if the citizen either feels able to complain about treatment at the hands of the official or can credibly threaten to go to another official who will provide the service for a smaller bribe.

The scale of the potential benefits from a continuing corrupt relationship may be such as to promise substantial returns from economising on transactions costs. By entering informal agreements to govern these relationships, the parties may be able to reduce the proportion of the rents going in transactions (or rent-seeking) costs. This kind of trust strategy underlies a lot of corruption, particularly in fields such as tax administration, procurement contracting and policing. Such conspiracies are, of course, illegal and unenforceable. But because they tend to be deeply rooted in social or family networks, they can be very difficult to uncover or counter effectively (Lambsdorff, 2002). Another development that high transactions costs may prompt is the emergence of a market for agents or intermediaries with specialist knowledge of the markets in question (Hasker and Okten, 2008). Closely related arguments underpin the emergence of multi-tier corruption of whole organisations (Tirole, 1986; Laffont, 1990; Kofman and Lawarree 1993).

To digress briefly from the field of corruption, we argue that there might be merit in including rent-seeking costs when looking at the costs of all or most offence types. In the context of burglary, for example, we could argue that real resource costs are entailed in the committing of the crime itself. Burglars spend time searching for appropriate targets, acquiring tools to speed entry, acquiring burglary-specific skills and so on. Clearly in the case of offences such as fraud and embezzlement, substantial resources may be invested by offenders in finding a *modus operandi* and in concealment and other activities that quite closely resemble the kinds of rent-seeking costs identified by Rose-Ackerman in her analysis of corruption. These costs are all real resource costs because the time and effort could otherwise be going into productive activity.

4.1.2 Victim costs The victim costs of street crime are usually fairly obvious: an identifiable person is injured, robbed or burgled or whatever. The victim costs of corruption are generally substantially more diffuse. In our visa example, they are shared by all the other citizens waiting to get a visa. This diffuseness impedes estimation of the extent of the victim costs. But the obvious importance of such costs for purposes of promoting economic development as well as evaluating anti-corruption policy has spurred the development of methods for inferring something about their scale.

The notion of 'victim costs' in the costs of crime literature is a fairly direct one: it refers to the impact of a particular offence and excludes the costs incurred though subsequent adjustments. So it could refer, in a corruption application, to the price paid over and above the lowest tender for a project, given that the two bids were similar in terms of the quality they offered. Or it could measure the loss of surplus to a group of citizens as a result of their paying a bribe for access to a service to which they were legally entitled to access at zero user cost. Or it could refer to the additional delay caused in getting a visa because an official had spent too much time on a prior corrupt transaction. It could even include losses from corrupt officials or politicians moving the proceeds off-shore to protect them, since this reduces the supply of funds available to domestic financial institutions for recycling into investment in the country.

Considerable care is needed at this point because much of the work on corruption does not distinguish very carefully between the harm to victims caused by corruption once it has occurred ('victim costs') and harm caused because of the effect on actions to mitigate losses from corruption that might occur in the future (costs in anticipation of crime). In some of the empirical literature, particularly cross-section analysis of the relationship between the extent of corruption and the rate of a country's economic growth, these two elements are clubbed together.

As in other areas of crime where victim costs have been estimated, the first task is to explore the extent of victimisation. This can generally be done either by looking at the incidence of the crime as recorded in official data or it can be estimated by using surveys. In the case of corruption it is this latter methodology that is most widely used for the simple reason that there are strong grounds for believing that officially recorded corruption will identify no more than a tiny proportion of the corruption going on. A number of international organisations, including Transparency International[4] and the World Bank,[5] publish findings from surveys of firms, citizens, experts and others asked about their experience of being asked for bribes. For example the World Bank survey asks about three aspects of corruption, namely: unofficial payments for a typical firm to get things done (percentage of sales); firms expected to give gifts in meetings with tax inspectors (per cent) and the value of gift expected to secure a government contract (percentage of contract). The survey findings do not generally give direct estimates of the costs of the corruption involved, but it is possible to imagine the sorts of questions that would need to be asked as a prelude to making such estimates.

As we will show below in Section 5, assessing victim costs will be substantially more complex than this when we move away from petty bureaucratic corruption to more elaborate corrupt edifices where the polity and bureaucracy have become entwined.

4.1.3 Criminal Justice System costs The costs of corruption to the criminal justice system (CJS) vary widely across countries, depending on how widespread corruption has been and how vigorously it has been pursued. Normally the three principal organisations whose costs contribute to CJS costs are the police, the courts and offender management services (prison,

---

4 For details see: http://www.transparency.org/policy_research/surveys_indices/cpi. In addition to the CPI, the organisation also produces a Bribe Payers Index and a Global Corruption Barometer.

5 The World Bank Enterprise Survey includes a section on corruption: http://www.enterprisesurveys.org/ExploreTopics/CompareAll.aspx?topic=corruption.

probation and so on). Substantial amounts of time are required for serious investigation of corruption by police (or commissions of enquiry) and prosecution. Terms of imprisonment may be lengthy, extending even to life imprisonment, and thus costly.[6] In practice the investigation work is often given to independent commissions, particularly if there is a suggestion that a country's police force is corrupt.

There are some data on the number of prosecutions being brought for corruption. In the US, the Transactional Records Access Clearinghouse (TRAC) publishes a monthly time series, taken from Justice Department sources, on new official corruption prosecutions. The monthly data, which run from October 2000, show the number of new prosecutions fluctuating between about 20 and 100 per month and suggest a slightly declining trend.[7] Although useful for certain purposes, such as exploring time trends within a country (Del Monte and Papagni, 2007), such data are clearly not a reliable guide as to how widespread corruption might be, particularly when making international comparisons. Variations in legal definitions of corruption, in the volume of law enforcement resources devoted to anti-corruption work and in the political will to explore corruption, may all play a significant role.

The possibility that prosecuting bodies, police or judicial authorities are themselves corrupt also influences the propensity to bring corruption charges. Further, there are countries where it is alleged that corruption charges are motivated purely by a wish to discredit political opponents.

It is probably fair to say that there are few countries where a substantial proportion of CJS resources is going into corruption. A few costly, high-profile cases can be identified, but the CJS costs are unlikely to represent more than a small proportion of the total costs of corruption.

4.1.4 Costs in anticipation of corruption The costs of burglary include the costs to householders of installing locks and bolts and taking other avoidance steps that are welfare-reducing. In the case of corruption, the corresponding avoidance measure may include the diversion of investment resources over the longer term away from sectors in which corruption is high. If the corruption becomes deeply embedded across many sectors in the economy, then there is a danger that investment resources will flow abroad or that consumption will rise at the expense of saving. Likewise, the prospect

---

[6] Some officials of China's State Food and Drugs Administration were recently sentenced to terms of between 13 years and life for taking bribes: *Financial Times*, 8 July 2007.

[7] http://www.trac.syr.edu/tracreports/bulletins/corruption/monthlyfeb07/fil/.

of high corruption may deter inward investment. The principal purpose of many indices of corruption is precisely to enable international investors to take an informed view about the countries and sectors to avoid.

Corruption prevention actions may also take the form of developing procedures and practices within organisations. Greater transparency brings its own potential costs to organisations but may also be used to strengthen a reputation for straight, honest dealing that is profitable over the longer term. Many large corporations have anti-corruption compliance programmes explicitly aimed at developing a good name on which they can trade. Likewise, accounting bodies may find themselves in a position to insist on strong enforcement of anti-corruption policy by their members as a means of improving their international standing.

Studies of international investment flows can be expected to give some indication of the extent to which countries with high corruption are losing out in the marketplace.

However, some care is needed with this argument lest greater corruption become an attraction to unscrupulous investors. If officials are prepared to take bribes in exchange for turning a blind eye to infringements of regulatory requirements, then this may reduce operating costs relative to those in competing locations. However, such advantages may be only skin deep because this same corruption can undermine significantly the quality of government services and infrastructure (Ogus, 2004). In any event, depressed investment inflows into a corrupt economy will help drive up interest rates and impoverish the economy and is thus a real cost of corruption to residents in the country.

An influential strand of the corruption literature seeks to relate national growth rates (and investment rates) to explanatory variables, including the extent of corruption in a country (Mauro, 1995; Keefer and Knack, 1997; Gyimah-Brempong, 2002) and the rate of growth of firms or the efficiency of firms to the amount of corruption (Fisman and Svensson, 2007; Boa and Rossi, 2007). These contributions typically find that corruption plays a significant role in retarding growth. Empirical estimates have been made of the strength of such effects but we do not document that here.

In extreme cases where political and government institutions have fallen prey to corruption, a widespread loss of trust can threaten social stability and even a government's own legitimacy. Citizens may become increasingly disinclined to pay taxes or to cooperate with state institutions, resulting eventually in revolution, a coup or military takeover.

One important conclusion we draw from this review of categories of the costs of corruption is that it is the costs in anticipation of corruption that may have the most serious economic consequences. In some ways, this reflects the position in relation to certain other kinds of crime types.

For example, terrorism derives a lot of its political leverage not from its immediate consequences for victims, devastating though these can be, but from the fear it creates and from the high costs that result as agents (and organisations) adjust their behaviour in line with events.

5. Political corruption

The political arena has historically been central to a great deal of what has been written about corruption, although it figures less prominently in a lot of the economics literature on the subject. Control of legislation and the granting of public office give politicians a great deal of patronage. This power can be used benignly and in the public interest or it can be misused for selfish gain. The temptations are obvious. Control of large public budgets makes a politician vulnerable to many sorts of pressure, ranging from a straight bribe to more subtle forms of influence such as offers of lavish hospitality from business leaders or lobbyists in exchange for opportunities to press a particular interest.

But there can be more subtle and sinister interpretations of corruption within the political sphere. Politicians have powers they may exercise to control key features of the landscape within which bribery occurs. In some countries, for example, they have influence over the appointment and transfer of civil servants, including tax inspectors, procurement officers and budget-controlling officials. In other countries, ministers may be in a position to approve special legislative provisions in the form of special tax exemptions, or special treatment for particular sectors or firms. Likewise, they may be able to make appointments to state-operated enterprises, such as financial institutions with discretionary powers to approve loans at special interest rates or to write off bad debts. All of these manifestations of weakness in governance arrangements have their dangers. The obvious danger is that the political will to remedy such weaknesses may itself be limited by the likelihood that it is political leaders themselves who have most to lose from reform.

There are echoes of these concerns in some of the models of corruption that explore the links between layers of hierarchical organisations (Bac, 1996). Managers of front-line bureaucrats taking bribes can usually ensure a cut for themselves. If politicians have control of the upper echelons of the bureaucratic triangle, then they too can join in. And if this is widely known, then it is only a short step to finding that the greediest will fight hardest for positions of political influence. The implication is that corruption can run very deep and result in contamination of the most central institutions. The most corrupt individuals will have an incentive to find their way to the most vital positions and exploit them for their own advantage.

Targeting enforcement efforts on front-line junior bureaucrats can thus rather miss the point. A deliberate blurring of distinctions between the branches of government, and gaining influence over critical points in the tax, procurement or budgeting systems of a country are the kinds of strategies that serious players may use. These ploys can be difficult to track. An anti-corruption prosecutor may yield, for whatever reason, to the temptation to go after the more amateurish front-line targets.

6. Anti-corruption policy

The breadth of the discussion of the design of policy to prevent or reduce corruption reflects the wide variation in the underlying analysis of corruption. The policy prescriptions produced by more abstract models are sometimes ambiguous (because optimal policy may be sensitive to parameter choice) and may have practical limitations.

One of the key lessons from observation of corruption is that great ingenuity may go not only into creating corrupt practices but also into defending the rents they generate. It is clearly essential, therefore, that the incentive structures within organisations are well understood before efforts to prevent corruption are implemented. But it is also clear that the corruption may spill over organisational boundaries, and that there may be scope for argument about the real source of corruption. For example, it is commonplace for government officials in low income countries to be very poorly paid. The responses by officials to this vary: they may spend afternoons away from the office tending market gardens, they may take bribes or whatever. The anti-corruption policy design problem is that just raising the salary levels of the officials to a reasonable level where they can survive without bribes is unlikely to be a sure-fire way of eliminating corruption (or moonlighting for that matter). The practices may have become deeply engrained in wider social relationships and networks and not susceptible to change overnight. The important point is that the 'engraining effect' is not accidental. It is of the essence of corrupt behaviour to want to compromise co-conspirators and to manoeuvre them into a position where they will hurt themselves more by confessing their corrupt involvement than by keeping it secret. The government of a country with a corrupt bureaucracy may, in any event, have insufficient resources to raise civil service income levels. By turning a blind eye to the corruption of department officials, a ruling party may be able to maintain civil service employment levels. Morally at least, the party has become involved in the corruption even if legally it has played no active part in its promotion. Of course it is a short step in this kind of setting for a politician to become directly implicated by taking a share of the bribe income from the top level of the civil service in exchange for protecting the status quo.

In many economic models of corruption the wage level of bureaucrats plays an important role in determining the propensity to engage in corruption. Particularly in developing countries suffering bouts of rapid inflation, public sector wages can fall to negligible levels, making jobholders highly vulnerable to bribe offers. Many models demonstrate, however, that a policy of raising wages in such circumstances is unlikely to be an effective form of corruption control (Mookherjee and Png, 1995; Besley and MacLaren, 1993; Van Rijckeghem and Weder, 2001).

Staff rotation is widely canvassed as a precautionary measure against corruption in public administration (Abbink, 2004; Rose-Ackerman, 1999), and is used by a number of governments, including the German federal government. To study the effect of this policy, an experiment was conducted where pairs of potential bribers and public officials were randomly re-matched in every round. A comparison of the outcome with the case where the identity of the pairs interacting remained fixed indicated that rotation of interacting pairs significantly reduced both the levels of bribes and the frequency of inefficient decisions due to bribery.

In a model of bribes paid for speeding up document processing, Bose (2004) shows that a reward/penalty scheme based on the average time taken to clear applications has superior properties to an enforcement-based approach.

From a business perspective, the attitude to corruption is generally rather pragmatic: if you have to pay a bribe to get a foreign contract, then that's what you do. This of course is a non-cooperative solution. It would be better for firms as a whole if none of them ever agreed to pay bribes. But if you are in a setting where you suspect other firms are paying bribes, then the profitable policy will often to be to join in with the corruption. Of course a superior solution may be to implement international agreements to outlaw bribery, but there are clearly instances where corruption goes on despite the existence of such agreements (Rose-Ackerman, 2002).

The effectiveness of measures against corruption can be difficult to gauge. Despite the existence of some tough national legislation, such as in the US, and despite there being a number of international agreements and conventions in place, it is suspected that a great deal of corruption continues to flourish. There are many possible reasons for this. Some are simple. For example, enforcers using powers under criminal law confront a high burden of proof. A corrupt individual with a good lawyer and the foresight to have maintained a degree of ambiguity in their corrupt dealings may often be able to escape conviction. Others are more complex.

Players in these kinds of positions take care to remove themselves from positions where there is a significant probability of being detected and prosecuted. There are many defensive moves they can make to avoid detection and skilful manipulators can find ways of weakening the capacity or will of anti-corruption enforcers to convict them. Standard devices include the use of off-shore bank accounts and complex corporate structures to make it difficult to track funds, operating through intermediaries who are compensated in a roundabout way, the mixing of legitimate and illegitimate sources of income, making counter-claims of victimisation, calling in political protection, threatening to reveal harmful details of an organisation's workings or connections and implicating co-conspirators in other illegal activities.

For the most part this multi-layering of corruption and subterfuge can successfully cover up corruption. But, particularly where corporate interests are concerned, there may be very powerful financial incentives for private or media investigation to uncover secrets that government-sponsored anti-corruption agencies cannot reach. Stock price movement analysis can sometimes be used to reveal the best informed market opinion about events behind the scenes.

As a first example, Fisman (2001) looked at Indonesian firms during the Suharto era to see whether, on days when scares about his health were made public, firms with close ties to Suharto would see their stock prices drop. The inference from the analysis of stock price movements drawn in the paper is that political connections accounted for a quarter of the value of well-connected Indonesian firms during the Suharto era.

Another intriguing example of the interplay between business and politics is the Al-Yamamah agreement signed between the governments of Great Britain and Saudi Arabia in 1985 for the provision of Tornado jets. Allegations had been made that corrupt payments, including commissions of around £1 billion, were made to intermediaries close to the Saudi government as part of the £40 billion deal. The British company at the centre of the deal, BAE Systems, claims it did nothing wrong and was working with the full knowledge of the British and US governments. An investigation of the deal by the UK's Serious Fraud Office (SFO) was discontinued at the end of 2006 by the British government's Attorney General, on the grounds that it represented a threat to national security and manufacturing jobs. This decision had followed a substantial dip in the firm's share price on worries that the Saudis might pull out of a deal to buy Eurofighters because of the SFO enquiry. The resulting sharp recovery of the firm's share price as the threat eased was reversed a few months later towards the end of June 2007 when it was announced that the Department of Justice would be pursuing BAE under anti-corruption laws[8] in the US. The dip, which reduced the firm's market capitalisation by

8 The 1997 Foreign Corrupt Practices Act, which was passed following Watergate.

11 per cent, or more than £1 billion, was triggered apparently mostly on the strength of fears that the US investigation might prejudice BAE's plans to expand its position as a defence supplier in the US. The US Congress had triggered the deal in the first place, some have argued, by their objections to the sale of F-15s to Saudi Arabia,[9] although there does not seem to be any suggestion that the new investigation is in any way a product of pressure from Congress. A question remains as to whether the British Ministry of Defence will comply with demands from US investigators to see confidential documents relating to the case.

Obviously this is a complex case, but it does have some interesting lessons. It shows that

- many stakeholders may be or become involved;
- political and corporate interests may become entwined (possibly deliberately);
- officials in one country may be reluctant to cooperate with their counterparts in another country;[10]
- uncovering a payment or a payment agreement is by no means sufficient to succeed with a corruption prosecution;
- players in the game seeing that the political and corporate stakes are high may, or may threaten to, increase them further as part of their strategy;
- delaying tactics may be deployed by players with short decision horizons, to the frustration of others who want to eliminate uncertainty and bring matters to a conclusion.

7. Concluding remarks

As we noted at the beginning of the chapter, corruption is believed to be very widespread. At a UN conference on corruption in 2003, Daniel Kaufman, director of global governance at the World Bank Institute, told reporters that the cost of corruption represents 5 per cent of the world economy – or more than 1.5 trillion dollars a year. Such measures are first approximations and often refer to estimates of the size of the resource

---

9 These various developments are a summary based on a series of newspaper articles in the *Guardian* ('Transatlantic Justice', Leader, 27 June 2007; 'Anti-bribery Watchdog Calls for Explanation of BAE Decision', 5 January 2007; and 'City Shrugs off Investigation at BAE as Earnings Soar to £1.2 b.') and the *Financial Times* ('BAE Faces Fines in US Bribery Probe', 26 June 2007 and 'Al-Yamamah: The Saudi Foreign Policy Connection', 1 July 2007).

10 That is despite the UK being a signatory of the OECD's 1997 convention on bribery.

transfers taking place rather than to the resource costs at stake. But they do give an indication that corruption is likely a source of significant welfare loss in the modern world. The research on which they are based also has the merit of helping identify sectors towards which anti-corruption investigations or measures might best be targeted.

Wealth-maximisation motives may lead individuals to contemplate seeking to corrupt other individuals, organisations, political parties or whatever. Looking more widely, the same motives may also lead to efforts to bring about self-serving legislative or procedural change or changes in law enforcement priorities. In some respects the dangers attending this kind of high-level hijacking of the key instruments of state power are much greater than those associated with low-level petty bureaucratic corruption. The political safeguards against such efforts need to be robust. Development agencies have rightly pressed for 'good governance' as a precondition for providing aid to countries. But countries throughout the world are vulnerable to pressures from individuals and organisations to implement political and administrative change that serves these special interests at the expense of the wider community. Constitutional protections have an important role to play and institutions such as the media may provide greater transparency, which can inhibit such abuses or distortions. But neither device provides guaranteed protection. Politicians may be able to force constitutional change and the media will, in the final analysis, follow the dictates of their owners. This makes political office and/or control of the media an obvious target for those seeking to manipulate political institutions for their private benefit at the expense of others.

The economics literature has explored many dimensions of corruption. It ranges from straightforward empirical studies of the link between corruption and growth to highly abstract models of organisations and incentive structures. This diversity reflects the intrinsic complexity of the phenomenon. But it has not as yet been sufficient to provide a complete understanding of corruption or to inspire a truly effective effort to prevent it.

Bibliography

Abbink, K. (2004), 'Staff Rotation as an Anti-corruption Policy: An Experimental Study', *European Journal of Political Economy*, **20** (4), November, 887–906.

Alam, S.M. (1995), 'A Theory of Limits on Corruption and Some Applications', *Kyklos*, **46**, 419–35.

Andvig J.C. (1991), 'The Economics of Corruption: A Survey', *Studi Economici*, **43** (1), 57–94, reprinted in Fiorentini and Zamagni (1999), *The Economics of Corruption and Illegal Markets*, 3 volumes, Cheltenham, UK and Northampton, MA, USA: Edward Elgar.

Azabou, M., and J.B. Nugent (1988), 'Contractual Choice in Tax Collection Activities: Some Implications of the Experiences with Tax Farming', *Journal of Institutional and Theoretical Economics*, **144**, 684–705.

Bac, M. (1996), 'Corruption and Supervision Costs in Hierarchies', *Journal of Comparative Economics*, **22** (2), April, 99–118.
Bac, M. and P.K. Bag (2006), Beneficial Collusion in Corruption Control: The Case of Nonmonetary Penalties', *Journal of Development Economics*, **81** (2), December, 478–99.
Bardhan, P. (2006), 'The Economist's Approach to the Problem of Corruption', *World Development*, **34** (2), February, 341–48.
Basu, K., S. Bhattacharya and A. Mishra (1992), 'Notes on Bribery and Control of Corruption, *Journal of Public Economics*, **48** (3), 349–59.
Becker, G. (1968), 'Crime and Punishment: An Economic Approach', *Journal of Political Economy*, **76**, 167–217.
Becker, G. and G. Stigler (1974), 'Law Enforcement, Malfeasance and the Compensation of Enforcers', *Journal of Legal Studies*, **3**, 1–19.
Besley, T. and J. MacLaren (1993), 'Taxes and Bribery: The Role of Wage Incentives', *Economic Journal*, **103**, 119–41.
Boa, E.D. and M.A. Rossi (2007), 'Corruption and inefficiency: Theory and Evidence from electric Utilities', *Journal of Public Economics*, **91** (5–6), 939–62.
Bose, G. (2004), 'Bureaucratic Delays and Bribe-taking', *Journal of Economic Behavior and Organization*, **54** (3), 313–20.
Bowles, R.A. (1999), 'Tax Policy, Tax Evasion and Corruption in Economies in Transition', in E.L. Feige and K. Ott (eds), *Underground Economies in Transition: Unrecorded Activity, Tax Evasion, Corruption and Organized Crime*, Aldershot: Ashgate.
Bowles, R. and N. Garoupa (1997), 'Casual Police Corruption and the Economics of Crime', *International Review of Law and Economics*, **17**, 75–87.
Brand, S. and R. Price (2000), 'The Economic and Social Costs of Crime', *Home Office Research Study 217*, London: Home Office.
Buscaglia, E. (1997), 'Corruption and Judicial Reform in Latin America', *Policy Studies Journal*, **17**, 273–95.
Cadot, O (1987), Corruption as a Gamble', *Journal of Public Economics*, **33**, 223–44.
Campos, E., D. Lien and S. Pradhan (1999), 'The Impact of Corruption on Investment: Predictability Matters', *World Development*, **27**, 1059–67.
Celentani, M. and J.-J. Ganuza (2002), 'Corruption and Competition in Procurement', *European Economic Review*, **46** (7), 1273–303.
Chang, J.-J., C.-C. Lai and C.C. Yang (2000), 'Casual Police Corruption and the Economics of crime: Further Results', *International Review of Law and Economics*, **20**, 35–51.
Cohen, M. (2000), 'Measuring the Costs and Benefits of Crime and Justice', *Measurement and Analysis of Crime and Justice: Volume 4 of Criminal Justice 2000*, Washington, DC: National Institute of Justice, available at: http://www.ncjrs.org/criminal_justice2000/vol_4/04f.pdf.
Cohen, M.A. (2005), *The Costs of Crime and Justice*, New York, NY: Routledge.
Cooter, R., and N. Garoupa (2000), 'The Virtuous Circle of Distrust: A Mechanism to Deter Bribes and Other Cooperative Crimes', Berkeley Olin Program in Law and Economics Working Paper no. 32, University of California, Berkeley, available at: http://repositories.cdlib.org/blewp/32/.
Djankov, S., R. La Porta, F. Lopez De Silanes and A. Shleifer (2002), 'The Regulation of Entry', *Quarterly Journal of Economics*, **117**: 1–38.
Del Monte, A. and Papagni, E. (2007), 'The Determinants of Corruption in Italy: Regional Panel Data Analysis', *European Journal of Political Economy*, **23** (2), 379–96.
Doig, A. (1995), 'Good Government and Sustainable Anti-corruption Strategies: A Role for Independent Anti-corruption Agencies?', *Public Administration and Development*, **15**, 151–65.
Doig, A., and S. Riley (1998), 'Corruption and Anti-corruption Strategies: Issues and Case-studies from Developing Countries', in *Corruption and Integrity Improvement in Developing Countries*, Paris: OECD/UNDP.
Doig, A., D. Watt and R. Williams (2005), 'Measuring "Success" in Five African Anti-Corruption Commissions: The Cases of Ghana, Malawi, Tanzania, Uganda and Zambia', U4 Research Report, Bergen: Chr. Michelsen Institute.

Dubourg, R., J. Hamed and Jamie Thorns (2005), 'The Economic and social Costs of Crime against Individuals and Households 2003/04', Home Office On-Line Report 30/05.

Fiorentini, G. and S. Zamagni (1999), *The Economics of Corruption and Illegal Markets*, 3 volumes, Cheltenham, UK and Northampton, MA, USA: Edward Elgar.

Fisman, R. (2001), 'Estimating the Value of Political Connections', *American Economic Review*, **91** (4), September, 1095–102.

Fisman, Raymond and Roberta Gatti (2002), 'Decentralization and Corruption: Evidence across Countries', *Journal of Public Economics*, **83**, 325–45.

Fisman, R. and J. Svensson (2007), 'Are Corruption and Taxation Really Harmful to Growth? Firm Level Evidence', *Journal of Development Economics*, **83** (1), 63–75.

Flatters, F., and W.B. MacLeod (1995), 'Administrative Corruption and Taxation', *International Tax and Public Finance*, **2**, 397–417.

Garoupa, N. (2000), 'The Economics of Organized Crime and Optimal Law Enforcement', *Economic Inquiry*, **38**, 278–88.

Garoupa, N. and M. Jellal (2007), 'Further Notes on Information, Corruption, and Optimal Law Enforcement', *European Journal of Law and Economics*, **23**, 59–69.

Garoupa, N. and D. Klerman (2001), 'Corruption and Private Law Enforcement, USC mimeograph.

Garoupa, N. and D. Klerman (2004), 'Corruption and the Optimal Use of Nonmonetary Sanctions'. *International Review of Law and Economics*, **24**, 219–25.

Gyimah-Brempong, K. (2002), 'Corruption, Economic Growth and Income Inequality in Africa', *Economics of Governance*, **3**, 183–209.

Hasker, K. and C. Okten (2008), 'Intermediaries and Corruption', *Journal of Economic Behavior & Organization*, **67** (1), 103–15.

Huther, J. and A. Shah (2001), 'Anti-corruption Policies and Programs: A Framework for Evaluation', World Bank Working Paper no. 2501, Washington, DC: World Bank.

Keefer, P. and S. Knack (1997), 'Why Don't Poor Countries Catch Up? A Cross-National Test of an Institutional Explanation', *Economic Inquiry*, **35**, 590–602.

Kingston, C. (2007), 'Parochial Corruption', *Journal of Economic Behavior and Organization*, **63** (1), May, 73–87.

Klitgaard, Robert (1988), *Controlling Corruption*, Berkeley, CA: University of California Press.

Kofman, F. and J. Lawarree (1993), 'Collusion in Hierarchical Agency', *Econometrica*, **61** (3), 629–56.

Kugler, M., T. Verdier et al. (2005), 'Organized Crime, Corruption and Punishment', *Journal of Public Economics*, **89** (9–10), 1639–63.

Laffont, J.-J. (1990), 'Analysis of Hidden Gaming in a Three Level Hierarchy', *Journal of Law, Economics, and Organization*, **6** (3), 301–24.

Laffont, J.-J., and Martimort, D. (1997), 'Collusion under Asymmetric Information', *Econometrica*, **65**, 875–912.

Laffont, J.-J., and J.-C. Rochet (1997), 'Incentives and Organization', *Scandinavian Journal of Economics*, **99** (4), 485–95.

Lambsdorff, J.G. (2001), 'Corruption and Rent-seeking', *Public Choice*, 1–29.

Lambsdorff, J.G. (2002), 'Making Corrupt Deals: Contracting in the shadow of the Law', *Journal of Economic Behavior and Organization*, **48** (3), July, 221–41.

Lambsdorff, J. Graf (2003), 'How Corruption Affects Productivity', *Kyklos*, **54**, 457–74.

La Palombara, J (1994), 'Structural and Institutional Aspects of Corruption', *Social Research*, **61**, 325–50.

Leff, N.H. (1964), 'Economic Development through Bureaucratic Corruption', *American Behavioral Scientist*, **8**, 8–14.

Lui, F. (1986), 'A Dynamic Model of Corruption Deterrence', *Journal of Public Economics*, **31** (2), 1–22.

Manion, M. (1996), 'Corruption by Design: Bribery in Chinese Enterprise Licensing', *Journal of Law, Economics, and Organization*, **12**, 167–95.

Marjit, S. and H. Shi (1998), 'On Controlling Crime with Corrupt Officials', *Journal of Economic Behavior and Organization*, **34**, 163–72.

Marjit, S., V. Mukherjee and A. Mukherjee (2000), 'Harassment, Corruption and Tax Policy', *European Journal of Political Economy*, **16** (1), 75–94.
Mauro, P. (1995), 'Corruption and Growth', *Quarterly Journal of Economics*, **110**, 681–712.
Mayhew, P. (2003), 'Counting the Costs of Crime in Australia', *Trends and Issues in Crime and Criminal Justice*, Canberra: Australian Institute of Criminology, available at: http://www.aic.gov.au/publications/tandi/ti247.pdf.
Mishra, A. (2002), 'Hierarchies, Incentives and Collusion', *Journal of Economic Behavior and Organization*, **47**, 165–78.
Mishra, A. (2006), 'Persistence of Corruption: Some Theoretical Perspectives', *World Development*, **34** (2), 349–58.
Mookherjee, D. and I.P.L. Png (1995), 'Corruptible Law Enforcers: How Should they be Compensated?', *Economic Journal*, **105**, 145–59.
Murphy, K.M., A. Shleifer and R.W. Vishny (1993), 'Why is Rent-seeking So Costly to Growth?', *American Economic Review*, **83**, 409–14.
Ogus, A. (2004), 'Corruption and Regulatory Structures', *Law and Policy*, **26** (3), 329–46.
Polinsky, A.M. and S. Shavell (2001), 'Corruption and Optimal Law Enforcement', *Journal of Public Economics*, **81** (1), 1–24.
Rasmusen, E. and J.M. Ramseyer (1994), 'Cheap Bribes and the Corruption Ban: A Coordination Game among Rational Legislators', *Public Choice*, **74**, 305–27.
Rose-Ackerman, S. (1978), *Corruption: A Study in Political Economy*, New York: Academic Press.
Rose-Ackerman, S. (1999), *Corruption and Government*, Cambridge: Cambridge University Press.
Rose-Ackerman, S. (2002), '"Grand" Corruption and the Ethics of Global Business', *Journal of Banking & Finance*, **26** (9), 1889–918.
Seligson, M.A. (2006), 'The Measurement and Impact of Corruption Victimization: Survey Evidence from Latin America', *World Development*, **34** (2), 381–404.
Shleifer, A. and R.W. Vishny (1993), 'Corruption', *Quarterly Journal of Economics*, **108**, 599–617.
Svensson, J. (2003), 'Who Must Pay Bribes and How Much? Evidence from a Cross Section of Firms', *Quarterly Journal of Economics*, **118** (1), 207–30.
Tirole, J. (1986), 'Hierarchies and Bureaucracies: On the Role of Collusion in Organisations', *Journal of Law, Economics and Organization*, **2** (2), 181–216.
Tirole, J. (1992), 'Collusion and the Theory of Organizations', in J.J. Laffont (ed.), *Advances in Economic Theory*, Cambridge: Cambridge University Press.
Treisman, D. (2000), 'The Causes of Corruption: A Cross-national Study', *Journal of Public Economics*, (3), 399–458.
Van Rijckeghem, C. and B. Weder (2001), 'Bureaucratic Corruption and the Rate of Temptation: Do Wages in the Civil Service Affect Corruption, and By How Much?', *Journal of Development Economics*, **65** August, 307–32.
Wu, S.-Y. (2006), 'Corruption and Cross-border Investment by Multinational Firms', *Journal of Comparative Economics*, **34** (4), December, 839–56.

12 Tax evasion and avoidance

Luigi Alberto Franzoni

1. Introduction

Collecting taxes from recalcitrant taxpayers requires effective enforcement rules and a dedicated administration. Over the last 40 years, a large body of literature has investigated the phenomenon of compliance to identify the forces that determine decisions to evade and to devise methods to raise compliance rates. The 'law and economics' approach to tax evasion is based on the hypothesis that compliance is essentially an economic decision and can thus be analysed using the tools of standard economic theory.

One of the first attempts to investigate tax evasion using the tools of economics was Cesare Beccaria's 'An Attempt at an Analysis of Smuggling' (1764). Beccaria developed a mathematical model to calculate the likely amount of goods smuggled, given the amount of goods recovered by customs officials. Further inquiries were carried out during the Enlightment by such precursors of the law and economics approach as Jeremy Bentham and Montesquieu. In that period, scholars sought to devise laws that could withstand rational scrutiny. Sanctions and enforcement were the object of special attention: they had to be such as to attain their purported goal without needless suffering. Law enforcement had to be taken out of the closet of arbitrary power and exposed to the light of reason and public accountability.

The rational approach of the Classical School was soon superseded by alternative theories of the biological and social roots of crime, driving a wedge between crime theory and economic theory. For a long time, the problem of law and tax compliance was separated from the mainstream of economics and essentially left to the police and the courts. The modern use of economic tools for the analysis of tax compliance can be credited to Allingham and Sandmo (1972), who extended Becker's influential work on law enforcement (1968) to taxation, applying modern risk theory.

In the decades since then, the literature on tax evasion has blossomed. Probably no aspect of tax compliance has escaped at least cursory scrutiny. Detailed introductions to this theme are now available, including notably the monographs of Cowell (1990; theoretically oriented) and Roth et al. (1989; an interdisciplinary perspective), and the surveys of Andreoni et al. (1998; including a thorough discussion of empirical results), Slemrod and Yitzhaki (2002; with large sections devoted to avoidance and administration), Cowell (2004; emphasising the limits of the traditional model), Marchese (2004; with special emphasis on public choice), and Slemrod (2007; focused on the US).

As a complex phenomenon, tax compliance needs to be addressed from a variety of perspectives. Taxpayers' behaviour is influenced by many factors, including their disposition towards public institutions, the perceived fairness of the taxes, prevailing social norms, and the chances of being detected and punished. Setting ethical and sociological motivations aside, the economic analysis of tax compliance has focused mainly on deterrence via detection and sanctions. The thesis is that the taxpayer's behaviour can be fruitfully seen as the result of a rational calculus, a careful assessment of the costs and benefits of evasion. Since even in the simplest tax and enforcement systems the incentive to comply is far from obvious, the economic perspective offers precious insights into proper policy design.

This chapter, which is an updated version of Franzoni (1999), surveys the theoretical and the empirical literature on tax evasion. Section 2 defines tax evasion as opposed to tax avoidance. Section 3 discusses Allingham and Sandmo's basic (1972) model of tax evasion, briefly reviewing its numerous extensions. Section 4 surveys the empirical evidence on taxpayer compliance. Section 5 deals with optimal enforcement policy and investigates some anti-evasion strategies. Section 6 examines additional policy issues, connected with the institutional and procedural aspects of tax enforcement. Section 7 provides some concluding observations.

2. Definition and extent of tax evasion

By distancing statutory taxes from effective payments, tax evasion defines a specific revenue deficiency, known as the 'tax gap'. For the 2001 tax year, for instance, the US overall gross tax gap in the United States was estimated at $345 billion, corresponding to a non-compliance rate of 16.3 percent. Similar measures – pointing generally to higher non-compliance rates – have been developed for most countries.

It must be understood from the outset that the tax gap is not equal to the additional revenue that would be collected by stricter enforcement. This is because perfect enforcement would significantly affect the economic scenario (some firms would go bankrupt, taxpayers would modify their labour supply, prices and incomes would change, etc.), so the tax base would surely be altered. As a result, at least in theory, net revenue could turn out to be even smaller. The standard gauges of tax gaps must be interpreted cautiously. They are only roughly suggestive of the likely immediate effects of marginal improvements in enforcement. One should also be wary of the cliché that statutory taxes represent the ideal world and tax gaps an intrinsic evil. This is not only because taxes may not necessarily be 'just', but also because statutory taxes themselves may be enacted by legislators who know they will be only partially enforced and so differ from what would be optimal under perfect enforcement.

On closer scrutiny, then, the estimated tax gap only shows the wedge between economic reality and a legal construct called 'statutory taxes'. Reality and its legal representation may differ for any number of reasons, among which, as we shall see, the wilful misrepresentation of tax liabilities is just one.

In economic terms, the problem of tax evasion originates in the fact that the variables that define the tax base (incomes, sales, revenues, wealth, etc.) are often not 'observable'. That is, an outsider cannot usually observe the actual magnitude of a person's tax base and hence cannot know the true tax liability. Sometimes this knowledge can be obtained by means of costly audits, in which case we say that the tax base is *verifiable* (at a cost). In other cases, as when it is related to cash payments, the tax base cannot be verified at all. Taxpayers can then take advantage of the imperfect information about their liability and escape taxation.

A related concept is *tax avoidance* (or reduction), by which persons reduce their own tax in a way that may be unintended by tax legislators but is permissible by law. Avoidance is typically accomplished by structuring transactions so as to minimise tax liability. In some cases, avoidance is encouraged by legislation granting particularly favourable tax treatment to specific activities. From a legal standpoint, evasion differs from avoidance in being patently unlawful, and hence punishable (at least in theory). From a functional standpoint, however, they obviously have very strong similarities; sometimes, indeed, they are practically indistinguishable (see, for instance, Slemrod and Yitzhaki, 2002).

Tax administrations and tax courts usually exert considerable effort to limit avoidance. This effort is usually made ex post, on a case-by-case basis, in an attempt to tailor general principles of taxation to specific situations. The standard approach here is to investigate the rationale for particular transactions, to see whether they are motivated by business reasons or by tax reasons ('business purpose' doctrine, 'economic substance' doctrine). The proper delimitation of these anti-avoidance efforts hinges on the suitable division of power between the legislature (which drafts the tax statute) and the courts (which interpret them and apply them to the individual case). As Weisbach (2002) argues convincingly, by drawing the line between admissible and inadmissible transactions, courts de facto determine the tax base. Thus, analysis of the proper scope of anti-avoidance doctrines to a large extent coincides with analysis of the optimal tax base.

Another problem with the measurement of tax evasion relates to its proper delimitation within the broader framework of the informal economy. No taxes are generally levied on transactions in the home and criminal sectors, which are usually beyond the reach of authorities and official statistics. Hence, proper determination of the boundaries of evasion is a formidable task, in that evasion is often inextricable from other illegal and unrecorded activities (see Gerxhani (2004) for a methodological discussion).

Aggregate estimates of evasion must overcome all these difficulties, in addition to the classic problem of lack of direct data. Various estimation methods have been devised, some based on data collected by fiscal authorities, others – less reliable – on data derived from national accounts and surveys. In Western industrialised countries, evaded taxes appear to amount to between 5–25 percent of potential tax revenue, depending on the country and the method used, with higher figures (up to 30–40 percent) for less developed countries (see Schneider and Enste (2000) and references therein).

As noted, these estimates must be treated cautiously. Essentially, they tell us that statutory taxes are not the whole story. From an economic perspective, what matters is *effective taxation*, that is, the net tax burden on individuals. This has major implications for the economic consequences of evasion: the main question is not how evasion distorts the statutory allocation of the fiscal burden, but how it constrains the set of possible public policies. When taxes can be evaded, taxation is an imperfect tool for pursuing government aims (be they redistribution, efficiency, or whatever), which will be only partly achieved. For instance, in a country where the more affluent have better opportunities for evasion (or avoidance), progressive taxation may not be an effective tool to pursue equality. Similarly, if the opportunity to evade varies substantially by occupation or business sector, formally fair taxes may result in large horizontal inequality. Empirical studies suggest that evasion is likely to have a strong impact on horizontal equity, a limited impact on vertical equity (see, for instance, Bishop et al., 2000; Galbiati and Zanardi, 2001). On top of horizontal inequality, the unequal distribution of opportunities to evade and of the willingness to seize them is likely to induce production inefficiencies, since evaders compete on unfair terms with tax-compliant firms.

In order to evaluate the way in which non-compliance affects the actual tax payments of individuals, one must examine compliance behaviour more closely. Theoretical models can help predict how taxpayers' behaviour will be affected by the relevant variables. Section 3 reviews some models and assesses their fit with observed practice.

3. The decision to evade

Compliance with the tax law typically means: (i) true reporting of the tax base, (ii) correct computation of the liability, (iii) timely filing of the return, and (iv) timely payment of the amounts due. The bulk of tax evasion involves the first point. Most evaders either do not declare their liability at all, or declare it only in part. In the following, we concentrate on the problem faced by an individual who has to decide how much, if any, of his aggregate tax liability to report. The focus is on income tax, but the insights apply to other taxes as well.

One of the earliest and most helpful models of tax evasion is that developed by Allingham and Sandmo (1972) and Srinivasan (1973), and revised by Yitzhaki (1974). The Allingham-Sandmo model (A-S) combines the pioneering insights of Becker (1968) on the economics of crime with an analysis of optimal portfolio allocation. It is based on a set of special hypotheses that are necessary to make it tractable. Although these assumptions have been extensively criticised in the literature, the A-S model remains the fundamental first step in understanding the basic issues involved in the evasion decision. For this reason, it is important to explain it in detail.

The main hypotheses underlying the model are the following:

(a) The taxpayer rationally decides the amount of income to report: the aim is to maximise the expected utility from net income. All factors not affecting the taxpayer's net income are ruled out.
(b) The taxpayer is averse to risk: uncertainty due to the randomness of tax enforcement (the return may or may not be audited) imposes a 'disutility' on the taxpayer. The taxpayer is not a 'gambler' who enjoys risky choices.
(c) The taxpayer's real taxable income y is known to the taxpayer but not to the tax administration, which observes only reported income, $y - e$ (where e denotes the amount of income not reported).
(d) Reported income is subject to a simple proportional tax with rate t. Thus, the taxpayer's upfront payment is $t(y - e)$. By underreporting, the taxpayer saves on the upfront tax payment.
(e) With probability a the tax return is subject to a perfect audit, able to reveal the taxpayer's true taxable income. If underreporting in the amount e is detected, then the taxpayer has to pay evaded taxes, te, plus a proportional fine fte, where f is the fine rate.

In light of these assumptions, the evasion decision becomes a matter of optimal 'portfolio allocation': taxpayers must decide what portion of their income to invest in the risky activity labelled 'tax evasion'. If there is no audit, net income is equal to true income less taxes on reported income: $y - t(y - e) = y(1 - t) + te$; if there is an audit, it is equal to true income, less taxes on true income, less the fine: $y(1 - t) - fte$.

The taxpayer's expected utility is thus:

$$EU(e) = (1 - a)u(y(1 - t) + te) + a\,u(y(1 - t) - fte),$$

where u is the taxpayer's utility function. This function captures the taxpayer's attitude towards risk (the more concave, the more risk averse).

To start with, let us calculate the return on the amount of underreported income, e. With probability $(1 - a)$, the taxpayer gets: $+te$; with probability a, the taxpayer gets: $-fte$. Thus, the expected return to the taxpayer is:

$$\textit{Expected return to evasion} = (1 - a)te - afte = [1 - a(1 + f)]te.$$

Thus for each dollar of unreported income, the taxpayer gets a net return equal to: $t[1 - a(1 + f)]$. The net return is positive only if $a(1 + f) < 1$, that is, only if the audit probability a and the fine rate f are small. If this condition is satisfied, evasion represents a profitable 'investment' opportunity.

Then the question arises: what share of their income will taxpayers conceal? Here, the taxpayer's attitude towards risk comes into play. In fact, the greater the tax evasion, the bigger the 'gamble' by the taxpayer. The gain may be very large, but the loss may also be very large. The reason for not evading one's entire income, given a positive return on evasion, has to do with the 'disutility' of the uncertainty associated with the evasion gamble. Technically, this 'disutility' is measured by the risk premium $RP(e)$ of the gamble, which is the amount that the taxpayer would be willing to pay in order to avoid the risk (read 'uncertainty') associated with the gamble. The risk premium depends on the taxpayer's attitude towards risk and increases (approximately) with the square of the tax evaded. Thus, an increase in the amount evaded has a linear impact on the monetary return, but a more than proportional impact on the 'disutility' of the risk.

If we account for the risk premium loss, the net benefit from evasion becomes:

$$\textit{Net evasion gain} = [1 - a(1 + f)]te - RP(e)$$

The optimal evasion decision will have to balance the gains from underreporting (the larger the amount 'invested', the greater the expected return) with the disutility due to the uncertainty attendant on the evasion

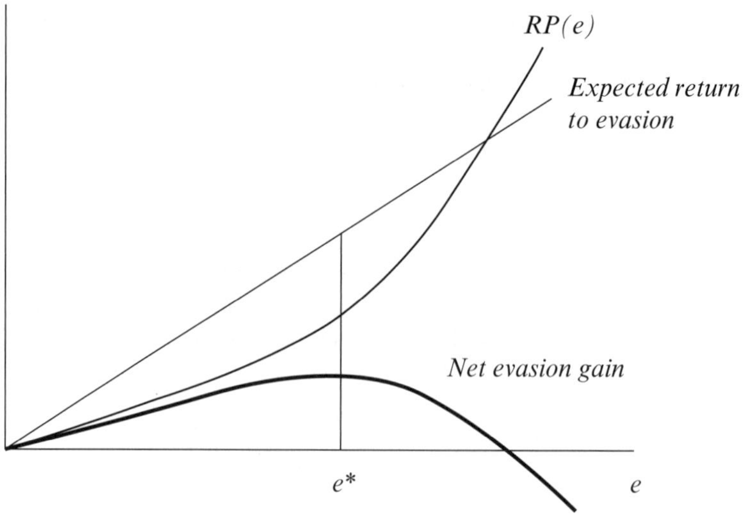

Figure 12.1 The net evasion gain as a function of the amount of income concealed

gamble (the larger the amount underreported, the greater the risk). Figure 12.1 illustrates.

The A-S model yields some important results.

(1) *Deterrence tools* As expected, the *amount* of tax optimally evaded by the taxpayer, te^*, depends negatively on the audit rate a and the fine rate f. Stricter enforcement (larger a and f) reduces the expected return to evasion and leads taxpayers to report a higher income.
(2) *Full deterrence* For moderately risk-averse taxpayers, evasion drops to zero only if the expected return to evasion is negative. In other words, the fine and audit rates must be sufficiently high: $a > 1/(1 + f)$.
(3) *Evasion and risk aversion* Taxpayers who are more averse to risk evade less. At the limit, the extremely risk averse behave 'as if' they were audited for sure. To them, the uncertainty created by the gamble is so costly as to completely offset the positive return to evasion: the net evasion gain becomes negative and the optimal evasion amount converges to nil.
(4) *Evasion and income* The impact of income level on evasion is less intuitive. As we have seen, the expected return on each dollar of taxes evaded depends only on the audit and the fine rates. But income level is likely to affect taxpayers' attitude towards risk and thus the size of the risk premium. More precisely, if taxpayers become less risk

averse as they become wealthier, then we should expect an increase in income to reduce the risk premium and to increase the optimal amount of income concealed. Technically, it can be shown that the amount of underreported income, e^*, increases with income if, and only if, the utility function displays decreasing absolute risk aversion, while the *share* of income underreported, te^*/y, increases with the income level if, and only if, the utility function displays decreasing relative risk aversion (see Cowell, 1990).

(5) *Evasion and the tax rate* A similar argument applies to the tax rate t. An increase in the tax rate makes the taxpayer worse off in real terms. Thus, it works like a reduction in income. So, as before, if the taxpayer becomes more averse to risk as he becomes poorer, a higher tax rate increases the disutility of risk and reduces the amount of evasion.

(6) *The excess burden of tax evasion* Let us consider the impact of underreporting on tax receipts. The net revenue loss is equal to evaded taxes, te, less expected recovery through auditing: $a(1 + f)\, te$. One can easily see that the net revenue loss for the tax administration exceeds the net evasion gain for the taxpayer: the wedge between the two is equal to the risk premium $RP(e)$, which represents an uncompensated loss. Intuitively, for one dollar of expected revenue obtained by the tax administration, the loss for the taxpayer is strictly greater than one dollar: the additional cost borne by the taxpayer is due to his uninsured risk (Yitzhaki, 1987).

Further considerations

The basic A-S model gives an account of taxpayers' evasion decisions in a very simple set-up: taxes and penalties are proportional, the audit rate is constant, and only one form of evasion is available. In addition, the taxpayer is assumed to rely on expected utility theory and to be perfectly amoral, that is, to make compliance decisions with exclusive reference to the consequences for net income. All these assumptions are open to criticism, and models based on alternative assumptions have been developed.

Ethical behaviour One standard criticism of the Allingham and Sandmo model is grounded in the belief that compliance decisions depend on moral views. This is clearly a problematic issue, one that cannot be easily captured by the consequentialistic set-up of standard decision theory. Bordignon (1993) makes an interesting attempt to account for non-self-motivated decisions in tax evasion. He develops a compliance model in which taxpayers are guided by suitably defined 'Kantian principles', which determine the amount that each taxpayer considers it fair to pay. Under this assumption, it turns out that tax evasion is generally lower than under selfish behaviour, that compliance depends on the level of public expenditure, and that evasion is likely to increase with tax rates.

Social pressure Other authors have stressed the 'social factors' underlying taxpayers' decisions (see Roth et al., 1989, for an excellent account of the sociological research). Economists have emphasised the 'stigma' attached to the violation of social norms and shown that tax evasion may have strong spillover effects. Social stigma is likely to give rise to a multiplicity of equilibria: when most people evade, the stigma effect is small and evasion is not in fact discouraged; when few evade, the stigma effect is great and evasion is discouraged. The transition from one equilibrium to the other takes the form of a 'non-compliance epidemic': if, for some reason, more people start to evade, the stigma decreases and evasion spreads to an ever larger fraction of the population (see Benjamini and Maital, 1985; Gordon, 1989; Myles and Naylor, 1996; Kim, 2003). Further empirical observations on the impact of sociological factors are reviewed in Section 4.

Risk allocation Alm and McCallin (1990), Landskroner et al. (1990), Yaniv (1990), and Wrede (1995) have extended the A-S approach with models in which taxpayers face more complex 'portfolio' set-ups offering other risky activities and alternative forms of evasion. Wadhawan (1992) posits that audits detect only a fraction of the taxpayer's evasion, while Das-Gupta (1994) analyses the case in which the income derives from a multiplicity of transactions.

Non-expected utility theory A major effort has been made to develop alternatives to expected utility theory to account for the behaviour patterns observed in experiments and other risk allocation contexts. This strand of research has been at once highly productive and somehow inconclusive: non-expected-utility models have proliferated, but none, so far, has clearly emerged as the definitive alternative to expected utility. Some have been fruitfully applied to the evasion gamble: see, among others, Bernasconi (1998), Eide (2002), and Bernasconi and Zanardi (2004). These models provide for a broader range of taxpayer responses to the evasion challenge, as they allow for the overestimation of low probabilities (for example, in rank dependent expected utility) or differential treatment of gains and losses with respect to a reference point (prospect theory). The comparative statics results of A-S have been shown to carry over to some important families of non-expected-utility models (Eide, 2002), but not to others (Dhami and Al-Nowaihi, 2007). Overall, the actual 'goodness' of these models can only be assessed with reference to their ability to fit observed behaviour in specific evasion contexts. An interesting insight from non-expected-utility theory is that advanced by Yaniv (1999): if taxpayers respond asymmetrically to gains and losses, as prospect theory hypothesizes, then compliance can be enhanced by changing the 'reference point' for the taxpayer's evaluation, for instance through a substantial tax payment on account. In this way, a taxpayer reporting his tax liability correctly gets a tax refund when he submits his tax return: compliance turns into a clear 'gain' and taxpayer attitude towards risk will change accordingly (in a beneficial way).

Tax uncertainty Alm (1988), Scotchmer and Slemrod (1989), Scotchmer (1989a), and Snow and Warren (2005) consider the effect of randomness in tax liability assessments. They all conclude that uncertainty over the true liability level or the outcome of the audit increases net tax revenue, either because greater uncertainty makes evasion more costly (when taxpayers are risk averse) or because it may induce taxpayers to underreport their income and so be fined, whereas overreporting yields only a tax rebate. This is not to suggest that the revenue service should deliberately create uncertainty over the application of the law, as this would surely increase the deadweight loss of tax enforcement (see Section 3) and possibly decrease social welfare. Also, vagueness in the formulation of the law would likely embolden confident taxpayers and eventually undermine the credibility of the system. For this reason, most revenue services provide advance rulings on request (OECD, 2007).

Labour supply Several authors have tried to extend the A-S model to include the labour supply decision, so as to endogenise taxpayers' gross income (see, among others, Andersen, 1977; Pencavel, 1979; Isachsen and Strom, 1980; Isachsen et al., 1985; and Cowell, 1985). The problem is that as soon as the decision to work is factored in, Allingham and Sandmo's simple comparative statics are lost. Depending on the taxpayer's marginal disutility from labour and risk attitudes, every outcome becomes possible. Usually, researchers overcome this problem by imposing strong restrictions on the utility function. Cowell (1985) takes a different course, assuming that decisions are made in two separate stages: first, the taxpayer decides how many hours to work; then he allocates this total labour supply between legal and illegal activities (alternatively, between reported and unreported income). On this assumption, Cowell shows that Allingham and Sandmo's results carry over (with some qualifications) to the extended set-up if the taxpayer's labour supply curve is upward sloping. Perhaps more importantly, he shows that the comparative statics results are strictly dependent on the nature of the evasion choice, as it can be tied either to the amount of income to report (for the self-employed) or to the amount of time spent in 'off-the-books' activities (for the moonlighter).

Evasion of indirect taxes The insights drawn from the analysis of income tax evasion usually fit other forms of evasion as well. Different considerations may apply, however, when the taxpayer is a firm subject to indirect taxation, for here tax evasion decision may affect output or pricing (tax shifting). However, Marrelli (1984), for the case of a monopolist, derives a result of separability: the evasion and shifting decisions are independent of one another as long as the audit probability is constant (see also Yaniv, 1995). The same result applies to oligopolistic markets when firms compete à la Cournot. The amount of evasion by each firm is shown to depend, aside from the enforcement parameters, on the degree of collusion and on market shares (Marrelli and Martina, 1988). The separability result does not hold, however, if there is free entry into the industry (Goerke and Runkel, 2007) or if the audit rate depends on comparative reporting (Bayer and Cowell, 2006).

Gordon (1990) offers an interesting insight into sales tax evasion. He suggests that under-the-counter cash sales may serve as a means of price discrimination: cash discounts are the best pricing strategy when the demand for cash purchases is highly elastic. He shows further that imposing a liability on detected cash customers could reduce cash sales, but only on condition that this is an *additional* liability, and not just the transfer of a part of the supplier's existing liability to the consumer.

Corporate tax evasion Tax evasion by corporations raises the important question of who makes the decision whether to comply with the law or not. In a publicly held corporation, this decision is usually delegated to a tax department headed by a specialized manager (chief financial officer (CFO), say, or a vice president for taxation). The problem here is the conflict of interest between shareholders and the officer in charge of the tax returns. Crocker and Slemrod (2005) develop an interesting extension of A-S in which the degree of non-compliance (the amount of illegal deductions claimed) is decided by a CFO whose remuneration depends on 'performance' (taxes saved). Only the CFO, however, knows the 'true' lawful level of deductions. Thus, his remuneration should give him an incentive to reduce the tax base (illegally), even if this may lead to a personal sanction. The authors show that under these conditions, a sanction on the CFO has greater deterrent power than a sanction on the corporation, since the latter can be passed on only very imperfectly to the party making the decision.

As we have seen, taxpayer non-compliance decisions may be very complex, and they are likely to be shaped by the practical framework of action. The empirical evidence in favour of this view, which we now briefly review, is quite abundant.

4. Empirical evidence on taxpayers' behaviour

Evidence on taxpayers' behaviour is notoriously difficult to come by. Data on the extent of evasion may be confidential (not available for external analysis) or not fully reliable (drawn, say, from national accounting sources). All the same, empirical studies on the determinants of taxpayers' compliance decisions have proliferated. The most important sources of empirical data are reviewed below.

Compliance measurement programmes

One of the most thorough investigations of tax evasion is the American Taxpayer Compliance Measurement Program (TCMP), conducted on a yearly basis by the IRS from 1963 to 1988 and based on a 'line by line' audit of a sample of 45,000 to 55,000 tax returns. This programme has now been replaced by the less ambitious National Research Program, which reviews some 46,000 returns, but not line by line. On the basis of this programme, the IRS estimates that for the 2001 tax year, the overall gross tax gap was $345 billion, corresponding to a non-compliance rate of 16.3 percent. After accounting for enforcement efforts and late payments, the amount was reduced to $290 billion, corresponding to a net non-compliance rate of 13.7 percent. *Underreporting* (unreported receipts and overstated expenses) accounts for 82 percent of the gross tax gap, *underpayment* for 10 percent and *non-filing* for 8 percent. Compliance rates vary widely across tax return classes. About 56 percent of the individual underreporting gap came from understated net business income (for example, unreported receipts and overstated expenses); 28 percent came from underreported non-business income, such as wages, tips, interest, dividends, and capital gains; and the remaining 16 percent came from overstated subtractions from income (that is, statutory adjustments, deductions, and exemptions) and from overstated tax credits (IRS, 2007a).

Ostensibly, compliance is highest where there is substantial reporting of information and substantial withholding of tax. Items subject to withholding and reporting, such as wages and salaries, have a misreporting rate of 1 percent; items subject to substantial information reporting (but no withholding), like interest and dividend income, have an average misreporting rate of 5 percent; items subject to some information reporting, like capital gains, show an average misreporting of 9 percent; while items subject to little or no information reporting, such as farm income and non-farm proprietor income, have an average misreporting rate of 54 percent (IRS, 2007b).

Audit returns were a prime source of data for the early investigations on the evasion phenomenon. In his pioneering analysis, Clotfelter (1983) uses TCMP data for 1969 to investigate the determinants of underreporting, defined as the difference between the income reported and that assessed by IRS examiners. He finds that both the marginal tax rate and after-tax income have significant effects on individual underreporting. In contrast to Allingham and Sandmo's prediction, he finds that elasticities with respect to marginal tax rates are positive and range from 0.5 for non-farm business to 0.8 for non-business returns. In line with Allingham and Sandmo, elasticities with respect to after-tax income are positive and range from 0.3 for non-business returns to 0.65 for farm returns. Also, wages, interest and dividends are associated with better compliance, while underreporting is higher for the youngest age groups.

Witte and Woodbury (1985) also analyse data from the TCMP for 1969, but focus on the effect of enforcement parameters. They find that the percentage of underreporting is related inversely to the probability of audit (with a lagged effect), and directly to the 'opportunities' for tax evasion (absence of withholding and information reporting) and to income, though in a decreasing way. Dubin and Wilde (1988) criticise these results and highlight the potential endogeneity of audit rates. The idea is that audit rates are decided by the IRS in view of their potential yield: a decrease in non-compliance rates reduces the net return from auditing and leads the IRS to devote less effort to auditing. Using the IRS budget per return as an instrumental variable for the audit rates, they find the audit rate to be endogenous in five out of seven audit classes. They also find that audits have a deterrent effect on evasion, and that non-compliance is positively related to the unemployment rate and the non-white fraction of the population. Feinstein (1991) uses a sophisticated estimation technique that allows for partial detection by IRS examiners. His results confirm the great unevenness in compliance attitudes between groups of taxpayers, with 'own business' and 'farm' filers scoring the lowest compliance rates. Using TCMP data for 1982 and 1985, Feinstein more easily disentangles the effects of marginal tax rates and gross income (taxpayers with identical incomes filing in different years face different marginal tax rates). He finds that the effect of marginal tax rates on evasion is negative and highly significant, while the effect of income is essentially nil. The former finding is consistent with Allingham and Sandmo's predictions, while the latter is not. Another finding is that a greater propensity to evade is accompanied by a higher detection rate (thanks to greater IRS examination effort).

Studies based on IRS data show that many factors come into the tax-compliance picture: income source, socio-economic group (age, sex, location, ethnicity), detection probability, marginal tax rate and income level. Strikingly, however, the severity of the sanction does not seem to play a significant role (perhaps because in the US sanctions are rarely inflicted).

One important lesson to be learned from the IRS data is that compliance rates vary enormously across categories and are strongly related to enforcement mechanisms such as withholding and information reporting. This result fits very well with deterrence theory, since it is easier to detect the evasion of liabilities subject to withholding and information reporting. Whether the compliance pattern fits with Allingham and Sandmo's theory is harder to tell. What one cannot do, in any case, is to take the average number of examinations per taxpayer (which would not exceed 1 percent), plug it into A-S model and claim that the predicted compliance rates are far below actual compliance rates (regrettably, this is a very common mistake). What evidence is available shows precisely this: information reporting and other enforcement mechanisms greatly reduce the chance that even tiny amounts of evasion will go undetected. Just to get a feel for the magnitude of the phenomenon, let us observe that in fiscal year 2007, about 1.82 billion reports were received by the US Internal Revenue Service and matched by computer with taxpayer records (IRS, 2007b). By no means can actual detection probabilities be proxied by the ratio between the number of audits and the total number of taxpayers.

Surveys

Another important source of information on taxpayers' attitudes is surveys. A good deal of work has been done in this area as well, and the results cannot be easily generalized (see, for instance, Richardson, 2006, and the literature cited therein). On the whole, these studies would appear to support the deterrence hypothesis. Specifically, the following factors have been found to be significant determinants of tax compliance: (1) the perceived probability of detection; (2) the severity of informal sanctions; (3) moral beliefs about tax compliance; (4) experience with other non-compliers and past experience with IRS enforcement (both encouraging evasion), (5) socio-demographic characteristics (older people and women tend to evade less, educated people tend to evade less), (6) the perceived complexity of the tax system (more complexity, more evasion), (7) the perceived fairness of the tax system (greater fairness, less evasion), (8) tax morale (high morale, low evasion). These findings are largely concordant with those based on the TCMP data. The main additional insight relates to the impact of sociological factors, which can hardly be detected by other means.

International comparative studies that try to relate observance of the law with the general cultural attitudes of individuals are most interesting in this regard. This line of research originates with the Weberian view that long-term factors like 'culture' or 'religion', in addition to, or despite, formal institutions (statute law, public governance), affect economic behaviour and possibly the extent to which people are law abiding.

Major surveys of people's cultural attitudes (for example, the *World Values Survey*) have found a great variety of attitudes around the world. Most of the axiological dimensions measured by the value surveys seem to be strongly correlated across cultural regions (see, for instance, www.worldvaluessurvey.org).

Several of the variables covered in these surveys are relevant to tax evasion. First, and most importantly, looking at responses to the question 'Is tax cheating justified?' in the *World Values Survey*, one can get a feel for 'tax morale' in different countries. In a comparison between the US and European states, for instance, Alm and Torgler (2006) find that US citizens have the highest tax morale, and that tax morale is strongly and negatively correlated with the size of the shadow economy.

A second interesting focus of research is the relationship between attitudes to obedience to the law and other cultural dimensions of individual countries. Using the Schwartz dataset, Licht et al. (2007) show that views on the 'rule of law' and 'corruption' are positively correlated with cultural attitudes relating to 'social embeddedness' (versus 'autonomy') and 'egalitarianism' (versus 'hierarchy'). The world thus seems to be divided into different cultural areas, some characterized by strong social embeddedness, strong hierarchical relationships, widespread corruption and weak rule of law. In turn, the level of the 'corruption' variable is shown to be strongly correlated with the size of the unofficial sector – and thus indirectly with tax evasion – in each country. The causal link seems to run from cultural-sociological factors to weak institutions and, finally, to a large unofficial economy.

One implicit lesson to be learned from this cross-cultural literature is that one should be wary of generalizing policy prescriptions. Legal and institutional provisions that work in one country may not work in another. For instance, stiff penalties for cheaters may not reduce tax evasion in a world where formal laws are not respected, and where social pressure and interpersonal relationships are the main forces driving compliance.

Experiments

A third, increasingly common empirical approach is based on 'laboratory' experiments (see, for instance, Baldry, 1987; Webley et al., 1991; Alm et al., 1993a; Alm et al., 1993b; Alm et al., 1995; Alm et al., 1999; Cadsby et al., 2006). The subjects participate in games simulating tax compliance, where they can underreport and incur the risk of a penalty. At the end, they receive a real reward proportional to their laboratory performance. The results tend to be highly sensitive to the design of the experiment. In general, this research suggests that audit rates play an important role in compliance decisions (especially for those who have already been audited) and that compliance is an increasing function of income and a decreasing function of the tax rate, while it is hardly affected by the size of fines (unless the audit rate is very high). These experiments also suggest that social norms and ethical attitudes play an important part in evasion choices, that individuals often take an all-or-nothing stance, that they tend to overweight low probabilities, that the structure of taxes is important. While the presence of an authority figure in the room increases compliance (Cadsby et al., 2006), direct appeals to taxpayers' conscience seem to have no significant effects (Blumenthal et al., 2001; Torgler, 2004).

Empirical investigations of the evasion phenomenon, carried out by economists, sociologists and psychologists, put the 'law and economics' approach into perspective. This approach emphasises the relationship between economic behaviour and legal rules, given the sociological and cultural environment (which is of course important, but not central to the analysis). The analysis investigates the impact of the enforcement process on an abstract 'rational man' pursuing self-interest. In this case, the rational man aims at minimising net payments to the tax administration (possibly allowing for risk aversion). Civic virtue, moral duty, social pressure, and other moral and social factors remain in the background. The fundamental hypothesis of the classic law and economics approach is that enforcement policy does not crowd out 'other' socio-psychological compliance factors. So far, this assumption has not been disproved by empirical research.

In the broad context of obedience to the law, tax compliance is probably one of the areas where the rationality assumption is most realistic. The benefits and costs of non-compliance can be evaluated in strictly monetary terms, possibly with the help of a tax expert; emotional considerations play a limited role – there is basically no 'victim' to imagine or sympathise with.

Note further that tax enforcement has traditionally relied on deterrence, rather than other, gentler tools. Since ancient times, taxation has been the visible outcome of the wielding of political and military power. Thus, unlike compliance with more culturally grounded norms – for instance those regulating sexual behaviour or neighbourly behaviour – tax compliance has constantly been anchored to the state's enforcement power.

The following section considers the question of the optimal design of tax enforcement policy, focusing on the detection and punishment of evaders.

5. Optimal tax enforcement

Let us go back to the model of Allingham and Sandmo. While it provides a fairly sophisticated description of taxpayers' evasion decisions, it leaves very little scope for enforcement policy, which is essentially reduced to two parameters: the penalty rate and the audit rate. The main policy prescription implicit in the model and most of its variants is that to curb evasion, audits have to be stepped up and fines increased. And given that raising the audit rate requires public resources while an increase in the penalty rate does not, the end result is likely to be one with Draconian but rare punishment, a rule such as 'hang evaders with probability (close to) zero'.

This is a difficult prescription to elude. But in fact it is not clear whether curbing or eliminating evasion is always a desirable goal. In general terms, the desirability of perfect enforcement depends on the 'goodness' of the tax to be enforced. For instance, when full enforcement of income tax would result in the collapse of an activity, one may well ask whether such unbearable tax rates represent the right policy.

Even if the tax is optimally designed, a Draconian sanction may not be a good policy, especially if the sanction is actually administered and not purely a deterrent. The following arguments against maximal sanctions have been advanced:

(a) *Imperfect adjudication* Innocent people may be convicted and guilty ones may be acquitted. In this case, very severe penalties are likely to create great ex-post inequality (unfairness), which may outweigh the beneficial effects of strong deterrence (see Cowell, 1990). The effect is even more problematic if individuals themselves include fairness in their utility function, as Polinsky and Shavell (2000) suggest.

(b) *Taxpayer's error* As before, if huge penalties are levied on taxpayers who have failed to comply merely by mistake, strong ex-post inequality is likely to arise. Thus, the penalty should be mitigated so as to account for good-faith non-compliance. Obviously, this argument presupposes that good faith cannot be faked.

(c) *Avoidance costs* If individuals actively seek to avoid conviction, the social cost of enforcement may increase with the penalty. In this case, a smaller penalty may be preferable (Malik, 1990). On the other hand, completely eradicating avoidance would not appear to be a practicable goal.

(d) *Reasonable doubt* If the sanction is administered by a body (a judge, a court, an officer) that makes its decision ex post on the basis of imperfect information, then large penalties may induce greater caution in convictions and possibly reduce the number of convictions (the standard of proof is likely to get tighter). As a consequence, larger sanctions may actually result in weaker deterrence (Andreoni, 1991a).

From a practical point of view, the major impediment to Draconian penalties stems from taxpayers' limited wealth. Since convicted evaders cannot be forced to labour, they can only pay a penalty as large as their own assets. The Draconian rule thus needs to be rephrased as follows: *in the presence of an infallible tax enforcer and perfectly knowledgeable taxpayers, the optimal penalty is that which expropriates the taxpayer of all his wealth ('maximal sanction').*

No such penalty is actually enforced. While practice varies greatly across countries, a common approach sees penalties for minor offences of the order of 10–30 percent of the tax evaded, while more serious offences involving deliberate evasion are sanctioned with penalties ranging from 40 to 75 percent of evaded taxes (OECD, 2007). Criminal tax fraud may lead to imprisonment.

Optimal auditing

Enforcement policies can be much more sophisticated than a mere combination of two variables, the penalty rate and the audit rate. The audit probability itself, for instance, need not be the same for all taxpayers. Indeed, a simple strategy is to base audits on information specific to the taxpayer, which may include any observable characteristic correlated with real tax liability, from compliance records to consumption patterns. Then, the relationship of an individual's reported tax liability to the average for similar taxpayers can be used to single out candidates for auditing.

In a classic article, Reinganum and Wilde (1985) show that by making audits conditional on the level of the reported liability, the enforcer can increase net revenue. They postulate a simple cut-off rule that triggers an audit only when reported income is 'too low'. They demonstrate that this rule is superior to the random audit rule considered by Allingham and Sandmo, and that it is the most economical way to foster truthful reporting when taxpayers are risk neutral and taxes and fines are lump sum. Scotchmer (1987) and Sanchez and Sobel (1993) extend this result and show that the cut-off audit rule is the *optimal* policy for a net revenue-maximizing enforcer when taxes and fines are proportional and taxpayers are risk neutral. These findings prompt a number of observations.

First, cost-efficient enforcement requires that audits be primarily deterrents, not a means to collect fines. Their function is to foster correct self-reporting by individuals. Indeed, under the optimal policy, audits will be performed only on people who are found (ex post) to be honest, so no fines will ever be collected.

Second, the optimal cut-off level is strictly dependent on the distribution of income among the population: effective auditing requires reliable information on taxpayers' liability.

Finally, optimal enforcement is likely to induce a strong regressive bias, as it provides high-income taxpayers with better chances to evade than low-income taxpayers. The idea is that high-income individuals have greater opportunities to misreport, and since it is more costly to deter them from evading, one should let them off the hook (on this, see also Scotchmer, 1992). This problem may be alleviated by shaping audit policy according to indexes correlated with true income (Scotchmer, 1987; Macho-Stadler and Pérez-Castrillo, 2002) and, to a lesser extent, by suitably adjusting the tax rate (Cremer et al., 1990).

A simple variation of the cut-off rule is represented by the FATOTA policy (fixed amount of taxes or tax audit) used in several countries and analysed by Chu (1990). Taxpayers can elect either to pay a fixed amount of taxes set by the tax administration and be exempted from auditing, or to pay only what they themselves claim to owe and be subject to standard tax audits (at a constant rate). This policy dominates the constant-audit rate policy à la A-S in a large variety of settings, including non-linear tax and penalty schedules and endogenous labour supply (see Ueng and Yang, 2001). One may wonder whether in practice this enforcement policy may not simply amount to a modification of the tax schedule, bringing the marginal rate on top incomes down to zero, as suggested by optimal tax theory. In fact, however, the FATOTA is not equivalent to a simple rescheduling of the statutory tax rates, because lower rates also reduce the penalty for underreporting (the penalty is usually proportional to the amount of taxes evaded), whereas the FATOTA reduces the upfront tax payment, but not the penalty (in case of detection, the liability is calculated with reference to the standard tax rate, not the fixed amount).

Border and Sobel (1987), Mookherjee and Png (1989), Marhuenda and Ortuno-Ortin (1997), Chander and Wilde (1998), Hindriks (1999) and Chander (2007) all address the problem of simultaneously setting optimal audit and tax schedules, assuming that taxpayers have limited liability and that the enforcer's objective is to maximise net tax revenue. The basic finding of this literature is that, at the optimum, effective taxation tends to be regressive and the audit function is non-increasing in reported income. Hence, the implications of non-compliance for effective taxation indicated by Scotchmer (1987) and Sanchez and Sobel (1993) carry over to this more general set-up. An interesting insight (Border and Sobel, 1987) is that when sanctions are upper-bounded and taxpayers are risk neutral, it is optimal to have a very small probability of auditing and to provide infinite rewards for truthful reporting.

The approach to enforcement discussed in the foregoing paragraphs is known as the so-called 'principal-agent' approach. It is one of the most general frameworks for analysing tax evasion and how it relates to public policy. Its shortcoming is that it makes extremely demanding assumptions concerning the enforcer's ability to devise and execute the optimal policy. Indeed, one may argue that the characteristics of actual tax enforcers do not always qualify them as 'rational'. They often have conflicting or ill-defined incentives, their rules may be oriented to 'process' rather than 'outcome', and they are likely to have short-sighted and perhaps multiple conflicting goals. This suggests that the enforcer may tend to behave myopically and just 'react' to impulses from the economic system. The enforcer may, for instance, take the amount of evasion in the economy as given and act only to maximise detection, while disregarding deterrence. This thesis, based on the assumption that the tax enforcer cannot credibly pre-commit to any specific auditing policy, is advanced forcefully by Graetz et al. (1986) and Reinganum and Wilde (1986). Their argument is that as actual audit rates are not observed by taxpayers, the enforcer has an incentive to relax any announced auditing policy once the tax returns are in, that is, once the policy has performed its deterrent effect. Since taxpayers will anticipate the enforcer's ex-post deviation, they will not believe the announced policy and will engage in greater evasion. The conclusion is that, in equilibrium, audits will be performed on likely evaders rather than on compliant (that is, deterred) taxpayers. This would appear to be a most reasonable prediction, and in fact it tallies with actual enforcement practices.

The insights of the two types of model on tax enforcement differ. 'Principal-agent' models (with commitment) are probably best used to define the constraints that tax evasion puts on the effective tax system. They neatly define the set of implementable allocations on the assumption that the enforcer performs at maximum capacity. The 'no-commitment' approach, with a lower profile, aims at capturing a version of tax enforcement closer to actual practice.

Several authors have considered the problem of optimal tax enforcement in a repeated-game setting (see, for instance, Landsberger and Meilijson, 1982; Greenberg, 1984; Harrington, 1988). The results are highly instructive. Greenberg (1984) proposes a simple enforcement scheme in which taxpayers are separated into three distinct groups depending on their 'criminal history'. If an individual is caught cheating once, he is relegated to a 'purgatory' state where he can redeem himself by not cheating and getting back into the 'paradise' of non-cheaters. If the individual in purgatory is recidivist and gets caught again, he is sent down to an 'inferno' where audits are carried out with a probability of one. The prospect of sure auditing for an infinite time horizon is sufficient to ensure compliance by (almost) everybody at a very low cost. This model shows that the intertemporal dimension, namely the ability to sort individuals according to past behaviour, greatly strengthens standard enforcement tools (the 'leverage effect'). This theory should be related to the literature on recidivism in criminal law enforcement.

6. Tax enforcement procedure

It is clear by now that compliance decisions in the real world are far more complex than in standard economic models and that enforcement unquestionably means more than the correct combination of the penalty and audit rates. The path from checking tax returns to the conviction of evaders is long and twisted. The process involves various bodies (tax administration, tax courts) and specific procedures (interviews, cross-examinations, settlements, etc.). The shape of the enforcement procedure affects taxpayers' attitudes towards compliance in two ways. First, it determines the actual probability that a sanction will be imposed on evaders and, possibly, innocent taxpayers; and second, it may affect the degree of 'hostility' in taxpayers' perception of the system.

We will touch briefly on some of these procedural and institutional aspects.

Compliance costs

According to a number of studies, the cost to the taxpayer of compliance with the most common taxes (income and VAT) in industrialised countries can be as high as 10 or 13 percent of the total tax liability (see Gale and Holtzblatt, 2000; Guyton et al., 2003; and references therein). High compliance costs, which may be due to complex tax schedules and rules, not only tilt the 'cost-benefit analysis' towards evasion, but may also cause resentment, weakening taxpayers' moral conscience or even prompting evasion as a form of 'retaliation' against the tax administration. Legislatures should accordingly avoid the vicious circle of countering evasion by increasing the complexity of tax regulations, further raising compliance costs with the risk of more evasion.

Tax experts

When tax law is very complicated, taxpayers usually have to turn to tax experts (CPAs or tax preparers), who exert considerable influence on their clients' attitudes towards evasion, thanks to their superior knowledge of enforcement patterns. An empirical study by Klepper and Nagin (1989) suggests that US tax preparers encourage compliance with regard to unequivocal items, and discourage it with regard to ambiguous ones. Other studies of this issue are Scotchmer (1989b), Reinganum and Wilde (1991), Erard (1993 and 1997), Franzoni (1998), Phillips and Sansing (1998) and Lipatov (2007).

Defence costs

Audits and tax litigation impose costs on taxpayers, whether compliant or not. According to deterrence theory, honest taxpayers should not bear any cost whatever. On the contrary, optimal enforcement would require that the taxpayer be rewarded when an audit finds that he is compliant (Border and Sobel, 1987; Boadway and Sato, 2000). Apart from the adverse impact on enforcement, defence costs might have the additional disadvantage of prompting 'nuisance' auditing by a greedy tax administration: lengthy and invasive auditing whose sole purpose is to extort money from the taxpayer, possibly in the form of a legal settlement (Franzoni, 2000) if not an illegal bribe (Hindriks et al., 1999).

Record-keeping

Costs are also entailed in mandatory record-keeping and reporting, whose role is to increase the visibility of offences, that is, the 'frequency and ease with which they come to the attention of and can be proved by enforcement officials' (Kagan, 1989). As noted in Section 4, non-compliance varies greatly with economic grouping, as tax violation by different groups has different degrees of 'visibility'. Unsurprisingly, therefore, evasion appears to be most widespread among independent contractors, professionals and farmers; compliance highest among payroll employees subject to withholding.

In a technical sense, greater visibility makes it easier both to 'observe' the real situation or behaviour of the taxpayer (by signalling potential violations) and to 'verify' it (prove it in court). Some forms of mandatory record-keeping, for example, serve a legal evidentiary function, constituting a de facto shift of the burden of proof. It is the taxpayer who has to prove his compliance with the law and bear the costs thereof. The optimal extent of compliance obligations is therefore bound up with the optimal allocation of the burden of proof. Generally, the efficient allocation is that which places the onus of the proof on the party for which it is least costly (given its level of informativeness).

Standard of proof

Another important factor in the 'visibility' of tax law violations is the standard of proof. Indeed, the difference between the 'observability' and the 'verifiability' of the tax base is precisely defined by the type of evidence that is necessary to assess it legally (and possibly prove that the original payments were not correct). In most countries, tax authorities have the power to estimate the liability by discretionary means when the information supplied by the taxpayer is insufficient or clearly incorrect (OECD, 2007). Clearly, under these circumstances, the standard of proof can be rather lax, and mere statistical evidence can be used as proof of taxpayers' liabilities. Presumptive taxation is a case in which statistical estimates and proxies are used *ab origine* to define the tax obligation, resulting in the automatic visibility of the activities covered and imposing virtually no compliance costs on taxpayers (see Tanzi, 1990). Note that simplifications and reductions in compliance costs will ordinarily be achieved only at the expense of a reduced ability to discriminate among taxpayers (for purposes of either vertical or horizontal equity). As Kaplow (1996) observes, there is likely to be a trade-off between compliance costs and accuracy of assessment.

Settlement

On the procedural side, another important consideration is the possibility of resolving tax disputes by amicable settlement. In most countries, taxpayers can make a 'deal' with inspectors and obtain substantial penalty discounts in exchange for collaboration. As the literature on pre-trial bargaining shows (see Chapters 5 and 6 in this Encyclopedia), settlements avoid adjudication costs. However, by reducing the expected payments of violators, settlements may undermine enforcement. For this reason, overall, their desirability remains dubious. Using different models, Macho-Stadler and Pérez-Castrillo (2002) and Franzoni (2004) argue that settlements allow tax inspectors to use their specific information ('professional judgement'). On this basis, they can 'price discriminate' among taxpayers. If the information is precise enough, settlement is unambiguously desirable in tax enforcement.

Tax amnesties

Some countries occasionally offer generalised pardons to taxpayers who agree to participate in amnesty programmes. The programmes vary enormously in nature and scope (see Das-Gupta and Mookherjee, 1996, and Franzoni, 1996, for general overviews). In the United States and most European countries, the amnesty programme generally gives taxpayers the chance to pay back taxes at a reduced rate, with no further benefits. In some Latin American countries and in Italy, amnesties can go so far as to provide participants with full indemnity against further liability. The amnesty thus works like a generalised tax settlement, open both to taxpayers who are already engaged in litigation with the tax administration and to taxpayers who could start litigation. The rationale for such measures is hard to determine, but can be ascribed to structural problems in the enforcement system (which might be unable to deal with massive non-compliance proceedings), short-sighted revenue needs of government (Stella, 1991) or an inability to lower excessively high tax rates (Franzoni, 2000).

Tax amnesties of narrow scope, like those allowing for the simple possibility of revising one's own tax return, may be a desirable feature of the enforcement system, as they offer taxpayers social insurance against unexpected shocks, allowing them to complete their payments after uncertainty (about their income or their true preferences) has been resolved (Andreoni, 1991b; Malik and Schwab, 1991).

Private enforcement

A fundamental problem for the optimal institutional design of tax enforcement is incentives for enforcers. Basically, the question is whether enforcement should be the job of public or private agents. First raised in general terms by Becker and Stigler (1974), the issue has been examined in the specific context of tax evasion by several authors. While in most countries taxes are collected by a public agency, in a few (for example, import duties in Indonesia), collection is delegated to private contractors. Melumad and Mookherjee (1989) show that the delegation of tax enforcement to a private party may be viable (that is, it can replicate the full-commitment solution) if it is backed by an incentive scheme based on publicly observable aggregate variables (audit expenditure, taxes filed and fines collected). This scheme rewards the agent for collecting fines, or, when no fine is collected, for meeting the target audit budget. Toma and Toma (1992) observe that different institutional arrangements may entail different agency costs, so that depending on their incidence, either public or private enforcement may be desirable,

Corruption

A key agency cost is generated by the danger of corruption. Since the personal interests of enforcement officers may not correspond to institutional aims, there is scope for collusion with taxpayers. This seriously complicates the analysis, as a third constraint (no collusion) must now be placed on the models. For while it may be contended that combating corruption can help control tax evasion, it may well be that anti-evasion measures as such just increase the scope for and the extent of corruption (see among others Chu, 1990; Chander and Wilde, 1992; Besley and McLaren, 1993; Mookherjee and Png, 1995; Flatters and MacLeod, 1995;

Hindriks et al., 1999). This only confirms that the institutional features of the enforcement system are a point of fundamental importance, as they define the incentive structure governing the conduct of enforcers and determine the actual functioning of all enforcement tools.

7. Conclusion

Of concern to all governments, tax evasion has been subjected to intense inquiry by economists and social scientists. A very large body of literature has been produced, both theoretical and empirical. This literature is of special interest to law-and-economics scholars interested in the mechanism of compliance with the law. Tax evasion, like such other economic crimes as corruption and fraud, can be suitably studied through the lens of the standard rationality assumption. This line of research has stressed the deterrent effect of the enforcement process, with special attention to audit policy and the penalty schedule.

Whereas in other fields of law and economics the insights of psychology and sociology have been applied only recently (Jolls, 2008), in the matter of tax evasion the social sciences have contributed from the earliest stages. Accordingly, no major behavioural revolution in the analysis of the phenomenon is to be expected. This does not mean, however, that there is no need for further research. Many features of the enforcement process remain unexamined, despite their great impact on the incentives for compliance. Among these, the most important are the structure of withholding and information reporting, the procedure for proof of violation (for example, the burden of proof and the standard of proof), the determinants of the taxpayer's culpability, the structure of the audit process and the litigation procedure, the actual powers of the tax administration to investigate and decide cases. There is a particularly great need for empirical inquiry into the impact of procedural specifications.

References

Allingham, M. and A. Sandmo (1972), 'Income Tax Evasion: A Theoretical Analysis', *Journal of Public Economics*, **1**, 323–38.

Alm, J. (1988), 'Uncertain Tax Policies, Individual Behaviour, and Welfare', *The American Economic Review*, **78** (1), 237–45.

Alm, J. and N. McCallin (1990), 'Tax Avoidance and Tax Evasion as a Joint Portfolio Choice', *Public Finance*, **45** (2), 193–200.

Alm, J. and B. Torgler (2006), 'Culture Differences and Tax Morale in the United States and Europe', *Journal of Economic Psychology*, **27**, 224–46.

Alm, J., M. Cronshaw and M. McKee (1993a), 'Tax Compliance with Endogenous Audit Selection Rules', *Kyklos*, **46** (1), 27–45.

Alm, J., B. Jackson and M. McKee (1993b), 'Fiscal Exchange, Collective Decision Institutions, and Tax Compliance', *Journal of Economic Behaviour and Organization*, **22** (3), 285–303.

Alm, J., I. Sanchez and A. de Juan (1995), 'Economic and Noneconomic Factors in Tax Compliance', *Kyklos*, **48** (1), 3–18.

Alm, J., G.H McClelland and W.D. Schulze (1999), 'Changing the Social Norm of Tax Compliance by Voting', *Kyklos*, **52**, 141–71.

Andersen, P. (1977), 'Tax Evasion and Labor Supply', *Scandinavian Journal of Economics*, **79** (3), 375–83.

Andreoni, J. (1991a), 'Reasonable Doubt and the Optimal Magnitude of Fines: Should the Penalty Fit the Crime?', *RAND Journal of Economics*, **22** (3), Autumn, 385–95.

Andreoni, J. (1991b), 'The Desirability of a Permanent Tax Amnesty', *Journal of Public Economics*, **45** (2), 143–59.

Andreoni, J., B. Erard and J. Feinstein (1998), 'Tax Compliance', *Journal of Economic Literature*, **36** (2), 818–60.

Baldry, J. (1987), 'Income Tax Evasion and the Tax Schedule: Some Experimental Results', *Public Finance*, **42** (3), 357–83.

Bayer, R. and F. Cowell (2006), 'Tax Compliance and Firms' Strategic Interdependence', mimeo.

Beccaria, C. (1764 [1968]), 'Tentativo analitico sui contrabbandi', *Il Caffè*, Brescia, Italy, pp. 118–19, translated as 'An Attempt at an Analysis of Smuggling', in W. Baumol and S. Goldfeld (eds), London: London School of Economics and Political Science, *Precursors in Mathematical Economics: An Anthology*.

Becker, G. (1968), 'Crime and Punishment: An Economic Approach', *Journal of Political Economy*, **76**, 169–217.

Becker, G. and G. Stigler (1974), 'Law Enforcement, Malfeasance, and Compensation of Enforcers', *Journal of Legal Studies*, **3** (1), 1–18.

Benjamini, Y. and S. Maital (1985), 'Optimal Tax Evasion and Optimal Tax Evasion Policy: Behavioral Aspects', in W. Gaertner and A. Wenig (eds), *The Economics of the Shadow Economy*, New York, Berlin and Tokyo: Springer.

Bernasconi, M. (1998), 'Tax Evasion and Orders of Risk Aversion', *Journal of Public Economics*, **67**, 123–34.

Bernasconi, M. and A. Zanardi (2004), 'Tax Evasion, Tax Rates, and Reference Dependence', *FinanzArchiv*, **60**, 422–45.

Besley, T. and J. McLaren (1993), 'Taxes and Bribery: The Role of Wage Incentives', *Economic Journal*, **103** (416), 119–41.

Bishop, J., J. Formby and P. Lambert (2000), 'Redistribution through the Income Tax: The Vertical and Horizontal Effects of Non-compliance and Tax Evasion', *Public Finance Review*, **28** (4), 335–50.

Blumenthal, M., C. Christian and J. Slemrod (2001), 'Do Normative Appeals Affect Tax Compliance? Evidence from a Controlled Experiment in Minnesota', *National Tax Journal*, **54** (1), March, 125–38.

Boadway, R. and M. Sato (2000), 'The Optimality of Punishing Only the Innocent: The Case of Tax Evasion', *International Tax and Public Finance*, **7** (6), 641–64.

Border, K. and J. Sobel (1987), 'Samurai Accountant: A Theory of Auditing and Plunder', *Review of Economic Studies*, **54** (4), 525–40.

Bordignon, M. (1993), 'A Fairness Approach to Income Tax Evasion', *Journal of Public Economics*, **52** (3), 345–62.

Cadsby, B., E. Maynes and V. Trivedi (2006), 'Tax Compliance and Obedience to Authority at Home and in the Lab: A New Experimental Approach', *Experimental Economics*, **9** (4), December, 343–59.

Chander, P. (2007), 'Income Tax Evasion and the Fear of Ruin', *Economica*, **74** (294), 315–28.

Chander, P. and L. Wilde (1992), 'Corruption in Tax Administration', *Journal of Public Economics*, **49** (3), 333–49.

Chander, P. and L. Wilde (1998), 'A General Characterization of Optimal Income Tax Enforcement', *Review of Economic Studies*, **65**, 165–83.

Chu, C. (1990), 'A Model of Income Tax Evasion with Venal Tax Officials: The Case of Taiwan', *Public Finance*, **45** (3), 392–408.

Clotfelter, C. (1983), 'Tax Evasion and Tax Rates: An Analysis of Individual Returns', *Review of Economics and Statistics*, **65** (3), 363–73.

Cowell, F. (1985), 'Tax Evasion with Labour Income', *Journal of Public Economics*, **26** (1), 19–34.
Cowell, F. (1990), *Cheating the Government: The Economics of Evasion*, Cambridge, MA and London: MIT Press.
Cowell, F. (2004), 'Carrots and Sticks in Enforcement', in H. Aaron and J. Slemrod (eds), *The Crisis in Tax Administration*, Washington, DC: The Brookings Institution.
Cremer, H., M. Marchand and P. Pestieau (1990), 'Evading, Auditing and Taxing: The Equity-compliance Tradeoff', *Journal of Public Economics*, **43** (1), 67–92.
Crocker, K. and J. Slemrod (2005), 'Corporate Tax Evasion with Agency Costs', *Journal of Public Economics*, **89** (9–10), September, 1593–610.
Das-Gupta, A. (1994), 'A Theory of Hard-to-tax Groups', *Public Finance*, **49**, 28–39.
Das-Gupta, A. and D. Mookherjee (1996), 'Tax Amnesties as Asset-laundering Devices', *Journal of Law, Economics and Organization*, **12**, 408–31.
Dhami, S. and A. Al-Nowaihi (2007), 'Why do People Pay Taxes? Prospect Theory versus Expected Utility Theory', *Journal of Economic Behaviour and Organization*, **64** (1), 171–92.
Dubin, J. and L. Wilde (1988), 'An Empirical Analysis of Federal Income Tax Auditing and Compliance', *National Tax Journal*, **41** (1), 61–74.
Eide, E. (2002), 'Tax Evasion with Rank Dependent Expected Utility', University of Oslo Working Paper.
Erard, Brian (1993), 'Taxation with Representation: An Analysis of the Role of Tax Practitioners in Tax Compliance', *Journal of Public Economics*, **52** (2), 163–97.
Erard, B. (1997), 'Self-selection with Measurement Errors: A Microeconometric Analysis of the Decision to Seek Tax Assistance and its Implications for Tax Compliance', *Journal of Econometrics*, **81**, 319–56.
Feinstein, J. (1991), 'An Econometric Analysis of Income Tax Evasion and its Detection', *RAND Journal of Economics*, **22** (1), 14–35.
Flatters, F. and B. MacLeod (1995), 'Administrative Corruption and Taxation', *International Tax and Public Finance*, **2** (3), 397–417.
Franzoni, L.A. (1996), 'Punishment and Grace: On the Economics of Tax Amnesties', *Public Finance/Finances Publiques*, **3**, 353–68.
Franzoni, L.A. (1998), 'Independent Auditors as Fiscal Gatekeepers', *International Review of Law and Economics*, **18** (4), 365–84.
Franzoni, L.A. (1999), 'Tax Evasion and Tax Compliance', in B. Bouckaert and G. De Geest (eds), *Encyclopedia of Law and Economics*, Cheltenham, UK and Northampton, MA, USA: Edward Elgar.
Franzoni, L.A. (2000), 'Amnesties, Settlements, and Optimal Tax Enforcement', *Economica*, **57**, 153–76.
Franzoni, L.A. (2004), 'Discretion in Tax Enforcement', *Economica*, **71**, 369–89.
Galbiati, R. and A. Zanardi (2001), 'The Redistributive Effects of Tax Evasion: A Comparison between Conventional and Multi-criteria Perspectives', SSRN Working Paper.
Gale, W. and J. Holtzblatt (2000), 'The Role of Administrative Issues in Tax Reform: Simplicity, Compliance, and Administration', in George Zodrow and Peter Mieszkowski (eds), *United States Tax Reform in the 21st Century*, Cambridge, UK: Cambridge University Press.
Gërxhani, K. (2004), 'The Informal Sector in Developed and Less Developed Countries: A Literature Survey', *Public Choice*, **120**, 267–300.
Goerke, L. and M. Runkel (2007), 'Tax Evasion and Competition', mimeo, available at SSRN.
Gordon, J. (1989), 'Individual Morality and Reputation Costs as Deterrents to Tax Evasion', *European Economic Review*, **33** (4), 797–805.
Gordon, J. (1990), 'Evading Taxes by Selling for Cash', *Oxford Economic Papers*, **42** (1), 244–55.
Graetz, M., J. Reinganum and L. Wilde (1986), 'The Tax Compliance Game: Toward an Interactive Theory of Law Enforcement', *Journal of Law, Economics and Organization*, **2** (1), 1–32.

Greenberg, J. (1984), 'Avoiding Tax Avoidance: A (Repeated) Game-theoretic Approach', *Journal of Economic Theory*, **32** (1), 1–13.
Guyton, J., J. O'Hare, M. Stavrianos and E. Toder (2003), 'Estimating the Compliance Cost of the U.S. Individual Income Tax', *National Tax Journal*, **56** (3), 673–88.
Harrington, W. (1988), 'Enforcement Leverage when Penalties are Restricted', *Journal of Public Economics*, **37**, 29–53.
Hindriks, J. (1999), 'On the Incompatibility between Revenue-Maximisation and Tax Progressivity', *European Journal of Political Economy*, **15**, 123–40.
Hindriks, J., M. Keen and A. Muthoo (1999), 'Corruption, Extortion and Evasion', *Journal of Public Economics*, **74** (3), 395–430.
IRS (2007a), *Reducing the Federal Tax Gap: A Report on Improving Voluntary Compliance*, Washington, DC: Internal Revenue Service, US Department of the Treasury.
IRS (2007b), *Data Book 2007*, Washington, DC: Internal Revenue Service, US Department of the Treasury.
Isachsen, A. and S. Strom (1980), 'The Hidden Economy: The Labor Market and Tax Evasion', *Scandinavian Journal of Economics*, **82** (2), 304–11.
Isachsen, A., S. Samuelson and S. Strom (1985), 'The Behaviour of Tax Evaders', in W. Gaertner and A. Wenig (eds), *The Economics of the Shadow Economy*, New York, Berlin and Tokyo: Springer.
Jolls, C. (2008), 'Behavioral Law and Economics', in P. Diamond and H. Vartianen (eds), *Behavioral Economics and its Applications*, Princeton, NJ: Princeton University Press.
Kagan, R. (1989), 'On the Visibility of Income Tax Violations', in J. Roth and J. Scholz (eds), *Taxpayer Compliance*, volume II, Philadelphia: University of Pennsylvania Press.
Kaplow, L. (1996), 'How Tax Complexity and Enforcement Affect the Equity and Efficiency of the Income Tax', *National Tax Journal*, **49** (1), 135–50.
Kim, Y. (2003), 'Income Distribution and Equilibrium Multiplicity in a Stigma-based Model of Tax Evasion', *Journal of Public Economics*, **87**, 1591–616.
Klepper, S. and D. Nagin (1989), 'The Role of Tax Preparers in Tax Compliance', *Policy Sciences*, **22** (2), 167–94.
Landsberger, M. and I. Meilijson (1982), 'Incentive Generating State Dependent Penalty System', *Journal of Public Economics*, **19**, 333–52.
Landskroner, Y., J. Paroush and I. Swary (1990), 'Tax Evasion and Portfolio Decisions', *Public Finance*, **45** (3), 409–22.
Licht, A., C. Goldschmidt and S. Schwartz (2007), 'Culture Rules: The Foundations of the Rule of Law and Other Norms of Governance', *Journal of Comparative Economics*, **37**, 659–88.
Lipatov, V. (2007), 'Corporate Tax Evasion: The Case for Specialists', mimeo.
Macho-Stadler, I. and D. Pérez-Castrillo (2002), 'Auditing with Signals', *Economica*, **69**, 1–20.
Malik, A. (1990), 'Avoidance, Screening and Optimum Enforcement', *RAND Journal of Economics*, **21**, 341–53.
Malik, A. and R. Schwab (1991), 'The Economics of Tax Amnesties', *Journal of Public Economics*, **46** (1), 29–49.
Marchese, C. (2004), 'Taxation, Black Markets, and Other Unintended Consequences', in J.G. Backhaus and R.E. Wagner, *Handbook of Public Finance*, Boston: Kluwer, pp. 237–75.
Marhuenda, F. and I. Ortuno-Ortin (1997), 'Tax Enforcement Problems', *Scandinavian Journal of Economics*, **99** (1), 61–72.
Marrelli, M. (1984), 'On Indirect Tax Evasion', *Journal of Public Economics*, **25** (1–2), 181–96.
Marrelli, M. and R. Martina (1988), 'Tax Evasion and Strategic Behaviour of the Firms', *Journal of Public Economics*, **37** (1), 55–69.
Melumad, N. and D. Mookherjee (1989), 'Delegation as Commitment: The Case of Income Tax Audits', *Rand Journal of Economics*, **20** (2), 139–63.
Mookherjee, D. and I. Png (1989), 'Optimal Auditing, Insurance, and Redistribution', *Quarterly Journal of Economics*, **104** (2), 399–415.

Mookherjee, D. and I. Png (1995), 'Corruptible Law Enforcers: How Should They Be Compensated?', *Economic Journal*, **105**, 145–59.
Myles, G. and R. Naylor (1996), 'Model of Tax Evasion with Group Conformity and Social Customs', *European Journal of Political Economy*, **12** (1), 49–66.
OECD (2007), *Tax Administration in OECD and Selected Non-OECD Countries: Comparative Information Series*, Paris: Centre for Tax Policy and Administration.
Pencavel, J. (1979), 'A Note on Income Tax Evasion, Labor Supply, and Nonlinear Tax Schedules', *Journal of Public Economics*, **12** (1), 115–24.
Phillips J. and R. Sansing (1998), 'Contingent Fees and Tax Compliance', *Accounting Review*, **73** (1), 1–18.
Polinsky, M. and S. Shavell (2000), 'The Fairness of Sanctions: Some Implications for Optimal Enforcement Policy', *American Law and Economics Review*, **2**, 223–37.
Reinganum, J. and L. Wilde (1985), 'Income Tax Compliance in a Principal-agent Framework', *Journal of Public Economics*, **26** (1), 1–18.
Reinganum, J. and L. Wilde (1986), 'Equilibrium Verification and Reporting Policies in a Model of Tax Compliance', *International Economic Review*, **27** (3), 739–60.
Reinganum, J. and L. Wilde (1991), 'Equilibrium Enforcement and Compliance in the Presence of Tax Practitioners', *Journal of Law, Economics and Organization*, **7** (1), 163–81.
Richardson, G. (2006), 'Determinants of Tax Evasion: A Cross Country Investigation', *Journal of International Accounting, Auditing and Taxation*, **15**, 150–69.
Roth, J., J. Scholtz and A. Witte (eds) (1989), *Taxpayer Compliance, volume 1: An Agenda for Research*, Philadelphia: University of Pennsylvania Press.
Sanchez, I. and J. Sobel (1993), 'Hierarchical Design and Enforcement of Income Tax Policies', *Journal of Public Economics*, **50** (3), 345–69.
Schneider, F. and D. Enste (2000), 'Shadow Economies: Size, Causes, and Consequences', *Journal of Economic Literature*, **38** (1), 77–114.
Scotchmer, S. (1987), 'Audit Classes and Tax Enforcement Policy', *American Economic Review*, **77** (2), 229–33.
Scotchmer, S. (1989a), 'Who Profits from Taxpayer Confusion?', *Economics Letters*, **29** (1), 49–55.
Scotchmer, S. (1989b), 'The Effect of Tax Advisors on Tax Compliance', in J. Roth and J. Scholz (eds), *Taxpayer Compliance*, volume II, Philadelphia: University of Pennsylvania Press.
Scotchmer, S. (1992), 'The Regressive Bias in Tax Enforcement', *Public Finance*, **47**, 366–71.
Scotchmer, S. and J. Slemrod (1989), 'Randomness in Tax Enforcement', *Journal of Public Economics*, **38** (1), 17–32.
Slemrod, J. (2007), 'Cheating Ourselves: The Economics of Tax Evasion', *Journal of Economic Perspectives*, **21** (1), 25–48.
Slemrod, J. and S. Yitzhaki (2002), 'Tax Avoidance, Evasion, and Administration', A. Auerbach and M. Feldstein (eds), *Handbook of Public Economics*, volume 3, Amsterdam: North Holland.
Snow, A. and R. Warren (2005), 'Tax Evasion under Random Audits with Uncertain Detection', *Economic Letters*, **88** (1), 97–100.
Srinivasan, T.N. (1973), 'Tax Evasion: A Model', *Journal of Public Economics*, **2** (4), 339–46.
Stella, P. (1991), 'An Economic Analysis of Tax Amnesties', *Journal of Public Economics*, **46**, 383–400.
Tanzi, V. (1990), *Public Finance in Developing Countries*, Aldershot, UK and Brookfield, US: Edward Elgar.
Toma, E. and M. Toma (1992), 'Tax Collection with Agency Costs: Private Contracting or Government Bureaucrats?', *Economica*, **59** (233), 107–20.
Torgler, B. (2004), 'Moral Suasion: An Alternative Tax Policy Strategy? Evidence from a Controlled Field Experiment in Switzerland', *Economics of Governance*, **5**, 235–53.

Ueng, K.L. and C.C. Yang (2001), 'Plea Bargaining with the IRS: Extensions and Further Results', *Journal of Public Economics*, **81**, 83–98.

Wadhawan, S. (1992), 'Evasion, Partial Detection and Optimal Tax Policy', *Public Finance*, **47**, 372–83.

Webley, P., F. Cowell, S. Long and J. Swingen (1991), 'Tax Evasion: An Experimental Approach', *European Monographs in Social Psychology*, Cambridge, New York and Melbourne: Cambridge University Press, Paris: Editions de la Maison des Sciences de l'Homme.

Weisbach, D. (2002), 'An Economic Analysis of Anti-tax-avoidance Doctrines', *American Law and Economics Review*, **4**, 88–115.

Witte, A. and D. Woodbury (1985), 'The Effect of Tax Laws and Tax Administration on Tax Compliance: The Case of the U.S. Individual Income Tax', *National Tax Journal*, **38** (1), 1–13.

Wrede, M. (1995), 'Tax Evasion and Risk Taking: Is Tax Evasion Desirable?', *Public Finance*, **50** (2), 303–16.

Yaniv, G. (1990), 'Tax Evasion under Differential Taxation: The Economics of Income Source Misreporting', *Journal of Public Economics*, **43** (3), 327–37.

Yaniv, G. (1995), 'A Note on the Tax-Evading Firm', *National Tax Journal*, **48** (1), 113–20.

Yaniv, G. (1999), 'Tax Compliance and Advance Tax Payments: A Prospect Theory Analysis', *National Tax Journal*, **52**, 753–64.

Yitzhaki, S. (1974), 'A Note on Income Tax Evasion: A Theoretical Analysis', *Journal of Public Economics*, **3** (2), 201–2.

Yitzhaki, S. (1987), 'On the Excess Burden of Tax Evasion', *Public Finance Quarterly*, **15** (2), 123–37.

13 Environmental crimes*
Michael Faure

1. Introduction

Economic analysis of law has long been applied also to the area of environmental law. Whereas traditional lawyers sometimes have difficulty applying economic notions to criminal behaviour, this is less so with respect to the area of environmental crime. The basic assumption of the economic model, that the behaviour of rational man will be influenced by specific costs and benefits, seems easier to accept when it concerns criminality by corporate actors, which is often the case with environmental crime. Many have therefore tried to apply the classic models of Gary Becker and George Stigler (Becker, 1962, 1968; Stigler, 1970) and further refinements thereof to environmental crime.

Applying these classic economic models to the area of environmental pollution does not provide specific difficulties. However, there are a few characteristics of environmental crime which make it worthwhile devoting a separate chapter to it. The field of environmental crime is different from traditional criminal law since in many legal systems the major part of environmental criminal law cannot be found in penal codes containing the principal offences;[1] the major part of environmental criminal law simply consists of provisions incorporated in environmental statutes of an administrative nature (for example, a Clean Water Act) and have as their main function the enforcement of compliance with administrative obligations. A great deal of environmental criminal law is therefore not formulated in an independent manner[2] but is rather formulated as accessory to regulation. In legal practice, an important part of environmental criminal law will therefore consist of violations of a regulatory nature. For example, the polluter will be prosecuted for discharging certain substances into the environment without a permit or for violating permit conditions. This

* I am grateful to Nuno Garoupa and Anthony Ogus for useful comments on an earlier version of this chapter.

1 There are a few exceptions: some countries (for example Germany, the Netherlands) have incorporated environmental criminal law in their penal codes. However, in legal practice the importance of those provisions is often limited.

2 Such an independent crime would for example be: 'He who pollutes the surface waters will be punished with . . .'.

so-called 'administrative dependence of environmental criminal law' has been extensively studied in legal doctrine (Faure and Visser, 1995; Heine, 1994), but is of importance in the economic approach to environmental crime as well. A consequence of this 'administrative dependence' is that administrative authorities have an important influence on the formulation of the contents of environmental criminal law and are also strongly involved in its enforcement and (dependent upon the legal system) in sanctions. This is therefore an area where the criminal law is strongly linked with regulation[3] and in this particular area of criminal law, the influence of administrative authorities will be far more important than in the traditional areas covered by the criminal law.

Given this background, we will of course not attempt within the scope of this chapter to repeat the application of the Becker/Stigler model to environmental crime, but rather we focus on the specific features of environmental criminal law which more particularly have to do with the important influence of the regulatory authorities in the phase of the formulation of the crime, monitoring and sanctioning. In that respect, we will focus on the main literature without attempting to be comprehensive.[4] The question of enforcement of environmental regulation (and thus environmental criminal law) was briefly discussed in a chapter on environmental regulation in the previous version of the Encyclopedia (Faure, 2000) and the classic references were (until 1992) provided in the contribution on criminal law in the *Bibliography of Law and Economics* (Faure, 1992). At the end of this chapter, a list of references is provided for the interested reader.

As indicated in this contribution, we will mainly focus on those areas where environmental criminal law differs from traditional criminal law from an economic perspective and which are thus addressed in the economic literature. We consider the question why environmental pollution needs to be enforced through the criminal law at all (Section 2), whether one could in certain circumstances use administrative rather than criminal law to enforce environmental regulation (Section 3) and the specific structure of environmental criminal law (Section 4). Next, we will discuss optimal sanctions for environmental crime (Section 5), specific problems arising in the case of corporate environmental crime (Section 6) and the effectiveness of environmental criminal law generally (Section 7), also

---

[3] The reader can therefore read this chapter in conjunction with Chapter 3 of this volume.

[4] The reader interested in further literature on compliance studies with respect to environmental regulation should consult a highly useful survey conducted by the US Environmental Protection Agency (2007).

taking into account the various possible enforcement strategies (Section 8).

This chapter merely focuses on the economic analysis of environmental crime and environmental criminal law. Other aspects of the economic analysis of environmental pollution are discussed in other volumes of the Encyclopedia. For example, environmental liability is discussed within the volume on tort law and economics, whereas environmental regulation generally is discussed within the volume on regulation. The reader who wishes for a more comprehensive insight into the general literature on the economics of environmental law can therefore refer to these other volumes.

2. Why environmental criminal law?

Of course, within the scope of this chapter, it is not useful to summarize the broad literature on criminalization, an issue which has been extensively discussed both from a legal (see, for example, Ashworth, 2000) as well as from a law and economics (Bowles et al., 2008; Faure and Visser, 2004; Ogus, 2004) perspective. For the sake of this contribution, it can just be argued that some of the arguments made in that literature in favour of criminal law do apply to the case of environmental pollution as well. However, one has to stress that much of the literature in fact provides arguments in favour of public enforcement or regulation rather than in favour of the criminal law.

One argument in favour of public enforcement is that private law remedies will not sufficiently deter (see, for example, Wilde, 2002, pp. 307–10). The arguments are well known: environmental pollution often has no individual victim that could file a liability suit; causation may be difficult to prove and the long time lapse may make it impossible to recognize that, for example, health damage has been caused through environmental pollution, let alone that a tort claim could still successfully be brought. These are arguments that are traditionally advanced in favour of regulation (see Shavell, 1984a, 1984b; and Chapter 3, this volume). This at least explains why public regulation and enforcement may be necessary from an economic perspective to cure the externalities caused by environmental pollution.

A second reason traditionally advanced in economic theory in favour of public regulation, but also to explain the use of the criminal law, is the low probability of detection (Posner, 1985; Shavell, 1985). In many cases of environmental pollution, the probability of being caught may not be 100 per cent, but may in fact be much lower. The result is that, according to the Becker model, the efficient sanction for deterring the potential polluter should be correspondingly higher. In general, this effect cannot be achieved with tort law, since tort law in principle only forces the injurer to compensate the victim for the amount of damage suffered and no more. This again shows the inappropriateness of civil law in cases where the probability of detection is less than 100 per cent. For optimal deterrence, a higher sanction has to be imposed in order to compensate for this low detection rate. This cannot be provided through private law, and hence explains the need for public sanctions which permit compensation for the lower detection rate (see also Skogh and Stuart, 1982; Skogh, 1973).

The low detection rate alone does not explain the need to use the criminal law to deter environmental pollution, but merely the need to use public sanctions. As we shall explain in the next section, it is, however, an important argument in favour of the criminal law in combination with the insolvency risk. Before discussing that aspect, it should be stressed that these traditional economic arguments in favour of criminal law or at least in favour of public enforcement may equally provide arguments in favour of decriminalization. It may be recalled that in the 1970s many criminal law scholars were sceptical about the effectiveness of criminal law and argued that it ought to be used more moderately or not at all. Although that radical view (sometimes referred to as abolitionism) has now been abandoned, it is still believed that the very costly institution of criminal law should be reserved for those cases where deterrence cannot otherwise be achieved. This also implies that the best way towards decriminalization is to improve the effectiveness of civil law. Hence, if the main problem with tort law is that it limits compensation to the amount of harm done to the victim, one way of counterbalancing the low detection rate is to increase the amount of compensation payable by the injurer under tort law. That is precisely the idea behind the concept of 'punitive damages' (see Cooter, 1982; Landes and Posner, 1981a).[5]

Another example, more specifically related to the issue at hand, refers to the argument that civil law will often not be useful as a deterrent against environmental pollution since damage may be widespread, the whole community victimized or the damage caused to collective goods that are not owned by one individual. In such cases, no one will bring a suit in tort. If, in these cases, one wishes to increase the effectiveness of the civil law, one way of doing so is to allow the use of civil law also when no individual victim is harmed, but where a (high) level of social harm is caused

---

[5] Nevertheless, punitive damages also seem to be applied, especially when the environmental harm is large (for example, with oil pollution) and where the probability of detection and conviction may in fact not be low at all. Punitive damages may therefore arguably be more necessary in the US than in Europe, possibly also due to different patterns of criminalization of environmental wrongdoing.

by the tortious act. One way of doing so is by allowing the state or other public authorities to act on behalf of the environment and to let them use tort law; another way is to grant non-governmental organizations or individuals the right to institute actions in tort, for example, to ask for an injunction to stop environmental pollution from occurring. Also class actions brought on behalf of a group of victims could be considered as a way to improve the functioning of private law, thus reducing the need for criminalization.

3. Administrative or criminal law?

So far, we have presented the traditional economic arguments to explain why environmental pollution cannot merely be remedied via private law and why public enforcement is indicated. The main reason is the low probability of detecting environmental crime. However, this does not necessarily explain why one should have to use the criminal law. Indeed, the low probability of detection could well be compensated by imposing a high fine on the polluter. Fines have always been considered the preferred sanction in economic theory, for the simple reason that the costs of imposition are low and fines in fact only generate money for the public budget (see, for example, Shavell, 1985; Posner, 1980). Monetary sanctions can, in principle, have both a criminal and an administrative nature. All things being equal, the administrative procedure has the major advantage that it is far less costly than the criminal procedure. Administrative fines can, within what is sometimes referred to as 'administrative penal law',[6] be imposed by administrative authorities after a relatively simple procedure and usually require a relatively low threshold of proof. Compared with the criminal law, the costs of the administrative procedure are substantially lower (see equally Chapter 3 of this volume). All things being equal, it can therefore be argued that if optimal deterrence can be achieved through fines, it seems desirable to use the less costly administrative law instead of the relatively more costly criminal procedure. This has led many scholars to argue that the imposition of relatively modest fines through the criminal procedure is inefficient, since a similar result could be achieved at lower cost through administrative law. More particularly, Ogus and Abbot have argued that in the UK more use should be made of administrative fines (and other administrative sanctions for that matter) to enforce violations of environmental regulations (see Ogus and Abbot, 2002a, 2002b). A clear

---

[6] The expression 'administrative penal law' may be confusing to some who consider 'penal' synonymous with 'criminal'. In the literature, this notion is used to refer to a system whereby administrative authorities impose penalties.

normative conclusion from this literature is therefore that in many more instances than is the case today, administrative law could be used to deter environmental pollution, especially when the penalties consist of relatively low fines or other (not too infringing) administrative sanctions.

However, there are two important reasons why not all efficient penalties necessary to deter environmental pollution can be imposed through administrative law and why criminal law therefore remains necessary. The first reason is that since the probability of detection of environmental pollution is in practice often very low, the optimal sanction to deter pollution may become very high as well. The likelihood that this optimal fine might outweigh the individual wealth of an offender is relatively high. Environmental polluters are often organized as corporate entities that benefit from limited liability (see Hansmann and Kraakman, 1991; Cortenraad, 1999). Hence, there is always a risk that environmental harm may cause costs that are higher than the assets of the firm or, in the criminal law context, that the optimal fine (to outweigh a low detection rate) will be much higher than the assets of the firm. Indeed, the optimal monetary sanction required for deterrence so frequently exceeds the offenders' assets that non-monetary sanctions, such as imprisonment, are necessary. The major advantage of the fine (lower administrative costs) therefore only leads to favouring this type of sanction when the risk of insolvency can be controlled. It should also be recalled that the probability of an administrative fine being imposed will be much higher (given a lower procedural threshold) than that of a criminal fine. As a result, the administrative fine should not necessarily be nearly so large as the criminal fine. This can again reduce the insolvency problem.

It should be recalled that the fact that the detection rate of environmental pollution is often less than 100 per cent was one of the reasons for introducing criminal law in the first place. This insolvency problem explains why increasing the amount of compensation due from a tortfeasor, for instance by introducing punitive damages (as in American tort law), will not eliminate the need for criminal sanctions. Indeed, the insolvency problem that arises if monetary sanctions are imposed would make the injurer judgment proof. Thus, non-monetary sanctions will often be needed to achieve deterrence.

There is a clear economic reason why society does not want to impose very stringent sanctions, such as imprisonment (but also high fines) through an administrative proceeding. The reason is that the costs of administrative proceedings may be lower than the costs of criminal proceedings, but the accuracy of the latter (where the investigations are often undertaken by professional lawyers) may be a lot higher as well.

This aspect is also important because a task of criminal law is not only to apply optimal sanctions to the guilty, but also to avoid punishing the innocent. This is referred to as the goal of reduction of error costs (see Miceli, 1990; and Chapter 3, this volume). The error cost is obviously a lot higher when very serious sanctions, like imprisonment, can be imposed, rather than monetary sanctions only. It is therefore understandable that less costly administrative proceedings are chosen in all cases where the consequences (and thus the error cost) will not be too high in the event of a wrongful conviction. Arguably, another goal of the administrative procedure is to avoid punishing the innocent (and thus reducing error costs), although they operate at a lower standard. That explains why administrative law (and the corresponding administrative procedure) will be reserved for cases where relatively low penalties can suffice to provide deterrence.

The policy lesson from this economic literature is therefore rather straightforward: in cases where optimal deterrence of environmental polluters can be achieved through relatively modest sanctions (like not excessively high administrative fines or other administrative sanctions), the use of less costly administrative penal law may be warranted. However, in cases where the probability of detection is relatively low, social harm and the potential gain to the polluter is high and thus a more severe sanction is needed, it may be warranted to use the more costly criminal procedure in order to reduce error costs. This is certainly the case when the optimal fine would reach the insolvency limit and non-monetary sanctions are thus needed for deterrence, but equally where for the same reason very high administrative fines have to be imposed. In reality, in many legal systems it is now possible to use either the criminal law or administrative penal law for particular environmental offences or in some cases even a combination of these. For a discussion of the optimal use of criminal sanction in addition to administrative penalties, see Garoupa and Gomez-Pomar (2004).

4. Structure of environmental criminal law

There is a great difference in the way criminal law is used to protect classical interests such as life, health or property and the way in which the environment is protected through the criminal law. Traditional interests enjoy far-reaching protection and every infringement is penalized as manslaughter, assault or theft. The environment does not enjoy such far-reaching protection as these traditional interests. The economic reason behind this is that many 'polluters' equally produce socially beneficial activities. An environmental criminal law which simply prohibited all pollution would therefore be socially wasteful. This explains the interweaving of criminal law with administrative law, which was mentioned in the introduction. Most environmental statutes provide administrative agencies with powers to decide upon the permitted degree of pollution. Thereby, it is these administrative authorities that determine the scope of environmental crime provisions.

Additionally, no general rule of criminal law prohibits polluting. Polluting only constitutes a crime when it violates an administrative norm, and even if a general prohibition exists, compliance with a permit is usually a sufficient justification. Because most environmental crimes consist of a violation of these administrative norms, the administrative agency that sets the (emission) standards determines what kind of behaviour is criminal.

This type of structure may be economically sound because the administrative authorities have an informational advantage over a judge in an individual criminal case. The alternative would be to consider all pollution a crime, leaving the judge to decide which acts warrant punishment. In most cases, a regulatory agency has either superior knowledge of, or far better access to, the relevant ecological and technological information than a judge does. Requiring a judge to acquire expert knowledge of chemical and toxic substances, and to keep up to date with recent developments in the field of environmental science, would be very inefficient, if not impossible. Moreover, administrative agencies acquire information that benefits a large number of people and therefore diminishes the costs of research for society.

Thus, the current structure of criminal environmental law, relying primarily on administrative agencies to determine environmental crimes, appears economically sound. Administrative law, however, cannot be the sole source of environmental criminal law since some serious cases of environmental pollution should be directly punishable, even if no violation of administrative provisions is at hand. This obviously raises a lot of questions as to how to formulate environmental criminal law from a legal perspective. To discuss this in detail would of course go beyond the scope of this contribution (see Faure and Visser, 1995). It should, however, be stressed that most environmental criminal law is merely an addition to a prior system of administrative decisions concerning the amount and quality of emissions into the environment. Traditionally, criminal law applied as soon as prior administrative decisions (like permit conditions) were violated, irrespective of whether this caused harm to the environment. Increasingly, one now notices that these mere administrative violations (for example, of permit conditions) are sanctioned with fines under administrative penal law. This corresponds with the economic reasoning explained above. Most offences are also strict liability offences, which require no specific intent or *mens rea*. This corresponds with a general trend to apply strict liability to regulatory offences (see Chapter 3 this volume). However, some legal systems make a distinction between these mere administrative violations on the one hand and situations where there is also an unlawful emission or even situations where there are serious consequences (like endangering of human health) resulting from environmental pollution. In those more serious cases, often criminal law applies and specific conditions apply with respect to *mens rea*. However, in a recent study, Babbitt, Cory and Kruchek hold that although the requisite criminal intent in case of environmental violations may have been modified (in the sense that it may to some extent have diminished), substantial defences and procedural safeguards still exist. Hence, they conclude that the danger of wrongful conviction is no greater in the area of environmental crime than in many other areas of criminal law (Babbitt et al. 2004, p. 61).

5. Optimal sanctions for environmental crime

Since it is not the purpose of this chapter to repeat the basic economic theory of crime, we can simply take the main conclusions from this literature and apply it to environmental crime.

When optimal deterrence can be achieved equally through fines and prison sanctions, fines are preferred since they are less costly to impose than prison sanctions (see, among many others, Polinsky and Shavell, 1991, 1979; and for a summary, Bowles, 1982). As was indicated above, many economists have for that reason shown themselves to be opponents of prison sanctions, simply because the costs of implementation of those sanctions are much higher than the costs of imposing fines. That is why the fine has been advanced as the ideal sanction in case of corporate crimes like environmental crime (Posner, 1980). This has, however, been criticized by Coffee (1980) as well as by Shavell (1985), who argued that fines can only work as an effective deterrent if there is no insolvency problem. As we have argued above, in the case of a low probability of detection and an insolvency risk, non-monetary sanctions will have to be applied (Polinsky and Shavell, 1979; Segerson and Tietenberg, 1992). This lesson from economic theory seems to be followed in legal practice as well: the available criminological studies report that the fine is the most commonly used sanction; the application of prison sanctions for environmental crime would be rare and would be limited to cases of fraud or serious environmental harm (see, for the situation in Europe generally, Heine and Meinberg, 1988; Meinberg, 1988; and for the situation of Belgium, Billiet and Rousseau, 2003).

A result of economic theory is that optimal sanctions in the case of environmental crimes depend upon a variety of elements, such as the probability of detection, the harm caused, the available assets of the polluter, the corresponding insolvency risk and the costs of the sanctions to be imposed. Optimal sentencing policy would consist of applying fines as long as possible (in the light of the insolvency risk) and to combine them in a differentiated manner with non-monetary sanctions where necessary (see Cooter and Ulen, 2004, p. 477). In reality, sentencing practice can be very different. This is more particularly the case in the US where strict sentencing guidelines apply, to which the judge in principle should adhere. In contrast to the economic model, the sentencing guidelines also provide quite often for incarceration as the main penalty in case of violation of environmental regulations. Frank Easterbrook has strongly opposed this idea of strict sentencing guidelines, arguing that 'there is no correct price for crime in the same way that there is no correct price for apples'. He holds that the price of (environmental) crime depends upon a variety of elements, indicated above, which enable the judge to determine the optimal penalty in a differentiated way (Easterbrook, 1983, pp. 295 and 325). Easterbrook therefore supports discretionary sanctioning powers for the judge, arguing that this will allow the judge to differentiate the sanctions in a more precise manner, taking into account the relevant economic criteria.

The economic lessons as formulated by Easterbrook seem to be followed in Europe where, if sentencing guidelines exist at all, they seem to provide sufficient flexibility for the judge to differentiate sanctions according to the economic criteria. Recently, the Department for the Environment, Food and Rural Affairs (DEFRA) in the UK published a *Review of Enforcement in Environmental Regulation* which provides for sentencing guidelines, but at the same time holds that this should not impose a rigid tariff but should merely provide a more systematic framework for more effective and consistent sentencing decisions (Parpworth, 2007, p. 21). Also, recent empirical evidence seems to support Easterbrook's criticism on the sentencing guidelines in the US. Barrett concluded in a study on the application of sentencing guidelines for environmental crime that 'the sentences imposed in the majority of cases reflected the reluctance of judges to impose significant incarceration for violations of environmental laws' (Barrett, 1992, p. 1421). Also, others have recently held that the sentencing guidelines lead to negative outcomes as far as enforcement and deterrence are concerned. Recent research by Babbitt et al. showed that the practice of lenient sentencing of environmental criminals, as a refusal to apply the guidelines, was well documented. Since the judiciary feels that the guidelines 'over criminalize' environmental violations, they may systematically sentence (even significant) violations too leniently, which may undermine the deterrent value of environmental enforcement and may trivialize environmental law itself (Babbitt et al., 2004, p. 63).

As far as non-monetary sanctions are concerned, there are, especially in modern environmental statutes, a variety of measures that can be imposed upon the convicted polluter, such as a duty to restore the harm committed, for example, by cleaning up a polluted soil or an order compensating pollution victims (independently of the latter's private law rights). Even though these measures are usually treated as non-monetary sanctions in legal doctrine (because they are different from a fine), many of these arguably have a monetary implication as well. In some cases, these measures can even go so far as an order to shut down a plant or to restore the damage that has been caused. In some cases, the legislator also provides the judge with the power to order the publication of the judgment in the mass media.

Even though the application of these special sanctions still varies between different legal systems, one can certainly note their increasing use. For example, if a polluter is prosecuted for illegally depositing waste, he will often be required also to clean up the waste he has discharged. In some legal systems, these orders can be enforced by means of a so-called penalty payment that will be due if the duties are not fulfilled within the time limit laid down in the judgment.

These specific duties seem to be effective penalties and lead to deterrence. The costs of soil clean-up can be substantial and thus provide additional deterrence. The publication of a judgment can lead to serious reputational loss.

One particular sanction which is increasingly gaining popularity in the fight against white-collar crime generally, but also in the area of environmental crime, is the forfeiture of illegal gains. From a legal perspective, this forfeiture of illegal gains rests on the notion that 'crime should not pay'. The gains obtained by the crime should be removed from the criminal in order to put him back in the *status quo ante* (for an overview of these legal foundations, see Faure, 2005, and for a comparative overview see Kilchling, 2002 and 1997). Recently, Bowles, Faure and Garoupa showed that the forfeiture of illegal gain can be efficient at providing additional deterrence in case of a low detection rate and low effective fines (Bowles et al., 2000, 2005). However, early empirical studies by German criminologists showed that the risk of removal of illegal gain had hardly any effect on potential criminals in their decision whether or not to commit the crime (see Smettan, 1992; Perron, 1993). Meanwhile, the possibilities of removing illegal gain as well as the practical application in the environmental area has spectacularly increased since these early studies of 1992–3 (for an overview of the practice in Belgium and the Netherlands, see Faure and De Roos, 1998). The additional deterrent effect, and therewith the effectiveness of the removal of illegal gains, in the case of environmental crime may well have substantially increased.

6. Corporate environmental crime

In the case of environmental pollution, the crime is often committed, not by an individual actor, but by persons acting on behalf of a company.

Many of the serious cases of environmental pollution have been committed within corporate entities. Therefore, unavoidably, the question arises whether the corporation, the employee or both should be held liable. At this point, we will not discuss the issue of corporate criminal liability in much detail, since one chapter in this volume deals specifically with the economics of corporate crime. We will merely briefly address the issue from the perspective of environmental crime.

From an economic point of view, designating the liable party is unimportant so long as sanctions are freely transferable and the parties are fully informed. With transferable sanctions, either the corporation charges the liable employee for the fine that it paid, or the employee asks the corporation for reimbursement of the fine that he paid. According to this line of reasoning, it is unimportant whether the fine is imposed on the corporation or the individual because the contractual relationship between the individual and the corporation governs these matters. This, obviously, is an application of the Coase theorem (Coase, 1960).

However, this Coasian solution to penalties within corporate entities may not always work in practice. One problem is that monetary sanctions are not always freely transferable between the employer (the corporation) and the employee, sometimes because the law prohibits paying someone else's fine. This is, for example, the case in Germany (see Faure and Heine, 1991, pp. 43–4). A contractual transfer of the fine may thus not always be possible. Therefore, in practice, it does matter at whom the penalty is directed (Segerson and Tietenberg, 1992, pp. 61–3). The argument for holding the employer liable is related to the insolvency problem mentioned above: when the corporation is held liable, the less costly fines can longer be applied in reaction to environmental crime; the corporation (employer) can in turn apply sanctions to the employee, such as refusing promotion or termination of the contract (compare with the principle of *respondeat superior* in tort law, Landes and Posner, 1981b, p. 914). Also, in the area of environmental crime, it is held that when the employee cannot bear the full burden of the optimal penalty, the government might still be able to impose the optimal penalty on the company (Cohen, 2001a, pp. 208–9).

However, the literature equally indicates that even though there are strong arguments for corporate criminal liability (Friedman, 2000; Kahan, 1998), there are reasons to apply criminal liability to individuals within the corporation as well. We have shown that non-monetary sanctions may have to be applied to environmental crime as well. Indeed, corporate entities may also be equally unable to pay for the damage caused by their pollution. A polluting corporation may escape a liability suit because the damage to the environment is widely dispersed and therefore difficult to trace. Monetary sanctions may exceed the corporation's assets and thus not be an effective deterrent. Because non-monetary sanctions are hard to apply to corporations (this is obvious for incarceration), they must also be applied to individual employees as well. Polinsky and Shavell have made a strong economic argument in favour of the individual criminal liability of the employee. One of the arguments they make is that monitoring by firms may often be imperfect: another problem is that if employees only face fines, they may not be induced to exercise socially optimal levels of care. Therefore they argue that non-monetary sanctions on employees (imprisonment) should be used in addition to fines applied on corporations (Polinsky and Shavell, 1993; Kornhauser, 1982).

This leads to the conclusion that corporate liability (leading to fines and non-monetary sanctions applicable to corporations) should be combined with the individual criminal liability of employees. However, some criticism has been formulated against corporate criminal liability, stressing even more the need to have individual liability on the part of the employee. Wheeler has argued that, in general, criminal statutes should not be used to regulate product safety (Wheeler, 1984). His arguments against criminal law are mainly arguments against punishing the corporation and are, to a certain extent, of interest for environmental crime as well. One of his points is that a civil lawsuit may be as much of a deterrent as criminal sanctions[7]. Another is that criminal law may lead to costly overdeterrence and that the costs of detecting, investigating, prosecuting and sentencing are much higher than the benefits of marginal deterrence. His argument that the existing market forces in place, such as private tort actions and civil regulatory systems, can better regulate product safety than criminal law might hold true for the field of product liability. However, it is obviously less convincing with regard to the area of environmental crime, precisely because this area requires *ex ante* regulation, without which potential polluters might otherwise escape liability.

Another criticism of the use of corporate criminal liability has been formulated by Jennifer Arlen. She argues that the traditional argument in favour of what is referred to as vicarious liability is seen as an indirect means of sanctioning wrongful employees, assuming that corporations subject to criminal liability will in turn sanction the wrongful agency. This regime can, however, according to Arlen, lead to potentially perverse incentives for the following reason: if a corporation is able to monitor its employees optimally, it will have to increase its level of corporate enforcement expenditures. This might reduce the number of agents who commit

---

[7] Powerful counter-arguments have been produced by Shavell (1984a, 1984b), who showed that in specific circumstances, tort law may lack a deterrent effect.

crime by increasing the probability of detection and thus reducing the costs of crime. On the other hand, the increased enforcement expenditures may also increase the probability that the government will detect those crimes, whereby the corporations' expected criminal liability for those crimes is increased. This means that additional enforcement by the firm only increases the firms' expected criminal liability. Thus vicarious liability could lead to the perverse incentive that the corporation will reduce the monitoring of its employees in order to avoid the detection of corporate (environmental) crime (Arlen, 1994).

7. Effectiveness of environmental criminal law?

The sparse empirical evidence that is available with respect to the probability of detection and the probability of being prosecuted and convicted shows, at least as far as Europe is concerned, that these are relatively modest, to say the least. Recent Belgian criminological research showed that around 74 per cent of all reports of violation of environmental laws are not prosecuted (Ponsaers and de Keulenaer, 2003). Moreover, there is of course a substantial part of violations that are not detected at all, which leads to a substantial dark number. Similar Belgian research also shows that when eventually a violation is detected, prosecuted and a sanction is imposed, average fines are relatively low. Research concerning the fines imposed by criminal courts in the region of Gent (Belgium) showed an average fine of 200,000 Belgian francs (Euro 5,000) (Billiet and Rousseau, 2003, p. 131). Similar research performed by German criminologists in the 1990s reveals a similar picture: many environmental crimes are, if detected and reported at all, not prosecuted and the penalties are generally relatively low fines (see, for example, Meinberg, 1988). Similar data are provided by Ogus and Abbot concerning the situation in the UK: prosecutions are conducted for less than a quarter of the worst environmental incidents and the amounts of the fines imposed are low relative to the profitability of the contravening activity (Ogus and Abbot, 2002a, pp. 497–8).

If one takes into account the fact that the economic gain resulting from a violation of environmental statutes can be substantial, it is not difficult to argue that current practice constitutes a serious problem of underdeterrence. In order to outweigh the potential gain to be made (for example, by deciding not to invest in a water treatment plant), detection and prosecution rates as well as effective sanctions should be substantially higher. Many have therefore held that by delaying an investment in environmental prevention equipment enterprises can save substantially on interest payments without additional risks (Nentjes and Hommes, 1990). Also, Cohen concluded from a review of empirical literature that there is little evidence of any preventive effect of increasing monetary sanctions and none on the role of criminal (non-monetary) sanctions (Cohen, 2000a, 2001a, p. 209). These results could lead to the depressing conclusion that environmental criminal law is apparently not able to provide any deterrence. One could even ask the question why many corporations comply relatively well with environmental law, given the fact that the benefits of violation are usually higher than the expected costs. A simple application of the Becker model teaches that there should in principle be much more environmental criminality than can be observed today. This has in the literature been referred to as the Harrington paradox, following a few papers by Winston Harrington, who identified this issue (Harrington, 1988; Harford and Harrington, 1991). The paradox is the following: the number of inspections (and hence detection) is low; even if violation is detected, sanctions are hardly ever imposed and yet, the level of compliance by firms seems to be relatively high. Apparently, firms may have an incentive to comply with environmental regulations, even if their costs of compliance exceed the expected penalty in case of violation. Some further literature which refines and tries to explain the Harrington paradox shows why firms may have these incentives. Heyes and Rickman (1999) show that enforcement agencies may use tolerance in some cases and for some types of violations in order to increase compliance in other contexts and for other violations. According to them, this type of regulatory dealing will improve both the rate of compliance and the individual performance of firms. Also others (for example, Nyborg and Telle, 2006) have held that the discovered pattern is less paradoxical than it seems. On the basis of enforcement data from Norway concerning compliance with environmental regulation, they show that enforcement of minor violations is indeed lax, but that serious violations on the other hand are subject to credible threats of harsh punishment and that as a result such violations are more uncommon. They therefore hold that these findings are actually consistent with standard theory.

In sum: these more recent studies show that even though in general the probability of detection for environmental offences may be low and on average the imposed penalties may also be low, that should not necessarily mean that firms would be better off with violation than with compliance. In order to analyse this behaviour by firms, not only should actual sentencing policy be addressed, but also enforcement strategy (which will be addressed below in Section 8). This corresponds with a review of empirical literature by Cohen, who showed that even though there is little evidence on the effect of increasing monetary sanctions, there is generally a deterrent effect from increased inspections and government enforcement actions (Cohen, 2000a; Cohen, 2001a, p. 209). There are, moreover, other reasons why firms comply, notwithstanding the Harrington paradox.

First, the traditional Becker model assumes the risk neutrality of the potential polluter. Violating polluters may well be risk averse. Even though the actual probability of detection, prosecution and conviction in the case of environmental crime may well be low, in theory the expected penalty can still be high. For most violations of environmental regulations, prison sanctions may be imposed, even though these are (at least in Europe) rare in practice. Risk aversion on the part of the potential perpetrator can thus provide additional deterrence (for a mathematical example, see Bowles, 1982, p. 59).

Second, the economic model of crime is based on available information by the potential perpetrator of the probability of detection and the expected sanction. Even though criminological research shows that both are relatively low, the relevant question is of course whether these are also perceived as such by (risk-averse) potential polluters (see also Ogus and Abbot, 2002b, p. 292). Also, the Harrington model discussed above assumes that the monitoring agency has information on the firm's compliance cost. In reality, this assumption may not hold and moreover, there may be a lack of information and also errors both on the part of the agency and on the part of the potential polluter.

Third, in the case of a prosecution before the criminal court, the polluter may be confronted by other costs which are added to the formal penalty which is imposed. For example, members of a board of directors may in some legal systems have to appear as defendants before a criminal court over a period of several weeks. This could be a very unpleasant experience, even if the sanction that is ultimately imposed (for example, a fine) is relatively low. The time spent and the loss of reputation involved in having pictures of those directors on trial appear in the press may also constitute an additional cost to the perpetrator. Moreover, a conviction for an environmental crime may lead to other costs to the firm. It may, for example, be more difficult to obtain a new permit since the convicted polluter may have lost goodwill with the administrative agency. Recent empirical research by Decker has shown that this is a realistic fear: companies that have complied in the past with environmental regulation more easily receive a new permit (Decker, 2003). A conviction may even lead to an increase in the insurance premium, which equally may lead to additional deterrence.

Fourth, a criminal prosecution and conviction may (of course depending upon the nature of the firm) lead to a significant loss of reputation. The reputational loss of being convicted as a polluter can lead to significant costs for a firm and thus constitute additional deterrence (Ogus and Abbot, 2002b, p. 292). This corresponds to the well-known idea that a criminal conviction may have the benefit of 'naming and shaming' (see generally on these notions, Braithwaite, 1989). The value of this 'shaming' approach to crime is debated. Posner does not believe that shaming would deter corporate crime since 'a corporation can act only through individuals, and there is a constant turnover of these individuals' (Posner, 1985, p. 1228). However, in a later publication with Rasmusen, Posner seems to recognize the value of shaming in enforcing specific norms (Posner and Rasmusen, 1999). Others are more optimistic and stress that a major advantage of 'shaming' is that it can achieve additional deterrence at relatively low costs (Morris and Tonry, 1990; Buell, 2006). The empirical evidence of the deterrent value of a reputational loss resulting from shaming is debated (X, 2003).

The issue has received some attention with respect to environmental crime: some hold that the mere fact of a criminal conviction can lead to a decrease of stock prices, which results in damage to the company which is substantially higher than the fine which was imposed (Karpoff and Lott, 1993). Cohen, however, comes to a different conclusion: he quotes various empirical studies that have demonstrated that the stock value of publicly traded firms is indeed reduced upon the announcement of a bad environmental outcome, such as an oil spill or criminal prosecution. However, quoting another study by Karpoff et al. (1998), Cohen holds that the stock price effects are approximately equal to government-imposed penalties, clean-up costs and private settlements, so that there is no additional reputational loss (Cohen, 2001a, pp. 213–14). Moreover, the mere fact of being labelled a 'criminal' violation did not cause any additional reputation loss.

Of course, the latter two effects play a role in the case of a criminal conviction, not when an administrative fine is imposed. The additional costs of going to trial may thus be an argument in favour of criminalizing environmental offences; it is doubtful whether this criminalization can also be based on the premise that a criminal conviction would lead to an additional reputation loss. There seems to be no empirical evidence to support this statement.

8. Enforcement strategies

In enforcement literature, not necessarily restricted to economic theory, a lot of attention has been paid to the type of strategy which has to be followed to induce compliance by polluters. The literature makes a distinction between two enforcement styles: the economic approach is qualified as the deterrence style, based on the idea that the authorities should be hard on polluters and should prosecute in all cases, preferably resulting in severe sanctions. A deterrence model, therefore, does not rely on agency discretion. A cooperation enforcement style relies more heavily on negotiations between the polluter and the agency, whereby the agency, through persuasion and by providing information, tries to bring the polluter to compliance. Within this cooperation model, punishment is not the appropriate instrument, but rather a method of last resort if other instruments (persuasion and information) have failed (Van Rooy, 2006, pp. 228–33).

At first blush, the cooperation model does not fit into the economic approach to enforcement. The classic Becker model assumes that the application of strict and deterrent sanctions, in combination with enforcement efforts to increase the detection rate, will provide incentives for the polluter towards compliance. If a cooperation model merely results in the risk that the polluter would, after being detected, still have to invest in abatement technology which he already had to do on the basis of a permit, deterrence will fail. Some economists therefore hold that the cooperation model (which was followed in the Netherlands in the 1990s) stimulates violations of environmental regulation since companies who comply after a first warning do not encounter any negative consequences of their violation (Nentjes and Hommes, 1990, pp. 1–7). Another problem with the cooperation model is that when a cooperative strategy has failed and the administrative agency has to change its position to a deterrence style, the cooperation and strong links between polluter and the agency may have made it difficult or even impossible to change to a deterrence approach when necessary. The cooperation strategy has the inherent risk that powerful and knowledgeable companies will de facto be able to control and 'capture' the agency. See, for example, a study of environmental law enforcement in Denmark, which showed that cooperative enforcement was undermined by capturing (May and Winter, 1999). There is hence always the danger that the cooperation model will lead to situations of collusion and corruption (Garoupa and Klerman, 2004), as a result of which compliance will fail.

However, notwithstanding these limits of the cooperation model, many have also pointed to the limitations of the deterrence approach. It has been argued that a strict deterrence approach which does not take into account the fact that, as a result of practical difficulties compliance is impossible, may lead to a refusal to comply because the deterrence approach is felt to be unreasonable (Hawkins, 1984). Moreover, enforcement agents may be unwilling to act as 'policeman' in an adversarial relationship with the polluter (Aalders, 2003; Aalders and Wilthagen, 1997). The cooperative strategy even receives some support from economists. It would indeed be too simple to reject the cooperation style entirely because of the danger of capture. An advantage of the cooperation model is that through persuasion, education and information companies can be lead towards compliance (Fenn and Veljanovski, 1988). One reason to follow the cooperation model can be related to the high costs for the enforcing agency in bringing a case to court (Ogus and Abbot, 2002b, p. 293). Those high costs may also explain why, in some cases, there is a seemingly high tolerance of non-compliance by the enforcing agency; this can be a strategic response by the agency to a difficult enforcement environment (Heyes and Rickman, 1999). This may hence provide a rationalization of 'regulatory dealing' between the agency and the polluter. Especially in cases where administrative authorities are well informed and small and medium-sized enterprises are not, a cooperative strategy could lead to a situation where the controlling agency in fact assists the enterprise towards compliance with environmental regulation (see also Johnston, 2001). This is also confirmed in a recent experimental study which found that there are substantial learning effects in the sense that compliance with the desired pollution reduction is substantially higher in a second period when the firm was informed about the content of their obligations (Alpízar et al., 2004). These results indicate that firms can understand and adapt their behaviour to elaborate regulatory contracts after a suitable learning period. This seems also to correspond with criminological research in the Netherlands which has confirmed that many violations of environmental regulation do not take place wilfully, but rather as a result of a lack of information or knowledge. In these cases, more particularly where first offenders are concerned, a cooperative enforcement style could probably be effective (Huisman, 2001; Huisman and van de Bunt, 1997).

Summarizing, there may not be such a strict distinction between the deterrence and cooperation styles. Proponents of the cooperative approach realize that coercion is also necessary in a cooperation model. Braithwaite therefore proposes a successful enforcement strategy that starts with informal and less intrusive enforcement options (persuasion, warnings), moving to more punitive options (fines or criminal prosecution) when cooperation has failed (Braithwaite, 2002).

In a powerful study, Lofton attributes the difference in enforcement styles between the US (which has a strongly deterrence-based enforcement style) and the UK (which has followed a cooperative strategy) to differences in cultural values and attitudes on social regulation (Lofton, 2001). Given the strong opposition of American business to environmental regulation, Lofton argues that only coercion or the threat of coercion would have worked to ensure compliance with environmental regulation in the US. Introducing a cooperative approach (which has worked in the UK) in the US context would, according to Lofton, have had disastrous consequences for environmental quality in the US. He therefore argues that varying enforcement styles are largely based upon cultural differences.

Hence, one can understand that, given the different cultural attitude of industry to environmental regulation in the US, the shift from traditional command and control to a more flexible system of industry self-regulation is described as a 'dangerous journey' by some American commentators (Steinzor, 1998).

In addition to this literature on enforcement styles, there is also some (partially empirical) related literature on the effectiveness of specific enforcement approaches. First, it can be recalled that an overview of the empirical literature shows that studies generally find a deterrent effect from increased inspections and government enforcement actions, but less so from increasing penalties (Cohen, 2000a; Cohen, 2001a, p. 209). However, a problem is of course that (as was already pointed out by Stigler) costs for increased monitoring can be high. Also, various empirical studies show that even in the absence of frequent prosecutions, inspections deter future violations (for an empirical study of the petroleum sector in Canada, see Eckert, 2004).

Several suggestions have been formulated and experiments executed to increase the effectiveness of monitoring and at the same time reduce monitoring costs. Arlen and Kraakman suggested a system whereby firms are required to self-report a violation of pollution standards; voluntary reporting would be rewarded with lenient treatment, whereas prosecutors would focus enforcement efforts on violations which are not self-reported. Thus, the most severe sanctions would be reserved for offenders who failed to report or who submit false reports (Arlen and Kraakman, 1997; Cohen, 2001a, p. 207). Innes has also shown that there may be substantial economic benefits from stronger incentives for environmental self-reporting, including saved avoidance costs, reduced enforcement costs and an increased frequency of appropriate remediation (Innes, 2001). One lesson from the work of Harrington, which we discussed earlier, is that it may be effective to divide firms into different classes on the basis of their compliance behaviour and to focus enforcement efforts correspondingly (Harrington, 1988; Harford and Harrington, 1991; Harrington and Heyes, 2001). This idea of targeted monitoring (whereby monitoring costs are mostly spent on those known to have a tendency to be in non-compliance) has been worked out, also empirically, by many. Friesen found that by targeting enforcement efforts on specific segments of the regulated community, greater compliance with environmental regulations could be achieved (Friesen, 2003). Also Heyes and Rickman showed that, given limited agency assets to spend on inspections, an enforcement agency may engage in 'regulatory dealing', using tolerance in some contexts and increasing compliance for other types of violations (Heyes and Rickman, 1999). They show that accepting a certain degree of tolerance with specific violations does not at all mean that the enforcement agency (in the particular case, EPA) is 'going soft' on pollution; it may rather be the result of a strategic choice to maximize the available budget and thus enforcement efforts (see also Heyes, 2002).

Also Rousseau recently showed that the Flemish Environmental Inspection Agency uses targeting to select firms it will routinely inspect and bases this selection on past compliance behaviour and on firms' capacity. Firms are inspected more frequently as long as the environmental problem persists. Once it is solved, firms only receive routine inspections. Hence firms move relatively easily back to the 'good' group. Rousseau argues that higher deterrence could be achieved by lowering the probability of escaping from the 'bad' group, which is effectively equal to one in Flanders. Thus, the deterrence potential of targeting could even be better exploited (Rousseau, 2007).

Bibliography

Aalders, M. (2003), 'Self-regulation and Compliance with Environmental Law from a Global Perspective', in N. Niessen and A. Bedner (eds), *Towards Integrated Environmental Law in Indonesia*, Leiden: CNWS, pp. 21–36.

Aalders, M. and T. Wilthagen (1997), 'Moving beyond Command and Control: Reflexivity in the Regulation of Occupational Safety and Health and the Environment', *Law and Policy*, **19**, 415–44.

Alpízar, F., T. Requate and A. Schram (2004), 'Collective versus Random Fining: An Experimental Study on Controlling Ambient Pollution', *Environmental and Resource Economics*, **29** (2), 231–52.

Arlen, J. (1994), 'The Potentially Perverse Effects of Corporate Criminal Liability', *Journal of Legal Studies*, 833–67.

Arlen, J. and R. Kraakman (1997), 'Controlling Corporate Misconduct: An Analysis of Corporate Liability Regimes', *New York University Law Review*, **72**, 687–779.

Ashworth, A. (2000), 'Is the Criminal Law a Lost Cause?', *Law Quarterly Review*, **116**, 225–56.

Babbitt, C.J., D.C. Cory and B.L. Kruchek (2004), 'Discretion and Criminalization of Environmental Law', *Duke Environmental Law and Policy Forum*, **15**, 1–64.

Barker, D.A. (2002), 'Environmental Crimes, Prosecutorial Discretion, and the Civil/Criminal Line', *Virginia Law Review*, **88** (6), 1387–431.

Barrett, J.J. (1992), 'Sentencing Environmental Crimes under the United States Sentencing Guidelines: A Sentencing Lottery', *Environmental Law*, **22**, 1421–49.

Becker, G.S. (1962), 'Irrational Behaviour and Economic Theory', *Journal of Political Economy*, 1–13.

Becker, G.S. (1968), 'Crime and Punishment: An Economic Approach', *Journal of Political Economy*, 169–217.

Billiet, C.M. and S. Rousseau (2003), 'De hoogte van strafrechtelijke boetes: Een rechtseconomische analyse van milieurechtspraak (1990–2000) van het Hof van Beroep te Gent', *Tijdschrift voor Milieurecht*, 120–34.

Bowles, R. (1982), *Law and the Economy*, Oxford: Martin Robertson.

Bowles, R., M. Faure and N. Garoupa (2000), 'Economic Analysis of the Removal of Illegal Gains', *International Review of Law and Economics*, 537–49.

Bowles, R., M. Faure and N. Garoupa (2005), 'Forfeiture of Illegal Gain: An Economic Perspective', *Oxford Journal of Legal Studies*, **25**, 275–95.

Bowles, R., M. Faure and N. Garoupa (2008), 'The Scope of Criminal Law and Criminal

Sanctions: an Economic View and Policy Implications', *Journal of Law and Society*, **35** (3), 389–416.
Braithwaite, J. (1989), *Crime, Shame and Reintegration*, Cambridge: Cambridge University Press.
Braithwaite, J. (2002),'Rewards and Regulation', *Journal of Law and Society*, **29**, 12–26.
Buell, S.W. (2006),'The Blaming Function of Entity Criminal Liability', *Indiana Law Journal*, **81**, 473–537.
Coase, R.H. (1960), 'The Problem of Social Cost', *Journal of Law and Economics*, 1–44.
Coffee, J.S. (1980), 'Corporate Crime and Punishment: A Non-Chicago View of the Economics of Criminal Sanctions', *American Criminal Law Review*, 419–76.
Cohen, M.A. (1999/2000), 'Monitoring and Enforcement of Environmental Policy', in T. Tietenberg and H. Folmer (eds), *International Yearbook of Environmental and Resource Economics*, Cheltenham, UK and Northampton, MA, USA: Edward Elgar, pp. 44–106.
Cohen, M.A. (2000a), 'Empirical Research on the Deterrent Effect of Environmental Monitoring and Enforcement', *Environmental Law Reporter*, **30**, 10.245–10.252.
Cohen, M.A. (2000b), 'The Economics of Crime and Punishment: Implications for Sentencing of Economic Crimes and New Technology Offences', *George Mason University Law Review*, **9** (2), 503–28.
Cohen, M.A. (2000c), 'Measuring the Costs and Benefits of Crime and Justice', *Measurement and Analysis of Crime and Justice, Criminal Justice*, **4**, 263–316.
Cohen, M.A. (2001a), 'Criminal Law as an Instrument of Environmental Policy: Theory and Empirics', in A. Heyes (ed.), *Law and Economics of the Environment*, Cheltenham, UK and Northampton, MA, USA: Edward Elgar, pp. 198–216.
Cohen, M.A. (2001b), 'The Crime Victim's Perspective in Cost-benefit Analysis: The Importance of Monetizing Tangible and Intangible Crime Costs', in D.P. Farrington, B.C. Welsh and L.W. Sherman (eds), *Costs and Benefits of Preventing Crime*, chapter 3, Boulder, CO: Westview Press, pp. 23–50.
Cohen, M.A. (2005), *The Costs of Crime and Justice*, New York: Routledge.
Cohen, M.A., R. Rust, S. Steen and S. Tidd (2004), 'Willingness-to-pay for Crime Control Programs', *Criminology*, **42** (1), February 86–106.
Cohen, M.A., R.T. Rust and S. Steen (2006), 'Prevention, Crime Control or Cash? Public Preferences towards Criminal Justice Spending Priorities', *Justice Quarterly*, **23** (3), 317–35.
Comte, F. (2003), 'Criminal Environmental Law and Community Competence', *European Environmental Law Review*, **18** (12), 147–56.
Comte, F. (2004), *Environmental Crime in Europe: Rules of Sanctions*, Groningen: Europa Law Publishing.
Comte, F. (2005), 'European Environmental Criminal Law: Recent Developments', *Yearbook of European Environmental Law*, 209–45.
Comte, F. (2006), 'Environmental Crime and the Police in Europe: A Panorama and Possible Paths for Future Action', *European Environmental Law Review*, **15** (7), 190–231.
Cooter, R.D. (1982), 'Economic Analysis of Punitive Damages', *Southern California Law Review*, 97–101.
Cooter, R.D. and T. Ulen (2004), *Law and Economics*, fourth edition, Boston, MA: Addison Wesley.
Cortenraad, W.H.F.M. (1999), *The Corporate Paradox, Economic Realities of the Corporate Form of Organization*, Boston: Kluwer Academic.
Decker, C. (2003), 'Corporate Environmentalism and Environmental Statutory Permitting', *Journal of Legal Studies*, 103–29.
de Prez, P. (2000), 'Excuses, Excuses: The Ritual Trivialisition of Environmental Prosecutions', *Journal of Environmental Law*, **12** (1), 65–78.
Dore, M. (2000), 'Limiting the Designated Felon Rule: The Proper Role of the Responsible Corporate Officer Doctrine in the Criminal Enforcement of New Jersey's Environmental Laws', *Rutgers Law Review*, **53** (1), 181–214.
Du-Rees, H. (2001), 'Can Criminal Law Protect the Environment?', *Journal of Scandinavian Studies in Criminology and Crime Prevention*, **2** (2), 109–26.

Easterbrook, F. (1983), 'Criminal Procedure as a Market System', *Journal of Legal Studies*, **12**, 289–332.
Eckert, H. (2004), 'Inspections, Warnings, and Compliance: The Case of Petroleum Storage Regulation', *Journal of Environmental Economics and Management*, **47**, 232–59.
Environmental Protection Agency (2007), Compliance Literature Search Results: Citations to over 200 Compliance-related Books and Articles from 1999 to 2007, April 2007, http://www.epa.gov/oecaerth/resources/reports/compliance/research/lit-results-2007.pdf.
Faure, M. (1992), 'Criminal Law, Enforcement of Crime and Law Enforcement', in B. Bouckaert and G. de Geest (eds), *Bibliography of Law and Economics*, London: Kluwer Academic Publishers, pp. 504–26.
Faure, M. (2000), 'Environmental Regulation', in B. Bouckaert and G. de Geest (eds), *Encyclopedia of Law and Economics*, Volume II, Cheltenham, UK and Northampton, MA, USA: Edward Elgar, pp. 443–520.
Faure, M. (2004), 'European Environmental Criminal Law: Do We Really Need It?', *European Environmental Law Review*, **18** (13), 18–29.
Faure, M. (2005), 'Gewinnabschöpfung und Verfall auf ökonomischen Prüfstand', in J. Arnold and others (eds), *Menschengerechtes Strafrecht: Festschrift für Albin Eser zum 70. Geburtstag*, Munich: Beck, pp. 1311–30.
Faure, M. and T. De Roos (eds) (1998), *De berekening van het wederrechterlijk verkregen voordeel uit milieudelicten*, The Hague: SDU Uitgevers.
Faure, M. and G. Heine (1991), 'The Insurance of Fines: The Case of Oil Pollution', *The Geneva Papers on Risk and Insurance*, **39**, 39–54.
Faure, M. and M.J.C. Visser (1995), 'How to Punish Environmental Pollution? Some Reflections on Various Models of Criminalization of Environmental Harm', *European Journal of Crime, Criminal Law and Criminal Justice*, 316–68.
Faure, M.G. and M. Visser (2004), 'Law and Economics of Environmental Crime', in H. Sjögren and G. Skogh (eds), *New Perspectives on Economic Crime*, Cheltenham, UK and Northampton, MA, USA: Edward Elgar, pp. 57–75.
Fenn, P. and C. Veljanovski (1988), 'A Positive Economic Theory of Regulatory Enforcement', *Economic Journal*, **98**, 1055–70.
Fortney, D.C. (2003), 'Thinking Outside the "Black Box" Tailored Enforcement in Environmental Criminal Law', *Texas Law Review*, **81** (6), 1609–35.
Friedman, L. (2000), 'In Defence of Corporate Criminal Liability', *Harvard Journal of Law and Public Policy*, **23**, 833–58.
Friesen, L. (2003), 'Targeting Enforcement to Improve Compliance with Environmental Regulations', *Journal of Environmental Economics and Management*, **46**, 72–85.
Garoupa, N. and F. Gomez-Pomar (2004), 'Punish Once or Punish Twice: A Theory of the Use of Criminal Sanctions in Addition to Regulatory Penalties', *American Law and Economics Review*, **6**, 410–33.
Garoupa, N. and D. Klerman (2004), 'Corruption and the Optimal Use of Non-monetary Sanctions', *International Review of Law and Economics*, **24**, 219–25.
Hansmann, H. and R.H. Kraakman (1991), 'Toward Unlimited Shareholder Liability for Corporate Torts', *Yale Law Journal*, 100, 1879–934.
Harrington, W. (1988), 'Enforcement Leverage When Penalties are Restricted', *Journal of Public Economics*, **37**, 29–53.
Harford, J.D. and W. Harrington (1991), 'A Reconsideration of Enforcement Leverage When Penalties are Restricted', *Journal of Public Economics*, **45**, 391–5.
Harrington, W. and A. Heyes (2001), 'The Theory of Penalties: "Leverage" and "Dealing"', in A. Heyes (ed.), *The Law and Economics of the Environment*, Cheltenham, UK and Northampton, MA, USA: Edward Elgar, pp. 185–97.
Hawkins, K. (1984), *Environment and Enforcement, Regulation and the Social Definition of Pollution*, Oxford: Clarendon Press.
Heine, G. (1994), 'Allemagne: Crimes against the Environment', *International Review of Penal Law*, 731–59.
Heine, G. and V. Meinberg (1988), *Empfehlen sich Änderungen im Strafrechtlichen*

Umweltschutz, Ins Besondere in Verbindung mit dem Verwaltungsrecht? Gutachten für den 57. Deutschen Juristentag, Munich: Beck.
Hendriks, L.E.M. (2002), *Milieustrafrecht*, second edition, Deventer: Kluwer.
Heyes, A.G. (2002), 'Eight Things about Enforcement that Seem Obvious but May Not Be', in T. Swanson (ed.), *An Introduction to the Law and Economics of Environmental Policy: Issues in Institutional Design*, Amsterdam: Elsevier, pp. 519–37.
Heyes, A. and N. Rickman (1999), 'Regulatory Dealing – Revisiting the Harrington Paradox', *Journal of Public Economics*, **72**, 361–78.
Hoffman, J. (2000), 'Sustainable Economic Development: A Criminal Justice Challenge for the 21st Century', *Crime, Law and Social Change*, **34** (3), 275–99.
Huisman, W. and H.G. van de Bunt (1997), 'Sancties, organisatiecriminaliteit en milieudelicten', *Ars Aequi*, 695–97.
Huisman, W. (2001), *Tussen winst en moraal, achtergronden van regelnaleving en regelovertreding door ondernemingen*, The Hague: Boom.
Innes, R. (2001), 'Self-enforcement of Environmental Law', in A. Heyes (ed.), *The Law and Economics of the Environment*, Cheltenham, UK and Northampton, MA, USA: Edward Elgar, pp. 150–84.
Johnston, J.S. (2001), 'The Law and Economics of Environmental Contracts', in E.W. Orts and K. Deketelaere (eds), *Environmental Contracts: Comparative Approaches to Regulatory Innovation in the United States and Europe*, The Hague: Kluwer.
Kahan, D.M. (1998), 'Social Meaning and the Economic Analysis of Crime', *Journal of Legal Studies*, **27**, 609–22.
Karpoff, J. and J. Lott (1993), 'The Reputational Penalty Firms Bear from Committing Criminal Fraud', *Journal of Law and Economics*, **36**, 757–802.
Karpoff, J., J. Lott and G. Rankine (1998), 'Environmental Violations, Legal Penalties, and Reputation Costs', John M. Olin Law and Economics Working Paper no. 71, second series, University of Chicago Law School.
Kilchling, M. (1997), 'Comparative Perspectives on Forfeiture Legislation in Europe and the United States', *European Journal of Crime, Criminal Law and Criminal Justice*, **5**, 342–61.
Kilchling, M. (ed.) (2002), *Die Praxis der Gewinnabschöpfung in Europa*, Freiburg im Breisgau: Max Planck Institute for Foreign and International Criminal Law.
Kochanowski, J., J. Czabanski and M.A. Cohen (eds) (forthcoming), *Economics of Crime*, Warsaw, Poland: Ius et Lex.
Kornhauser, L.A. (1982), 'An Economic Analysis of the Choice between Enterprise and Personal Liability for Accidents', *California Law Review*, **70**, 1345–92.
Kritikos, A.S. (2004), 'A Penalty System to Enforce Policy Measures under Incomplete Information', *International Review of Law and Economics*, **24** (3), 385–403.
Landes, W. and R. Posner (1981a), 'An Economic Theory of Intentional Torts', *International Review of Law and Economics*, 127–54.
Landes, W. and R. Posner (1981b), 'The Positive Economic Theory of Tort Law', *Georgia Law Review*, **15**, 851–924.
Landes, W.M. and R.A. Posner (1986), 'New Light on Punitive Damages', *Regulation*, 33–6.
Lofton, J.A. (2001), 'Environmental Enforcement: The Impact of Cultural Values and Attitudes on Social Regulation', *Environmental Liability*, **4**, 167–81.
May, P.J. and S. Winter (1999), 'Regulatory Enforcement and Compliance: Examining Danish Agro-Environmental Policy', *Journal of Policy Analysis and Management*, **18**, 625–51.
McDougall, C., M.A. Cohen, A. Perry and R. Swaray (2006), 'Costs and Benefits of Sentencing', in B.C. Welsh and D.P. Farrington (eds), *Preventing Crime: What Works for Children, Offenders, Victims, and Places*, Dordrecht, the Netherlands: Springer, chapter 8, pp. 117–27.
McDougall, C., M.A. Cohen, R. Swaray and A. Perry (2003), 'The Costs and Benefits of Sentencing – A Systematic Review', *Annals of the American Academy of Political and Social Science*, **587**, 160–77.

Meinberg, V. (1988), 'Empirische Erkenntnisse zum Vollzug des Umweltstrafrechts', *Zeitschrift für die Gesamte Strafrechtswissenschaften*, 112–57.
Miceli, T. (1990), 'Optimal Prosecution of Defendants Whose Guilt is Uncertain', *Journal of Law, Economics and Organisation*, **6**, 189–201.
Morris, N. and N. Tonry (1990), *Between Prison and Probation: Intermediate Punishment in a Rational Sentencing System*, New York: Oxford University Press.
Nentjes, A. and J. Hommes (1990), 'Handhaving van het Milieurecht', *Tijdschrift voor Milieuaansprakelijkheid*, 1–7.
Nyborg, K. and K. Telle (2006), 'Firms' Compliance to Environmental Regulation: Is There Really a Paradox?', *Environmental and Resource Economics*, **35**, 1–18.
Ogus, A. (2004), 'Enforcing Regulation: Do we need the Criminal Law?', in H. Sjögren and G. Skogh (eds), *New Perspectives on Economic Crime*, Cheltenham, UK and Northampton, MA, USA: Edward Elgar, pp. 42–56.
Ogus, A. and C. Abbot (2002a), 'Pollution and Penalties', in: T. Swanson (ed.), *An Introduction to the Law and Economics of Environmental Policy: Issues in Institutional Design*, Amsterdam: Elsevier, pp. 493–516.
Ogus, A. and C. Abbot (2002b), 'Sanctions for Pollution: Do We Have the Right Regime?', *Journal of Environmental Law*, **14**, 283–300.
O'Hear, M.M. (2004), 'Sentencing the Green-collar Offender: Punishment, Culpability and Environmental Crime', *Journal of Criminal Law and Criminology*, **95** (1), 133–276.
Parpworth, N. (2007), 'Enforcement in Environmental Regulation: The Defra Review', *Environmental Liability*, 15–26.
Perron, W. (1993), 'Vermögensstrafe und Erweiterte Verfall', *Juristenzeitung*, 919–20.
Polinsky, A.M. (2006), 'Optimal Fines and Auditing When Wealth is Costly to Observe', *International Review of Law and Economics*, **26** (3).
Polinsky, A.M. and S. Shavell (1979), 'The Optimal Trade Off between the Probability and the Magnitude of Fines', *American Economic Review*, 880–91.
Polinsky, M. and S. Shavell (1991), 'A Note on Optimal Fines When Wealth Varies among Individuals', *American Economic Review*, **81**, 618–21.
Polinsky, A.M. and S. Shavell (1993), 'Should Employees be Subject to Fines and Imprisonment Given the Existence of Corporate Liability?', *International Review of Law and Economics*, **13**, 239–57.
Polinsky, A.M. and S. Shavell (1998), 'Punitive Damages: An Economic Analysis', *Harvard Law Review*, 869–962.
Ponsaers, P. and S. de Keulenaer (2003), 'Met strafrecht tegen milieudelicten? Rol en functie van bijzondere inspectiediensten in de strijd tegen milieucriminaliteit', *Panopticon*, 250–65.
Posner, R. (1980), 'Optimal Sentences for White-collar Criminals', *American Criminal Law Review*, 400–18.
Posner, R. (1985), 'An Economic Theory of the Criminal Law', *Columbia Law Review*, **85**, 1193–209.
Posner, R.A. and E.B. Rasmusen (1999), 'Creating and Enforcing Norms, with Special Reference to Sanctions', *International Review of Law and Economics*, **19**, 369–82.
Roef, D. (2001), *Strafbare overheden: een rechtsvergelijkende studie naar de strafrechtelijke aansprakelijkheid van overheden voor milieuverstoring*, Antwerpen: Intersentia; Maastricht: Groningen.
Rousseau, S. (2007), 'Timing of Environmental Inspections: Survival of the Compliant', *Journal of Regulatory Economics*, **32**, 17–36.
Segerson, K. and T. Tietenberg (1992), 'Defining Efficient Sanctions', in T.H. Tietenberg (ed.), *Innovation in Environmental Policy*, Aldershot, UK and Brockfield, USA: Edward Elgar, pp. 63–5.
Selin, C. (2001), 'Your Money or Your Life: A Look at the Convention on the Protection of the Environment through Criminal Law', *RECIEL*, **10** (1), 106–14.
Shavell, S. (1984a), 'Liability for Harm versus Regulation of Safety', *Journal of Legal Studies*, 357–74.

Shavell, S. (1984b), 'A Model of the Optimal Use of Liability and Safety Regulation', *RAND Journal of Economics*, 271–81.
Shavell, S. (1985), 'Criminal Law and the Optimal Use of Non-monetary Sanctions as a Deterrent', *Columbia Law Review*, **85**, 1232–62.
Shover, N. (2005), 'Environmental Crime', *Crime and Justice: A Review of Research*, **32**, 321–71.
Skogh, G. (1973), 'A Note on Gary Becker's Crime and Punishment: An Economic Approach', *Swedish Journal of Economics*, 305–11.
Skogh, G. and C. Stuart (1982), 'An Economic Analysis of Crime Rates, Punishment and the Social Consequences of Crime', *Public Choice*, 171–9.
Smettan, J.R. (1992), *Kriminelle Bereicherung in Abhängigkeit von Gewinnen, Risiken, Strafen und Moral*, Freiburg im Briesgau: Max Planck Institute for Foreign and International Criminal Law.
Steinzor, R.I. (1998), 'Reinventing Environmental Regulation: The Dangerous Journey from Command to Self-Control', *Harvard Environmental Law Review*, **22**, 103–202.
Stigler, G. (1970), 'The Optimum Enforcement of Laws', *Journal of Political Economy*, 526–36.
Van Rooy, B. (2006), *Regulating Land and Pollution in China, Law Making, Compliance, and Enforcement: Theory and Cases*, Dissertation, Leiden: Leiden University Press.
Watson, M. (2005a), 'Environmental Crime in the UK', *European Environmental Law Review*, **14** (7), 186–92.
Watson, M. (2005b), 'Organised Crime and the Environment: The British Experience', *European Environmental Law Review*, **14** (8–9), 207–13.
Watson, M. (2006), 'The Use of Criminal and Civil Penalties to Protect the Environment: A Comparative Study', *European Environmental Law Review*, **15** (4), 108–13.
Wheeler, N. (1984), 'The Use of Criminal Statutes to Regulate Product Safety', *Journal of Legal Studies*, 593–622.
Wilde, M. (2002), *Civil Liability for Environmental Damage: A Comparative Analysis of Law and Policy in Europe and the United States*, The Hague and London: Kluwer Law International.
X (2003), 'Shame, Stigma and Crime: Evaluating the Efficacy of Shaming Sanctions in Criminal Law', *Harvard Law Review*, **116**, 2186–207.

14 Cyber crime

*Mark A. Cohen**

1. Introduction

The purpose of this chapter is to examine the economic theory and empirical evidence on crime and punishment for economic crimes (for example, fraud and tax evasion) and new technology offenses (for example, computer hacking and viruses), with reference to the role of the United States Sentencing Commission ('Commission') in affecting individual behavior.[1] This chapter relies upon the economic theory of individual behavior known as the rational actor paradigm. Under this theory, it is assumed that white-collar criminals are no different from most law-abiding citizens. They are rational decision makers acting in what they perceive to be their own best interest.[2] Although one might question whether offenders who engage in crimes of passion are rational, there should be little controversy in this view of offenders who commit economic crimes such as fraud and tax evasion. As rational decision makers, white-collar criminals base their decision to commit an economic crime upon their subjective evaluation of the expected costs and benefits of committing the crime. Even if actions appear irrational, they may be based on the offender's perception of risk and opportunities. Of course, potential white-collar criminals are not the only decision makers that affect the crime rate. Others who play a role are

* Professor of Management and Law, Vanderbilt University and Vice President for Research, Resources for the Future.

[1] This chapter is based largely on a paper entitled, 'Economic Theories of Crime Control: Implications for Federal Sentencing Policy', presented at the Symposium on Federal Sentencing Policy for Economic Crimes and New Technology Offenses, sponsored by US Sentencing Commission and George Mason University Law School, October 12–13, 2000. That paper was subsequently published as, 'The Economics of Crime and Punishment: Implications for Sentencing of Economic Crimes and New Technology Offenses', *George Mason University Law Review*, **9** (2), 503–28 (winter 2000). The *George Mason University Law Review* has granted permission to reprint (and update) this article.

[2] See Mark A. Cohen and Sally S. Simpson, 'The Origins of Corporate Criminality: Rational Individual and Organizational Actors', chapter 2 in *Debating Corporate Crime*, edited by William S. Lofquist, Mark A. Cohen and Gary Rabe (Cincinnati, OH: Anderson Publishing Co. and Academy of Criminal Justice Sciences, March 1997).

law enforcement officials, judges, victims, and society as a whole (that is, potential victims).

Section 2 of this chapter examines the incentives that each faces and identifies the interactions between them. This first part provides a 'systems' approach to thinking about crime control that takes into account the actions of each decision maker. Section 3 outlines the implications for this 'systems' approach to crime control. Finally, Section 4 considers some of the major issues that the Sentencing Commission dealt with in revising its Guidelines for sentencing white-collar offenders for economic crime and new technology offenses.

2. Optimal level of crime and crime control: a systems approach

Although crime itself is socially harmful, the costs of devoting resources to catching criminals and punishing them also creates social harm, in that the resources could have been put to a different, socially beneficial use.[3] Thus, the economic approach to crime control is concerned with finding the optimal combination of preventing, detecting, enforcing, and offending behavior. Put differently, although we would all like there to be zero crime, economic theory recognizes that this is an unattainable goal – primarily because of the costs involved in preventing, detecting, and punishing criminal activity.[4]

What role does sentencing have in this system? Certainly, we cannot expect the Commission – and sentencing policy – to solve all of the problems of the criminal justice system. Moreover, it is important to understand the interrelationship between the various actors in the criminal justice system, since the actions of one might affect the behavior of the others. Thus, for example, if the Commission were to dramatically increase the penalty for computer-based consumer fraud relative to other forms of consumer fraud, one effect of this policy might be to shift some of the 'offender talent' away from computer crime into other forms of consumer fraud. Although the goal of the stricter sentencing policy might

---

[3] See Gary S. Becker, 'Crime and Punishment: An Economic Approach', *Journal of Political Economy*, **76**, 169, 171 (1968) (hereinafter 'Crime and Punishment') ('Public expenditures in 1965 at the federal, state, and local levels on police, criminal courts and counsel, and "corrections" amounted to over $4 billion, while private outlays on burglar alarms, guards, counsel, and some other forms of protection were about $2 billion'); see also David A. Anderson, 'Aggregate Burden of Crime', *Journal of Law and Economics*, **42**, 611, 612 (1999) ('Overt annual expenditures on crime in the United States include $47 billion for police protection, $36 billion for correction, and $19 billion for prosecution (the legal and judicial costs) of state and local criminal cases').

[4] See 'Crime and Punishment', *supra* note 3, at p. 180.

clearly have been to reduce computer crime, its net effect might be only a minimal reduction in the overall consumer fraud rate. Alternatively, it might simply induce offenders to use more sophisticated and costly forms of evasion. Ultimately, how much (if any) the overall consumer fraud rate will decrease will depend in part on the cost of committing a crime using a computer versus other fraud vehicles and the cost to consumers of avoiding victimization on the computer.

The concept of an 'optimal' level of crime may appear to be morally repugnant to people who believe the government should attempt to eradicate all social evils.[5] In particular, it might be difficult to accept the fact that there will always be some crime and that public policymakers will in effect tolerate some crime. Yet, both private citizens and policymakers make such difficult decisions every day.

For example, storeowners must choose how best to cope with the problem of shoplifting. By employing elaborate security measures, they can reduce the level of this crime or if security is sufficiently onerous, perhaps eliminate it completely. Consider the example in a retail store of locked chains used to protect expensive leather jackets from being stolen. Although the use of chains may virtually eliminate shoplifting of these leather jackets, it also imposes very real costs on storeowners, including the cost of the security device and the lost revenues from customer dissatisfaction that results from having to wait for a salesperson to unlock each coat and supervise the entire purchase process. These costs could exceed the store's losses due to shoplifting, in which case the storeowner might forego this form of crime prevention. Ultimately, the storeowner selects a level of security, and hence implicitly, a positive level of crime, that she believes will maximize net profits.

Of course, the storeowner is not the only actor in this drama. Shoplifting is a crime, and one that results in punishment for the offender who is convicted. Part of the decision calculus of the storeowner and the potential shoplifter is knowledge about what the criminal justice system will do. What is the likelihood that the shoplifter will be caught? If caught, how much time will it take the storeowner to deal with the criminal justice system? How expensive is it to prosecute and convict the shoplifter? What sanction will the judge impose for this offense? All of these questions are important and interrelated. For example, if judges are reluctant to impose any significant sanctions on shoplifters, prosecutors might decline those cases or accept minimal plea bargains or pre-trial diversions. However,

---

5 See Kenneth G. Dau-Schmidt, 'An Economic Analysis of the Criminal Law as a Preference-Shaping Policy', *Duke Law Journal*, **I**, 11–12 (1990).

that does not necessarily mean shoplifting will increase dramatically. If the risk of being penalized by the criminal justice system decreases, storeowners may increase their surveillance and prevention measures, as these forms of preventive expenditures become more cost effective relative to punishment. However, if the sanction is very severe – so that shoplifters are guaranteed a year in prison, for example – store owners will shift some of the cost of prevention onto the criminal justice system. Thus, fewer storeowners will purchase costly security systems that help reduce crime, and instead they will rely on the deterrent effect of strict sentencing to reduce shoplifting.

The lessons learned from the shoplifting example can be applied to economic crimes as well. As individual consumers or business people, we take all kinds of precautions against fraud. We hang up on telephone sales persons even if we might otherwise be interested in the product being offered, since we are concerned that the party on the other end – whom we do not know – is attempting to swindle us out of our hard-earned money. Similarly, on the Internet, we are reluctant to deal with merchants we are not familiar with since it is much easier to 'move' on the Internet than to close up a store and open in another town where nobody knows the storeowner's reputation. We are reluctant to give out credit card information over the Internet because unauthorized eyes can easily intercept our transmissions. We are reluctant to bid in online auctions because we do not know if the seller is trustworthy and will deliver what he promises. Of course, purchasing products over the Internet and bidding in online auctions are both relatively safe activities with low frequencies of fraud. Why? Both individuals and businesses take costly actions to prevent and/or raise the costs to potential offenders from committing these frauds. Thus, many consumers will not give out their credit card information on the Internet unless they know that the company uses appropriate encryption technology. Similarly, many consumers will not bid in an online auction unless they know that the auction company has a feedback mechanism to check on the reputation of the seller, and/or they offer insurance against fraud. Finally, many consumers will also look for a well-known, established firm that has an existing reputation. All of these prevention activities are costly – to businesses and ultimately to consumers. In some cases, where these protections are not available, consumers will decide that taking these actions are too costly relative to the benefits, and they will decide either to take a chance or to forego the transaction altogether – perhaps taking a costly trip to a 'bricks and mortar' retail store instead.

Moreover, the availability of criminal remedies might have an effect on the amount of prevention expenditures undertaken by businesses and consumers. If I know that the penalty for computer fraud, for example, is very severe and that the chance of getting caught is very high, I might be less reluctant to use the Internet to make purchases. However, I might also take less care in avoiding a potentially fraudulent vendor. The question then becomes whether it is more cost effective to rely upon prevention or punishment to deter fraud. At the same time, if enforcement is very stringent and penalties are severe, in a climate of rapidly changing technology and intellectual property, some marginal companies might decide that the risk of being labeled a criminal is too great a risk to go into that line of business altogether.[6] Thus, some 'innocent' individuals or companies might not engage in the socially beneficial activity at all.[7]

More formally, there are several types of costs associated with economic crimes: (1) social harm[8] which is often equated with the term 'loss' that is used in the fraud guidelines of the Commission,[9] (2) the cost of apprehending and convicting offenders – law enforcement and the criminal justice system, (3) the cost of imposing sanctions – collecting fines, constructing and maintaining prisons, probation officers, etc., (4) the cost to potential victims who take preventive measures to avoid being a victim, (5) the cost to innocent individuals who are or may be charged with crimes they did not commit, and (6) the resources devoted to committing the crime itself (for example, telephones, computers, mailing list rentals). Under an economic approach to crime, the goal of society is to minimize the sum of all six of these costs.

Although I am framing the question of writing sentencing guidelines in

---

6 See Jeffrey S. Parker, 'Criminal Sentencing Policy for Organizations', *American Criminal Law Review*, **26**, 513, 554–63 (1989) (discussing optimal penalties and overdeterrence).

7 See Daniel L. Rubenfeld, 'Econometrics in the Courtroom', *Columbia Law Review*, **85**, 1048, 1051 (1985) ('Type 1 errors involve the cost of concluding that an activity was illegal – for example, that there was discrimination amounting to a violation of Title V11 – when in fact it was not. Type 2 errors involve the cost of wrongly concluding that an activity was not illegal, when in fact it was'). We are seeing this to some extent in the area of privacy rights on the Internet.

8 Technically, 'social cost' and 'loss' are not the same thing. Loss is closer to the concept of an 'externality' than to a social cost, since the former may include private losses (for example, transfers from victim to the offender) that are not always considered to be social losses. For a discussion of these concepts in the context of crime, see Mark A. Cohen, *The Costs of Crime and Justice* (New York, NY: Routledge, 2005).

9 See *US Sentencing Commission Guidelines Manual* (hereinafter *Guidelines*), § 2B1.1 – Larceny, Embezzlement, and Other Forms of Theft, Offenses Involving Stolen Property; Property Damage or Destruction; Fraud and Deceit; Forgery; Offenses Involving Altered or Counterfeit Instruments Other than Counterfeit Bearer Obligations of the United States.

terms of an 'optimal' level of crime, this goal is not necessarily incompatible with the traditional goals of sentencing. Instead, it helps to operationalize the often conflicting goals of deterrence, incapacitation, rehabilitation, and retribution.[10] For example, although the optimal crime control model is similar to a deterrence model, it recognizes that deterrence comes at a price – and that its benefits should be balanced against its costs. Similarly, incapacitation makes sense when the cost of imprisonment is less than the expected harm caused by recidivism, and rehabilitation is good when its costs are outweighed by its crime control (or other social) benefits.

Complicating the picture, there are at least five distinct decision makers: (1) potential offenders, (2) potential victims, (3) law enforcement, (4) the courts, and possibly (5) individuals potentially accused of committing a crime they did not commit. It is important to understand the interrelationships between these parties. To do that, we must first ask what motivates their actions, and how we can predict the effect of changing sentencing policy on the actions of each of these five categories of decision maker.

2.1 Potential offenders

We are all potential offenders.[11] Ultimately, while this is often an 'implicit' decision, we each weigh the benefits of evading or breaking any particular law against the cost of being caught. The expected benefits from committing an economic crime are generally monetary. However, it is also possible that offenders receive psychic benefits from economic crimes – such as peer approval, a feeling of importance, or 'getting back at the system'. Many computer crimes appear to be motivated more by these psychic benefits than by pure monetary benefits. How else do you explain most computer viruses and hackers? Although some of this activity is motivated by money, such as extortion, it seems that some computer crime is perpetrated for the psychic rewards that the offender receives from crashing other computers.

---

[10] For a description of the goals of sentencing in the criminal law, see *Model Penal Code* § 1.02(2)(a–d) (1985).

[11] For example, although I do not think I would ever be tempted to commit a fraud or evade taxes, the reason I am not so tempted is not that I am inherently any different from someone who does. Instead, the perceived costs of evading taxes, for example, far outweigh any benefits I can see from doing so. In other words, in choosing what is best for me, I weigh the benefits from tax evasion – saving money – against the costs of tax evasion – which include the expected penalty, possible prison sentence, and moral outrage I would expect to endure from my family, friends, and community. On April 15 every year, I choose to honestly report my taxes. However, for someone who chooses otherwise, they perceive the expected benefits from tax evasion to exceed the expected cost to them.

The expected costs to the offender include the expected sanction – which depends on the risk of being caught, indicted, and convicted, as well as the expected severity of punishment if convicted. It might also depend on the extent to which the potential offender believes his standing or reputation in the community will be affected. Will this reduce his long-term opportunities for employment? Will this reduce his stature among family and friends? These are all expected costs that the potential offender will weigh against the potential gain from committing the crime.

Notice that I have used the terms 'expected' costs and 'expected' benefits. The expected cost from criminal action includes both the negative value (utility) to the criminal of the expected sanction from committing the crime and the foregone opportunities that the criminal gives up in order to pursue criminal activity. The expected sanction is calculated as the probability of apprehension and conviction multiplied by the sanction that the offender expects to be imposed. Thus, in order to fully understand the potential offender's decision calculus, one should look at the offender's personal perception of variables such as the likelihood of apprehension, conviction, and imprisonment, even if that differs from actual rates. For example, if all potential embezzlers believe there is a 100 percent chance of being apprehended and convicted, even if the truth were that only one in ten embezzlers were caught – this crime would probably be non-existent.

Although all potential criminals may face the same expected sanction for the same crime, different people may value that expected sanction differently. For example, an individual who is risk averse (that is, prefers certain outcomes to gambles) will react differently to a 50 percent chance of being convicted than an individual who prefers risk.[12] All else equal, the risk-loving individual will be more likely to commit the crime, since he or she is less responsive to the chance of being convicted than the risk-averse individual. Not only do people differ in their preferences toward risk, but they may also differ on such dimensions as moral standards, family responsibilities, concern for the social stigma of having a criminal record, and tolerance toward living in a prison environment. Differences in these and other individual dimensions will yield differences in the value the individual places on being sanctioned and thus on the degree of responsiveness to those sanctions.

In addition to the negative value of the expected sanction, the potential criminal must consider the foregone legitimate and criminal opportunities

---

[12] See generally Kenneth W. Simons, 'Assumption of Risk and Consent in the Law of Torts: A Theory of Full Preference', *Boston University Law Review*, **67**, 213 (1987) (providing a detailed explanation of risk preference theory).

as a cost of criminal activity.[13] Foregone legitimate opportunities from engaging in criminal activity include: current wages that the criminal could be earning if he or she did not engage in criminal activity, the value of leisure time the criminal gives up while engaging in criminal activity, and the value of future earning opportunities that may be lost if the individual develops a criminal record. Foregone criminal activity includes the other crimes that the criminal could commit instead of the current one. That is, the potential offender not only considers whether or not to commit a crime, but which crime to commit. This decision will again be based on the (perceived) expected costs and benefits of each type of crime.

Not all potential criminals have the same opportunities. People differ in their ability, training, and access to criminal opportunities. For example, increased computer literacy will inevitably increase the rate of crime committed through the use of a computer. In addition, increased opportunities to earn money in legitimate occupations will reduce the crime rate.

Given our understanding of the costs and benefits of criminal activity, in order to reduce the propensity of potential offenders to commit crimes, we need to raise the expected cost of the criminal activity and/or reduce the expected benefits. There are many different actions that society can undertake to affect the crime rate, including: making it more technologically difficult and thus more expensive to commit a crime,[14] providing more non-criminal opportunities to earn a legitimate income,[15] increasing the psychic costs of crime through public information and education campaigns, encouraging negative peer pressure and other forms of social stigmas,[16] and increasing the expected punishment through increasing the probability of detection or increasing the severity of punishment.[17]

---

[13] See David J. Elbaz, 'The Troubling Entrapment Defense: How About an Economic Approach?', *American Criminal Law Review*, **36**, 117, 141–2 (1999) (explaining how criminals consider opportunity costs when contemplating criminal activity).

[14] See Jonathan Todd Laba, 'If You Can't Stand the Heat, Get Out of the Drug Business: Thermal Imagers, Emerging Technologies, and the Fourth Amendment', *California Law Review*, **84**, 1437, 1441 (1996) (providing examples of new crime fighting technologies).

[15] See generally Sylvia G. McCollum, 'Mock Job Fairs in Prison–Tracking Participants', *Federal Probation* **64**, 13 (2000) (describing an in-prison job fair program in Texas).

[16] See generally Dan M. Kahan, 'Social Influence, Social Meaning, and Deterrence', *Virginia Law Review*, **83**, 349 (1997) (describing how stigmatizing crime reduces criminal activity).

[17] See Laba, *supra* note 14; see also Miriam A. Cavanaugh, 'If You do the Time, You Will do the Time: A Look at the New "Truth in Sentencing" Law in

2.2 Potential victims

Each potential victim decides what level of resources to devote to avoidance or prevention activities by examining the perceived expected costs and expected benefits of prevention. The expected benefits of prevention consist of the harm caused by the criminal act that is avoided, multiplied by the reduced probability of becoming a victim. The costs of prevention include the physical costs such as security systems, software programs, and auditors. But the costs of prevention also include more subtle costs and foregone opportunities such as the cost of not engaging in an online auction due to fear of being defrauded.[18] The cost of prevention is likely to differ by considerable amounts by the type of potential victim. More sophisticated computer users are likely to be able to avoid becoming fraud victims at a much lower cost than others. More vulnerable victims, such as the elderly, might have a higher cost of prevention.

Potential victims will react to changes in the expected costs and benefits of prevention. Elderly individuals have extremely low victimization rates[19] among both street crimes and white-collar crimes (with some apparent important exceptions such as telemarketing fraud). The reason is that they generally realize they are especially vulnerable and take added precautions to avoid situations that put them at risk. A sudden change in the crime rate will also affect the costs and benefits of preventive measures by potential victims. For example, increased access to private information on the Internet that lowers the cost of committing identity theft or credit card fraud also increases the expected benefit to potential victims from taking preventive or avoidance measures. Thus, if the government now takes actions that otherwise decrease the crime rate – such as significantly increasing the sanction for identity theft or credit card fraud – this will decrease the expected benefit of taking private preventive actions. Hence, potential victims will respond to the increased probability of detection or increased severity of punishment by reducing their own preventive or avoidance activities. Similarly, increased restitution will decrease the incentive for potential victims to take preventive measures.

Michigan', *University of Detroit Mercy Law Review*, **77**, 375 (2000) (describing Michigan's new sentencing regime that sets stricter sentences for criminals).

18 See Elbaz, *supra* note 13.

19 See for example, Mark Warr, 'Public Perceptions and Reactions to Violent Offending and Victimization', in *Understanding and Preventing Violence: Consequences and Control of Violence*, volume 4. edited by Albert J. Reiss, Jr and Jeffrey A. Roth, Committee on Law and Justice, Commission on Behavioral and Social Sciences and Education, National Research Council (Washington, DC: National Academy Press, 1994), pp. 11–15.

That does not mean restitution is bad or that the government should not increase the sanction for identity theft. Simply, we need to recognize the interrelationships between the actions of each actor in this system. By doing so, we can determine how to prioritize crimes in terms of government enforcement and sentencing policy. Finally, victims can affect the probability of conviction by the amount of cooperation they give to government officials.[20] This will depend on their treatment in the criminal justice system, including the amount of time they must spend resolving legal controversies.

As noted above, the cost of prevention is likely to differ among potential victims. Thus, the elderly or mentally handicapped might be more vulnerable to telemarketing fraud, for example, which might justify more punitive sanctions where vulnerable victims are included. In addition, the government might have a higher cost of prevention than the private sector, as individual decision makers within the government do not have the same private incentives that their private sector counterparts have to help prevent the government from becoming a victim. This might justify more punitive sanctions for economic crimes against the government relative to crimes against private businesses.

2.3 Law enforcement

Law enforcement agencies – both investigative and prosecutorial – are obviously key actors in the criminal justice system. To the extent that devoting more attention to one type of crime increases the probability of detection, conviction, and punishment of criminal wrongdoing, this will result in a deterrent effect for that crime.[21]

Although we would like to think that all alleged crimes are given equal treatment in both investigation and prosecution, the reality is that government resources are limited and each agency must establish enforcement priorities.[22] Those priorities might depend on the perceived harm caused by certain types of crimes, the difficulty of establishing criminal liability, community standards, and even the political aspirations of individual

---

[20] See Deborah Kelly, 'Victim Participation in the Criminal Justice System', in *Victims of Crime: Problems, Policies, Programs*, edited by Arthur J. Lurigo, R.C. Davis and W.G. Skogan (1990), pp. 172–3 (noting that lack of victim cooperation results in high dismissal rates for criminal prosecutions).

[21] However, it may also increase the rates of other crimes on the margin.

[22] See G. Robert Blakey, 'Federal Criminal Law: The Need, not for Revised Constitutional Theory of New Congressional Statutes, but the Exercise of Responsible Prosecutive Discretion', *Hastings Law Journal*, **46**, 1175, 1246 (1995) (discussing prosecutorial enforcement priorities in the federal system).

prosecutors.[23] Given scarce resources and the need to prioritize workloads, one factor that inevitably affects investigators and prosecutors is the ultimate punishment the alleged criminal offender can expect to receive. Sentencing guidelines can send strong signals to prosecutors about which crimes should be the highest priority and which should be placed lower on the priority list. Thus, when the Commission increased the probability and severity of punishment for white-collar offenders in 1987, it should have had two effects. First, it should have deterred and incapacitated offenders, and second, it should have shifted the priorities of some law enforcement officials towards white-collar crime. Both of these effects tend to reduce white-collar crime.[24]

2.4 Courts

As should be clear by now, sentencing guidelines can have an important effect on the incentives of the other actors – and not just the criminals – in this 'system'. Sentences issued by courts provide signals to all parties about the 'price' that one will have to pay for committing a crime that is detected and successfully prosecuted. Such potential offenders may be deterred if the sanction is severe enough. However, as indicated above, there are other effects from raising sanctions. Potential victims might take less care to prevent or avoid crimes as they benefit from the increased deterrent effect of more severe sanctions. Potential offenders might shift to other crimes that have relatively less onerous sanctions attached to them. Prosecutors might move certain crimes up or down their priority list as they adjust to these signals about the 'payoff' from their prosecutorial efforts.

Although most of these effects are intended, one must also be careful about unintended consequences. For example, courts setting very high penalties on crimes where innocent individuals are easily mistaken might deter socially beneficial activity as well as criminal activity. This is of particular concern for offenses that might be committed by legitimate businesses as opposed to businesses largely established for the purposes of committing criminal activities.

2.5 Potential mistaken offenders

Unfortunately, there is always the possibility that an innocent individual will be charged with a crime. There are many safeguards in our legal system

---

23 Id.

24 See Mark. A. Cohen, 'Sentencing Guidelines and Corporate Criminal Liability in the United States', *Business and the Contemporary World*, **4**, 140, 150 (1992) (noting that increasing sanctions for certain crimes provides an incentive for the government to search for and prosecute those types of crimes).

to prevent such mistakes from happening – and in reality, it is probably a rare event. However, in some cases – especially in the area of economic crimes – the fact that there is always a possibility that an innocent person will be charged with a crime can have important behavioral consequences on the innocent.[25]

The concern over mistaken offenders is a particular problem in the area of economic or regulatory offenses involving commerce.[26] For example, although stringent copyright protection laws are important, suppose copyright violations were a strict liability offense with severe punishments for offenders. This would certainly deter copyright violations and have a positive effect on innovation and creativity. Yet, there is also the possibility that well-meaning, law-abiding individuals and businesses who might otherwise use copyrighted material legally will decide that the risk of making a mistake and violating the law outweighs the potential gain from engaging in that line of business. Thus, there will be some negative effect on innovation and creativity. This is just one example, and even if this particular example is stretched, the concern is real. Anytime an illegal activity may come about as a result of a normal business activity, stringent penalties run the risk of deterring both the illegal and legitimate business activity. This is the 'overdeterrence' problem that economists often talk about in the context of corporate crime.[27] It is a particular problem in emerging areas of criminal law where the scope of the law and definitions of illegal activity are largely untested.[28] Thus, it is of particular concern in the area of new technology crimes. It is also why we often resort to civil sanctions for these types of offenses, where the remedy is injunctive relief and perhaps some monetary compensation. Thus, for example, the Federal Trade Commission's (FTC) mandate to control misleading and deceptive advertising generally involves this form of sanction instead of more punitive approaches.[29] Legitimate firms that want to try new advertising messages know that they will generally have the first bite of the apple, so that

---

[25] See Michael L. Travers, 'Mistake of Law in Mala Prohibita Crimes', *University of Chicago Law Review*, **62**, 1301, 1325 (1995).

[26] See Jeffrey S. Parker, 'The Economics of Mens Rea', *Virginia Law Review*, **79**, 741, 757 (1993) (describing the effects of overdeterring crime).

[27] See id.

[28] See Kathyleen A. O'Brien, 'Strategies for Successfully Defending against Federal Trade Commission Investigations of False and Deceptive Advertising', 1010 Practising Law Institute PLI Order No. B407202, 269, 312–26 (1997).

[29] See *Porter & Dietsch, Inc. v. FTC*, 605 F.2d 294, 309 (1979) (citing case law supporting the proposition that the FTC has discretion over what punishment to issue in cases of deceptive advertising, depending on the knowledge of the deception).

if a new practice is deemed to be misleading, the repercussions to the firm acting in good faith are not devastating.

Recently, this concern about overdeterrence has come to the forefront in efforts to control money laundering through wire transfers and prepaid credit cards. Reportedly, several companies left the wire transfer business following new rules enacted after 9/11, and there is concern that the same might happen with prepaid card providers if money-laundering rules and penalties are further tightened.[30]

3. Implications of the economic model of criminal justice

There are many ways which society can reduce crime and its effects. To the extent that we can educate, exert social pressures, and increase the stigma associated with certain activities, we might be able to reduce the propensity of potential offenders to commit crime. Potential victims might be able to do a better job of protecting themselves by taking more precautions, buying encryption software, asking more questions and otherwise taking private actions to reduce their probability of being victimized. We might spend more on law enforcement by hiring new Federal Bureau of Investigation (FBI) agents, more United States Attorneys, or better equipment to increase the productivity of our existing officers. This will raise the probability of detection and hence increase the deterrent effect of our law enforcement efforts. Finally, we might increase the severity of sanctions to deter potential criminals and/or incapacitate known criminals from committing repeat offenses. This chapter focuses on the implications of this economic model for setting rational sentencing policy. That means I will assume all of the other actors' actions remain unchanged, except to the extent that sentencing behavior influences them.

3.1 Offenders should be held accountable for all losses and costs associated with their actions

Since the goal of the economic model is to optimally deter illegal behavior, and rational potential criminals take into account the expected punishment they will receive from their actions, we want to set penalties based on the losses caused by their criminal actions. This result follows from the 'optimal penalty' model of Gary Becker, which calls for a sanction equal to the harm divided by the probability of detection.[31] Thus, all else equal,

---

30 See 'Prepaid Cards: The Cleanup', *Business Week*, March 3, 2008, p. 32.

31 See 'Crime and Punishment', *supra* note 3, at 172–80. A more detailed discussion of how the Becker model applies to corporate crime and punishment in the context of regulatory offenses can be found in Mark A. Cohen, 'Environmental Crime and Punishment: Legal/Economic Theory and Empirical Evidence on

the severity of punishment should increase with the size of the loss.[32] The difficulty in implementing this simple notion will become evident in a later section of this chapter, when I discuss the 'foreseeability' standard in defining loss.[33] In addition, the severity of punishment should increase with the cost of apprehension, conviction, and the cost of imposing a penalty.[34]

3.2 Crimes that are difficult to detect or prosecute should be punished more severely

Becker's model supports the theory that crimes which are difficult to detect or prosecute should be punished more severely.[35] Potential offenders weigh the expected punishment against the expected gain they will receive from committing the crime. Since expected punishment is smaller when the risk of detection is small, potential offenders will tend to commit crimes that are relatively more difficult to detect and/or prosecute. Thus, the optimal penalty should increase in order to take this into account.

3.3 Certain punishment has a deterrent effect even if average punishment is unchanged

One of the most important insights of the economics of crime model is that if sanctions are set sufficiently high, only people who prefer risk can be expected to commit crimes.[36] Empirical evidence supports this finding.[37] Given this fact, one of the best ways to deter risk-preferring individuals from committing crimes is to impose a certain punishment that those individuals will foresee as being likely. Sentencing guidelines are a step in the right direction provided that they do not contribute to uncertainty.

Enforcement of Federal Environmental Statutes', *Journal of Criminal Law and Criminology*, **82**, 1054–108 (1992).

32 Id., at pp. 170–71.

33 See *infra* Section 4.2.

34 See Mark A. Cohen, 'Optimal Criminal Fines for Organizations', working paper prepared for US Sentencing Commission (January 1988); A. Mitchell Polinsky and Steven Shaven, 'Enforcement Costs and the Optimal Magnitude and Probability of Fines', *Journal of Law and Economics*, **35**, 133–48 (1992) (including formal models that argue enforcement costs should be included in the penalty calculation).

35 See 'Crime and Punishment', *supra* note 3, at p. 174.

36 See id. at p. 180.

37 See Michael K. Block and Vernon E. Gerety, 'Some Experimental Evidence on Differences between Student and Prisoner Reactions to Monetary Penalties and Risk', *Journal of Legal Studies*, **24**, 123–38 (1995) (providing experimental evidence that prisoners respond more to the certainty of punishment than students, who respond to the severity of punishment).

Thus, sentencing guidelines should not be based on random events that are beyond the control of the individual offender.

3.4 Reputation loss from conviction might be more important than prison sentence

The criminal sanction is only one of a myriad of punishments that might be imposed on criminal offenders.[38] In addition to civil or administrative penalties, criminals might suffer the wrath of their community in terms of future employability. Doctors or lawyers might lose their licenses to practice their professions.[39] Others will be kept away from positions of importance that rely upon trust or otherwise involve some type of fiduciary duty. Indeed, there is empirical evidence that criminal offenders with higher legitimate pre-conviction earnings pay a much more serious price in terms of post-conviction earnings.[40] There have also been calls for increasing the use of 'shaming' as a form of punishment itself.[41] From a policy perspective, criminal sentencing should take into account all of the other penalties – both government and market imposed – on the offender. Prison time is a last resort and is called for if the others do not adequately deter or there is a need for incapacitation to decrease the risk of recidivism.

3.5 Monetary sanctions are preferable to prison

Another important implication of the Becker model is that because prisons are costly, we should resort to less costly means of punishment to the extent that they offer adequate deterrence and otherwise serve the goals of punishment.[42] Thus, if monetary penalties adequately deter and punish offenders, that is the preferred method. The difficulty in implementing this as policy is that the fine for many such offenders would easily exceed their assets; thus prison is necessary.[43] To take a simple example, if there is a one in five chance of detecting and convicting a person who fraudulently obtains $1 million in a credit scam, the optimal penalty would be $5 million ($1 million of which might be used for restitution). In reality,

---

[38] See 'Crime and Punishment', *supra* note 3, at pp. 179–80.

[39] See John R. Lott, Jr, 'Do We Punish High Income Criminals Too Heavily?', *Economic Inquiry*, **30**, 583–608 (1992); John R. Lott, Jr, 'The Effect of Conviction on the Legitimate Income of Criminals', *Economic Letters*, **34**, 381–5 (1990).

[40] See id.

[41] Dan M. Kahan and Eric A. Posner, 'Shaming White-Collar Criminals: A Proposal for Reform of the Federal Sentencing Guidelines', *Journal of Law and Economics*, **42**, 365–91 (1999); John Braithwaite, *Crime, Shame and Reintegration*, New York: Cambridge University Press (1989).

[42] See 'Crime and Punishment', *supra* note 3, at p. 180.

[43] Id., at pp. 197–8.

in most cases, these scam artists have few assets remaining, and prison may be the only form of punishment available.

3.6 Need to take into account interdependencies of crimes and actors
For example, as discussed above, although potential victims can take precautions against victimization, the cost of avoidance might vary across individuals. In some cases, it might cost less for potential victims to avoid victimization than it does for law enforcement agencies to prevent the crime from occurring. However, in other cases, the cost of avoidance might be prohibitive. In those instances, where crimes impose higher avoidance costs or where it is more difficult for potential victims to avoid victimization, offenders should be punished more severely relative to crimes where potential victims can cheaply avoid the crime.

The fact that the criminal justice arena is an interdependent system also suggests that before a policy is developed, the behavior of other actors is considered. Indeed, there is some evidence that while the Commission increased corporate criminal sanctions in 1990, this increase was partly offset by reducing other monetary sanctions – hence, the overall effect was not as punitive as envisioned.[44]

4. Application of economic crime control model to sentencing of economic crimes

The US Sentencing Commission published their first set of Guidelines in 1987 following passage of The Crime Control Act of 1984 which established the Commission as an independent regulatory body to write guidelines for sentencing all federal criminal offenders.[45] In addition to the overall goal of reducing disparity through restricting judicial discretion, Congress specifically called for increased sanctions for white-collar offenders.[46] The Commission followed this mandate by increasing both the probability of imprisonment and the length of the sentence for most white-collar offenses. It also increased monetary penalties significantly.

Generally, the Guidelines are based on 'offense levels', where each crime is given a base level and increases or decreases from that level are based on various elements of the offense (for example, whether a weapon

---

[44] See Cindy R. Alexander, Jennifer Arlen, and Mark A. Cohen, 'Regulating Corporate Criminal Sanctions: Evidence on the Effect of the U.S. Sentencing Guidelines', *Journal of Law and Economics*, **42**, 393–42 (1999).

[45] Comprehensive Crime Control Act of 1984, Public Law 98-473, October 12, 1984. The Guidelines, which were first issued in 1987, are updated annually.

[46] See US Sentencing Commission, *Supplemental Report on the Initial Sentencing Guidelines and Policy Statements* (1987), p. 18.

was present, if there was a particularly vulnerable victim, or the dollar magnitude of the loss or gain). These offense levels, coupled with information on an offender's prior criminal history, determine whether or not any prison time is warranted, and if so, the appropriate length (expressed in a range where the judge has some discretion). Offenders are virtually always required to pay restitution if there is a readily identifiable victim. Monetary penalties for corporations convicted of federal crimes are based on a 'multiple' of up to four times the maximum of 'loss' or 'gain'.

The remainder of this section applies the economic crime control model to several specific proposals that were under consideration in 2000 by the Commission when revising their guidelines for economic crimes. Section 4.1 considers the overriding question of whether the overall punishment for economic crimes should be increased. A variation on this proposal was to increase the punishment only for frauds involving very large losses. Section 4.2 examines whether the offense level should be based on 'actual' versus 'intended' loss and the extent to which foreseeability should be used in defining loss. Finally, Section 4.3 considers whether or not interest should be included in the loss definition used to calculate the monetary fine.

4.1 Increased offense levels for fraud

One proposal considered by the Commission was to increase the relationship between monetary losses and the offense level – which would ultimately increase the length of prison sentences for larger frauds. One commentator, the Judicial Conference's Committee on Criminal Law ('Judicial Conference Report'), indicated that the fraud and theft guidelines were too lenient relative to street crime, and that the slope of the loss table was not steep enough.[47] In support of that position, they noted that there was no 'proportionality' between dollar losses and offense levels. For example, while there is a three-level difference between a $10,000 fraud and a $70,000 fraud, there is only a one-level difference between and a $1.5 million and a $2.5 million fraud.[48]

Although the jury is still out on the need to increase the loss tables, there is no compelling evidence that such changes are necessary or even prudent. First, sanctions have increased dramatically for economic crime offenders relative to pre-Guideline sanctions.[49] Second, the effect of inflation on

---

[47] Memo from Honorable J. Phil Gilbert, Committee on Criminal Law of the Judicial Conference of the United States, to Honorable Richard P. Conaboy, Chairman, US Sentencing Commission, April 3, 1998.

[48] See Guidelines, § 2B1.1(b)(1)(f–i), (o-p).

[49] See Stephen Breyer, 'The Federal Sentencing Guidelines and the Key Compromises upon which they rest', *Hofstra Law Review*, **17**, 1, 20–22 (1988).

the loss tables has increased (and will continue to increase) the severity of punishment.[50] Third, there is no empirical evidence that economic crimes have been increasing in number or severity. Fourth, the notion of proportionality is not one that should be operationalized by simple statistics. In addition to considering these arguments below, this section proposes reforms that would address some of the concerns of proportionality in a manner that is more consistent with economic theory and the concept of 'marginal deterrence'.[51]

4.1.1 Sanctions have increased in severity compared to pre-guideline sanctions When the Commission first promulgated the Guidelines in 1987, it made a conscious effort to increase both the percentage of white-collar offenders who spend time in prison and the average length of prison terms for those who are sentenced to prison.[52] In addition, just two years later the Commission changed the fraud loss table and increased the severity level for all frauds greater than $40,000.[53]

According to Commission data, sanctions have become increasingly severe for economic crime offenders (defined as including fraud, tax evasion and embezzlement).[54] In fact, as shown in Table 14.1, the rate of imprisonment has increased from 39 percent in 1984 to 61 percent in 1999 – a 50 percent increase. Of those who received prison sentences, the average length for economic crime offenders increased slightly from about 14 months to 18 months. The reason the average sentence length for economic crimes did not increase very much was primarily due to the fact that many offenders who previously would have received probation now spend some time in prison. However, the short prison sentences that these offenders received offset the increased sentence length that the Guidelines imposed on other economic crime offenders. Thus, the Guidelines did increase the severity of punishment for economic crimes. More importantly, the 'expected' prison sentence (probability of serving

---

50 See infra Section 4.1.1.

51 The theory of marginal deterrence focuses on the incentives, created by particular schemes of punishment, for similarly situated offenders. See David D. Friedman and William Sjostrom, 'Hanged for a Sheep: The Economics of Marginal Deterrence', *Journal of Legal Studies*, **22**, 345 (1993).

52 See Guidelines, Chapter 1 introduction.

53 Guidelines amendment 154 (effective November 1, 1989).

54 See US Sentencing Commission, *The Federal Sentencing Guidelines: A Report on the Operation of the Guidelines System and Short-term impacts on Disparity in Sentencing, Use of Incarceration, and Prosecutorial Discretion and Plea Bargaining* (1991), p. 368 (hereinafter, *Report on Operation of the Guidelines System*) (defining economic crimes as including fraud, tax evasion and embezzlement).

*Table 14.1 Prison Time for Economic Crime Offenders Sentenced under Federal Sentencing Guidelines, 1984–1999**

	Percent prison	Average time served (for those serving time)	'Expected prison'
1984	39%	14 months	5.5 months
1990	51%	14 months	7.1 months
1999	61%	18 months	11.0 months

Note: * See *Report on the Operation of the Guidelines System, supra* note 54, at 377, 379. See also US Sentencing Commission, *Sourcebook of Federal Sentencing Statistics* (1999), pp. 20, 28.

time multiplied by the average time served) has doubled, from 5.5 months pre-Guidelines to 11.0 months today.[55]

4.1.2 Inflation has increased the severity of punishment The Guidelines first went into effect in 1987. Although the inflation rate in the US has been relatively low since then, time does take its toll. For example, $100 in 1987 had the same buying power as $150 in the year 2000. Thus, if we compare the 'seriousness' of two frauds, each involving $6,000, for example, but one being committed in 1987 and another in the year 2000, the 1987 fraud was much more serious in terms of victim and social harm. Yet, if we look at the loss tables, both frauds of $6,000 earn base offense levels of eight (six plus two for the $6,000 loss).[56] In fact, if we convert the 1987 fraud into year 2000 dollars, it would be the equivalent of a $4,000 fraud in 2000. However, a $4,000 fraud only receives an offense level of seven.

The effect of inflation has therefore been to increase the severity of the fraud, theft and tax loss tables by approximately one level between 1987 and 2000. Furthermore, this inflationary creep in the Guidelines will continue every year into the future, eventually increasing severity by another level and onward. This inflationary creep affects the entire loss table. However, it does not affect the monetary fine calculation for organizational defendants, since inflation does not affect the multiple that is applied to the loss.

4.1.3 No empirical evidence that economic crimes are on the rise Although there is anecdotal evidence that economic and white-collar crime is on the

[55] Id.

[56] See Guidelines, §2B1.1(b)(1) – Fraud Loss Table. Note that this table has still not been updated as of 2008.

rise, there is no empirical evidence to support this claim. As one who has studied white-collar and corporate crime for years, I know the difficulty of measuring crime rates. Unlike street crimes, there are no comprehensive government surveys or systematic collection agencies that report on the incidence of white-collar or corporate crime. Often, victims are unaware or misinformed about their victimization, making any such estimates suspect.

What evidence do we have that fraud is on the rise? We are commonly told that health-care fraud is an increasing problem. A poll by the AARP in 1999 found that 90 percent of respondents believed health-care fraud was steady or increasing.[57] Yet, according to government estimates, Medicare 'actually lost about seven cents of every dollar to fraud, waste and mistakes in 1998. . . [which is] only half of what was lost by the government's health insurance program for the elderly and disabled just two years ago'.[58] This reduction in fraud was attributed to stepped-up enforcement.[59] This is just one example of how there is misinformation about the growth in fraud.

What about fraud convictions? According to IRS data, criminal prosecutions were recommended in 3,526 cases in 1987,[60] compared to an almost identical number (3,427) in 1998. However, the number of convictions per year appears to have increased from about 2,500 to 3,000 per year.[61] Similarly, the number of convictions for financial fraud reported by the United States Department of Justice (DOJ) Criminal Division increased slightly from 2,309 in 1987 to 2,613 in 1998.[62] According to Commission data, the number of fraud offenders sentenced under the Guidelines has remained relatively stable, with 5,905 offenders sentenced in 1995 and 6,199 in 1999.[63] Embezzlement increased from 809 to 949, while tax offenses have decreased from 737 to 722 over the same time

---

57 AARP, *America Speaks out on Health Care Fraud: A Consumer Survey*, Washington, DC: AARP (1999) p. 5.

58 Eileen O'Connor, 'Federal Campaign Enlists Seniors as Medicare "Fraud Busters"' (February 24, 1999), available at http://www.cnn.com/ALLPOLITICS/stories/1999/02/24/medicare.oconnor.

59 Id.

60 US Department of Justice, Bureau of Justice Statistics, *Sourcebook of Criminal Justice Statistics* (1999), p. 474, available at http://www.albany.edu/sourcebook.

61 Id.

62 Id., at p. 314.

63 US *Sentencing Commission, Sourcebook of Federal Sentencing Statistics* (1996), p. 7 (hereinafter 1996 Sourcebook); US Sentencing Commission, *Sourcebook of Federal Sentencing Statistics* (1999), p. 12 (hereinafter 1999 Sourcebook).

period.[64] None of these figures indicates a significant increase in cases tried in Federal courts between 1987 and 2000.

As noted above, the Guidelines significantly increased the likelihood that white-collar offenders would spend time in prison – and increased the average time served. Recall from the model that an increase in expected punishment is likely to have several effects. Although it might deter potential offenders from committing the crime, it might also spur law enforcement agencies and prosecutors to pursue more cases against those offenders since the 'payoff' is now greater. Therefore, even if there is a deterrent effect from the higher punishment, the 'detection' effect might offset, and even overwhelm, any reduction in crime. That is, even if the crime rate is going down, we might observe more convictions. Thus, it is generally not appropriate to draw inferences about the rate of crime from sentencing data alone. Dramatic changes in sentencing policy are only justifiable for addressing to dramatic increases in fraud or the rate of crime in general. Currently no persuasive evidence of such increases exists.

4.1.4 Proportionality requires more than simple statistics As noted above, the loss tables that determine the offense level were criticized for being 'flat'. For example, while there is a three-level difference between a $10,000 fraud and a $70,000 fraud, there is only a one-level difference between a $1.5 million and a $2.5 million fraud. The Commission originally set the loss table for fraud by empirically estimating the relationship between loss and prison time from past practice and using that as a guide.[65]

At a minimum, we should note that the 'flat' structure was consistent with judicial preferences. Is there any reason why doubling the dollar value of a fraud at low levels should result in the same increase in offense level as it does at high levels of loss? Is there any reason why a doubling of the dollar value of a fraud should double the length of a prison sentence? The answer to both these questions is 'no'.

In theory, there are several reasons why the loss table should be 'flat'. First, larger frauds are generally easier to detect since they involve more victims, larger losses per victim, and/or victims who are more eager to obtain restitution and retribution. Second, the fact that criminals tend to be risk preferring suggests that a more certain punishment has more of a

---

64 US Sentencing Commission, *Sourcebook of Federal Sentencing Statistics* (1995), p. 7 (hereinafter 1995 Sourcebook); 1999 Sourcebook, *supra* note 63, at p. 6.

65 This is based on the author's understanding of conversations with Commission staff at the time the Guidelines were adopted in 1987.

deterrent effect than a more severe punishment. Thus, we should be willing to trade off reduced sentences at the upper end of the distribution for more certain – but shorter-sentences for most white-collar offenders. Third, individuals (especially criminal offenders) are likely to have very large discount rates (that is, they put a large premium on current consumption and less weight on their future).[66] This reduces the deterrent value of long prison sentences.

In addition to proportionality across the fraud loss table, the Judicial Conference noted that there is no proportionality between street crimes and economic crimes.[67] However, it is difficult to compare the severity of punishment across crime types unless factors such as harm and detectability are compared as well. Presumably, someone who sells $10,000 worth of cocaine or takes $10,000 by threat of physical harm causes more social harm than someone who embezzles $10,000 from a bank. Accordingly, a small fraud starts with a base offense level of six, while the small-time cocaine dealer receives a base level of 12 and a robbery has a base offense of 20 (or 22 for a bank robbery).[68] Even burglary has a higher base level (17 for burglary of a residence or 18 for a burglary of $10,000).[69] Note that the commentary to the Guidelines indicates that residential burglary has a higher base level than other burglaries because of the increased risk of physical or psychological harm.[70] To the extent that fraud involves victims who suffer serious psychological trauma or financial hardships, one might want to increase the base offense level. The current Guidelines do this with a provision for a two-point increase for vulnerable victims, or a four-point increase for a large number of vulnerable victims.[71]

At lower levels of sales, it appears there is actually some comparability across drugs and fraud values. According to the 1995 Commission Report on Cocaine and Sentencing Policy, a marijuana defendant selling $42,000 worth of drugs would receive an offense level of 14.[72] This is only one offense level higher than a fraud defendant with a loss of $42,000

---

66 See Richard A. Posner, 'An Economic Theory of Criminal Law', *Columbia Law Review*, **85**, 1193, 1213–14 (1985).

67 Memorandum from Honorable J. Phil Gilbert, Chair, Committee on Criminal Law of the Judicial Conference of the United States to Honorable Richard P. Conaby, Chair, United States Sentencing Commission (April 3, 1998).

68 See USSG §§ 2D1.1(c)(14), 2F1.1(a), 2B3.1(a).

69 USSG § 2B2.1(a)(1).

70 Guidelines, § 2B2.1.

71 See Guidelines, § 3A1.1(b).

72 US Sentencing Commission, 'Special Report to the Congress: Cocaine and Federal Sentencing Policy', (February, 1995), available at http://www.ussc.gov/crack/exec.htm.

and more than minimal planning would receive.[73] The difference in base sentences is only about three months. However, the larger dollar values of between \$500,000 and \$8 million (depending on the drug) would have a base offense level of 32.[74] The highest offense level for fraud with more than minimal planning is 26.[75] Of course, the difference between an offense level of 26 and 32 is five years – the former being slightly higher than five years, while the latter is greater than ten years.

Therefore, it does appear that both the offense level and prison sentence increase faster for drug offenses than they do for comparable dollar values of fraud. But there are other reasons why the large fraud offender might be dealt with less severely than the large drug dealer. First, it is much more difficult to detect and convict a large drug dealer. They have sophisticated networks of workers who shield them from legal culpability. More important, perhaps, is the fact that there are generally few readily identifiable victims who would complain about the drug dealer. On the other hand, large frauds are likely to be exposed, as victims or class action lawyers will no doubt seek out legal authorities to remedy their concerns. Thus, I would expect frauds to be much more easily detected and a perpetrator convicted than in the case of drug offenses. Recall, in the model, that more detectible crimes require less severe sanctions for optimal deterrence.

4.1.5 Proposal for differentiating between temporary and permanent losses A fraud that results in victim losses and ultimate restitution paid of \$1 million is different from a fraud that results in \$1 million where no restitution is ever paid. Yet, the current Guidelines treat these offenses as being identical. Restitution is generally required where victims and losses are identifiable.[76] However, the judge is free to reduce restitution below victim loss based on financial considerations and the assets of the offender.[77] Further, there is no penalty to the offender if the amount of restitution ordered does not fully cover victim losses. The result of this anomaly is that there is an incentive built into the Guidelines to hide assets or squander them on a high style of living. An alternative rule would differentiate between offenders that can afford to pay restitution and those that cannot.

Although there are many ways that one could implement such a proposal, one method might be to add the uncompensated amount to the

---

73 Guidelines, § 2F1.1.
74 Guidelines, § 2D1.1(a)(1–3).
75 Guidelines, § 2F1.1(b)(2).
76 Guidelines, § 5E1.1(a)(1).
77 Guidelines, § 5E1.1(f).

loss calculation for purposes of calculating an appropriate offense level. Alternatively, the Commission might spell out specific offense characteristics leading to an increase in the offense level depending on how much of the victim loss is not recoverable.

This proposal would partly address one of the concerns over the severity of the loss tables that was mentioned in the Judicial Conference Report. The report took note of *United States v. McDowell*, where all but $8,000 of a $300,000 fraud had been spent and was not recoverable for victim restitution.[78] The concern expressed by the Judicial Conference centered on what it considered a low offense level of 15 and a resulting guideline range of 18 to 24 months. This range was based on an offense level calculation of six for the base fraud, eight for the dollar loss, and one additional net point for offense and offender adjustments. The trial judge ignored the Guidelines and imposed an upward departure to a level 19 and a sentence of 37 months. The trial judge's reasoning was overturned, but the sentencing departure was upheld on other grounds. The proposal by the Judicial Conference was to raise the severity of the loss tables so that a loss of this magnitude would yield a level 18, which provides for 27 to 33 months.[79] However, that approach would also increase the sanction for the fraud offender who did not spend the money and was able to pay restitution. My proposal would treat these two offenders differently. For example, if the Commission were to simply add uncompensated losses to the existing loss estimate, the offender who paid back the $300,000 in restitution would still receive a level 15 with a range of 18 to 24 months. However, the offender that squandered all but $8,000 would be charged with a loss of $592,000 ($300,000 fraud plus $292,000 unpaid restitution), for an offense level of 17 and a sentence of 24 to 30 months. Alternatively, specific upward adjustment could be built into the Guidelines to increase the offense level for such cases accordingly.

4.2 Intended versus actual loss and the issue of causation

One of the most difficult issues in drafting Guidelines is whether to use intended or actual loss as the basis for computing an offense level. Related to this question is what standard of 'causation' should be used in determining loss. To answer these questions, recall the purpose of sanctions – to provide foreseeable consequences for illegal behavior that will optimally

[78] 109 F.3d 214 (5th Cir. 1997).

[79] Memorandum from Honorable J. Phil Gilbert, Chair, Committee on Criminal Law of the Judicial Conference of the United States to Honorable Richard P. Conaboy, Chair, United States Sentencing Commission (April 3, 1998).

deter potential offenders from committing crimes. In other words, potential offenders should be able to anticipate the punishment they will receive if they commit an act.

From a pure deterrence standpoint, if an individual offender is risk neutral, it does not matter whether the penalty is based on intended or actual loss. Before deciding on whether or not to commit a crime, the 'expected' loss is all that can be estimated, and thus the potential offender relies upon that measure in determining whether or not to commit a crime. The fact that will be punished on the realization of actual loss does not change that decision calculus if he is risk neutral. However, if the potential offender is risk preferring (as, I argued earlier, criminal offenders tend to be), he prefers the gamble to the expected value of the outcome. This means that a penalty based on the expected value of the outcome will have a greater deterrent effect than one that is based on the actual outcome.

Although 'expected loss' is the appropriate criterion for determining offense levels, note that if a loss is not foreseeable, it cannot be part of the expected loss calculation. That is, if the potential offender does not foresee the possibility of an outcome occurring, it is not taken into account in the decision calculus about whether or not to offend. Thus, a 'foreseeability' standard that ignores such losses would be appropriate. The difficulty is in determining which losses are foreseeable.

Consider two different offenders, both of whom commit insurance frauds that take $100,000 from customers with no intention of paying claims. Total claims by customers of the first fraud are $50,000, while customers of the second fraud incur $10 million in losses following a disastrous hurricane. Under most definitions of 'foreseeable', one would argue that the first offender's customer claims of $50,000 were foreseeable. However, even in the second case, courts have ruled that such losses were indeed caused by the fact that there was no insurance and hence the full value of the victim losses is the proper measure of loss.[80] I believe these courts are largely correct in considering the loss foreseeable as long as there is some estimable chance that a hurricane would hit the area being insured. The problem is in the current rule that calls for calculation of actual instead of expected loss for purposes of determining the offense level – irrespective of whether the loss was foreseeable.

Under the current loss rules, the first offender is likely to be held liable for $150,000 in losses ($100,000 in fraudulent premium plus $50,000 in claims not paid), while the second will be held accountable for $10,100,000

---

[80] See *United States v. Neadle*, 72 F.3d 1104, 1108–9 (3d Cir. 1996), amended by 79 F.3d 14 (1996).

in losses ($100,000 in fraudulent premium plus $10 million in unpaid claims). This effectively means that offenders are entering a lottery, where they know that if they get caught, they will be held accountable for lost premiums plus any actual losses that occur. As noted above, the ideal way to handle these two cases would be to sanction them the same – based on the 'expected loss'. In this case, expected loss would equal the premiums ($100,000) plus the average payout of insurance policies of this type. Thus, if 90 percent of premiums normally go to pay claims, the expected loss in this case would be $190,000. This is higher than the loss for the first offender, but lower than the loss for the second one.

Note that I have not argued for $190,000 in restitution. Restitution has a completely different goal than efficient crime control – making the victim whole. In this example, the restitution amount for the first offender should be $150,000, while the second offender would be entitled to $10,100,000. Even if an 'intended loss' standard is adopted for purposes of computing an offense level, actual loss plays an important role in sentencing the fraud offender. Moreover, note that in the previous section, I proposed that the unpaid restitution be used to increase the offense level of the crime in the case wherein the second offender does not pay full restitution, thus preserving marginal deterrence.

My analysis of these two insurance frauds is contrary to both the current approach and the proposed changes to loss rules. Furthermore, I realize that there are many potential objections to my proposal. First, it might be unworkable in practice, as it is often more difficult to estimate the expected loss in a case than to observe actual loss. A careful analysis of recent cases and perhaps some boilerplate provisions to reduce the burden on the sentencing court could overcome some of these objections. Second, because of the manner in which we communicate crimes and punishment, concern might be expressed that it would send a bad signal to potential criminals if the sanction for imposing a loss on victims of over $10,000,000 appears to be a slap on the wrist. Third, by imposing higher sanctions when actual loss is greater, one might argue that we provide an incentive for offenders to avoid these more costly outcomes. Thus, for example, if potential offenders were contemplating setting up a fraudulent insurance scheme, they might think twice about locating the operation in Florida, and instead move to an area where extreme outcomes are much less likely. Thus, to the extent that offenders can reduce the likelihood of some of these 'controllable events', using an actual loss standard is likely to lower actual losses. My response to these latter two concerns, however, is that the requirement that restitution be imposed, coupled with my proposal to increase loss by any unpaid restitution, largely overcomes these concerns and preserves marginal deterrence.

4.3 Interest

Currently, the loss rules for fraud exclude 'interest the victim could have earned on such funds had the offense not occurred'.[81] Similarly, in a fraudulent loan case, the rules appear to exclude interest payments a lender might have received and instead focus on 'the amount of loan not repaid at the time the offense is discovered, reduced by the amount the lending institution has recovered. . .'.[82] That is, although lending institutions might incur significant foregone interest income on a fraudulent loan, this amount is not included as a loss.

Apparently, there is disagreement among the courts over how to interpret the current Guidelines, as many circuits have decisions that explicitly include interest that had been bargained for, but exclude other interest calculations based on the opportunity cost of the fraudulent losses. For example, courts have included late fees and interest in cases involving unauthorized use of credit cards or specific investment returns that were promised but not delivered.[83] However, they have refused to permit similar lost profits in fraudulent investments when interest payments were not specified.[84] The distinction is supposedly between contractually promised interest and the opportunity cost or time value of money.

Economic theory would tell us that interest is an important component of loss. The time value of money is well established in economics as being worthy of consideration in all areas of cost-benefit analysis and policy analysis in general.[85] From the perspective of the victim, there is no doubt that foregone interest is a loss. Moreover, from the perspective of the potential offender who is deciding whether or not engage in a fraudulent activity, the time value of money will certainly play a role.

For example, an offender who defrauds victims out of $1 million and is able to hold that amount for several years before being sentenced will have

---

81 Guidelines, § 2F1.1, comment note 8.

82 Guidelines, § 2F1.1 n. 8(b).

83 See *United States v. Lowder*, 5 F.3d 467, 471 (10th Cir. 1993).

84 Id. (distinguishing 'opportunity cost' interest losses versus specific interest rates promised but not delivered, as in *United States v. Bailey*, 975 F.2d 1028 (4th Cir. 1992)). In *Bailey*, investors were never promised a specific return on investment. See id. Thus, the court ruled that any lost profits would amount to the opportunity cost or time value of money, which is not to be considered under the Guidelines. However, in *Lowder*, investors were told they would earn a guaranteed 12 percent rate of return and had been issued statements to that effect. *Lowder*, 5 F.3d at 471. Thus, the court considered this to be a contractual obligation that was fraudulent.

85 See, for example, *Chicago Board of Realtors Inc. v. City of Chicago*, 819 F.2d 732, 741 (7th Cir. 1987) (Posner, J, concurring).

earned (or been able to earn) hundreds of thousands of dollars in interest. The fact that this is not considered a loss for purposes of sentencing means that the offender has an incentive not to plead guilty and settle the case, since he has use of those resources for a longer period of time at no real cost to himself. Of course, interest may be charged in restitution orders at the discretion of the judge.[86] Therefore, to the extent that restitution with interest is ultimately ordered, some of the incentive for delay is reduced.

Interestingly, the Staff Report summarizing the comments of interested parties on this matter found near agreement that interest should generally be excluded from the loss calculations.[87] The reasons appear to be more on practical than theoretical grounds. Essentially, the arguments are: (a) interest would only be a small part of loss and hence not have a significant impact on sentencing outcomes, and (b) estimating interest would be a burden. To the extent that these concerns are valid, one possibility would be to allow the sentencing court to consider interest if it believes that doing so would more adequately reflect the severity of the offense and where estimating interest is not deemed by the court to be too burdensome.

5. Conclusion

Economic theory, empirical evidence, and social science in general, can play an important role in developing guidelines for sentencing offenders convicted of economic crimes. The Guidelines were originally written with the goal of reducing disparity while imitating past practice. However, punishment for economic crimes was made more punitive by increasing the likelihood of a prison sentence as well as the average length of prison for those who are incarcerated. Aside from notions of fairness or justice, one of the benefits of reduced disparity is the fact that 'certainty of punishment' has crime control benefits. That observation is largely based on the fact that criminal offenders tend to be risk-loving and would prefer the gamble of a prison sentence to a certain punishment. As a result, the original Guidelines – coupled with upward revisions in 1989 and the built-in inflationary impact of the loss tables – resulted in a significant increase in the severity of criminal sanctions for economic crime offenders.

The rational actor paradigm helps explain the behavior of potential offenders, potential victims, law enforcement agencies, and courts. Understanding the behavior of these actors provides important insights

---

[86] See *United States v Johannsen*, 36 F. Supp. 2d 1135, 1136 (SD Iowa 1999) (interest may also be mandatory in some cases).

[87] United States Sentencing Commission, 'Staff Working Paper: Loss Issues' (May 2000), at p. 10.

into the effect that proposed changes in sentencing policy would likely have on crime rates. Key to this understanding is awareness that sentencing policy should not be viewed in isolation, but instead as part of an interdependent crime and punishment system. Increasing the severity of punishment might deter crime, but it might also have other unintended consequences such as making other crimes more attractive, causing offenders to take more expensive and elaborate activities to evade detection, causing potential victims to take less care in preventing victimization, and encouraging law enforcement officials to prosecute more cases of that nature. In some cases, increasing the severity of punishment might even stifle legitimate behavior. Thus, it is important that the Commission work through the implications of any Guideline revisions on the likely actions of other parties.

15 Terrorism*

Nuno Garoupa, Jonathan Klick and Francesco Parisi

1. Introduction

Until recently, economic analysis of terrorist behavior was relatively underdeveloped.[1] However, given the recent focus of policymakers on measures to fight terrorism, it may be useful to examine what insights the field of economics has to offer to inform the development of counter-terrorism policy. One of the most fruitful areas within economics to mine for insights in this regard is the law and economics of criminal behavior. In many (but certainly not all) ways, terrorist activities resemble criminal activities, and so it might be useful to apply (and modify where necessary) the economic models of crime in this area.

This chapter attempts to lay out the implications of the law and economics literature on crime as they relate to terrorism.[2] The economic model of crime and law enforcement relies on the balance between the benefits from offending and the respective costs in terms of probability and severity of punishment, with respect to individuals (decision whether or not to commit a crime) and society (design of optimal law enforcement) to achieve efficient deterrence.[3] The preferences of terrorists are very important to an understanding of the benefits from offending (even if these

* This chapter updates a previous version published by the three authors in *Public Choice*; N. Garoupa, J. Klick and F. Parisi (2006), 'A Law and Economics Perspective on Terrorism', *Public Choice*, **128** (1), 147–68, reproduced with kind permission from Springer Science and Business Media. The usual disclaimers apply.

1 See a recent survey by Fernanda Llussa and Jose Tavares (2007), 'The Economics of Terrorism: A Synopsis', *The Economics of Peace and Security Journal*, **2**, 62–70.

2 The seminal paper is by G.S. Becker (1968), 'Crime and Punishment: An Economic Approach', *Journal of Political Economy*, **76**, 169–217.

3 For a criticism of the deterrence literature in terrorism, see B.S. Frey (2004), *Dealing with Terrorism: Stick or Carrot?* (Edward Elgar, Cheltenham, UK and Northampton, MA, USA); B.S. Frey and S. Luenchinger (2003), 'How to Fight Terrorism: Alternatives to Deterrence', *Defense and Peace Economics*, **14**, 237–49; B.S. Frey and S. Luenchinger (2004), 'Decentralization as a Disincentive for Terror', *European Journal of Political Economy*, **20**, 509–15.

preferences are not well understood generally by others) as well as for establishing effective punishment.[4] Penalty enhancements only make sense in the economic model if perceived as more severe by potential and actual offenders, and not just by society (including victims) generally. Although many commentators suspect that ordinary punishment is inappropriate because terrorists have peculiar preferences, the fact of the matter is that there has been no empirical assessment of preferences for terrorism, and governments suspect that terrorists care about the severity of ordinary punishment to the same extent.[5]

Another strand of the economic literature looks at criminal incapacitation rather than deterrence. Efficient incapacitation is achieved by eliminating opportunities for terrorism at minimum cost to society. One possibility is simply to eliminate the physical ability to commit offenses by imprisonment or by imposing the death penalty. Another possibility is to reduce assets made available for terrorism by cutting terrorists off from their funds. A third alternative is to increase the distance between terrorists and potential victims by imposing harsher immigration laws, including deportation.[6]

Having in mind the nature of terrorism, we should look at efficient legal policies at the individual and organization levels. Financial penalties are unlikely to play any substantive role with respect to individual terrorists (most of them are indigent anyway), but may play a larger role regarding fund-supporting organizations. The effectiveness of deportation is enhanced when applied to well-known leaders (for example, radical clerics) rather than minor and obscure members of the organization.

We begin our analysis by discussing what insights are available from models that focus on corporate or collective crimes as they relate to terrorism. We then discuss the basic rational agent model of crime in the context of terrorism, pointing out the assumptions that might need to be changed in this new area of application. We then present a sampling of anti-terror measures enacted by different countries, highlighting how the details of the laws correspond to the insights from economic models of crime.

---

4 See, on terrorist preferences and rational behavior, P. Bernholz (2004), 'Supreme Values as the Basis for Terror', *European Journal of Political Economy*, **20**, 317–33.

5 Examples include the IRA and ETA as we will see when we discuss anti-terrorism legislation in the UK and Spain in Section 8.

6 In this line of reasoning, see A. Ogus (2007), 'Responding to Threats of Terrorism: How the Law can Generate Appropriate Incentives', *Journal of Interdisciplinary Economics*, **19**, 35–55. The author argues that ex post deterrence is likely to be less cost-effective than ex ante preventive measures.

Our chapter does not address legal international cooperation on anti-terrorism measures.[7] The current economic literature on cooperation at the level of criminal prosecution and criminal law is extremely underdeveloped and seems to support the comparative federalism paradigm (in the context of this chapter, jurisdictions should compete by means of tougher legislation to avoid terrorism attacks), which is not very appealing in the context of terrorism (given external costs).[8]

2. Communal liability: identifying the relevant unit

While an individual may independently carry out an act of terrorism, the nature, the goal and the magnitude of terror crimes make terrorism more like corporate crime and organized crime than individual crime. Honor, pride and family status limit the persuasive power that individual punishment will have on a potential terrorist, while the continuity and long-term goals of the terrorism organization enhance the effects that group liability may yield. While preventing terrorist acts requires the deterrence of those individuals who would otherwise commit the acts, the role of terrorist organizations and networks suggests that anti-terrorism policy must focus incentives and punishment on the terrorist group as well as the individual terrorist. Notice we focus on two distinct aspects. We consider the most obvious case of liability for active supporters of terrorism, but also the less obvious case of liability for those who benefit indirectly from terrorism or are passive supporters of terrorism, that is, those who are in a better position to deter terrorism and fail to do so.

There are two different rationales for group liability. The first is based on the idea that terrorism has a 'constituency' that benefits from terrorist acts. Group liability would target the constituency that benefited from the terrorist act. This is similar to the foundation of vicarious liability of the principal for the acts of the agent (that is, enterprise liability). This is a rationale that focuses on the wrongdoers' external benefits. The second rationale instead focuses on the identification of superior enforcers. Liability is imposed on the wrongdoer's group not because the group benefits from the terrorist acts, but because the group can monitor and prevent terrorist acts more effectively. Large financial liability of groups

[7] See, for example, T. Sandler (2005), 'Collective versus Unilateral Responses to Terrorism', *Public Choice*, **124**, 75–93.

[8] See N. Garoupa (1997), 'Optimal Law Enforcement and the Drug Market: Some Comments on the Schengen Agreements', *International Review of Law and Economics*, **17**, 521–35, and D. Teichman (2005), 'The Market for Criminal Justice: Federalism, Crime Control and Jurisdictional Competition', *Michigan Law Review*, **103**, 1831–76.

and families that provided support, or could have prevented the commission of a terrorist act, serves this purpose. In certain settings, this form of 'communal liability' might prove more effective than individual criminal liability of those who were directly involved in the terrorist activity. This claim, based on Becker's analysis, supposes that spreading liability to the members of the group or family infrastructure will provide some level of internal monitoring, and eventually ex post sanctions on members of the group that occasioned the imposition of financial liability on the group as a whole.

Within this framework of group-wide liability, family or group members of a terrorist become quasi-enforcers. Since groups and families are held (strictly[9]) liable for their members' actions, the government delegates to the family or group infrastructure the task of monitoring and controlling potential offenders. It lowers the cost of enforcement to the government, but it increases the monitoring costs to such local groups. In doing so, the government must make sure the group has the appropriate incentives to monitor and eventually penalize its members for engaging in criminal activities that lead to liability for the group.

It should be remembered that the imposition of group liability for crimes that are not easily preventable or detectable from outside the group is not a novel idea. Historically, groups and clans were liable for the wrongs committed by group members and this ensured effective internal monitoring of the troublemakers within the group. Parisi and Dari Mattiacci (2004) show that the law applicable to inter-group wrongdoing was often characterized by rules of absolute and collective responsibility.[10] Historically, communal liability thrives in social contexts where local groups and families have better information than potential

---

[9] For the implications of strict versus negligence-based vicarious liability on the economic incentives to monitor potential wrongdoers, see G.D. Mattiacci and F. Parisi (2003), 'The Cost of Delegated Control: Vicarious Liability, Secondary Liability and Mandatory Insurance', *International Review of Law and Economics*, **23**, 453–75.

[10] Most relevant is the recent work by F. Parisi and G.D. Mattiacci (2004), 'The Rise and Fall of Communal Liability in Ancient Law', *International Review of Law and Economics*, **24**, 489–506. In ancient societies, rules of communal responsibility permitted the imposition of sanctions (both physical and pecuniary) on a wrongdoer's clan. These rules followed the collective ownership structure of early communities. The authors provide an economic explanation for the widespread use of communal liability rules in ancient law, considering the factors that determined the rise and subsequent abandonment of communal liability. See also F. Parisi (2001), 'The Genesis of Liability in Ancient Law', *American Law and Economics Review*, **3**, 82–124.

victims and central enforcement authorities, thus providing less expensive preventive measures.[11] Local groups could be superior enforcers because their enforcement measures are more credible and effective.[12] Obviously, in the case of terrorist activities, local monitoring should be augmented with central enforcement. Through communal liability, local groups and families should be given incentives to cooperate with central enforcement authorities in the prevention of terrorist activities.

The creation of internal monitoring incentives created by communal liability should be evaluated against the common pool effects that such a system creates. The history of communal liability rules in ancient law can be used to illustrate this tension. Historically, the boundaries of the 'group' for communal responsibility purposes tend to narrow over time. The system of communal responsibility was never extended beyond the closer family (that is, a group that recognized a common ancestor within the last three, or at most four, generations).[13]

---

[11] Early rules of communal liability were an effective instrument for restoring the equilibrium between groups and to promote intra-group monitoring incentives, in an environment characterized by limited access to information outside the group and underdeveloped discovery systems. Second, these societies were characterized by a substantial lack of privacy and this facilitated the opportunities for cross-monitoring members within the group. R.A. Posner (1980), 'A Theory of Primitive Society, with Special Reference to Law', *Journal of Law and Economics*, **23** (1), 1–54, considers the function of privacy, or lack thereof, in a system characterized by communal responsibility and collective ownership. He maintains that the characteristics of strict and communal liability for injuries, and collective guilt, fundamentally derive from the high information costs of ancient society. A way of limiting these costs is by maintaining crowded living conditions that deny privacy, thereby increasing the production of information (but at the same time reducing the production of some socially useful information by failing to assign a property right in such information). Because of the limited extent of personal privacy, detection of crimes is high and so is the probability of punishment. This in turn serves to keep the required level of sanctions low and to moderate the lack of individual incentives to contribute to the common good.

[12] Inducing optimal monitoring and ensuring internal sanctioning (that is, credibility of a firm's enforcement policy) is also not immune to controversy. Arlen (1994) identifies a 'potentially perverse effect' by which holding firms (vicariously) liable for offenses committed by its employees can increase enforcement costs. If the information that the firm acquires can be used to increase its own probability of incurring liability, the firm will not monitor optimally. In order to tackle this effect, a composite liability regime where some duty-based liability or mitigation provisions are included has been proposed. However, it has been noted that when information costs are high, strict liability could be preferable. See J.H. Arlen (1994), 'The Potentially Perverse Effects of Corporate Criminal Liability', *Journal of Legal Studies*, **23**, 833–67.

[13] Exodus 20: 5 and Deuteronomy 5: 9. Parisi and Dari Mattiacci (2004) show

The implementation of legal policies designed to create widespread monitoring incentives should obviously be attentive to the respect of other important legal safeguards. There are in fact different ways in which families, groups or even states can 'foster' terrorist activities. Arend and Beck's (1995) distinction between toleration, support and sponsorship becomes relevant in the context of legal policies of communal liability.[14] Liability on the group can be imposed on a strict basis, regardless of the group's involvement in the terrorist activities. But if strict group liability is found inappropriate, a specification of the standard becomes necessary. At the most conservative end of the spectrum, liability of the group may be imposed only in the case of active involvement of the group, through sponsorship. This form of liability would not substantially depart from existing criminal rules. At the other end of the spectrum, group liability may be imposed even if the evidence reveals only passive acquiescence or toleration. This standard may be coupled with an inversion of the burden of proof. For example, rules could be designed to exclude the imposition of liability for groups and families that cooperated with central enforcement authorities, reporting suspect group members, even if criminal activities were not successfully prevented. Finally, intermediate solutions could also be possible, imposing liability for groups that provided any form of support to individuals that were involved in terrorist acts.[15]

3. Terrorism as crime: new dimensions

The standard crime model provides valuable insights when considering terrorist groups as cohesive units. However, terrorism represents a peculiar form of crime which poses several difficulties in the application of

---

that early clans tended to remain relatively small in size (and to become even smaller, as group wealth increased), in spite of the forgone economies of scale in external security. External security was obtained through coalitions of clans, but the boundaries of the group for purposes of joint ownership and communal responsibility never extended beyond the closer family. This still characterizes the domain of vicarious liability of the family in the Romanistic legal systems, where the finding of a common ancestor within the last three generations serves as the general threshold for establishing a family link.

[14] A.C. Arend and R.J. Beck (1995), *International Law and the Use of Force,* p. 142 (Routledge, London), distinguish three different levels with which a group or state can foster terrorist activities: (1) toleration, (2) support; or (3) sponsorship. Higher levels of involvement also include lesser forms.

[15] J. Murphy (1989), *State Support of International Terrorism: Legal, Political and Economic Dimensions,* pp. 32–3 (Westview Press, Boulder, CO) distinguishes 12 ways in which support to terrorism can be given, including assets, financial support, territory, training, intelligence, weapons and explosives, transportation, technology, and rhetorical support.

neoclassical models of crime. Crimes of terrorism are not committed by individuals acting in isolation, without regard to other possible actors. In the context of terrorist organizations, the crime results from the concerted or interdependent action of various actors committing – or possibly preventing – offenses. Agency problems, including coordination or team issues, are thus likely to be pervasive in the case of organized terrorist activities. Further, families of terrorist members may directly or indirectly support terrorist activities, concealing the whereabouts of members or providing practical or financial assistance.

When agency problems are considered, the standard crime model needs to be extended to maintain its descriptive power. The adoption of a principal-agent framework can provide useful insights into terrorism, helping predict criminal behavior by terrorist organizations.[16]

3.1 Spreading the incentives: insights from the economics of corporate criminal liability

The economics of corporate criminal liability provides important insights into the punishment of terrorist groups, since some of the problems that have been identified in the literature are easily recast in terms of terrorists. Ideally, with complete contracting and without liquidity constraints, individual liability alone would induce efficient behavior. Consequently, corporate and organizational liability would not be necessary and the classical economic model of crime would be enough to prescribe efficient policies.

Models of corporate liability apply when contracts are incomplete or when solvency matters. In the context of terrorism, models of corporate liability may be predictive. Individual terrorist actors may not be entirely responsive to incentives, as with suicidal bombers who are not afraid of jail sentences or have not enough assets to make financial penalties effective. On the other hand, supporting organizations usually have extensive funds and most individual members (who are not suicidal bombers) care about imprisonment.

In the case of corporate or organizational criminal liability, the existence of different interests within the organization can be exploited for the purpose of deterrence with a choice of appropriate remedies. With respect

---

16 See, for example, T.J. Miceli and K. Segerson (2007), 'Punishing the Innocent along with the Guilty: The Economics of Individual versus Group Punishment', *Journal of Legal Studies*, **36**, 81–106. They show that group punishment can never dominate individual punishment on pure deterrence arguments. See also the application to terrorism by L. Gan, R.C. Williams and T. Wiseman (2004), 'A Simple Model of Optimal Hate Crime Legislation', NBER Working Paper 10463.

to corporations, appropriate incentives are created to deter business offenses, that is, offenses committed by agents with or without the shareholders' consent. In this context, the literature has examined whether or not it is desirable to hold an employee liable for corporate crimes committed by managers,[17] and what the structure of optimal corporate sanctions should look like.[18]

Applying by analogy the results of corporate criminal liability, it could be claimed that a socially optimal criminal sanctioning policy would favor large financial liability of groups and families that provided support, or could have prevented the commission of a terrorist act, over criminal liability (and jail sentences) for those individuals directly involved in the terrorist activity.

3.2 Agency costs and group liability

Agency costs play a central role in assessing efficient policies. In a world where the alignment of interests is costless, it is not relevant who is actually punished, since terrorists and supporters (including relatives) can bargain ex ante and reallocate sanctions. Individual liability of terrorists alone induces efficient behavior. However, in the particular case of terrorist activities, agency costs exist and can be significant. Usually, there is asymmetric information because active members of a terrorist group have more and better information concerning terrorist activities than other members of their family or support group.

One consequence of the asymmetry between these actors is that communal liability will distort incentives inside the group. On the one hand, it will deter those harmful activities that are easily observable, but it will induce active terrorists to engage relatively more in those harmful activities that are hardly observable and controllable by their families and group members. On the other hand, spreading of liability might affect productive activities that are somehow correlated with but not easily separable from terrorist activities (for example, money laundering).[19]

---

[17] See, among others, K. Segerson and T. Tietenberg (1992), 'The Structure of Penalties in Environmental Enforcement: An Economic Analysis', *Journal of Environmental Economics and Management*, **23**, 179–200; A.M. Polinsky and S. Shavell (1993), 'Should Employees be Subject to Fines and Imprisonment Given the Existence of Corporate Liability?', *International Review of Law and Economics*, **13**, 239–57; S. Shavell (1997), 'The Optimal Level of Corporate Liability Given the Limited Ability of Corporations to Penalize their Employees', *International Review of Law and Economics*, **17**, 203–13.

[18] See J.H. Arlen (1994), 'The Potentially Perverse Effects of Corporate Criminal Liability', *Journal of Legal Studies*, **23**, 833–67.

[19] See N. Garoupa (2000), 'Corporate Criminal Law and Organization

In an ideal world, in which the individual terrorist bears the full burden of the sanction, group and individual sanctions are substitutes. In the case of terrorist activities, it is very unlikely that any substantial portion of the sanction can be passed along to the actual wrongdoer. This is because the group is often unable to shift the penalty to the actual wrongdoers, who often sacrifice their lives to carry out a terrorist act. When the penalty cannot effectively be placed directly on the wrongdoer, the group must monitor the member's actions to prevent any potential wrongdoing.

These arguments suggest that, in spite of the general skepticism of law and economics scholars on the issue of corporate criminal liability,[20] there may be valid considerations in support of group liability for the wrongdoing of one of its members. Aligning the interests of the group with those of the government by making use of the spreading of liability can be potentially effective.

4. Terrorism as organized crime

The organization of terrorist activities bears some resemblance to that of organized crime. Organized crime can be characterized as exhibiting economies of scale, undertaking violence against other legal and illegal business, creating a hierarchy which internalizes negative externalities and manages a portfolio of risky activities, and avoiding resource dissipation through competitive lobbying and corruption.[21]

We emphasize the following differences between organized crime (including terrorism) and corporate crime: (i) organized crime is carried out by illegal organizations (usually without legal entity, but not always), the criminal market being their primary market and legitimate markets being secondary markets; (ii) corporate crime is carried out by legal firms (with legal entity), the legitimate output market being their primary market and the criminal market being their secondary market. Whereas organized crime exists to capitalize on criminal rents and illegal activities, corporations do not exist with the purpose of violating the law. Organized crime and terrorists get into legitimate markets in order to improve their standing in the criminal market, corporations violate the law so as to improve their standing in legitimate markets.

Incentives: A Managerial Perspective', *Managerial and Decision Economics*, **21**, 243–52.

[20] See M. Block (1991), 'Optimal Penalties, Criminal Law and the Control of Corporate Behavior', *Boston University Law Review*, **71**, 395–419.

[21] See G. Fiorentini and S. Peltzman (1995), 'Introduction', in G. Fiorentini and S. Peltzman (eds), *The Economics of Organised Crime* (Cambridge University Press and CEPR, London).

There are different reasons for the existence and persistence of organized crime and terrorist organizations in different societies. In general, we can say that organized crime emerges because there is an absence of state enforcement of property and contractual rights, which can also include the collapse of legitimate business institutions. Organized crime provides primitive state functions, but at a cost that is typically much higher than modern governance. Thus, its control is necessary, since it can easily corrupt existing institutions and business environments.[22] This characterization can easily be applied to terrorism, the Taliban government of Afghanistan being the obvious example.

The economic literature on organized crime is quite limited when compared to the work on individual crime and criminal law. Economic analysis of organized crime has stressed welfare comparisons between different market structures (monopoly versus competitive supply) of offenses. Crimes are economic bads, not goods. A monopolistic market is more efficient than a perfectly competitive one in the presence of bads because the output is smaller.[23] Besides monopoly power, transaction costs also determine the activities of organized criminal firms, being more successful when there is a production cost advantage. That explains, for example, why organized crime supplies protection to illegal firms dealing with victimless activities where the activities are easily observable, while self-protection is the rule for organizations involved in appropriation.[24] Certainly terrorism fits better with the former rather than the latter.

The criminal organization can be modeled as a vertical structure where the principal extracts some rents from the agents through extortion.[25] As long as extortion is a costless transfer from individuals to the criminal organization, it has been shown not only that the existence of extortion is social welfare improving because it makes engaging in a criminal offense less attractive, but that it also allows the government to reduce

---

[22] See S. Skaperdas (2001), 'The Political Economy of Organized Crime: Providing Protection when the State does Not', *Economics of Governance*, **2**, 173–202.

[23] See, among others, J.M. Buchanan (1973), 'A Defense of Organized Crime?', in S. Rottenberg (ed.), *The Economics of Crime and Punishment* (American Enterprise Institute, Washington, DC); J.F. Reinganum (1993), 'The Law Enforcement Process and Criminal Choice', *International Review of Law and Economics*, **13**, 115–34; N. Garoupa (2000), 'The Economics of Organized Crime and Optimal Law Enforcement', *Economic Inquiry*, **38**, 278–88.

[24] See A.R. Dick (1995), 'When does Organized Crime Pay? A Transaction Cost Analysis', *International Review of Law and Economics*, **15**, 25–45.

[25] See K.A. Konrad and S. Skaperdas (1997), 'Credible Threats in Extortion', *Journal of Economic Behavior and Organization*, **33**, 23–39.

expenditure on law enforcement (the government free-rides on the entry barriers created by criminal organizations). However, when extortion is costly because the criminal organization resorts to threats and violence, the existence of extortion is social welfare diminishing and may lead to more expenditure on law enforcement. Extortion in the context of terrorism is costly (for example, the revolution-supporter taxes extorted by ETA in Spain or by Colombian terrorist groups) because they are enforced by kidnapping and murder.

Illegal organizations, however, are not just the kind of firms that operate in the criminal market or commit business crimes. They also operate in legitimate input and output markets and compete with the state in the provision of public services (two good examples are the extensive parts of Colombia controlled by left and right terrorist groups or the former Taliban government of Afghanistan). They exist as an alternative provider of goods and services to the private sector and compete with the government in terms of tax rates and provision of public goods. Their existence can have a beneficial effect because the 'kleptocratic' tendencies of the government are moderated.[26] However, they may distort legal markets (for example, money laundering, control of unions, unfair competition) and create inefficiencies.[27] Incorporation into legitimate business can be a problem, but at the same time a solution, by making detection easier (because activities in legitimate markets are easier to monitor and be detected).

The institutional environment of organized crime (and terrorism) has not been analyzed by economists with the attention it deserves. One major issue that constrains the relationship between those involved in organized crime, in particular terrorism, is that contracts are not enforceable in court. That is not to say that illegal contracts are not enforceable. One mechanism to enforce an illegal contract is the threat and use of violence. The participants in illegal markets lack access to state-provided facilities for settlement of disputes. Consequently, violence can be an effective method to resolve disagreements. Furthermore, victims of violence are disadvantaged in seeking police protection: the process of providing an informative complaint will convey information to the police about the illegal activities of the complainant.

---

26 See H.I. Grossman (1995), 'Rival Kleptocrats: The Mafia versus the State', in G. Fiorentini and S. Peltzman (eds), *The Economics of Organized Crime* (Cambridge University Press and CEPR, London).

27 See D. Gambetta and P. Reuter (1995), 'Conspiracy among the Many: The Mafia in Legitimate Industries', in G. Fiorentini and S. Peltzman (eds), *The Economics of Organized Crime* (Cambridge University Press and CEPR, London).

Violence further arises when the criminal organization wants to monopolize the market or avoid competitive entry. Moreover, in the long run, the violent gang and terrorist group can usually replace internal violence by reputation, increasing profits and saving on labor costs.[28] The threat of violence also affects the organization of the market ex ante by avoiding misunderstandings and controlling the degree of subjective uncertainty as well as investment in reputation.[29]

A second mechanism to enforce an illegal contract is reverting to arbitration. Seeking the Mafia's arbitration can be of advantage to criminal firms because violence is costly and uncertain: the cost of acquiring reputation is high in an environment where disputes are frequent. Moreover, there is a complete absence of feasible symbols of quality and reliability. On the supply side, allowing the Mafia to act as a referee solves the problem of defining property rights. In the context of terrorism, a similar argument applies to the unitary leadership of the terrorist organization (for example, internal rifts within the IRA or ETA were dealt with swiftly and without mercy by the leadership every time they arose).

Given that enforcing criminal contracts is expensive, either because violence is not inexpensive (even if only at a threat level) or because solving the matter within the Mafia's institutional system is not costless (it may include costs of arbitration, rents to be paid as subscription, bribes), one might think that a criminal organization would prefer an employment relationship rather than subcontracting. Monitoring and enforcing a contract is relatively easier in an employment relationship. The cost of monitoring subcontractors is augmented because there is no book-auditing and record-keeping must be minimal to reduce evidence.

The problem posed by an employee is that his detection can compromise the whole organization with higher probability than an external subcontractor. Employees can provide information about past and future deals, leading to arrest and seizure of assets involved in the transaction. Therefore, the entrepreneur aims to structure the relationship so as to reduce the amount of information available to employees concerning his own participation, and to ensure that they have minimal incentive to inform against him. Moreover, employees are afraid of other employees. Thus dispersion and monitoring naturally emerges as a way of controlling individual risk.

One consequence of these observations is that illegal firms should be

---

[28] See P. Reuter (1983), *Disorganized Crime* (MIT, Cambridge, MA).

[29] See, on the subject, K.A. Konrad (2004), 'The Investment Problem in Terrorism', *Economica*, **71**, 449–59.

smaller than where the product is legal. In policy terms, sanctioning the organization more severely affects not only the dimensions but also the characteristics of a criminal network. Severe punishment reduces the dimensions of the network, but it might increase the effectiveness (criminal productivity) of its members. Eventually smaller firms are easier to manage and consequently fewer mistakes are committed, diminishing the likelihood of detection.

This last point is especially salient with respect to terrorist groups to the extent that they too face organizational problems that are more easily managed in smaller groups. Also, given the public nature of the good they produce, a smaller group may be more effective since there will be less free-riding.[30] To effectively monitor and provide adequate incentives to workers, terror groups tend to tap into existing social networks such that they can select for high demanders of the public good. They also use the social network to provide incentives in cases where standard labor incentives are not possible (for example, when success requires that the worker dies). So, for example, if organized crime and terror organizations each draw their employees from cohesive communities, the value of status (even past death) is greater, and there can be strong expectations that rewards and punishments will be visited upon surviving individuals about whom the worker cares a great deal. Also, especially in the context of terror activities, it makes sense that workers are often selected on the basis of their religiosity since expectations regarding the afterlife can provide strong incentives and can allow for very effective monitoring.[31]

Terror groups also seem to build counterparts in legitimate markets, just as we see with organized crime. As with organized crime, these legitimate businesses or political groups serve to help fund the terror activities (for example, Sinn Fein and the IRA, some of the Islamic charity groups that have come under suspicion in recent years, religious schools in Afghanistan, Batasuna and ETA, etc.). This vertical integration arises given the high transactions costs terror groups would have in dealing with completely legitimate businesses.[32]

Given the relatively undeveloped state of economic analysis of organized crime, the literature does not offer huge insights into the nature of terrorist organizations. However, it would seem that the similarities of the

---

[30] See M. Olson (1971), *The Logic of Collective Action* (Harvard University Press, Cambridge, MA).

[31] See J. Klick (2006), 'Salvation as a Selective Incentive', *International Review of Law and Economics*, **26**, 15–32.

[32] See L. Iannaccone (2004), 'The Market for Martyrs', unpublished manuscript, available at http://www.mercatus.org/pdf/materials/822.pdf.

two institutions, in particular the observation that terror groups generate public goods, could generate a number of interesting empirical predictions and policy recommendations.

Law enforcement can also benefit from the insights of the principal-agent set-up. Terrorism is usually a cooperative (even if not organized in the sense of a vertical hierarchy) crime in the sense that it involves more than one individual. In this context, distrust between agents and principals may deter crime ex ante and reveal information and evidence ex post. Legal mechanisms that create distrust between different parties (for example, plea-bargaining or leniency programs) generate a chilling effect, so that the different parties are less likely to violate the law (since each party is afraid that the other will make a deal with the authorities and provide incriminatory evidence). In the case where a violation does happen, the same legal mechanism is useful to get information and evidence from the different parties. Naturally, well-designed plea-bargaining or leniency programs increase the effectiveness of law enforcement and reduce enforcement costs. However, if not well designed, plea-bargaining could be counterproductive because it diminishes the expected cost of illegal activities and thus it generates more terrorism.[33]

The reputation of the terrorist group is very important in undermining law enforcement efforts. The conventional model assumes a never-capitulate enforcement policy which hinges on the government's ability to fully control deterrence with full credibility. By allowing reputation costs and limits, including budget constraints and electoral cycles, to the government's choice of legal policy, we can see how a pre-commitment not to negotiate can become a liability in law enforcement. Nevertheless, making concessions under plea-bargaining can also limit the credibility of the government's policy.[34]

5. Terrorism as crime: revisiting the basic crime model

Traditionally economic analysis of crime has been concerned with individual deterrence from the viewpoint of cost-benefit analysis. In the usual Becker-Polinsky-Shavell set-up, potential criminals compare the illegal gain from committing an offense with the expected cost, including

---

[33] See N. Garoupa (2007), 'Optimal Law Enforcement and Criminal Organization', *Journal of Economic Behavior and Organization*, **63**, 461–74.

[34] See, among others, H.E. Lapan and T. Sandler (1988), 'To Bargain or not to Bargain: That is the Question', *American Economic Review*, **78**, 16–20; H.E. Lapan and T. Sandler (1993), 'Terrorism and Signalling', *European Journal of Political Economy*, **9**, 383–97; T. Sandler and W. Enders (2004), 'An Economic Perspective on Transnational Terrorism', *European Journal of Political Economy*, **20**, 301–16.

expected punishment. The theory of optimal law enforcement has emerged as a normative comprehensive framework to prescribe optimal legal policies when individuals behave rationally.[35]

In the standard models of crime, offenses are committed by rational individuals who decide whether or not to commit the crime based on the probability and severity of punishment. Some of the insights provided in the context of the rational individual can be usefully carried over into the terrorism context. For example, it has been noted in the literature that expected punishment should increase with the harmfulness of the criminal act.[36] One can argue that terrorism is usually associated with more socially costly offenses and much more serious consequences, and so enforcement should be harsher.

Further, it has been shown that when the government observes how difficult it is to apprehend individuals, involving the expending of considerable enforcement resources, the optimal sanction should be maximal for those most difficult to apprehend.[37] If apprehension rates for terrorists are lower (low probabilities of detecting, apprehending and punishing criminals), this model of optimal sanction would provide an additional justification for harsher punishment.

One could also argue that punishment should be more severe in the context of terrorism if it is found that terrorists (including supporting organizations) are on average wealthier or hold more assets than other categories of criminals.[38]

To the extent to which financial penalties are imposed on terror group

---

[35] Useful surveys can be found in N. Garoupa (1997), 'The Theory of Optimal Law Enforcement', *Journal of Economic Surveys*, **11**, 267–95; A.M. Polinsky and S. Shavell (2000), 'The Economic Theory of Public Enforcement Law', *Journal of Economic Literature*, **38**, 45–76.

[36] See A.M. Polinsky and S. Shavell (1992), 'Enforcement Costs and the Optimal Magnitude and Probability of Fines', *Journal of Law and Economics*, **35**, 133–48.

[37] See L. Bebchuk and L. Kaplow (1993), 'Optimal Sanctions and Differences in Individuals' Likelihood of Avoiding Detection', *International Review of Law and Economics*, **13**, 217–24.

[38] Note, however, the debate concerning the efficiency of wealthier individuals being more or less severely punished. See D.D. Friedman (1981), 'Reflections on Optimal Punishment or Should the Rich Pay Higher Fines?', *Research in Law and Economics*, **3**, 185–205; J.R. Lott (1987), 'Should the Wealthy be Able to Buy Justice?', *Journal of Political Economy*, **95**, 1307–16; N. Garoupa (2001), 'Optimal Probability and Magnitude of Fines', *European Economic Review*, **45**, 1765–71; N. Garoupa and H. Gravelle (2003), 'Efficient Deterrence does Not Require that the Wealthy Should be Able to Buy Justice', *Journal of Institutional and Theoretical Economics*, **159**, 545–52.

assets, the relevance of risk profiles come into play. Economic theory usually treats organizations as risk neutral and individuals as risk averse. According to the prevailing theory of optimal penalties, risk-neutral terrorist groups should be more severely punished than risk-averse individuals. Higher penalties would in turn allow lower enforcement probabilities, a predicate that is consistent with the empirically observable lower apprehension rate.[39]

The economic models of marginal deterrence could become a serious concern for terrorism. Marginal deterrence becomes relevant when criminals choose their criminal conduct from a range of harmful acts to commit (for example, whether to commit rape or also to kill the victim). In such contexts, the threat of sanctions plays a dual role. Sanctions should aim at deterring the lesser crime, but for individuals who choose to commit the lesser crime, there should be a sufficient escalation in the threat to deter the commission of the more serious crime. Marginal deterrence pursues deterrence of a more harmful act by threatening a higher sanction than that imposed for a less harmful act. In the case of terrorist acts, the issue of marginal deterrence could be of critical importance. For example, penalties for the bombing of a building should be high enough to deter the act, but maximal penalties should only be imposed for the most harmful terrorist activities.[40]

A similar logic applies to the case of attempted terrorism.[41] The sanction for attempts should never be larger than the sanction for causing harm. Further, attempts should be severely punished when the government cannot determine the probability of harm but does know the magnitude of the potential harm.[42] This result is important for the context of terrorism, where the likelihood of success is relatively low.

At the individual level, the standard crime models may need to be modified slightly to generate useful predictions and policy prescriptions in the terrorist context. For example, some terrorists may gain utility from the prospect of receiving certain punishments (for example, the death penalty) if they wish to be viewed as martyrs for their cause. Incorporating this

---

[39] See A.M. Polinsky and S. Shavell (1979), 'The Optimal Trade-off between the Probability and Magnitude of Fines', *American Economic Review*, **69**, 880–91.

[40] See, among others, G.J. Stigler (1970), 'The Optimum Enforcement of Laws', *Journal of Political Economy*, **78**, 526–36; L.L. Wilde (1992), 'Criminal Choice, Nonmonetary Sanctions and Marginal Deterrence: A Normative Analysis', *International Review of Law and Economics*, **12**, 333–44.

[41] Obvious examples are the failed July 21, 2005 bombings in London.

[42] See S. Shavell (1990), 'Deterrence and the Punishment of Attempts', *Journal of Legal Studies*, **19**, 435–66.

concern into the crime model is not straightforward. Presumably, the desire to be a martyr is subordinate to the desire to be effective in carrying out the terror activity.[43] If it were not, terrorists would not spend resources in planning and carrying out their attacks, since they could achieve martyrdom relatively easily without any preparation. For example, it would be quite simple to become a martyr by charging toward a well-protected enemy target with a weapon. Since execution or imprisonment will preclude the terrorist from engaging in future terror activities, it would appear that increasing punishments or the probability of apprehension will have a deterrent effect, even if the terrorist gets some value out of martyrdom. However, on the margin, this factor might imply that some forms of punishment will be more effective than others. For example, shaming mechanisms that are likely to lower the terrorist's status among his network could be relatively effective.

Another issue, which is addressed more fully below, involves the public good nature of the terrorist's activities. In other words, the benefits of the crime (that is, the costs inflicted on individuals constituting the enemy of the terrorist group), in this context, accrue to many individuals beyond those directly involved. Thus, policy prescriptions can profitably exploit the problems that arise from the provision of public goods.

6. Implications for the security of victims

In the previous sections we have discussed terrorism if committed by individuals in a set-up without agency costs (classical theory) and in a set-up with agency costs (importing insights from corporate criminal liability). In these discussions, the behavior of victims was implicitly exogenous. However, a more general model needs to incorporate incentives faced by victims as well.

Potential victims can exercise security measures in order to reduce the probability of victimization. Nevertheless, it is not clear if these security measures are part of efficient deterrence, let alone whether the government should encourage them.[44] Security measures are chosen by potential

---

[43] Evidence to this effect can be found in *Military Studies in the Jihad Against the Tyrants* (translation available at http://www.thesmokinggun.com/archive/jihadmanual.html), which describes among the qualifications necessary for its members, 'Sacrifice: He has to be willing to do the work and undergo martyrdom for the purpose of achieving the goal and establishing the religion of majestic Allah on earth'. Further evidence can be found in the requirement that members be cautious and prudent.

[44] For a general discussion, see W.K. Viscusi and R.J. Zeckhauser (2003), 'Sacrificing Civil Liberties to Reduce Terrorism Risks', *Journal of Risk and*

victims for private reasons; hence the choice of precaution is generally not socially optimal.[45]

Within the economic literature on private precaution, we can distinguish three arguments against the efficiency of security or victimization avoidance measures. Even though developed in the context of the classical model, these arguments can easily be extended to terrorism.

The first argument against the efficiency of private precaution goes along the following lines: victims are expected to over-invest in precaution because they do not take into account the gains for the perpetrator. The argument that a victim, whether an individual or a group, ignores criminal gains implies that the private value of precaution is higher than its social value.[46]

A second argument predicts over-investment based on a different rationale. Faced with a victim who takes security measures, the perpetrator will prey on the individual who has taken fewer precautions. As a consequence, security measures divert rather than deter crime. However, because victims do not care about overall deterrence, but only about their own likelihood of victimization, they over-invest in precaution.[47]

The last argument goes in the opposite direction: victims will tend to under-invest in precaution because they anticipate that the government will reduce public enforcement accordingly. Alternatively, they over-rely on governmental law enforcement. The private value of precaution is lower than its social value.[48]

The problem of inefficient behavior by potential victims has led Harel to argue for a 'contributory fault' rule in criminal law.[49] In tort law, contributory negligence and comparative negligence rules are rules by which responsibility for an accident is apportioned between the tortfeasor and

---

Uncertainty, **26**, 99–120; W.K. Viscusi and R.J. Zeckhauser (2005), 'Recollection Bias and the Combat to Terrorism', *Journal of Legal Studies*, **34**, 27–55; C.R. Sunstein (2007), 'On the Divergent American Reactions to Terrorism and Climate Change', *Columbia Law Review*, **107**, 503–57.

[45] See S. Shavell (1991), 'Individual Precautions to Prevent Theft: Private versus Socially Optimal Behavior', *International Review of Law and Economics*, **11**, 123–32.

[46] See the article by O. Ben-Shahar and A. Harel (1995), 'Blaming the Victim: Optimal Incentives for Private Precautions against Crime', *Journal of Law, Economics and Organization*, **11**, 434–55.

[47] See the article by K. Hui-Wen and I.P.L. Png (1994), 'Private Security: Deterrent or Diversion?', *International Review of Law and Economics*, **14**, 87–101.

[48] See K.N. Hylton (1996), 'Optimal Law Enforcement and Victim Precaution', *Rand Journal of Economics*, **27**, 197–206.

[49] See A. Harel (1994), 'Efficiency and Fairness in Criminal Law: The Case for a Criminal Law Principle of Comparative Fault', *California Law Review*, **82**,. 1181–229.

victim. Damages are rendered non-recoverable or are reduced when the victim was also negligent. A similar interpretation is proposed for criminal law: if a victim satisfies the standard precaution, the offender faces a high sanction; if a victim fails the standard precaution, the offender faces a low sanction. Offenders have some information on potential victims' private precautions and will search for victims who fail to take the standard precaution. This obviously induces victims to choose the standard precaution.

Cohen presents a similar, though less radical idea with respect to sentencing of economic crimes and new technology offenses.[50] Economic crimes against victims with higher costs of prevention should be more severely punished. In fact, if it is usually more difficult for the government to prevent business crimes than for the private sector (essentially due to asymmetries of information), offenders should be more severely punished when the victim is the government rather than the private sector.

Certainly, the choice of targets by terrorists seems to be related to the degree of self-protection by victims, with the obvious examples of the attacks in New York (September 11, 2001), Madrid (March 11, 2004), and London (July 7 and 21, 2005), and more commonly in the case of Palestinian suicide bombers in Israel. The economic approach suggests that bombing trains or buses and killing innocent civilians could be more effective from the viewpoint of terrorists due to the high security protection offered to public officials and buildings.

In order to achieve more security, potential victims may have to help authorities to detect and punish crime. Usually, a victim decides to report suspicious behavior and help enforcers by considering several aspects: the cost of reporting, including reputation and possible effects on utility; the consequent increase in the likelihood of recovery if a crime has already been committed, in particular compensation; the effect on deterrence and incapacitation of future crimes (future security); and legal obligations that must be fulfilled (depending on which criminal liability rules are in place).

Strict monetary compensation for reporting would cover some of the costs borne by the actual or potential victim. However, it might create moral hazard by reducing the appropriate incentive to self-care for security ex ante (in a way, this monetary compensation would play the role of insurance).[51]

---

[50] See M.A. Cohen (2000), 'The Economics of Crime and Punishment: Implications for Sentencing of Economic Crimes and New Technology of Offenses', *George Mason Law Review*, **9**, 503–28.

[51] See N. Garoupa (2001), 'Optimal Law Enforcement when Victims are Rational Players', *Economics of Governance*, **2**, 231–42.

7. Political economy of anti-terrorism legal policy

Special attention should be devoted to the political economy aspects of terrorism. So far we have analyzed how legal policy, including criminal liability and security measures, deters crime. Now we look at the other side of the coin: how criminal organizations affect legal policy. In that respect, crimes committed by organizations differ substantially from individual crime because organizations have a particular ability to influence, and eventually shape, the preferences of the criminal justice authorities.

First, terrorism-supporting organizations can more easily corrupt enforcers, regulators and judges. They are better organized, are wealthier and benefit from economies of scale in corruption. Corruption is especially problematic because it diminishes deterrence of the underlying criminal behavior.[52]

These organizations are also better placed to manipulate politicians and the media. By making use of large grants, generous campaign contributions and influential lobbying organizations, they may directly (via legislator) or indirectly (via opinion makers) push for changes in the law and legal reforms that benefit their illegal activities.

Finally, terrorist-supporting organizations benefit more from globalization and free movement of capital in order to better hide their illegitimate activities than individuals. Corporate avoidance activities are more effective. Avoidance activities generate waste and reduce the effectiveness of law enforcement.[53]

These characteristics affect the design of optimal law enforcement. Within the classical model, some of the aspects we have pointed out have been addressed: for example, how enforcement should change when avoidance activities become quite frequent or how enforcement should be designed in an environment with corruption.

Another problem posed by terrorism is its power to redistribute future income in favor of the terrorist-supporting group. There are two

---

[52] See R. Bowles and N. Garoupa (1997), 'Casual Police Corruption and the Economics of Crime', *International Review of Law and Economics*, **17**, 75–87; J.-J. Chang, C.-C. Lai and C.C. Yang (2000), 'Casual Police Corruption and the Economics of Crime: Further Results', *International Review of Law and Economics*, **20**, 35–51; A.M. Polinsky and S. Shavell (2001), 'Corruption and Optimal Law Enforcement', *Journal of Public Economics*, **81**, 1–24; N. Garoupa and D. Klerman (2004), 'Corruption and the Optimal Use of Nonmonetary Sanctions', *International Review of Law and Economics*, **24**, 219–25.

[53] See A.S. Malik (1990), 'Avoidance, Screening and Optimum Enforcement', *Rand Journal of Economics*, **21**, 341–63; H. Gravelle and N. Garoupa (2002), 'Optimal Deterrence with Legal Defence Expenditure', *Economic Inquiry*, **40**, 366–79.

important transaction costs to be considered: direct (greater loss of income in successful attacks) and indirect (legislative and law enforcement costs). A balance between these direct and indirect costs must be achieved in order not to leave everyone worse off.[54]

8. A sampling of anti-terror measures

In the US, the September 11, 2001 attacks prompted lawmakers to re-examine their ability to detect and prosecute terrorist activities effectively. The primary result of this effort was the USA Patriot Act. A number of other countries, which had their own experiences with terrorism, already had anti-terror laws in place.[55] Here we give a brief overview of a number of different countries' responses to terrorism, highlighting details that relate to the discussions above.[56] Specifically, we look at how anti-terror measures incorporate the factors discussed above: (i) penalty enhancement for terrorist crimes or for crimes with terrorist motivation (severity and probability of punishment); (ii) special provisions against organized terrorism crime and supporting organizations, in particular cutting terrorists off from their funds; (iii) special provisions regarding voluntary surrender (to make cooperation in crime more difficult).

8.1 United States

US anti-terrorism measures focus primarily on raising the probability of detection and punishment of planned terror activities, as opposed to using punishment enhancements to raise the expected marginal cost terrorists face. While constitutional and procedural safeguards in US criminal law generally pre-suppose a suspect's innocence (presumption of innocence) and make it relatively difficult for prosecutors to rebut such a presumption through restrictive rules regarding the detention of suspects, the admissibility of evidence and a host of other avenues, laws enacted to combat terrorism and prosecutorial practice in the wake of the September 11, 2001 attacks have effectively moved toward a default that is much more neutral if not reversed in its presumptions regarding the guilt of terror suspects, at least those without US citizenship. Effectively, if the general presumption

---

54 See M.R. Garfinkel (2004), 'Global Threats and the Domestic Struggle for Power', *European Journal of Political Economy*, **20**, 495–508.

55 Before 2001, there were already several international conventions on terrorism, such as against the taking of hostages (1979), suppression of terrorist bombings (1997) or suppression of the financing of terrorism (1999).

56 Other examples of similar legislation include the Australian Anti-terrorism Act of 2005 (and other statutes), the Canadian Anti-terrorism Act of 2001 and the Japanese Anti-terrorism Special Measures Act of 2001.

of innocence in the US can be seen as an attempt to minimize Type II errors (that is, the guilty go free) conditional on fulfilling a constraint regarding Type I errors (that is, a minimum number of innocent people are wrongly apprehended and convicted), anti-terror policies seem to flip the optimization problem to one in which the constraint involves Type II errors (that is, very few guilty individuals go uncaptured) and we optimize over Type I errors.

From a mechanism design standpoint, such a switch could be optimal if the expected costs of damage done by free terrorists are quite large relative to the expected damage associated with a free non-terrorist criminal, assuming that society's estimate of the cost of wrongful punishment remains unchanged. Also, from the standpoint of marginal deterrence, it may be more effective to vary the probability of detection/punishment in cases where the level of punishment has an effective upper bound (for example, execution).

One of the most visible attempts to reduce Type II errors has been the adoption of the Terror Alert System by the US Department of Homeland Security. The Terror Alert System serves to place the population on guard when intelligence suggests that the likelihood of a terrorist attack has risen. In addition to alerting the citizenry to be on the lookout for suspicious activities, the Terror Alert System serves as a coordination mechanism by which federal authorities can easily signal the need for additional protective measures, such as increased police presence and surveillance of high-profile targets, to state and local authorities.[57]

In terms of procedural reforms meant to improve public law enforcement's ability to identify and capture potential terrorists, the USA Patriot Act[58] contains a number of provisions that expand the scope of government surveillance powers, especially as they relate to telecommunications.[59]

The Patriot Act also contains a handful of provisions affecting penalties for those engaged directly or indirectly in terrorist activities:

8.1.1 Penalty enhancement for terrorist crimes or with terrorist motivation The Patriot Act also includes provisions which increase the maximum term of imprisonment for terrorist activities to life in prison

---

[57] See J. Klick and A. Tabarrok (2005), 'Using Terror Alert Levels to Estimate the Effect of Police on Crime', *Journal of Law and Economics*, **48** (1), 267–80.

[58] Uniting and Strengthening America by Providing Appropriate Tools Required to Intercept and Obstruct Terrorism Act of 2001 (Public Law 107–56).

[59] For a good discussion of the degree to which the Patriot Act expands the government's surveillance powers, see *Northwestern University Law Review*, **97**, 607.

under some circumstances. Further, for non-life terms, the Act allows for a period of post-release supervision that can extend for the rest of the individual's life.[60]

8.1.2 Special legislation/provisions to tackle group or organized individuals in terrorist activities The Patriot Act provides for federal prosecution of any individual who harbors or conceals or provides any material support to an individual he knows or has reason to know has or is about to commit a terrorist activity. These actions can be punished with both fines and imprisonment,[61] with the sentence increased to life in prison in some cases for those who provide material support to a terrorist. It also provides for the forfeiture of any assets held by an individual or organization that perpetrates or plans to perpetrate any act of terrorism.[62]

8.1.3 Special issues regarding the provision of information regarding terrorist activities In the money-laundering provisions of the Patriot Act, financial institutions are protected from any liability with respect to their customers, arising from regulatory or contractual obligations, if they voluntarily report potential violations of US money-laundering laws by organizations involved in supporting terrorist activities.[63]

8.1.4 Other aspects The Patriot Act gives the Attorney General the responsibility to hold in custody any alien about whom there is a reasonable suspicion of involvement in terrorist activities, until the alien can be removed from the United States.[64]

8.2 United Kingdom

Much of the UK's anti-terror legislation stems from difficulties with the IRA. However, in the aftermath of the September 11 attacks, attention shifted to the presence of foreign nationals who might be involved in international terrorism while residing in the UK. New legislation was prepared in the aftermath of the July 7 bombings and the failed July 21 attacks in 2005.[65]

---

60 18 USCA § 3583.
61 18 USCA § 2339.
62 18 USCA § 981.
63 31 USCA § 5318.
64 8 USCA § 1226a.
65 The Terrorism Act 2000 (TACT) came into force on February 2001 in response to the changing threat from terrorism, and replaced previous temporary anti-terrorism legislation that dealt primarily with the IRA. Just after the

8.2.1 Penalty enhancement for terrorist crimes or with terrorist motivation Individuals convicted of engaging in terrorist activities can be sentenced to life in prison. Further, the Terrorism Act 2000 (TACT) created new criminal offenses for anyone who incites a terrorist act, provides terrorist training, or provides training in the use of firearms, explosives, or chemical, biological, or nuclear weapons. The Act also provides for the forfeiture of any money or property held by an individual who violates the anti-terrorism laws if the money or property was going to be used to support terrorist activities.

8.2.2 Special legislation/provisions to tackle groups or organized individuals in terrorist activities The UK's Prevention of Terrorism Act (first passed in 1974) essentially allowed the UK government to declare certain groups suspected of engaging in terrorist activities illegal, implying that membership in those groups is an offense for which someone could be arrested. Fines and prison sentences could also be levied if an individual was found to have provided financial support to a proscribed group.

New provisions to reduce the possibility of terrorists making money through organized crime and disrupt financial operations supportive of terrorism have been implemented by the Proceeds of Crime Act 2002.

8.2.3 Special issues regarding the provision of information regarding terrorist activities Under the Terrorism Act 2000 (TACT), individuals who reasonably suspect that someone will engage or has engaged in a terrorist offense, but do not report this suspicion to law enforcement officials, can be fined or imprisoned.

8.2.4 Other aspects In the wake of the September 11 attacks in the US, the UK passed the Anti-terrorism Crime and Security Act (ATCSA) which allowed for the detention of foreign nationals who were suspected of but had not been convicted of involvement in international terrorism but could not be deported because they faced the prospect of torture or

---

September 11 attacks, new legislation was passed, the Anti-terrorism Crime and Security Act 2001 (ATCSA). Two later legislative pieces were introduced, the Prevention of Terrorism Act 2005 (this act brings about a new system of control orders to fight terrorism that replaces the controversial section 4 of ATCSA 2001) and the Terrorism Act 2006 following the July 2005 bombings (this act develops a range of measures to enhance enforcers with further power to investigate and arrest suspects of terrorism, including dissemination of publications or encouragement of terrorism, as well as training of terrorists).

inhumane treatment in their country of origin.[66] After the recent terrorist attacks in London (July 7 and 21, 2005), further legal reforms that provide the police and the courts with adequate and more effective instruments (which could include access to email and mobile phonecalls without previous judicial control) and tighter immigration laws (including deportation of radical clerics) have been passed (the Terrorism Act 2006).[67]

8.3 Spain

Given the activities of the Basque terrorist group ETA since the early 1970s, Spain has passed several anti-terrorism laws. Nowadays Articles 571 to 580 of the Penal Code regulate the crime of terrorism, and several other pieces of legislation provide further restrictions on individuals or organizations suspected of terrorism.[68] The conflict between anti-terrorism

---

[66] The Anti-terrorism, Crime and Security Act 2001 (ATCSA) was repealed by the House of Lords by December 2004 under the notion that it was discriminatory and not proportionate to the threat the UK faced from terrorism. Deportation in such instances is prohibited under Article 3 of the European Commission on Human Rights (ECHR). This provision was found to be incompatible with the ECHR's Articles 5 and 14 due to the differential treatment of foreign nationals relative to citizens of the UK. A compromise was reached in which the same prohibitions would be applied to UK citizens and foreign nationals alike, whereby individuals who are suspected of engaging in terrorist activities can be subjected to curfews, limitations on their use of telecommunications equipment, limitations on what individuals they may associate with, etc. The government introduced a new Prevention of Terrorism Bill to overcome the problem; the aim of the Prevention of Terrorism Bill was to put in place measures which are fully compatible with the European Convention of Human Rights and which are applicable to both British and foreign nationals regardless of the type of terrorism involved (whether it is domestic or international). The bill become the Prevention of Terrorism Act 2005 by March 2005. However, the Act was challenged by the courts in April 2006 (it was declared incompatible with the ECHR's Article 6 on the right to fair proceedings), a decision partially reversed by the Court of Appeals in August 2006.

[67] The Terrorism Act 2006 was as controversial as the previous legislation. It was introduced in October 2005 and raised serious criticism. In particular, the extension of the period of detention without charge to 90 days was defeated and amended to 28 days.

[68] Law 3/1988, dated May 25, develops the legal definition of crimes by terrorist organizations (on top of crimes by individual members), including the crime of membership of a terrorist organization; Law 4/1988, dated May 25, introduces a more flexible system of procedural guarantees for those accused of terrorism; Law 7/2000, dated December 22, regulating hate speech; Law 6/2002, dated June 27, effectively illegalizes the political wing of terrorist groups (hence, also cutting access to public funding for legally constituted political parties); Law 7/2003, dated June 30, allows penalty enhancement for terrorist crimes and reduces the possibility of parole. The specific enforcement of this legislation has become a hot

laws and procedural guarantees for the accused has been assessed several times by the Constitutional Court, recognizing that a balance between them is hard to achieve.[69]

8.3.1 Penalty enhancement for terrorist crimes or with terrorist motivation The current legislation imposes longer imprisonment sentences for terrorist acts than for similar offenses without terrorist motivation; it reduces the possibility of parole or any other mechanism that could undermine the effective duration of the sentence; it allows under exceptional circumstances the maximal sentence to be 40 rather than the usual 30 years in prison.

Anti-terrorism law enforcement benefits from a special regime that allows custody for a longer period of time and grants the police extra powers of investigation and monitoring. Hence, we can conjecture that law enforcement is more effective for terrorist crimes than otherwise.

8.3.2 Special legislation/provisions to tackle groups or organized individuals in terrorist activities An organization that is hierarchical, apparently stable, uses weapons, and practices violent acts against individuals or property, including murder or kidnapping, can be prosecuted as a terrorist group. Membership of a terrorist organization is punished as such (that is, independently of the crimes committed), including not only the direct members of the organization and those hired or contracted by the organization to pursue their interests, but also pure collaborators that favor in some respect the activities of the organization. Consequently, individuals who inform the organization about potential victims, who help in the escape of members of the organization, or who offer any kind of help to the organization are liable under penal law. Sentences can range from five to ten years in prison plus fines.

A particular point concerns those who individually or in a group (political parties) promote and justify terrorist crimes and terrorists, or engage in hate speech against the victims of terrorism. Not only are they also liable,

political issue during the last couple of years when the socialist government opened unsuccessful negotiations with the Basque terrorists without the support of the conservative opposition.

69 For example, the following decisions of the Constitutional Court: STC of December 16, 1987 (on delimiting the elements that should be used to characterize a terrorist organization); STC of March 12, 1993 (on the comprehensive meaning of membership of terrorist organizations); STC of March 3, 1994 (on the possibility of a longer period of custody); STC of July 20, 1999 (on the punishment for collaboration with terrorist organizations).

but political parties that openly support terrorism or include convicted or suspected terrorists in their leadership are forbidden.

8.3.3 Special issues regarding the provision of information regarding terrorist activities Self-reporting terrorists will benefit from special treatment under three conditions: (i) the individual has voluntarily abandoned any kind of involvement with terrorism, (ii) the individual self-reports to the authorities and confesses his or her own crimes, (iii) the individual actively cooperates with the authorities to produce evidence to convict other terrorists or stop terrorist activity. The reduction in the sentence is, however, not very significant and it is up to the judge, not the prosecutor, to take such a decision.

8.3.4 Other aspects The legislation recognizes convictions for terrorism or membership of terrorist organizations abroad as automatically equivalent to convictions in Spain for the purposes of penalty enhancement for recidivism.

8.4 Israel

Israel has had anti-terrorist legislation in place since 1948. In recent years, the country has become involved in international anti-terror efforts, enacting a law in 1994 which allows officials in the country to confiscate property in Israel belonging to any individual or organization declared by another country to be involved in terrorist activities, even if those activities were not directed toward Israel.

8.4.1 Penalty enhancement for terrorist crimes or with terrorist motivation In the 1948 law, any individual involved in the planning, implementation or direct support of a terrorist organization or activity can be imprisoned for up to 20 years. Further, under the 1994 law, the payment of any compensation or support to the families of suicide bombers or others involved in terrorist activities is prohibited.

8.4.2 Special legislation/provisions to tackle groups or organized individuals in terrorist activities Indirect support for terrorist organizations, such as the provision of funds, allowing the organization to use a residence for meetings, publication or broadcast of words of praise, sympathy or encouragement of terrorist activities, and the solicitation of funding for terrorist activities, is punishable by prison and fines.

8.4.3 Other aspects In a holdover from British mandatory law, the Israeli government retains the right to demolish any real property owned by members of the nuclear family of a terrorist, presumably increasing the incentive for relatives to monitor the activities of potential terrorists. Interestingly, in the original British law, this collateral punishment could be inflicted at the village level, but current Israeli practise limits the punishment to close family members only.[70]

9. Conclusion

Even though economic analysis of terrorist activities and groups is relatively underdeveloped, we can gain some insights into these activities by looking at economic models of crime. Clearly, some modification of these models is necessary in the terrorism context, but it would seem that the existing models can serve as a guide to understanding terrorist activities, as well as being beneficial to the development of anti-terror measures. In this chapter, we have reviewed the existing law and economics literature on crime, noting where various models might apply (with some modifications) to the terror context. We then looked at a sample of anti-terror laws, highlighting the measures that are implied by the economic models.

---

70 U. Amit-Kohn, J. Renato, C.B. Glick and J. Biton (1993), *Israel, the 'Intifada' and the Rule of Law* (Israel Ministry of Defense Publications, Tel-Aviv), p. 12.

16 Behavioral criminal law and economics

Richard H. McAdams and Thomas S. Ulen***

Introduction

The standard theoretical law-and-economics account of criminal behavior begins from the observation that potential criminals are rational decisionmakers (Becker, 1969). The theory assumes that potential criminals compare the expected costs and benefits of criminal activity, where the expected benefits include the anticipated monetary and nonmonetary returns to the crime, discounted by their probabilities of realization, and the expected costs of the crime, which include formal and informal sanctions (the latter including loss of lawful employment opportunities, social stigma, and guilt), discounted by the probabilities of detection. If the expected benefits exceed the expected costs, then the rational potential criminal commits the crime; otherwise, he or she does not. Moreover, the rational potential criminal compares the expected costs and benefits of criminal activity with those of legitimate activity and rationally allocates her time and other resources between those alternatives so that the marginal net benefit is equated.[1]

Similarly, the standard law-and-economics account of other participants in the criminal justice system – police, judges, prosecutors, defense attorneys, juries, and legislators – also presumes rational decisionmaking. So, the police – both individually and collectively – may choose to allocate their limited resources according to rational calculations about costs and benefits, choosing, for example, between the investigation of detected

* Bernard D. Meltzer Professor of Law, University of Chicago Law School, 1111 E. 60th Street, Chicago, IL, 60637; USA, tel. (773) 834–2520; rmcadams@uchicago.edu.

** Swanlund Chair, University of Illinois at Urbana-Champaign, and Professor of Law and Director, Illinois Program in Law and Economics, University of Illinois College of Law, 504 E. Pennsylvania Ave., Champaign, IL, 61820; USA, tel. (217) 333–4953; tulen@law.illinois.edu.

[1] Suppose that there is a negative marginal net benefit from legitimate activity from criminal activity and a positive marginal net benefit from criminal activity. The rational potential criminal should shift time and other resources from legitimate to criminal activity until the further reassignment of those resources yields no net gain in total net benefits – that is, until the marginal net benefit of resources used in criminal and legitimate activities is identical.

crimes and prevention of crimes so that the marginal productivity of additional resources devoted to either activity is equal.

Not only has this account received theoretical elaboration and extension, it has also been tested empirically. For a review, see Levitt and Miles (2007). The early empirical literature – that of the 1970s – was often done in alternating turns by those favorably disposed toward the rational-choice-theory account and those critical of that theory. In the late 1970s a panel of the National Academy of Sciences surveyed the empirical literature and reached the conclusion that 'deterrence works' – that is, that the predictions of the rational choice theory explain observed patterns of criminal behavior.

These theoretical accounts of decisionmaking by criminals and other participants in the criminal justice system have had a profound influence on legal scholarship over the past 40 years and an equally important impact on criminal justice policy. For example, the United States Sentencing Commission, created by Congress in the early 1980s, was charged with rationalizing federal criminal sentencing by, among other things, reducing the variability of sentences on the ground that indeterminate sentencing was not as deterring as determinate sentencing. And in the debates to explain the remarkable decline in crime that began in the early 1990s, some have argued that that decline is partly attributable to the deterrence-based policies of the 1980s and 1990s, such as the remarkable increase in the frequency with which criminals have been incarcerated. (Levitt, 2004b).[2]

But at the same time as these rational choice theory-based arguments have become so important, a significant and broad criticism of rational choice theory and of its application to issues of criminal law has been made. That criticism is called 'behavioralism'. Importantly, behavioralism is not a *theoretical* criticism of rational choice theory. Rather, it is a criticism based almost entirely on experimental and other empirical studies that find the predictions of rational choice theory to be inaccurate. To illustrate with one example, rational choice theory predicts that in making decisions under uncertainty, decisionmakers accurately ascertain the probabilities of the various alternatives open to them, apply those probabilities to payoffs of the alternatives, and choose that alternative that maximizes their expected subjective utility. But psychologists and economists have discovered that most decisionmakers facing an uncertain set of options use far simpler heuristics to make a decision, such as choosing that alternative that is most 'salient'.

---

[2] The number of persons incarcerated in jails and prisons in the United States increased from about 500,000 in 1980 to over 2 million by 2002.

The findings of behavioralism have become so thorough and well established as to make it difficult to begin any analysis of decisionmaking from the position of rational choice theory. This, of course, has profound implications for many areas of law and public policy, including criminal law. Many of the policy changes championed or implemented after the impact of Becker's revolutionary insight stand or should stand on less firm foundations than had been previously thought to be the case. The central purpose of this chapter is to indicate how some of the central findings of the behavioral literature erode the rational-choice-theoretic foundations of criminal law and policy and to show how a recognition of the behavioral literature might lead to a rethinking of the legal and policy conclusions of the past 30 or so years.

In deciding what topics to consider, we are motivated by two desires – (1) to give an accurate, positive account of human decisionmaking with respect to matters of criminal law and policy, and (2) to analyze legal and policy instruments in accordance with their ability to minimize the social costs of crime as committed by the real decisionmakers we identify in point (1).

This chapter proceeds as follows. In Section 1 we briefly summarize behavioral economics, citing some applications to show how those behavioral considerations might affect some standard law-and-economic analyses. Then, in Section 2 we focus on the behavioral analysis of the decision to commit a crime by an individual in order to show how behavioral considerations amend the standard, rational-choice-theory account. In Section 3 we extend this behavioral analysis to the decisionmaking of other actors in the criminal justice system (potential victims, prosecutors, judges, and others). Then we conclude and summarize.

1. Background on behavioral economics

Behavioral economics has its origins in experiments and empirical research addressed at testing the predictions of rational choice theory. The result of those experiments and empirical research is a body of findings that is highly critical of rational choice theory. In this section, we categorize and summarize those findings.[3]

1.1 Deviations from perfect rationality

The gist of the behavioral literature can be conveyed quickly. Rational choice theory holds, generally, that human decisionmakers are close

---

[3] We recognize that our background on behavioral economics will be selective and, therefore, incomplete. For a general survey of these and other topics in the behavioral literature, see Korobkin and Ulen (2000).

calculators of the costs and benefits of the options open to them; that they do not make mistakes in choosing courses of action or goods and services that might maximize their well-being or profit unless they have been systematically misled. The findings of the behavioral literature are that human beings make *systematic* mistakes in their decisionmaking. These are not randomly distributed mistakes around a predictable and relatively constant mean, but clear and persistent deviations away from the predictions of rational choice theory. To foreshadow some examples that we will discuss, human beings seem to attach far more value to the way things are (to the status quo) than we would have expected to have been the case; they are far more optimistic about themselves, their talents, and their prospects for the future than experience or the facts warrant; they rely on readily available evidence rather than investigation; they put more credence in evidence that confirms their prior beliefs than in an alternative belief; and they pay closer attention to fixed costs in making current decisions than rational calculation suggests than they should.

Let us consider some examples – overoptimism and the availability heuristic.

There is ample evidence that individuals are overoptimistic when it comes to assessing their own abilities, their prospects, or other matters associated with themselves (see Weinstein, 1980; Plous, 1993). For instance, researchers have asked those getting a marriage license to estimate the likelihood that their marriage will end in divorce, given that nearly 50 percent of all US marriages end in divorce. Not surprisingly, the mean estimate is zero (Baker and Emery, 1993).

Another example of a systematic deviation from the assumptions of rational choice theory is the 'availability heuristic'. A 'heuristic' is a decision rule; the 'availability heuristic' describes the situation in which an actor overestimates the relevance of salient or memorable incidents at the expense of base rates. Tversky and Kahneman (1982, p. 164) explain: 'A person is said to employ the availability heuristic whenever he estimates frequency or probability by the ease with which instances or associations could be brought to mind'. If memorable events are memorable precisely because they are common or representative, then this mental shortcut can often lead to estimates that approximate statistical probabilities. But memorable events can also be memorable for reasons having nothing to do with their general prevalence – for example, because they are vivid, well-publicized, or more prevalent among a particular actor's friends and acquaintances. Actors often estimate these available events as being much more common than they actually are. For example, most people believe that words beginning with the letter 'k' are more prevalent than words in which 'k' is the third letter, although the latter set of words is actually twice as large as the former (Tversky and Kahneman, 1982, pp. 166–8). Presumably, this is because it is easier to bring to mind words that begin with the letter 'k' than those that have 'k' as their third letter (such as 'ark' and 'ankle'). Similarly, most people believe that homicides and car accidents kill more Americans than diabetes and stomach cancer – presumably because of the greater media coverage provided to the former – although the two diseases kill far more people than do auto accidents.

The point, generally, is that criminals may not use objectively verifiable evidence of frequency and severity, as rational choice theory implicitly assumes that they do (for example, Wilson and Abrahamse, 1992). We explore the specific implications below.

1.2 Deviations from expected utility theory

Rational choice theory has an extension for explaining and predicting decisionmaking under uncertainty: subjective expected utility (SEU) theory. According to that theory, decisionmakers make choices among uncertain courses of action so as to maximize their expected utility. This involves their estimating the probabilities of the various possible outcomes of a course of action, such as success and failure, multiplying each probability times the utility of the outcome, and summing all the possibilities:

$$E(U) = p_1 U(O_1) + p_2 U(O_2) + \cdots + p_n U(O_n),$$

where the p's sum to 1.

Decisionmakers facing an uncertain actual outcome are thought to have three possible attitudes toward risk: (1) risk aversion, (2) risk neutrality, or (3) risk preferring or seeking. Risk aversion means that the decisionmaker would be willing to pay to avoid assuming a risk; a person with that taste or preference would prefer a certain to an uncertain prospect of equal expected value. Risk neutrality means that the decisionmaker is indifferent to risk: he seeks to maximize expected value. Risk preferring means that the decisionmaker would pay to assume a risk; she prefers an uncertain to a certain prospect of equal expected value.[4]

Compound tastes are possible: a person may be risk averse at low levels of income or for low-stakes gambles and risk seeking at high levels of income or for high-stakes gambles. But it is more conventional in SEU

---

4 There is also an important connection between a decisionmaker's attitudes toward risk and her marginal utility of income. A risk-averse individual has declining marginal utility of income; a risk-neutral individual has a constant marginal utility of income; and a risk-seeking individual has an increasing marginal utility of income.

theory to assume that a decisionmaker's risk attitude is consistent across different levels of income and size of gambles.

There is, however, ample psychological evidence to suggest that in making decisions under uncertainty, people behave in a manner that is predictable but systematically different from that suggested by SEU theory. Daniel Kahneman and Amos Tversky (1979) proposed an alternative to SEU called 'prospect theory' that was consistent with the behavioral evidence. For our purposes, there are two aspects of this theory that are notable. The first is the notion of 'framing': how a decisionmaker deals with an uncertain prospect depends not only on the absolute value of the possible outcomes but also on how it is perceived to deviate from a baseline or reference point. Subsequent research has shown that the 'frame' within which a decisionmaker operates is fluid and easily manipulable[5] (see Tversky and Kahneman, 1986; Korobkin and Guthrie, 1994).

The second is that most people's attitude toward uncertain gains is different from their attitude toward uncertain losses. In brief, when a decision option is perceived to be a 'gain' from a baseline or reference point, people are risk averse, but when a decision option is perceived to be a 'loss' from a baseline or reference point, people are risk seeking. Below, we explain the significance of these findings for criminal law.

1.3 Hedonic adaptation and patterns of remembering

Within the last two decades a new literature has appeared on the psychology and economics of happiness (see, for example, Layard, 2005; Gilbert, 2006; Frey, 2008). That literature has highlighted some aspects of decisionmaking that bear upon criminal law and punishment. Particularly, we

---

[5] Kahneman and Tversky illustrated the effects of framing through the 'Asian disease' problem. Participants in a study were told that 'the US is preparing for the outbreak of an unusual Asian disease, which is expected to kill 600 people'. Two alternative programs have been proposed to deal with the outbreak. Under Program A, 200 people will die. Under Program B, 'there is a one-third possibility that 600 people will be saved, and a two-thirds possibility that no one will be saved'. Kahneman and Tversky asked participants in an experiment to choose between A and B; 72 percent preferred A.

The investigators asked a second group of participants to choose between two other programs. Under Program C, 400 people will die. Under Program D, 'there is a one-third probability that nobody will die, and a two-thirds probability that 600 people will die'. 78 percent of participants preferred Program D.

This change in choice behavior is apparently due to the manner in which the choices were presented or framed because, using the expected value calculus, the choices between A and B and between C and D are functionally the same choices, so that those who prefer A to B should prefer C to D.

are referring to literature that finds that humans adapt to changes in their circumstances relatively quickly and make predictable mistakes in recalling affective experiences.

1.3.1 Hedonic adaptation 'Hedonic adaptation' refers to a process in which decisionmakers return to a 'set point' of happiness when events push them away from that set point. The notion of a 'set point' refers to the default level of happiness that a person has, analogous to the default setting of a thermostat. Just as a thermostat controls the environmental heating and cooling so as to bring the temperature back to the default setting, so, too, do the 'set point' and hedonic adaptation theories of happiness suggest that we have a 'default setting' of happiness to which we return if circumstances push us away from that set point. For example, very happy occurrences increase our happiness levels, but only temporarily. Within a relatively short period of time (a year), that increase will dissipate so that the person returns to their good-fortune level of subjective well-being.

The classic study that established this remarkable pattern appeared in 1978. Brickman et al. (1978) interviewed those who had won lotteries, those who had suffered significant accidental harm (quadriplegia or paraplegia), and a control group and found that all three groups had returned to their pre-experience levels of subjective well-being within a relatively short time. For a review, see Bagenstos and Schlanger (2007, pp. 761–6). That is, those who had won lotteries experienced an increase in well-being, but then drifted back down to their pre-winning state of well-being. And those who suffered horrible injuries experienced a significant decline in well-being, but then rose back to their pre-accident level of well-being.

The strong implication of this literature is that the episodic circumstances of our lives play a transitory role in our long-term well-being. Our subjective well-being is deeply influenced by whatever factors determine our 'set point' of well-being.

There have been many elaborations on the Brickman-Coates-Janoff-Bulman findings since that article appeared. For example, one strand has developed the idea, implicit in the adaptation finding, that human beings do not accurately forecast the things that will make them happy or sad. We are bad at what is referred to as 'affective forecasting' (Wilson and Gilbert, 2003; Blumenthal, 2005). Our beliefs that we would be truly happy if only we could live in California rather than Ohio or that we would be miserable if we had to move from California to Ohio are simply not true (Schkade and Kahneman, 1998). In both instances, we adapt back to our set-point level of happiness.

The most recent scholarship on hedonic adaptation – or the 'hedonic treadmill'[6] – has confirmed the basic findings but has added some important nuances. For example, recent experiments suggest that, among other findings, individuals may have multiple set points, that different individuals have different set points, that some individuals alter their set points in response to some life events, and that different individuals may adapt at different rates and to different extents. Diener et al. (2006). It appears, to take but one example, that Germans do 'not get lasting boosts in happiness from marriage', and that 'widows and widowers, people who were laid off from work, and individuals who divorced all reported long-lasting, changes in life satisfaction after these life events' (Diener et al. 2006, p. 312).

1.3.2 Patterns of remembering Daniel Kahneman (2000) and others have been exploring the difference between how people experience events as they are occurring and how people remember those same events later. The central conclusion of their work is that there are systematic differences between the actual experience of events and what people remember of them later. In brief, we tend to summarize our remembered experiences by averaging the peak (or bottom) event with what happened at the end during the remembered experience – called by Kahneman the 'peak-end rule' – and by ignoring the duration of the experience. We do not remember experiences by recalling the moment-by-moment events and computing a running total of the good and bad aspects of those recollections.

To illustrate, suppose that you have recently gone on a vacation. While you were on vacation, suppose that the weather was delightful; your companions were relaxed and enjoyable; the food was good but not great; and you slept very well. However, on the return journey there was a violent thunderstorm, making the plane flights scarifying, and the airline lost your luggage. Kahneman and his co-investigators suggest that in recalling the vacation, we would average the best day and the unhappy occurrences at the end and ignore the facts that the duration of the apparently good days far outweighed that of the apparently bad homeward experience.

Kahneman first noticed these patterns in asking those who had just been through a colonoscopy to recall their experiences.[7] He also did a series of

---

[6] The phrase 'hedonic treadmill' refers to an implication of the adaptation finding: in order to rise to higher levels of well-being (or avoid returning to their set point), people must continually engage in ever-bigger or more stimulating consumption or experiences.

[7] One of us can testify that these results would no longer be found because doctors routinely prescribe an amnesiac as a part of the procedure.

brilliant experiments in which the subjects were asked to go through three tests. In the first test, the subject was to hold his hand in a bucket of very cold water until the experimenter instructed him to pull his hand out of the water. During the time that the hand was submerged, the subject was to use a dial calibrated from 1 (the lowest) to 10 (the highest) to indicate how much pain he was experiencing. Unknown to the subject, the experiment would allow the immersion to continue for 60 seconds. Almost all subjects found that by the end of the experiment the pain was intense. After the conclusion of the experiment, the subjects were allowed to dry and warm their hands.

The second experiment also involved the same subjects' submerging their hands in a bucket of very cold water and recording the pain they were feeling. There were, however, two important differences in the second experiment. First, the submersion was going to last 90 seconds, 30 seconds longer than in the first experiment, and, unknown to the subjects, after exactly 60 seconds the experimenter turned a valve that released slightly warmer water into the bucket. The temperature during the first 60 seconds was just as cold as it had been in the first experiment. But the introduction of the hotter water for the last 30 seconds raised the temperature by 2° C. The researchers found that the peak amount of pain was the same in both experiments and occurred near the end of the first 60 seconds of the experiment.

The third experiment consisted of the subjects' choosing to repeat either experiment 1 or 2. Even though the second experiment lasted longer than the first and, therefore, had a greater total amount of pain than the first experiment, almost three-quarters of the subjects chose to repeat the second experiment over the first one.

Kahneman and his co-authors hypothesized that 'duration neglect' explains that people do not recall the duration of the experience as a key factor in remembering it. Rather, they remember the peak intense moment and what was happening to them at the end of the experience. The peak intensity of the two experiments was an identical level of pain, so that on that basis there was no reason to prefer one experiment to the other. But there was a difference in what the subjects remembered about the end of the experience. The end of the first experiment was a painful time. The end of the second experiment was, however, less painful and, therefore, more enjoyable.

One might hypothesize that if, in remembering an experience, people apply the peak-end rule and ignore the duration of the experience, then one might manipulate someone's likely remembrance of an event by keeping it short and making the end pleasant (if one would like the subject to have a happy remembrance) or unpleasant (if one would like the subject to have a distasteful remembrance).

1.3.3 Criticisms of the behavioral literature Not all serious scholars have accepted the findings of the behavioral literature. Several believe that the legal and economic professions have been too quick to abandon the rational choice theory of human decisionmaking or that the behaviorists have oversold their findings.

For example, John List (2003) has argued, on the basis of experimental results involving sports memorabilia and collector pins, that as participants gain experience in market transactions, some of the findings of the behavioral literature disappear (see also List, 2006; Levitt and List, 2006). Specifically, List found that the endowment effect, which holds that people place an irrationally higher value on the status quo than on a seemingly more attractive alternative, vanishes with increasing market experience.[8] In a theoretical argument that reaches a similar conclusion, Alan Schwartz (2008) suggests that where there are two types of consumers – naïve and sophisticated – and where firms compete for consumer business by offering either exploitative or naïve contracts, competition can cause the number of exploitative contracts to decline or even vanish.

We think, however, that these criticisms have far less force in the context we explore here – criminal law. As Jolls et al. (1998, pp. 1486–7) first observed, the market for crime gives far less feedback to participants than legal markets. '[T]he decision to enter a life of crime is not one that is made repeatedly with many opportunities to learn. Once a teenager has dropped out of high school to become a drug dealer, it is difficult to switch to dentistry.' Nor is 'arbitrage . . . possible in this situation. If someone is unfortunate enough to commit a crime with a negative expected value, then there is no way for anyone else to profit directly from his behavior.' Thus, unlike the optimistic stock purchaser who sees very quickly his fortune decline, the optimistic criminal who underestimates the probability of his detection may offend for years before ever being detected and receiving contrary information. Even then, being caught once after several years may not be incompatible with his optimistic estimate of the detection probability.[9]

---

[8] List reports that 'across all consumer types, marketlike experience and the magnitude of the endowment effect are inversely related. In addition, within the group of subjects who have intense trading experience (dealers and experienced nondealers), I find that the endowment effect becomes negligible.' Id., at 42–3. Kathy Zeiler and Charles Plott (2006) have also argued that both the endowment effect and the findings of prospect theory are misinterpretations of experimental evidence.

[9] Amitai Aviram (2007) proposes that politicians and other opinion leaders can engage in a type of 'bias arbitrage', gaining by exploiting the biased beliefs

Mitchell (2002a, 2002b) has argued that behaviorists have not provided a comprehensive and empirically sound account of human decisionmaking that warrants abandoning rational choice theory. Moreover, he argues, there is substantial empirical evidence that, at least with respect to some explicit economic decisions, people behave as rational choice predicts that they will. Oldfather (2007) makes the different point that, even if one takes behavioral biases to be true of the average member of the population, we know that criminals differ from the average in many ways; so, absent experiments focused on criminals, we cannot assume the applicability of the behavioral literature to this unusual subpopulation. Both points are well taken. We are still at an early stage of our knowledge of human decisionmaking – one might say that the behavioral findings are strong and suggestive but not complete. Noting this caveat, however, we believe there is enough consensus about some of the findings of the behavioral literature to warrant our taking the rational choice theory-based predictions and explanations of criminal behavior less seriously and in exploring alternative explanations and predictions. That is the task to which we now turn.

2. Behavioral economics analysis of potential criminal offenders

Deterrence is a central concept in the economic theory of criminal law. This section addresses two ways in which behavioral insights are important to this concept. First, we consider the challenge behavioral findings pose to deterrence theory, the claim that marginal changes in the severity of criminal punishment will not actually influence the decision to offend. Second, assuming that the challenge fails – that deterrence theory is essentially correct – we consider how behavioral research nonetheless recommends modifying the economic model of the decision to offend, which in turns affects the optimal use of criminal sanctions.

2.1 The behavioral challenge to deterrence theory

The empirical evidence supporting deterrence theory consists mostly of macro-level regressions between the inputs of certainty (arrest and conviction data) and severity (criminal sentencing data) and the output of crime rates. For reviews, see Levitt (2004a), Nagin (1998), and Paternoster (1987).[10] By contrast, some of the behavioral empiricism focuses on more

---

of the public. But the arbitrage here works through the political system, not an explicit price mechanism, so it does not really contradict the point in the text that criminal markets work less efficiently than others.

[10] Some recent work, for example, Kessler and Levitt (1999), carefully distinguishes this deterrent effect from the incapacitation effect.

specific causal steps necessary for deterrence. Robinson and Darley (2004) offer perhaps the most aggressive critique of deterrence in recent years. See also Darley (2005) and Robinson (2006). They focus on three links in the theory: (1) that potential offenders know that the law punishes certain acts; (2) that they (at least implicitly) calculate the costs and benefits of those acts; and (3) that criminal sanctions make the costs outweigh the benefits. We identify the behavioral research relevant to each claim.

The first step in deterrence theory is a link between criminal sanctions and the perception of criminal sanctions. By hypothesis, the objective fact that the state punishes criminals causes people to update their beliefs about the probability of being punished for a future crime. Yet Robinson and Darley (2004) claim that '[p]otential offenders commonly do not know the legal rules, either directly or indirectly, even those rules that have been explicitly formulated to produce a behavioral effect'. For example, Robert MacCoun et al. (2008) report on survey data regarding sanctions for possession of small amounts (one ounce) of marijuana. Almost one-third of respondents say they do not know whether the maximum penalty is a fine or a jail term. Among those who provide a specific answer, respondents in states where the maximum penalty is a jail term were more likely to report that jail is the maximum than those who live in states where the offense is fine-only, but the magnitude of the difference is quite small – 30.7 percent of fine-only state residents (incorrectly) identify jail as the maximum while 33.1 percent of those in states authorizing jail identify (correctly) that maximum. Six percent report that there is a minimum jail sentence, though this is not true in any state. See also Roberts (1992).

Similarly, a major study by Kleck et al. (2005) examines the relationship between the perception of punishment practices and actual punishment for four crimes – homicide, aggravated assault, robbery, and burglary. The authors surveyed 1,500 respondents in 54 urban counties, inquiring about five punishment variables for each crime – the probability of arrest, conviction, and incarceration, the maximum authorized punishment, and the swiftness of punishment. They then compared these estimates to actual punishment practices. Of the 20 possible correlations, there was no statistically significant relationship in 17 cases, with or without controls, and even excluding the 15–20 percent of respondents who refused to give any estimate because they said they did not know. Of the remaining three cases, where the correlation was significant, two were positive but one was negative, (Kleck et al., 2005, p. 647). Among respondents who had been arrested for a non-traffic offense, the correlations were even weaker (only one positive and significant correlation out of the 20) (Kleck et al., 2005, p. 647).

Deterrence theory also assumes that potential offenders rationally (though not necessarily consciously) consider and weigh the costs and benefits of committing a crime. Robinson and Darley's (2004) second criticism is their claim that individuals who commit crime do not rationally assess the costs and benefits of their criminal acts. Here, they advert to a behavioral bias discussed below in section 2.2.3 – that individuals are impulsive in the sense of having inconsistent discount rates that favor immediate consumption – along with a variety of other psychological points: that criminals do not appear to calculate, are under the influence of drugs at the time of their offense, and are driven principally by emotion or peer approval that frames their actions and not by rational calculation. Darley (2005, pp. 195–6) reports:

> One well-supported theory of criminal behavior holds that many crimes are committed by persons with somewhat disordered personalities who are characterized by a predilection for impulsive behavior. . . . These are the sorts of crimes that become semi-humorous reports in newspapers. Like the bank robber who passes his demand for money on material that reveals his identity, prison inmates report that they were not thinking of the possibility of prison when they committed their offense.

Anderson (2002, p. 308) reports on a survey finding that, '[a]t the time of their offenses, 76% of the criminals in the sample and 89% of the most violent offenders were incognizant of either the possibility of apprehension or the likely punishments associated with the crime'.

Robinson and Darley's third criticism is that the prospect of punishment is not likely to outweigh the perceived advantages of offending. Here, they rely on a number of behavioral observations described above: that people may perceive a low probability of punishment, like other low-probability events, as zero; that hedonic adaptation and duration neglect weakens or reverses the effect of severity of punishment; and that given hyperbolic discounting,[11] the delay in punishment severely weakens the effect of severity.

The second and third criticisms are significantly weakened by a key feature of deterrence theory: the success of deterrence is not measured by those who commit crimes but by those who do not. Perhaps the reason those who commit crimes appear to be irrational is that the expected sanctions are sufficient to deter the rational, which explains why most

---

[11] According to experimental findings, people experience 'hyperbolic discounting' in that they prefer a smaller and sooner payoff to larger and later payoffs if the smaller payoffs are nearly immediate. But when the smaller and sooner payoff and the larger and later payoff are both fairly distant from the decision point, the larger and later payoff is preferable.

individuals are deterred from committing serious offenses. Thus, punishing individuals who commit crimes under various defects of rationality may work by enhancing the state's credibility in threatening to punish more rational individuals if they commit an offense. By contrast, those studies that focus on prisoners are by definition focusing on individuals for whom deterrence failed, who may not be representative of those for whom it works.

Robinson and Darley might respond that some of their points apply not just to some special subset of the population – such as the imprisoned or the drug addicted – but to everyone. Consider the effect of hedonic adaptation and duration neglect. As explained above, happiness studies suggest that, after a major event, most people adjust back to their base rate of happiness more quickly than they expected; and when remembering positive or negative experiences, most people fail to account sufficiently for the duration of the experience (and unknowingly give special weight to its peak and end points).

Yet the correct inference to draw from these points is complex. Robinson and Darley are right that incarcerated individuals will adapt to prison more quickly than they anticipate and, after being released from prison, will not fully remember the duration or the pain of incarceration. Consequently, incarceration will produce less specific deterrence than a model of perfect rationality predicts. But these points need not affect general deterrence. At least for the majority of individuals who are never incarcerated, what matters for deterrence is their *anticipated* loss from prison. If individuals never have occasion to learn how quickly they will adjust to prison and how much they will forget its duration, then they remain as deterrable by the anticipation of long prison terms as someone not subject to these psychological effects. Their point has force principally with respect to recidivism: incarceration, once experienced, may not have the deterring effect that it might have for those who have never been incarcerated. Yet, even here, the happiness literature finds not only that people fail to predict their adjustment to negative situations, but that they also fail to remember their adjustment later (when one compares contemporaneous accounts to later memory of the same events). See Bronsteen et al. (2008).

In the end, however, the question is empirical and subject to further inquiry. Some economic work supports behavioral skepticism of the deterrence theory by studying the perceptions of juveniles upon reaching the age of majority. When an individual becomes an adult in the eyes of the criminal law, he is immediately subject to much higher punishments (being no longer eligible for the juvenile justice system). The advantage of studying such individuals is that it is unlikely that other variables change very much the week before and after an individual's 18th birthday. Yet Lee and

McCrary (2005) find that this discontinuous jump in penalty levels has almost no effect on the teenager's willingness to offend. Looking at weekly Florida crime data from 1989 to 2001, they find that 'the drop in arrests at [age] 18 is small in magnitude and statistically insignificant' across a range of specifications. They conclude that teenagers are either badly informed of the objective changes in punishment severity, are irrational, or subject to hyperbolic discount rates, which makes them impulsive. Other studies, however, reach partially or entirely different conclusions (see Levitt, 1998; Lochner, 1997).

2.2 Behavioral adjustments to deterrence theory

In this section, we assume that deterrence theory is basically correct and ask what adjustments behavioral findings imply for an economic model of crime. In other words, we assume that marginal changes in the expected sanction do affect the crime rate, but we ask how the 'standard' economic model of crime changes if people are not perfectly selfish or rational. The critical variables in the baseline economic model of crime are the probability of being sanctioned, which requires detection of and conviction for the crime, and the magnitude of the sanction. Other standard variables are risk aversion and the discount rate, since criminal penalties are imposed with some probability less than one and frequently at a time after the criminal receives the benefits of the crime. What happens to the standard model if we take cognitive biases into account? We consider first the cognitive biases, then prospect theory, then motivational departures from simple selfishness.

2.2.1 Deviations from perfect rationality: the effect of cognitive biases on the decision to offend

OPTIMISM OR OVERCONFIDENCE Nuno Garoupa (2003) and Christine Jolls (2004) observe that the optimism bias weakens deterrence by making potential offenders underestimate the probability of their violation's being detected (including arrest and conviction) and punished. One might add that the optimism bias would also cause criminals to overestimate the expected benefits of crime, such as the amount of money held by an intended robbery or fraud victim. In each case, instead of mistakes being randomly distributed around a mean, optimism skews the beliefs in one direction. Thinking that the costs are lower and the benefits are higher than they actually are, the overly optimistic potential criminal commits more offenses than the rational criminal. As a result, optimal deterrence requires higher sanctions or higher probabilities, unless there is some way to educate or 'debias' the potential criminals.

Garoupa (2003), however, also notes a potentially offsetting effect. If the overly optimistic offender underestimates the probability of detection, he will reduce his investment in taking care to prevent detection, as by narrowing the timing or location of his crimes to avoid witnesses or cameras. Taking fewer precautions would bolster the true probability of detection, which partially offsets the dilution of deterrence that excess optimism causes and enhances the incapacitation effect, as it will be easier to apprehend an optimistic than a rational offender. The stronger incapacitation effect could conceivably entirely offset or even reverse the effect of weakened deterrence, allowing for lower penalties. The issue is empirical, but the analysis illustrates the importance of considering *all* the ways that some bias could affect the decision to offend. Indeed, we note below that the optimism bias could cause potential victims to underestimate their chances of being victimized and therefore to take too few precautions against crime.

THE AVAILABILITY HEURISTIC Jolls (2004) also observes that the availability heuristic has two effects on the decision to offend. First, the perceived probability of detection will depend not only on how frequently offenses are detected but also on how salient or vivid the method of detection is. For example, if traffic cops issue bright orange tickets for illegal parking, these may generate more deterrence than beige tickets, holding constant the objective probability of detection, merely because the vividness of the orange tickets makes them easier to recall (see also Jolls et al., 1998, p. 1538).

Second, the actual frequency of detection may have non-linear effects on the perceived probability of detection. Some evidence suggests that people underestimate the probability of infrequent events, while other evidence suggests that people overestimate the probability of infrequent events. Potentially, the availability bias changes the basic economic prescription because the evidence of a given context may suggest that people will underestimate the probability of detection if it is below some critical level, but correctly estimate it (or overestimate it) at some higher level, which means there may be efficiencies to raising the probability of detection.

In general, if criminals are biased by availability when calculating (no doubt in an informal sort of way) the expected costs of crime, the rational choice theory-based analysis of deterrence could change radically, depending on what types of events are more salient to potential criminals. In order to determine which deterrence mechanism will be most efficient, policymakers need to understand whether criminals are likely to over- or underestimate the frequency and the severity of punishment that is actually meted out. If punishments are so severe that some sentences become shocking and publicized, increasing severity could be the more efficient deterrence strategy. Otherwise, increasing the frequency of punishment is likely to be more efficient, under the assumption that if a criminal knows or knows of someone who has been imprisoned for a particular crime, this information is likely to be available and cause him to overestimate the likelihood that he will be arrested and convicted if he commits the same crime.

PESSIMISM AND PROJECTION General biases may in turn lead to more specific biases. Cooter et al. (2006) discuss two biases they term 'pessimism' and 'projection', in each case a distortion arising from a more fundamental process. By pessimism, also known as the 'uniqueness bias', they refer to the fact that individuals 'tend to overestimate the violation of social norms by other people'. Pessimism might be the result of the availability bias, given that the news media give more attention to, and make more salient, stories of wrongdoing. Or pessimism might occur because of the fundamental attribution error (see Jones and Harris, 1967; Ross, 1977): if people over-attribute observed bad behavior to the character of the actors (and under-attribute the cause to external circumstances), then they will expect more unobserved bad behavior than actually occurs. In other words, they will tend to overlook how much bad behavior is caused by people occasionally 'lapsing'.

Projection bias – also known by the related term 'false-consensus bias' (see Ross et al., 1977) – refers to the tendency of individuals to 'overestimate how many other people act [in] the same manner as he does'. Projection may occur because of the availability bias; if people tend to associate with like-minded individuals, they will find it easier to recall instances of behavior or statements like their own. In each case, there are possible emotive causes that are not linked to the cognitive biases we are discussing.

In any event, pessimism and projection have effects on the perceived probability of detection. Although they also consider the opposite case, Cooter et al. (2006) reasonably assume that the effect of believing there are more violations is to lower the perceived probability of detection. The pessimism bias causes all individuals to believe there are more violations than there actually are, which by assumption increases violations. The projection bias causes only *wrongdoers* to believe there are more violations, which increases their existing tendency to violate norms (either making them violate more frequently or merely pushing them farther away from the margin). But the projection bias causes *rightdoers* to believe there are fewer violations, which increases their existing tendency to obey norms (pushing them farther from the margin). Cooter, Feldman, and Feldman then consider the combined effects. For rightdoers, pessimism and projection push in opposite directions and may cancel each other out or at least offset each other. For wrongdoers, however, both effects push in the same direction – believing there are more violations than there actually are, which lowers the perceived probability of detection and leads to more crime or at least makes current crime levels more stable and crime harder to deter. Cooter, Feldman, and Feldman's paper illustrates the importance of considering the *combined* effects of different biases on one decision, rather than the easier work of identifying the effect of one bias across multiple decisions (as most papers do).

FRAMING Some psychological evidence suggests that an individual's choice between two options can be influenced by the presence of a third, unchosen option. The consumer's choice between goods *A* and *B* may switch depending on whether the individual is also given the choice of good *C*, even though *C* is never chosen. As explained above, option *C* somehow 'frames' the other options by drawing attention to comparative advantages or disadvantages. Meares et al. (2004) have proposed that criminal sentences may have a similar effect. Where *A* is the choice of selling or using heroin and *B* is the alternative of committing no crime, the harsh punishment of *C* – selling or using crack cocaine – might make *A* look 'cheaper' and therefore better by comparison. Substitution is always a concern of the economics of crime, but the framing point suggests that apparently irrelevant alternatives can affect the selection of substitutes for the criminal offense.

THE ILLUSION OF CONTROL Some psychological evidence suggests that individuals suffer from an 'illusion of control', overestimating their ability to control risks and therefore distinguishing to a greater degree than is rational between risks that are and are not in their control (see Langer, 1975). For example, Guttel and Harel (2008) point to studies finding that an individual tends to be willing to bet more on predicting the roll of dice that the individual rolls, than the same dice rolled by others. The same illusion causes individuals to be more willing to bet on the outcome of dice they have not yet rolled than the as-yet-unrevealed outcome of dice they have already rolled. The psychological literature shows that this preference generalizes: people 'have a strong preference for guesses of future contingencies over guesses of past contingencies', or as Guttel and Harel put it, they have greater confidence in their *predictions* than their '*postdictions*'. The illusion of control is probably connected to the self-serving bias, in which individuals tend to over-estimate their abilities. Because people believe they can still influence a future outcome but not the past, they are more confident about future than past outcomes.

Guttel and Harel (2008) then explore how the distinction matters to optimal public enforcement. One example is the choice between rules and standards. Suppose the actor knows there is a rule or standard but does not know of its exact content. Guessing whether one has violated a rule often involves postdiction because the rule specifies some specific fact that already does or does not exist. For example, the rule against drunk driving specifies a blood alcohol content that one either has or has not reached. Estimating the probability of detection here involves *postdicting* this specific fact. By contrast, a standard (for example, where 'under the influence' means an influence imposing an 'unreasonable' risk) may not identify any determinative fact. In this case, estimating whether one has violated a standard may involve *predicting* how the enforcer will apply the standard (that is, what fact will turn out to be determinative). Rules therefore have a greater deterrent than standards, though the true probability of being punished is the same.

Guttel and Harel's (2008) second example is the difference in certain law enforcement strategies. Consider IRS enforcement policy. Current IRS policy is to select tax returns for an audit *after* the return is filed. Thus, individuals complete their tax forms while *predicting* whether they will be audited. But if the IRS announced that it had already selected the taxpayers it would audit *before* the returns were filed, then individuals would complete their tax forms while *postdicting* whether they would be audited. Given the bias, the policy of announcing that certain taxpayers have been selected for auditing before any returns have been submitted would generate more deterrence than the policy of selecting auditees only after the returns have been submitted, holding constant the actual probability of an audit.

Guttel and Harel's (2008) final example involves sentencing facts. Making a sentence depend on facts that exist only after the crime occurs, such as whether an attempt succeeds or what degree of bodily harm the crime causes, involves prediction. By contrast, making a sentence depend on facts that existed at the time the crime was committed, such as the value of the item stolen or the age of the victim, involves postdiction. Holding constant the actual probabilities, the individual will be less confident and therefore more deterred in the latter case than the former.

2.2.2 Deviations from expected utility theory (prospect theory) Jolls (2004) describes two consequences that prospect theory has on the standard economic model of crime. First, 'agents exaggerate the difference between a small probability of a particular event and a zero probability of that event'. This appears to work as if people overestimate infrequent events (although it is alternatively possible they misperceive the effect of zero probability events). If so, then it would appear that, contrary to the optimism bias, individuals will be more deterred by a low probability of detection than under expected utility theory.

Second, 'changes far from an individual's reference point matter relatively little'. Thus, 'the deterrent effect of increasing the magnitude of penalties will have a strongly diminishing effect'. For example, 'the difference between a fine of $8000 and $10,000 . . . will be far less than the difference between a fine of $0 and $2000'. See also Lattimore and Witte (1986).

Harel and Segal (1999) describe how prospect theory affects the optimal use of uncertainty in criminal punishment. The state would seem to gain the most deterrence by selecting the types of certainty or uncertainty that are most dispreferred by potential criminals. There are two policy instruments, the magnitude of punishment and the probability of punishment.

Regarding the magnitude of punishment, expected utility theory is consistent with potential criminals' being risk neutral, risk averse, or risk preferring. Prospect theory more definitively says that most people are risk preferring regarding losses, so potential criminals may be risk preferring regarding criminal sanctions. If so, then they would prefer that the magnitude of sanctions be uncertain, as where the punishment is allowed to vary randomly around some mean. Therefore, holding constant the expected punishment, the state generates more deterrence by making the magnitude of sanctions certain. Harel and Segal observe that this result favors the use of sentencing guidelines that render the magnitude of fines or imprisonment as predictable as possible.

Yet, Harel and Segal (1999) note, this recommendation is complicated by the idea of ambiguity, as distinct from risk. Risk involves future contingencies whose probabilities are known, whereas ambiguity (or uncertainty) involves future contingencies whose exact probabilities are unknown. Empirical evidence suggests that even those individuals who prefer risk are averse to ambiguity. What we don't know is whether their aversion to ambiguity is so great that they would prefer a determinate sentence to an ambiguous sentencing lottery, in which case the latter would be a more efficient deterrent than the former (contrary to the prior paragraph). We require additional empirical evidence to assess whether the preference for risk is of a larger or smaller magnitude than the aversion to ambiguity (see Segal and Stein, 2006).

In addition to the magnitude of punishment, the state selects a probability of punishment (which depends on the probability of detection and conviction). Presumably there is no practical way to remove risk from the system because that would require the expense of detecting all violations or detecting none of them. Because risk is inherent in any practical detection policy, the potential criminal's aversion to ambiguity provides a determinate policy recommendation: introduce ambiguity by preventing the potential criminal from knowing the precise probability of punishment. Harel and Segal (1999) note that society does in fact introduce ambiguity by constantly changing enforcement priorities in a way that obscures the exact probability of detection at any given time. One might add that the discretionary interaction between different types of law enforcers – local and national police, local and national prosecutors – also obscures the exact probabilities.

2.2.3 Deviations from perfect self-control: inconsistent discount rates and impulsiveness Jolls et al. (1998) use criminal law as their main example of 'bounded self-control', where poor impulse control leads to crime. The relatively new economic literature on 'hyperbolic discount rates' (for example, Frederick et al., 2002; Laibson, 1997; O'Donoghue and Rabin, 1999) finds dynamic inconsistency of discount rates over time, specifically, that individuals apply a different and higher discount rate when choosing whether to defer immediate consumption by a certain time than when comparing two future consumption choices by the same amount of time. Crime usually has immediate benefits for the criminal, while most costs are delayed, so the effect of impulsiveness is more crime.

Even before much of the behavioral literature existed, Robert Cooter (1991) modeled the problem of 'weakness of will' or impulsiveness by assuming that an individual's discount rate fluctuates. He begins his model with preferences for risk rather than discount rates. For each time period, an individual draws a risk preference for that period from a probability distribution of risk preferences for that individual (which models mood fluctuations). The farther from one's mean preference, the lower the probability that one draws a particular rate. Thus, there will be a set of risky decisions in which most of an individual's possible risk preferences will cause him to avoid the risk. Yet where the individual, with low probability, draws a preference unusually favorable to risk, he 'lapses' by taking the gamble. Cooter then notes that the model works identically if we substitute 'discount rates' for 'risk preferences' and imagine the individual chooses between present and future consumption. An individual may usually draw discount rates that favor future consumption, but on occasion may draw an unusually high discount rate and 'lapse' by deciding in favor of immediate consumption. In either case, when such an individual later draws a more common risk preference or discount rate, he experiences costly 'regret' at his prior decision.

Cooter (1991) then applies this model to the decision to commit a crime (or a tort). Where one's discount rate fluctuates, one may 'lapse' into committing the crime because the benefits from crime are enjoyed immediately, while the potential sanctions are delayed. The policy implication here concerns the advantage of narrowing the time between the crime and the punishment. To some degree, this simply points to the obvious advantage of having police solve crimes sooner rather than later. But Cooter (1991) observes that this point and the original model on risk preferences may also justify ex ante criminal regulation rather than ex post criminal liability. Rather than creating criminal (or tort) liability only after a harm occurs, intervening before harm occurs may narrow the temporal gap between the benefit and the cost and make it more likely that punishment would occur. Cooter does not give an example, but consider the use of criminal sanctions for mislabeling over-the-counter drugs. There might be a considerable delay after labeling before the drugs are put in circulation and could cause harm; so punishing for the mislabeling (in addition to harms caused by mislabeling) narrows the relevance of the discount rate. Also, it may be easier to detect mislabeling than to determine the causally responsible party for the resulting injuries, which narrows the importance of risk preferences. As an extension, one might use Cooter's model to justify attempt liability and punishment for other forms of criminal preparation. Punishing speeding and drunk driving allows the law to intervene more quickly and with greater certainty than punishing only negligent driving that causes death or injury. See also Utset (2007).

No discussion of hyperbolic discounting's role in crime should ignore its relevance to the problem of addiction (see Garoupa, 2003, 7–8; Bowers, 2008; Ainslie, 2000; Corrado, 2006; Bickel and Marsch, 2001). Addiction is important to crime for at least two reasons. First, the possession and distribution of certain addictive substances (for example, heroin and cocaine) are among the most significant modern crimes. Second, addicts are often unable to hold lawful jobs and therefore commit a significant amount of property crime to finance their addiction. The theory of hyperbolic discounting (perhaps along with the optimism bias) provides perhaps the only economic theory of addiction other than Becker and Murphy's (1988) theory of 'rational addiction'. The benefits of drug use are immediate; because purchase often precedes use by only a short time, one can also say that the benefits of purchase are fairly immediate to the purchaser. Yet, excepting the purchase price (which may not exist when people get the drug as a gift or on credit), the costs of addictive substances are deferred: not only the health consequences of long-term use but the risk that use will lead to addiction and all the costs that entails. Thus, if there is hyperbolic discounting, then addiction may occur despite the individual perceiving the costs as exceeding the benefits.

One particularly interesting implication of hyperbolic discounting is the alternative to criminal prohibition that Leitzel (2008) calls 'self-exclusion'. Leitzel addresses the practise primarily in the context of gambling, where some casinos and lotteries allow individuals to sign up for exclusion, which bars them from entering gambling facilities and sometimes permits the facility or the state to confiscate any winnings, should they manage to gamble anyway. This form of self-control mechanism – metaphorically, Ulysses tying himself to the mast – makes sense given hyperbolic discounting: when focused on the distant future, one prefers to exclude oneself from gambling even though one knows that when the time comes, one would prefer to gamble. Leitzel also explores whether 'self-exclusion' could be used as an alternative to criminal drug prohibition.

2.2.4 Deviations from perfect selfishness: concern for others and for fairness What difference would it make for criminal law if individuals have other-regarding preferences or preferences for fairness? The issue receiving the most attention is the effect of the public's fairness preferences on optimal punishment. There is evidence that people view proportionate punishments as fair and disproportionate punishments as unfair. If individuals incur costs from their state imposing 'unfair' punishments, then there are new costs to implementing what might otherwise be efficient punishment, such as those minimizing the probability of detection and maximizing the sanction. See Polinsky and Shavell (2000).

More generally, however, any preference for the welfare of others will increase the costs of behavior that is harmful to others, which should work to decrease crime. At the same time, a preference for fairness may underlie certain crimes of 'self-help' retaliation against others. Garoupa (2003) notes that much of the recent work suggests that people are reciprocators who gain utility by acting altruistically toward those who treat them fairly but also by acting spitefully against those who treat them unfairly. If so, then when individuals feel themselves treated unfairly by another, including not only being the victim of a crime but being offended by, say, insulting behavior, the aggrieved individual will perceive new benefits to harming their tormentor. Retaliation of this sort is frequently the cause of crime, such as vandalism and assault (for example, Black, 1983), though this is generally ignored by economists.

Moreover, preferences for fairness suggest an entirely different basis for legal compliance that psychologists emphasize: that the perceived fairness or legitimacy of a legal rule or legal regime determines how much individuals will defer to and act in conformity with the rules or regime. The literature on this claim is broad and deep, but somewhat outside the scope of this chapter (see, for example, Meares et al., 2004; Murphy, 2004; Paternoster et al., 1997; Tyler, 1990; Tyler and Fagan, 2006).

Funk (2005) offers what might be thought of as an economic account of these legitimacy claims by examining how deviations from perfect selfishness interact with bounded rationality. She posits that there are internal, moralistic costs to committing crimes, such as guilt, shame, or remorse. One incurs these costs only if one believes oneself to have acted badly. Yet self-serving biases and cognitive dissonance allow people to believe, to some degree, 'what they want to believe'. Consequently, the moralistic costs are 'state dependent' so that they are lower in the state of one's being a criminal than in the state of one's being a law abider. As a result, there are multiple equilibria and 'there may be greater and longer-lasting effects of crime-enhancing shocks than of crime-reducing shocks'.

An increase in the external conditions for crime causes more crime, which works via cognitive dissonance and self-serving biases to lower the actual moralistic costs of crime, so the norm against crime has less effect for the new criminals, making the crime increase more severe and stable. A decrease in the conditions for crime causes a decrease in crime, but does not have the reverse effect. Because there is no general moral norm favoring crime, there is no 'dissonance' created by not committing a crime and no need to engage self-serving biases. There is therefore no change in beliefs that increases the moralistic costs of crime. As a result, the best policy may be a 'big bang' shock in the direction of greater enforcement, rather than incremental increases.

3 Behavioral economic analysis of other decisionmakers in the criminal justice system

Garoupa (2003, p. 12) notes the fundamental point that, 'once criminals are not fully rational, so are not victims, enforcers, and politicians'. In this section, we consider the effect of behavioral assumptions on the economic analysis of the other actors involved in crime and public law enforcement. Specifically, we address the behavioral economics of potential crime victims, legislators, prosecutors (and defendants), judges, and juries.

3.1 The behavior of potential victims and legislators

To our knowledge, no one has yet systematically considered the effect of the behavioral findings we have discussed on potential crime victims. The optimal level of precaution by potential victims is itself a complex subject, even if victims are rational.[12] But consider what changes if potential

[12] Some precautions displace crime rather than decrease it. If the car thief sees an alarm system or steering wheel lock on a car, he may just move on to another vehicle. Such devices mostly redistribute crime, so their social costs may exceed their social benefit. By contrast, other precautions primarily decrease crime. For example, 'Lojack' allows electronic tracking of a stolen car and because the device is not visible to the thief, its presence enhances the deterrence of all car theft. Ayres and Levitt (1998).

victims are not rational. What happens to our predictions if victims are subject to the behavioral patterns discussed in this chapter?

The optimism bias may obviously cause potential victims to underestimate the odds of being victimized and therefore to take fewer precautions against crime than a purely rational actor. Yet optimism might itself have offsetting effects if optimism makes a potential victim think that a given precaution will generate more protection from crime than it actually will. By contrast, the availability heuristic might cause potential victims to overestimate the odds of being victimized – because examples of crime are often vivid and easy to recall, especially given media attention to the issue – and therefore to take more precautions than a purely rational actor. The evidence of crime 'scares' or 'panics' is more consistent with this availability effect (see Burns and Crawford, 1999; Thompson, 1998).

The literature on victim precautions refers to private actions as distinct from public law enforcement. But we can think of precautions as including political action favoring candidates who will take stronger (more costly) measures to fight crime. If so, then the availability heuristic implies that biased members of the public will fear crime more and demand stronger anti-crime measures than a purely rational member of the public. Some evidence suggests (for example, Hipp, 2007) that the public's estimates of the amount of crime in an area are largely determined by the amount of one vivid type of crime – robbery – in that area. Other citizen beliefs about crime are influenced by local television news (Gilliam and Iyengar, 2000). Many specific legislative actions seem to respond to vivid examples of crimes rather than any broader defect in existing laws. For example, Congress enacted laws against 'car-jacking' even though the behavior at issue already consisted of several crimes (theft, robbery, kidnapping, etc.) subject to serious punishment (see Aviram, 2007). If the effect of optimism dominates availability, however, then these effects are reversed: the optimistic citizen expects less crime than the rational citizen.

3.2 The behavior of police

The most obvious concern for police is the confirmation bias, the tendency of individuals to search for new evidence and to interpret ambiguous evidence only in a way that confirms their existing beliefs (all without consciously aiming to do so) (Nickerson, 1998; Friedrich, 1993; Simon et al., 2001). This bias makes police errors more likely, as police continue to focus attention on their initial suspect even when a rational observer would find new evidence or interpret old evidence to suggest the suspect's innocence (O'Brien and Ellsworth, 2006). The error not only leads to the arrest and possible conviction of an innocent individual, but the focus on the innocent makes it unlikely that the police will ever apprehend the guilty. O'Brien and Ellsworth (2006) ran two experiments finding evidence of confirmation bias in the context of mock police investigations. Stating a hypothesis early in the review of evidence in a mock police file led to more errors.

Psychologists also find the confirmation bias affects the course of police interviews or interrogations, where those who believe in guilt will fail to ask the kind of questions that might uncover evidence of innocence, as well as to interpret ambiguous evidence consistently with the guilt hypothesis. Most recently, Hill et al. (2008) have found similar results in their study of interrogation – that independent of actual guilt, interrogators with a hypothesis of guilt frame questions, the answers to which seem more corroborative of guilt (see also Kassin et al., 2003; Meissner and Kassin, 2004). Findley and Scott (2006) examine how institutional pressures and legal rules magnify the effect of confirmation bias.

A behavioral approach might also be relevant to assessing and understanding claims of racial profiling or, more generally, race discrimination in the criminal justice system. The psychological literature on 'implicit bias' claims that bias exists at a subconscious level, as measured by studies showing that many white people take longer to perform classification tasks if those tasks run counter to negative stereotypes of black people than if they conform to such stereotypes. Jolls and Sunstein (2006a) provide a review. One study finds, for example, that in a computer simulation of the decision to fire a weapon, where the goal is to shoot at armed individuals but not unarmed individuals, white participants made the decision to shoot armed black individuals faster than the decision to shoot armed white individuals and were more likely to err by shooting unarmed black individuals than unarmed white individuals (Correll et al., 2002). These results have been linked to implicit bias or stereotyping, but there are also implicit restraints – a negative attitude towards prejudice – that may operate to control the behavioral effects of the bias (Glaser and Knowles, 2008; Mitchell, 2009). Implicit bias might also explain findings that police tend to enforce the law more stringently – making more arrests or searches – when the enforcement target is a different race (black or white) than the police officer (Antonovics and Knight, 2004; Donohue and Levitt, 2001).

3.3 The behavior of prosecutors and defendants

Most criminal cases are resolved by a guilty plea negotiated between the prosecutor and the defendant (note the shift here from the language of a 'potential offender'; the defendant is either an actual offender or, if innocent, a non-offender). Consider how behavioral effects influence this negotiation.

On the civil side, many scholars have noted that optimism bias may impede settlement, as each party believes it is more likely to win at trial than is actually the case, thus shrinking or eliminating any settlement range. Rachlinski (1996) uses prospect theory and loss aversion to suggest another way that behavioral bias may impede settlement. For the plaintiff, the choice between suit and settlement is between the uncertain value of a trial and a certain outcome (the settlement amount). This being a choice involving a sure gain against a probabilistic gain, the plaintiff is likely to be risk averse and to find the sure gain (the settlement) more attractive than trial. By contrast, the defendant sees the choice between suit and settlement as one between an uncertain loss (trial) and a certain loss (the settlement amount). The experimental results suggest that people choosing between a certain and uncertain loss of roughly equal value will prefer the uncertain loss – that is, will behave in a risk-preferring manner. As a result, defendants may prefer trial to settlement.

For criminal law, we may use Rachlinski's insight to help understand plea bargaining between prosecutors and criminals. Prosecutors may be analogous to plaintiffs in Rachlinski's model and prefer a plea bargain to trial (assuming all other incentives facing the prosecutor are held constant), while defendants may be analogous to the defendants in Rachlinski's civil trials and prefer a criminal trial to a sure criminal sanction. These preferences may produce different plea bargains than would occur between rational prosecutors and rational defendants. Other things equal, loss aversion would require that prosecutors offer better deals than they would offer rational defendants in order to induce a guilty plea.

Birke (1999) notes the tension between loss aversion causing defendants to favor trial and the fact that more than 90 percent of cases are resolved by a guilty plea. Burke (2007) notes also that biases such as optimism may also affect prosecutors and make them less inclined to accept settlement rather than trial. So how do we explain high plea-bargaining rates? Birke (1999) notes but rejects the most obvious account – that prosecutors offer sufficiently good deals that even loss-averse defendants are better off accepting the deal. He claims instead that defendants are making mistakes and would gain utility from rejecting most of the agreements they accept. Bibas (2004) also suggests that various biases prevent criminal defendants from making choices that maximize their utility.

Covey (2007) agrees that loss aversion, optimism bias, and other limitations on rationality all work against defendants' accepting plea bargains. Unlike Birke and Bibas, however, Covey believes criminal defendants do generally advance their interests by accepting pleas, given the features of the criminal justice system designed to overwhelm the natural reluctance of defendants to accept guilty pleas. Indeed, Covey says we can understand the function of these features better as devices to overcome the impediment to plea bargaining that defendant biases otherwise create: (1) very high plea discounts and trial penalties offset loss aversion; (2) informal 'open-file' discovery practices and sentencing guidelines minimize the uncertainty of trial and sentencing outcomes, thus giving less room for the optimism bias to operate; (3) pre-trial detention re-frames prison as the baseline and the plea discount as a gain rather than a loss; (4) defense lawyers can provide information and perspectives that 'de-bias' the defendant's decisions. The third point is particularly interesting, but as Burke (2007) notes, if pre-trial detention reverses the frame for defendants, it may also do so for prosecutors, who may then perceive the defendant's release from incarceration as a loss and prefer the uncertain loss of trial to the certain loss of a plea bargain.

Most of the analysis here has focused on the ways that cognitive bias or other behavioral findings affect the actors at issue. But Aviram (2008) notes that bias might matter not because it infects prosecutorial decisions but because prosecutors aware of cognitive bias should allow that fact to influence their enforcement decisions. Regarding corporate securities fraud, Aviram notes that investors subject to the availability bias will underestimate the risk of fraud when the market is doing well but overestimate the risk of fraud when the market is doing badly. If so, then prosecutors should offset the bias by counter-cyclical enforcement, bringing more prosecutions during booms than immediately after busts. Conspicuous enforcement when the market is up may also offset the availability bias by providing vivid examples of fraud. By contrast, prosecutions are less useful when investors already overestimate the probability of being defrauded because conspicuous enforcement exacerbates the availability bias. In general, conspicuous enforcement provides information that can exacerbate or ameliorate the availability bias and the prosecutor should adjust his or her actions to account for this effect. Aviram's point might be extended to other crimes if the availability bias causes potential victims to take too much or too little private precaution and enforcement decisions can reduce the bias.

3.4 *The behavior of judges in criminal cases*

One group of scholars has systematically investigated the degree to which judges exhibit the biases that psychologists have found in other populations (see Guthrie et al., 2001, 2007; Wistrich et al., 2005). One particularly relevant finding is the hindsight bias – 'the well-documented tendency to overestimate the predictability of past events' (Guthrie et al., 2007, p. 24). This bias may figure in criminal cases when judges are asked to decide whether the police had probable cause (or in some cases, reasonable suspicion) at the time of a search, when the judge knows that the search produced incriminatory evidence. The assessment should be made solely on the basis of evidence known at the time the search commenced, which could not include the results of the search. But in the vast majority of cases the judge decides the issue only when evidence is discovered and the defendant moves to suppress it from the criminal prosecution. If the judge is subject to the hindsight bias, he or she will overestimate the predictability of finding the evidence, which means finding probable cause (or reasonable suspicion) when the rational judge would find otherwise.[13]

Some scholars have justified the warrant requirement on these grounds – it requires the judicial assessment of probable cause *before* the search, thus avoiding hindsight bias. Such a theory might help to explain when courts require warrants. For example, the Supreme Court generally requires a warrant to search a house, but not for a public arrest (although it does require judicial assessment of the probable cause determination for arrest within 48 hours after the arrest). Note that former searches are more likely to be subject to the hindsight bias than the public arrest. One expects the search of a house to reveal itself as warranted (evidence is discovered) or unwarranted (no evidence is discovered). By contrast, the failure to find evidence on a person arrested does not prove the arrest invalid, but leaves the probable cause determination just as it was before the arrest. Of course, there is the possibility that the search of the body of the arrestee will produce incriminating evidence, which then could induce the hindsight bias. But this risk is less than with a house search, arguably providing a weaker need for a warrant.

In any event, it remains uncertain if the hindsight bias is a genuine problem. Although Guthrie et al. (2001, pp. 801–3) found evidence that judges exhibit the hindsight bias when they employed criminal scenarios involving searches, Wistrich et al. (2005, pp. 1313–18) found no hindsight bias. One possibility is that judges manage in some kinds of familiar cases to structure their reasoning so as to avoid the bias, although the authors speculate about various alternative explanations. More empirical research would be useful.

3.5 The behavior of criminal juries

There are only a few law and economics models of jury behavior (for example, Schrag and Scotchmer, 1994) and no standard theory of jury

---

[13] The less common cases are civil rights actions for damages. In these cases, if the search revealed no incriminating evidence, the hindsight bias produces the opposite problem – overestimating the lack of probable cause.

behavior, so we cannot systematically examine the way that behavioral findings vary economic analysis. But several scholars have examined how the behavior literature predicts mistakes that juries will likely make in criminal cases. Sunstein et al. (2002) examine how bounded rationality causes decisionmakers such as juries to make predictably incoherent or inconsistent judgments. Rachlinski and Jourden (2003) apply this to the criminal jury, studying the role of 'contrast effects', where logically irrelevant contrasts produce different decisions. Interestingly, their experimental study finds contrast effects in jury sentencing for a term of years, but not for death penalty determinations. Prescott and Starr (2006) discuss behavioral effects – such as framing, anchoring, and deliberative polarization – on jury sentencing determinations.

Conclusion

As with other areas of law, the effect of behavioral assumptions on the economic analysis of criminal law is substantial. The empirical testing of behavioral claims continues, but the best available evidence at this point demands some revision of the positive description and normative recommendations economics makes for criminal law.

References

Ainslie, G. (2000), 'A Research-Based Theory of Addictive Motivation', *Law and Philosophy*, **19**, 77.

Anderson, D.A. (2002), 'The Deterrence Hypothesis and Picking Pockets at the Pickpocket's Hanging', *American Law and Economics Review*, **4**, 295.

Antonovics, K. and B.G. Knight (2004), 'A New Look at Racial Profiling: Evidence from the Boston Police Department', NBER Working Paper no. W10634.

Aviram, A. (2007), 'Bias Arbitrage', *Washington and Lee Law Review*, **64**, 789–828.

Aviram, A. (2008), 'Counter-cyclical Enforcement of Corporate Law', *Yale Journal on Regulation*, **25**, 1–33.

Ayres, I. and S.D. Levitt (1998), 'Measuring Positive Externalities from Observable Victim Precaution: An Empirical Analysis of Lojack', *Quarterly Journal of Economics*, **113** (1), 43–77.

Bagenstos, S., and M. Schlanger (2007), 'Hedonic Damages, Hedonic Adaptation, and Disability', *Vanderbilt Law Review*, **60**, 745.

Baker, L.A. and R.E. Emery (1993), 'When Every Relationship is Above Average: Perceptions and Expectations of Divorce at the Time of Marriage', *Law and Human Behavior*, **17**, 439.

Becker, G. (1969), 'Crime and Punishment: An Economic Analysis', *Journal of Political Economy*, **76**, 169.

Becker, G.S. and K.M. Murphy (1988), 'A Theory of Rational Addiction', *Journal of Political Economy*, **96** (4), 675–700.

Bibas, S. (2004), 'Plea Bargaining Outside the Shadow of Trial', *Harvard Law Review*, **117**, 2463–547.

Bickel, W.K. and L.A. Marsch (2001), 'Conceptualizing Addiction: Toward a Behavioral Economic Understanding of Drug Dependence: Delay Discounting Processes', *Addiction*, **96**, 73.

Birke, R. (1999), 'Reconciling Loss Aversion and Guilty Pleas', *Utah Law Review*, 205–54.

Black, D. (1983), 'Crime as Social Control', *American Sociological Review,* **48,** 34–45.
Blumenthal, J.A. (2005), 'Law and the Emotions: The Problem of Affective Forecasting', *Indiana Law Journal*, **80***,* 155.
Bowers, J. (2008), 'Contraindicated Drug Courts', *UCLA Law Review* **55**, 783.
Brickman, P., D. Coates and R. Janoff-Bulman (1978), 'Lottery Winners and Accident Victims: Is Happiness Relative?', *Journal of Personality and Social Psychology*, **36**, 917.
Bronsteen, J., C. Buccafusco and J. Masur (2008), 'Happiness and Punishment', *Columbia Law Review*, **108** (forthcoming).
Burke, A.S. (2007), 'Prosecutorial Passion, Cognitive Bias, and Plea Bargaining', *William and Mary Law Review*, **91**, 183–211.
Burns, R. and C. Crawford (1999), 'School Shootings, the Media, and Public Fear: Ingredients for a Moral Panic', *Crime Law and Social Change*, **32** (2), 147–68.
Cooter, R.D. (1991), 'Lapses, Conflict, and Akrasia in Torts and Crimes: Towards an Economic Theory of the Will', *International Review of Law and Economics*, **11**, 149–64.
Cooter, R.D., M. Feldman and Y. Feldman (2006), 'The Misperception of Norms: The Psychology of Bias and the Economics of Equilibrium', unpublished manuscript.
Corrado, M.L. (2006), 'Behavioral Economics, Neurophysiology, Addiction and the Law', University of North Carolina Legal Studies Research Paper no. 892007.
Correll, J., B. Park, C.M. Judd and B. Wittenbrink (2002), 'The Police Officer's Dilemma: Using Ethnicity to Disambiguate Potentially Threatening Individuals', *Journal of Personality and Social Psychology*, **83**, 1314–29.
Covey, R. (2007), 'Reconsidering the Relationship between Cognitive Psychology and Plea Bargaining', *Marquette Law Review*, **91**, 213–47.
Darley, J.M. (2005), 'On the Unlikely Prospect of Reducing Crime Rates by Increasing the Severity of Prison Sentences', *Journal of Law and Policy* **13**, 181–247.
Diener, E., R.E. Lucas and C.N. Scollon (2006), 'Beyond the Hedonic Treadmill: Revising the Adaptation Theory of Well-being', *American Psychologist,* **61***,* 305.
Donohue, J.J. III and S.D. Levitt (2001), 'The Impact of Race on Policing and Arrests'. *Journal of Law and Economics* **44**, 367–94.
Findley, K.A. and Michael S. Scott (2006), 'The Multiple Dimensions of Tunnel Vision in Criminal Cases', *Wisconsin Law Review*, 291.
Frederick, S., G. Loewenstein and T. O'Donoghue (2002), 'Time Discounting and Time Preference: A Critical Review', *Journal of Economic Literature*, **40**, 351–401.
Frey, B. (2008), *Happiness: A Revolution in Economics*, Cambridge, MA: The MIT Press.
Friedrich, J. (1993), 'Primary Error Detection and Minimization (PEDMIN) Strategies in Social Cognition: A Reinterpretation of Confirmation Bias Phenomena', *Psychological Review,* **100** (2), 298–319.
Funk, P (2005), 'Government Action, Social Norms and Criminal Behavior', *Journal Institutional and Theoretical Economics* (forthcoming).
Garoupa, N. (2003), 'Behavioral Economic Analysis of Crime: A Critical Review', *European Journal of Law and Economics*, **15**, 5–15.
Gilbert, Daniel (2006), *Stumbling on Happiness*, New York: Alfred A. Knopf.
Gilliam, Jr, F.D. and S. Iyengar (2000), 'Prime Suspects: The Influence of Local Television News on the Viewing Public', *American Journal of Political Science*, **44**, 560–73.
Glaser, J. and E.D. Knowles (2008), 'Implicit Motivation to Control Prejudice', *Journal of Experimental and Social Psychology*, **44**, 164–72.
Guthrie, C., J.J. Rachlinski and A.J. Wistrich (2001), 'Inside the Judicial Mind', *Cornell Law Review*, **86**, 777–829.
Guthrie, C., J.J. Rachlinski and A.J. Wistrich (2007), 'Blinking on the Bench: How Judges Decide Cases', *Cornell Law Review* **93**, 1–43.
Guttel, E. and A. Harel (2008), 'Uncertainty Revisited: Legal Prediction and Legal Postdiction', unpublished manuscript.
Harel, A. and U. Segal (1999), 'Criminal Law and Behavioral Law and Economics: Observations on the Neglected Role of Uncertainty in Deterring Crime', *American Law and Economics Review*, **1**, 276–312.

Hill, C., A. Memon and P. McGeorge (2008), 'The Role of Confirmation Bias in Suspect Interviews: A Systematic Evaluation', *Legal and Criminological Psychology*, **13** (2), 357–71.
Hipp, J.R. (2007), 'Resident Perceptions of Crime: How Similar are they to Official Crime Rates?', CES Paper 07–10.
Jolls, C. (2004), 'On Law Enforcement with Boundedly Rational Actors', Harvard Law and Economics Discussion Paper no. 494.
Jolls, C. and C.R. Sunstein (2006a), 'The Law of Implicit Bias', *California Law Review*, **94**, 969–96.
Jolls, C. and C.R. Sunstein (2006b), 'Debiasing through Law', *Journal of Legal Studies*, **35**, 199–241.
Jolls, C., C.R. Sunstein and R. Thaler (1998), 'A Behavioral Approach to Law and Economics', *Stanford Law Review*, **50**, 1471.
Jones, E.E. and V.A. Harris (1967), 'The Attribution of Attitudes', *Journal of Experimental Social Psychology*, **3**, 1–24.
Kahneman, D.A. (2000), 'Experienced Utility and Objective Happiness: A Moment-based Approach', in D. Kahneman and A. Tversky (eds), *Choices, Values, and Frames.*
Kahneman, D. and A. Tversky (1979), 'Prospect Theory: An Analysis of Decision under Risk', *Econometrica*, **47**, 263.
Kassin, S.M., C.J. Goldstein, and K. Savitsky (2003), 'Behavioral Confirmation in the Interrogation Room: On the Dangers of Presuming Guilt', *Law and Human Behavior*, **27**, 187–203.
Kessler, D. and S. Levitt (1999), 'Using Sentence Enhancements to Distinguish between Deterrence and Incapacitation', *Journal of Law and Economics*, **42**, 343–63.
Kleck, G., B. Sever, S. Li and M. Gertz (2005), 'The Missing Link in General Deterrence Research', *Criminology* **43**, 623–60.
Korobkin, R.B. and C. Guthrie (1994), 'Psychological Barriers to Litigation Settlement: An Experimental Approach', *Michigan Law Review*, **93**, 107.
Korobkin, R.B. and T.S. Ulen (2000), 'Law and Behavioral Science: Removing the Rationality Assumption from Law and Economics', *California Law Review* **88**, 1251.
Laibson D. (1997), 'Golden Eggs and Hyperbolic Discounting', *Quarterly Journal of Economics*, **112**, 443.
Langer, E.J. (1975), 'The Illusion of Control', *Journal of Personality and Social Psychology*, **32**, 311.
Lattimore, P. and A. Witte (1986), 'Models of Decision-making Under Uncertainty: The Criminal Choice', in D.B. Cornish and R.V. Clarke (eds), *The Reasoning Criminal: Rational Choice Perspectives on Offending*, Springer-Verlag.
Layard, Richard (2005), *Happiness: Lessons from a New Science*, New York: The Penguin Press.
Lee, D.S. and J. McCrary (2005), 'Crime, Punishment, and Myopia', NBER Working Paper.
Leitzel, J. (2008), 'Self-exclusion', unpublished manuscript.
Levitt, S.D. (1998), 'Juvenile Crime and Punishment', *Journal of Political Economy*, **106**(6).
Levitt, S.D. (2004a), 'Deterrence', in James Q. Wilson and Joan Petersilia (eds), *Crime: Public Policies for Crime Control*, pp. 435–50.
Levitt, S.D. (2004b), 'Understanding Why Crime Fell in the 1990s: Four Factors that Explain the Decline and Six that Do Not', *Journal of Economic Perspectives,* **18** (1), 163–90.
Levitt, S.D. and J.A. List (2006), 'What do Laboratory Experiments Measuring Social Preferences Reveal about the Real World?', *Journal of Economic Perspectives*, **21**, 153.
Levitt, S.D. and T.J. Miles (2007), 'The Empirical Study of Criminal Punishment', in A. Mitchell Polinsky and Steven Shavell (eds), *The Handbook of Law and Economics*, pp. 453–95.
Levitt, S.D. and Thomas J. Miles (2006), 'Economic Contributions to the Understanding of Crime', *Annual Review of Law and Social Science*, **2**, 147–64.
List, J.A. (2003), 'Does Market Experience Eliminate Market Anomalies?', *Quarterly Journal of Economics*, **118**, 41.

List, J.A. (2006), 'The Behavioralist Meets the Market: Measuring Social Preferences and Reputation Effects in Actual Transactions', *Journal of Political Economy*, **114**, 1.
Lochner, L. (1997), 'Individual Perceptions of the Criminal Justice System', *American Economic Review*, **97**(1).
MacCoun, R., R.L. Pacula, J. Chriqui, K. Harris and P. Reuter (2008), 'Do Citizens Know Whether their State has Decriminalized Marijuana? A Test of the Perceptual Assumption in Deterrence Theory', unpublished draft.
Meares, T.L., N. Katyal and D.M. Kahan (2004), 'Updating the Study of Punishment', *Stanford Law Review*, **56**, 1171–210.
Meissner, C.A. and S.M. Kassin (2004), 'You're Guilty, So Just Confess! Cognitive and Behavioral Confirmation Biases in the Interrogation Room', in G.D. Lassiter (ed.), *Interrogations, Confessions, and Entrapment,* New York: Kluwer Academic, pp. 85–106.
Mitchell, G. (2002a), 'Why Economists' Perfect Rationality Should Not be Traded for Behavioral Economics' Equal Incompetence', *Georgia Law Journal*, **91**, 67.
Mitchell, G. (2002b), 'Taking Behavioralism Too Seriously?: The Unwarranted Pessimism of the New Behavioral Analysis of Law', *William and Mary Law Review*, **43**, 1907.
Mitchell, G. (2009), 'Second Thoughts', *McGeorge Law Review* (forthcoming).
Murphy, K. (2004), 'The Role of Trust in Nurturing Compliance: A Study of Accused Tax Avoiders', *Law and Human Behavior*, **28**, 187.
Nagin, D. (1998), 'Criminal Deterrence Research at the Outset of the Twenty-first Century', *Crime and Justice: A Review of Research*, **23**, 1–42.
Nickerson, R.S. (1998), 'Confirmation Bias: A Ubiquitous Phenomenon in Many Guises', *Review of General Psychology,* 2 (2), 175–220.
O'Brien, B. and P.C. Ellsworth (2006), 'Confirmation Bias in Criminal Investigations', September 19, available at http://papers.ssrn.com/sol3/papers.cfm?abstract_id=913357.
O'Donoghue, T. and M. Rabin (1999), 'Doing it Now or Later', *American Economic Review*, **89**, 103–24.
Oldfather, C.M. (2007), 'Heuristics, Biases, and Criminal Defendants', *Marquette Law Review*, **91**, 249–62.
Paternoster, R. (1987), 'The Deterrent Effect of the Perceived Certainty and Severity of Punishment: A Review of the Evidence and Issues', *Justice Quarterly*, **4**, 173–217.
Paternoster, R., R. Bachman, R. Brame and L.W. Sherman (1997), 'Do Fair Procedures Matter? The Effect of Procedural Justice on Spouse Assault', *Law and Society Review*, **31**, 163.
Plous, Scott (1993), *The Psychology of Judgment and Decisionmaking*.
Polinsky, M. and S. Shavell (2000), 'The Fairness of Sanctions: Some Implications for Optimal Enforcement', *American Law and Economic Review,* **2**, 223–37.
Prescott, J.J. and S. Starr (2006), 'Improving Criminal Jury Decision Making After the Blakely Revolution', *University of Illinois Law Review*, 301–56.
Rachlinski, J. (1996), 'Gains, Losses, and the Psychology of Litigation', *South California Law Review*, **70**, 113.
Rachlinski, J.J. and F. Jourden (2003), 'The Cognitive Components of Punishment', *Cornell Law Review*, **88**, 457–85.
Roberts, J.V. (1992), 'Public Opinion, Crime, and Criminal Justice', in Michael Tonry (ed.), *Crime and Justice: A Review of Research,* **16**.
Robinson, P. (2006), 'How Psychology is Changing the Punishment Theory Debate', in Belinda Brooks-Gordon and Michael Freeman (eds), *Law and Psychology: Current Legal Issues*, **9**, 94–104.
Robinson, P. and J.M. Darley (2004), 'Does Criminal Law Deter? A Behavioral Science Investigation', *Oxford Journal of Legal Studies.*
Ross, L. (1977), 'The Intuitive Psychologist and His Shortcomings: Distortions in the Attribution Process', in L. Berkowitz (ed.), *Advances in Experimental Social Psychology*, Vol. 10, New York: Academic Press, pp. 173–230.
Ross, L., D. Greene and P. House (1977), 'The False Consensus Effect: An Egocentric Bias in Social Perception and Attribution Processes', *Journal of Experimental Social Psychology*, **13**, 279–301.

Schkade, D.A. and D. Kahneman (1998), 'Does Living in California Make People Happy?: A Focusing Illusion in Judgments of Life Satisfaction', *Psychological Science*, **9**, 340.
Schrag, J. and S. Scotchmer (1994), 'Crime and Prejudice: The Use of Character Evidence in Criminal Trials', *Journal of Law Economics and Organization*, **10**, 319–42.
Schwartz, A. (2008), 'How Much Irrationality does the Market Permit?', *Journal of Legal Studies*, **37**, 131.
Segal, V. and A. Stein (2006), 'Ambiguity Aversion and the Criminal Process', *Notre Dame Law Review*, **81**, 1495–551.
Simon, D., L.B. Pham, Q.A. Le and K.J. Holyoak (2001), 'The Emergence of Coherence over the Course of Decision Making', *Journal of Experimental Psychology: Learning, Memory, and Cognition*, **27** (5), 1250–60.
Sunstein, C.R., D. Kahneman, D. Schkade and I. Ritov (2002), 'Predictably Incoherent Judgments', *Stanford Law Review*, **54**, 1153.
Thompson, K. (1998), *Moral Panics*, London: Routledge.
Tversky, A. and D. Kahneman (1982), 'Availability: A Heuristic for Judging Frequency and Probability', in Daniel Kahneman et al. (eds), *Judgment under Uncertainty: Heuristics and Biases*.
Tversky, A. and D. Kahneman (1986), 'Rational Choice and the Framing of Decisions', *Journal of Business*, **59**, 251.
Tyler, T.R. (1990), *Why People Obey the Law*, New Haven, CT: Yale University Press.
Tyler, T.R. and J. Fagan (2006), 'Legitimacy and Cooperation: Why do People Help the Police Fight Crime in their Communities?', unpublished manuscript.
Utset, M.A. (2007), 'Hyperbolic Criminals and Repeated Time-inconsistent Misconduct', *Houston Law Review*, **44**, 609–76.
Weinstein, N. (1980), 'Unrealistic Optimism about Future Life Events', *Journal of Personality and Social Psychology*, **39**, 806.
Wilson, J.Q. and A. Abrahamse (1992), 'Does Crime Pay?', *Justice Quarterly*, **9**, 359.
Wilson, T. and D. Gilbert (2003), 'Affective Forecasting', in Mark Zanna (ed.), *Advances in Experimental Social Psychology*.
Wistrich, A.J., C. Guthrie and J.J. Rachlinski (2005), 'Can Judges Ignore Inadmissible Information? The Difficulty of Deliberately Disregarding', *University of Pennsylvania Law Review*, **153**, 1251–345.
Zeiler C. and C. Plott (2006), 'Exchange Asymmetries Incorrectly Interpreted as Evidence of Endowment Effect Theory and Prospect Theory?', California Institute of Technology Social Science Working Paper no. 1230.

Index

Aalder, M. 337
Abbink, K. 283
Abbot, C. 324, 333, 335, 338
Aboody, David 242
Abrahamse, A. 407
acquittals, mistaken *see under* errors
Adelstein, Richard 127, 133, 134
administrative fines *see under* fines
adversarial systems 71, 146, 157, 165
Afghanistan 384, 385, 387
agents, principals and *see* principal-agent
Aghion, P. 61, 62
Agrawal, Aunp 246
Ainslie, G. 424
Albrecht, Hans Jorg 149
alcohol 28, 115, 260, 421
Alexander, Cindy 223, 239
Allen, T. 82
Allingham M. 290, 291, 294–300, 302–3, 306–8
Alm, J. 298, 299, 304
Al-Nowaihi A. 298
Alpizar, F. 338
Alschuler, Albert 149, 153–4, 156, 158, 160, 161, 164
Al-Yamamah agreement 284
Anderson, David 182, 415
Anderson, P. 299
Andreoni, J. 290, 307, 313
Andvig, J.C. 273
Anti-terrorism Crime and Security Act (2001) 398–9
antitrust 60, 61, 62, 93–4, 385
  corporate crime, and 225, 234–5, 241
  private claims 67–70, 74, 80–81
Antonovics, K. 429
Aoki, M. 63
appeals 139–40, 164, 178, 201–2
Aranson, P. 105
Arend, A.C. 380
Arlen, Jennifer 234, 237, 242, 249, 332, 333, 339
arms and guns 82, 212, 258, 260, 265, 266, 398
Arya, Anil 244
Ashe v Swenson (1970) 210
Ashurst Report (European Commission) 69, 80
Ashworth, A. 100, 322
Asia 69
assets *see* wealth
Attempt at an Analysis of Smuggling, An (Beccaria) 290
Aubert, C. 79, 80, 235
audits 292, 296, 299, 302, 305–6, 307–10, 311, 450
auditors 33, 60, 233, 235, 244, 247, 354
availability heuristic *see under* behavioural criminal law
Avio, Kenneth 210
Aviram, A. 427, 430
Ayres, I. 98, 106, 134
Azabou, M. 274

Babbit, C.J. 328, 329
Babcock, Linda 165
Bac, M. 273, 281
BAE Systems 284–5
Bagenstos, S. 409
bail system 134, 153, 154, 162
Bail Reform Act (1984) 134
Baiman, Stanley 243
Baker, L. 406
Baker, Scott 156
Baldry, J. 304
Baldwin, R. 91, 95
Bank of America 240
Bardach, E. 97
Bardhan, P. 272
Bar-Gill, Oren 157, 242, 243, 244, 247, 249
Barrett, J.J. 329
Batasuna 387
Bayer, R. 300
Beattie, J.M. 145

Bebchuk, Lucian 242, 243, 244, 247
Beccaria, C. 1, 290
Beck, R.J. 380
Beckenstein, Alan 241
Becker, G.S. 1
  behavioural criminal law and economics 403, 405, 424
  corporate crime 228
  corruption 275
  cyber crime 358, 359, 360
  environmental crimes 320, 321, 322, 334, 335, 337
  private law enforcement 60, 63
  tax evasion and avoidance 290, 294, 313
  terrorism 378, 388
behavioural criminal law and economics 403–32
  availability heuristic 406–7, 418–19
  behavioural adjustments to deterrence theory 417–26
  behavioural economics, background to 405–13
  cognitive bias 165, 417–22, 430
  control, illusion of 420–22
  criticisms of behavioural literature 412–13
  detection 406, 417–18
  deterrence theory 413–17
  deviations, perfect rationality from 406–8
  fairness 425–6
  finding of systematic mistakes 406
  framing 408, 420
  hedonic adaptation 408–10, 416
  hyperbolic discounting 423–5
  overoptimism 406, 417–18, 429–30
  pessimism and projection 419–20
  police 428
  potential criminal offenders, analysis of 413–26
  prosecutors and defendants 429–30
  prospect theory 407–8, 422–3
  remembering, patterns of 410–12
  victims 426–7
Belgium 328, 330, 333
Benabou, Roland 244
Beneish, Messod 246
Benjamini, Y. 298
Bentham, J. 1, 64, 76, 290
Berk, Richard 215
Bernasconi, M. 298
Besley, T. 274, 283
bias 165, 406, 417–22, 428–32
Bibas, Stephanos 153, 158, 159, 161, 430
Bibliography of Law and Economics (Faure) 321
Bickel, W.E. 424
Bierschbach, R.A. 95
Biggar, D. 112, 117
Billiet, C.M. 328, 333
Birke, Richard 160, 429, 430
Bishop, J. 293
Bishop, W. 105
Bjerk, David 141, 148, 163
Black, D. 425
Black, T. 210
Blackstone, William 103, 114, 177, 179, 206
Blockburger v United States (1932) 199, 200, 201
Blumberg, Abraham 160
Blumenthal, J.A. 409
Blumenthal, M. 305
Boa, E.D. 280
Bohm-Bawerk, Eugen von 63
Bordens, Kenneth 156
Border, K. 308, 311
Bordignon, M. 297–8
Bose, G. 283
Bosnian war crimes 83
Bowen, Robert 235
Bowers, Josh 154, 158, 424
Bowers, W.J. 208, 210
Bowles, R.M. 99, 105, 273, 275, 322, 328, 330, 335
Boylan, Richard 158
Braithwaite, J. 98, 106, 336, 338
Branch v Texas (1972) 208
Brand, S. 276
Brazil 69, 80, 259
Breit, W. 68, 74
bribery and extortion 44–6, 94, 206, 222, 271
  organized crime 268, 384–5, 386

private enforcement of law 71, 72, 81
rent-seeking 186, 187, 191–3, 196
see also corruption
Brickman, P. 40
Broadway, R. 311
Brokelmann, H. 80
Bronsteen, J. 416
Brosi, Kathleen 151
Brown, R.M. 98
Brumm, H.J. 21
Buell, S.W. 336
Bunt, H.G. van de 338
Bureau of Justice Statistics 148
Burke, A.S. 429, 430
Burns, Natasha 246
Burns, R. 427
Busch, L.A. 61
business purpose doctrine *see under* tax evasion

Cadot, O. 275
Cadsby, B. 304, 305
Calfee, J.E. 96
Call, Andrew 235
Cameron, S. 210
Canada 66, 69, 339
capital punishment 66, 195, 207–17
brutalization effect 208
deterrent, examined as 207–16
moratorium, impact of 213
sensitivity analysis 214–16
testing for deterrence 211–13
history 208–9
terrorism 376, 390, 391
see also homicide
Capone, Al 262
Carney, William 242
Carver, T. 259
Cassone, Alberto 241
causation and loss determination 369–71
Ceausescu, Nicholae 83
Chadha, Sahiba 246
Chander, P. 308, 313
Chang, J. 273
charge-bargaining 147–8, 157, 164
Chen, Z. 79, 80
Chhaochharia, Vidhi 248
Chicago v Morales (1999) 206
Chicago school of antitrust 69, 74
Chicano gangs 261
China 75, 79, 185
Choi, Stephen 248
Chressanthis, G.A. 210
Chu, C.Y. 228, 234, 237, 308, 313
Church, Thomas 153, 156
civil cases 82, 91, 94, 113, 120–22, 136, 357–8
civil law countries 132, 146–7, 165–6
Clark, J.B. 63
Classical School 290
Clawson, P.L. 260, 263
Clay, K. 76
Clayton Act (1914) 68, 80
Clean Water Act (1972) 83
Cloniger, D.O. 210, 211, 213, 217
Clotfelter, C. 302
Coase, R. 70, 72, 120, 227, 331
Coates, D. 409
Coates, John 247
Cockburn J.S. 145
Coffee, John 233, 328
Cohen, Mark 221, 223, 276, 331, 333–4, 336, 339, 393
Cohen, Stanley 153
Coke, Edward 177
Colander, D. 63
Cole, H. 68
Columbia 257, 259, 263, 385
combined sanctions 9–10, 19
Commission Report on Cocaine and Sentencing Policy 367–8
Committee on Capital Markets Regulation 247 (2006)
common law 63, 112–13, 115, 120, 122–3, 145–6
corporate crime, and 232, 236, 240
countries 112–23, 123, 146–7, 148, 166
companies *see* corporate crime
competition *see* antitrust; *see under* organized crime
compliance
programmes *see under* corporate crime
tax regimes, with *see under* tax evasion
compulsory prosecution 133, 134, 147, 166

computers and computer crime *see under* sentencing guidelines
conflict of interests 300
Congress, United States 134, 242, 285, 361, 404, 427
contributory negligence 112, 392
convictions, mistaken *see under* errors
cooperation enforcement approach 336–40
Cooter, R.
  behavioural criminal law and economics 419, 420, 423, 424
  criminal procedure 130, 132
  economics of capital punishment 208
  environmental crimes 323, 329
  private enforcement of law 70, 72
Core, Robert 246, 247
corporate crime and torts 220–49, 280, 357, 362, 383
  equity holdings, effect of 223
  monitoring *see under* monitoring
  nature of 220–23
  sanctions 223–36
    compliance programs 223, 280
    harm, equal to 227–9
    irrelevance principle 226–7, 229
    judgment-proof firms 223, 229–30
    limited liability 223, 228
    self-reporting 223, 233–6
    structure 236–42
      agent indemnification 239–40
      civil versus criminal penalties 237–8
      reputational penalties 238–9
      strict liability and negligence 236–7, 238
    targets of 220–21, 230–33
  securities fraud 242–8
  see also environmental crimes; terrorism
corporate finance and securities *see* securities
Corrado, M.L. 424
Correll, J. 428
corruption 44–6, 100, 104, 105, 106, 206, 271–86, 394
  anti-corruption policies 282–5
  corporate crime 222, 235
  costs 274–81
    anticipation of corruption, in 278, 279–81
    criminal justice system 278–9
    rent-seeking 276–7
    victims 277–8
  definition 271–2, 279
  environmental crimes 337
  nature 273–6
  organized crime 268
  political 281–2
  rent-seeking 186–8, 193–5, 276–7
  tax evasion 313–14
  see also bribery; rent-seeking
Cortenraad, W.H.F.M. 325
Cory, D.C. 328
costs 3, 9, 74 , 104, 132, 134
  administrative procedures 324–6
  anticipation of corruption, in 278, 279–81
  criminal offences, of 91–5, 105, 127, 332, 338, 347–58
  deterrence 179–83, 189–90, 351
  disutility 179–83
  errors 99, 102, 105, 107, 177, 179–81
    criminal procedures minimizing *see* procedure
  excessive sanctions 152
  fines, imposing 31–2, 328
  imprisonment 20–21, 48, 95, 328, 351, 360
  indignation 97
  information 101, 103, 105
  marginal deterrence 35, 332
  monitoring 97, 333
  observation of wealth 48–50
  offenders, incurred by 95, 351–3, 358–9
  prevention *see* prevention *under* individuals
  psychic 274–5, 353
  regulation 103, 104–5
  rent-seeking *see under* rent-seeking
  sanctioning 179–83
  saving 43, 61, 121–2, 133
    plea bargaining by 150–52
    settlements by 38–9, 125–6
    under-deterrence by 11–13, 41
  self-reporting, reduced by 40
  tax evasion 306, 310, 311, 313

trial and litigation 38, 150, 163
under-deterrence 182
Courage v Crehan (2001) 69–70, 73, 80
Cover, J.P. 210
Covey, R. 430
Cowell, F. 290, 291, 297, 299, 300, 306
Craswell, R. 96
Crawford, C. 427
Cremer, H. 308
Crime Control Act (1984) 361
Crime Control Model 174–5
crimes 1, 21, 34–6, 37–9, 40, 48, 112, 357, 359
detecting *see* detecting offenders
economic *see* tax evasion; sentencing guidelines
organized *see* organized crime
prevention *see* prevention of crime
street *see* street crimes
white-collar *see* white collar crime
see also corporate crime; cyber crime; environmental crime; tax evasion; terrorism
Criminal Justice Agency, New York City 154
criminal justice, economic model *see under* cyber crime
criminal law
behavioural *see* behavioural criminal law and economics
procedure *see* procedure; procedural protections
regulation, and *see under* regulation
torts, and *see* torts
Crocker, K. 300
Cronshaw, M. 304
Crow, Jim 185
cruel and unusual punishments *see under* sanctions; *see also* fairness
cyber crime 346–74
criminal justice economic model 358–61
certainty of punishment 359
interdependencies, crimes and actors of 361
offenders accountable for all costs 358–9
sanctions 360–61
sentencing economic crimes, and *see* sentencing guidelines
optimal level and crime control 347–58
law enforcement and resources 355–6
mistakes 356–8
offenders, potential 351–3, 356
victims, potential 354

dangerousness 41–2, 47, 134
Darley, J.M. 414, 415, 416
Das-Gupta, A. 298, 312
Davis, Michael 224
Dawson, Robert 136
De Roos, T. 330
Dechow, Patricia 246
Decker, C. 335
Del Monte, A. 279
Democracy and Distrust (Ely) 175–6
democracy-forcing theory 175–6
Denmark 337
Department for Environment, Food and Rural Affairs 329
Department of Homeland Security 396
Department of Justice 65, 234, 236, 279, 284, 365
Depoorter, B. 80
deportation and removal 376, 397, 399
Desai, Hemang 246
detecting offenders 20, 53–4, 116, 359, 385, 389
behavioural analysis 417–19, 422
environmental crimes 322–6, 328, 333–4
marginal deterrence, increased probability and 35
probability 20, 42–3, 326, 359
resources 4, 10–19
self-reporting 39–40
deterrence 21–2, 33–4, 43–6, 127, 139, 233, 330, 332
certainty of punishment 359–60, 366–7
crime 95–6, 111, 114–16, 363–6
criminal procedure 126, 140–42
environmental crimes 323–6, 330, 332–4

errors diluting 29–31, 141
fines and imprisonment 21, 22, 48, 113, 116
insurance premiums 335
plea bargaining and settlements 38–9, 150–52
police and prosecution 142, 164
principal-agent relationships 37
regulation, and 92, 98–9
rent-seeking 189
risk aversion 335
sentencing 41, 349–50
tax evasion 296, 303, 306–7, 311
theory 413
see also costs; marginal deterrence; over-deterrence; stigma; under-deterrence
deterrence style approach 336–40
Dezhbakhsh, H. 211, 213, 217
Dhami, S. 298
Diamond, Douglas 243
Diaz v United States (1912) 199, 200
Diener, E. 410
discretion 42, 43, 95, 99, 106, 126–7, 141
see also judges; juries; prosecutors
discrimination 52, 134, 162, 185, 208, 217, 262, 428–9
Dixit, Avinash 264
Djankov, S. 84
Dnes, A. 111, 118, 119
Doig, A. 271
Donaldson, William 240
Donohue, John 183, 216, 217, 429
Doob, Anthony 153
Dostoevsky, Fyodor 64
double jeopardy 115, 122, 172, 178, 197, 199–203
Drew, K.F. 62
drugs 222, 367–8, 415, 416, 424–5
offences 65, 111, 114, 412, 414, 415
organized crime, and 257, 259, 260, 261, 268, 269
Dubin, J, 302
Duborg, R. 276
Due Process Model 174–5
duration neglect 411, 415, 416
Dyck, Alexander 235
Dye, Ronald 243, 244
Easterbrook, Frank 126, 127, 133, 151, 156, 329
economic crimes *see* tax evasion; sentencing guidelines
economic substance doctrine *see under* tax evasion
Eckert, H. 339
Ecuador 259
Efendi, Jan 24
Ehrlich, I. 105, 209, 210, 215
Eide, E. 298
Ekelund, R. 214
Elder, Harold 132
Ellickson, Robert C. 76
Ellis, Christopher 234
Ellsworth, P.C. 428
Ely, John Hart 175–6
Elzinga, G. 68, 74
Emery, R.E. 40
enforcement, law *see* private enforcement; public enforcement
enforcement pyramid 98
Enriques, Luca 247
Enron 221, 242, 245
Enste, D. 293
entrapment 139
Environment Agency 96
environmental crimes 39, 60, 61, 67, 83–4, 320–40
administrative or criminal law 324–6
corporate crime, and 225, 230, 239, 330–33
dependence of law, administrative 320–22
environmental criminal law 326–8, 333–6
enforcement strategies 336–40
optimal sanctions for 328–30
public enforcement, arguments in favor of 322–4
Erard, B. 311
Erickson, Merle 246
errors 28–32, 76, 82, 83, 125, 139–41, 306
costs *see under* costs
environmental crimes 325–6
mistaken acquittals 28–31, 102, 125, 132–3, 142, 179, 306, 395–6
mistaken convictions 28–31, 102–3,

125, 131–3, 140, 142, 179, 306, 356–8
reduction 31, 102–3, 131, 133
Escobar, Pablo 263
ETA 385, 386, 387, 399
Europe 62–4, 66, 69–70, 75, 76, 259, 304, 312
environmental crimes 328, 329, 333–5
plea bargaining 133, 146–7,
European Commission 69
European Court of Justice 69, 70, 73, 80
European Union 69–70, 80
evidence 102–3, 125, 136–9
ex post facto rule 172, 178–9, 195, 197, 204–5
ex post facto tax recovery 292, 306–7
excessive punishments *see under* fairness
see also cruel and unusual punishments
exclusionary rule 125, 137, 162
extortion *see* bribery; corruption

Fagan, J. 214, 215, 426
fairness 53–4, 126–7, 139, 141, 209, 303, 306
behavioural analysis, and *see under* behavioural criminal law
sanctions 52–4, 141, 163, 179, 196–8
fault based liability 1, 3, 20, 31–4, 52–4
optimal magnitude when enforcement certain 5–6, 8–9, 10
optimal magnitude when enforcement uncertain 13, 15, 16–17, 18, 19
Faure, M. 111, 321, 322, 327, 330, 331
Fearon, G. 61
Federal Bureau of Investigation 358
Federal Civil False Claims Act (1863) 235
Federal Trade Commission 357
Feeley, Malcolm 154
Feess, Eberhard 234
Feinstein, J. 302
Feldman, M. 419, 420
Feldman, Y. 419, 420
Fenn, P. 97, 160, 337
Findley, K.A. 428
fines 3, 21–2, 29, 33–4, 37, 122, 195, 360–61
administrative 324–6, 327, 336
cheaper sanctions providing 19, 21–2, 328
costs of imposing 31–2, 328
environmental crimes 324–6, 328
imprisonment and, *see* combined sanction
optimal magnitude 4–6, 11–15, 32, 42–3, 45
Finkelstein, C. 101
Fiorentini, G. 273
Fiorina, M.P. 105
firms, sanctioning of 53–4
first best behaviour 20, 23–4, 33, 35, 41, 49
sanctions 5–6, 8–9, 11–13
first time offenders 40
Fischel, D.R. 237, 238
Fisher, George 149
Fisman, R. 280, 284
Fixed Amount of Taxes or Tax Audit 308
Flatters, F. 313
Fleming, Charles 240
Flemish Environmental Inspection Agency 340
foreign crimes *see under* torts
forfeiture 330, 397
Forst, Brian 15
framing and framing related extortion 44–5
France 63, 148
Franzoni, L.A. 291, 311, 312
Frederick, S.
freedom, defendant's right to 134
Frey, B. 408
Frick, K. 96
Friedman, D.
criminal law procedure 173, 195, 196
criminal law and regulation 95
criminal law and torts 111, 112
environmental crimes 331
plea bargaining and prosecution 145, 146

private law enforcement 62, 65–6, 74, 75, 81
Friedrich, J. 428
Friesen, L. 339
Fudenberg, Drew 243, 244
Funk, P. 95, 426
Furman v Georgia (1072) 208, 209

Gabel, H. 241
gain 5–6, 7–8, 326, 333
Galbiati, R, 293
Gale, W. 310
Gambetta, D. 261
gambling 222, 257, 260, 425
Ganuza, Juan Jose 233
Garoupa, N.
corruption 275
criminal law and regulation 106
environmental crimes 337
private enforcement of law 75, 76, 81
gate-keepers 60, 235, 244, 247
Gazal-Ayal, Oren 157
Geller, A. 214
Gellhorn, W. 93
Genesove, David 235
Germany 148–9, 165, 283, 330, 331, 333
Gerschenkron, A. 63
Gerxhani, K. 293
Gibbons, J. 210
Gideon v Wainwright (1963) 172
Gidi, A. 69, 80
Gilbert, Daniel 408, 409
Gilliam, F.D. 427
Gilmore, Gary 209
Ginsberg, D. 80
Gittings, R.K. 212, 215, 216
Glaeser, E. 62, 75
Glaser, J. 428
Glover, Jonathan 244
Goerke, L. 300
Goldman, Eitan 243, 244
Gomes, Fernando 233
Gomez-Pomar, F. 99, 326
Gordon, J. 298, 300
Graetz, M. 309
Grande, Elisabetta 147
grand juries 146, 151
Gray, A. 160
Gray, W.B. 96
Green Gang 257, 263
Greenberg, J. 309
Greenstone, Michael 248
Gregg v Georgia (1976) 209
Gregory, W.L. 156
Greif, A. 63, 76
Grinstein, Yanif 248
Grogger, J. 210
Grossman, Gene 131, 155
Grossman, H.I. 264
Grossman, Sanford 242
Guinchard, A. 101
Guthrie, C. 408, 431
Guttel, E. 420, 421
Guyton, J. 310
Gyimah-Brempong, K. 280

Halcrow Group Ltd. 99
Hanlon, Michelle 246
Hamdani, A. 101
Hampton, P. 91
Handelman, S. 260
Hansmann, H. 325
Harel, A. 420, 421, 422, 423
harm 21–2, 33–6, 40, 45, 47, 49, 93, 114–15
social and environmental 323–4, 326, 327, 328, 347, 350
Harrington, J. 234, 240
Harrington, S. 240
Harrington, W. 97, 309, 334, 335, 339
Harris, V. 419
Hart, Oliver 243
Harvard school of antitrust 69, 74
Hasker, K. 277
Hawkins, G. 209
Hawkins, K. 337
Hay, J. 84
health and safety *see* safety
Healy, Paul 242, 246
hedonic adaptation *see under* behavioural criminal law
Heine, G. 321, 328, 331
Helland, Eric 238
Herzog, Sergio 153
Hess, H. 263
Heyes, A.G. 334, 338, 339
Hill, C. 428
Hindriks, J. 308, 311, 313

Hinloopen, Jeroen 234
Hipp, J.R. 427
Hirart, Y. 78, 83
Hochberg, Yael 248
Hoenack, S.A. 210
Holderness, Cliff 241, 242
Holtzblatt, J. 310
homicide 115, 116–17, 122–3, 199–200, 268, 407
  see also capital punishment
Homicide Act (1957) 122
Hommes, J. 333, 337
Hong Kong 257
Huisman, W. 338
human rights 60, 61, 101–2
human trafficking 260
hybrid cases and regimes 120–22, 237
Hylton, K.H. 104
hyperbolic discounting *see under* behavioural criminal law

illegal contracts 385–6
Immordino, Giovanni 244
imperfect knowledge of sanctions and detection 42–3
'impossibility theorem' 72, 74
imprisonment 21, 33–4, 94, 113, 183, 195, 360–61, 416
  corruption for 45, 279
  costs *see under* costs
  environmental crimes 325, 326, 328–9, 332, 335
  fines, and, *see* combined sanctions
  life 7, 279
  mistakes diluting deterrence 29–30
  optimal magnitude 6–9, 16–19, 20
  population 164, 183
  pre-trial 134, 153, 154, 430
  principal-agent relationships 37
  repeat offenders 37, 42, 46–8, 360
  settlements 38, 39
  standard of proof 136
  stigma *see* stigma
  United States, in 65, 76
  white collar crime 363–6
incapacitation 42, 46–8
incentives 45–6, 72–3, 74–5
individuals 32, 41–3, 47, 96–7
  prevention of crime 54, 348–9, 350, 354–6, 358, 361, 391–3
  private protection 54, 82, 279
  risk, and *see* risk averse; risk neutral; risk preferring
  wealth *see* wealth
Indonesia 284
inflation 363, 364
  information 114, 140, 242–4
  asymmetric 127, 131, 155, 335, 338
  costs *see under* costs
  private enforcement of law 61–3, 67–8, 70, 73–5, 77–84
  public agents 2–3, 70, 77–8, 80–82
Inland Revenue Service 301, 302, 303, 365
Innes, Robert 233, 339
innocence 138–9, 428
  plea bargaining, and 153–7, 158, 159, 161, 163
  presumption of 134, 175, 395–6
inquisitorial systems 132–3, 146
insolvency 325–6, 328, 331
inspectors 60, 67
insurance 335, 349, 393
interest 372–3
Introduction to the Principles of Morals and Legislation (Bentham) 64
investing funds 61, 67, 68, 81–3
IRA 386, 387, 397
irrelevance principle *see under* corporate crime
Isachsen, A. 299
Israel 165, 393, 401–2
Italy 147, 148, 167, 257, 259, 312
Iyengar, S. 427

Jackson, B. 304
Jackson, John 149, 159
Jackson, Justice Robert H. 145
Jackson v Georgia (1072) 208
Jain, Pankaj 248
James, Annabelle 238
Jankowski, M.S. 259, 261, 262, 267
Janoff-Bulman, R. 409
Japan 66, 257
Jellal, M. 75, 275
Johnson, M. 248
Johnson, S. 106
Johnston, J.F. 240
Johnston, J.S. 106, 338
Jolls, C. 314, 412, 417, 418, 423, 428

Jones, C. 80
Jones, E. 419
Jourden, F. 432
Journal of Economic Literature 272
Juan, A. de 304
judgment-proof offenders 61, 81, 82
  firms and corporations *see under* corporate crime
judges and judicial 61, 67, 136, 137, 327
  bias and corruption 188, 279, 394, 431
  discretion 126–7, 141
  plea bargaining, and 147–8, 157, 160, 164–5
  refusing access to public infrastructure 61
  resources 126, 132, 141
  sentencing, and *see under* sentencing guidelines
Judicial Conference's Committee on Criminal Law 362, 367, 369
judicial review 105, 122, 151
Jurek v Texas (1076) 209
juries 104, 136, 138, 141, 146, 151, 202–3, 432
  rent-seeking, and 198–9
  trial by, right to 178

Kagan, R.A. 97, 311
Kahan, D.M. 331, 420
Kahneman, D. 406, 407, 408, 409, 410–11
Kambhu, J. 106
Kaplow, L. 233, 312
Karpoff, J. 95, 239, 247, 336
Kassin, S.M. 428
Kasznik, Ron 242
Katyal, N. 420
Katz, L. 212
Katz, Michael 131, 155
Kaufman, Daniel 285
Kedia, Simi 246
Keefer, P. 280
Kellough, Gail 154
Kemper 240
Kepner v United States (1904) 201–2
Keulenaer, S. de 333
Khalil, Fahad 231
Khanna, V.S. 104
Kilching, M. 330
Kim, Y. 298
Kingston, C. 271
Kirkbride, James 238
Kleck, G. 414, 415
Klees, A. 80
Klein, Susan 111, 115, 122
Klepper, S. 322
Klerman, D. 75, 81, 106, 337
Knack, S. 280
Knight, B.G. 429
Knowles, E.D. 428
Kobayashi, B.H. 103, 155
Kofman, F. 273, 277
Kokott, Juliane 103
Konrad, K.A. 267
Kornhauser, L.A. 224, 226, 332
Korobkin, R.B. 408
Kovacic, W. 235
KPMG 236
Kraakman, Reinier 221, 232–4, 236, 237, 241, 249, 325, 339
Krishnamurthy, Srinivasan 246
Kruchek, B.L. 328
Kugler, M. 273
Kunruether, Howard 418

La Porta, Rafael 248
labour market 67, 299–300
Laffont, J.J. 64, 78, 79, 80, 273, 277
Laibson, D. 423
Lambert, Richard 244
Lambert v Lewis (1981) 118
Lambsdorff, J.G. 277
Landa, J. 76
Landes, W.
  criminal law and torts 112
  criminal procedure 128–9, 134
  economics of capital punishment 212
  environmental crimes 323, 331
  plea bargaining and prosecution 150, 151, 154, 155, 157
  private enforcement of law 70, 72–4, 77
Lando, H. 102, 135
Landreth, H. 63
Landsberger, M. 309
Landskroner, Y. 298

Langbein, John 133, 149, 150, 173, 174
Langer, E.J. 420
Langer, Maximo 149, 166
Laroque, Guy 244
Latin America 66, 69, 76, 312
Lattimore, P. 422
Law, M.T. 106
Lawarree, J. 273, 277
Layard, Richard 408
Layson, S. 210
Leamer, E. 210
Lee, D. 246, 417
Lee, R.W. 260, 263
legality principle 146–7
Leitzel, J. 425
Letza, Syeve 238
Levitt, Steven
  behavioural criminal law and economics 404, 412, 413, 417, 429
  corporate crime 233
  criminal procedure 183
  economics of capital punishment 212
  organized crime 261, 262
Lewis, T. 103
Li, Haidan 248
Liberty, Susan 243
licences 93–4, 335, 360
Licht, A. 304
Lieven, Anatol 259
limited liability 62, 325
  corporate crime, and *see under* corporate crime
Lipatov, V. 311
List, John 412
litigation 78–9
  see also under costs; *see* private enforcement
Liu, Z. 215
Lloyd's of London 240
lobbying 185–6, 187–91
Lochner, L. 417
Loewenstein, George 165
Lofton, J.A. 338
London, attacks on 393, 397, 399
Long, Cheryl 158
Lopez-de-Silanes, Florencio 248
Lott, John 155, 221, 239, 249, 336
Lucas, R.E. 410
Lynch, Gerard 238

Macaulay, S. 76
MacCoun, Robert 414
Macho-Stadler, I. 308, 312
MacLaren, J. 274, 283, 313
MacLeod, B. 313
MacMinn, Richard 229
Macrory, R. 91, 98, 99
Madrid attacks 393
mafia 257, 259–63, 265, 267, 386
Magna Carta 196
Maital, S. 298
Malik, A.S. 93, 233, 306, 313
Malthus, Thomas 63
Manion, M. 94
manslaughter 117, 118, 119
Marchese, Carla 241, 291
Marchesini, R. 213, 217
marginal deterrence 34–6, 46, 95, 390
Marhuenda, F. 308
Marrelli, M. 300
Marsch, L.A. 424
Martimort, D. 78, 79, 80, 231, 273
Martin, B.G. 263
Martin, Gerald 246
Martina, R. 300
Mashaw, J. 105
Mattiacci, Guiseppe Dari 233, 378
Maurizi, A. 93
Mauro, P. 280
May, P. 96, 337
Maydew, Edward 246
Mayhew, P. 276
McAleer, M. 210
McCallin, N. 298
McCannon, B.C. 97
McClelland, G.H. 304
McCrary, J. 417
McGeorge, P. 428
McKee, M. 304
McManus, W. 210
McNulty Memorandum (2006) 236
Meares, T. 420, 426
Medellin cartel 263
Medicare 365
Meilijson, I. 309
Meinberg, V. 328, 333

Meissner, C.A. 428
Melumad, N. 313
Memon, A. 428
mens rea 100–101, 113, 114, 327–8
Merry, S. 62–3
Mexico 257
Mezzetti, Claudio 156
Mialon, Hugo 138
Miceli, T. 76, 103, 126, 133, 135, 141, 326
Miles, T.J. 404
Milgrom, P. 76
Miller, Nathan 235
Ministry of Defence 285
Miranda v Arizona (1966) 172
Mishra, A. 273
Misner, Robert 164
misreporting *see* securities fraud
mistrials 202–3
Mitchell, G. 413
Mitnick, B.M. 90
Mnookin, Robert 165
Mocan, H.N. 212, 215, 216
Mollenkamp, Carrick 240
monetary sanctions *see* fines
money laundering 358, 385, 397
Mongerald, Eric 83
monitoring 36, 72, 92–3, 97–8, 104, 176
  corporate crime 228, 231–8, 241, 248
  environmental crimes 332–5, 339
  public agents, of 72, 76, 161, 164
  terrorism 378–80, 383, 386–7, 400, 402
Montesquieu 1, 290
Mookherjee, Dilip 62, 95, 283, 308, 312, 313
Moore, Michael 160
Moore, T. 92
morality *see* social norms
Morris, N. 336
Morse, Adair 235
Motta, Massimo 234
Mullin, Wallace 235, 240, 241
Murphy, K.M. 273, 274, 424, 426
Mussolini, Benito 83
Myerson, Roger 244
Myles, G. 298

Nagin, D. 311, 413
naming and shaming *see* stigma
Narayan, P.K. 215
National Academy of Sciences 210, 404
National Advisory Commission 150
National Research Programme 301
Naylor, R. 298
Nelson, Karen 248
Nentjes, A. 333, 337
Netherlands 330, 337, 338
New York, 9/11 attacks on 393, 395, 398
Newman, H.A. 224, 228
Nickerson, R.S. 428
Niehaus, Gregory 240
non-monetary sanctions 329–30
  imprisonment *see* imprisonment
normative analysis as positive theory 111, 118, 119, 123
Norway 334
Nugent, J.B. 274
Nussim, J. 93
Nyborg, K. 96, 334

O'Brien, B. 428
O'Donoghue, T. 423
offenders 40, 352–3, 358–9, 414–15
  behavioural analysis of *see under* behavioural criminal law
  detecting *see* detecting under resources
  potential *see under* cyber crime
Ogus, A. 272, 280
  criminal law and regulation 90, 91, 92, 93, 96, 98, 103, 106
  environmental crimes 322, 324, 333, 335, 338
Ohanian, L. 68
Okten, C. 277
Oldfather, C.M. 413
opportunity principle 146–7
Organization for Economic Co-operation and Development 271, 299, 307, 312
organized crime 257–69, 383–7, 398
  economic consequences 266–8
  internal organization and market structure 262–6
  origins 258–61, 384

protection, sale of 257–8, 384
terrorism as 383–8
Origins of Adversary Criminal Trial, The (Langbein) 174
Orsagh, T. 210
Ortuno-Orton, I. 308
over-deterrence 8, 41, 95–6, 238, 332, 357, 358
Oyer, Paul 248

Packer, Herbert 171–2, 174–5
Pagano, Marco 244
Palepu, Krishna 242, 246
Palestine 393
Palim, M. 69
Papachristou v City of Jacksonville (1972) 205
Papagni, E. 279
Parigi, Bruno 231
Parisi, F. 80, 233, 378
Parker, J.S. 101, 103, 238
Parpworth, N. 329
Passel, P. 210
Paternoster, R. 414, 426
Patriot Act (2001) 395, 396–7
peak end rule 410
Pearce v Secretary of State for Defence (1988) 118
pecuniary legal claims 61, 62, 81
Penal Code (1988) 399
Pencavel, J. 299
Perez-Castrillo, D. 308, 312
Perron, W. 330
Persson, M. 76, 83
Peru 259
Phillips, J. 311
Physiocrats 63
Pierce, J.L. 208, 210
Pigouvian tax system 64
Pincus, Morton 248
Pitchford, Rohan, 228, 229
plea bargaining 128–34, 141, 145–66
behavioural analysis 429–30
comparative jurisdictions 132–4, 165–6
discretion, prosecutors of 145, 146–7, 161–4, 348
history 145–6, 149–50
judicial participation 164–5
mistaken convictions, and 153–7
nature 147–9
private litigation settlements, compared with 152–3
resources, constraints, and 150–52
screening mechanism, as 155–7
Plous, Scott 406
Png, I.P.L. 95, 283, 313
Poitevin, M. 103
Polanyi, K. 75
police 28, 33, 35, 60, 67, 71, 104, 142, 162
behavioural analysis of *see under* behavioural criminal law
bribery *see* bribery
corruption 279
entrapment 139
marginal deterrence 35
sexual assault cases 81–2
tax evasion 290
policies 31, 43, 282–5
Polinsky, M.
behavioural criminal law 425
corporate crime 221, 224, 228–9, 249
corruption 273, 275
criminal law and regulation 98, 102, 103, 106
environmental crimes 328, 332
plea bargaining and prosecution 146
private enforcement of law 76
public enforcement of law 60
tax evasion and avoidance 306
terrorism 388
political economy
anti-terrorism legal policy *see under* terrorism
criminal procedure, of *see* procedural protections
pollution 326–7, 328
Polo, Michele 234
Ponsaers, P. 333
Posner, R.
criminal law and torts 111, 112, 119, 120
criminal procedure 128, 129, 134, 136, 137, 140, 141
criminal law and regulation 93, 100, 101, 102, 103, 105, 107

economics of capital punishment 212
environmental crimes 322, 323, 324, 328, 331, 336
plea bargaining and prosecution 150, 151, 154, 155, 157
private enforcement of law 70, 72–4, 77
Pouyet, J. 78
precautions 24–5, 26–7, 30
individuals by *see under* individuals
Prescott, J.J. 432
presumption of innocence 134, 175, 395
pre-trial bargaining *see* settlements
pre-trial detention *see under* imprisonment
Prevention of Terrorism Act (1974) 397
Price, C. 83
Price, R. 276
prices 60, 64–7, 69, 80
principal-agent 36–7, 62, 105–6, 309, 381–3
prison over-crowding 164, 183
Prisoner's Dilemma 233–6
Pritchard, A.C. 248
private enforcement of law 54–5, 60–84, 313
antitrust and competition 67–70, 80–81
blackmail, as 70, 73, 77
corporate finance 84
costs 61, 75
criminalization 65–7
definition 60
environmental pollution 83–4
ex ante regulations and ex post litigation compared 78–9, 83
history 62–3
martial law 83
models 70–77, 77–81, 81
pecuniary legal claims 61, 62, 81
privatization 67–70
prosecutors and regulators 61–2, 64, 67
public law enforcement, and 60–64, 70–80
resources 63, 75
sexual assault and domestic abuse 81–2
Private Securities Litigation Reform Act (1995) 248
Privileggi, Fabio 241
probation 65, 136, 153, 238, 279, 350, 363
procedural protections, criminal 171–206
applications of 199–206
core protections 177–83
double jeopardy prohibition *see* double jeopardy
reasonable doubt *see* reasonable doubt
public choice approach, procedure to *see* public choice
procedure, criminal 125–42, 161–4
definition 125
economic objectives 127–8
errors *see under* errors
evidence, rules of *see* evidence
nature of 126–7
pre-trial bargaining *see under* settlements
procedural protections 133
see also appeals; bail; discretion; plea bargaining; prosecutors; standard of proof
Proceeds of Crime Act (2002) 398
Profitt v Florida (1976) 209
prosecutors 31, 38–9, 60, 61, 157–9, 164, 356
bribery *see* bribery
corruption *see* corruption
discretion 60, 126–7, 136, 141, 146–7, 149, 161–4, 191–5
see also plea bargaining; private enforcement of law; public agents
prospect theory *see under* behavioural criminal law
prostitution 65, 257, 260, 268
protection, private *see under* individuals
protection, sale of *see* organized crime
psychic benefits 351
public agents 45–6, 61–2, 81, 191
salaries and rewards 45, 62, 282–3

public choice theory 171–206
  applications of 199–206
  criminal procedural protections 183–206
    rent-seeking in law enforcement *see* rent-seeking
  Ely 175–6
  Langbein 174
  Packer 174–5
Public Company Accounting Oversight Board 247
public enforcement of law 1–55, 60
  coexisting with public law enforcement 60–64
  detection of offenders *see* detecting offenders
  errors *see* errors
  fines, costs of imposing *see under* fines
  general enforcement and optimal sanctions 33–4
  general problem of 3–4
  incapacitation *see* incapacitation
  individuals' imperfect knowledge 42–3
  marginal deterrence *see* marginal deterrence
  optimal enforcement, theory of 4–10, 10–21
  principal-agent relationship *see* principal-agent
  private enforcement compared *see under* private enforcement
  repeat offenders *see* repeat offenders
  sanctions *see* sanctions
  self-reporting *see* self-reporting
  settlements *see* settlements
  social norms *see* social norms
public interest 92, 105–6, 115, 119, 123, 146, 151–2
punitive damages 112, 323, 325, 355

Qian, Yingyi 228, 234, 237

Rabin, M. 423
Rachlinski, J.J. 429, 431, 432
Racketeer Influenced and Corrupt Organization Act (1970) 268
Rajgopal, Shiva 235
Rasmusen, Eric 136, 336
rational actor paradigm 346–7, 389, 403–5
  see also behavioural criminal law and economics
reasonable doubt 158, 177–9, 180–83, 194–5, 197
  definition of varying 134
  function 172, 177, 184
  standard of proof *see* standard of proof
  substitution effects *see* substitution effects
  tax evasion 306–7
Rego, Sonja 248
regulation and breaches
  administrative sanctions 96–100, 102–3
  costs *see* criminal; regulation *under* costs
  criminal law, and 90–107
  ex ante and ex post litigation compared 78–9, 83
  ex post deterrence, ex ante prevention and 91–4
  institutional processes 104–7
  mens rea see mens rea
  over-deterrence 95–6
  procedural arrangements 101–4
  public interest 119–20
  sanctions 94–100
  settlements *see under* settlements
  standard of proof 103
regulators 1, 60
  private enforcement of law, and *see* private enforcement
  refusing access to public infrastructure 61
  settlements *see under* settlements
  see also public agents
rehabilitation 351
Reinganum, Jennifer 130, 141, 155, 307, 309, 311
remembering *see under* behavioural criminal law
rent-seeking behaviour 184
  constraints on 191–9
    juries 198–9
    penalty restrictions 195–8
    procedural protections 191–5
  corruption, and *see* corruption

costs, criminal process in 187–91
direct costs 188
crime as 117
law enforcement, in 184–7, 205
corruption 186–7
inter-group wealth expropriation 185–6
private 71, 75
regulation 92, 104, 106
repeat offenders 40–42, 47, 96–7, 141, 360, 362, 416
reputational damage *see* stigma
resources *see under* cyber crime; judges; plea bargaining; *see* procedure
respondent superior 232, 331
restitution 368–9, 371, 373
retroactive punishments *see ex post facto*
Review of Enforcement in Environmental Regulation (DEFRA) 329
rewards 2, 45
Rey, P. 235
Rezaee, Zabihollah 248
Rhodes, William 151
Richardson, G. 303
Richardson, Scott 246
Richman, Daniel 159, 164
Rickman, N. 334, 338, 339
rights of access *see* private enforcement of law
Ringleb, A.L. 230
risk 38, 39, 46, 298
risk averse individuals 3, 158
behavioural criminal law 407–8, 422–3
detection probability 13–15, 17–18, 19–20
environmental crimes 335
errors 29–30
magnitude of fines, and 13–15, 46
plea bargaining 132, 155
principal-agent relationships 37
sanctions, and 352, 390
self-reporting 40
settlements 38, 39, 152
tax evasion 296–7, 299
risk neutral individuals and organisations
accidental harm 23
behavioural criminal law 407–8, 422–3
corporate crime, and 228, 390
detection probability 11–13, 16–17, 19–20, 43, 45–6
deterrence, and 370
environmental crimes 335
errors 28, 30
fairness of sanctions 53–4
general enforcement 33–4
magnitude of fines 11–13, 43, 45–6
precautions 25
self-reporting 40
settlements 38
tax evasion 307, 309
terrorist groups 390
risk-preferring individuals
behavioural criminal law 407–8, 422–3
certainty of punishment 359–60, 366–7
detection probability 18–19
deterrence, and 370
plea bargaining, and 150
sanctions, and 352
Roach, K. 69
Roberts, J. 80, 414
Robinson, P. 414, 415, 416
Romano, Roberta 247
Rose-Ackerman, S. 77–8, 105, 276, 277, 283
Ross, L. 419
Rossi, M.A. 280
Roth, J. 290, 298
Rousseau, S. 328, 333, 340
Rubin, P.H. 211, 217
Rubinfeld, Daniel 130, 132
Runkel, M. 300
Russia 259

safety regulations and breaches 22, 27, 39, 332
Salop, S.C. 68
Sanchez, I. 304, 307, 308
sanctions 1–2, 195
combined *see* combined
corporate crime and torts for *see* corporate crime
costs *see* costs
criminal law 94–100

cruel and unusual 195, 196–7, 208
discretionary *see under* discretion
environmental crimes *see* environmental crimes
excessive *see under* fairness
fairness *see under* fairness
fines *see* fines
first time offenders 40
general enforcement 33–4
imprisonment *see* imprisonment
incapacitative *see* incapacitation
incentive as *see under* incentives
indirect *see* stigma
individuals' imperfect knowledge of 42–3
inefficient 195, 196
levels compared 2, 64–7, 71, 73, 76
magnitude 3, 35–6
optimal, plea bargaining and 150
principal-agent, allocation between 37
purpose 369–70
rent-seeking, reduced by 189
repeat offenders 40–42
restrictions on 195–8
retroactive *see ex post facto*
self-reporting, reduced for 39–40
settlements, in 39
severity increasing 359, 363–4
stigma and reputational damage *see* stigma
terrorism 389–91, 396–402
threat as deterrence *see* deterrence
wealth of individuals, and *see* costs *under* wealth
Sanders, Andrew 148, 165
Sandmo, A. 290, 291, 294–300, 302–3, 306–8
Sansing, R. 311
Sapienza, Paula 248
Sarbanes-Oxley Act (2002) 114, 221, 242, 247–8
Sato, M. 311
Saudi-Arabia 284, 285
Schaefer, H. 106
Schinkel, Maarten 241
Schkade, D.A. 409
Schlanger, M. 409
Schneider, F. 293
Scholz, J.T. 96
Schrag, J. 103, 432
Schulhofer, Stephen 126–7, 150, 151, 154, 156, 158, 161
Schulze, W.D. 304
Schwab, R. 313
Schwartz, A. 412
Schwartz, E. 105
Schwartz, S. 304
Scollen, C.N. 410
Scotchmer, S. 103, 299, 307, 308, 311, 432
Scotland 160
Scott, Michael 428
Scott, Robert, 150, 154, 161
Scottish Enlightenment 63
search and seizure 137
Seaton, J. 111, 118
securities 61, 67, 84, 239, 242–8, 336
Securities and Exchange Commission 245
Segel, V. 422, 423
Segerson, K. 231, 328, 331
Seidmann, Daniel 138
self-incrimination, rule against 138
self-regulation 104, 105–6
self-reporting 39–4, 223, 233–6, 339, 401
Seligman, Joel 247
Selznick, P. 96
sentence-bargaining 147–8, 164–5
Sentencing Commission, United States 40–41, 221–3, 238, 346–74, 404
sentencing guidelines, 163, 164, 222, 238, 329, 346–74
certainty of punishment 359–60, 366–7
computer crime 346, 349–50, 351, 353, 354
corporations 362
economic crime control model, and 361–73
Federal crimes 40–41
fraud and embezzlement 346, 348, 349–50, 354, 362–8
goals and role 347–8, 351
guidance to prosecutors 356
inflation 363, 364
intended and actual loss, causation and 369–71

interest 372–3
judges 163, 329, 348, 362, 373
offense levels 361–3
sanctions, increased severity of 363–4
tax evasion 346
temporary and permanent losses 368–9
victims 247, 355
see also cyber crime
Serious Fraud Office 284
settlements 37–9, 106, 112, 132, 141, 146
plea bargaining *see* plea bargaining
pre-trial bargaining 125
private enforcement of law, and 70–72, 152–3
tax evasion 311, 312
Shaked, A. 106
Shanghai 257, 263
Shavell, S.
behavioural criminal law 425
corporate crime 221, 224, 228–9, 231, 233, 236, 249
corruption 273, 275
criminal procedure 140
criminal law and regulation 92, 98, 102, 103, 106
criminal law and torts 111
environmental crimes 322, 324, 328, 332
plea bargaining and prosecution 146
public enforcement of law 60
tax evasion and avoidance 306
terrorism 388
Shepherd, Joanna 126, 136, 141, 208, 212, 213, 214, 216, 217
Sherman Antitrust Act (1890) 68, 69, 80
Shleifer, A. 62, 75, 84, 248
Shustorovich, E. 212
Sicily 259, 261, 263
Siegelman, Peter 183
silence, right to 138, 139, 162
Simon, D. 428
Simpson, Sally 238
Sinn Fein 387
Siven, C.H. 76, 83
Sjostrom, W. 95
Skaperdas, Stergios 262, 267
Skogh, G. 323
Slemrod, J. 290, 291, 292, 299, 300
Slezak, Steve 243, 244
Slaon, Richard 246
Smettan, J.R. 330
Smith, Adam 63
smuggling 290
Smyth, R. 215
Snow, A. 299
Snyder, Christopher 233, 240, 241
Sobel. J. 307, 308, 311
social norms 51–2, 298
social welfare 3–5, 7
ex ante preventive regimes 91–4
bail 134
corporate crime 226, 228, 229, 243
corruption, and 46
environmental crimes, and 326–7
fairness of sanctions 52–4
industrial and commercial undertakings 96
marginal deterrence 35
maximizing when enforcement certain 3–10
mistakes diluting deterrence 29–31
optimal level of crime and crime control 347–58
organized crime 384–5
principal-agent relationship, and 36–7
repeat offenders, sanctions for, and 41–2
rent-seeking, effects of *see* costs under rent-seeking
securities fraud 243
self-reporting, benefits on 40
settlements, effects on 37–9
social norms 51–2
tax evasion 299
Solnick, S.L. 260
Sourcebook of Federal Sentencing Statistics 221–2
South Africa 66, 76, 259
Soviet Union, former 75, 259–60
Spagnolo, Giancarlo 234
Spain 399–401
Spiller, P.T. 105
Srinivasan, T.N. 294
Srivastava, Anup 246

standard of proof 129, 177, 238, 307
administrative procedures 324, 325
civil cases 112, 135, 136, 178, 180–83, 238
corporate crime, and 238
crimes 31, 103, 112–13, 125–6, 238
tax evasion 311–12, 314
torts 112–13
trial at 134–6
standards of care
safety regulations 27
tax evasion 307, 311–12
Starr, S. 432
Stein, A. 95, 423
Steinzor, R.I. 339
Stella, P. 313
Stephen, Frank 127, 133, 158, 160, 161, 165
Stephenson, M.C. 105
Stigler, G.
corruption 275
criminal law and torts 119
environmental crimes 320, 321, 339
private enforcement of law 71, 72, 73, 74, 81
tax evasion and avoidance 313
stigma and reputation 94–5, 103, 115, 153, 179, 183, 360
corporate crime 238–9
environment crime 330, 335–6
fines, and 136
imprisonment, and 94, 136, 360
increasing 358
murder, and 208
offender's perception of 352
rent-seeking, and 180, 190–91
tax evasion 298
terrorism, and 391
Stocken, Phillip 244
Stone, Christopher 241
street crimes 354, 362, 365
strict liability 3, 20
administrative sanctions 96
corporate crime, and *see under* corporate crime
environmental crimes 327–8
errors *see* errors
general enforcement 33–4
mens rea see mens rea
optimal magnitude when enforcement certain 4–5, 6–8, 9–10,
optimal magnitude when enforcement uncertain 11–15, 16–19, 19
precautions, and *see* precautions
Strom, S. 299
Stuart, C. 323
Stuntz, William 150, 154, 158, 160–64
subjective expected utility 407–8
substitution effects 189, 197
Sunder, Shyam 244
Sunstein, C.R. 412, 423, 428, 432
Supreme Court, United States 114, 121–2
Sutton, J. 106
Svensson, J. 280
Svorny, S. 92, 94
Swanson, Edward 246
Sweeney, Amy 246
Swiss Re 240
Sykes, Alan 224, 237, 238
Syropoulos, C. 262

Tabbach, A.D. 93
Taliban 384, 385
Tanzi, V. 312
Tata, Cyrus 160
tax evasion and avoidance 20–22, 33, 42, 46, 60, 66, 290–314
avoidance, definition of 292
business purpose doctrine 292
corporate tax 300–301
decision to evade 294–301
Allingham-Sandmo model 294–300
definition and extent 291–3
economic substance doctrine 292
enforcement procedure 310–14
amnesties 312–13
compliance costs 310
corruption 313–14
defence costs 311
experts 310–11
private enforcement 313
record-keeping 311
settlements 312
standard of proof 311–12
ethical behaviour 297–8
evasion, definition of 291–2

indirect taxes 300
labour supply 299–300
non-expected utility theory 298–9
optimal tax enforcement 306–10
optimal auditing 307–10
sanctions 363–4
social pressure 298
sentencing *see* sentencing guidelines
tax gap 291–2
tax shifting 300
taxpayers' behaviour 291, 301–6
uncertainty 299
Taxpayer Compliance Measurement Programme 301–2
Taylor, J.B. 210
Telle, K. 97, 334
Terror Alert System 396
terrorism 281, 375–402
anti-terrorism measures 395–402
Israel 401–2
Spain 399–401
United Kingdom 397–9
United States 395–7
communal liability 377–80
crime, as 388–91
incapacitation 376
organized crime, as 383–8
political economy, anti-terrorism legal policy of 394–5
preferences of terrorists 375–6
principal-agent framework 380–83
victims, security of 391–3
Terrorism Act (2000) 398
Terrorism Act (2006) 399
Thaler, R. 412, 423
Thistle, P.D. 210
Thompson, K. 427
Thompson Memorandum (2003) 236
three-strike laws 141, 163
Tietenberg, T. 231, 328, 331
Tirole, J. 61, 62, 243, 244, 277
Tona, E. 313
Toma, M. 313
Tonry, N. 336
Tor, Avishalom 156, 157
Torgler, B. 304, 305
torts 111–23
corporations by *see* corporate
criminal boundary, empirically testing 118–19
foreign crimes and long arm crimes 122–3
hybrid cases 120–22
intentional and unintentional 112–13
recklessness and gross negligence 114, 116, 117
traffic control and violations 20, 21, 22, 39, 40, 46
Transactional Records Access Clearinghouse 279
Transparency International 278
Trebilcock, M. 69
Triads 257
Tuinstra, Jan 241
Tullock, G. 117
Tuna, Irem 246
Tuohy, C. 105
Turner, Jenia Iontcheva 149, 164
Tversky, A. 406, 407, 408
Two Models of Criminal Procedure (Packer) 174
Tyler, T.R. 426

uncertainty 407–8
see also certainty *under* risk preferring individuals
Ueng, K.L. 308
Ulen, T. 70, 72, 208, 329
under-deterrence 8, 20, 33, 41–2, 189, 333
costs 11–13, 41–2, 49, 182
United Kingdom 91, 115, 122–3, 132, 284
environmental crimes 329, 333, 338
evolution of legal procedures 62–4, 75, 145, 196
plea bargaining 145, 148, 164
terrorism measures *see under* terrorism
United Nations 285
Convention against Corruption 271
United States 83–4, 115, 122–3, 134, 185, 242, 364, 417
antitrust 67–9, 74, 80
Constitution 122, 137, 138, 176, 178, 197, 208, 209
corporate crime and torts 220, 235
corruption 279, 283, 284
environmental crimes 329, 338–9

evidence, rules of 136–9
evolution of legal procedures 62–4, 65–6, 67–9, 112, 145–6, 208–9
organized crime 257, 261, 264, 268
plea bargaining and settlements 125–6, 132–3, 145–6, 148, 163–5
prosecutors 158–9
tax evasion 291, 301–3, 304, 311
see also imprisonment; terrorism
United States v McDowell (1997) 369
Utset, M.A. 424

Van Aaken, Anne 159
Van der Wyngaert, Christine 148
Van Rijckeghem, C. 281
Van Rooy, B. 337
Veall, M.R. 210
Veljanovski, C. 97, 338
Venkataraman Kumar 246
Venkatesh, Sudhir 261, 262
Verrecchia, Robert 243
victims 2, 354–5, 391–3,
behavioural analysis of *see under* behavioural criminal law
sentencing, and *see under* sentencing guidelines
vulnerable 354, 355, 362
Viscusi, K. 111
Visser, M. 321, 322, 327
Vissing-Jorgensen, Annette 248
void-for-vagueness doctrine 205–6
Voigt, Stefan 159
Volpin, Paolo 247

Wadhawan, S. 319
Waldfogel, Joel 134
Walters, D. 96
Walzl, Markus 234
Warren, R. 299
Warren Court innovations 172
wealth and assets of individuals 33, 34, 37, 48–50, 113, 116, 134, 389
inability to pay 132, 146, 153, 160, 162, 325, 360
fines, and 21–2, 195
lawyers 159–60
optimal magnitude of sanctions, and, 4, 5, 9, 12–13, 15, 19, 25
tax, and 292, 297, 307
wealthy defendants 153, 159–60
Weber, Max 61, 62, 63, 261, 304
Webley, P. 304
Weder, B. 283
Weisbach, D. 292
Wehrly, E.W. 239
Weiler, W.C. 210
Weimer, David 151
Weinstein, N. 406
wheel-clamping 94, 99
Wheeler, N. 332
whistle-blowing 234–6
White, James. J, 229
White, L.J. 68
white-collar crime 330, 354, 356, 361, 363–7
Whitman, J.Q. 99
Wiggins, Steven 230
Wilde, L. 302, 307, 308, 309, 311, 313
Wilde, M. 322
Wiley, J.S. 96
Williamson, O. 63, 81
Wilson, J.Q. 407, 409
Wilson, T. 409
Wilson, Wesley 234
Winship, Re (1970) 172–3, 177–81, 183
Winter, S. 337
Wistrich, A.J. 431
Witte, A. 302, 422
Wolf, E. 62–3
Wolfers, J. 216, 217
Wolfson, A. 105
Wood, R. 96
Woodbury, D. 302
Woods, M. 91, 98
World Bank 271, 278, 285
World Values Survey 304
Worldcom 221, 240
Wortley, Scot 154
Wrede, M. 298
Wright, David 224, 228
Wu, Min 246
Wurmnest, W. 80

Yakuza 257
Yang, C.C. 308
Yaniv, G. 298, 299, 300
Yeung, K. 106
Yitzaki, S. 291, 292, 294, 297

Young, Richard 148, 165
young offenders 65
Yuesheng, Du 263
Yunker, J.A. 210

Zamagni, S. 273
Zanardi, A. 293, 298
Zhang, Q. 93, 248
Zimmerman, Jerold 243
Zimmerman, P.R. 212–13, 214
Zimring, F.E 209, 214
Zingales, Luigi 235
Zitzewitz, Eric 247